OWLS OF EUROPE

White owls seem not (but in this I am not
positive) to hoot at all: all that clamorous hooting
appears to me to come from the wood kinds. The
white owl does indeed snore and hiss in a
tremendous manner; and these menaces well
answer the intention of intimidating: for I have
known a whole village up in arms on such an
occasion, imagining the churchyard to be full of
goblins and spectres.

GILBERT WHITE, *The Natural History of Selborne*
(first published 1789): from a letter to the Hon.
Daines Barrington, Selborne, July 8th, 1773.

Owls of Europe

by HEIMO MIKKOLA

Illustrated by
IAN WILLIS

T & A D POYSER
Calton

© by Heimo Mikkola and Ian Willis 1983

ISBN 0 85661 034 8

First published 1983 by T & A D Poyser Ltd
Town Head House, Calton, Waterhouses, Staffordshire, England

Plates printed by Wood Westworth
and Co., St Helens, Merseyside

Text set in 9/11pt Linotron 202 Plantin,
printed and bound in Great Britain
at The Pitman Press, Bath

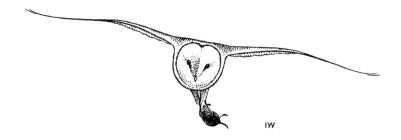

IW

Contents

5

Colour Plates I–VIII

The Plates appear between pages 96 and 97. The birds are grouped, loosely, by size, colour and general appearance, rather than in any particular order of species. Plates I–V show perched birds; Plates VI–VIII show birds in flight.

List of Photographs

List of Figures

List of Tables

Dedicated to
Diane and Kyllikki

Introduction

Owls are successful birds and they have dispersed to all continents except Antarctica and some remote ocean islands. The great majority of species occur in the tropics and subtropics. North America and the Palearctic zone of the Old World (Europe, Asia, except the southern-most tropical parts, and northern Africa) are inhabited by 33 species of owls, of which eight species occur both in North America and Eurasia. Thirteen regularly breeding species of owl are known from Europe, ten of which are on the British list.

The basic aim of the book has been to review the available knowledge of the 13 owl species of Europe, and four additional species from countries adjoining the Mediterranean, some of which species may occasionally occur in Europe. This work, therefore, deals with 17 species out of the 134 world species at present known.

The sequence and scientific nomenclature of Professor K. H. Voous in his *List of Recent Holarctic Bird Species* (1977) has been followed with some minor differences in English vernacular names. To avoid obvious confusion the older name of African Marsh Owl is preferred to Marsh Owl and Hume's Owl seems more suitable than Hume's Tawny Owl. In his article 'More about Desert Liliths: Hume's Tawny Owl' in the journal *Israel Land and Nature*, summer 1977, M. C. Jennings suggested that Hume's Tawny Owl should be called Desert Tawny Owl, but this name, unfortunately, gives the impression that this very distinctive owl is no more than a desert form of the Tawny Owl, as I wrongly suggested myself in *Owls of the World* in 1973.

The main body of the book consists of species descriptions, and preceding these are general summaries covering the most important features that distinguish owls from other groups of birds. The 17 species accounts each contain the following sections: *Description; In the field; Voice; Behaviour; Food; Breeding biology; Distribution.*

The distribution of each species is shown by two maps, one for Europe, North Africa and the Middle East, the other for the world. Whilst I have tried to present as accurately as possible the current state of the existing knowledge of west Palearctic owls' ranges, it should be remembered that many species, such as Great Grey, Snowy, Hawk, Tengmalm's and Short-eared Owl, tend to be nomadic, nesting where food animals are most abundant. The maps for such species are, therefore, only a guide based on nests discovered in recent years, though they should give a good indication of the regions normally inhabited by each species.

Part three of the book deals primarily with ecological relationships among European owls, and attempts to answer the question of how different owl species manage to live alongside each other. This question can be raised in a more general way: why are there only thirteen regularly breeding owl species in Europe? This has been and still remains a complex ecological problem in which many more questions may be posed than can be answered. In this part I have, however, tried to explain the complex interactions between predators and their prey. I have also included an analysis of sexual dimorphism, which is obviously a morphological isolation mechanism to reduce possible intraspecific competition. Part three also deals with the interspecific relationships among European owls and other birds of prey, including all recorded number of instances in which an owl species has killed or been killed by other owls or raptors.

At the end there is a final chapter on conservation and protection of European owls, especially with regard to intra- and interspecific competition, and a summary of the legal status of owls in Europe.

Ian Willis has painted the series of colour plates depicting the most important plumages of all 17 species and their distinctive races covered in the book. The series includes flight plates of all the aforementioned species, for although some of them rarely fly by day it was felt that it would be of interest to show all species in flight postures.

The figures on each colour plate are to scale. Ian Willis also drew all the many vignettes, line drawings, graphs and maps, which add so much to this book.

It was February 1975 when I started to plan and compile the data for this book with Ian Willis. Now more than seven years later new literature and new observations still provide potentially new material for the book. However, one has to stop somewhere and, in the main, observations and published data in this book do not extend beyond October 1980.

I am well aware that many owl enthusiasts have first-hand experience of the ecology of European owls, and that their views on many aspects of ecology might differ from those presented in this book. It would be a pleasure to receive their comments and criticisms on this and any other matter connected with European owls. Any photographs of the less well-known species or races, particularly of the Brown Fish Owl *Ketupa zeylonensis*, would be similarly welcomed. All correspondence should be addressed to Heimo Mikkola, c/o T. & A. D. Poyser Ltd.

Acknowledgements

The present book could not have been written or illustrated without the help of numerous friends, colleagues and institutions.

Very special thanks are due to Professor Ossi V. Lindqvist, University of Kuopio, for constant encouragement and for offering detailed comments, criticism and advice in preparing the first drafts of this work. The University Library of Kuopio has kindly made it possible to build up a collection of existing owl studies, hundreds of which have been consulted when writing this book.

My special gratitude for constructive criticism goes primarily to my colleague Ian Willis, who has been much more than the illustrator of this book. Ian has scrutinised the entire manuscript whilst improving my often inadequate English and adding small items of information. Ian, as a specialised ornithological artist, sees live and stuffed owls in greater detail than I do, as an ecologist. Thus he often felt it necessary to revise my sections 'Description' and 'In the field', for which I am very grateful. During the last five years he has also supplied me with many relevant reprints on owls and made all his ornithological contacts available for me as well.

My grateful thanks are due to Mrs Diane Willis, BA, who has meticulously eradicated my inconsistencies whilst tackling the tedious job of typing the various drafts of the manuscript. Her enthusiastic response provided incentive when it was badly needed, and several passages owe much to her fine judgement. She also gave me valuable help with translations of various owl studies from the French.

I am also indebted to my wife, Kyllikki Mikkola, MSc, for assisting me in many ways in all stages of this work. Without her constant companionship in the field between 1966 and 1976 it would not have been possible to devote so much of my time to watching owls, and later I could never have finished the writing of this book without her understanding and forbearance.

Messrs J. A. Alcover, C. C. Barnard, G. F. Date, L. Davenport, A. Hakala, P. Helo, K. Huhtala, A. Kaikusalo, J. Koivusaari, A. Leinonen, M. Rikkonen, C. Riols and S. Sulkava generously made available their unpublished notes to me, and I am obliged to Messrs P. Alaja and H. Kangasperko, who collected the stomachs whose contents were analysed for knowledge of autumn and winter food. Drs E. Antikainen, S. Klaus and J. Wiesner kindly provided useful translations of some Russian publications.

Both Ian Willis and I would like to thank Dr David Snow and the staff at The British Museum (Natural History), Ornithological Department, Tring, Hertfordshire, for permission and help in examining skins, skeletons and literature. A number of people from Britain showed interest and helped, especially, Ian during various stages of his work, and these include the late Cyril Helyer, Alan Kitson, Richard Porter, Raymond Hawley, Donald A. Smith and Donald Watson. Mr and Mrs G. R. Roper-Caldbeck provided Ian Willis with a suitably rural studio where much of his work was completed in the hot Galloway summer of 1978, and his thanks are due to them for their kindness.

Our thanks are due to those who provided photographs, sketches or slides upon which certain of Ian Willis's text figures were based. In this context we would like to mention Messrs O. Eskelinen, R. Fritz, S. Grönlund, P. Hublin, L. Lyytinen, J. Steenhart and J. Väisänen. Many photographers responded to our requests for black and white prints and we thank them all; choosing the selection that appears in this book from the large amount of first-class work available proved a very difficult task.

For locating certain papers, statistics and other information on matters connected with conservation and legal status, we much appreciate the help given by two staff members of the RSPB, Richard Porter and Michael Everett.

In preparing the maps, the following persons kindly provided many details of the recent distribution and populations of west Palearctic owls in the various countries:

AUSTRIA: H. Frey, W. Scherzinger and W. Wruss
BELGIUM: G. Huyskens
BULGARIA: S. Dontchev and S. Simeonov
CZECHOSLOVAKIA: Z. Bárta and L. Kučera
CYPRUS: L. I. Leontiades
DENMARK: S. Rosendahl
ESTONIA: T. Randla and L. Rootsmäe
FINLAND: K. Hyytiä

FRANCE: H. Baudvin, C. Frelin, C. Riols, M. C. Saint Girons and L. Yeatman

GEORGIA, CAUCASUS: Z. Zhordania

GERMANY (EAST) DDR: S. Klaus, M. Melde, R. Oeser, F. Ritter, S. Schönn and J. Wiesner

GERMANY (WEST) FDR: H.-H. Bergmann, P. Bühler, B. U. Meyburg, J. Weiss, V. Wendland and K.-H. Wickl

GIBRALTAR: C. Finlayson

GREAT BRITAIN: G. Beven and R. Spencer

GREECE: B. Antipas and H.-J. Böhr

HUNGARY: L. Horváth

ICELAND: S. A. Bengtson and F. Gudmundsson

IRAN: D. A. Scott

IRELAND: J. S. Fairley and D. Scott

ISRAEL: J. Leshem and H. Mendelssohn

ITALY: M. Bonora, S. Lovari and E. Moltoni

LEBANON: A. M. Macfarlane

MOROCCO: M. Thévenot

NETHERLANDS: L. Brussaard and R. M. Texeira

NORWAY: Y. Hagen, N. Røv and J. F. Willgohs

OMAN: M. D. Gallagher

POLAND: L. Tomialojć

PORTUGAL: R. M. A. Delgado Rufino, J. R. Santos Junior and R. O. Vicente

RUMANIA: D. Munteanu

SAUDI ARABIA: M. C. Jennings

SPAIN: C. M. Herrera, F. Hiraldo, F. J. Purroy and V. Sans-Coma

SWEDEN: K. Bylin, B. Frylestam and Å. Norberg

SWITZERLAND: A. Schifferli

SYRIA: A. M. Macfarlane

TURKEY: Ornithological Society of Turkey

YUGOSLAVIA: V. F. Vasić

USSR: V. Galushin and O. Semenov Tian-Shansky

PART I

SPECIAL CHARACTERISTICS OF OWLS

1: The origin of owls

Birds are poorly represented as fossils, compared with fish, reptiles and mammals, partly because bird bones are thin-walled, hollow, fragile and easily destroyed by predators or scavengers. Often they are so badly damaged during the process of fossilisation that they cannot be identified. That is why palaeornithology remains one of the most neglected of natural history subjects. However, we know that in geological terms, birds are relative newcomers to the earth's fauna. *Archaeopteryx lithographica*, the first known birds, appeared in the Upper Jurassic about 170 to 160 million years ago, but it is not possible to say how soon after this some sort of owl evolved. Rich and Bohaska (1976) recently published their discovery of what they believed to be the oldest known owl, *Ogygoptynx wetmorei*, which lived in North America during the mid-Paleocene (about 60 million years ago). This owl clearly does not belong to any of the known families of *Strigiformes* and may represent a new higher category of owls that provides a link between the *Strigidae* and the *Tytonidae*. However, Walker (1973) has suggested that, in Europe, the modern families of owls or owl-like birds had already evolved during the latter half of the Mesozoic era, between 135 and 70 million years ago. At least two tarsometatarsi found in the Upper Cretaceous deposits of Rumania have *Strigiform* characters. If this identification is correct, it will prove to be the earliest known owl in the world.

There is good evidence that between 70 and 50 million years ago, when southern England and parts of France were covered with sub-tropical or tropical forest, and temperate plants grew in what is now the Arctic, a larger number of owl species lived in Europe. Two tarsometatarsi bones found in the phosphorite deposits of Gernay, France, appear to belong to the *Strigiformes* (Walker 1973). They seem to be leg bones of a large owl similar to and about the size of the present-day Eagle Owl. Seven further species were recorded from phosphorite deposits in Quercy, France, but the exact strata were not noted when specimens were collected, rendering it impossible to date them precisely, although their age is probably between 45 and 27 million years as shown in Table 1. By the early Eocene (53 to 47 million years ago) a number of other strigiforms had made their appearance in North America. *Protostrix* and *Eostrix* owls, in the family *Protostrigidae*, are known from a number of localities in the American West (Rich and Bohaska 1976).

During the Miocene period (27 to 8 million years ago) the climate became cooler, and temperate flora replaced the subtropical ones. It is probable that the owl species placed in extant genera (*Bubo, Otus, Strix* and *Tyto*) are the first true examples of their type. Earlier specimens described from Upper Eocene/Lower Oligocene deposits have been ascribed to the genera *Bubo* and *Asio*, but they need to be re-examined before either genus can be accepted as having existed before the Miocene (Table 1).

The Pleistocene period, often referred to as the Great Ice Age, ended about 10,000 years ago. Owl fossils from this period are relatively plentiful when compared with earlier times. Fourteen of the existing species of owls have been discovered in many parts of Europe. In addition, the now extinct *Tyto melitensis* inhabited Malta (Table 1A). The Great Grey Owl once ranged as far south as Rumania, where it no longer exists. Likewise, the Spotted Eagle Owl *Bubo africanus*, a present-day African species, has been found as a fossil in Sardinia, though it no longer occurs in Europe.

One feature which all fossil owl remains have in common is that they represent true owls. So far no owl-like fossils have been discovered which could give us any hints as to what birds might share a common ancestor with the *Strigiformes*. From what is known so far, it does seem likely that the *Caprimulgiformes* (oilbirds, potoos, nightjars and nighthawks) are the owl's nearest living relatives and that they may have evolved from a common, nocturnal ancestor, perhaps not more than 100 million years ago.

Owls have also been grouped with the *Coraciiformes*, particularly with the goatsuckers, but Dement'ev *et al* (1951) consider this groundless. On the other hand, Koenig (1973) has confirmed similarities between *Coraciiformes* and owls by a comparison of bee-eaters (*Meropidae*) and the Scops Owl. Owls do possess many characteristics in common with other birds of prey, but they are best regarded as a distinct and sharply differentiated order.

2: Taxonomy

Although the members of the *Strigiformes* may be easily distinguished from those of other orders, the familial, subfamilial and generic relationships within the order are much less certain. Owl taxonomy is currently in a state of flux. For instance, Norberg's (1977, 1978) studies on the occurrence and evolution of bilateral ear asymmetry in owls will almost certainly bring about some revision.

Peters' (1940) owl classification is the most widely used. He separated modern owls into two families: the typical owls, the *Strigidae*, and the barn owls, the *Tytonidae*.

Tytonidae

The skull is long and narrow, the orbits small and the furcula unpneumatic (Fig. 2). The rear edge of the sternum has one pair of notches. The bill is elongated and relatively slender. The coccygeal gland is plumose. The ears are symmetrical in shape and size, but the left one, together with the skin flap in front of it, is located higher than the right ear-hole and skin flap. There does not seem to be any individual difference in this asymmetry (no left- or right-eared owls) and it is restricted to the ear-opening without affecting the middle and inner ears. The second and third toes are of equal size. The claw of the middle toe is serrated along the inner edge and the tarsometatarsus is elongated. Postembryonic development consists of two downy plumages, as in diurnal raptors, but a mesoptile stage is lacking. The eggs are elongated.

The *Tytonidae* is subdivided into the *Tytoninae* and the *Phodilinae*. In the *Tytoninae* there is one genus *Tyto* consisting of eight species, of which only one, *Tyto alba*, occurs in Europe. The *Phodilinae* has one genus *Phodilus* which contains two species, one occurring in south-east Asia and the other in Africa. The last taxon has been the source of debate for many years, with some authors choosing to ally *Phodilus* with the strigids rather than the tytonids. Recently Feduccia and Ferree (1978) have shown similar derived bony stapes (*Columella*) occurring in *Tyto* and *Phodilus* supporting the concept of their close affinity.

Strigidae

The skull is round, the orbits large, the furcula is pneumatic and the rear edge of the sternum has two pairs of notches (Fig. 2). The bill is strong, short and sharply decurved. The coccygeal gland is naked. The ears are frequently asymmetrical in shape and size, the right ear being larger than the left (see Fig. 1), with the asymmetry also extending to the bones of the skull. However, Norberg (1978) has stressed that the outer ears are perfectly symmetrical in the majority of *Strigidae* genera, and that an asymmetrical arrangement is known to involve parts of the skull in four species only: Ural Owl, Great Grey Owl, Tengmalm's Owl and Saw-whet Owl *Aegolius acadicus*. Moreover, both the *Tyto* and *Pholidus* genera of the *Tytonidae* show a clear bilateral asymmetry of the external ears. It must be concluded that these parts of the owl's skull are unreliable factors in separating the *Strigidae* and the *Tytonidae*.

The third toe is longer than the second, with smooth cutting edges to the claw of the middle toe. The tarsometatarsus is short. Postembryonic development consists of a single downy plumage and a mesoptile stage. The eggs are round.

The latest review of the world's owls is presented by Clark *et al* (1978) in their *Working Bibliography of Owls of the World*. They recognise 23 genera in the *Strigidae* family: *Otus, Mimizuku, Lophostrix, Bubo, Ketupa, Scotopelia, Pulsatrix, Nyctea, Surnia, Glaucidium, Xenoglaux, Micrathene, Uroglaux, Ninox, Sceloglaux, Athene, Ciccaba, Strix, Rhinoptynx, Asio, Pseudoscops, Nesasio* and *Aegolius*. The genus *Xenoglaux* is a new one, containing but one species, the recently discovered Long-whiskered Owlet *Xenoglaux loweryi*, found in 1976 by O'Neill and Graves (1977) in the Peruvian Andes. The total number of species generally recognised today is 124, although Clark *et al* accept only 123 because they combine Striated Scops Owl *Otus brucei* with Oriental Scops Owl *Otus sunia*. We have chosen to follow those who separate Striated Scops Owl as a distinct species and therefore 17 species are covered by this book.

In Europe the taxonomic position of the 13 regularly breeding species is clear, but there are many different opinions on the names and even the genera of the other four species. As stated above, Clark *et al* (1978) include Striated Scops Owl *Otus brucei* in Oriental Scops Owl *Otus sunia*, while Hume's Owl (or Humes' Tawny Owl) *Strix butleri* has often been suspected of being no more than a race of Tawny Owl *Strix aluco* (even Mikkola in Burton *et al* 1973). A most radical revision of owl systematics was offered by Eck and Busse in their publication of 1973 in which they listed only 24 genera and 109 species in the world. They included African Marsh Owl *Asio capensis* as a race of Short-eared Owl *Asio flammeus* and completely eliminated the genus *Ketupa* (fish owls), combining it with *Bubo* (eagle owls). If we were to recognise these authors, Brown Fish Owl *Ketupa zeylonensis* would be *Bubo zeylonensis*.

Nevertheless, this book regards the Striated Scops Owl as a distinct species from the Oriental Scops Owl *Otus sunia*, thus agreeing with Pukinskii (1977). Moreover, it recognises Hume's Owl *Strix butleri* as a quite separate species from Tawny Owl *Strix aluco*, which is in agreement with substantial new information from the Middle East (see Hume's Owl in Part II). Furthermore, the African Marsh Owl *Asio capensis* has not been included in the Short-eared Owl *Asio flammeus*; nor has Brown Fish Owl *Ketupa zeylonensis* become a member of the *Bubo* genus, the majority view having been preferred (cf. Voous 1977, Clark *et al* 1978) to that of Eck and Busse (1973).

3: Anatomical characters

This book is primarily a description of the ecology of owls and will therefore offer only a summary of the main anatomical characters, for the most part listed in *Birds of the Soviet Union* (Dement'ev *et al* 1951).

The skull of a typical owl is desmognathic and holorhinal. The vomer is usually

Snowy Owl

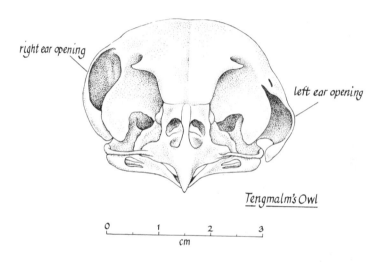

right ear opening

left ear opening

Tengmalm's Owl

0   1   2   3

cm

Fig. 1 (above) Ear-opening of Snowy Owl, after Portenko 1972. Edge of facial disk has been raised to expose aperture, though normally it would be hidden. (below) Skull of Tengmalm's Owl, showing the right ear-opening positioned about 6mm (average) higher than the left, after Nordberg 1968. The Snowy Owl drawing is not to scale

absent. Basipterygoid processes are functionally developed. The number of cervical vertebrae is 14. The neck is of medium length. The thoracic vertebrae are free and are not ankylosed with the os dorsale. The sternum has a large keel (carina) with one (*Tytonidae*) or two (*Strigidae*) pairs of emarginations at the posterior edge. The skeleton of the extremities is structurally similar to that of diurnal raptors but with various segments displaying different proportions; the wing skeleton with the antebrachium (ulna and radius) constituting the longest portion, and the humeral longer than the carpal, with the last constituting the shortest segment. Bock (1968) described an osseous arch on the radius, which is unique to owls. Two muscles partly attach to the arch, and a proprioreceptive organ is located beneath it. In a subsequent study, Bock and McEvey (1969) concluded that the osseous arch of the radius provides a strong case for a monophyletic origin of all owls. On the other hand, the study of the leg musculature of owls carried out by Berlin (1963) revealed that there is a close parallel between the *Strigiformes* and the *Falconiformes*, the owls lacking just two muscles, the ambiens (*Mm. ambiens*) and the *peroneus longus*. The musculature of the feet is powerfully developed (flexors). The toe structure is also very similar to that of diurnal birds of prey, the third and fourth toes having short, proximal phalanges.

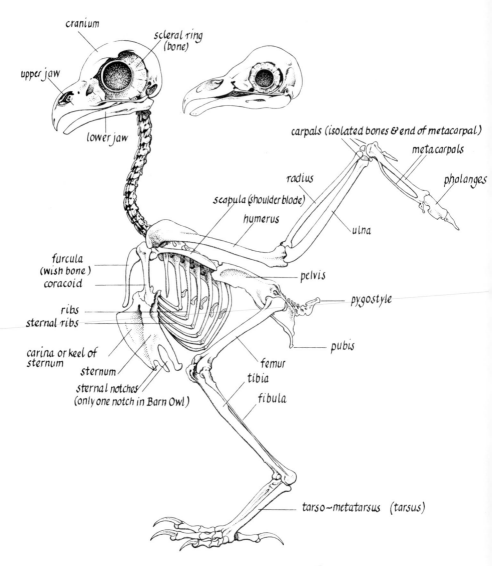

Fig. 2   *Skeleton of typical owl – in this instance Tawny Owl – with skull of Barn Owl for comparison, showing larger and more finely built bill, and smaller orbits that characterise the Tytonidae*

The brain is of the occipito-temporal type and is relatively large. In some owl species the external ears are very large and have a complicated geometry. The large apertures are frequently surrounded by a fold of skin with a highly developed system of motor muscles.

A most remarkable aspect of the external ear geometry is the bilateral asymmetry exhibited by species of nine genera: *Tyto, Phodilus, Bubo, Ciccaba, Strix, Rhinoptynx, Asio, Pseudoscops* and *Aegolius* (Norberg 1977). This asymmetry means that one ear is much larger than the other, often as much as 50% in some species; in addition it is usually placed higher on one side of the head than the other, the right ear usually being the larger and higher. The bilateral ear asymmetry extends to the temporal parts of the skull in only four owl species (Ural, Great Grey, Tengmalm's and Saw-whet Owl) and lies in the soft anatomy of the other owl species having asymmetrical ears. It involves the external ear only and has never been reported to extend to the middle or internal ear. The bilateral asymmetry of the external ears in owls is related to directional hearing or sound localisation ability (Norberg 1977). It should be emphasised, however, that the outer ears are perfectly symmetrical in the majority of owl species, in fact, as far as is known, in all species of the other 16 owl genera.

The feathers lack after-shafts but have long, downy bases. The ends of the barbicels are elongated, non-interlocking and produce soft plumage. Down is found solely on the *alar pterylae*. The coccygeal gland is naked (*Strigidae*) or nearly so (*Tytonidae*). The lower trachea (syrinx) has a single pair of muscles, frequently with a well-developed vocal membrane, which causes the wide variety of sounds emitted by owls. The tongue is fleshy, the crop is absent and the cecum is functional.

Fig. 3   Outer end of primary feather of typical owl, to show softened edges

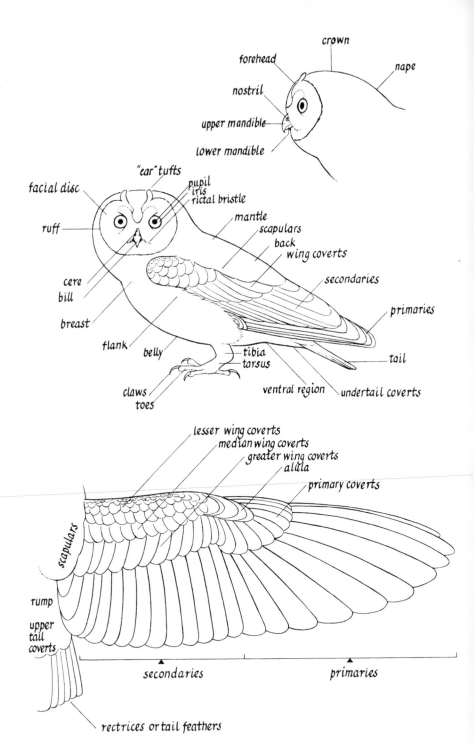

crown

forehead

nape

nostril

upper mandible

lower mandible

"ear" tufts

facial disc

pupil
iris
rictal bristle

mantle

scapulars

back

wing coverts

ruff

secondaries

primaries

cere
bill

breast

flank

belly

tibia

tarsus

claws

toes

ventral region

undertail coverts

tail

lesser wing coverts

median wing coverts

greater wing coverts

alula

primary coverts

scapulars

rump

upper
tail
coverts

secondaries

primaries

rectrices or tail feathers

Topography of a typical owl – the features shown are based on short-eared owl

4: External features

The feathering of the owls is soft and loose, with only certain northern species (Snowy Owl and Hawk Owl) having relatively stiff feathers clinging closely to the body. The feathers usually cover not only the tarsus (= tarsometatarsus) but also the toes. The unfeathered parts are the cere, which is covered with long, thick vibrissae or bristles pointing anteriorly, the lower surface of the toes, and sometimes the internal or rear surface of the tarsus. Certain exceptions to this rule occur, and these include the Brown Fish Owl which has bare tarsi and toes.

Camouflage, or cryptic coloration as it is often called, is a feature of most owls' plumage, and helps concealment when resting during the day. Woodland owls tend to be brown or grey in basic coloration and, as a general rule, birds found in coniferous woodland tend to be greyer than those inhabiting broad-leaved trees. Owls living in open habitats are typically paler, and those inhabiting desert country are distinctly sandy-coloured. Hume's Owl and the desert races of Little and Eagle Owl are in this category. Members of the same species can differ markedly in colour depending on the type of terrain they inhabit. Some types of owls are dimorphic, that is to say, the adult plumage has two basic colour variations, e.g. the Tawny Owl is typically brown but also has a rarer grey phase. Both variations of a dimorphic species have survival value, but in different habitats. Sexual colour dimorphism is usually absent with a few exceptions; for example, in the Snowy Owl, the female is barred whereas the male is pure white. Differences between juvenile and adult plumage are also usually absent, but there are some noticeable exceptions, such as Tengmalm's Owl. In such cases a plumage more or less, or exactly, resembling the adults is attained in October or November of their first year of life. The young Snowy Owl, however, which is very heavily barred, does not lose this plumage until considerably later. Many species tend to become paler or more whitish in old age.

The facial feathering forms the so-called facial disc, and is composed of disconnected feathers placed concentrically around the eyes and separated from the frontal, auricular and throat feathers by dense, short feathers. The remiges and rectrices are relatively soft, particularly their outer edges, which form a softened fringe (Fig. 3). This feature was thought to assist the owl in flying silently, but a recent study revealed that the removal of this fringe made no difference to the wing noise of the Tawny Owl (Neuhaus, Bratting and Schweizer 1972). All the same, owls do fly silently, which is a necessary asset for a group of birds that hunts its prey, by sound as well as sight, close to the ground. There are ten primary feathers, not including the rudimentary first primary concealed beneath the coverts, and twelve rectrices.

The bill is short, with a sharply decurved upper mandible displaying a terminal hook, with sharp cutting edges. The tarsometatarsus is relatively long. The toes have sharp, markedly curved, raptorial claws, and are used for striking and gripping the prey, the inner surfaces of the toes being equipped with pads with hard papillae. The feet are always four-toed, with the fourth toe reversible.

Most owls have relatively large, rounded wings which are somewhat shorter in those species which hunt in cover, and much longer in those which hunt in open country or are highly migratory. Owls' wings are broad, with a large area in comparison to the weight of the bird, or, in aeronautical terms, they have a low wing-loading (cf. Table 2). The higher the wing-loading, the more effort is required for the bird to support itself in the air, and the more noise the hard-working wings are likely to make. Owls with their low wing-loadings fly very buoyantly and effortlessly, without too much flapping and loss of energy. It enables them to glide easily and to fly slowly for long periods at a time.

A feature of owls is their big eyes. Their forward position on the face, together with their ability to blink with the upper eyelids, give owls a semi-human appearance, in which lies much of their appeal to man. The eyeballs of some large owls are, in fact, larger than our own.

Owls probably have the most frontally situated eyes of all birds, and the effect is heightened by the fact that their bills, unlike those of other raptors, are deflected more or less downwards to clear their field of vision. They have a rather narrow visual field of 110°, of which about 60° to 70° is overlapping; man, in comparison, sees a total field of 180°, of which about 140° is covered by both eyes (Fig. 4).

Like man, owls employ binocular vision, looking at an object with both eyes in order to judge its position accurately. This is known as the parallax method and becomes more effective the farther apart the eyes are placed. Larger owls have their

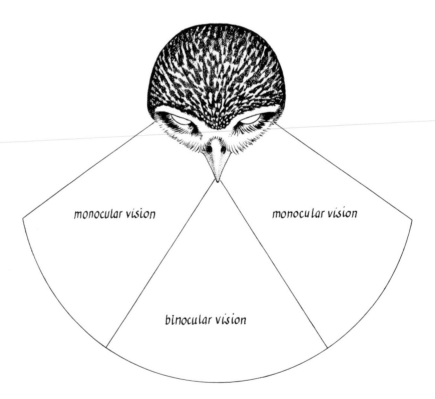

Fig. 4   Head of an owl, showing overall visual field and extent of binocular vision

Head-bobbing (left) and head-weaving (right) movements of owls

eyes well spaced, and it seems that the smaller species, by having flatter skulls, have developed as far as is physically reasonable in order to achieve wide spacing. Owls can further improve this three-dimensional vision by constantly moving and bobbing their heads, so that each eye sights the object under scrutiny from a variety of minutely different angles (see drawing above). The head-bobbing movements of some of the smaller owls may be amusing, but it is only the process of assessing as fully as possible what it sees before deciding what action to take.

The eyes themselves are immobile due to the fusing of the sclerotic ring with the skull. Optical immobility is compensated for by an exceptional ability to rotate the head (up to 270°), and by an extraordinary acuteness of hearing. This is made possible by adaptations in ear structure, which have modified the skull as profoundly as those of the eyes. The most obvious of these adaptations is the sheer size of the ear openings. Instead of fairly small round openings as in most birds, owls have surprisingly large, half-moon-shaped vertical slits, nearly as deep as the head itself. The facial discs, so characteristic of owls, are fringed by stiff, short feathers which border the openings, and are carried upon flaps, front and back, which can move to control the size of the ear opening. At the present stage of research the exact amount of muscular control that the owl has over the facial disc and the skin flaps of the ear openings is not known. However, this aural dexterity enables owls to scan different parts of their environment for sounds in the same way that many mammals can move their external ears. The 'ear-tufts' which many species possess, have, in fact, nothing to do with the sense of hearing. Ear-tufts only express mood and act as night-time recognition signals. They may also aid camouflage by breaking the outline of the owl's head.

5: Some unique aspects of the owl physique

Owls are largely nocturnal and have well-adapted eyes to hunt their prey in poor light. As in all nocturnal birds, the retina has many more rods than cones. Rods are sensitive to poor illumination, but give an imperfect colour vision, or none at all, and a poor ability to distinguish fine details. Cones, on the other hand, of which diurnal birds have a predominance over the whole of the retina, as well as the central area where rods are absent, are associated with colour vision and good visual acuity. The eye of an owl has become elongated by the development of a greatly enlarged cornea and lens. In this way the maximum amount of light enters the eye and a brighter image falls on the retina. Some of the resolution is lost, however, because this light is falling on rods which are not sensitive to fine image details. Another adaptation to poor illumination is that the retina and lens have been brought closer together. Thus the image is less dispersed and consequently brighter. However, as a result the image is smaller, being spread over fewer retinal cells, though this is partly compensated for by the large size of the eye. In its turn, the greater size is at the expense of a wide field of vision, but, as previously stated, owls can rotate their heads 270° to compensate for this disadvantage. The eye of an Eagle Owl (Fig. 5) shows a relatively shortened retina and a huge, highly convex lens. In all birds, the eyeball is protected by a ring of small bony plates (scleral ossicles) and in owls these form a long, bony tube. In many hawks the eye is superficially similar. They, as most predatory birds, need high resolution from great distances. They have as large an eye as possible, with a somewhat flattened lens and no proportionate enlargement or reduction of the retinal area. The lens is therefore at a greater distance from the retina and provides a larger image on the retina, while the highly curved cornea allows plenty of light to enter the eye, and with the image falling mainly on cones, this means a good resolution (Fig. 5) (cf. Burton 1973 and Katharine Tansley, in Landsborough Thomson *et al* 1964).

A popular misconception is that owls are blind by daylight. This is patently untrue, because many owls are able to hunt in daylight and none are helpless. Eagle Owls have been found to possess vision more acute in daylight than man. This is made possible by an exceptional range of aperture (pupil size) controlled by the iris.

As the eyes of owls have to operate by day and night, the range of adjustment called for by the iris must be correspondingly great. By day the iris muscles constrict to shut down light to the sensitive retina. When needed for the dark this shield is drawn right back, and in species which have yellow or orange irises, these are reduced to thin, narrow rings surrounding the shiny, black pupils so that the lens is exposed to catch every possible ray of light.

It is always difficult to prove whether an animal can perceive colour. As owls have some cones in their retina, it seems likely that they can do so when the light is good – like diurnal birds whose colour vision is exceptionally good compared with others in the animal kingdom. However, experiments on a crepuscular Little Owl, which was taught to distinguish colours against a series of greys matched for their luminance, showed beyond reasonable doubt that it could perceive yellow, green and blue; red and the darkest grey were confused (Sparks and Soper 1970).

Lindblad (1967) has studied how much light owl species need to find their prey by sight (Table 3). These experiments showed that Tawny, Ural and Long-eared Owls are able to see and to approach dead prey, directly, from a distance of two metres or more under an illumination calculated to be as low as 0.000 000 16 to 0.000 000 25 foot candle. So these owls can see their prey readily, even in a dark forest where the light

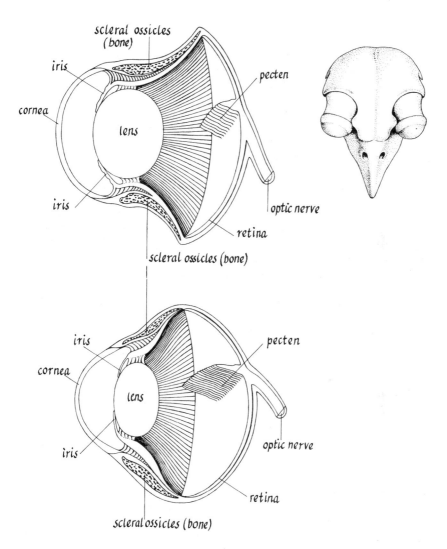

Fig. 5   Cross-sections of eye of Eagle Owl (top left) *and Golden Eagle* (below). *The smaller drawing shows the tubular eyes of a typical owl within the eye sockets of the skull*

may be 0.000 000 4 foot candle. Man, Tengmalm's Owl and Pygmy Owl can see nothing in such light. The Pygmy Owl's sight in darkness was the poorest of the owls studied, its sight being twice as poor as in man.

Assertions that the owl is visually sensitive to infra-red radiation given out by the body of a prey animal have been proved incorrect (Payne 1962, Konishi 1973).

HEARING

An owl's sense of hearing is no less remarkable than its exceptional sight, the two working in conjunction to enable the bird to penetrate darkness.

The inner ear of owls is very large, and the auditory region of the brain is provided with many more nerve cells than in other birds of comparable size, which explains why owls have such exceptionally sensitive hearing although some songbirds may be able to hear frequencies as high as can, for example, the Barn Owl (Konishi 1970). The same authority (Konishi 1973) compared the hearing of man, the domestic cat and the Barn Owl (see Fig. 6). It seems that the cat and the owl have very similar auditory sensitivities up to about 7 kHz, beyond which the cat continues to be sensitive, whereas the owl's sensitivity starts to decline sharply. Both animals are much more sensitive than man in the frequency range of about 500 Hz to 10 kHz.

How does the owl locate a moving animal in the dark? Small rodents obviously make noises when moving about and such sounds provide all the information needed for the owl to locate it. On first hearing a rustle from an animal, in complete darkness, the owl turns its head towards the sound source. The facial disc may act as an amplifier, collecting and focussing sound from a large area. Once the owl has faced its intended prey, it needs to hear at least one additional sound before striking. By moving its head around until the sound registers equally in both ears, the owl will be facing its prey, which is an obvious advantage when the prey cannot be seen. A special factor, which is clearly important in many species, is the asymmetrical placing of the ear openings (Payne 1962). This means that a sound will be perceived by one ear fractionally before the other. The minute time difference, some 0.00003 seconds, is sufficient to be perceived by the owl and to indicate the direction of the sound source. The sound will also be louder in the ear nearer the sound source, at least for sounds with the wavelength equivalent to or shorter than the width of the head.

What happens if, after the owl takes off, the prey moves or stops making any sounds? The experiments of Konishi (1973) with trained Barn Owls reveal that the owl can make course corrections in mid-flight (as in man's moon shots) in order to strike the target accurately. The minute adjustments necessary to bring the head into line again should the prey move, will be made in flight as the owl swings down, gently flapping, towards the sound source. As the owl comes within a range of about 60 cm from the prey, it brings its feet forward and spreads the talons in an oval pattern. Just before striking the prey, it stretches its legs forward ahead of its face and wings, often closing its eyes during this last phase of the strike.

It would seem that an owl is capable of locating and striking an unseen living prey animal in complete darkness, using only its acute sense of hearing for guidance. However, in the wild, conditions are rather different and there is never total darkness where an owl is likely to hunt. It is possible, therefore, though not proven, that the night-time hunting owl combines its acute visual and aural abilities.

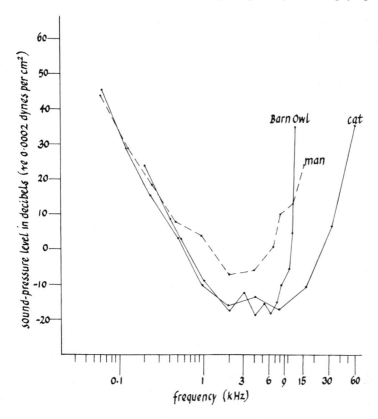

Fig. 6 Comparison of minimum audible fields of man, cat and Barn Owl. The cat and owl can hear faint sounds undetected by man. (From M. Konishi, American Scientist, *Vol 61, 1973)*

GASTRIC DIGESTION

Except for the very largest items, owls usually swallow their prey whole, unlike the diurnal raptors, which tend to dismember it and swallow selected parts. In owls, the process of sorting out what is nourishing and what is not takes place internally. An owl retains its animal meal within the ventriculus by closure of the sphincter between the ventriculus and proventriculus; the pyloric opening, which is small and arises superiorly, probably remains open during most of the digestive process. In this contracting and relaxing pouch enzymatic secretions collect, arising from the glands of the proventriculus, small intestine and pancreas.

As digestion proceeds, the nutrient effluent is pumped into the small intestine by ventricular contractions. Indigestible solids, e.g. bone, fur, teeth, nails and chitinous materials, collect in the inferior portion of the ventriculus and are gradually forced into a tight pellet form. The length of time between feeding and regurgitation of a pellet is subject to internal and external factors (cf. Chitty 1938). In a hungry Great Horned Owl *Bubo virginianus* studied by Grimm and Whitehouse (1963) in their laboratory, pellet formation was essentially complete eight hours after feeding.

Before regurgitation, an event Guérin (1928) held to be voluntary, the pellet lies in the superior portion of the ventriculus immediately below the sphincter. At expulsion the sphincter is relaxed and ventricular contraction, with accessory contractions of the abdominal wall and proventriculus, forces the pellet upwards in a series of steps until it is finally discharged; the process in the Great Horned Owl taking approximately four minutes (Grimm and Whitehouse 1963).

Although the general enzymatic action in digestion is little known, there is evidence that in young owls the gastric pH is distinctly acidic, becoming more neutral in older birds. Higher pH excludes pepsin as the active proteolytic enzyme, thus indicating that the food digestion ability of young owls should be more efficient than that of adults. The importance of pH becomes clearer if we compare the basal pH of owls and diurnal raptors studied by Duke *et al* (1975).

The basal pH for the owls is about 2.35 (range of means = 2.2–2.5) compared with that of diurnal raptors which averages about 1.6 (range of means = 1.3–1.8). Therefore, owls have about six times less hydrogen ion per ml in their basal gastric secretion than diurnal birds of prey, a physiologically significant difference.

The low pH of the stomach is undoubtedly more vital to bone digestion than proteolytic activity. Therefore, the low pH of the *Falconiformes'* gastric juices appears to explain the more successful digestion of their food compared with that of owls, by virtue of their greater ability to digest bones. The average proportion of bones in the pellets was strikingly more in owls than in *Falconiformes*, namely 45.8% and 6.5% respectively. The proportion of ingested food appearing as pellets was considerably more in owls than in hawks and eagles, averaging 12.5% and 5.2% respectively (cf. Duke *et al* 1975).

Apparently, owls digest soft foods approximately as well as hawks, but not mineral nutrients, and, therefore, owls receive about equal caloric benefit from their diet. Food intake (g/day per kg) is generally less in owls than in the *Falconiformes* (Duke *et al* 1975).

Unlike diurnal birds of prey, owls have no crop in which to store their food. Instead, they must catch small amounts of food at regular intervals.

6: Owl pellets

The undigested portions of food consumed by owls are not excreted in the normal manner as faeces, but are compressed into compact masses and ejected through the mouth as the owl makes retching movements. These castings or pellets usually contain the bones, claws, bills or teeth of mammals, birds, reptiles, amphibians and fishes, fragments of the external armour of insects, and even identifiable remains from worms and other invertebrates. These hard parts are usually enclosed by softer, but indigestible, substances such as the fur of mammals, bird feathers and vegetable fibres. Where captive owls are unable to collect sufficient binding materials in the food supplied, they turn to substances quite unrelated to their normal foodstuffs. Glue (1969) relates that captive Barn and Little Owls have produced pellets bound with polythene, paper, paper clips and rubber bands.

Generally speaking, the largest owls produce the largest pellets (Table 4). On average, those of the Eagle Owl are 77 × 31 × 28 mm (100 pellets) whereas the Pygmy Owl's pellets are only 27 × 11 × 9 mm (100 pellets). The sizes of Scops and Little Owl pellets are missing from Table 4 because I have been unable to measure any of their fragile pellets. However, Géroudet (1965) gave some dimensions for Little Owl and März (1972) listed some for Scops Owl: Little Owl pellets 20 to 40 mm in length and 10 to 20 mm across and those of Scops Owl 20 to 30 mm in length and 10 to 12 mm in thickness. On average, Little Owl pellets measure 37 × 15 mm (Mebs 1966) and Scops Owl pellets 25 × 10 mm (Baudvin 1976).

Strong winds and rain are known to affect the hunting success of open country species like the Barn Owl, which may produce a small pellet in consequence; and wet conditions often result in Tawny Owls casting up small, brown, hard pellets. These fibre pellets contain the remains of earthworms, beetles, slugs or other invertebrates, which are often readily available prey in wet weather (Glue in Burton 1973).

The dimensions (weight, length and diameter) of pellets ejected by captive individuals of Tengmalm's Owl and Short-eared Owl showed a considerable seasonal variation; the pellets being twice as large in spring and autumn as in summer and winter (Erkinaro 1973). The author explained this variation on the basis of the owl's daily activity rhythm and its seasonal changes. In spring and autumn, when the pellets were at their largest, the owls maintained a long, almost uninterrupted rest phase by day, whereas in summer and winter their activity was spread evenly throughout the 24 hour period.

During his laboratory experiments with Tengmalm's Owl and Short-eared Owl, Erkinaro (1973) came to another interesting conclusion that there is no correlation between the amount of food taken in and the size of the pellet produced, although this was true only of these laboratory experiments quoted here. Occasionally, after feeding on large prey such as the Brown Rat *Rattus norvegicus*, Water Vole *Arvicola amphibius* or young Rabbits *Oryctolagus cuniculus*, Tawny Owls may produce pellets as large as 80 mm × 30 mm (Witherby *et al* 1940). Similar Barn Owl pellets, produced after a successful night's hunting, have contained up to 13 Pygmy Shrews *Sorex minutus*, 9 Common Shrews *Sorex araneus* and 7 Short-tailed Voles *Microtus agrestis* (Glue 1969).

The shape and even the colouring of pellets is sometimes diagnostic of the species that produced them, although their properties will naturally depend to some extent upon the owl's diet at the time. Normally it is not too difficult to distinguish Barn Owl and Tawny Owl pellets. Those of the Barn Owl are compact, often rounded, hard and commonly blackish, even when dry, with a characteristic varnished appearance. Tawny Owl pellets are grey when dry and of a very friable consistency (Witherby *et al* 1940).

Two pellets are usually formed each day and these are often deposited at daytime roosts, or at nest-sites, but their accumulation varies from species to species. The habits of two of the more widely studied owls, the open country Barn Owl and the woodland-dwelling Tawny Owl, illustrate this point. Barn Owls tend to remain faithful to their hideouts year in and year out, so that a large number of pellets may accumulate in one place. Tawny Owls, on the other hand, tend to change their roosting sites quite often, and so the indigestible remains of their meals will be accordingly dispersed. In fact, Tawny Owls release their pellets while flying in search of prey (Guérin 1932), making the task of collecting them in quantity rather time-consuming.

Although sophisticated techniques can be used to assess the contents of intact pellets, such as X-ray photography or chemicals (for example, boiling them in NaOH (sodium hydroxide)), the best method is to break them down in a dry state with dissecting needles or forceps. The hard parts (bones and chitinous fragments) are separated from the softer substances (fur, feathers and fibre), and individual prey items are examined under a good pocket lens or a low power microscope.

Mammals can usually be identified quite easily from their skulls, jaws or teeth. Birds' bills provide helpful clues to their identity, as do their skulls, sterna and pelvic girdles, but these may not always be intact.

Some owls, like the Tawny Owl, may render the task of pellet analysis more difficult because they do not always bolt their food whole. The skulls of their victims may be crushed before they are swallowed and very fragile crania, or brain cases, may not withstand the acidic stomach juices of the owls. Soft-bodied foods, such as nestling birds and certain invertebrates, are easily overlooked or not properly identified. Small mammals or birds may be decapitated or larger food items may be partially consumed (often when parent owls are feeding their young), thereby complicating any analysis.

The number of small mammals is frequently deduced by counting the skulls, but this method usually results in an underestimate during the breeding season, since the male often eats the fore part of the prey and takes only the remainder to the nest. In such cases, mammal leg bones and those of birds (ulna, humerus and tarsus) aid the calculations.

Are the results of pellet analysis a reliable guide to the food intake of owls? It would seem that insufficient attention has been given to the possibility that the number of animals in an owl pellet, calculated from the skeletal remains, may be smaller than the actual number of individuals originally consumed. The frequently absent portions of the skulls of voles and mice in Tawny Owl pellets were found by V. P. W. Lowe in his experiments of feeding these birds in captivity. Detailed data have not been published but some figures are given in a paper by Southern (1970). Raczyński and Ruprecht (1974) have made a comprehensive study on the effect of digestion on the osteological composition of owl pellets. By analysing owl pellets, determinations were made of the elements missing from skeletons of birds and mammals fed to three species of owls

(Tawny, Long-eared and Barn Owl). It was discovered that the pelvic girdle is most often missing (up to 80%), with skulls (up to 35%) and mandibulae (maximum 25%) less often; the reason for their disappearance being the digestion of these bones. In general the largest number of missing portions of the skeleton occurred in the Tawny Owl (51%), and the Long-eared Owl (46%), with the smallest number in the Barn Owl (34%). Losses in the number of individuals identified in owl pellets were correspondingly: 16% for Tawny, 20% for Long-eared and 8% for Barn Owl. The number of missing elements of the skeleton was in reverse proportion to the age of the owls and their prey.

The high degree of digestion of bones observed in young Tawny and Long-eared Owls can be explained by the relatively short period of time they remain in the nest. Unlike those two species, the Barn Owl, whose young remain in the nest for seven to eight weeks, digested bones to a lesser extent.

Raczyński and Ruprecht's observations reveal (if the birds used in their experiments were behaving as they would in the wild) that one should allow for intensive digestion of bones, even in the case of owls, and also that this process is probably strictly physiological in character. Nevertheless, it should be pointed out that there are many differences in the digestive abilities of individual owls, especially between different owl species, and one should neither dismiss nor undervalue studies which are based upon pellets.

A number of short experiments of up to two months' duration, which I carried out with Tengmalm's, Hawk, Short-eared, Long-eared, Ural and Great Grey Owls, indicated that the animal remains found in their pellets reflected exactly the animals fed to them. Other experiments conducted with owls also suggest that if they are fed a number of rodents a corresponding number of skulls, or matching sets of jaws, can be recovered from the subsequently ejected pellets (Oleś 1961, Short and Drew 1962, Hagen 1965, Wolk 1965 and others).

Pellets remain a useful source of data. Careful searching in the field, patient analysis in the laboratory and careful interpretation of findings can provide a wealth of information about the feeding habits of owls.

It should also be remembered that not only the ornithologist can derive data from examining owl pellets. What we find in them can sometimes produce very useful information on the distribution of the prey animals themselves. Small mammals are sometimes a difficult subject to study and any knowledge of their distribution is welcome to the mammalogist.

Sometimes pellets yield very interesting information about the behaviour of mammals that is not easily obtainable by other means. For example, moles occur regularly in the menus of Tawny and Barn Owls. Indeed, in one owl study they accounted for nearly half the food intake, by weight, of Tawny Owls between May and October. Clearly, the owls do not hunt moles underground and it seems probable, therefore, that moles visit the surface, or scrape around beneath the moss or leaf litter, rather more often than might have been supposed (Sparks and Soper 1970). Data obtained from owl pellets have also been used in a wide variety of ecological studies. For instance, on a count of *ossa innominata* (hip bones), calculations have been made of numbers and density of species forming the chief component of owls' food, and of sex proportions in the populations of some mammal species. Recently, owl pellets collected under field conditions have been used for bioenergetic evaluations to define food requirements and to determine the energy budget of owls. A circumstance (in addition to bone losses) rendering elaborations of this kind difficult, is the fact that the collection of owl pellets is probably incomplete, as some are usually dropped away from the owl's day-time roosting place. Attempts have also been made to define the effect of owl predation on numbers for various common species of Micromammalia. The results of Raczyński's and Ruprecht's studies, however, require a critical evaluation of the use hitherto made of owl pellets, both for ornithological and theoretical purposes.

PART II

SPECIES DESCRIPTIONS

7: Barn Owl *Tyto alba*
(Scopoli)

DESCRIPTION

The upperparts are orange-buff, spotted with dark grey and white, mainly in the form of variable patches. The face is white, as are the underparts, although the latter may sometimes be speckled with a few black spots. Occasionally there is an orange-buff tinge on the breast, sometimes restricted to the sides only. Females usually have a greater number of dark spots, even when their underparts are pure white. The primaries and secondaries are pale orangey-buff on the outer webs with much white on the inner webs. They are tipped with soft edgings, speckled grey and barred with three to four narrow dark bars, these markings being very fine on the palest individuals. The tail is medium or pale orangey-buff with four dark bars and a pale grey, finely speckled tip. The underwing is white with a few faint greyish bars on the primary-tips. The bill is ivory-coloured and the relatively small eyes are black. A variable purplish-brown wash spreads downwards from the lower, inner corner of each eye. The long slender legs are covered with narrow white feathers and the dirty yellow-brown feet are bristled. The claws are black and the middle one is comb-like.

The above description applies only to the nominate or typical race *T. a. alba* inhabiting Britain and parts of western and southern Europe. This white-breasted Barn Owl is replaced to the north and east by the dark-breasted Barn Owl *T. a.*

guttata, which is a much darker subspecies. It has generally dark buffish-brown and heavily spotted underparts and dark grey and orange upperparts, the grey being heavily speckled and more predominant than in the nominate race. The flight-feathers and tail are similar to, but darker and more orange than those of *T. a. alba*. The underwing-coverts are the same colour as the underbody, liberally covered with dark spots and the undersides of the flight-feathers are dirty grey with dark barring on their outer halves and sooty brown speckled tips to the primaries. The facial disc is vinous or whitish with a distinct purplish-brown patch spreading out in front of the eye. The facial ruff is brownish-chestnut with black tips. Voous (1950) has shown that intermediates between this race and *T. a. alba* occur in the Alps, Rhine Valley, The Netherlands, Belgium, Luxembourg and northern and central France, and Barn Owls in these areas do manifest an extremely wide range of individual variation and an independent inheritance of all variable characteristics. Hybridisation between *alba* and *guttata* takes place continuously and the genes inducing the brown coloration of the underparts have spread at the expense of the white colouring. Females of either race tend to be darker than the males in all European and North African populations, but there is much variation in both sexes.

Unlike other European owls the young Barn Owl has two downy stages and does not develop a mesoptile plumage. The first natal down is short and pure white, sparse on the belly, lacking on the sides of the neck though it covers the legs down to the claws except for the back of the tarsus. A second coat of down replaces the first within 12 to 14 days; it is long, thick, buffish-cream in colour with the first down clinging to its tips (Harrison 1975). Because of the absence of a mesoptile plumage immatures are almost identical to adults in appearance.

The overall length of European Barn Owls varies between 330 and 390 mm in either sex (Géroudet 1965). Voous (1950) lists the wing length of males as 259–309 mm (average 286 mm from 174 birds) and of females as 263–305 mm (average 287 mm from 164 birds). Much data was collected in Britain, southern Scandinavia, central and southern Europe and North Africa (see below) and the wing measurements themselves do not apparently correlate in any significant way with geographical origin (number of birds in brackets).

	Sweden	Britain	C. Europe	S. Europe	N. Africa
Wing length (mm)	289 (27)	287 (75)	286 (221)	286 (15)	292 (8)

However, Prestt and Wagstaffe (1973) pointed out that the wing of the dark-breasted Barn Owl is slightly larger than that of the nominate race and some of Baudvin's (1975) measurements support their view. The average 'fresh' wing length was 297 mm for *guttata* and 291 mm for *alba*, the average from 22 measurements being 294 mm for either race. It is interesting to note that the average of Baudvin's measurements is much higher than any in Voous' material, in which the average for France was 285 mm (N=8). The reason seems to be that Baudvin measured living birds and not museum specimens, whereas some of the latter were probably measured after natural shrinkage had occurred.

Males weigh between 280 and 365 g (average 312 g from 17 birds) and females between 290 and 450 g (average 362 g from 55 birds) (Baudvin 1975). These figures show the female to be 50 g heavier, a strange fact when one remembers that on average the sexes have equal wing lengths. Perhaps the width of the wing differs, although no comparative study appears to have been made on this subject. Weights also demonstrate that the dark-breasted Barn Owl is slightly larger than the White-breasted subspecies but, unfortunately, Baudvin (1975) did not take into consideration the known sexual differences in his comparison:

Tyto alba alba	337 g (N=63)
Tyto alba guttata	346 g (N=32)
Total	340 g (N=95)

The North American Barn Owl *T. a. pratincola* is generally similar to the European races and includes light and dark forms, but is of notably larger size. The average weight of 16 males given by Earhart and Johnson (1970) was 442 g and that of 21 females 490 g.

IN THE FIELD

The white-breasted race is the only owl with a white heart-shaped facial disc, dark eyes and no ear-tufts, with golden-buff above and white below. The dark-breasted race is darker above and on the facial disc, and brownish-buff below, including the underwing-coverts. The flight-feathers are dull greyish on the underside. As indicated by its long wings, the Barn Owl is a bird of open habitats. The Short-eared Owl, another open-country owl of about the same size, is easily distinguished from the Barn Owl by its striped underparts, well-feathered legs and toes, yellow eyes and a darker, very differently-shaped facial disc. When flying the Barn Owl appears more markedly 'owl-like' due to its large head and light, moth-like flight. It appears very buoyant as it sweeps backwards and forwards over the ground seeking its prey.

It is normally most active in the evening or at night, when it can be found on its regular hunting grounds, but it will also hunt by day in the winter or when feeding young. It roosts in dark places in ruins, churches, barns and lofts of old houses, in holes and crevices in cliffs and caves, in hollow trees and, more rarely, conifers. In spite of its light coloration it is not easy to find a roosting owl, which, for instance, may stand bolt upright, pressed into a dark corner under a barn roof. If disturbed while roosting it flies only a short distance before re-alighting.

The ample proportions of a Barn Owl's wings mean that in flight the bird's weight is well supported by air flowing over relatively large surface areas. In fact, the dumpy, barrel-shaped appearance of a Barn Owl, in common with many other owls, is the result of loose, deep plumage covering a surprisingly small body. Sparks and Soper (1970) described a Barn Owl, weighing 500 g, as having a wing area of about 1,700 cm^2, which means that the wing loading was only 0.29 g/cm^2 (also Brüll 1964). By comparison a male and female Tawny Owl that I studied were only slightly heavier (male 580 g and female 600 g) than the Barn Owl but had a wing-loading of 0.40 g/cm^2 (Table 2). With their low wing-loading Barn Owls glide easily and can fly leisurely through woodlands, or quarter the ground at comparatively low speeds. Buoyant flight, which is a result of low wing-loading, has an important survival value for Barn Owls, as they are more adept than other medium-sized owls in avoiding their raptor and owl enemies, even in open spaces.

VOICE

The Barn Owl's 'song' is a loud, drawn-out, hissing scream *shrrreeeeee* with a marked gargling or tremulous effect. A typical scream lasts about two seconds and is often uttered in flight. The female's full screech usually has a different tone from the male's and is not so perfectly delivered, tending to break off into a less tremulous scream (Bunn 1974).

Before emerging from its day-time roost, the male frequently gives a series of subdued screeches. If the female is present screeching duets are regular, the screech being repeated with great regularity every fourth second (Witherby *et al* 1952).

Besides the screeching 'song', the Barn Owl emits purring, wailing, screaming, hissing, snoring, chirruping, twittering and squeaking notes. During coition the male will utter a repeated staccato squeaking, plaintive in tone and quite different from the ordinary squeaking notes. The young have a series of chittering or twittering sounds peculiar to them and very characteristic of their first month of life. They have also been recorded uttering some of the adults' calls while still in the nest. A highly distinctive, fast, chattering twitter stimulates the owlets to beg for food. The male uses it during the food presentation and the female will use it at the nest from the day before the first egg hatches until the young are able to feed themselves unassisted. Bunn (1974) has described and interpreted in fuller detail all the above-mentioned calls, which were heard during his long-term study of the Barn Owl voice.

In Witherby *et al* (1940) it is stated that, like other owls, the Barn Owl snaps its bill when angry. However, during his long study of this species Bunn (1974) was not satisfied with this explanation. He suggested that the closing of the bill is too gentle to create such a hard sound and maintained that it is actually produced by the movement of the back of the tongue in the muscular pharynx as the organ is withdrawn. Therefore, instead of 'bill-snapping' perhaps the term 'tongue-clicking', as coined by Bunn, ought to be adopted when describing this sound, which is common to all European owls.

Outside the breeding season the Barn Owl is largely silent although a single screech may be frequently uttered at dusk as it flies from its roost. Throughout the year the paired male will greet his mate with a squeaky chirrup whenever he looks at her, to which she responds by squeaking (Bunn and Warburton 1977).

BEHAVIOUR

The Barn Owl is predominantly sedentary and many birds retain essentially the same territory throughout the year. The size of the territory depends greatly on the availability of nest sites and food, a fact which sometimes leads to the creation of loose breeding colonies. Smith *et al* (1974) studied a colony of 28 owls, in which two pairs occupied in effect the same home range, whilst the home ranges of three additional pairs showed an approximate 55–70% overlap. Pairs with greatly overlapping home ranges were weak territorily and commonly defended a patch of ground only 5–10 m around the nest.

Most adults remain paired throughout the winter when they are frequently to be found roosting side by side. Mutual preening is the main form of pair-bonding behaviour at these roosts. Weather influences the choice of roosting sites and a pair will move into the most protected recesses during the coldest months (Smith *et al* 1974).

Weather also has an effect on the start of courtship activities, which in a mild winter may commence as early as February, when the male begins to exhibit marked territorial behaviour by increased screeching. Occasionally, trespassing males will be driven off with furious, harsh screeches. The male adopts a kind of 'song flight' to mark the boundaries of his territory, which consists of flying backwards and forwards while repeatedly screeching. A display flight which includes wing-clapping sometimes occurs in the female's presence, the male hovering momentarily in front of her clapping his wings either softly or loudly. The male will often pursue his mate around the nesting area, sometimes with great vigour, both sexes typically uttering the most unearthly screeches and wails, although occasionally silent flights may take place. Frequently, the male will suddenly swoop into the nesting barn whence his screeching attracts the female. Bunn and Warburton (1977) believe this behaviour to be particularly important in pair formation comparing it to the 'in and out flights' of some hole-nesting passerines.

In March the female becomes sexually active, greeting the male with 'snores' and regularly emitting this sound in his presence. This has an effect of stimulating the male, being in essence a juvenile call, and he responds by bringing her prey items. Copulation almost always follows food presentation and is accompanied by the female, still holding the prey in her bill, snoring loudly while the male utters a staccato squeak (Bunn 1974).

A good description of the early breeding period has been written by Bunn and Warburton (1977): 'From the onset of breeding activity until the eggs are laid, the male frequently searches the roosting barn for suitable nesting sites and, having found a dark corner or crevice, crouches and begins purring, revolving round, poking about with his bill and stamping or scraping with his feet to form a nest hollow. This invariably attracts the female and the two crouch down together, with lowered wings, the female snoring and tongue-clicking in excitement. This behaviour nearly always culminates in copulation, which is extraordinarily frequent: from early March until the first egg is laid, it occurs every few minutes during the evenings.'

As with most owls abroad by day, the Barn Owl is frequently mobbed by small birds. In its turn this owl will tolerate the immediate presence of smaller birds but will avoid the Beech Marten *Martes foina* (Baudvin 1975). House Sparrows *Passer domesticus*, Jackdaws *Corvus monedula* and Kestrels *Falco tinnunculus* frequently share the same nest site entrance as Barn Owls with no apparent complications (Fellowes 1967, Baudvin 1975).

In the presence of an observer the adults are usually shy at the breeding site, slipping out before the intruder can approach closely, and the young can often be handled without difficulty. On occasions the young will take up a defensive attitude which is somewhat different from other owls, by crouching or lying flat on the ground stretching the head forward with wings spread horizontally. This posture is also adopted in the presence of a cat (Hubl 1952). Anger is expressed by lowering the head, swinging it from side to side close to the ground with wings drooped, and simultaneously hissing and clicking the tongue (Witherby *et al* 1940).

The Barn Owl's breeding activity was studied almost fifty years ago in 1935 by Bussmann using an automatic device to register the adults' movements to and from the nest. By attaching his terragraph to a nest containing four young, Bussmann found the feeding activity of the parent owls began between 20.50 and 23.25 hr (average 21.43 hr in 26 days between 31st May and 30th June), and ended between

Defensive posture of Barn Owl

00.25 and 04.15 hr (average 03.17 hr). Bussmann's birds therefore spent anything from an hour to almost seven-and-a-half hours hunting every night (an average of a little over five-and-a-half hours per night). In July and August of the following year, again at a nest with four young, Bussmann (1937) calculated from his evidence that the adults made an average of 11.3 feeding visits per night, spanning a hunting period averaging 5 hr 33 min.

More recently in East Germany Ritter and Görner (1977) studied the Barn Owl's feeding activity at a nest with five young (only one fledged) between 9th June and 14th September. The mean number of daily visits with food was 3.3 during the incubation period and 4.1 in the remainder of the breeding season. The number of feeding visits per day decreased whenever the weather deteriorated into periods of rain or strong wind. In fact Barn Owls do not hunt at all during heavy rain and will commence later or finish earlier if the wind is too strong.

These same two ornithologists found that the birds' circadian rhythm exhibited two phases during nights of normal weather conditions. Hunting commenced shortly after sunset and the first peak of activity occurred about an hour later, between 21.00 and 22.00 hr at the East German nest site (Fig. 7). Around midnight activity waned slightly and the second peak (as high as the first one) was between 01.00 and 02.00 hr. Only occasionally did hunting continue after sunrise (Fig. 7).

An interesting Egyptian record of hunting by artificial light has recently been published (Short and Horne 1981). The authors write that 'Barn Owls several times foraged in the floodlights of the Sound and Light show at the Gizeh pyramids, in the period 1976–1979.'

Barn Owls frequently hunt in daylight, especially in the winter. Dickson (1972) has seen a Barn Owl hunting 66 minutes before sunset in November and in December five owls observed by Bunn (1972) in Yorkshire, England, continued to hunt up to two hours after sunrise. Throughout the first two months of 1979 in the Loch Ken valley, in south-west Scotland, during a period of exceptionally severe frosts and heavy snowfall, Barn Owls could be seen at almost any time of the day, quartering the snowbound field edges and frozen marshes. Ian and Diane Willis often travelled up and down the valley at this time and never failed to see a hunting owl, sometimes several in a few kilometres, from an hour and a half after sunrise until late afternoon. It seems likely that the very low temperatures, which fell to −18.5°C in the district on some nights, and froze the snow-covered herbage solid for weeks on end, created great difficulties for the hunting birds, forcing them to hunt for longer periods than usual. But this cannot be the only reason for daylight hunting in winter because IW has witnessed it in the same locality during fairly mild spells.

In the summer months adult Barn Owls emerge from their nesting places well before dusk in order to find enough food for their growing young. In his study areas in northern England Bunn (1972) found that some Barn Owls often hunted in daylight at all times of the year. Hunger is probably the main factor determining whether a bird hunts by day or not and at what time it does so, but as already mentioned, weather affects hunting in that continuous rain prevents hunting and strong winds will curtail it.

Laboratory tests carried out by Erkert (1969) have shown that Barn Owl activity reaches a peak at a certain light intensity. According to his researches, the optimum activity lies at 0.4 lux for Barn and Long-eared Owls and is between 4.6 and 155 lux for the Little Owl, revealing that the owls' circadian rhythm is directly influenced by light. Even the distance that the Barn Owl flies, as well as the speed of its flight, are directly related to the degree of illumination.

Dice (1945) calculated that the Barn Owl can approach dead prey from about two metres when the illumination is 0.000 002 foot-candle but that it has some difficulties

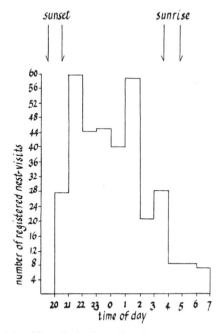

Fig. 7   Feeding activity of Barn Owl at Jena, East Germany (Ritter and Görner 1977) on 88 days between 9th June and 14th September

in seeing carcasses even under otherwise favourable conditions when the incident light is reduced to 0.000 000 53 foot-candle. A Barn Owl is therefore inadequately equipped for the poor light conditions of a dark wood, where the light registers a mere 0.000 000 4 foot-candle, and it would be unable to see mice moving about in the leaf litter, unlike more keenly-sighted species such as Long-eared, Tawny and Ural Owls. Some difficulty might even be experienced in open areas on cloudy, moonless nights.

However, the Barn Owl's extraordinary hearing fully compensates for its relatively poor eyesight. It can recognise and locate its prey by hearing alone in complete darkness (Payne 1971, Konishi 1973). The acoustical recognition of prey is based on the owl's ability to remember and distinguish their rustles from other sounds. The Barn Owl can memorise single frequencies and detect minute deviations from them (Quine and Konishi 1974). Laboratory experiments suggest that the Barn Owl can learn to remember complex noise spectra and distinguish them from slightly different spectral patterns (Konishi and Kenuk 1975).

Certain questions about the Barn Owl as a hunter have yet to be answered. It is not known, for example, to what extent they rely on the faint light of dawn and dusk, or moonlight, or how much hunting is done in more or less total darkness. As a predator it is certainly a diligent, active bird, whether searching for its prey from a low perch or hunting post or, as it more usually does, on the wing. Its hunting flights often follow regular beats. On several evenings in June 1977, Ian and Diane Willis observed a breeding male hunting in Parham Park, Sussex. This male hunted mainly along the edges of fields up to 400–500 m from the nest. The bird would emerge to commence hunting at about 20.30 hr each evening, that is to say, about two hours before dusk. In one 30-minute period it carried five separate voles and mice back to the nest in a hollow tree, where there were young to judge by the noise as food was brought in. On one occasion the hunting bird hovered briefly for four seconds over a spot at the edge of a field before plunging into the long herbage where it caught a rodent. Another hunting technique involved flying low along a field edge and, on spotting a likely prey animal, it would make an immediate twist or cartwheel in the air so that in a moment it was facing in the opposite direction. This manoeuvre would instantly be followed by a drop into the grass, though it was not always successful in catching its intended victim.

On another occasion in March 1979, some 90 minutes before sunset, the same observers found a pair of Barn Owls hunting over newly-planted conifers by a remote hill cottage in Galloway, south-west Scotland. In the half-hour while they watched, one bird was seen to hover above a particular spot for 35 seconds with a beautifully controlled Kestrel-like action, though with rather heavier wing movements. During the last moments of its hover it stretched its legs fully downwards far farther than normal, and began to descend slowly before plummeting quickly into the grass head-first with wings held back like a swimmer in a butterfly stroke. On another occasion it hovered for six seconds over one spot, whilst on two further occasions it fluttered briefly over different places.

A Barn Owl, originally discovered by Peter Martin, and watched by Ian and Diane Willis on a bright sunny winter afternoon as it hunted at Bracklesham Bay, Sussex (14th February 1978) adopted still-hunting and flight-hunting techniques. Its hunting patch was a tall grassy embankment skirting a wide dyke. It would spend much time perched on top of a fence post, craning its head forward and apparently listening and watching for animals in the grass. Occasionally it would fly from the fence post and drop onto something in the vegetation. At other times it would fly slowly just above the tall grass with legs dangling and, on spying a movement, it would suddenly drop into the grass.

The hunting examples described above show that most prey is taken on the ground, although roosting passerines may be snatched from bushes or ivy and, like Tawny Owls, Barn Owls have been observed beating their wings against bushes, apparently with the intention of flushing roosting birds (Witherby *et al* 1940).

A series of excellent photographs taken by Payne (1962) in laboratory conditions have demonstrated that there are behavioural differences between strikes in light and darkness. In adequate lighting the owl first turned its head to face the prey, a mouse, then crouched and leaned forward. It lifted from the perch with one stroke of its wings and then glided towards the mouse without further wing-flapping. Its feet were held well back until, just before striking, it raised its wings and brought its feet forward, throwing back its head at the same time. At this point it presented the appearance of a projectile, its claws as the tip. At the moment of impact its eyes were closed.

A further set of photographs showed the same owl performing rather differently in darkness. When the mouse first rustled the leaves, the owl turned its head towards the sound, exactly as it did when it could see the animal. Once the owl faced the mouse, it had to hear at least one additional sound before striking. It again leaned forward and flew. However, this time it did not glide smoothly but flapped its wings quite violently and continuously all the way to the animal and, with each stroke, its feet swung back and forth beneath it like a pendulum. When it was just over the mouse, it again brought its feet forward and threw back its head, thus bringing its widely spread talons into the same path that its head had taken a moment before. The considerable

Spread of Barn Owl's talons at moment of striking prey (after Payne 1962)

area (roughly 60 cm², as calculated by Payne) covered by the fully spread talons at the moment before impact is indicated by the drawing based upon the holes made by the talons of a Barn Owl in a piece of paper at the moment of striking (cf. Payne 1962).

Its silent flight enables the Barn Owl both to hear its prey's movements and calls and to approach within striking distance without itself being heard. Prestt and Wagstaffe (1973) suggested that its sudden silent appearance and its shriek may make its prey too terrified to move.

After capture the prey is often devoured at once or carried only a short distance to a more sheltered place before being swallowed. In order, perhaps, to hide its prey from other predators, a daylight hunting Barn Owl will mantle the newly killed animal with spread or partly spread wings. D. and I.W. watched a bird do just this when it had caught a rodent (vole?) one winter afternoon near Loch Ken, southwest Scotland. Two nearby Carrion Crows immediately took a great interest in the mantling owl, and due to their persistent, close, unwanted company the owl finally took its intended meal into a nearby bramble and hawthorn brake where it swallowed the animal. If it is feeding young the owl will take the prey directly to the nest site, flying fairly low, the prey hanging from one foot.

FOOD

Barn Owl pellets are relatively conspicuous objects due to their black, characteristically shiny appearance and large size (average dimensions $50 \times 27 \times 22$ mm, see Table 4). They are compact and slow to decompose. The Barn Owl's digestive system is inefficient in dealing with bones, with the result that its pellets contain almost all the skeletal material of the prey consumed (Glue 1967). In the case of young Barn Owls, analysing their pellets must be undertaken with greater care than usual since the adult owls frequently decapitate prey before giving them to the owlets, and the skulls of the prey animals simply do not appear in their pellets (Festetics 1968).

Favoured roosting sites include agricultural buildings, especially barns and outbuildings, disused houses and ruins. Because such places are relatively dry and well-protected, they tend to preserve pellets, unlike natural sites such as hollow trees or rock cavities. Some nest sites have been occupied for a great many years and, several sites, for more than 100 years (Glue 1969). The large numbers of castings which accumulate on roost and nest site floors enable regular samples to be collected for analysis.

The daily food intake of Barn Owls in the wild is 70–104 g (average 94 g per day), from which the owl produces an average of 1.4 pellets/day (Schmidt 1977). Glue (1973) stated that small pellets are formed and regurgitated at night while hunting, and larger second pellets are later cast up at the daytime roost, which the owl may frequent for months, even years, if not disturbed excessively.

The Barn Owl's food has been studied throughout almost the whole of its world-wide range, indeed, in Europe a great deal of material had already been collected by the end of the last century. Uttendörfer (1952) summarised most of the data collected before 1947 from Germany, France, Italy and Crete, totalling not less than 77,964 prey items. In this mass of evidence voles constituted 50.9%, shrews 26.0%, mice 17.2%, other small mammals up to the size of the Rabbit *Oryctolagus cuniculus* 0.9%, birds 3.1%, frogs and lizards 1.2% and insects 0.7%. The proportion of insects and other invertebrates in Uttendörfer's list is, however, unduly low because they were, unfortunately, not included in some of the studies he was analysing.

Since Uttendörfer (1952) the food of the Barn Owl has remained the most thoroughly studied aspect of owl ecology in western Europe. Table 5 lists the main results from Denmark (Lange 1948), East Germany (Haensel and Walther 1966), Britain and Ireland (Glue 1974), France (Thiollay 1968), Spain (Herrera 1973) and Italy (Lovari *et al* 1976). This material involves the remarkable total of 145,373 prey items.

The Barn Owl feeds almost exclusively on small mammals in every part of its European range. Members of the three mammal families *Soricidae* (shrews), *Cricetidae* (voles) and *Muridae* (mice and rats) formed 85.9–98.6% of the total prey in seven European countries, according to the figures in Table 5. The remaining proportion of the diet comprised of birds, bats, moles, a few medium-sized mammals such as rabbits, hamsters, weasels or stoats, dormice, birchmice, amphibians, lizards and invertebrates. Only in Spain did these items make up more than 10% (14.1%). By concentrating entirely upon Spanish material Herrera (1974) generalised that Mediterranean Barn Owls manifest a greater trophic diversity than ones from more temperate regions; in other words, they feed more often upon prey other than small mammals. However, this generalisation does not appear to be valid in Italy, where small mammals were taken about as often as in Denmark or France.

It has been well documented that the Barn Owl does not prey selectively on small mammals but takes all species according to their availability (e.g. Schmidt 1970, Vernon 1972). This suggests that the study of the Barn Owl's diet is suitable for determining the presence of nocturnal small mammal species within its hunting territory. Non-selective predation could also explain why shrews form between 12.9 and 38.0% of its prey, when, for example, a vole and mouse specialist like the Long-eared Owl consumes only 0.1 to 7.0% of shrews (Tables 5 and 41), even though this species hunts at night, usually over open fields as does the Barn Owl.

Shrews may even constitute the main species in some Barn Owl populations. In an examination of 34,866 prey items in Belgium, Straeten and Asselberg (1973) identified the Common Shrew *Sorex araneus* as the most important prey species at 36.8%. Pygmy Shrew *Sorex minutus* and White-toothed Shrew *Crocidura russula* made up a further 16.3%, the total proportion of all voles being only 32.0%, mice and other small mammals 7.7% and birds 2.9%. Interestingly, in Tanzania, Africa, Laurie (1971) also reported that shrews are the commonest prey, these mammals constituting a similar proportion (55.8%) as in the Belgian study. Unfortunately, it is not known if the availability of shrews in itself explains why they dominate the Barn Owl's menu in Belgium and Tanzania or if this owl has, after all, certain preferences when selecting its food. At least the above examples prove that the Barn Owl does not dislike shrews, unlike many carnivores such as domestic cats, foxes and jackals (Laurie 1971).

Table 5 demonstrates clearly that all the Barn Owl populations under scrutiny regularly took small numbers of birds but only in the Danish material did they form slightly more than 5% of the prey items, whereas in France they constituted a mere 0.6%. According to Glue (1972), in no single British diet did birds form more than 8% of the vertebrate prey totals. However, in Hungary (Schmidt 1968) and Poland (Ruprecht 1964) the House Sparrow *Passer domesticus* and the Tree Sparrow *Passer montanus* formed 19.4 and 18.4% respectively of the Barn Owl's diet. Schmidt (1972) identified no less than 5,888 birds eaten by Barn Owls in Hungary, 93% of which were House Sparrows and 5% Tree Sparrows. In Britain, in the food remains, there were 194 House Sparrows out of 314 birds (62%) and only three Tree Sparrows, but 38 (12%) Starlings *Sturnus vulgaris* (Glue 1972).

Frogs and lizards are even more rarely preyed upon than birds but it is worth noting that some of the lizards taken are diurnal, which confirms that Barn Owls may sometimes hunt in the daytime. Herrera (1973) turned this the other way round by suggesting that the occurrence of lizards in the owl's diet is possibly new evidence for lizards' nocturnal life in southern Spain! A total of 119 lizards were counted in his information.

The percentage of insects and other invertebrates in the Barn Owl's diet varied between 0.1 and 4.3 (Table 5), decreasing markedly from south to north, as already suggested by Uttendörfer (1952). In the British studies beetles formed the main constituent of all invertebrates taken, whereas in Italy large crickets and grasshoppers *Orthoptera* were the most common invertebrate prey, beetles occurring very rarely (Lovari *et al* 1976).

My own unpublished examination of Barn Owl's food in southern England indicates that the amount of insects consumed should not be underestimated, even though they do seem to form a rather insignificant part of the total amount of food taken. 1973 was a good year for some species of butterflies in southern England (Len Mummery and Ian Willis, *pers. comm.*) and the Barn Owl pair I studied had consumed at least 34 Small Tortoiseshell *Aglais urticae* and 24 Peacock Butterflies *Inachis io* as well as 2 Herald Moths *Scoliopteryx libatrix*. In addition the remains of 3 beetles, 2 unknown worms and 1 Common Earwig *Forficula auricularia* have appeared among 1,033 prey animals so far identified from their pellets. Likewise, Buckley and Goldsmith (1972) found one butterfly, a Peacock, in pellets plus the much-

Small Tortoiseshell butterflies

fragmented wings of Ghost, Swift or Drinker-type moths *Noctuidae*. A single Damsel-fly *Zygoptera* was the only other day-flying insect discovered by them.

Burton (ed. 1973) states that there are no carrion-feeding owls but this does not mean that owls entirely shun this source of food. Christine and Bob Dunsire (1978) recently observed a Barn Owl, in their car headlights, perched on a dead Hedgehog *Erinaceus europaeus* in the road. The Hedgehog appeared fully grown and freshly run over, and from its position the owl looked as if it had been, or was about to commence, eating from the Hedgehog's underside but, naturally enough, it flew off when interrupted.

It should be remembered throughout this book that the 'average' diet of a European owl does not exist elsewhere than in my tables, unless an 'average' locality can be defined. In reality the composition of an owl's diet is rarely identical from one place to another, nor from one year to another, varying with changes in the habitat and the availability of small mammals. While there is clearly no dramatic seasonal variation in the Barn Owl's prey, there is a suggestion of seasonality at some sites. Frogs are taken more often in the spring when they are travelling in large numbers towards the breeding ponds (Buckley and Goldsmith 1972, Fairley and Clark 1972). Brown Rats *Rattus norvegicus* tend to appear more frequently as a prey animal during the autumn after harvest, and substantially more birds are consumed in January, February and May than at other times.

Buckley and Goldsmith (1972) remark that at some sites large prey species are taken in greater numbers during the breeding season, suggesting selection by the Barn Owl, as is the case with the Tawny Owl. Glue (1971) has compared the changes of the Barn Owl's diet in relation to the habitat exploited. Short-tailed Voles *Microtus agrestis* formed the bulk of the Barn Owl's food in rough grassland, scrub, young forestry plantations and wetland habitats, with Common Shrew consistently the important secondary prey. In well-wooded habitats Wood Mice *Apodemus sylvaticus*, Short-tailed Voles and Brown Rats were nutritionally the more important prey, with Common Shrews, House Mice *Mus musculus* and Bank Voles *Clethrionomys glareolus* of lesser importance. The Water Vole *Arvicola amphibius* was locally a valuable prey item in wetland habitats. On British farmland Short-tailed Voles again were consistently the main prey consumed but they formed a greater proportion of the diet on pastoral rather than on arable farmland where the Brown Rat was nutritionally important.

BREEDING BIOLOGY

Of all European owls the Barn Owl is to be found particularly in the proximity of man. It likes nothing better than to roost or nest in a farmstead, castle, ruins of all kinds, even occasionally in the middle of a town or village. Few habitats below the tree-line are resisted by this species and it will not scorn copses and woodland edges if there is plenty of old timber, or remote fells provided there are shepherds' cottages, farms and barns in which to shelter. However, in the desert areas of North Africa and the Near East it often lives in remote desert or semi-desert regions far from human habitation. Its main requirement seems to be plenty of open ground over which it can hunt. The nest may be in an artificial site, such as an old barn, minaret, derelict building, ruin, down a well or in a haystack, or in a natural site such as a hollow tree or a cavity in a cliff face. No less than 1,238 Barn Owl nesting sites have been described in Holland (Braaksma and de Bruijn 1976). As breeding places, Dutch Barn Owls seem to prefer farms and barns, churches taking second place (Table 6). Other important breeding sites are castles, artificial nest boxes, windmills, and house chimneys. Urban nest sites clearly dominated the Dutch findings (96%), instances of breeding in hollow trees and other natural sites being very rare (4%). Table 6 shows that a considerable urbanisation has taken place in recent years. In the nesting information gathered before 1963 natural nest sites still made up 6% but thereafter they decreased to only 2%.

In England the Barn Owl chiefly occupies agricultural habitats, particularly where areas of rough waste ground and suitable nesting places occur. Bunn *et al* (1982) suggest that nest sites are not generally to be found above 1000 feet (330 m) altitude. Nesting in hollow trees is much more common in England than Holland, 39% of 282 sites on nest record cards being in hollow trees (Sharrock comp. 1976). A slight urbanisation might have also taken place in England in recent years because before 1932 about 43% of 915 registered breeding pairs were nesting in hollow trees (Haverschmidt 1934), though nests in old trees are still common. The old trees are usually isolated rather than in dense woodland. The occupation of man-made nest boxes has become more common in recent years both in Holland (12% vs. 4%, Table 6) and England (Sharrock comp. 1976).

Normally owls do not include nest-building among their skills but Barn Owls are known to use their own pellets (often in great numbers) as lining material in existing nests. For example, Kaus (1977) in West Germany witnessed two or three cases where the owls built a heap of fresh pellets (height 10 cm and width 20 cm), on which they later raised young.

The first egg is usually laid in April, but at times as early as February and, very commonly, a second clutch is laid in July. In northern Europe the breeding season is much shorter than in southern Europe, as shown below:

First egg laid:	Feb	March	April	May	June	July	Aug
	%	%	%	%	%	%	%
Denmark (56 nests)	—	1.8	23.2	66.1	8.9	—	—
France (504 nests)	0.2	5.4	37.5	17.3	12.3	21.4	5.9

In Denmark (Trap-Lind 1965) data from 56 nests show that over 66% of the clutches are laid during May, whereas in France (Baudvin 1975, 1976) most of the first broods have been started in April and the second ones in July.

Sometimes the breeding season extends until the end of the year; for example, in

West Germany Kaus (1977) observed a third brood. The second brood of another Barn Owl pair consisted of six three- or four-week old chicks on 7th September 1974, whilst on 19th October the same pair had five fresh eggs. Haverschmidt (after Makatsch 1976) discovered a winter nest in Holland in December which had small young fledging during the first half of January. Wallace (1948) suggested that Barn Owls may breed continuously during periods of high prey density. Normally the laying season spans February to October but even then the Barn Owl has the longest breeding season of any owl.

The eggs are the typical dull white colour common to all owls but differ in being elliptical in shape. The interval of laying between two eggs is an average of 2.5 days (Baudvin 1978). Usually, incubation duties are performed by the female alone, often starting with the first egg, but it is not uncommon for the male to incubate during the female's short evening absence. Smith *et al* (1974) frequently observed both adults side by side on a clutch.

The clutch size is very variable, usually 4–7, occasionally 2–13. In East Germany Hummitzch (1950) found two nests containing 16 and 18 eggs respectively. In such cases one should always suspect two females of having laid in the same nest. The variation in the number of eggs tabulated by Hummitzch (1953) is as follows:

Clutch size	2	3	4	5	6	7	8	9	10	11	12	13	16	18
Number of nests	3	13	22	37	35	17	5	4	5	1	1	1	1	1

The average clutch size does not seem to decrease southwards, unlike that of most European owls. In most northern areas (Sweden, Denmark) the averages are 4.63 and 5.55, whereas in France it is 6.22 (Table 7). On the other hand the average clutch size in Holland is lower (4.03) than in Sweden, making any geographical trend difficult to assess.

Baudvin (1975, 1976) has shown that during years of abundant prey animals the clutch size is higher: 6.08 (107 nests) in 1972; 3.75 (4 nests) in 1973; 6.82 (103 nests) in 1974; 5.56 (55 nests) in 1975. There were also marked differences in the monthly average clutch sizes during March to August, as shown below:

	Av. clutch size	No. of nests
March	5.39	18
April	5.40	63
May	6.13	24
June	8.06	35
July	7.31	54
August	5.05	16

From this evidence it can be seen that, in France, the larger clutches were laid in June and July. This is because the first brood is always smaller than the second. In West Germany, Kaus (1977) discovered that the average clutch size of the first brood was 5.4 eggs (158 nests) and that of the second brood 7.2 eggs (69 nests). He also noted that all unusually large clutches (one of 14 eggs, one of 12, one of 11 and two of 10 eggs) were either in very late nests or in those which were proven to be second broods.

Estimates of the length of the incubation period vary (e.g. 32–34 days, Witherby *et al* 1940; 30–31 days, Bunn and Warburton 1977), the recent study of Smith *et al*

(1974) showing that the incubation periods of eleven marked eggs averaged 30.8 days (range 27–34 days). During this time the female leaves the nest for brief periods only, relying on the male for her food. Bunn and Warburton (1977) timed her longest period of absence as ten minutes.

Hatching usually takes place in the small hours of the morning, the first small hole appearing in the egg shell during the previous evening. The female can hear the young calling from inside the egg at least 24 hours before hatching. Bühler's observations (1970) of hand-raised Barn Owls showed that the female is in a position actively to help her young while they are hatching. Without damage to the young the female breaks off shell chips with her bill and removes any shreds of the membrane from the chicks, the allantois and larger pieces of eggshell. Once the young chick is free the mother then plucks off the remains of the embryonic sac and other bits of material and pecks her offspring clean. Bühler's owls swallowed the smaller fragments immediately after removing them and either left the larger pieces at the edge of the nest or, holding them in one talon, broke them up and ate them piecemeal. This kind of help to the young whilst hatching may also exist in other owl species as it has a clear selective advantage by increasing the hatching rate.

East German information (Hummitzch 1950, 1953) shows that the number of young hatched is commonly from three to six:

Brood size	1	2	3	4	5	6	7	8	9	12	18
Number of nests	5	11	21	38	28	26	8	2	5	1	1

In one nest all 18 eggs hatched but in another of 16 eggs only 12 hatched.

The newly-hatched young are covered in thick greyish-white down with thinner patches on the sides of the neck and belly. During the first 15 days this is gradually replaced by a longer pure white down. At this stage (mesoptile plumage) the young bird no longer relies on the female for warmth and can swallow whole the common prey species such as voles and shrews.

It seems likely that the Barn Owl may remove its young from the nest in response to disturbance at the moment of hatching, though this has not yet been fully proven (Baudvin 1975). After the young have hatched, the female becomes very attentive, continually using the fast, chattering note to stimulate the young to beg. They do not gape but readily take food from her when she dangles strips of meat that touch the bristles around the base of their bills. When feeding small young, the female raises herself slightly from the brooding position and straddles them (Bunn and Warburton 1977).

Shortly after hatching, the young weigh about 14 g (Schneider 1964). Between 6th and 15th day the young increase their weight by approximately 12 g per day; between 16th and 25th by 8 g and between 26th and 30th day by 4 g (Baudvin (1975). Bunn and Warburton (1977) logged the development of the primary feathers as follows: 3rd week primary quills about 2.5 cm long, 5th week primaries about 7.5 cm, 7th week primaries 12.5 cm long and in the 9th week the owlet flies perfectly. Given a young Barn Owl's weight and wing length its age can readily be calculated.

The number of fledged young increases very clearly towards the south, indicating that the Barn Owl is not well adapted to the climate of northern Central Europe (Table 8). The mean brood size in southern Sweden is 2.15, whereas in France it is 4.54, the average for the whole of Europe being 4.00 young in 1,732 nests. In Sweden the brood size is 46% of the average clutch size, in Germany 66–79.5%, in Holland 79%, in Switzerland 84% and in France 73% (Tables 7 and 8).

The usual three to four year cycle of the Common Vole seems to have a strong influence on the average number of fledged young, as shown below in data from Germany (Kaus 1977) and France (Baudvin 1975, 1976):

Year	Germany	France	Total	Nests
1971	4.25	5.09	4.58	59
1972	4.34	4.16	4.24	235
1973	3.05	1.75	2.82	23
1974	6.28	5.19	5.47	274
1975	—	3.99	3.99	148

The years 1971/72 and 1974/75 were periods of increase in Common Vole populations, thus matching peaks in the size of Barn Owl broods. The asynchronous hatching of the eggs is a natural adaptation which offers the optimum survival of young, given an uncertain food supply. In the event of shortage the stronger members of the brood will survive at the expense of the weaker. Baudvin (1978) states that cannibalism is the principal cause in nestling mortality, his study revealing that 430 (16%) young were consumed by siblings. Cannibalism arises because of a lack of food, due to various causes, some of which might be, alone, or in combination: that the male is not in good physical condition; that prey is not sufficiently abundant; or that climatic conditions are not favourable for hunting in two out of three days. If one of the above-mentioned conditions is not fulfilled, cannibalism is an alternative solution.

Because of the two- to three-day intervals between each hatching, it is usually the more vigorous older chicks that claim and obtain food first. Once they are full, they no longer accept food. The others can then partake of their share, and so on for as long as there are young and prey items. If there is a lack of prey to feed the younger two or three chicks, these will weaken. At several days' old they can sustain a fast for one or two nights but if unfavourable conditions persist these ever-weakening runts will stop cheeping for food and eventually die. The adult will then no longer consider them as young since they do not move nor emit any sound. Taking them for prey the adult tears them up and feeds them to the older young – a natural adaptation which permits part of the clutch to survive in transitorily bad conditions.

Generally the death and absorption of one or two young is sufficient to see the survivors through the period of shortage which, Baudvin (1978) suggests, is usually due to poor weather conditions, especially rain, which renders prey less accessible to the Barn Owl. Baudvin (1978) has also shown that the size of the clutch has no marked influence on the risks of cannibalism. The larger clutches (ten or eleven young) do not suffer more than the smaller (three or four young). This is natural when we remember that the larger brood sizes are common during peak vole years.

After fledging, when they are between seven and eight weeks old, the owlets gradually discover how to catch prey although still supported by their parents. Approximately three weeks later they either leave the territory of their own accord or are tolerated for a further week or two before being driven away by one of the adults (Bunn and Warburton 1977).

The available ringing recoveries show that the first-year bird seldom flies far, the majority of recoveries being obtained less than 20 km from the nest site (Frylestam 1972). Fledged birds will disperse in all directions and sibling birds show no tendency to keep company. This behaviour may be useful in filling vacancies in suitable breeding habitats. Both sexes are known to breed in their first year. In England one female of a 1971 brood laid a total of 16 eggs in a well 25.5 km from her birthplace in the following year (Bunn and Warburton 1977). However, three out of four fledged young will die during their first November to February; the commonest cause of death being lack of food associated with low temperatures and snow cover. Thus only 24% (Sweden, Frylestam 1972) to 26% (Switzerland, Glutz von Blotzheim 1964) of ringed Barn Owls have been recovered after their second year, although the oldest known Barn Owl in Switzerland reached the age of 21 years.

DISTRIBUTION

The Barn Owl belongs to the cosmopolitan faunal type but extends into temperate regions only in North America and Europe and is essentially restricted within latitudes 40°N and 40°S of the equator. The Barn Owl's tropical and sub-tropical background may explain why it often suffers considerable losses during severe or long winters. The northernmost Barn Owls in the world are those living in Scotland. They belong to the nominate race *T. a. alba* which was first described in 1769 from specimens collected in Italy. *T. a. alba* is widespread in Britain, Ireland and most of western and southern Europe and countries bordering the Mediterranean except the Balkan Peninsula. This 'Common' or 'White-breasted' Barn Owl is replaced by the dark-breasted *T. a. guttata* in southern Sweden and Denmark and from Germany, Poland and western Russia south into Austria, Hungary, Romania and Yugoslavia. Along the western edge of its distribution, in eastern France and western Germany, intermediates between this race and *T. a. alba* occur. A third race in Europe, found in Corsica and Sardinia, is *T. a. ernesti*. This subspecies is very pale above and its pure silvery underparts are rarely spotted.

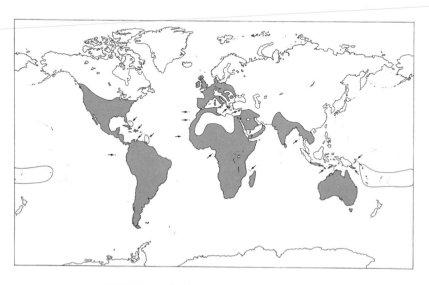

BARN OWL – shaded area indicates breeding distribution

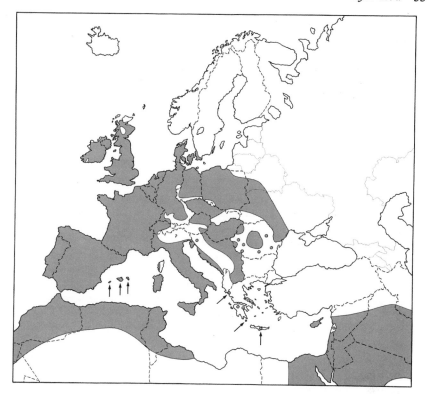

BARN OWL – resident, though may wander, especially when food is scarce

Outside Europe, geographical distances have produced at least 31 races: seven in Africa and the Middle East, eleven in South and East Asia and Australasia and thirteen in North and South America. In addition to *T. alba* and its large number of associated races, there are a further seven species of barn owl, six of which occur in the Australasian region (Burton ed. 1973). The Barn Owl is mainly sedentary but northern populations especially may move south or west in winter. This is certainly true in North America where southward migration occurs chiefly through the period August to December, northward migration taking place during March and April (Stewart 1952). An average southward migration rate of 28 km per day was shown by three birds. One averaged 42 km per day during 13 days. In Europe there seems to be no special trend in the direction of Barn Owls movements. Only certain topographical features, especially large areas of water, have restricted the dispersal of birds. Movements between mainlands and islands are therefore rare. Thirteen recoveries of Dutch Barn Owls have been made in France and one in England, Spain, Switzerland and Poland (Braaksma and de Bruijn 1976). As well as these, four Barn Owls ringed in Switzerland have been recovered in Holland (Glutz von Blotzheim 1964). It is clear then that there is some exchange of breeding owls between neighbouring European countries.

Short term fluctuations caused by hard winters, or by variations in the density of small rodents, tend to mask long term trends but there seems no doubt that the Barn Owl has continued to decline in most parts of Europe during this century.

The most drastic decline in numbers has taken place in The Netherlands. Before the severe winter of 1963 the national population fluctuated between 1,800 and 3,500 pairs, but during the years 1967–74 the numbers ranged from only 200 to 400 pairs (Braaksma and de Bruijn 1976). The loss of food supply due to changing agricultural practices is believed to be a major factor causing this decline. Further important causes are increased road casualties and the taxidermist trade. Despite legal protection in Holland since 1912, more than 10,000 legally stuffed Barn Owls make this the most commonly stuffed bird in the country since 1945.

In England and Wales long term fluctuations have been attributed largely to loss of habitat, human disturbance, severe winters and (in eastern England during the late 1950s and early 1960s) toxic chemicals, i.e. pesticides. However, only a few estimates are available to show the extent of the fall in the British population. In 1932 Blaker (1934) estimated the Barn Owl population of England and Wales to be about 12,000 pairs. In Ireland the number of breeding Barn Owls is now between 1,500 and 3,000 pairs (D. Scott, *in litt.*), the density being only a fraction of what it used to be (Ogilvie 1976). The current total for the whole of Britain and Ireland has recently been estimated at between 4,500 and 9,000 pairs (Sharrock comp. 1976).

In France the Barn Owl is apparently more frequent in the northern half of the country, though it is present over the whole country including Corsica. Baudvin (*in litt.*) attempted to estimate the current French population and arrived at a figure of between 20,000 and 50,000 pairs.

In the Iberian Peninsula the Barn Owl is common or moderately common throughout, but in southern Spain it is very likely experiencing a decrease in population, as revealed from many reports in localities where the bird was common a few years ago and is now, apparently, non-existent (Herrera, unpublished data). Alcover (*in litt.*) states that this owl breeds on all the larger Balearic Islands (Mallorca, Menorca and Ibiza) also on the smaller Cabrera (16 km^2) and on some other small islands.

It seems probable that the Barn Owl breeds in all the countries bordering the Mediterranean, though our knowledge regarding its distribution in Albania, Greece and Turkey is very limited. It must be pointed out, however, that in Turkey, in the absence of breeding records (although many ornithologists have visited or resided in Turkey in recent years, often for months or even years at a time), it is reasonable to suppose that Barn Owls do not regularly breed and are only a rare vagrant to that country. The only recent records are of a bird recorded at Çamlica, on the eastern side of the Bosphorous opposite Istanbul, between 10th August and 30th September 1971, whilst perhaps the same bird was seen taking House Sparrows from trees near the ferry terminal at Uskudar on 1st September, a distance of 5 km from the other sightings (The Ornithological Society of Turkey, Bird Report 1970–73). Böhr (*in litt.*) found this owl in Greece between 1961 and 1976 in five different areas marked on the map. In Cyprus the Barn Owl is said to be a scarce resident (Leontiades, *in litt.*).

Because of its wide distribution the Barn Owl must be one of the best known owls in the world (Burton ed. 1973). It is unfortunate that our existing knowledge of its southern and especially eastern European distribution and population is as limited as shown in these paragraphs. Not even the latest European Atlas report (Everett and Sharrock 1980) has added anything new to our knowledge of the Barn Owl's distribution in Europe. It has only confirmed the opinions of Dontchev and Simeonov (*in litt.*) that the Barn Owl does not breed in Bulgaria but is only a winter visitor. In Romania it is a scarce breeding bird but may be more widespread than our map indicates, particularly in the north and west of the country (Munteanu, *in litt.*).

According to the distribution map of Burton (ed. 1973), this owl should be breeding in the Crimea, Bulgaria and Romania but Flint *et al* (1968) gave a much more limited distribution for the USSR. The latter information has been used as a basis for the Russian distribution on the map accompanying this text.

Although the Barn Owl has been observed on nine occasions in Norway between the years 1900 and 1962 (according to stuffed specimens) (Barth 1963), and twice (1935 and 1963) in Finland, it has never nested further north in Fennoscandia than in the most southern part of Sweden. In 1955 the estimation for southern Sweden was about 100 breeding pairs (v. Haartman *et al* 1967), although the recent estimate of Ulfstrand and Högstedt (1976) is about 10 pairs. The decline has apparently continued, for during the last few years (up to 1980) only a few pairs have bred in the south-west part of Scania (Frylestam, *in litt.*).

8: Striated Scops Owl *Otus brucei*
(Hume)

Adult males and females are a pale greyish-sand colour with indistinct markings of a lighter hue and pronounced dark shafts and streaks. The outer scapulars are light creamy-buff with a slight rufous tinge, the whole effect being of a pale area down the outer scapulars containing some dark markings. The dark shafts are particularly broad on the forehead and the sides of the breast and are somewhat narrower on the upper parts, and still narrower on the wings. The lesser wing-coverts lack a russet tinge, and differ in this respect from the Scops Owl.

The primaries are brown with greyish tips and faint light markings on the internal vanes, with three or four whitish patches on the external vanes forming bars on the open wing. The underparts are similar to the upperparts in fundamental tones but are somewhat paler. The feathers of the legs are rufous-buff usually with dark vermiculated streaks. The bill and claws are horn-coloured and the iris is yellow. In the hand the length of the first flight-feather (not counting the bastard feather) is situated between the 5th and 7th (in the Scops between the 4th and 6th), the 3rd and 4th are the longest (whereas it is sometimes the 2nd in the Scops). It therefore differs from the Scops Owl on the basis of the wing formula i.e. it has a less pointed wing for only short migrations. The best character for separating the two in the hand is said to be the length of the third primary, which is equal to or less than the sixth in *Otus brucei*, but distinctly larger than the sixth in the sympatric subspecies of *Otus scops* (Abdulali 1972 in Gallagher 1975). A quicker way of separating them, apparently, is to look at the feet, *Otus brucei* being feathered on the first two phalanges in contrast to the bare toes of *Otus scops* (G. P. Hekstra in Gallagher and Rogers 1980).

Striated Scops Owl exhibits a whole cline of colour variation from sandier to greyer birds. Most birds appear to be somewhat intermediate between the two extremes though there is by no means the same dramatic spectrum of colour as in Tawny Owl. This information is based upon a thorough examination of all the skins of this species in the British Museum (Nat. Hist.), Tring, by Ian Willis.

Measurements from Dement'ev *et al* (1951) are as follows: the length of two males 210 mm and 211 mm, and that of two females 207 mm and 210 mm. The wing span of each male was 540 mm, and 575 mm for one female. One male weighed 110 g. The wing measurements of males varied between 150 mm and 165 mm (average 158.8 mm from 24 birds) and that of females between 155 mm and 168 mm (average 161.1 mm from 11 birds). The sexual dimorphism of size is therefore negligible.

IN THE FIELD

The Striated Scops Owl superficially resembles the Scops Owl but is paler and sandier (from which is derived its Russian name 'Yellowish Owl'), with precise blackish stripes at close quarters and a noticeable lack of horizontal dark streaks and vermiculations. Its voice is very different from Scops. Pukinsky (1977) describes it as a long sequence of *kuh-kuh-kuh-kuh* notes sometimes lasting up to half an hour.

VOICE

Almost all authors seem to disagree on the call of *Otus brucei*. Meinertzhagen (1954) writes in *Birds of Arabia* that its voice is identical to the Scops Owl's, but according to Etchécopar and Hüe (1970) the song is reminiscent of Scops and Tawny Owls. It has the soft, piping note of the former but this is extended and finishes by rising with the tremulous sonority of the Tawny Owl. Dement'ev *et al* (1951) describe the same voice as *tsirr-va-vaa* which begins with a warble, and also a nuptial call, *ukh-ukh*, which is persistently repeated.

Gallagher (1975) describes the song as 'a long sequence of short, soft, single notes, *wup-wup-wup*, like a distant well-pump; individual birds having different tones'. This call appears to be similar to the persistent *ukh-ukh* (Dement'ev *et al* 1951) and the short monotonous *boo-boo* (Ticehurst, cited in Ali and Ripley 1969) for this species. Pukinsky (1977) has recently been able to explain more thoroughly the call of *Otus brucei*, the song being as stated above, a monotonous *kuh-kuh-kuh-kuh*. During warm nights it will sing continuously, like the Nightjar *Caprimulgus europaeus*. During courtship it uses the voice *tsipp-va-va-vau*, which has a slight bronze-like quality. Sometimes this voice can be heard together with the song described by Dement'ev *et al*, *tsirr-va-vaa*, and Pukinsky (1977) maintains that this is often uttered as a response to sudden human disturbance at the breeding sites. In addition, this owl has a dog-like barking note, *an*, which is used as a warning signal during the nestling period.

BEHAVIOUR

Little is known about the behaviour of this species. It is likely to be less migratory than its closest relative the Oriental Scops Owl *Otus sunia*, for it has shorter wings than this species. Also, Oriental Scops Owl prefers forest and thick woodland whereas *Otus brucei* favours more open habitats. Striated Scops Owl commences breeding earlier than Oriental Scops Owl. These differences render the possibility that the western *brucei* and the eastern *sunia* populations can be considered as separate species (Pukinsky 1977).

In the Middle East, where Scops and Striated Scops Owls overlap in range, the former species (*Otus scops*) prefers mountain woodland whilst the Striated favours riverine woodland. Meinertzhagen (1954) regarded this owl as a species of arid regions but Etchécopar and Hüe (1970) realised that it was also found outside desert areas.

In the USSR this owl is also called 'Desert Owl', but Pukinsky (1977) does not approve this name because he maintains that, where it can, the Striated avoids deserts. It lives chiefly in woods near rivers and often near cultivated places, being a typical owl in abandoned gardens, vineyards and roadside groves. However, it avoids direct contact with man and human settlements.

In the Amu-Darja jungle area, N. A. Poskevits discovered that the population density of this owl was 0.3–0.8 pairs per 3 km transect. In Tigrovaja, R. L. Potanov studied an area of 40,000 ha for several years and found a range of 9–12 pairs of Striated Scops Owls. A. N. Shinin studied a desert area near the Afghanistan border and found only two Striated Scops Owls' nests, although at the same time he knew of 50 Little Owl nests. This seems to confirm that desert is not favoured by *Otus brucei* (Pukinsky 1977).

FOOD

There are some detailed studies of Striated Scops Owl's food in the USSR but I have only a very general translation of them available at present. Spangenberg and Feig have found remnants of insects, small passerine birds, bats and small rodents at the nests of *Otus brucei* along the lower Syr-Darja river. Among the birds taken they mention Tamarisk Bunting *Emberiza* spp. and for rodents the House Mouse *Mus musculus*. The insects were mainly beetles *Coleoptera*, grasshoppers *Acrididae*, locusts *Tettigonidae* and bees *Apidae*. Insects form the main diet, though this owl takes small mammals and birds more often than *Otus sunia* (Pukinsky 1977). According to Dement'ev *et al* (1951) the Striated Scops Owl's diet consists chiefly of insects but also bats and small passerines. It is also known to take lizards.

BREEDING BIOLOGY

The nests are usually in holes of trees, including woodpecker holes, with no additional nesting material. It will also use magpies' nests. A. M. Mambetshumaer found not less than 31 nests in Amu-Darja in the USSR in 1962 and 1963, of which 27 were in old magpie nests (Pukinsky 1977). In addition to holes in trees, nests have been found in riverside holes, rock caves, nest boxes intended for Starlings *Sturnus vulgaris*, and in other man-made holes and structures.

The clutch size is normally between four and five eggs but varies from two to six. The eggs are larger than those of Scops Owl: 28.6–34 mm × 26–29.4 mm, the average of 60 eggs being 31 × 27 mm. The weight of a fresh egg is about 12–13 g but during incubation it decreases by more than 1 g. Apparently the eggs are laid either in 24 hour (P. L. Potanov) or 48 hour (S. Bakaev) intervals. Only the female undertakes the incubation and the male regularly feeds her. Incubation can begin from the first egg but usually the intensive incubation starts after two or three eggs have been laid. The highly attentive incubation lasts 21–22 days for the last egg (S. Bakaev). The weight of newly-hatched young varies between 8.5 g and 10.5 g. During the third night the chick's eyes will open and at the age of seven days the young show signs of their first feathers. Two days later the first primaries are beginning to show and the nestling period lasts only four weeks. Both parents bring in food (Pukinsky 1977).

The young are independent about seven weeks after first leaving the nest (before being able to fly properly) and remain in close proximity to one another for a while (Harrison 1975).

The southern non-migratory populations of the Striated Scops Owl start to breed at the end of February but populations living north of the January 0°C isotherm are migratory and breed a month or two later. In Samarkand, A. N. Bogdanov noted that migrating owls return not earlier than 11–15th April, and the latest nest he found containing unincubated eggs was 15th June. However, in the south the eggs are hatched before the monsoons begin and owlets fly before the rains cease. Usually the development of the young coincides with the maximum supply of insect food.

DISTRIBUTION

According to Vaurie (1965), the Striated Scops Owl occurs in Asia where it lives in riverside woodland from Palestine to the Aral Sea, Iran and Turkestan.

Etchécopar and Hüe (1970) seem convinced that this owl is much less rare in the Near and Middle East than was thought until recently. This may be true in Iran, where it is commonly heard in spring and summer in woodlands and gardens of the Southern Zagros and other mountain ranges south and east of Shiraz (Scott, *in litt.*). On the other hand there have been no records of this owl from Syria or Lebanon since 1919 (Macfarlane, *in litt.*). Meinertzhagen's contention (1954) that it was distributed in Palestine and Syria was probably based on old information. S. Vere Benson (1970)

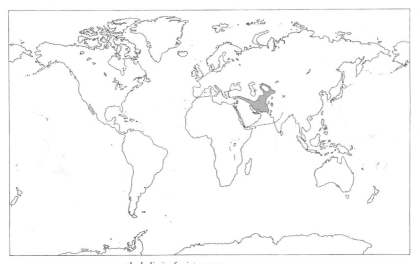

------   *southerly limit of winter range*

×   *recorded from the Kun Lun, Chinese Turkestan*

STRIATED SCOPS OWL – as it is resident in Iran and the Gulf States, it seems that only the northerly populations are migratory

mentions Striated Scops Owl as a breeding bird in Jordan but gives no other information.

The species is resident in the United Arab Emirates and northern Oman and has been collected on migration in Bahrain (Jennings 1981). One was caught, presumably on migration, in southern Oman in October 1978 (Walker 1981). Jennings believes that the owl might be a migrant and winter visitor throughout Saudi Arabia, though evidence is flimsy at present. However, it is known to winter in western, and probably north-western, India and Pakistan (Vaurie 1965).

There is a specimen in the British Museum (Nat. Hist.) that was collected near Ludd (Lod near Tel Aviv?) on 5th April 1920; and whilst in Israel, in March 1976, I. W. was told by a ringing team from Beersheba University operating at Eilat that this species was occasionally caught in the nets. One such bird was caught and ringed there on 23rd February 1979 (S. Christensen, *in litt.*). The status of Striated Scops Owl in the Near East appears to be imperfectly known at present.

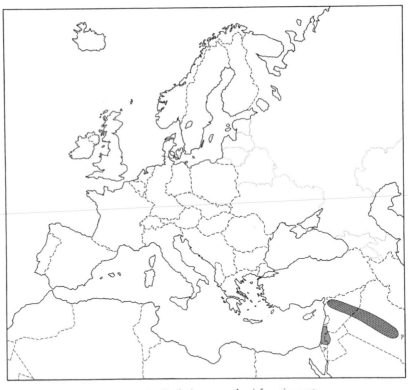

◑ *probable breeding distribution – up-to-date information scanty*
◐ *no recent breeding records*

STRIATED SCOPS OWL

9: Scops Owl *Otus scops*
(Linné)

DESCRIPTION

The whole of the upperparts are greyish-brown, fringed rufous at the sides of the mantle and the edges of the facial disc. The overall appearance is delicately patterned with blackish-brown shaft-streaks, wavy barring and 'pepper' speckling. The reddish-brown feathers surrounding the lower part of the facial disc are tipped with black and form a distinct dark border to the face. A line of creamy-white oval patches along the scapulars is conspicuous. The underparts are paler and greyer with the shaft-streaks more pronounced, particularly on the upper breast. The tail- and flight-feathers are barred with whitish, buff and grey.

The iris is pale yellow in immatures and orange- or lemon-yellow in adults. The bill is blackish and the yellowish-brown feet are unfeathered. The sexes are alike but there is much individual colour variation, primarily in the different intensity of russet shades in the plumage with two types of colour variations distinguishable: grey and rufous. The former employs its camouflage to roost against the trunks of trees while the latter does so in thick foliage.

The foregoing description applies to the nominate race *Otus scops scops* which only occurs in the Mediterranean area on passage. The other six races occupying the area covered by this book do not greatly differ from this subspecies. But it is worth noting that two races *O. s. majorcae* of the Iberian Peninsula and the Balearic Island and *O. s. cyprius* of Cyprus show little colour variation. As for *O. s. turanicus*, which inhabits Iraq through Iran to Pakistan and Uzbekistan, an examination of the skins at the British Museum (Nat. Hist.), Tring, by I.W. revealed that it is neither pale nor more silvery-grey than other races as suggested by Vaurie (1965). On average they are colder in coloration, less warmly grey-brown, but the differences are slight.

Koenig (1973) found that the female is slighly larger and heavier than the male and the few measurements to be gleaned from Dement'ev *et al* (1951) are as follows: total length of males 201–206 mm, females 208–210 mm. Wing length of males 143–161 mm (average 151 mm from 11 birds); females 146–163 mm (average 154 mm from 11 birds).

During migration the Scops Owl loses a substantial amount of its weight, which in April varies between 66 g and 92 g (average 79 g from 54 birds), but this is regained during the summer. Its autumn weight varies between 60 g and 145 g, the average being 93 g from 111 birds (Géroudet 1965).

IN THE FIELD

In Europe this is the only small owl with ear-tufts, though these are not always conspicuous. It usually adopts a slim, elongated posture when alarmed and, even when relaxed, looks quite unlike a Little Owl, being slimmer, greyer, with a quite different shape to its slimmer 'face', and with shortish, broad 'ears'. When disturbed or alarmed the Scops Owl may hold its elongated posture for many minutes. In this position the eyes narrow to slits and the area above the bill becomes broader and flatter, resembling a slab of bark. The whole effect is to lessen the appearance of a 'face' and provide no focal point for the eye of an intruder. The bark-coloured plumage and the 'ear'-posture give camouflage during the day while it roosts in a tree close up against the trunk, and it can be almost impossible to detect. Occasionally one may disturb a roosting bird and it flutters off with a silent, wavering action quite unlike the bounding, undulating flight of the Little Owl.

VOICE

The Scops Owl's 'song', chiefly uttered during warm, calm nights, is a very distinctive low, short whistle on a seemingly single, but actually disyllabic, note *tyeu*, repeated at intervals of three seconds for tens of minutes or even hours on end. This call is not unlike the single note of the Redshank *Tringa totanus*; it is musical and yet melancholic and monotonous. In certain regions bordering the Mediterranean, for example, Spain and Turkey, this strange little call is a highly characteristic night-time sound in the summer, interrupting the endless chirruping of the cicadas. Sometimes it is uttered over two tones when two birds reply to each other. Also, the male and female may 'sing' in a duet, the female's part being higher-pitched and less regular, longer and more disyllabic. This 'song' is uttered from a perch in a tree from dusk onwards through the night, but occasionally it may be heard during the day (Witherby *et al* 1942).

To the unskilled ear the 'song' is sometimes confused with that of the Midwife Toad *Alytes obstetricans*, which also calls at night. The toad's voice, however, is purer and more electronic, shorter and more monosyllabic but, except at close range in ideal conditions, it can be difficult to distinguish.

Notes similar to those of the 'song' of the Scops Owl may be used as calls (Witherby *et al* 1942), and during the breeding season, both adults and young use a great variety of hissing, chirruping and trilling calls, in addition to bill-snapping when irritated (Koenig 1973).

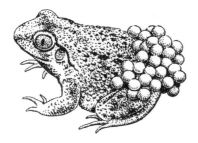

BEHAVIOUR

The resounding pipe of a stationary male attracts females and wards off rivals. Single females call loudly like males, but paired females call softly in turn with their partner. There is a short period at the beginning of the breeding season when the pair will sit together, conspicuously, near the intended nest-site. The male presents various nesting-holes to the female, and she will demonstrate her preference for one by using it as a resting place during the day. A pair copulates up to ten times a night outside the nesting-hole, the male uttering the copulation twitter. The female stays with one partner only, but the male tends to be polygynous and in captivity may maintain two broods simultaneously. The pair bond is strengthened by contact calls, mutual feeding and preening (Koenig 1973).

The Scops Owl hunts by night and sometimes by day, although it usually spends the day well-concealed in a tree or building, beginning to hunt at dusk after a good deal of piping. Scops Owls locate their prey from a vantage point and catch it on the ground; flying prey is forced down. The prey is usually carried in the bill but may be held in the talons when speed is called for. The normal flight is direct and rapid.

Scops Owls feed their young more frequently than other European owls, because the insect prey does not have a very high nourishment value. In Germany, parents brought bush-crickets to the nest every eleven minutes during the first half of the night (Mebs 1966). Both parents defend eggs and chicks vehemently (Koenig 1973).

FOOD

Scops Owl pellets are rarely found as their high content of insect remains render them very fragile. Average dimensions of pellets are given by Baudvin (1976) as 25 × 20 mm, but März (1972) records minimum and maximum dimensions as 20–30 mm × 10–12 mm.

Koenig (1973) remarked that the Scops Owl is more insectivorous than any other European owl. Mebs (1966) also noted that in south Germany and west Switzerland the food brought to nestlings consisted almost entirely of Great Green Bush-crickets *Tettigonia viridissima*, which were easy to locate and catch because of their chirping.

Meinertzhagen (1959) writes that this owl preyed upon moths in Crete, especially the Oleander Hawk Moth *Daphnis nerii*. He never saw the Scops Owl attempt to take small bats although they were common in the neighbourhood.

In addition to bush-crickets and moths the Scops Owl eats beetles, grasshoppers, crickets and caterpillars. Occasionally, it also takes mice, shrews, lizards and such small birds as finches, buntings and tits, though the birds may be sick or injured.

A quantitative study has recently been made in Spain of the breeding season food of the Scops Owl, and of 159 prey items, 1.2% were small mammals (mice, *Murinae*), 0.6% small birds, 1.2% amphibians, 2.5% reptiles and 94.3% invertebrate prey (Hiraldo and Herrera, unpublished).

BREEDING BIOLOGY

The Scops Owl's favoured breeding habitat is areas of scattered broad-leaved trees. It also occurs in orchards, olive groves, parkland and open woodland, or occasionally, in thick hedgerows with isolated trees and old ruins. In desert oases it lives in clumps of palms. On the other hand, in the northern and eastern parts of its Asiatic range it nests both in birch and coniferous forests, whilst in southern Europe it is often found in avenues and gardens of villages and towns.

No materials are added to the nest which is usually a hole in such trees as cork oaks, olive and date palms, from near ground level to 9–12 m high; and occasionally in walls and ruins, on the ground or in old nests of magpies and other corvids. Three to six, usually four, eggs are laid at two-day intervals, in southern Europe mostly in early May.

Incubation is by the female, for 24 to 25 days, and she remains with the young while they are small. Until their 18th day the young are fed only by the female, the male bringing the food to her. Later, both adults bring food, mostly at dawn and dusk.

The owlets' eyes begin to open on the third day; the head-bobbing, sighting movements begin on the fifth day, and later are used in food-begging after the young have left the nest. The ear is open and functioning from the moment of hatching and the olfactory sense is probably well developed.

The down dries within 8–12 hours of hatching; the first quills appear on the sixth day, and on the 50th day the contour plumage is complete. In full juvenile plumage they resemble the adults more closely than most young owls.

The young leave the nest after about 21 days and their first attempts at flight are made on about the 24th day, although their flying ability is not fully developed until around the 33rd day. Their first attempts at catching prey are usually from the 17th day onwards, and this behaviour is fully developed by the 45th day. The first regurgitated pellets appear on the sixth day, and later, every 1–3 days. At first the pellets contain no bones. Bone fragments appear after 16–28 days, and whole bones from the fifth to the eighth week onwards. After the 14th day the faecal sac is deposited in a hole dug by the nestling itself in the nest floor (Koenig 1973).

The family remain together on migration and the young reach sexual maturity when they are eight months old, the females becoming sterile at six years and males at ten. The maximum age recorded is twelve and a half years (Koenig 1973).

DISTRIBUTION

The Scops Owl belongs to the Old World faunal type and represents the Mediterranean distribution element. According to Voous (1960), the northern limit of distribution approaches the July isotherm of 60°F, which means that in southern Germany the Scops Owl nests only during unusually hot summers (Mebs 1966), and in southern Poland it has nested only once, in 1900 (Tomialojć, *in litt.*).

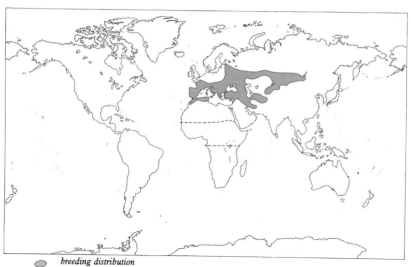

breeding distribution

- - - approximate north and south limits of main wintering area

SCOPS OWL

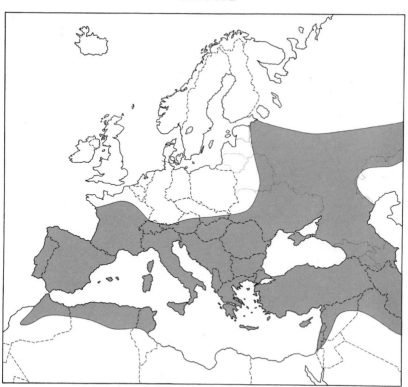

SCOPS OWL – breeding distribution – some birds remain to winter in Mediterranean region, including all birds of the Cyprus race, O. s. cyprius

In most of Europe the Scops Owl is a summer visitor only, although it was once much more numerous. Ern (1958–59) found it well distributed in the coastal areas of Yugoslavia; Krampitz (1956) stated that it was the most common owl in Sicily; in the South Tyrol, Psenner (1960) counted up to five breeding Scops Owls per hectare, with the shortest distance between two occupied nests only 50 m.

In France, since the 1939 Inventory, it is reported to be 'breeding in the whole country except the far north and north-east.' It is one of a number of species in France whose ranges have shrunk southwards. The reasons for this are unclear. It may be the decrease in populations of large insects (Coleopters, Sphynx, Bombyx) in the northernmost part of the country where large-scale farming is widespread. Another possibility may be a reduction in the number of hollow trees. The species no longer breeds in Britanny (north of the Loire), Normandy, Picardy and Lorraine, and it is accidental in Île-de-France and Champagne. Its reappearance since 1973 in southern Alsace is the only sign of a local improvement. In southern France it is common and widespread, and there are frequently several pairs in one village. Elsewhere in France there is often only one pair for an area of about 500 km^2. The total population is probably a little less than 10,000 pairs (Yeatman 1976).

The Scops Owl is widespread in Spain, although in some areas it occurs infrequently. It is locally abundant in parks in Granada, Córdoba, Sevilla, Jaén, Badajoz and Cáceres, though there are none in the city of Almería and they are scarce in the surrounding countryside. They are especially numerous in the foothills and lower slopes of the Cantabrians, and I.W. found them to be quite common in the foothills of the Pyrenees. Generally speaking, they are more abundant in the south, judging from birds illegally shot that Hiraldo (*in litt.*) obtained from taxidermists.

In Italy the Scops Owl is absent from the mountainous regions but is present along the Adriatic and Tuscany coasts (Bonora, *in litt.*).

The Scops Owl breeds regularly in Greece and is locally quite common. It is more abundant in the south than in the north where it is only a summer visitor (Bauer, *in litt.*).

In Turkey it is a fairly widespread and not uncommon summer visitor to Western Anatolia and the southern coastlands, and is locally distributed across the rest of the country (Orn. Soc. of Turkey, Report for 1970–73).

In Bulgaria and Rumania this owl is common in the plains and foothills up to 1,000 m (Donchev and Munteanu, *in litt.*), but in Hungary it breeds only sporadically and is fairly uncommon (Horváth, *in litt.*). Rough estimates suggest a breeding population of 50–150 pairs in Austria (Wrüss, *in litt.*), and of 50 pairs in Czecho-slovakia (Bárta, *in litt.*).

The European Scops Owl is largely migratory, spending the winter in the African savannahs between the Sahara and the rain forests. The Cyprus race *cyprius* is resident, as are some birds elsewhere in the Mediterranean. Owls from Siberia travel to Ethiopia, a journey of 7,000 to 8,000 km that may take two months to cover. Unfortunately their migration routes take them over countries where many are shot; Scops Owls are regularly for sale in the market of Valetta, Malta. The long journey also depletes their fat reserves; and pesticides that they have accumulated from contaminated insect food may reach fatal levels (Burton ed. 1973).

Non-breeding summer visitors have been found in southern Scandinavia, even in Iceland four or five times, and around Moscow, USSR.

10: Eagle Owl *Bubo bubo*
(Linné)

DESCRIPTION

The whole of the upperparts are brown-black and tawny-buff, showing as dense freckling on the forehead and crown, thick streaks and delicate wavy barring (the latter dark on pale ground colour) on the nape, sides and back of the neck, and dark splotches, freckles and vermiculations on the pale ground colour of back, mantle and scapulars. On the darkest individuals the dark of the back areas is very extensive, tending to cover much of the back, although on paler birds it takes on the appearance of a patchwork of dark and light splotching. A narrow buff band, freckled with brown buff, runs up from the base of the bill, above the inner part of the eye and along the inner edge of the black-brown, erectile 'horns' or 'ear-tufts'. A similar, sometimes paler, narrow band, with some cream or creamy-white admixed, runs down the outer edge of the scapulars. The rump and upper tail-coverts are much more delicately patterned with dark vermiculations and fine wavy barring.

The facial disc is less well-defined than in species such as Tawny Owl but decidedly more so than in Brown Fish Owl. The loral semi-circle is pale cream while the rest of the facial disc is tawny-buff, liberally 'pepper-speckled' with black-brown, so densely on the outer edge of the disc as to form a vague frame to the face. A dark line also borders the outer edge of the buff bill-to-'ear-tuft' line between the base of the 'ear-tuft' and the eyelid. Chin and throat are white continuing down centre of upper breast, partially and variably dividing the thick black-brown streaking thereon. A tawny-buff and black-brown marked band continues the effect of the dark facial frame across the throat. The dark streaking of the underparts is densest and thickest across the upper breast, less prominent on rest of breast and entirely lacking on remainder of underparts. The whole of the underparts except for chin, throat and centre of upper breast is, however, covered with fine dark wavy barring, on a tawny-buff ground colour. Legs and feet are likewise marked on a buff ground colour but more faintly.

The primaries and secondaries are dark tawny-buff, mottled with grey-brown and patterned with about five blackish-brown bars. On the basal half of two-thirds of the primaries the mottled tawny-buff portions of the wing pattern give way to a much more uniform dull orangey hue, which is quite striking in the spread wing. The tail is tawny-buff, mottled dark grey-brown with about six black-brown bars. The outer tail feathers are paler than the inner ones due to the fainter dark mottling on the tawny-buff ground colour. The underwing-coverts are buff entirely covered with black-brown vermiculations. The longest primary coverts are tipped black-brown forming a dark crescent near wing bend. Underside of flight-feathers grey with brownish tinge, the same tone as the coverts. Tips of flight-feathers washed dark grey-brown, particularly noticeable on primaries. Dark grey-brown barring on outer halves of flight-feathers. Bill and claws are black. Iris orange (yellow in palest desert race *desertorum* and almost yellow in *ascalaphus*).

Certain authors, for example Witherby *et al* (1943) have suggested that there are no sexual differences on the basis of colour in this species, but Blondel and Badan (1976) in their extensive studies of the large Eagle Owl population of Provence, southern France, noted that, 'In all the observed pairs the females, distinctly more massive than the males, seemed darker to us, . . .'

The nestling is covered with an abundance of short, soft down which is buffish-white, buffest on the forehead, rump, wings and below eyes.

The mesoptile, or downy juvenile plumage, is darkish buff, completely barred darkish brown. The legs and toes, wholly feathered, as at all stages of growth, are buff, unbarred.

Within the geographical area covered by this book ten highly variable races of Eagle Owl occur, perfectly reflecting the wide range of habitats and the huge region that they inhabit.

The nominate race *Bubo bubo bubo*, whose full description has been given above, is found in Europe from Fenno-Scandia and North Russia south to the Pyrenees (but excluding the British Isles) and the Mediterranean.

The Iberian Peninsula is inhabited by *B. b. hispanus* which is very similar to the preceding race, the only colour differences being the paler ground colour and the rather more sharply defined dark markings below. It intergrades with *bubo* in the Pyrenees.

In north-western Russia *B. b. ruthenus* appears as a distinct form from the nominate *bubo* in a zone stretching from the Pechora Basin to the lower Volga. It is paler and greyer than more westerly European populations with much more white in its plumage. However, it is only a half-way stage to the magnificent giant of the Urals and beyond, the strikingly white and grey *B. b. sibiricus* (see colour plates and photos). At rest this splendid resident of the taiga is glowingly pale, the dark markings being much reduced both above and below. Strangely enough, the open wing displays a great area of brown colour on the flight-feathers and primary coverts, very similar to that of the nominate *bubo* except that is is rather paler and more obviously barred across the flight-feathers (see colour plate). This bird must count as one of the splendours of the North Eurasian fauna. Judging from skins examined by Ian Willis at The British Museum (Nat. Hist.), Tring, it is the largest race in the western Palearctic, distinctly larger than *bubo*.

From Asia Minor and southern Russia eastwards occurs the rather yellowish-brown, crisply patterned *B. b. interpositus*, paler and less warm brown than *bubo*, with which it hybridises in the northern Ukraine. In the south of its range another zone of hybridisation exists with *ascalaphus* in western Syria, Lebanon and Israel, while it may also interbreed with *nikolskii* in southern Iraq.

The previous race grades into another rather pale but dull ochre-brown race *B. b. turcomanus* in the steppes between the lower reaches of the Volga and Ural rivers. It ranges eastward across Kazakhstan through steppe, semi-desert and hill country to Lake Balkhash in Central Asia.

Less pale than *turcomanus* and rather more pinky-brown in ground colour is *B. b. gladkovi*, which has the smallest range of any of the 20 or 21 races* of Eagle Owl, extending from the east coast of the Caspian from Cape Tyub Karagan across the sandy desert of the Aral-Caspian depression to the escarpment of the Ust Urt Plateau.

With a westernmost extension only just within the area covered by this book (Luristan in the Zagros) the pale sandy-brown *B. b. nikoslkii* has a full range extending over the rest of Iran and most of Afghanistan.

Lastly, there is the perplexing problem of the desert Eagle Owls of North Africa and Arabia *B. b. ascalaphus* and *B. b. desertorum*. Vaurie (1965) considered them to represent a border line case between species and subspecies and he grouped the two subspecies together in a single form. He lists various morphological characteristics which differentiate these birds from the *bubo* group of Eurasia, although his assertion that they all have less feathering on tarsi and toes has not been borne out by an examination of skins by Ian Willis at the British Museum (Nat. Hist.), Tring, where typical *ascalaphus* show more or less the same amount of feathering as races from further north. A single hybrid specimen *interpositus × ascalaphus* in the museum at Tring (from northern Syria and labelled *aharonii*) has more sparsely feathered toes, whilst the very small sandy-coloured *desertorum* has the feathering confined to the upper side of the toes, which are otherwise dirty yellowish-brown in colour.

The problem of these two subspecies arises from the fact that, although typical examples of each are distinctly different from one another, birds right through the range from lighter to darker coloration have been found breeding in the same localities in Egypt.

Meinertzhagen (1954) regarded *desertorum* as living 'in absolute desert under the most arid conditions.' Clearly there is much to be discovered about the status of these two very interesting desert and semi-desert races, and current ideas on the problem are not helped by a recent general lack of published information on subspecific status of birds recorded in North Africa and the eastern Mediterranean (see colour plates for colour and pattern of these two subspecies). In March 1982 Robert Fryer (*in litt.*) had superb views of a very pale Eagle Owl which showed the characters of the race *desertorum* at 24°N 42°E in western Saudi Arabia.

The wing lengths of the nominate race *Bubo b. bubo* have been recorded in Norway (Hagen 1942), Sweden (Glutz von Blotzheim and Bauer 1980), East Germany (März and Piechocki 1976), Switzerland and Austria (Glutz von Blotzheim and Bauer 1980) and from western parts of the USSR (Dement'ev *et al* 1951). The averages are shown

---

* Depending on whether one accepts Vaurie's (1965) view on the status of *B. b. desertorum*.

below in millimetres (numbers of owls in brackets):

	Female	*Male*
Austria and Switzerland	478.2 (25)	445.1 (12)
East Germany	478.5 (19)	448 (4)
Norway	476 (10)	449 (14)
Sweden	472 (16)	447 (8)
West Russia	485 (20)	453 (29)

Eagle Owls in the western parts of USSR have clearly longer wings than those in western Europe. In addition, Dement'ev *et al* (1951) and Vaurie (1965) have, between them, listed wing lengths for the 21 different races (Table 9). It is clear that owls living in Siberia (namely *B. b. sibiricus, yenisseensis* and *yakutensis*) have long wings when compared with the races of central Asia such as *B. b. interpositus, turcomarus* and *omissus*. However, the races *B. b. hemachalana* and *B. b. auspicabilis* of the high mountain areas of southern USSR have wings almost as long as northern populations of the nominate race, whilst the Eagle Owl found in the very high plateaux of east Central Asia, *B. b. tibetanus*, has even longer wings than the great *B. b. sibiricus* of the northern forests.

Unfortunately, weight measurements for all these races are unavailable but it is generally known that the females average larger than males in all races. There is a distinct decrease in size from the birds of northern Eurasia to those of the southern Sahara and Arabian deserts. The largest is *sibiricus* in which large females are almost twice the size of small males of the race *desertorum* (see Table 9 for detail of wing lengths of all Eagle Owl races over the whole of the species range).

Weights (in grammes) for the nominate race *B. b. bubo* are available from West Germany (Mebs 1966), Norway (Hagen 1942), Finland (v. Haartman *et al* 1967) and from the western parts of USSR (Dement'ev *et al* 1951), as follows:

	Female				*Male*			
	Max	*Min*	*Aver.*	*N*	*Max*	*Min*	*Aver.*	*N*
West Germany	3,200	2,500	2,600	?	2,500	2,000	2,100	?
Norway	4,200	2,280	2,992	12	2,810	1,835	2,448	13
Finland	4,000	2,200	3,025	21	3,000	1,620	2,225	22
West Russia	3,260	3,075	3,164	6	2,700	2,100	2,458	6

Although this sample is small it seems likely that these owls are on average heavier in western parts of the USSR in comparison with those of West Germany. There seems to be no clear difference between Fenno-Scandian and Russian owls.

IN THE FIELD

A large bulky owl with prominent 'ear-tufts' that are held upright in the male and typically more horizontally, or even drooping, in the female (Blondel and Badan 1976). Most races are twice as large as the Long-eared Owl, though the smaller desert races may be closer to the latter's size, and it seems that birds approaching Long-eared in size are generally much paler and sandier than that species. The Snowy Owl is almost equal in size to the Eagle Owl but its white colouring is unmistakable and its small 'ear-tufts' are frequently imperceptible. Snowy Owls are always birds of open country, and it is possible that they need outline recognition signals, in the form of 'ear-tufts', less than their woodland-living relatives.

Over most of Europe, Eagle Owls are essentially tawny-buff, heavily mottled black-brown on the upperparts and thickly dark-streaked on the tawny-buff breast. The eyes are large and orange. Birds in the more arid parts of its Eurasian range become generally paler, yellowish- or cinnamon-brown in ground colour according to the race, with less conspicuous streaking below, and the dark markings above become smaller and more streaked. The desert races of the Middle East are similar, but mottled with dark above rather than streaked. In the palest subspecies *desertorum* of the cream and cinnamon rocks and sands of the Sahara and Arabian deserts, the plumage perfectly matches its surroundings, the ground colour of the underparts being whitish on some individuals, tinged sandy-rufous across the sparsely but clearly streaked breast. This race has golden-yellow, not orange, eyes.

The massive Siberian race *sibiricus* is impossible to confuse with any other Palearctic owl, being strikingly pale milky-buff on underparts, densely but neatly streaked blackish across breast and more buff-grey on underparts, with much dark mottling and speckling and off-white in the greyish areas. There are large paler areas on scapulars, wing-coverts and rump/upper tail-coverts. The flight-feathers, in striking contrast to the distinctly grey shades of the body and wing-coverts, are sandy-orangey-brown, washed grey-brown on secondaries and tips of primaries, thus ensuring a brighter rufous-orange patch over most of primaries. The flight-feathers and the dull rufous-buff tail are barred dark brown. The pale grey-buff face and the orange eyes heavily rimmed with black, add to the majestic appearance of this owl.

A superficial similarity to the Brown Fish Owl could be confusing but the Fish Owl has an ill-defined facial disc and always has yellow eyes without black rims, shorter and more triangular-shaped 'ear-tufts', narrower but overall dark streaking on the underparts, and completely bare legs and feet of a dirty grey hue.

In flight the huge barrel-shaped body, great wing area and powerful, majestic wing-flapping (reminiscent of a Buzzard *Buteo buteo*) are unmistakable. It is not a strictly nocturnal owl, usually hunting in the twilight of dusk or the grey of dawn, and it may also be seen by day, especially during spring and in winter.

VOICE

The Eagle Owl's monotonous call is well known over much of mainland Europe, a continuous *oohu-oohu-oohu* which has given rise to its German name of 'Uhu'. The call is one of the best aids to locating the bird, being audible at great distances, in all conditions up to 1.5 km, but during good weather up to 4 km (Glutz von Blotzheim and Bauer 1980). The Eagle Owl may call throughout the year, but vocal activity is at its highest in the six weeks before egg-laying. During that period the owl may call up to 600 times a night (Desfayes 1951).

In East Germany, König and Haensel (1968) monitored the resumption of calling throughout a single year. Figure 8 shows that calling usually began before sunset, though often half an hour earlier. Intensive calling normally lasted no longer than 70 minutes, thus ending approximately half an hour after sunset, but single calls could be heard before and after this period.

In my own small samples (Mikkola 1970) the first call took place at 17.50 hr and the

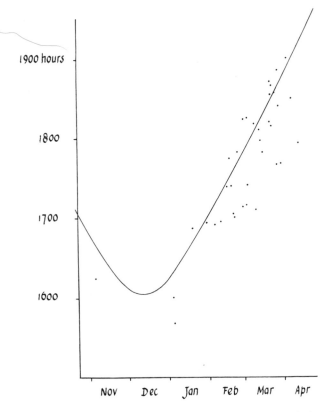

Fig. 8 *Commencement of Eagle Owl's calling activity in East Germany (König and Haensel 1968). Solid line shows approximate times of sunset; dots show start of calling*

last one at 09.45 hr, the calling being more often heard during calm and cloudless nights when the temperature was between 0° and −5°C.

When the Eagle Owl 'sings' it holds itself horizontally (head, body and tail on the same axis) and rocks backwards and forwards on its extended feet to the rhythm of its bitonal song (Blondel and Badan 1976). These two authors never heard the Eagle Owl singing from the roost site, nor from the nest, but they found several special song posts inside the owl's territory. The Eagle Owl would also call in flight, notably as it moved between song posts.

When the adults are excited, they reply to each other from ridge to ridge. The voice of the female during this duetting is about a third higher than the male's, making it possible to sex birds at the peak of the mating season (cf. Leibundgut 1973).

At the time of mating other sounds are made which can be almost terrifying to a person walking in the forest and unaware of the owl's presence. These sounds suggest the moaning of a baby or a grisly guffaw with rattling and grating (Brdicka 1969).

The food-begging calls of the young are very characteristic, a *chwätsch* or a longer *chjüjöo*, uttered every ten seconds, according to Blondel and Badan (1976). These hootings can be heard up to 1 km away on calm nights (Frey 1973).

In Sweden, Kranz (1971) calculated that owlets made 2,000 to 2,500 food-begging calls a night, with a maximum of 550 calls an hour in June. In July the maximum rose to 600 calls an hour and in August 900 calls an hour, reaching a total of 5,000 calls a night.

During feeding sessions the young owls give a repeated, specific call, a sort of *bibi-bibi*, reminiscent of the Little Grebe *Podiceps ruficollis*. When the owlets are more than two weeks old they may snap their bills loudly in anger or agitation (Blondel and Badan 1976).

When an adult female reacts to intruders, she growls and barks in a most impressive manner, but one that is phonetically impossible to describe (cf. Blondel and Badan 1976).

BEHAVIOUR

Like many other owls, the Eagle Owl is sedentary and strongly territorial throughout the year, except for some mountain populations which may be forced to descend to lower ground in winter. For instance, all Swedish recoveries of older birds are in the vicinity of the ringing place. One Eagle Owl ringed as an adult was found at the same locality 20 years later (Lettesjö 1974). The average size of an Eagle Owl's territory, and its hunting range around the nest site, depends mainly upon the amount of available prey in the area. In Provence, France, a sector of 140 km^2 studied by Blondel and Badan (1976) contained ten certain pairs, perhaps 12, making an average territory per pair of about 1,400 ha.

Mebs (1972) arrived at a similar average size (1,500 ha) for Franconia in West Germany, whereas März (1958) believed an average territory in central Europe to be between 8,000 and 15,000 ha. In Sweden, Olsson (1979) found the mean distance between 29 nest sites to be 8.5 km, with a territory radius of about 4–5 km. This gives an area somewhat between the sizes mentioned by Mebs and März.

If the habitat is favourable, pairs may be relatively close to each other. In France, Blondel and Badan (1976) found occupied nests at less than 2 km apart (1.2, 1.4 and 1.6 km) and once three territories within 3.7 km. In the Auvergne region, Choussy (1971) found two Eagle Owl nests only 300 m apart and Blondel and Badan (1976) mentioned another record from the Massif Central where two nests were 400 m apart.

In Sweden, where the average territory radius is 4–5 km, Olsson (1979) believes it is unlikely that Eagle Owls would attack intruders at that distance. Their vigorous calls are quite capable of keeping other Eagle Owls away. On the other hand, if one of the paired adults is lost for any reason, territorial calls reaching up to 4 km will attract surplus owls to restore the pair. This shows how regular spacing is maintained by intraspecific competition and territorial behaviour, as Southern (1970) demonstrated with the Tawny Owl.

Blondel and Badan (1976) noted that Eagle Owl territories are bounded with song posts, which are assiduously frequented, sited on ridges, mountain peaks and rocky points. The bird sings and moves from post to post, marking out its territory. It rarely stays more than 5 to 10 minutes in the same place.

Faithful to their territory throughout the year, Eagle Owls also pair for life. Choussy (1971) has noted that the white marking on the throat serves as a recognition sign for the two sexes as they display to each other. Blondel and Badan (1976) once witnessed a pair mating. After singing for a time on a mountain peak, the male went to join the female, perched a little way off. The male landed beside her and then mounted her immediately with flapping wings. The act was very quick and the female crouched silently under the weight of her partner. After mounting, the male flew away. The female straightened herself slowly and remained immobile and silent for a long time, as if waiting for the male to return with food.

In earlier Scandinavian accounts authors seem to agree on the importance of the great forests to the Eagle Owl. However, nowadays the majority of Eagle Owls breed in well-cultivated districts dotted with human settlements. It is likely that the forests are no longer able to provide the Eagle Owl with sufficient food due to the recent extensive decline in small game, and this could explain the alteration in habitat selection. Indeed, Olsson (1979) has shown that Eagle Owls in Sweden take a major part of their food from two minor habitats, namely cultivated areas and wetlands. Although woods still form 60% of Eagle Owl biotopes in inland habitats, only 20% of the owl's food is found in woodland. The Austrian, Frey (1973), has shown, similarly, that the Eagle Owl's territory in central Europe has three essential components: rocks, forests and fields. As a result, Eagle Owls often live unconcernedly close to man according to Frey (1973). The Eagle Owl's fearlessness, or even aggressiveness towards man, shows considerable individual variation, and perhaps some geographical differences. In Finland, I have visited many Eagle Owl nests and have never been troubled by any of the adults. On most occasions I have found it difficult even to catch sight of them. On the other hand, in central Europe it is widely believed to be dangerous to visit an Eagle Owl's nest, and adult birds are said to attack anyone who tries to get too near the young (cf. Brdicka 1969).

In France, Blondel and Badan (1976) have noted that the intensity of aggression is variable from one individual to another, and that the male never shows aggression, even if the young are in danger. One female they studied for several years was particularly fearless, and in broad daylight flew to a perch quite close to one of the observers and scolded loudly and long. At night she was even more fearless and brushed against him, uttering harrowing cries. Once, when the young were close to fledging, she launched a direct attack and struck Badan on the neck. The blow was violent, like a strong punch, which left him stunned for several seconds. Fortunately, it seems that some Finnish Eagle Owls are becoming more aggressive towards intruders, like their central European cousins. Martti Lagerström and his owlwatching companions have encountered some angry Eagle Owls in recent years in southern Finland; whereas Prof. Merikallio knew of only one such observation in Finland in all the decades he was collecting his material.

It is generally accepted that the Eagle Owl is largely nocturnal, but its diurnal activity has been closely studied in Sweden by Kranz (1971). In 1969 he spent about 225 hours at a nest in Sörmland between June and September. His results are shown in Figure 9. It reveals how the owlets begin their food-begging or hunger calls near sunset, and before sunset in June because of the short nights. Similarly, hunger calls were recorded in June well after sunrise, although in July, August and September they ceased more or less at sunrise. All of the 22 feeding visits recorded took place between 21.00 and 04.00 hr, the peak activity being seven feeds between 23.00 and 24.00 hr. In June the nest contained three young but later one died. Only one feed per observation night was recorded in June, whereas later it varied from two to three per night. In France, Blondel and Badan (1976) found that three to four meals per night was usual. The first meal was always at nightfall. Towards 22.00 hr there was often an

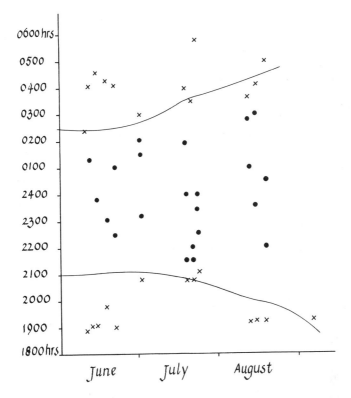

Fig. 9   Activity of a family of Eagle Owls in Sweden during 13 nights between June and September 1969 (Kranz 1971). x = start and finish of hunger calls of young; o = feeding visits of adults. The solid line indicates approximate times of sunrise and sunset at the study area

'optional' meal, a further one at times between 01.00 and 0.300 hr, and then a meal shortly before dawn. The period of darkness in France is much longer than in Sweden, allowing the French Eagle Owls more hunting time. In Sweden, activity was mainly concentrated in the hours just before midnight, giving a more or less monophasic pattern of activity.

An Eagle Owl's hunting ground is extensive, often as much as ten or more kilometres in diameter, depending upon the density of prey species in the area. For example, in Sweden, Olsson (1979) studied one territory where adult Eagle Owls brought several young herons to their nest from a heronry 4.1 km distant, and in another territory Eagle Owls brought in young Buzzards from a Buzzard's nest 4.8 km away.

Buzzards and other birds of prey including smaller owls are frequently preyed upon by the Eagle Owl as is described in greater detail in the chapter 'Interspecific aggression among European owls and raptors'. Only the Golden Eagle and the White-tailed Eagle seem to be possible rivals for the Eagle Owl. However, the White-tailed Eagle has also demonstrated a high degree of tolerance in Sweden by nesting on one occasion only 600 m from an Eagle Owl's nest, and in two other cases

900 m away (Olsson 1979). Blondel and Badan (1976) maintain that in Provence the Eagle Owl did not disturb the other raptor species, Bonelli's Eagle *Hieraaetus fasciatus* and Egyptian Vulture *Neophron percnopterus*, which also favour rocky surroundings. But they did acknowledge that nest site competition might occur between the Eagle Owl and the Peregrine *Falco peregrinus* (see Conservation chapter). Olsson (1979) noted that predation from foxes *Vulpes vulpes* and badgers *Meles meles* seems to be the greatest natural danger to Eagle Owl nestlings in Sweden. Eleven such cases were proven by Olsson and there was evidence that several others may have occurred. In one instance a large dead owlet was found half-way into a fox's den. Although an adult Eagle Owl may catch a young fox, it seems incapable of defending its young against such large mammal predators. On the other hand, of the large rupestral birds of prey, the Eagle Owl is the only species whose older nestlings display elaborate intimidation behaviour when faced with a possible predator. The owlet gets to its feet, fixes the enemy with its immense eyes, puffs out its feathers and stretches its wings to a maximum to increase its size, and blows and clicks its bill while rocking from one foot to the other. Blondel and Badan (1976) have witnessed owlets click their bills and take up their intimidation posture when faced with a toad, a large *Coleoptera* insect, a fieldmouse and a Serin *Serinus serinus*. The Serin came on several consecutive days in search of down for its own nest.

The older owlet's intimidation posture should be effective in dissuading predators such as foxes or badgers which are not aware of the owlet's inoffensive and helpless state, lacking the adult's powerful bill and claws. Up to the age of four weeks the owlets attempt to flatten themselves in an attempt to hide, contenting themselves with bill clicking and blowing. This is the period when they are very vulnerable and fall victim to predators such as foxes and badgers, and even martens (Frey 1973). Adoption of a defensive posture is not the only means of outwitting an enemy. It is almost certain that the Eagle Owl will carry its young away if the nest is seriously disturbed. Choussy (1971) has deduced this in two cases in France. Once, an owlet disappeared from a nest that he visited regularly and was later found in another valley about 900 m away. Choussy could only surmise that the adult owl had carried its unfledged young to the new place. At another nest the female appeared alarmed and distressed by his visits and most probably carried her three young away between 12th–13th April when he discontinued his observation of the nest site. The transporting of young has more or less been proven with the American Eagle Owl *Bubo virginianus*. Brady (1976) concluded that a Great Horned Owl transported two unfledged owlets from their nest because of an unusual windstorm. The owlests were found the following day about 9 m up a tree about 70 m away, beyond a 6 m wide stream. Other owls such as Barn and Tawny Owls will also move their owlets if the nest is disturbed (cf. Choussy 1971).

The Eagle Owl has various hunting techniques and will take prey on the ground or in full flight. Its food is varied, ranging from *Coleoptera* insects to foxes. The owl may hunt in forest, but it prefers open spaces. From the beginning of egg-laying to the time when the chicks are half-grown the male alone hunts, but once the chicks are aged a month or more, the female will help. As with many other birds of prey, the male never stays at the nest but leaves the prey item then departs immediately. The female distributes the food to the chicks and feeds herself at the nest. Blondel and Badan (1976) noted that in a period of superabundance of food the female carefully hides left-over prey items under a bush or in a rock crevice. During the chicks' first four weeks the female remained in the nest and surplus food was placed at the back of the nest against a rock. One evening they saw the female remove an entire fox cub from beneath a neighbouring plant *Smilax*, having concealed the cub the day before or that same morning. The fox was not completely eaten that night and its remains were hidden again in the same place at the end of the meal. The next day, the operation was repeated. This food storage behaviour is, according to Blondel and Badan (1976), regular, notably for large, freshly-killed prey animals. It is not until they are six weeks old that the young owls begin effectively to feed themselves. By then they have the strength to tear a rabbit to pieces, whereas hitherto prey items were dismembered by the female (Blondel and Badan 1976).

FOOD

Because of their large size, Eagle Owl pellets are relatively easy to collect in quantity at diurnal roosts, at special plucking posts or at and near nest sites. There is usually a tree near the nest with a favoured branch where the male has regularly perched. Under such a roosting place there will be plenty of pellets and droppings, but rarely any other food remains because the Eagle Owl does not eat at its roosting place. Feathers, bones and other food remains will be found, instead, on rocks and on ridges where the owl feeds. During the incubation and early nestling periods the female leaves her pellets at the bottom of the nest. After breeding, this thick pellet carpet containing the food of the female and her young can also be collected. The size and shape of the pellets vary considerably, depending on structure, contents or age. In Sweden (Höglund 1966), Norway (Willgohs 1974) and in Finland (K. Huhtala, *in litt.*) pellet dimensions were recorded as follows:

	Sweden	Norway	Finland
Number of pellets	25	210	100
Maximum length (mm)	120	178	129
Maximum width (mm)	41	60	44
Minimum length (mm)	46	30	36
Minimum width (mm)	27	20	22
Average size (mm)	76×32	72×34×26	77×31×28

In Sweden, Höglund recorded the average dry weight of pellets as 14.2 g of which 6.98 g (49%) was bones. The shape of most pellets is somewhat compressed, irregularly cylindrical or conical (Willgohs 1974). When feeding on frogs or fish, and thus lacking the pellet-forming feathers and fur, the owl may assist pellet production by eating vegetable matter such as grass, moss or bits of heather. According to Willgohs these types of 'frog pellets' are smaller in size; two he measured were 52 × 39 mm and 47 × 32 mm. Another form of pellet has been recorded several times on inshore islands off western Norway where, after eating *Carcinus maenas* crustaceans, owls have produced 'crab pellets', irregular in shape and 40–80 mm in length.

Hedgehog spines are found in pellets less often than one might expect. The reason is that the owl has learned to prepare the hedgehog by tearing off the skin and spines of the back before eating the flesh (cf. März 1958 and Willgohs 1974).

The Eagle Owl's food has been well studied and dcoumented throughout its wide distribution range. Janossy and Schmidt (1970) complied Eurasian and North African results, giving, especially, an excellent account of Russian work. Since 1970, several new food studies have been published in Spain (Hiraldo *et al* 1975), in France (Blondel and Badan 1976), in Austria (Frey 1973, 1976; Frey and Walter 1977), in Germany (Bezzel *et al* 1976 and Wickl 1979), in Poland (Banz and Degen 1975), in Bulgaria (Baumgart *et al* 1973; Baumgart 1975) and in Mongolia (Piechocki *et al* 1977). For this book I have collated the less known but recent studies from northern Europe (Table 10). This large list (17,615 prey items) shows that the Eagle Owl will eat almost anything, from *Coleoptera* beetles to roe deer fawns *Capreolus capreolus*. As shown in Table 10 the major part of the Eagle Owl's diet consists of mammals, but birds of all kinds are also taken, including crows, ducks, grouse, seabirds, and even other raptors and owls. Snakes, lizards, frogs, fish, crabs and beetles are eaten occasionally. In northern Europe the most preyed-upon mammal species were ground voles *Arvicola terrestris*, (24%), *Microtus* voles (12%) and brown rats *Rattus norvegicus* (11%). Seabirds and ducks were the main avian prey (18% together). It is interesting to note that hares and grouse form only 2.7% and 3.1% respectively of the prey items, although most hunters are convinced of its game-killing habits and are still killing Eagle Owls. In Finland, killing Eagle Owls has been legal during hunting seasons and winters until this year (1983) when the law, hopefully, will finally be changed. The proportion of hares is highest in the Swedish results and even there Olsson (1979) estimated that hares formed only 9% of the prey biomass. In Canada, the situation seems to be completely different with the closely-related Great Horned Owl. For instance, McInvaille and Keith (1974) found that in Alberta as much as 77% and 81% of the owl's food is composed of snowshoe hares *Lepus americanus*. The Great Horned Owls in their study area manifested marked functional (dietary) and numerical responses to a cyclic increase of snowshoe hares. In northern Europe the Eagle Owl clearly has a similar relationship with the cyclic occurrences of *Microtus* and *Arvicola* voles.

I have studied one Eagle Owl pair in Kuopio for several years and noted remarkable differences in the diet from one year to another. During good ground vole years (for example 1981) the voles made up two-thirds of the diet, but when the voles were less numerous (for instance between 1972 and 1974) the proportion fell to between 5% and 16%. During these latter years the Eagle Owl preyed entirely upon brown rats living in a rubbish dump nearby. The rats then formed 66%–86% of the owl's food (Mikkola 1974). This example seems to indicate that these Eagle Owls prefer to hunt ground voles if they are numerous, and turn to brown rats when voles are scarce, because the rubbish dump always has plenty of rats. North European studies, too, show that there are large local differences in the owl's diet. In Norway the Eagle Owls studied were mainly coastal birds and these owls took relatively few mammals, preying on other birds, namely ducks and seabirds, this category comprising about 51% of the food items. In Estonia the owls studied were mostly forest birds, consuming over 83% mammals and only about 14% birds. The Finnish material, also, is mainly from inland habitats and is similar to the Estonian situation. The Swedish material is derived from a mixture of coastal and inland owls, the results being somewhere between those of Finland and Norway.

These studies indicate that the composition of the Eagle Owl's diet largely depends on the relative abundance and accessibility of mammal and bird prey, and that the Eagle Owl may, depending on the ecological situation, be either a food generalist or a food specialist. Spontaneous specialisation on abundant prey species probably favours successful hunting. The exploitation of few but abundant prey species enables the Eagle Owl to hunt in intensively-used areas of monoculture (cf. Bezzel *et al* 1976). Baumgart (1975) proposed that the Eagle Owl's preferred prey animals are not necessarily the most abundant, but those that are the most accessible (relative availability) and also the most economic (cf. Blondel 1967). Local variations in the owl's diet may likewise reflect accessibility of prey animals rather than their abundance.

BREEDING BIOLOGY

Eagle Owls occupy a variety of habitats from coniferous taiga forests in the north to warm deserts in the south. An adequate supply of food and good nesting places are probably the most important prerequisites for the Eagle Owl. In former times this owl nested mainly in inhospitable or inaccessible places, preferring regions that were remote from man's cultivations and settlements. Nowadays, there are more and more Eagle Owls which will tolerate human neighbours now that the forests of their breeding territories are being managed and altered. In North America particularly, and some parts of Europe, there are urban Eagle Owls which readily breed near human settlements and motorways (cf. Blondel and Badan 1976).

Olsson (1979) listed 199 Eagle Owl nest sites in Sweden, where this owl is a bird of wooded mountains, rocky woodland, and cliffs in the archipelagoes. The frequency of use of the various types of nest sites was as follows:

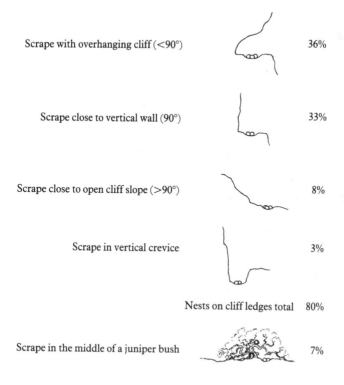

Scrape with overhanging cliff (<90°)	36%
Scrape close to vertical wall (90°)	33%
Scrape close to open cliff slope (>90°)	8%
Scrape in vertical crevice	3%
Nests on cliff ledges total	80%
Scrape in the middle of a juniper bush	7%

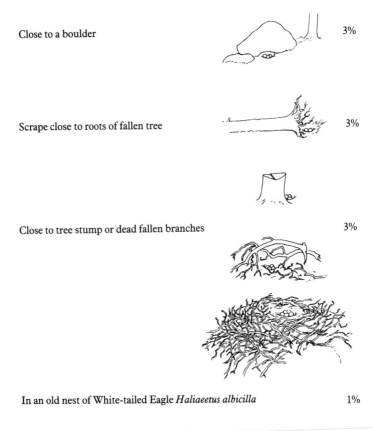

Close to a boulder   3%

Scrape close to roots of fallen tree   3%

Close to tree stump or dead fallen branches   3%

In an old nest of White-tailed Eagle *Haliaeetus albicilla*   1%

Close to a tree   3%

Olsson also listed the heights of 177 cliff nests. As Fig. 10 shows, the majority of the nests are located in the two middle quarters of the rock face.

Frey (1973) stated that Eagle Owls in Lower Austria prefer a cliff location that gives a clear field of view from the nest. This preference also seems common among Swedish owls in the light of Olsson's information above. Eagle Owls in Finland frequently inhabit low-lying woods and marshy forests where there are no rocks or cliffs available for breeding. In such areas, as in Pohjanmaa, the Eagle Owl usually breeds close to a tree, often an uprooted one, but they also use other nest sites not noted in Sweden. Prof. Merikallio listed five Eagle Owl tree-nests: two in an old Golden Eagle's *Aquila chrysaetos* nest, one in a nest originally built by a Buzzard *Buteo buteo*, and two in a large hollow of a tree. My colleague, Juhani Koivusaari, recently

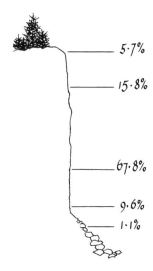

Fig. 10   Placing on rock face of 177 cliff nests at various sites (Olsson 1979)

found an Eagle Owl breeding in one of his White-tailed Eagle nests. In two different areas in Pohjanmaa the Eagle Owl has bred on hay in a barn and once in the attic of a forest cottage. In the 1960s in Oulu, Dr Seppo Sulkava and I studied an Eagle Owl which bred in a temporary shelter of poles and branches which foresters had erected during the winter to protect them from wind and rain.

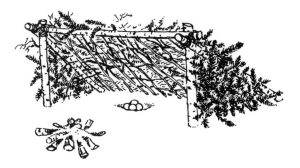

In recent years Risto Saarinen has built similar shelters in some of his Eagle Owl territories where no protected nest site had existed, and they have twice (1979) been adopted by Eagle Owls. One autumn a Finnish bird photographer built a hide preparatory to filming the mating display of Capercaillie *Tetrao urogallus* the following spring. On visiting the hide later he found three young Eagle Owls in a nest scrape inside (Saarinen 1979). The most curious nest site I know of is at Oulu, and concerns an Eagle Owl which we call 'anthill breeder'. For several years this owl has bred in hollows she has made in various anthills. I do not know whether the owl finds a

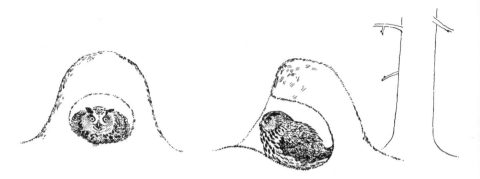

disused anthill or whether the anthill is occupied when she excavates it in early spring. I have seen at least five different anthills which this female has used.

In eastern Finland, Eagle Owls usually nest in rocky surroundings, and one of my favourite Eagle Owls at Kuopio has two high, rocky hills in its territory, about 1.5 km apart, which she uses alternately. I know of eight different nest sites (four on each hill) which she has used since 1973. It seems that the Eagle Owl rarely occupies the same nest site in consecutive years but will remain two or three years on the same hill. Blondel and Badan (1976) also stated that a female they came to know very well over a period of seven years, occupied eight different sites in the same territory. However, in some territories the most favoured scrapes are used for several years. Olsson knew a territory where the same scrape was used 15 times during his 16 years' study period. Only once during this time did the owl breed in another scrape.

It is possible to help Eagle Owls breed by improving nest sites on rocky cliffs. Frey *et al* (1974) have done so successfully in Austria and so has Olsson (1979) in Sweden. One of Olsson's owls was using an extremely open nest close to a vertical face and to give the nest some shelter, an old juniper bush was placed over the nest scrape. The BBC wished to film my Eagle Owl in Finland, so in the autumn I made a nest scrape beside a large flat rock in an ideal place for filming from a hide. Somewhat surprisingly the owl nested in this man-made scrape and, for the first time in my study period, she had four young all of which fledged successfully. Unfortunately, the BBC team was too busy filming elsewhere and unable to take advantage of this fantastic opportunity.

The Eagle Owl does not construct a true nest but makes a hollow in the ground (or even excavates anthills). After preparing the scrape no material is brought to the nest, but this does not mean that there is no bedding. During the incubation and nestling period, the female breaks up her pellets and arranges them carefully in the nest to form a soft pad for the young chicks (cf. Blondel and Badan 1976).

The early breeding stages of the Eagle Owl should not be studied at all. If the bird is disturbed at the nest in early spring, it often abandons eggs and even small nestlings. However, it seems that we have plenty of data on the egg-laying of the Eagle Owl both in northern and southern Europe. In Spain the first layings take place as early as the end of January, the laying period extending to April (Morillo 1976). In southern France the average date of the first egg laid was 27th January, the extremes being 27th December and 23rd February. Three replacement clutches were known to have been laid on 7th, 10th and 16th March (Blondel and Badan 1976). In West Germany the average commencement of incubation was 25th February (Rockenbauch 1978). In Sweden, Olsson (1979) has noted the dates of egg-laying at 83 nests (Fig. 11). The main period is the last ten days of March with an approximately even spread before and after this time. Two egg-layings in May were known to be replacement clutches and although many other eggs have been laid in May, it is not known whether these were first clutches or replacement ones. In Finland, early visits to nests containing eggs have been avoided and we have no recent information on first-laying dates. From earlier data of egg-collectors, egg-laying starts in southern Finland at the end of March and in the north around mid-April, extending to the end of May in Lapland. Some late nests with eggs have been found even at the beginning of June (v. Haartman *et al* 1967).

When the Eagle Owl starts breeding early in northern Europe its eggs are laid on snow, or at least the nest is surrounded by snow. Olsson (1979) stated that most of the eggs in Sweden were laid while the snow cover was still 10–20 cm deep. This is possible only because of the careful nest site selection by Eagle Owl, though we have one observation in Finland to the contrary. In the middle of April an Eagle Owl laid one egg in the snow in a mixed forest in Mustasaari. The depth of snow was 35 cm. The snow melted under the female and the egg sank until it rested on a small stump, which caused the bird to desert. Later this female made a new nest on snowless ground about 100 m from the snow nest. On this occasion two eggs were laid at the base of a large boulder and both hatched successfully (Pulliainen and Rajala 1973).

Eggs are laid at 2–4 day intervals, a clutch of three eggs usually taking 7–8 days. The clutch size of the European Eagle Owl varies from one to six, the average as shown below being 2.6 for 481 nests.

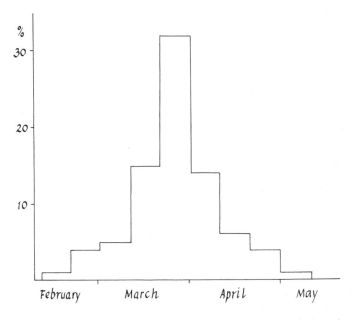

Fig. 11   First-egg-laying dates of Eagle Owl in southeast Sweden. One exceptionally late brood (26th May) has been omitted (after Olsson 1979)

Eggs	1	2	3	4	5	6	X̄	No. of nests
Sweden (Olsson 1979	1	19	6	1	–	–	2.26	27
Curry-Lindahl 1950)	7	56	41	12	–	3	2.59	119
Finland (Merikallio Archives)	–	97	74	24	1	–	2.64	196
Estonia (Randla 1976)	–	10	11	2	–	–	2.65	23
E. *Germany* (Knobloch in Glutz v. Blotzheim and Bauer 1980)	–	37	29	10	2	–	2.71	78
W. *Germany* (Förstel 1977)	2	6	8	5	2	–	2.96	23
France (Blondel and Badan 1976)	–	1	11	3	–	–	3.13	15
Total	10	226	180	57	5	3	2.64	481

This list would seem to show that the clutch size increases from north to south, being 3.1 in France and only 2.3 in Sweden. Prof. Merikallio stated that in his material the clutch size was slightly more (2.7) in south Finland than in Lapland (2.5 from 5 nests). In Sweden clutches are, it seems, smaller than about 30 years ago (Curry-Lindahl 1950), the average clutch size having decreased from 2.6 to 2.3. In Finland Korpimäki (1981) has noted recent clutch sizes for 43 nests and has similar results (average 2.6) to Prof. Merikallio. Leibundgut (1973) has noted that young captive females laid 2 to 3 eggs, while older owls laid 3 to 5 eggs. The older females also started to breed earlier, at the end of March in Zürich, and the younger ones at the end of April or the beginning of May.

Incubation begins when the second egg is laid and is for 32–35 days, being undertaken almost entirely by the female. The chicks hatch at intervals over several days. The newly-hatched nestling is altricial and downy, the down being short, thick and soft, buffish-white, with more buff on the forehead and under the eyes, and on the wings and rump (cf. Harrison 1975). Scherzinger (1974) has studied the development of young Eagle Owls in captivity, and noted that at hatching the chick weighs 52 g. At between 28 and 35 days old the owlets weigh about 68% of the adult weight (2,300 g). At this age, although unable to fly, the owlets leave the nest. Their first attempts at flight take place when they are 52 days old and after a further eight days or so the owlets can fly well. Several days later, at about 70 days, they begin to catch their first food items independently. According to Morillo (1976), the family group remains in the breeding territory until October when the immatures disperse.

The breeding success of the Eagle Owl has been studied in Sweden, Finland and West Germany as recorded below:

	Sweden	Finland	W. Germany
Number fledged/successful nests	1.6	1.7	1.8
Number of nests	87	54	261
Author	Olsson 1979	Korpimäki 1981	Wickl 1979

If we compare the number of eggs with the number of fledged young, we see that on average one egg or one owlet disappears, even in successful nests. The last-hatched chick is often considerably smaller than the first-born and may fall victim to its siblings who, with help from the female, show no hesitation in eating it if food is short. The real breeding success is however much lower than the list suggests. In

Sweden, Olsson (1979) has shown that from 219 occupied nesting territories only 87 nest attempts (i.e. 40%) were successful, the number of fledged young per occupied nest averaging only 0.6. Olsson (1979) also showed that without an abundance of rodents, Eagle Owls in south-east Sweden may not begin breeding, but that the clutch size or the number of fledged young was not affected to any high degree by this factor. Haftorn (1971) stated that in the mountainous forests of eastern Norway the Eagle Owls breed almost only in peak rodent years. On the other hand in southern Europe the Eagle Owl breeds successfully every year. In France, Blondel and Badan (1976) calculated an average of 2.7 young from 13 clutches, which is very high compared with results for Sweden and Finland. In Austria, Frey (1973) also found no evidence that his Eagle Owls ceased breeding in some years and he maintained that this was due to the varied choice of prey there, as did Blondel and Badan (1976) in France.

The causes of death of fledged Eagle Owls have been recorded in Finland (Saurola 1979), Sweden (Olsson 1979) and in West Germany (Wickl 1979, including Obst *et al* 1977). Although the samples are very mixed, and in many cases the real cause of death has not been stated at all, Table 11 still gives some idea of the dangers faced by this owl from man. Electrical constructions, traffic and direct killings by shooting, trapping or otherwise, together caused death in 61.1% of the 296 cases where the cause was known. And in Finland and Germany some of the 'found' casualties were most likely killed by man. Known cases of natural deaths are not numerous, but interesting. In Sweden, a 30 cm long adder *Vipera berus* was found in the stomach of a dead Eagle Owl and the adder had probably bitten the owl before dying itself. Another dead Eagle Owl had had its oesophagus perforated by the ingested leg of a raptor (Olsson 1979). Bochenski (1960) mentions a case from Poland where an Eagle Owl was killed by a protruding hedgehog spine.

As so many owls die from electrical installations it is important, and surely also possible, to render such installations less dangerous. On the other hand, Blondel and Badan (1976) have noted that in southern France several Eagle Owl pairs have nested in the immediate vicinity of high tension cables, and that the birds (at least the experienced adults) know how to avoid them even at night. In Sweden, owls under the heading 'poisoned' are all poisoned by mercury. Olsson (1979) suggests that this figure is a minimum because starved Eagle Owls often had high mercury residues. Since 1966 the most fatal mercury compound has been banned in Sweden, so the risk of poisoning is now lessening.

In Europe, the Eagle Owl is highly sedentary. All the Swedish ringing results show that ringed birds have kept close to their hatching place. Seventy-five per cent have been found less than 50 km away, and none farther than 86 km (Olsson 1979). Rockenbauch (1978) recorded one recovery in West Germany where the owl had travelled 205 km from its nest during its first winter.

DISTRIBUTION

The Eagle Owl belongs to a cosmopolitan group of very large owls, of which the Great Horned Owl from America and the Cape Eagle Owl *Bubo capensis* from Africa are also members. Eck and Busse (1973) treated this group as Eagle Owl, *Bubo bubo*, naming a total of 43 subspecies, but Great Horned Owls and Cape Eagle Owls are more usually considered to be separate species on grounds of plumage colour and marking. However, in evolutionary terms the ecological separation of these species

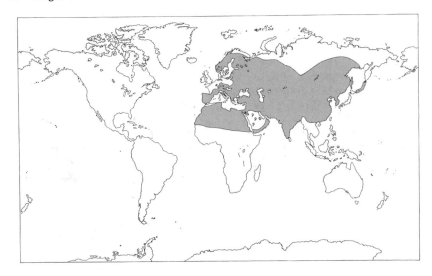

EAGLE OWL – mainly resident but has wandered to Britain, Holland, Denmark and Japan

occurred quite recently. If one takes the Eagle Owl, *Bubo bubo*, as a separate species its faunal type is palearctic and its distribution trans-palearctic, oriental and discontinuously Ethiopian, in boreal, temperate, Mediterranean, steppe, desert and tropical winter-dry climatic zones (Voous 1960).

The area range of this book encompasses the ten races described at the beginning of this species chapter. This versatile and widespread owl has declined markedly in western and northern Europe due to human persecution in various forms (see Conservation chapter), disturbance, habitat change and, probably, toxic chemicals (cf. Everett and Sharrock 1980). This drastic decline has been well documented in Sweden where three countrywide surveys on the status of the Eagle Owl have been made since 1943. The list below shows the number of breeding places with one or a pair of Eagle Owls present at the three surveys between 1943 and 1975 (cf. Olsson 1976).

	Year of survey			Difference between
Area	1943–48	1964–65	1974–75	1st and 3rd survey
Götaland	68	56	46	− 22
Svealand	94	28	68	− 26
Norrland	293	91	57	−236
Whole country	455	175	171	−284

The most alarming situation is in Norrland where the Eagle Owl population has shown a steady and rapid decline. Olsson believes that active persecution is still going on in this part of Sweden. The European Atlas (Everett and Sharrock 1980) stated that the Eagle Owl is certainly the most endangered European owl, although it still breeds over the larger part of continental Europe from about 70°N in Norway, 68°–69°N in Sweden and Finland and the southern Kola Peninsula, southwards throughout Russia, central and south-east Europe as far as the German Rhineland,

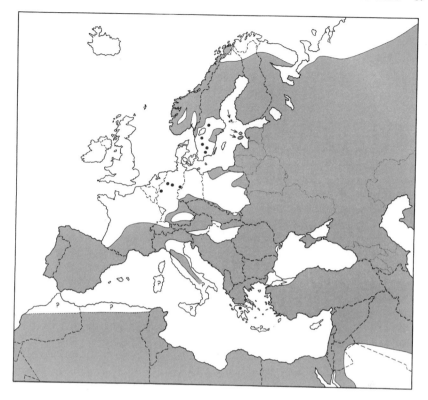

EAGLE OWL – mainly resident

eastern and southern France, Iberia, Italy and the Balkans. It is probable, but not certain, that its present absence in Great Britain and Ireland is the result of persecution by man, as in western Europe and parts of Italy and the Balkans.

Approximate population estimates from northern and central Europe show that there are between 4,500 and 6,500 Eagle Owl pairs in the countries listed in Table 12. But the Table lacks information from Portugal and the Balkan countries, and the estimation for Spain seems rather high in comparison with other European countries. In Portugal, the Eagle Owl is said to be resident but very rare (R. Vicente, *in litt.*), though a little less so in the north-east corner of the country (Delgado Rufino, *in litt*). In Spain, Morillo (1976) stated that its numbers have diminished during the last few years, making it rare in the Iberian continent. On the other hand, F. Hiraldo (*in litt.*) has more recently found relatively dense Eagle Owl populations in parts of Spain, as many as four pairs in 3 km² in some favourable sites of Sierra Morena and Montes de Toledo. In the rest of the country the population is less numerous but the Eagle Owl is still well distributed, absent only in wide valleys and some mesetas.

In Italy, Mario Bonora (*in litt.*) has studied Eagle Owls in Bologna where he has discovered seven territories in an area of 2,000 km². His owls have been regularly shot by Italian hunters despite the law that has protected all owls in that area since 1963! In Greece the Eagle Owl is said to be rare and irregular, but birds are thought to be killed for taxidermy in many parts of the country (cf. Bauer *et al* 1969). There seem to be few, if any, owlwatchers in Greece and so no counts of breeding birds are known. In Yugoslavia, the Eagle Owl occurs throughout the country but the numbers are not known (V. Vasic, *in litt.*). In Turkey this owl is sparsely but widely distributed, being most common on the Central Plateau. It is almost certainly absent from Thrace (cf. O.S.T. Reports). The Eagle Owl seems to be absent from all the Mediterranean islands and the Canaries. Morillo (1976) has confirmed its absence in the Balearics and the Canaries and the French Atlas shows none in Corsica. Bonora gave no Eagle Owls for Sardinia or Sicily, nor did Böhr for Crete or Leontiades for Cyprus. Macfarlane (*in litt.*) stated that the Eagle Owl is resident in Syria and Lebanon but in very small numbers. Scott (*in litt.*) wrote that this owl is common in Iran and widespread, occurring throughout the country in forests, mountains, deserts and the more humid lowlands.

11: Brown Fish Owl *Ketupa zeylonensis*
(Gmelin)

Bright brown above with wide black streaks. The upper back and the wing coverts are very mottled with brown and fawn. There are some buff and white spots on the shoulders and there is a pale edging to the scapulars. The flight and tail feathers are strongly barred with black-brown and pale buff. The underneath is a warm fawny-buff, distinctively marked with black-brown longitudinal streaking. Each feather is marked with fine wavy barring noticeable only at close range. The iris is bright yellow, the bill is dirty greenish-horn-coloured and the legs are lead grey. The tarsus is bare, the feathers are replaced by granular scales and the sole is covered with small scales. The claws are very curved. The facial disc is only slightly developed and fawny-brown in colour, but the feather tufts forming 'ears' are broad and long. Natal down and mesoptile plumage have not yet been described.

There seem to be colour differences between widespread populations. In the arid areas of Palestine and Iraq, the Brown Fish Owls collected have been very pale and buff, but they are a richer yellow-brown in the humid forest areas of India and Indo-China. There are no measurements available from the western birds but Dement'ev *et al.* (1951) have some measurements from the eastern birds *Ketupa z. doerriesi*. Length of males 710 mm, wingspan 1780 mm; length of females 710 mm, wingspan 1890 mm. Wings of males 510–550 mm (average 530 mm from 7 birds); females 538–560 mm (average 548 mm from 9 birds). The females tend to be slightly larger than males, but otherwise the sexes are believed to be similar.

IN THE FIELD

They are large, nocturnal owls, with an external appearance generally similar to the

Eagle Owl, with which they are often mistaken, although they differ in three main respects. Firstly, their feet are devoid of feathers; secondly, they have an even less prominent facial disc; thirdly, they lack soft plumage and silent flight. (See also penultimate paragraph of 'In the field' description for Eagle Owl.)

VOICE

As with most owls, the Brown Fish Owl is particularly noisy before breeding, and pairs sometimes indulge in bouts of duetting which may continue for many minutes. Etchécopar and Hüe (1970) maintain that its call is unlike that of an owl, being a mewing rather reminiscent of the Stone Curlew *Burhinus oedicnemus*. Other calls are a lugubrious *haou-haou-haou-ha* and a deep triple note *hou-hou-hou*.

BEHAVIOUR

The Brown Fish Owl is strongly territorial and is always found near water where it seeks its food. It rarely hunts before dusk, being thoroughly nocturnal. Usually, it hunts from a tree stump, a dead branch or some other vantage point overlooking the water's edge. It catches its prey in the same manner as a fish-eagle, by swooping and snatching it from the surface of the water with its talons, and not by plunging bodily into the water in the manner of the Osprey *Pandion haliaetus*.

FOOD

The Brown Fish Owl feeds primarily on fish. The feet of fish-owls, like those of fish-eagles and the Osprey, are beautifully adapted to grip a wriggling, slippery, loose-scaled fish. However, the Brown Fish Owl will also take almost any other prey that comes its way, including small mammals, birds, snakes, frogs, crayfish, crabs and sometimes insects. Mammals recorded in its diet include a small porcupine; and birds include species up to the size of junglefowl and pheasants. It also scavenges to some extent. One Brown Fish Owl has been recorded feeding on the carcass of a crocodile (Burton ed. 1973).

BREEDING BIOLOGY

Brown Fish Owls use a variety of nest-sites, including holes in trees and riverbanks, ledges in cliffs and ruins, hollows in the forks of trees, and the old nests of crows, vultures and eagles. Tolerance of the nearby presence of humans whilst breeding is suggested by the nest in a hollow of a large tree in a Canal Department bungalow in India, photographed by Lowther. Clutch sizes of from one to three eggs have been recorded.

It is thought to breed between November and May throughout its range. In India and northern Indo-China this is the dry season, which suggests that the breeding season might be timed to coincide with the period when river levels are low, the water clear, and fish therefore easier to catch. Nevertheless, the same period is the wet season in the Middle East and a more satisfactory explanation needs to be found (Burton ed. 1973).

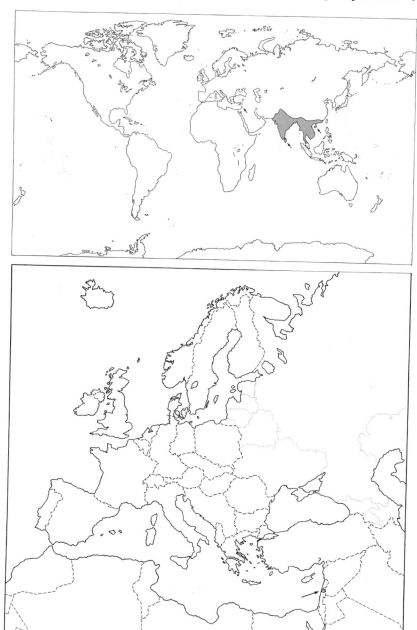

BROWN FISH OWL – arrow points to breeding area in lower map

DISTRIBUTION

Etchécopar and Hüe state that the Brown Fish Owl has been found locally in the south of Turkey, Palestine, perhaps Syria, the hills south of the Zagros in Iraq and the south-west of Iran, also in India, Ceylon, southern China and the Himalayas up to 3,000 m. Nowadays its status is uncertain in Turkey, but it may still breed beside rivers along the Mediterranean coast. Macfarlane (*in litt.*) has not seen this bird in Syria nor in Lebanon, and Mendelssohn (*in litt.*) says it is decreasing in Israel. He writes: 'Formerly this species occurred in western Galilee and around Lake Tiberias. Now it occurs only in some valleys on the eastern shore of Lake Tiberias. The reason for its decline is the use of thallium sulphate as a rodenticide in the [nineteen] fifties and the drying up of the stream in a valley in western Galilee where this species occurred. The water from this stream is now being used for human settlements.' Scott (*in litt.*) states that it is very rare in Iran if not extinct. It was formerly reported in forests along rivers in the south-west Zagros mountains, but it has not been reported in the last 20 years.

12: Snowy Owl *Nyctea scandiaca*
(Linné)

DESCRIPTION

The general coloration of the Snowy Owl is white, barred and spotted to a varying extent with dark brown. The upper part of the facial disc is incomplete, the feathers above the golden- or lemon-yellow eye being normal and not radiating. It has very small ear-tufts, each consisting of ten to twelve small short feathers, but these are seldom visibly erected above the normal layer of head feathering. As one would expect with a bird capable of surviving throughout the high Arctic year the Snowy Owl has had to adapt to the severities of climate and habitat. The plumage is exceptionally dense and downy in comparison with some southern owls, and the feather cells are filled with air for additional insulation. In addition, the short black bill and the legs of the Snowy Owl are both largely concealed by feathers, which are very long and dense on the legs and extend right down to the black claws.

Sexual colour dimorphism is usually absent in owls, but the Snowy Owl is an exception. The adult male is almost pure white and the adult female is predominantly white marked with dark brown. This colour dimorphism has survival value during the breeding season, as the barring on the female provides excellent camouflage when nesting on hummocky or rocky ground in partially snow-covered tundra.

The Snowy Owl also differs from many other owls by having clear differences between first-year and fully adult plumages. The first-year plumage of both sexes is distinctly darker than the adult plumages, due to the much heavier barring of the young birds. The female first-year plumage is white with dense black-brown regular cross-barring below, and more U- or V-shaped barring above, except on the lower nape which appears as a white collar. The top of the head is densely flecked and spotted black-brown. The face and upper breast are unmarked white. This is the darkest and most heavily barred plumage in the Snowy Owl, and is illustrated in the chapter heading.

First-year males also have dark brown markings and cross-barring, but their plumage is much less contrasted than that of young females; and although the distribution of barring is about the same as in females, it is browner and less distinct. Tulloch (1969) describes the males as having, from a distance, a fawn appearance, whereas young females look grey.

The definitive plumage of second-year and older birds is basically snowy-white in the male, usually marked only by a few dark brown spots on the nape, back, scapulars and wings, and small bars or patches on the tips of the remiges. Occasionally, its overall appearance is even whiter, but conversely some birds may be more marked with fine dark brown bars, or transversely extending patches on the scapulars, wing-coverts, underparts, remiges and rectrices. From their second year adult females have a white ground colour, against which are fairly extensive, though rather broken, brown cross-bars on the underparts, upperparts, remiges and rectrices. The feathering of the face, throat, upper breast, wing lining and legs is always white.

The female has four to six brown cross-bars on its tail, whereas the male has either none or up to three corresponding bars. The fine bars of the male's underparts are not more than 3 mm in breadth, whilst those of the female are over 3 mm (Portenko 1972).

During their first ten days the nestlings are covered with white down but this soon changes to sooty-grey except for the throat, legs and toes and the striking facial disc. The mesoptile plumage is brown with white tips (remnants of down) on the under parts, and the scapulars are brown with whitish bars, the facial disc is whitish, and the remiges and rectrices are white with brown cross-bars and brown vermiculations in the form of speck-like marbling.

Portenko (1972) listed the following measurements: total length of males varies 525–640 mm (average 585 mm from 9 birds); females 590–650 mm (average 617 mm from 9 birds), revealing that the females are noticeably larger.

Dement'ev et al (1951) noted the wing length for 86 males as 384–423 mm (average 405 mm). The wing length of 63 females measured was 428–462 mm (average 438 mm).

The weight of males is 1,280–2,300 g (average 1,726 g from 13 birds) and that of females 1,700–2,950 g (average 2,239 g from 27 birds), the measurements of these 40 owls emanating from studies in Finland (v. Haartman et al 1967) and the USSR (Dement'ev et al 1951). Watson (1957) weighed a larger number of individual owls in Canada, and gave the weight of 36 males as 710–2,500 g (average 1,730 g), and that of 23 females as 780–2,950 g (average 2,120 g). There seems to be no noticeable size difference between Eurasian and North American Snowy Owls (see also Portenko 1972).

IN THE FIELD

This very large, white, round-headed bird is unmistakable. Barn Owls are also white-breasted in the West European race, but the Snowy Owl is much larger in size, and its upper parts are white and its eyes are yellow. The Snowy Owl is almost as large as the Eagle Owl but is easily distinguished from most races of this latter bird, apart from its whiteness, by its smaller eyes, a fairly long tail and an absence of ear-tufts. In the whitish Siberian race of the Eagle Owl the pattern is vermiculated and streaked rather than barred as in the Snowy Owl.

Usually the Snowy Owl perches on the ground or upon a rock, sometimes on a post or stump, and only occasionally does it perch in trees. It is extremely shy during the

Hawk Owl *Surnia ulula*

Barn Owl *Tyto alba guttata*

Barn Owl *Tyto alba alba*

Snowy Owl
Nyctea scandiaca ♂

Snowy Owl *Nyctea scandiaca* ♀

Ian Willis 1976

Eagle Owl *Bubo bubo sibiricus*

Eagle Owl *Bubo bubo bubo*

Eagle Owl
Bubo bubo desertorum

Eagle Owl
Bubo bubo ascalaphus

Ian Willis 1976

Great Grey Owl *Strix nebulosa*

Brown Fish Owl
Ketupa zeylonensis

Long-eared Owl *Asio otus*

Short-eared Owl *Asio flammeus*

African Marsh Owl *Asio capensis*

Ian Willis 1976

IV

Ural Owl
S. u. uralensis

Ural Owl
Strix uralensis liturata

Tawny Owl *Strix aluco*
(rufous end of colour spectrum)

Tawny Owl *Strix aluco*
(grey end of colour spectrum)

Hume's Owl *Strix butleri*

Ian Willis 1976

Tengmalm's Owl
Aegolius funereus
(adult)

Tengmalm's Owl
Aegolius funereus (juvenile)

Little Owl
Athene noctua lilith
(palest desert race)

Little Owl
Athene noctua vidalii

Scops Owl
Otus scops

Striated Scops Owl *Otus brucei*

Pygmy Owl
Glaucidium passerinum

Ian Willis 1976

VI

Eagle Owl
Bubo bubo sibiricus

B. b. bubo

B. b. desertorum

Snowy Owl
Nyctea scandiaca
♀

Great Grey Owl
Strix nebulosa

Brown Fish Owl
Ketupa zeylonensis

Snowy Owl *Nyctea scandiaca* ♂

IW 1976

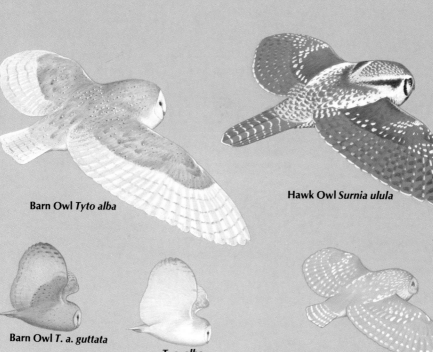

Barn Owl *Tyto alba*

Hawk Owl *Surnia ulula*

Barn Owl *T. a. guttata*

T. a. alba

Little Owl
Athene noctua lilith

Tengmalm's Owl
Aegolius funereus (adult)

Little Owl *A. n. vidalii*

Scops Owl *Otus scops*

Tengmalm's Owl (juvenile)

Striated Scops Owl *Otus brucei*

Pygmy Owl *Glaucidium passerinum*

IW 1978

VIII

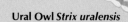

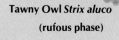

Ural Owl *Strix uralensis*

Tawny Owl *Strix aluco*
(rufous phase)

Hume's Owl *Strix butleri*

Tawny Owl *Strix aluco*
(grey phase)

Short-eared

Long-eared

Long-eared Owl *Asio otus*

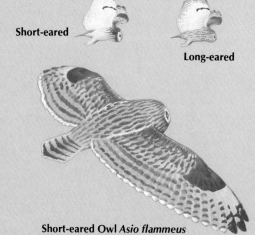

Short-eared Owl *Asio flammeus*

Marsh Owl *Asio capensis*

IW 1976

breeding season, and, for example, in Portenko's experience (1972), it normally takes to the wing when the intruder is still 200–300 m away, though at other times in the year it will sit boldly on telephone poles or on the top of a house, even if people are walking about nearby. This may explain why so many Snowy Owls have been killed during their invasions to more southerly latitudes. Like so many birds reared in the fastnesses of circumpolar regions, they are largely or completely ignorant of the ways of man.

The flight of the Snowy Owl is more hawk-like than owl-like. It glides slowly like a Buzzard *Buteo buteo*, but it can also fly remarkably fast. Sometimes it hovers whilst searching for small rodents.

VOICE

The usual call of the male in Shetland was a loud, harsh, grating bark, which Tulloch (1968) noted as *ergh-ergh-ergh-ergh*, while the female had a higher-pitched *eergh-eergh-eergh*. This is probably the same call as that quoted by Witherby *et al* (1938–41) as *rick, rick, rick*, and by Watson (1957) as *kre, kre, kre, kre, kre*, though there may be some individual variation.

In Shetland the male often hooted a low, deep, rough *hoorh*. Also recorded is a sound resembling the *aaow* of a Great Black-backed Gull *Larus marinus*. Bill-snapping expresses irritation, as in other owls.

Scherzinger (1974) has made an extensive study of Snowy Owls in captivity, and concludes that the voices of both sexes are closely similar and of a simple sound structure. When excited the owl utters a cackling note which is intensified into the barking territory-call which becomes a warning when uttered as a single call.

Very small chicks utter a faint cheeping sound and later will snap their bills if handled. After one week, the begging-call of the owlets is a high-pitched, penetrating, whistling squeal similar to that of the female during the breeding season. The young still utter this noise when they have been flying for over a month, by which time they can be heard over 1.5 km away (Tulloch 1968).

Outside the breeding season Snowy Owls are generally silent (Scherzinger 1974).

BEHAVIOUR

The Snowy Owl is said to be predominantly sedentary. Indeed, in Shetland it is thought that one pair bred in the same area on the small island of Fetlar for at least eight consecutive years (Tulloch 1975). Nevertheless, like many northern owls, the Snowy Owls leads an essentially nomadic life in the Arctic regions, erupting across the treeless tundra westwards as well as southwards in response to food availability, and thus to climatic conditions. Climate also influences the start of courtship, which, for example, in Novaya Zemlya does not begin until April (Portenko 1972). Courtship consists of territory-call, demonstration of nest-site, presentation of prey, display followed by copulation. The male adopts a remarkable posture before copulation, with head lowered and wings half-raised in an 'angel' position (see drawing below). This distinctive ritualised gesture to the female derives from the movements of nest-building and perhaps feeding young. Copulation takes place on the ground. When the male is presenting food to the female, both will make continuous guttural clucking and croaking noises. Similarly, when encouraging the young to feed, the

Nest-enticement – 'angel position' of male (after Scherzinger)

female utters a version of this clucking which is reminiscent of a broody hen (Tulloch 1968).

Faithfulness between pairs has been little studied, but it would seem that Snowy Owls only rarely remain paired for life. Snowy Owl males are known to be polygamous. Hagen (1960) was the first ornithologist to discover one bigamous male controlling two neighbouring territories. The two females nested about 1.35 km apart and one laid her eggs about 16 days in advance of the other. Similarly, in Shetland the male had two females in 1973, but he was not prepared to feed his two mates and after a while the younger female lost heart and deserted her eggs (Tulloch 1975).

Unfaithfulness is not confined to males. In Norway, Schaanning (1916) noted a female which accepted three different males within 18 days, but on her behalf it must be said that the first two males were killed one after the other near the nest. And Høst (1935) relates that two different males were feeding the same female and her brood at a nest in Norway.

It is difficult to discover the normal sizes of territories, because Snowy Owl numbers fluctuate according to the abundance or scarcity of an erratic food supply, but in years when lemmings are abundant a territory can be as small as 0.75 km² (Watson 1957) in suitable terrain.

In its territory the Snowy Owl normally shows little or no interest in other birds except those which it kills while hunting (Tulloch 1968). When confronted with an enemy the owl adopts a camouflage posture, closing its eyes to a slit and erecting its body, or it may feign yawning followed by wing-spreading, and as a final gesture it intensifies its erect pose and ruffles its feathers (Scherzinger 1974). A Snowy Owl has also been observed to thrust its wings forward and flap them in this position as a defence against Arctic Skuas *Stercorarius parasiticus* (Witherby *et al* 1940). There is a known instance of terns mobbing and killing a Snowy Owl in Greenland (Meinertzhagen 1959).

When the nest is disturbed, the male tends to hoot, either in flight or whilst making the threat posture, whereas the female will feign injury. In her distraction display she utters a squealing note and thrashes about on the ground with wings spread, twisting and dragging them (Tulloch 1968).

The nest is more vigorously defended by the male when the young are small but with older young the female becomes bolder. Both adults will deliver attacks, rattling their bills loudly as they dive. After the young are outside the nest the female will defend them, mostly alone, by diving so closely that the intruder is touched by a wing (Tulloch 1968).

Nestlings remain motionless when handled, but after one month the young owlets begin to defend themselves with bill and claws. The young will also use an exaggerated threat posture when approached, raising their body feathers and wings to make themselves look huge. They may also turn onto their backs to display their talons and gape, hissing and snapping their bills at the same time (Tulloch 1968).

In the Arctic summer when darkness is almost non-existent, Snowy Owls must, inevitably, be active in daylight, even though they prefer to be crepuscular. In southern Norway the breeding owls studied by Hagen (1960) were most active, vocally and in hunting, between 21.00 and 06.00 hours, that is to say, during the 'night'. These 'nocturnal' owls brought the first prey item to the nest at 23.00 hours, and afterwards one prey animal every 10 to 15 minutes until 01.00 hours. Less intensive feeding continued until 03.00 hours, but the adults showed no signs of hunting after this time or before 23.00 hours.

The light and darkness cycle is more or less the same in Shetland as in southern Norway, and the Snowy Owls' activity pattern is also similar. In Shetland, of 100 prey items brought to the young, 91% were brought between 18.00 and 06.00 hours, and 60% were between 21.00 and 03.00 hours (Tulloch 1969). Portenko (1972) concludes in his Snowy Owl book that activity is not so much dependent on the time of day, but is directly regulated by the activity of the main prey species (lemmings, etc).

Nagell and Frycklund (1965) studied the Snowy Owl's activity during the winter in Sweden and discovered that it is least active between 10.00 and 15.00 hours.

In Austria, Scherzinger (1974) found that the birds he kept in captivity had alternate periods of resting and movement throughout the 24 hour period. They were most active at dawn and least active at noon and midnight, but some movement, including hunting, feeding and display took place at all hours.

Hunting flights take place from low perches and the owl will perch for long periods on hummocks, fence posts or ruined buildings, evidently waiting for prey to move, but it will also hunt small mammals on foot. It kills its prey by pecking, biting and kneading. Its initial catching posture is retained as long as the prey shows vigorous resistance. The owl eats its food on the ground, small animals being gulped down whole, larger species or individuals piece by piece.

Stores of surplus food are laid down throughout the year (Scherzinger 1974). In Shetland these depôts were all within about 180 m of the nest and the male often left surplus prey at them, particularly when the female refused it at the nest. Some prey remained at food depôts until it became rotten. The female, too, frequently took surplus food from the nest and deposited it at one or other of the caches (Tulloch 1968).

Meinertzhagen (1959) describes the methods this owl employs when attacking the large Arctic Hare *Lepus timidus*. The owl will grasp the hare with one foot and use the other as a brake in the snow or herbage; it will also use its wings as brakes when being dragged along by its victim. The Snowy Owl has also been observed fishing; for example, Mr Millais (cited in Meinertzhagen 1959) records seeing a male in Iceland which caught a Char *Salvelinus alpinus* in the same manner as an Osprey *Pandion haliaetus*.

FOOD

At Kuopio University we have recently studied the Snowy' Owl's food consumption and the suitability of pellets for food analyses. During the feeding tests one captive Snowy Owl consumed white laboratory rats and mice at a rate of 338 g per day. From the 26 food items consumed the bird produced 16 pellets, at an average of 1.3 per day. The average daily weight of dry pellets was 13.4 g, and the size of the pellets was smaller than those collected in the wild (Table 13). The smaller size of the pellets produced in the laboratory suggests two possibilities: either the efficiency of food digestion was higher in the laboratory, or, as seems more likely, the food intake in the wild is greater.

In the laboratory tests all the large bones of the prey animals were found completely undigested in the pellets, which means that this type of analysis can give an accurate picture of the Snowy Owl's food (cf. Koivusaari et al 1977).

The Snowy Owl's diet has been studied during the breeding season in Norway (Løvenskiold 1947, Hagen 1960), in Sweden (Andersson and Persson 1971) and in Finland (A. Hakala, A. Kaikusalo and M. Rikkonen, in litt.). As shown in Table 14, various small and medium-sized rodents form the Snowy Owl's staple food in this Fenno-Scandian information.

Most (50.6%) of the 2,726 prey items consumed were *Microtus* voles and the majority of these were Root Voles *Microtus ratticeps*, while the Norway Lemming *Lemmus lemmus* constituted only 34.3%. These analyses reveal that the importance of lemmings in the Snowy Owl's diet has been over-estimated in most previous books, in which the lemming has always been quoted as an outstandingly important food source for the Snowy Owl. This relative unimportance is further demonstrated by the fact that Snowy Owls have bred, or continue to breed, in Iceland or on Fetlar in the Shetland Islands, where lemmings or lemming-like rodents are absent. Only in a small-scale Swedish study has the Norway Lemming been proved to be the principal food item, constituting 90.3% of 206 prey animals.

The food of the Snowy Owl has been studied on Fetlar during the breeding season by direct observations, especially in 1968 when observers in a hide were able to identify 116 prey animals (Tulloch 1969). The main food was Rabbit *Oryctolagus cuniculus* (72%), and the remaining 28% consisted of fledgling birds: 23 Oyster-catchers *Haematopus ostralegus*, 3 Curlew or Whimbrel *Numenius sp.*, 1 Lapwing *Vanellus vanellus*, 1 Arctic Skua and 4 unidentified birds.

In the Fenno-Scandian material summarised in Table 14 there were 38 birds out of 2,726 different prey items, including 10 Willow Grouse/Ptarmigan *Lagopus sp.*, 4 plovers *Charadrius sp.*, 1 Snipe *Gallinago gallinago*, 1 thrush *Turdus sp.*, 1 young Snowy Owl (cannibalism), 8 small birds such as buntings and finches and 13 unidentified species. Some frogs *Rana sp.*, fish *Salmo sp.* and insects *Coleoptera sp.* were found in castings.

In Finland the Snowy Owl's food has been studied during the autumn and winter period near breeding sites in Lapland, as well as in southern Finland during invasions (Table 15). In Lapland, winter food contained only one bird (*Lagopus sp.*) among 226 prey items, whereas studies in southern Finland recorded 8 birds out of 95 prey animals. It would seem that this essentially Arctic owl has to change its diet to a quite remarkable extent when invading southwards outside the breeding season. Nevertheless, in both areas voles (*Microtus and Clethrionomys*) formed the main part of the diet, although the Norway Lemming was the commonest prey item in Lapland. In both areas the predator's choice depended, of course, on the availability of various species of small and medium-sized rodents. The nine birds taken in Finland were: Black Grouse *Tetrao tetrix*, Willow Grouse/Ptarmigan *Lagopus sp.*, Mallard *Anas platyrhynchos*, a single unknown duck, one gull and four unidentified small birds.

Facial patterns of young Snowy Owl – at 10 days (left), at 18 days (right)

BREEDING BIOLOGY

The typical nesting habitat of the Snowy Owl is high or low Arctic tundra, preferably hummocky or rolling, and the owl tends to select a breeding site with a good view over the surrounding countryside.

The nest is on the ground, and is usually no more than a slight depression, often thinly lined with moss or grass, at a high point on rolling tundra. Male and female both form the nest hollow by scraping, burrowing and gyrating. Typical nest hollows are about 50 cm in diameter and 10–15 cm deep (Hagen 1960, Portenko 1972).

Watson's researches (1957) revealed that most first eggs are laid between 10th and 22nd May at nearly 30° of latitude in Canada, Alaska, Siberia and Scandinavia. The white eggs, rounded and elliptical in shape, are usually laid at intervals of about two days, but sometimes at intervals of up to five days, as on Fetlar when bitter north winds, to which the nest was exposed, coincided with a gap of four or five days in egg-laying (Tulloch 1968).

The clutch size of the Snowy Owl varies from 4 to 9 or 10, but exceptionally 11 or 14 eggs are laid (Witherby *et al* 1940). Professor Merikallio analysed 66 nests from Finnish Lapland and in these the clutch size varied as follows:

Eggs per clutch	5	6	7	8	9	10	11	12	13	14
Number of clutches	9	14	10	12	11	3	1	3	2	1

The average clutch size, based on these 66 nests, is 7.74, but it is known to be larger in years of lemming abundance (Portenko 1972).

The female alone incubates, for a period of 32 to 34 days according to most writers (e.g. Scherzinger 1974), beginning with the first egg, so that the subsequent nestlings are of markedly different ages (see photo). Newly-hatched owlets weigh 42–45 g (Hagen 1960), and develop quickly in response to the exposed ground nest-site. The downy neoptile covers the nestling from the moment of hatching and protects it during the whole nestling period. The eyelids open on the fifth day, and the pinions appear with their quills on the eighth day and are fully grown by the eighth week. The white feathers of the final plumage cover the mesoptile from the 45th day (Scherzinger 1974, Busse and Busse 1976).

At ten days old the young Snowy Owl has a characteristic white 'X' in the centre of the slightly darker mesoptile covering its face, but by its 18th day the owlet has a distinctly darker mask with rather differently-shaped and more generously distributed white markings (see drawing on the previous page).

The female alone feeds the young, which, in their first few days, gape in a half-upright posture. Initially, they take only small pieces of food from their mother's bill, but from the 12th day they gulp down whole mice, and from the 38th day they dismember larger prey without assistance (Scherzinger 1974).

When the chicks are older they will often rush to the male and take prey from him on his arrival at the nest-site. On Fetlar, on one occasion when the young were still in the nest, the male arrived while the female was absent and attempted to feed the young. The female came winging back and snatched the rabbit from him, proceeding to feed the young herself. At the same nest, when the young were scattered and nearly ready to fly, the usual procedure continued with the male being met by the female, who took the prey to one or other of the young (Tulloch 1969).

Soon after hatching the young owls can crawl and sit, and when twelve days old they are able to walk. They leave the nest between the 15th and 20th day, climb over obstacles when 20 days old and are able to fly at 50 to 60 days. The owls reach sexual maturity at the end of the first year (Scherzinger 1974).

DISTRIBUTION

The Snowy Owl belongs to the Arctic faunal type having circumpolarly holarctic distribution in the tundra climatic zone. Voous (1960) places the northern limit of distribution slightly north of the 1°C (34°F) July isotherm, with the southern limit approaching the 15°C (57°F) isotherm.

Snowy Owls winter within their breeding range and south to central Europe, central Asia, and the northern United States. Due to the highly nomadic life-style of the entire Snowy Owl population in the holarctic zone, no subspecies seems to have evolved there or elsewhere despite its huge distributional range (Portenko 1972).

In Europe the Snowy Owl breeds in Iceland, the mountains of Fenno-Scandia, Lapland, and northernmost Russia. Strangely enough, it does not breed on the Kola Peninsula, despite the fact that lemmings occur in this large tundra area (Semenov-Thian-Shanski, *in litt.*). Since 1967 a pair has nested on Fetlar in the Shetlands, the male pairing with two females in 1973 and 1974 (Hudson 1975). However, the male failed to appear in 1976 and since then no nesting has taken place in this locality (Sharrock 1976). In Iceland the Snowy Owl is very scarce and may only be nesting sporadically around the ice-caps in the Central Plateau (Gudmundsson, *in litt.*), while Bengtson (*in litt.*) maintains there are nowadays not more than ten pairs.

The numbers of Snowy Owls breeding in Norway are unknown, but the species occurs in rodent years and regularly breeds in the coastal and western part of Finmark. In southern Norway the owl seems now to be less abundant than some decades ago, although it is still found sporadically in most parts of the mountain

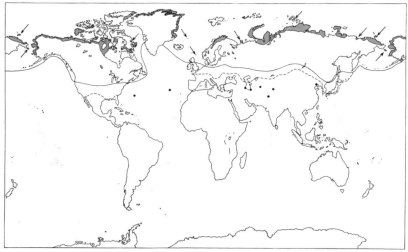

——— approximate southward limit of its more or less regular wanderings or migrations
------ limit of area in which it occurs as a vagrant
• most southerly records of stray birds
⬭ breeding distribution

SNOWY OWL

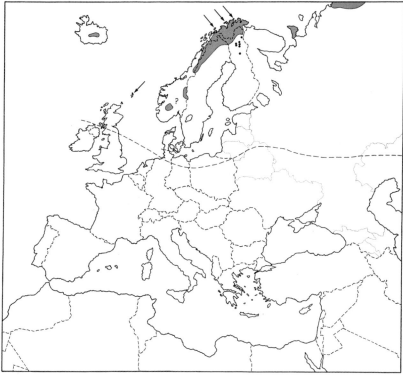

⬭ breeding distribution
˜˜˜ approximate southernmost limit of more or less regular invasions
• localities where breeding observed in Finland in 1974 outside normal breeding
range (30–35 pairs discovered) – nesting occurred in Fetlar (Shetlands) 1967–75
and summering birds are regularly seen on Scottish mainland and islands

regions (Røv, *in litt.*). Johnsen (1933) suggested that Snowy Owls might also breed in Spitzbergen, but, as happens in other regions, one can only hope to find the nests in the birds' special breeding years.

In Sweden Snowy Owl numbers fluctuate from nil to over 100 pairs, according to the scarcity or abundance of its normal food species (Ulfstrand and Högstedt 1976). Indeed, in 1978, approximately 100 nests of Snowy Owls were recorded in the district of Norrboten, Sweden (Persson 1978).

In Finland this owl was quite common in the Arctic areas of the country at the beginning of this century. In 1907 about 800 Snowy Owl eggs were collected from 100 nests in Finnish Lapland (Merikallio). Intense trapping and egg-collecting were reputed to be the primary reasons why the Snowy Owl became so rare in Finland. However, in the early spring of 1974 several sightings were again reported. In most cases, the owl had been seen in the north-western 'arm' of the country. Hakala *et al* (1974) estimated that about 30 to 35 Snowy Owl pairs nested within the Finnish borders in the summer of 1974. Before that date the last published report of a breeding Snowy Owl in Finland had been in 1932. The summer of 1974 was a good lemming season but that does not explain the absence of Snowy Owls between 1932 and 1974. Lemmings were even more numerous in 1969 and 1970 than in 1974 although no Snowy Owls bred in Finland. Hakala *et al* (1974) suggest that their appearance in 1974 was related to a recent decline of rodent populations somewhere in Siberia.

The above example from Finland demonstrates the difficulty of detecting any long-term trends in Snowy Owl populations, which live an essentially nomadic existence similar to Great Grey and Hawk Owls. Merikallio in his unpublished work speculates that the Snowy Owl population has generally decreased in Europe. His reasoning was based on the fact that peak years are not as spectacular as they were before 1945. Widespread trapping and egg-collection do not solely explain this decline, if at all, and the reasons for it presumably involve some climatic factors (see Great Grey Owl).

The Snowy Owl is considered an endangered species because of its scarcity (Hudson 1975), and its killing is now prohibited in all the west European countries in which it breeds. Furthermore, no photographs may be taken at the nest without a special licence in Scotland and Iceland.

13: Hawk Owl *Surnia ulula*
(Linné)

Adult Hawk Owls are brownish-black above, with heavy white spotting and streaking on the head, back and wings, and white bars across the tail. The face pattern, whitish with a heavy black border to the facial disc, is distinctive. The underparts are white, closely and heavily barred with grey-black.

Juveniles in the first few weeks after leaving the nest have short tails, a blackish mask surrounding the eyes which joins with black borders to the facial disc that are much wider than on the adult. The whole effect gives the young owl a different appearance to the more familiar adult plumage. I was approached fairly recently by two young Finnish birdwatchers who thought they might have discovered a new owl for Finland. It was described as resembling an adult Spectacled Owl *Pulsatrix perspicillata*, a South American species with a distinctive black facial mask. They were quickly put right, but the story does serve to emphasise the unusual appearance of the young Hawk Owl.

Many of the features which characterise the owl family are reduced or lacking in this species. It has a relatively flat-topped head with a small facial disc. The wings are large and taper to a point; the tail is long and graduated towards the tip; the bright yellow eyes are relatively small; and the ears are placed symmetrically. The plumage is more compact than in other owls and the soft, sound-deadening filaments at the feather-tips, which assist the noiseless flight of the typical owls, are poorly developed.

The total length of males is 360–390 mm (average 371 mm from 11 birds); females 372–410 mm (average 396 mm from 10 birds). The wing length of males is 222–244 mm (average 235 mm from 22 birds); females 224–250 mm (average 237 mm

Newly-fledged Hawk Owl

from 27 birds). The weight of males is 215–375 g (average 282 g from 22 birds); females 270–380 g (average 324 g from 20 birds). The Hawk Owl would seem, therefore, to be dimorphic in body weight and total length, but almost monomorphic in wing length. There can also be differences in the colour of the sexes, as Bottomley (1972) pointed out: 'Although we could not be sure which sex was which, there was a marked difference in the plumages of the two adults: one had blackish-brown barring and mottling above and narrower barring below, while the other was so lightly marked all over as to appear almost white at a distance.' However, this kind of difference can be due to ageing, older owls often being whiter.

IN THE FIELD

Hawk Owls are usually seen perched in exposed positions on the tops of trees, bushes and posts. Most are fearless of man and this boldness usually enables a close approach. Identification, in any case, is not difficult. Unlike most owls, which sit bolt upright, Hawk Owls normally perch in an inclined, falcon-like position, sometimes with the long tail cocked at an angle.

The bird's flight is swift and direct, the pointed wings and long tail giving a hawk-like effect.

VOICE

The display call of the Hawk Owl is a trilling whistle *ululululululululululu* . . . which usually lasts more than ten seconds. It is rather similar to the long, bubbling note of the Whimbrel *Numenius phaeopus* or the female Cuckoo *Cuculus canorus*. Helo (1971) maintained that it is possible to imitate the Hawk Owl's call with a referee's whistle. This territory call is very weak and during calm weather it can be heard at a distance of 500 m.

The so-called hunting call is an often-repeated series of three, four or more loud querulous syllables *queep-queep-queep* or *kleep-kleep*. The typical alarm call is a rapid, strident, hawk-like series of similar syllables *kee-kee-kee-kee* or *kip-kip-kip-kip*, usually uttered in flight. A more frequent distress call is the raspy, rising, two-part screech *screeeeeeee-yip*, the emphasis on the last syllable. This is the call usually given from a nearby perch by an adult owl when the observer is near the nest. It is also used when the male brings food to the female, and the female utters this call when communicating with the young, especially when they have left the nest (Leinonen, *in litt.*). The female has a special voice *srii-srii* when feigning injury. On one occasion a male made the same noise when a Greenshank *Tringa nebularia* mobbed the female (Leinonen, *in litt.*).

The young have a shrill, hissing call, which is longer than that of Tengmalm's Owl or owls of the *Strix* genus.

Von Haartman *et al* (1967) cite several observers' descriptions of about seven more calls in addition to those described above. This lends weight to the conclusion that the Hawk Owl seems to be a versatile vocalist.

BEHAVIOUR

The nesting behaviour of the Hawk Owl is not well known, but it is clear that territories are established a few weeks before the start of nesting. In central Finland during 1970, Hawk Owls were heard calling from as early as 17th February until 13th April (Mikkola 1970). The male is said to make display flights over the tree-tops of the territory, and wing-clapping as the bird flies among the trees has also been described. Hawk Owl territories are probably quite large, since two nests have never been found close together; the area of 200 km² that Hagen covered in Norway held four pairs. Certainly the hunting ranges are extensive: in Russia Bianki and Koshkina found the remains of 13 Root Voles *Microtus ratticeps* at a nest more than 1 km from the nearest habitat suitable for this mammal.

The Hawk Owl seems to be tolerant of other birds of prey nesting in their territories: Honey Buzzards *Pernis apivorus*, Sparrowhawks *Accipiter nisus*, Short-eared Owls, Ural Owls and Great Grey Owls have been found breeding within 500 m of a nest, although the last three species are direct competitors for food and may hunt at the same time as the male Hawk Owl. On the other hand, in Finland during the winter, Hawk Owls have been recorded taking Tengmalm's Owls on three occasions.

Despite its relatively small size, this owl can be dangerous at the nest, because both parents will attack intruders, particularly after the young have hatched. It seems that the male is the more aggressive, especially when the female is incubating or brooding.

The Hawk Owl is diurnal and will hunt in bright sunlight. One male in 1970 was vocal between 06.00 and 20.00 hours in spring, and was only once heard to call at night. In Lapland, in June 1970, a female ceased to attack observers after 23.00 hours, although it was still light (Mikkola 1970). In Sweden a pair fed their young hourly during a bright day; after 17.00 feeding was less frequent, but visits were recorded in daylight between 02.00 and 03.00 (P.O. Swanberg, after Hagen and Barth 1950).

In its hunting technique the Hawk Owl resembles a shrike, using a high vantage point as a look-out and swooping down on its prey. It flies fast and low, swooping up to a perch at a new vantage point. Hawk Owls have also been known to hover like a Kestrel *Falco tinnunculus*.

FOOD

Present information on the food of the Hawk Owl in northern Europe during the breeding season has been collected in Norway (Hagen 1952), in Kantalahti, Murmansk Province, northern Russia (Bianki and Koshkina 1960), and in Finland (Mikkola 1972, and Hublin and Mikkola 1977). These studies were based on analyses of pellets or other food remains from 17 nest sites (Fig. 12).

Pellets were usually found within 70–150 m of the nests, frequently underneath the habitual perch of a male. Forty pellets collected in Finland were intact: their dimensions varied from maxima of $7.6 \times 1.8 \times 1.8$ cm and $5.8 \times 2.2 \times 2.1$ cm to minima of $3.0 \times 2.1 \times 2.0$ cm and $3.3 \times 1.7 \times 1.3$ cm, the average being $4.1 \times 2.2 \times 1.9$ cm. Remains of up to four animals were present in each pellet and the average number was 1.7.

The percentages of the main groups of prey animals are given in Table 16. During the breeding season voles (*Microtidae*) are the main prey, forming between 93.5% and 98.3% of prey analysed in the three countries. Those of the genera *Clethrionomys* (34.1%–75.9%) and *Microtus* (7.4%–57.1%) were easily the most numerous at every site. Shrews (*Soricidae*) of the three species made up 1.4%; the remaining 2.9% comprised eleven other mammals (mice, Weasels *Mustela nivalis* and Flying Squirrels *Pteromys volans*), two frogs, one fish, one beetle, and birds ranging from thrushes to game-birds (Willow Grouse *Lagopus lagopus* and Hazel Hen *Bonasia bonasia*). In the northern parts of the region *Microtus* voles appear to have been relatively scarce, and *Clethrionomys* voles formed the majority of the food. In southern and central Finland, however, the former were the more numerous, accounting for 90.2% of the prey taken (Mikkola 1971).

In general, the availability of prey directly governed the predator's choice. In northern Russia, however, the contents of pellets differed from expectations based on nearby trapping. Shrews were trapped but were not present in the pellets, and Grey-sided Voles *Clethrionomys rufocanus* occurred marginally more often in the pellets than in the traps (Bianki and Koshkina 1960).

The population dynamics of the Norway Lemming *Lemmus lemmus* can no longer be regarded as the factor governing the fluctuations of Hawk Owl numbers, as earlier studies had suggested. Only 43 lemmings (2.9%) were found in all the reports. Only four lemmings were found in three nests in Lapland in 1970, and this was in the most remarkable year for lemmings since the 1930s.

In Finland, stomach analyses were conducted on 35 Hawk Owls outside the breeding season by the Departments of Zoology, at the Universities of Oulu and Kuopio, and on two in Kantalahti, Russia (Table 17). The remains of up to five

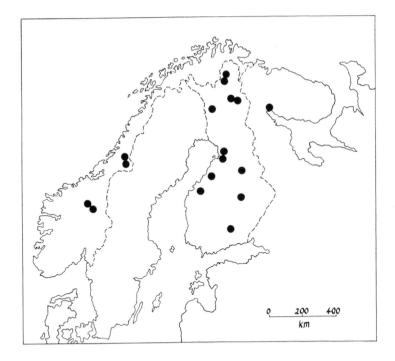

Fig. 12 Localities of Hawk Owl nests from which pellets or other food remains were collected for analysis in Norway (1949), northern Russia (1957) and Finland (1958–76)

animals were present in each stomach and the average number was 1.2. Four stomachs of Finnish specimens were empty.

The results agree with earlier reports of winter food (Vladimirskaya 1948, Uttendörfer 1952): the proportion of voles dropped to 57%, but birds, especially Willow Grouse, rose to 29.5% nearly 16 times greater than in the breeding season. This was to be expected, since most of these owls were collected during winters when vole populations were low, and in areas where the snow-cover was so thick that small mammals were difficult prey. Clearly, the Hawk Owl's predilection for voles does not signify an exclusive specialisation, but given that climatic conditions determine their distribution or availability, vole populations do account directly for the movements and breeding density of the owls to the exclusion of all other factors.

BREEDING BIOLOGY

The favoured breeding habitat is dense coniferous or mixed forest on the edge of marshes or areas cleared by felling, sometimes quite near human habitation (twice recorded within 100 m). The proximity of the nest-site to open ground is indicative of the owl's hunting methods.

Holes in trees and the tops of stumps, nest-boxes and occasionally old nests of raptors or crows are used. The Hawk Owl does not bring fresh material to the nest. Dates of egg-laying vary considerably: for example, Merkallio found eggs on the extreme dates of 30th March and 23rd June. His records of the sizes of 135 completed clutches may be tabulated as follows:

Eggs per clutch	3	4	5	6	7	8	9	10	11	12	13
Completed clutches	5	16	31	27	23	17	8	3	4	0	1

The average clutch size, which was 6.31 over the whole series, seemed to decrease southwards: in Lapland it was 6.56 (101 clutches), in central Finland 5.94 (18) and in south Finland 5.13 (16). The number of eggs in 17 nests found in Lapland during 1903–16 varied from 5 to 13, with an average of 7.5. It is interesting that the five clutches found in 1907, a good vole year, had between 8 and 13 eggs and the average was 10.2 (Montell 1917).

Eggs are laid at intervals of one or two days and incubation starts from the first egg and lasts not more than 30 days. The female alone incubates and she is fed by the male. The young leave the nest when they are between three and five weeks old. In northern Russia the youngest fledgling at one nest left a week after the oldest (Bianki and Koshkina 1960). The owlets are reluctant fliers at first, and spend much time moving about the branches of the nest tree. Even after six to eight weeks they are usually found in the vicinity of the nest. They keep together and may stay within the territory for many weeks.

DISTRIBUTION

The Hawk Owl is a representative of the Siberian-Canadian faunal type, belonging to the fauna of the boreal climatic zone in the holarctic region. Hawk Owls are found mainly in the northern coniferous forests, and those in Fenno-Scandia are the most

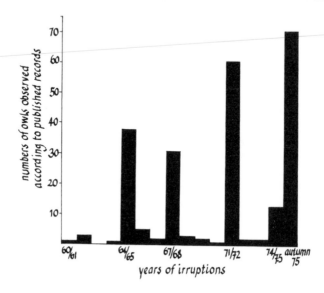

Fig. 13   Number of Hawk Owls recorded in southern Sweden beyond the normal distribution range during the winters 1960/61, 1974/75 and autumn 1975, according to published records (after Kjell, Bylin, in litt.)

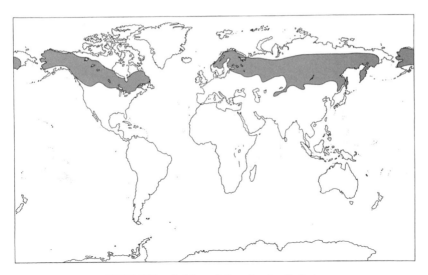

HAWK OWL – shaded area indicates breeding distribution

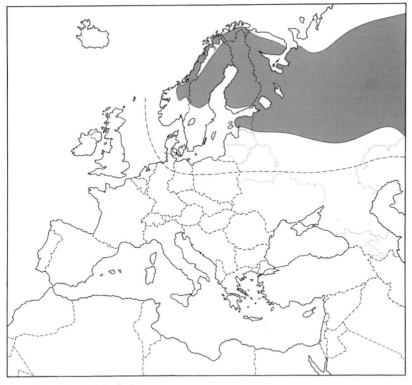

〜〜 breeding distribution
〜—〜— maximum southerly extent of normal invasions

HAWK OWL

westerly part of a population distributed throughout the taiga of Eurasia east to Anadyr, Kamchatka and Sakhalin. The southernmost nest ever found in Europe was at about 55°N in central Russia (Mebs 1966).

Hawk Owls, like Great Grey Owls, lead an essentially nomadic life, irrupting through the coniferous zone westwards as well as southwards in response to food availability, and thus to climatic conditions (Mikkola and Sulkava 1969).

Hawk Owl irruptions follow the same pattern as those of Snowy Owls when populations of voles (*Microtidae*) are normal, most of the owls wintering in the north, but in peak vole years remarkable invasions may occur, birds penetrating central Europe, and, rarely, crossing to Britain. Most recent invasions, in the autumns and winters of 1957/58, 1961/62, 1964/65 and 1971/72, have been on rather a small scale compared with earlier ones in 1881/82, 1898/99, 1914/15, 1928/29, 1930/31, 1931/32, 1942/43 and 1950/51, probably because the population in Fenno-Scandia had suffered a general reduction during that whole period (Table 18).

An example of a westward irruption from Russia into Fenno-Scandia occurred in 1957. In northern Russia this was an excellent vole year and Hawk Owls nested in large numbers (Bianki and Koshkina 1960), but in Finland only three nests were found (von Haartman *et al* 1967). During the following autumn and winter, however, Finland witnessed a sizeable influx of Hawk Owls, and numbers of them reached West Germany (Berndt 1959). Clearly, these had come from the east. The spring of 1958 was very cold in Finland, and voles were numerous, so that the wintering owls remained to breed throughout the country. Hagen's (1956) earlier assertion that the Hawk Owls which invaded Scandinavia in large numbers in 1950 had originated from within Fenno-Scandia is thus open to question. Edberg's (1955) previous suggestion that they had irrupted from the east seems to have been correct, since the size of the invasion approached that of 1914, the largest on record, in spite of the fact that the Fenno-Scandian population had considerably decreased by 1950.

Interestingly, there was a particularly large invasion in autumn 1975 throughout Fenno-Scandia, which suggests that the population of Hawk Owls in western Eurasia is experiencing a resurgence of its former numbers (Fig. 13).

14: Pygmy Owl *Glaucidium passerinum*
(Linné)

DESCRIPTION

Adult plumage is dark grey-brown above with light mottling, and buff-white below mottled and streaked dark brown, especially across the upper breast (mottling), and sides of the body (streaking). There is a prominent, white half-collar around the back of the neck. The head is rounded and lacking a well-defined facial disc and is small for an owl. It has a whitish face with small brown markings, mainly in the form of two to three broken, concentric rings around each eye. It has yellow irides and a yellowish bill.

The wings are short and rounded, the wing coverts having light patches at the tips of the external webs in the form of spots, which are smallest on the lesser coverts. The remiges are earth-brown, with faint, narrow, pale bars (two to three in number) lightening into whiter patches at the web edges, and there is a very narrow white border to the rear edge of the wing. The rectrices have three or four narrow white bars and narrow whitish tips. The tail is quite long for an owl. The legs and feet are well covered in whitish feathers with only the dark brown claws visible.

The sexes are said to be similar, but Klaus *et al* (1965) maintain that the male has much fewer whitish markings on the head and back, making it appear much darker, and that the male's light-coloured half-collar on the back of the neck is more prominent than the female's. Some of these differences could, however, be due to the different age of the sexes studied. Juveniles are darker and largely unmarked above and have brown blotches on the under parts.

The total length of males varies 152–170 mm; that of females 174–190 mm (Dement'ev *et al* 1951, Mebs 1966). Dement'ev *et al* gave the wing length of males as 92–102 mm (average 97.8 mm from 29 birds); females 100–112 mm (average 103.8 mm from 41 birds).

The weight of males is 47–62 g (average 56.8 g from 7 birds); females 55–79 g (average 67.2 g from 14 birds). These measurements were taken from birds which died or were killed during irruptions. In his study of this owl Scherzinger (1970) discovered that during the breeding season the weight of females varied 74–83 g, and that of males 65–72 g, making an average of 73 g for the adult Pygmy Owl. Unfortunately, he gave no details of how many were weighed, but the female would seem to be at least 10 g (15%) heavier than the male. The difference in size between the sexes is generally not difficult to see.

IN THE FIELD

As its English name suggests, the Pygmy Owl is the smallest of the European owls. Only the Scops Owl approaches it in size, but this latter species, as well as being larger, can be distinguished by its different habits and voice, and by certain characteristic physical differences. The Pygmy Owl has a relatively small head with no ear-tufts and its facial disc is less well-marked, being more rounded and less upright in shape. As the bird alights, the tail is cocked like a Wren's *Troglodytes troglodytes*, and when perching, it frequently flicks its tail from side to side.

Outside the breeding season the Pygmy Owl is relatively easy to study, at least in Fenno-Scandia, because it leaves the forest depths in autumn to winter near human settlements. It is often seen during daylight hours, especially when attempting to catch small birds on the wing in gardens. During this period it is audacious, perching conspicuously on the crown of small conifers. In flight the wings appear very rounded and its progress is noisy and undulatory. The Pygmy Owl's habits are reminiscent of shrikes, particularly when it flies from a look-out on the topmost branches of small trees.

VOICE

The Pygmy Owl is highly vocal. Its territorial song *peeu-peeu-peeu* is like the call of the Bullfinch *Pyrrhula pyrrhula*, and when given from a perch seems to come from different locations as the bird turns its head. In addition, it has a vibrating song, consisting of *peeu* calls coupled with a vibrating *py-py-pyp*. The female sometimes utters a similar, but higher and more cackling song (cf. König 1968).

The territorial calls are given almost throughout the year, but they are more likely to be heard from March to May. Occasionally, a pair will duet.

A special feature of the Pygmy Owl is its strong reaction to imitated alluring calls. By imitating its hoot it can even be coaxed into attacking (cf. Jussila 1974).

Apart from the two territorial songs, König (1968) has listed many other types of whistles. A *kiu* often has an alarm function, but it is also a sign of excitement. Each sex has an increasingly excited *kiu-kiu-kyugyugyugyug*, and the female often importunes the male for copulation with this sequence of calls.

The excited male, while offering prey to his female, *bibbers*, and she will respond with either a high-pitched *seeht* or a suppressed *zeweek*. During the copulation the female twitters *kjikjikji* . . .

A high and weak *tsilp-tsilp* (somewhat resembling the song of the Chiffchaff *Phylloscopus collybita*) seems to be a sign of uneasiness or alarm. Contact calls are low *peeu* and *pyip* calls. The male calls the female from the nest-hole to take prey from him, mostly during the incubation and hatching period, with a long *zhew* instead of a song.

Peeu calls on an ascending scale, often heard from both sexes in autumn, have been described as 'autumnal song'. König (1968) however, thinks that the 'scale' is a high-intensity call that enables the birds (which are only loosely associated after the breeding season) to maintain contact. The songs given in autumn are the same as the spring songs. In autumn the birds are, probably, loosely paired.

The young birds beg with a high-pitched *seeh*, sometimes in two syllables. When disturbed, they snap their bills or make high *chirking* sounds (König 1968).

BEHAVIOUR

In Central Europe the Pygmy Owl occupies a territory of 1.0 to 1.4 km² throughout the year (Scherzinger 1970, 1974), but in Fenno-Scandia the owls are less sedentary. Each autumn they leave their territory in the dense forest and move near to human habitation, where food is more readily found during the very cold winter.

Weather influences the start of the courtship, but it usually begins around mid-March, with hole demonstrations, presentation of prey and copulation. A sudden physical approach or touch may create conflict between the male and female, and her copulation posture is not necessarily an invitation to the male (cf. Scherzinger 1970, 1974).

The male calls to mark the boundaries of his territory, which is subdivided into roosting area, hunting ground and nesting area. The latter usually has at least two holes. During fights between males over territory, they exchange calls and fly after each other in turn (cf. Schönn 1976).

When threatened the Pygmy Owl's behaviour is characterised by conflict sleeping, camouflage posture and threat posture. Near the nest the owl will even attack humans. Alarmed young owls press themselves to the bottom of the nest-hole.

The owl holds its plumage close to the body in all displays except when threatening, when the feathers are ruffled, and when dozing, sunbathing or breeding. The facial feathers lie flat when in the camouflage posture, or when the bird is preening or is afraid. It bathes regularly in water, sun, rain and even snow (Scherzinger 1970).

The Pygmy Owl requires a similar habitat to Tengmalm's Owl, but it is not clear to what extent the latter is an enemy of the Pygmy Owl. Two different Tengmalm's Owls attacked Scherzinger (1970) during four nights when he imitated the territorial song of the Pygmy Owl. In addition, Scherzinger (1970) and Schönn (1976) have each seen an attack by a Tengmalm's Owl on a Pygmy Owl, and in Finland the remains of a Pygmy Owl were once found in a Tengmalm's Owl nest. On the other hand, there is one record in Finland of both species breeding in the same tree, the two nest-holes being only about 4 m apart. During the night the owls were never seen out of the nest-holes at the same time, but by day it was always the female Pygmy Owl that was aggressive towards the female Tengmalm's Owl when both were out of their holes. The latter was often forced to fly back to its nest, but it never made any movement against the Pygmy Owl (Hautala, *in litt.*).

Martens, larger owls (especially Tawny and Ural) and raptors are far more dangerous enemies of the Pygmy Owl than Tengmalm's Owl. Even the Nuthatch *Sitta europaea* is a potential threat because it may wall up the openings of suitable holes, which the owl is then unable to open. Dormice are also competitors as they nest in the same type of holes, filling them with grass, etc., so that the owl may be unable to use them.

The owl's appearance and call stimulate mobbing behaviour in small birds. König (1972) found that mobbing in response to the Pygmy Owl's calls was not an inherited habit of small birds, but that small passerines in the Pygmy Owl's territory learned that the voice came from an enemy. Tits, Chaffinches *Fringilla coelebs*, treecreepers and similar species showed the mobbing reaction only where Pygmy Owls regularly occurred. Mobbing is thus a valuable aid to finding Pygmy Owls. Scherzinger (1970) stated that mobbing had no effect on the Pygmy Owl, but König (1972) seemed to believe that mobbing caused a decrease, or even led to the owl's extinction, in the Black Forest (south-west Germany).

Pygmy Owl activity during the breeding season has been studied in Sweden (Bergman 1939, Jansson 1964), in Norway (Seierstad *et al* 1960), in Finland (Mikkola 1970) and in Austria (Bergmann and Ganso 1965, Scherzinger 1970).

In Austria the Pygmy Owl was most active during the breeding season between 03.00 and 05.00 hours and 19.00 to 21.00 hours (Fig. 14). Of 138 feeding visits between 26th May and 30th June, 51 took place between 03.00 and 05.00 hours and 45 between 19.00 and 21.00 hours (cf. Scherzinger 1970 and Fig. 14). There was also a slight increase in the owl's feeding activity between 08.00 and 10.00 hours. In Austria, the owl's favourite hunting times seem to be just before dawn and at dusk. The owl sleeps at night like other day-active birds (cf. Scherzinger 1970).

Some 1,300 km to the north of Austria, in southern Norway and central Sweden, the duration of Pygmy Owl activity is more than 22 hours daily, compared to less than 18 hours in Austria. In southern Norway the owl rests only during the darkest hours of the night, between 23.00 and 01.00 hours, the most active periods occurring on either side of these resting hours. In southern Norway between 09.00 and 11.00 hours the owl is even busier than in Austria.

In central Finland the Pygmy Owl is most active between 22.00 and 01.00 hours and from 09.00 until 10.00 hours (Fig. 14). During a period of 15 days there were 43 nest visits between 22.00 and 01.00 hours, and 12 visits from 09.00 to 10.00 hours. Thus in Austria and southern Norway there were two clear peaks of activity: late evening and early morning, with a lesser peak before midday. In central Finland, however, the peaks of morning and evening have combined to cover the short summer twilight, but as in Austria and southern Norway there is also a lesser peak in day activity between 09.00 and 10.00 hours. The activity of Pygmy Owls before midday could be explained by the fact that the young become hungry at that time (cf. Bergmann and Ganso 1965).

It is known that the Pygmy Owl's night vision is one of the poorest of the owls (Lindblad 1967). This explains why Pygmy Owls were found to be inactive in Austria and southern Norway around midnight. The position is somewhat different in Finland due to the lighter summer nights. Oulu, for example, in western Finland, where I studied the Pygmy Owl's activity, is only 172 km south of the Arctic Circle, and the light intensity on bright nights at the beginning of June, is 50 lux at midnight and 100 lux in midsummer (Erkinaro 1969). In such light the Pygmy Owl can readily see its prey, an important prerequisite when hunting is almost exclusively visual (Scherzinger 1970).

Scherzinger (1970) has also studied the Pygmy Owl outside the breeding season and has found that the day activity continues all the year round, in two phases. Activity would usually begin 40 minutes before sunrise and end 35 minutes after sunset. Thus the owl's working day in winter in central Finland is not more than six hours, which is

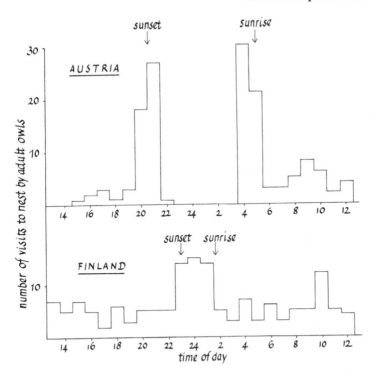

Fig. 14 *Comparison of feeding activity of Pygmy Owls in Austria and Finland*

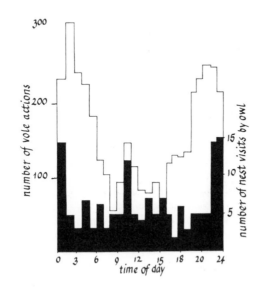

Fig. 15 *Comparison of Pygmy Owl and Bank Vole activity in Finland*

why it must be active throughout that period. However, during spring and autumn courtship there is much more activity after sunset, especially if there is a moon.

It is interesting to compare the activity of the Pygmy Owl with that of its prey animals. The peaks in Bank Vole *Clethrionomys glareolus* activity at Valtimo in east central Finland, coincided with those of the Pygmy Owl in Oulu in western Finland (Fig. 15). Both species were mainly nocturnal and each had a clear peak between 09.00 and 10.00 hours. Bergstedt (1965) has studied the activity of the Bank Vole in southern Sweden, and his results show that the peaks in the circadian rhythms of the Bank Vole and the Pygmy Owl are also the same in the south. Similarly, Short-tailed Voles *Microtus agrestis* are most active at night in summer when the Pygmy Owl is also hunting. In winter, Short-tailed Voles are diurnal like the Pygmy Owl. The change-over occurs in spring and autumn (Erkinaro 1969). On the other hand, small birds preyed on by the Pygmy Owl are mostly diurnal species. The peaks of their activity do not match the Pygmy Owl's.

During the breeding season almost all hunting is by the male, but at the end of the nestling period the female also hunts. Usually, the male does not carry prey animals to the nest but passes them to the female some 10 to 30 m from the nest.

When attacking or when catching prey the owl uses the glide and the dive technique, similar to that of Tengmalm's Owl. However, Pygmy Owl hunting attacks are triggered by optical stimuli, and like the Sparrowhawk *Accipiter nisus*, the owl makes only surprise attacks; if unsuccessful, it does not pursue the prey further (Kellomäki 1966). Characteristically, the owl flicks its tail and rattles its wings during the take-off for a surprise attack. The owl seizes its quarry with the talons of both feet. Mice are paralysed by a bite to the snout, a neckbite being inflicted only on dead animals. The owl's catching posture adjusts to the motions of the living prey. Having secured its prey the owl strikes at the apertures or the thinner parts of the skull. Typical pellets contain splintered bones, although during their first days of life, young owls drop boneless pellets. Food supplies are stored by the owl at all times of year. In summer, the forks of twigs and branches serve as a larder, holes being used in winter (cf. Scherzinger 1970).

FOOD

The Pygmy Owl differs from all other hole-nesting European owls in that it keeps the nest cavity clear of prey remains. Only at the end of the nestling period do sanitary arrangements lapse, and scraps of fur, feathers and bones will be found in the bottom of the nest after the birds have departed. Nonetheless, because the female drops most of the prey remains under the nest tree or under trees nearby, food remains are readily collected by the researcher.

I have measured 132 pellets collected in the breeding season. The average size was 26 × 11 mm, which is about the same average that Bergmann and Ganso (1965) obtained from 74 pellets in Austria. During the winter, Pygmy Owl pellets are slightly larger, the average of 40 pellets being 28 × 12 mm (Kaakinen and Mikkola 1972). This is due to the fact that pellets ejected by the young, included in the summer analysis, are smaller than those of the adults (cf. Mikkola 1970).

From food remains collected at 34 nests in Finland, between 1962 and 1973, we have been able to identify 2,761 individual prey animals eaten by Pygmy Owls during the breeding season (cf. Kellomäki 1969, Mikkola 1970, Mikkola and Jussila 1974 and Kellomäki 1977).

The food of Finnish Pygmy Owls consists of shrews *Soricidae*, voles *Cricetidae*, mice *Muridae*, bats *Vespertilionidae*, lizards *Lacertidae*, birds *Aves*, fish *Pisces* and insects *Insecta*. The proportions of different groups by numbers are given in Table 19. Voles formed the most abundant food item group (49.5%), the numbers of Bank Voles exceeding those of Short-tailed Voles. Small mammals formed altogether 54.2% of the food of the Pygmy Owl.

Avian prey comprised at least 37 species, forming 44.0% of the prey by number. The most abundant species were Chaffinch, leaf warblers *Phylloscopus sp.*, Siskin *Carduelis spinus* and Pied Flycatcher *Ficedula hypoleuca*. The heaviest prey animals were Great Spotted Woodpecker *Dendrocopos major*, Song Thrush *Turdus philomelos* and Red-wing *Turdus iliacus*. Each of these last three species may sometimes approach the Pygmy Owl in size.

Other prey species, including Common Lizards *Lacerta vivipara*, a Perch *Perca fluviatilis* and insects (all of them *Coleoptera*), are known to have been consumed, but their proportions in the diet were small (1.8%).

Small variations occur during the year in the types of food taken to the nest in different regions, depending on the prey species available (Mikkola 1970). In addition, the Pygmy Owl's diet varies from year to year, again depending on variations in small mammal populations (Kellomäki 1969).

When the vole populations in central Finland were at their maximum numbers in 1962, 1965–66 and 1969, the proportion of voles in the Pygmy Owl's diet was 78.8, 71.0, 76.7 and 65.6%. The diversity of their avian prey and the proportions of adult and young birds increase towards the end of the breeding season. This is probably due to the increased difficulty of catching small mammals in the taller vegetation of the field layer, and the greater availability of birds, especially fledglings (Kellomäki 1977).

In Sweden, data on the Pygmy Owl's food has been published by Bergman (1939), Curry-Lindahl (1958, 1960), Bengtsson (1962) and Jansson (1964). Of these authors, Jansson gives most information. During one breeding season 215 prey animals were brought to an observed nest; 63% were small mammals and 37% birds. Most of the mammals were voles, only one shrew being definitely identified.

The Pygmy Owl has also been studied in Norway by Lund (1951), Seierstad *et al* (1960) and Sonerud *et al* (1972). In the two first-mentioned studies the samples were rather small, but in the study by Sonerud *et al*, 108 prey animals were analysed at one nest site; 56% were birds (13 different species), and only 27% were mammals (3 species), the remainder being lizards (4%) and unidentified animals (13%). It was found that the proportion of birds in the nesting owl's diet was 20% before hatching and 71% after hatching, the increase thus being very high. This was caused by a marked reduction in the small rodent population during the nesting period. From seven eggs only three young owls reached the fledging stage.

Many records relating to diet of the Pygmy Owl in Central Europe have been published. März (1964) analysed 162 prey animals at five nest sites in West Germany in 1962–63. Broken down into their various components, they consisted of 19% small mammals, 80% birds and 1% lizards. In this investigation the percentage of mammals had been calculated from the numbers of skulls, but this would be perhaps four to five times too small a percentage for the breeding season, because the male often eats the fore part of a small mammal, taking only the hind part to the nest (cf. Mikkola 1970). This can easily be seen from the studies of Bergmann and Ganso (1965). They analysed the diet of the Pygmy Owl at one nest site in Austria, from prey remains and by direct visual observations. Of 86 prey remains identified, 20% were mammals (counted from the numbers of skulls) and 80% were birds. Of the 32 prey animals recorded by direct observations, only 9% were birds and 91% were mammals. Lately, Schönn (1976) has recorded the same kind of results in East Germany. Of 218 prey remains from four nests, 64.7% were birds, 34% small mammals and 1.3% lizards. However, of 241 prey items recorded when the nests were under observation, 65.1% were small mammals, 33.6% birds and 1.2% reptiles. It is therefore difficult to compare Finnish results with those obtained in other areas because of the different methods used. A number of studies of the Pygmy Owl's diet have been made in Russia, where it has been found that, during the breeding season, the Pygmy Owl is capable of killing all, or almost all, small female birds which attempt to breed within 250 to 300 m of the owl's nest-hole (cf. Ptušenko and Inozemcev 1968).

The Pygmy Owl is not a food specialist in the same sense as many other owls, miscellaneous food items also being eaten in good vole years. The reason for this is that the productivity of the habitats occupied by the owl is quite poor, and therefore all available prey must be taken (cf. also Kellomäki 1977).

It is comparatively easy to study the Pygmy Owl's diet outside the breeding season because of its habit of laying down food caches. In late autumn and early winter, especially, the Pygmy Owl stores its prey in hollow trees or, nowadays, more often in nest-boxes. By studying these stores we can obtain a good picture of its diet during the period.

In Finland we have identified 1,297 prey items of the Pygmy Owl outside the breeding season (Table 19). The proportion of voles eaten was almost the same (48.0%) in the winter as it was during the breeding season, but there were fewer birds. Instead, the owl consumed more shrews, which made up 12.4% (only 3.6% during the breeding season). However, birds still formed 32.1% of the owl's food. This decrease of 11.9% is due to the scarcity of birds during the Finnish winter when most birds will have migrated. This is also the reason why the numbers of bird prey, outside the breeding season, is even lower in the Moscow region as shown in Table 20.

According to Lichačev (1951), Vorob'ev (1952), Voroncov et al (1956) and Šilov and Smirin (1959), birds form only 5.1% of prey numbers in the owl's diet outside the breeding season in the area of Moscow, whereas the corresponding percentages in the forest of Bielowieza in USSR and in Central Europe were 21.9 and 61.6 respectively (Table 20). In Norway the owl apparently consumes more shrews (44%) than in Finland (cf. Hagen 1952), but this seems to be due to the different phases in vole population cycles in Norway during the investigation years, rather than the geographical location. Except in the breeding season, the composition of the Pygmy Owl's diet relates directly to vole populations (cf. Kellomäki 1969, Kaakinen and Mikkola 1972).

We can conclude from the results of Table 20 that, outside the breeding season, the Pygmy Owl compensates for the lack of voles by catching more shrews, which may then form numerically more than half its diet (cf. Bielowieza, Goloduško and Samusenko 1961). These results also demonstrate that birds are a more difficult prey for the owl except in the breeding season, when it captures with relative ease many species which are roosting in holes; hence, tits usually form the greater part of the owl's bird-diet during this period.

BREEDING BIOLOGY

In Central Europe the Pygmy Owl lives in mountain forests up to 1,650 m altitude. The biotope ranges from richly structured virgin coniferous forest (from which mature trees are regularly removed by man), clearings and forest-islands,* to completely deforested areas; which means that the species occurs in all types of woodland. Scherzinger (1974) stated that in Central Europe (Bayerischer Wald, West Germany) the area of mature timber forest in twenty territories varied between 3.9% and 86.7%, and the size of Pygmy Owl territories in different types of forests ranged from 0.2 to 1.7 km², the average of 50 territories being 1.4 km².

On the west coast of Sweden the habitat most frequently chosen by the Pygmy Owl is oak forest with dense areas of spruce. It also favours gardens and parks with nest boxes. Part of the attraction of such places may be the frequency of holes suitable for food-hoarding, and partly the greater supply of rodents and passerine birds (Lindberg 1966).

In Finland the Pygmy Owl can be found in conifer areas all over the country, but Kellomäki (1970) suggested that the most favoured habitats are the mature spruce forests, where he once found two nests only 450 m from each other.

Like most other small owls, the Pygmy Owl nests in holes or hollows in trees. In Finland 47% of the nests have been in spruces, 39% in aspen, 12% in pine and only 2% in birch trees. Eight of the 58 nests have been in nest-boxes and 50 in holes made by either the Great Spotted Woodpecker, the Three-toed Woodpecker *Picoides tridactylus* or the Grey-headed Woodpecker *Picus canus*. Most (70%) of the nests have been at least 1 km from the nearest house, but the lack of natural holes can bring the Pygmy Owl to a nest-box in a farmhouse garden. This is known to have happened at least three times in Finland (cf. Kellomäki 1970).

Weather influences the start of breeding activities and late snowfalls, that may cause even advanced broods to be abandoned (Scherzinger 1974), mean that the Pygmy Owl in Finland can hardly commence breeding before late April, and this explains why hatching usually coincides with that of most of its prey birds. Kellomäki (1977) thought that this owl's late breeding is probably an adaptation which helps ensure successful fledging even in poor vole years.

The pair clean the nest-hole before the eggs are laid. An egg is laid every second day and weighs about 8.7 g. The Pygmy Owl is one of the few owl species which does not start incubation before the clutch is completed, the incubation lasting 29 days (Scherzinger 1970).

All available records of the sizes of the Pygmy Owl's clutches may be tabulated as follows:

Eggs per clutch	3	4	5	6	7	8	9	10	Average
Finland	4	8	6	5	1	4	1	1	5.4
Sweden		1	5	1	6				5.9
Austria		4	1	1					4.5
Completed clutches	4	13	12	7	7	4	1	1	5.4

* Small clumps of trees isolated after the surrounding ones have been felled.

In Finland a normal clutch contains three to eight eggs, but one nest was found with nine eggs in Oulu, and another with ten eggs in Kajaani (Merikallio). As shown in the above Table, the average was 5.4 eggs for 30 clutches. In Sweden the average is even higher, being 5.9 eggs in 13 nests, the range extending from four to seven eggs (Rosenius, according to Merikallio). The clutch size is lower in Central Europe, because Scherzinger (1970) had an average of only 4.5 eggs in his six nests in Austria, the range there being from four to six eggs. There are no reported instances of clutch sizes larger than seven eggs for Central Europe.

There is certainly a noticeable difference in the number of nestlings per brood between Finland and Germany. Kellomäki (1977) noted an average of 5.1 nestlings (range from 3 to 7) in his 16 nests in Finland, although Scherzinger (1974) found an average of only 4.3 nestlings in his 13 nests in the Bayerischer Wald, and no more than an average of 3.3 nestlings survived until the end of the breeding season.

Kellomäki (1977) found a positive correlation between the clutch size and the proportion of mammals in the Pygmy Owl's diet, and a negative correlation between the clutch size and the proportion of birds in the diet. This indicates that the clutch size of the Pygmy Owl is determined by the availability of small mammals before egg-laying.

In poor vole years many young seem to die of hunger or from related cannibalism (cf. Sonerud et al 1972, Jussila and Mikkola 1973), and breeding success is much better during good vole years. This seems to demonstrate that the Pygmy Owl is highly dependent on voles for the success of its young, and is unable to exploit birds sufficiently to supplement its diet in poor vole years, as Kellomäki (1977) put forward in his thesis.

The weight of the newly-hatched Pygmy Owl is about 5.6 g and at this stage it is covered with whitish down. The male responds to the discovery that the first young has hatched by providing more food for the female, but she alone feeds the young whilst they are in the nest-hole. The aggressive behaviour of the female towards the male seems to stimulate him into bringing food more often (cf. Scherzinger 1970, Schönn 1976).

Whilst the young occupy the nest the female endeavours to keep it free of waste material such as pellets, droppings and feathers. Young owls form balls of excrement when still fledglings and adult owls spray out liquid dung (Scherzinger 1970). At three days the young form regular pellets (Jansson 1964). Starting on the sixth day the original nestling down plumage, the protoptile, is pushed out by the second of such downy plumages, the mesoptile. The eyes are opened on the ninth day. When two weeks old, the young have already gained about 60% of the 58–70 g of weight that they will acquire before leaving the nest. At 25 days the nestling is fully feathered and it leaves the nest finally at 30 days, being then able to fly. Parental protection ends three to four weeks later. In contrast to owls that hatch in unprotected nests, the Pygmy Owl nestling has a smooth plumage and has no specialised climbing behaviour (Scherzinger 1970).

The owls become sexually mature as early as five months, but in the beginning they show sexual ambivalence (Scherzinger 1970).

DISTRIBUTION

The Pygmy Owl belongs to the Siberian-Canadian faunal type and its distribution is

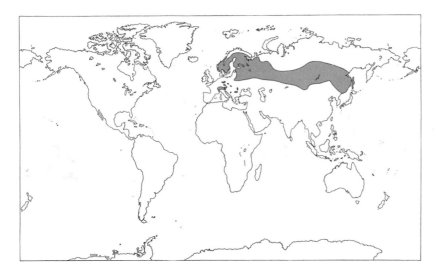

PYGMY OWL – shaded area indicates breeding distribution

thus Holarctic in boreal climatic zones and mountain regions. But the Pygmy Owl forms one part of a species group with an almost cosmopolitan distribution, absent only from Australia, the relationship to its geographical representatives being problematical and its distribution history obscure (Voous 1960).

In Eurasia the Pygmy Owl lives in a broad belt 600 to 1,000 km wide across Europe and Asia from Norway to Sakhalin. Like Tengmalm's Owl, the Pygmy Owl is a taiga element with post-glacial relics in the mountains in Central Europe. Only two subspecies or races are recognised; the eastern form (*G. p. orientale*) of East Siberia, Manchuria and Sakhalin is reported to be slightly paler and greyer, rather more noticeably spotted with purer white, and a little larger than the western stocks (*G. p. passerinum*), and so undoubtedly the variation in this continuous range is clinal (cf. Dement'ev *et al* 1951, Vaurie 1965).

In Central Europe the population of the Pygmy Owl is mainly resident (cf. Scherzinger 1970) but in winter some individuals move southwards or down from the mountains, usually in response to bad weather (cf. Mebs 1966).

In Northern Europe the Pygmy Owl is subject to periodic movements, but these are not as regular as those of the Tengmalm's Owl. Remarkable irruptions by Pygmy Owls have taken place during the following winters in Fenno-Scandia:

1903/4, 1907/8, 1914/15, 1918/19, 1921/22, 1926/27, 1931/32, 1932/33, 1934/35, 1935/36, 1938/39, 1942/43, 1946/47, 1947/48, 1949/50, 1950/51, 1954/55, 1955/56, 1960/61, 1963/64, 1965/66, 1968/69, 1969/70, 1970/71, 1971/72.

Most of these irruptions have been quite small but, for example, in the years 1955/56, 1963/64, 1968/69 and 1971/72 Pygmy Owls have even been seen in Denmark (cf. Rosendahl 1973), where this owl is only an occasional visitor after large invasions from the north. From the evidence of a few ringing recoveries, the Pygmy Owls' direction of invasion in autumn is from north to south or south-east, and Lindberg (1966) noted that the owls which had wintered in suitable places in southern Sweden

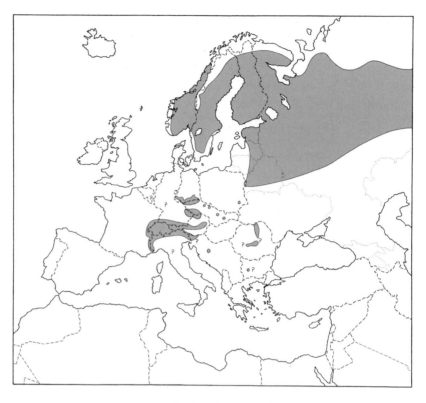

PYGMY OWL – shaded area indicates breeding distribution

in 1963/64 disappeared in March, and the northbound flight seems, according to observations, to have been in a north-easterly direction.

The Pygmy Owl is reluctant to fly over open water, and the sea will usually inhibit further advance, the Scandinavian population mostly moving back and forth between north and south within this section of the continent. A mixture of cold weather and a very poor year for small mammals (including shrews) triggers off a large irruption of Pygmy Owls, and these movements are therefore more irregular than those of the Hawk, Snowy, Great Grey and Tengmalm's Owls, which occur after a crash of the vole or lemming populations.

Throughout its European range the Pygmy Owl is less numerous than Tengmalm's Owl. Merikallio (1958) thought that there were 200 to 300 breeding Pygmy Owl pairs in Finland, which is surely too low a figure for today and, possibly, in the lifetime of that authority, because Ulfstrand and Högstedt (1976) estimated 20,000 pairs for Sweden, although this is perhaps too high a figure. Even in Estonia, USSR, which has a relatively small land area, there may be between 100 and 200 pairs (Randla, *in litt.*). Schönn's estimate (*in litt.*) for East Germany is 40 to 60 pairs, and Scherzinger (1974) found 50 pairs in the Bayerischer Wald in West Germany.

In Czechoslovakia there are at least 25 to 35 pairs (Bárta, *in litt.*) and in Rumania the Pygmy Owl has bred infrequently in the dense coniferous forests. During the last century this owl was apparently more common in Rumania (Munteanu, *in litt.*), as was also the case in Poland, where it may have been widespread over the whole country (Tomialojć, *in litt.*). Nowadays it is numerous only in the forest of Bielowieza.

In Bulgaria the Pygmy Owl nested in the Rila mountains in 1950 and perhaps in 1955 (Dontchev and Simeonov, *in litt.*).

There is a forest area in the most easterly part of Belgium where this owl may exist in small numbers, but there are no conclusive records probably because too few ornithologists visit the area (Huyskens, *in litt.*).

15: Little Owl *Athene noctua*
(Scopoli)

The upperparts are dark brown, splotched with white; the underparts are pale, off-white, broadly streaked with dark brown, most heavily on the upper breast. The crown and nape have elongated white speckles and the neck has larger white markings. There are similarly shaped but even larger white splotches, partly covered by the basic brown colour, on the scapulars, upperparts and wings. The remiges are brown with whitish bars and greyish tips. The rectrices are brown with four to five ochre-white crossbands.

The ill-defined facial disc and the pale 'eyebrows', combined with the low forehead produce a frowning, disapproving expression. The eyes are bright yellow, pale yellow in juveniles. The bill is wax-yellow and the claws black. The toes have greyish-white bristles and the feathers on the tarsometatarsus are white without patches.

The above description applies to the western and central European birds. Taxonomists distinguish eleven subspecies or races, based mainly on colour and size differences, although the characteristics of one race generally grade into those of the neighbouring races. The darkest race *A. n. vidalii* occurs in western Europe, including Britain. The palest *A. n. lilith*, which is a ghostly sandy-buff, inhabits the dry, sandy region at the eastern end of the Mediterranean. Keve *et al* (1960) separated three different populations in south-east Europe: *A. n. noctua*, *A. n. daciae* and *A. n. indigena*. The largest wing measurements are those of the Balkan owls (*A. n. indigena*), the smallest those from Transylvania (*A. n. daciae*), whose population, however, showed the biggest difference between the sexes. Keve *et al* (1960) listed the following measurements of the nominate form *A. n. noctua*. The wing length of males was 151–170 mm (average 160.9 mm from 20 birds) and that of females 152–170 mm (average 162.9 mm from 23 birds). The weight of males was 108–210 g (average 171.7 g from 17 birds) and that of females 120–207 g (average 174.9 g from 16 birds). The differences between the sexes is thus very small.

126

Dement'ev *et al* (1951) also give measurements for the same race. In the Russian data the overall length of males was 232–250 mm (average 241.6 mm from 5 birds) and that of females 243–275 mm (average 252.6 mm from 7 birds). The wing length of males was 152–169 mm (average 160.2 mm from 37 birds) and that of females 158–177 mm (average 168.4 mm from 26 birds). Sexual dimorphism would therefore seem to be more marked in this Russian data than in Keve's which was collected from south-east Europe.

I have found that the tarsus of the Little Owl is much longer than that of Tengmalm's Owl, being 29–34 mm and 20–23 mm respectively (cf. Géroudet 1965). Presumably the Little Owl's terrestrial habits (cf. *Behaviour*) have led to this noticeable increase in leg length.

IN THE FIELD

A rather small owl, as its name implies, about the size of a Song Thrush *Turdus philomelos*. It is compact and plump, with a flat-headed appearance emphasised particularly by the broad, whitish 'eyebrows', which give the bird a frowning expression. Confusion may be possible with Tengmalm's Owl, but the shape of the facial disc is quite different, lacking the high arched areas over the eyes that are so distinctive of Tengmalm's. The present species less often perches in an upright posture, and the feet are not as feathered as Tengmalm's, though a fairly close view is needed to see the latter feature.

The wings are broad and rounded with the numerous whitish spots on the upperwing showing up particularly well in flight which, by day, is deeply undulating. This dipping flight may aid the bird in evading hunting raptors. At night it flies straight and low over the ground.

VOICE

The voice is very varied. Two calls predominate – a ringing, plaintive *kiew, kiew*, repeated at intervals of a few seconds, and a rapidly repeated loud, yelping *wherrow*, the sharp emphasis being placed on the first syllable. Less frequent calls are a soft whistle and notes such as *ivid* and *i-it*. When disturbed, the Little Owl utters complaining, trilling notes. As in most owls, bill-snapping occurs and is usually a sign of stress or anger. A continuous wheezing call is made by the young when hungry.

Various 'songs' have been recorded, perhaps the most common being an erratic sequence of *kiew, kiew* notes and variations, sometimes sounding like the beginning of the Curlew's *Numenius arquata* song. Others are a sharp chattering and rattling.

In spring the male and female may duet using these songs and calls, and at this time of the year a faint snoring is sometimes heard during the day. Another distinct call is reminiscent of a person breathing out in deep sleep (A. Hibbert-Ware, Witherby *et al* 1940).

BEHAVIOUR

The male Little Owl usually begins to mark its territory at the beginning of February by singing from some favourite tree, telegraph post, or fence post within its territory. The main courtship generally begins in March, when it is possible to hear as many as six competing males. During the courtship the male utters a loud *hooo-oo, hooo-oo* and the female shrieks and yelps in answer. The courtship consists of nest-hole demonstrations, prey presentations and copulations. Before copulation the male usually flies round and round the perching female, often quite close to their nest site. They then face each other on a tree branch or a fence, where the male bobs up and down, weaving and dancing before her. She in turn bobs up and down and then slightly opens and flutters her lowered wings before copulation. Occasionally, the two owls pursue one another in flight with great agility, the male sometimes hovering above the sitting female (Glue and Scott 1980). Haverschmidt (1946) noted a pair which copulated almost every day in March and April. Although there are no long-term marking studies available, it seems likely that the nest site tenacity is strong and the pair-bond is unbroken as long as both partners survive. In England and Wales certain nest sites have, to date, held Little Owls for over 25 years (Glue and Scott, 1980). According to Mebs (1966) a pair will live together outside the breeding season. Well before egg-laying the couple spend much time near the chosen nest hole (Ullrich 1973).

No determined attempt at nest construction has been witnessed, but before egg-laying the hole is cleaned and a hollow is scraped. Some males remain in the nest hole with the female during the laying period. During the incubation, and from hatching to the fourteenth day, the female leaves the nest for brief periods only, relying on the male for food (Glue and Scott 1980). The Little Owls' territory is usually quite small. Eight territories on water-meadows in Hampshire averaged 35 ha and eleven on mixed farmland in Warwickshire 38 ha each. It is not unusual for pairs to breed in close proximity. Glue and Scott (1980) knew of two nests in England only 240 m apart, and another two nests 320 m apart.

In Germany, Ullrich (1973) found four nests within 1 km^2, the distances between breeding pairs being 300 m, 500 m, 750 m and 750 m. In 1952 Mebs (1966) even found 16 to 20 pairs per km^2 in some suitable areas in Germany, and he maintained that the typical hunting territory of a Little Owl is about 0.5 km^2.

The Little Owl avoids inter-specific competition with the Tawny Owl, the smaller bird being more common in open habitats, but it is not known whether and to what extent inter-specific competition occurs with the Scops Owl in habitat common to both species. However, the Little Owl inhabits the more open and less mountainous and hilly regions, nor has it such strictly nocturnal habits as the Tawny and Scops Owl. On the other hand the Little Owl often nests and hunts over much the same ground as the Barn Owl, even sharing the same nest tree on occasions and breeding successfully as little as 2 m away. Hollow trees may be shared by other species, too, a point well illustrated by a decaying ash tree in Nottinghamshire, where three species bred successfully in 1968: Kestrels occupied a hole near the tree crown (10 m), Little Owls a hole in the side of the trunk (4 m), and Wrens *Troglodytes troglodytes* the ivy *Hedera helix* near the tree base (Glue and Scott 1980).

The Little Owl is normally most active around dawn and at dusk, but it frequently suns itself, and will also hunt by day. It often hunts by perching on a post or similar vantage point, watching for movement on the ground below. It is able to run quite rapidly whilst chasing prey, being rather more terrestrial than most owls, and showing an ecological similarity to the American Burrowing Owl *Athene cunicularia*, a highly specialised terrestrial species (Voous 1960).

Little Owls frequently perch in the open by day, on a post, tree, or telegraph wire,

or even a building, particularly an isolated one. The habit is evident in warm as well as temperate climates, even in desert areas, where in the bright light of midday the birds will close one or both eyes to slits. The example of the race *lilith*, seen by Ian Willis and portrayed in the colour plate, was perched on a pile of rubble on the northern edge of the Sinai Desert, one very hot and brilliant midday in March. Little Owls may often be seen bobbing up and down in such positions in a rather comical fashion, and this may indicate anxiety.

FOOD

Pellets of the Little Owl are comparatively small, on average $25 \times 14 \times 14$ mm (Festetics 1959), and 20–40 mm in length and 10–20 mn across (Géroudet 1965). They are usually rounded at each end, but occasionally they may be tapered to a point at one end, thus leading to confusion with similarly-shaped Kestrel pellets, particularly as both predators use similar vantage points (Glue 1969).

Fewer studies have been published on the Little Owl's diet than on that of other European owls, except for the results of a thorough inquiry on the ecological niche that this owl occupies in Britain (Hibbert-Ware 1938). These results showed that its staple diet throughout the year consisted of insects (including adult and immature earwigs, craneflies, Cockchafers *Melolontha melolontha* and other beetles (*Coleoptera*)) and small rodents. Birds are an important food only during the nesting season, the species most commonly taken being Starlings *Sturnus vulgaris*, House Sparrows *Passer domesticus*, Blackbirds *Turdus merula* and Song Thrushes. Game chicks are occasionally taken by Little Owls. However, one game chick and seven poultry chicks (the latter from one Little Owl's nest during two seasons) was the total obtained by field workers and the analyst during the 16 months of the Little Owl Food Inquiry (Hibbert-Ware 1938).

The Little Owl's food has also been studied in Moldavian SSR (Ganya and Zubkov 1975), in East Germany (Haensel and Walther 1966), in Holland (Haverschmidt 1946), in France (Thiollay 1968), in Spain (Herrera and Hiraldo 1976) and in Italy

(Lovari 1974). In East Germany the amount of insects and other invertebrates eaten was 72.3%, in Holland 89.2%, in France 94.4%, in Spain 95.9% and in Italy 97.6% (Tables 21 and 22). It is clear that the amount of invertebrate food increases gradually from mid-Europe to the Mediterranean. This is probably due to the increasing scarcity of vole (*Microtus*) prey in the Mediterranean community (cf. Herrera and Hiraldo 1976).

Recent pellet analyses confirm a seasonal pattern in the importance of small mammals and frogs in the Little Owl's diet (Tables 21 and 22). In Moldavian SSR small mammals (bats, moles, shrews and rodents up to the size of young hares) formed 40.7% of the prey numbers in spring and summer, and the percentage increased in autumn and winter to 72.9. Frogs are taken mainly in the breeding season (max. 6.9% in Holland). According to Glue (1972), the majority of birds are taken whilst they are breeding (mid-April to mid-July) but in Moldavia birds are more commonly taken in the autumn/winter (Tables 21 and 22).

In Italy during the winter (December 1970–72, January to March 1971–73) Lovari (1974) found that there was an increase in small mammals of up to 4%, although earwigs remained the staple food and *Coleoptera*, too, were frequently taken. A small amount of vegetable matter was also consumed. The Little Owl seems to be the only European owl which regularly takes plant food, especially outside the breeding season (cf. Thiollay 1968); but Haverschmidt (1946) and Festetics (1959) also found grass and seeds in every pellet during the breeding season.

BREEDING BIOLOGY

The Little Owl is found in a variety of habitats, ranging from parkland, orchards and cultivated fields with hedges, to rocky, semi-desert regions and steppes, but it generally avoids mountainous, hilly and densely wooded areas. Glue and Scott (1980) have listed the breeding habitats of Little Owls in Britain between 1939 and 1975 (Table 23). Although this owl has been successful in occupying a wide range of habitats in England and Wales, it prefers to breed on agricultural land, especially where there are plenty of well-established hedgerows, copses, orchards or woods. Those birds which occupy residential or industrial land require suitable ground nearby, such as playing fields, cemeteries or waste ground. Elsewhere in Europe the Little Owl is frequent around parks and gardens.

It readily accepts artificial nesting holes as breeding sites. Natural breeding cavities in trees are usually roomy, but the female usually does not brood immediately below the entrance hole but in an adjoining cavity. Other cavities are often used, such as holes in old buildings, in walls and cliffs. Occasionally a nest has been located in hay or corn stacks, or in rabbit burrows. The disused nests of birds such as Jackdaws *Corvus monedula* and Stock Doves *Columba oenas* have also been used.

Glue and Scott (1980) found that the most frequently used nesting places in lowland Britain were holes in deciduous trees (Table 24). In fact, 92% of the 526 nests examined in detail were in trees; man-made structures of various types accounted for 7%, six nests were in rock clefts or rabbit burrows, and three were in gravel- and sand-pit tunnels and inside stacked peat on moorland.

Data from 357 British nests showed that laying is almost exclusively confined to April and May, 83% of the clutches being started between 11th April and 10th May (mean 28th April, including any repeats). The laying season spans 16th March to 19th

June (Glue and Scott 1980). In 17 nests studied in Germany the first eggs were laid between 15th April and 20th May (Ullrich 1973, 1975). Thus, it seems that the Little Owl has a highly synchronised laying period and the shortest breeding season of any owl species breeding regularly in Europe.

Second broods are rare and lost clutches are not often replaced. At one nest site in Lincolnshire, three owlets fledged from the first clutch started on 12th April, then a further two young hatched from a second clutch in the same nest on 18th July and left on 19th August (Glue and Scott 1980).

Little Owl eggs are white, with no gloss, and broadly elliptical in shape. The available records of the clutch size may be tabulated as follows:

Eggs per clutch	1	2	3	4	5	6	7	Average	Source
Denmark	—	—	—	33	29	12	2	4.8	Rosendahl 1973
W. Germany	—	—	3	8	3	—	1	4.2	Ullrich 1973, 1975
Switzerland	—	—	8	13	8	2	1	4.2	Géroudet 1965
Britain	3	26	95	105	35	2	2	3.6	Glue and Scott 1980
Completed clutches	3	26	106	159	75	16	6	3.9	

Clutches of three to five eggs came from 340 nests; clutches of two and six eggs were occasional, one and seven rare, though clutches of eight eggs have been recorded (Witherby *et al* 1940). In Britain, replacement clutches were of three (on five occasions) and four (once) eggs. In West Germany one replacement clutch had four eggs (Ullrich 1975). The average clutch size of 391 broods was 3.9 eggs, and as with many other owls the number seems to decrease southwards and westwards.

Eggs are often laid on consecutive days or at two-day intervals, but sometimes, especially between the final two eggs, there may be up to a week's interval. Incubation is by the female alone, and normally begins as soon as the first egg has been laid but, unlike most owls, incubation may also be delayed until the clutch is completed. Some authors claim that the male participates in incubation, but this requires confirmation.

The incubation period is said to be 24–25 days (Campbell and Ferguson-Lees 1972) and 27–28 days (Ullrich 1975), but the more recent study of Glue and Scott (1980) indicates that the eggs will hatch between 28 and 33 days.

Newly-hatched young weigh about 11 g and, in contrast with many owls, the female and male may both feed them (Haverschmidt 1946). However, according to Glue and Scott (1980), the male rarely feeds the newly-hatched young, but will bring the food to the female, which leaves the nest only for brief periods from the time of hatching until between the fourteenth and sixteenth day. From about the fourteenth day until fledging both sexes share the feeding. The main feeding time is from dusk to midnight, with a break of two hours before a resumption of feeding activity until dawn. Little hunting takes place during the day, and food items are rarely brought to the nest in daylight (Glue and Scott 1980). The owlets rapidly increase in weight up to the tenth day, and by the 16th day they have attained approximately 64% of their fledging weight (170 g). During the second and third week this weight increase is reduced to about 3 g per day (Ullrich 1973).

After about 12–14 days, the young will produce hunger cries, a continuous wheezing sound. Later, they make tongue-clicking noises similar to those produced by other owls. The young owls leave the nest-hole as a rule after 30–35 days, although the clutch size and the general availability of food cause some variation in timing. Young owlets may remain in the breeding hole by day far beyond this age.

In England and Wales of 477 eggs laid, at least 269 (56.4%) hatched, and 234 young (49.1%) fledged (Glue and Scott 1980). The average brood size of 241 nests was 2.4, one, two or three young being usual, five the maximum. Cannibalism is not rare, especially when food is short, but when food is abundant even large clutches may be safely reared.

In a study in West Germany there was an average of 4.2 eggs per clutch and two to three young (average 2.4) left the nest-hole, the breeding success being 58.2%. Ullrich (1973) stated that the Little Owl's breeding success is generally better than that of Tengmalm's Owl, which is only 44.2% in West Germany (König 1969). The reason may be that Tengmalm's Owl lives in deep forests where it is more vulnerable to the attentions of Eagle and Tawny Owls, and pine martens *Martes martes*.

Glue and Scott (1980) listed the known causes of 52 breeding failures in Britain. Little Owl's eggs were taken by man (14 times), Magpie *Pica pica* (1), fox *Vulpes vulpes* (1), stoat *Mustela erminea* (1), hedgehog *Erinaceus europaeus* (1); young taken or killed by man (6), fox (1), stoat (1), rat *Rattus norvegicus* (1); adult owls shot by man (4), killed by stoat (1), domestic cat *Felis domestica* (1); nest chamber deliberately blocked by man (4), tree felled (3), eggs infertile or addled (2), nest cavity collapsed (2), hay bales dislodged (2), eggs and young saturated by rain (2), deserted after disturbance by machinery (2), nest tree struck by lightning (1), and nest in willow taken over by Shelducks *Tadorna tadorna* (1). Thus, man caused directly or indirectly the failure of 35 breeding attempts (67%). It is interesting to note that other owls or raptors do not appear among the causes of failure.

When the owlets first leave the nest they can flutter only a few metres, but successful young are able to fly well within a week of leaving the nest. The parents continue to feed the young for up to one month after fledging. The family may stay together until September, though dispersal of juvenile Little Owls usually takes place within four or five weeks of fledging. The exact age that the young bird reaches sexual maturity is not known, but the recovery of ringed Little Owls at the nest during their first summer indicates maturity within one year (Glue and Scott 1980). According to Glue (1971), about 60% of Little Owls ringed as nestlings die within four months of fledging; but in terms of longevity the species has been known to survive 17 years (Rosendahl 1973).

DISTRIBUTION

Voous (1960) asserted that the Little Owl belongs to the Turkestanian-Mediterranean faunal type having a trans-palearctic distribution, with a limited southern extension in the Ethiopian region. The distribution limits approach the July isotherm of 63°F in the north and of 88°F in the south. However, Meinertzhagen (1959) has remarked that the Little Owl is a direct relative of the American Burrowing Owl *Speotyto cunicularia*, which therefore should be named *Athene cunicularia*; furth-

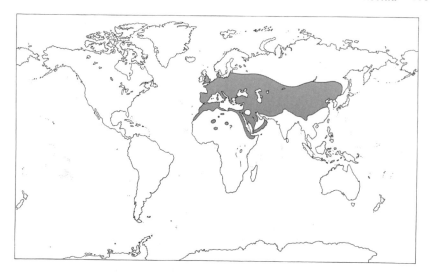

LITTLE OWL – mainly resident – shaded area indicates breeding distribution

ermore, Voous (1977) treats the two specific Latin names synonymously. Hence, the little owl group would seem to have an holarctic distribution as do the groups of *Glaucidium* and *Aegolius*.

Lambrecht (1917) believed that as early as the Pleistocene era Little Owls inhabited Hungary, Bohemia, France, Belgium, the Appenines and even England. It became extinct in England with the glaciation, but it was successfully reintroduced to Britain in the nineteenth after a number of failed attempts. The first, which was unsuccessful, was by C. Waterton, who in 1842 released five Little Owls in Walton Park in Yorkshire. Later, between 1874 and 1880 E. B. Meade-Waldo released 40 birds in Kent. This had some success, but other birds set free in Norfolk and Sussex in the 1870s were not so successful. During 1888–90 Lord Lilford introduced Little Owls from Holland into areas near Oundle, in Northamptonshire, and this resulted in the Little Owl spreading its breeding range to Rutland by 1891 and to Bedfordshire by the following year. Despite further attempts in Yorkshire, Hampshire and Hertfordshire in the 1890s, regular breeding of this bird was established only in the counties of Kent, Bedfordshire, Northamptonshire and Rutland by the end of the century. However, further releases were made and Little Owls began to spread so rapidly that 20 years later there were Little Owls in every county to the south of the Humber. By 1923 the species could be found as far south as Land's End and northwards to the Scottish border, which it crosssed in the following 12 years. This colonisation in Britain is an example of how the Little Owl spreads in general (cf. Sharrock 1976, Keve *et al* 1960).

In the 1940s its range in Britain was still expanding northwards, but decreases were recorded in some counties in the south and west of Britain, such that between 1956 and 1965 the numbers of Little Owl fell sharply in many areas. The numbers were especially low after the hard winters of 1946/7 and 1962/3 and the decreases may have been due to these periods of very cold weather. There have been further decreases between 1955 and 1961 and this may be partly due to the chemical contamination of

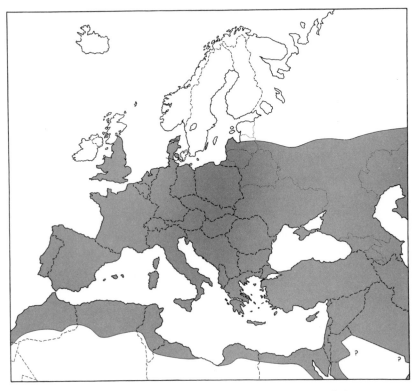

LITTLE OWL – mainly resident – shaded area indicates breeding distribution

prey (cf. Parslow 1973, Sharrock 1976). Signs of a slight recovery have been noted in some areas of England where the total numbers of breeding Little Owls, as calculated in *The Atlas of Breeding Birds in Britain and Ireland*, is about 7,000–14,000 pairs (Sharrock 1976); Parslow (1973) included the Little Owl in the range of 1,000 to 10,000 pairs.

Fenno-Scandia is much too cold for the Little Owl. It has been found only once in Finland, on 15th September 1901, in Muurame (Lönn, in the collection of the Department of Biology, University of Jyväskylä). The Little Owl appears to be an extremely rare species in Estonia, the only reliable record dating from 1885 (Randla 1976). In Sweden the species has not bred since 1941 and has not been recorded since the 1950s (Bylin, *in litt.*).

In central and southern Europe the Little Owl is common everywhere except in high mountains, dense woods or the central areas of towns. For instance, in France, the Little Owl was found nesting in 74% of the squares of the French breeding bird atlas grid and in all Departments, including parts of Corsica. Roughly speaking, the French population can be placed between 30,000 and 80,000 pairs, which means that it is scarcer than the Tawny Owl but much more numerous than other species of *Strigidae* (Yeatman, *in litt.*). However, Terrasse, writing in the ICBP Vienna Conference Report (1977), states that this common species has greatly decreased in France since 1964.

In south-east Europe and in Turkey, Syria, Lebanon, Iran, and other parts of the region, the Little Owl is the commonest owl, or at least the most often seen. Throughout their broad range, Little Owls are sedentary and do not undertake regular migrations, although some individuals disperse and wander outside the breeding season up to 300 km from the natal site (Mebs 1966).

16: Tawny Owl *Strix aluco*
(Linné)

DESCRIPTION

Two colour types occur, one being rich chestnut-brown, the other having greys in place of deep browns. Intermediate birds are variously tawny-buff, buff-brown or greyish-brown in coloration. The greyest, lightest birds are by far the least common in Britain.

The upperparts of the brown birds are of a rich tawny or, less frequently, a rather more tawny-chestnut hue, streaked, mottled and vermiculated with dark brown and blackish-brown, and mottled with lighter brown or tawny-buff. Buff or whitish-buff mottling forms bands running back and outwards across the crown from the central upper edge of the facial disc. Dense black-brown mottling adjacent to these bands usually highlights this pattern, though in the more tawny-coloured birds the pale bands are buffer and less conspicuous. The outermost scapulars are variably tipped and edged whitish, forming ragged pale 'braces'.

The face is either pale rufous-buff, or deep buff with only a tinge of rufous. The loral semi-circles and narrow ring surrounding the eyes are buff. The facial 'ruff' is densely flecked and edged dark brown, forming a very narrow, but quite well-defined dark edge to facial disc, widest at top of disc. Underparts are whitish or buff, each feather with a central streak and variable cross-bars of dark brown or black-brown, densest across breast, but absent on middle of belly and, usually, on lower throat. Primaries and secondaries barred tawny-buff or buff and blackish-brown with brown or smoky brown mottling on the buff areas, though mottling almost or completely lacking on buff of outer webs of primaries. Buff is distinctly lightest on basal areas of central primaries. Tips of remiges greyer, mottled darker. Primary coverts barred brown (rufous- or buff-brown) and black-brown with some dark brown mottling. Wing-coverts much as scapulars, though dark brown cross-barring particularly well-marked on greater coverts which have variable white spots on distal portion of outer webs. Sometimes these form quite large white blobs on dark brown wing, especially on outer greater coverts and even occasionally the odd outer median covert and bastard wing feather. Tail feathers tawny to tawny-chestnut, central pair with some dark mottling, but otherwise unmarked, outer feathers barred dark brown, and remaining rectrices barred only across inner webs. All tail feathers tipped greyish-white or buffish. The underwing is creamy-buff with a dingy brown wash across distal parts of remiges and broad grey-brown bars across outer primaries and narrower ones on distal portions of inner primaries and secondaries. Rufous-yellow wash on tips of underwing-coverts which are lightly streaked dark brown with broad black-brown tips to primary coverts forming a dark semi-circular mark near bend of wing.

The bill is pale olive-yellow and the very large eyes have bluish-black irides. The wholly-feathered tarsi and feet (except for distal part of toes) are white with some brownish speckling. The claws are blackish with dirty white bases.

Grey-brown birds have the same basic pattern as brown birds, though all the browns are replaced by a much greyer hue. In extreme examples the overall ground-colour of the upperparts is greyish-white, streaked and mottled black-brown, while the underparts are white with black and black-brown markings.

There appears to be no sexual difference on the basis of colour and pattern, although there is a great deal of individual variation.

The down of the Tawny Owl nestling is white, fairly short, thick and soft, entirely covering the owlet to the base of the claws, except for the bare patch at the back of the tarsal joint.

The mesoptile plumage is so similar to that of the young Ural Owl as to be almost indistinguishable (see also that species). The nestlings are rather round and woolly-looking, the feathers being of a very loose structure. They are entirely covered with slightly wavy greyish-white and dirty brown-buff barring apart from the centre of the belly, tarsi and feet which are grey-buff. The centre of the facial disc lacks barring and is greyish-buff in colour. Like the adults they have livid pink, wax-like edges to the eyelids. Photographs taken by Scherzinger (1980) of owls in captivity show, however, some differences between the Tawny and Ural Owl nestlings. Already at the age of two days the down of the Ural Owl is less white than that of the Tawny Owl, which has a relatively larger head and smaller more slender bill and weaker claws. At the age of 28 days the Tawny Owl has a much less developed facial disc, a clearly smaller bill and generally lighter and more striped appearance.

Many years ago, Sten Bergmann (in one of his excellent but largely unknown Swedish animal books) wrote that the growing feathers of the young Tawny Owl are brownish, whereas those of the Ural Owl nestlings are blackish-grey. He also remarked that the bill and claws of the Ural Owl are much larger than those of the Tawny Owl young. In the field these differences have value only for birdwatchers who are wholly familiar with both species, or for those able to compare young Ural and Tawns Owls at the same time. This problem of identification occurs only at the nest when the parent owl has not been seen.

Altogether six subspecies were recognised by Vaurie (1965) as inhabiting the regions covered by this book. They vary according to size and coloration, and the above descriptions apply to birds of the races *sylvatica* inhabiting Great Britain, southern and western France and the Iberian Peninsula, and *aluco* which ranges over continental Europe and Sicily east to the Urals and Lebanon. The nominate race *S. a. aluco* differs from *sylvatica* in being more consistent in individual plumage, but grey birds predominate over brown ones, the reverse of the situation in the westernmost parts of Europe.

The Siberian race *S. a. siberiae* of westernmost Siberia and the Urals is only found in a pale grey colour form. Its ground-colour is whiter than *aluco* and the dark markings on upper- and underparts are reduced.

A dark and highly variable race *S. a. willkonskii* inhabits the Caucasus and northern Iran. It exhibits grey and brown 'phases' but, additionally, an apparently rather rare colour form exists which is chocolate- or coffee-brown in hue.

The very pale *S. a. sancti-nicolai* of Iraq and southwest Iran is confined to a grey ground-colour, or at most brown-grey.

Lastly, the race of north-west Africa *S. a. mauritanica* is very constant in its coloration, which is always dark grey-brown, heavily marked above and below with black-brown.

It is obvious from these descriptions that some races are much less variable individually than others. In this context it must be realised that the so-called grey and brown 'phases' form a complete range of intermediates within the populations displaying such colour differences. The possible exception is the very dark and rare form *willkonskii*.

The measurements of the nominate race *aluco* given by Dement'ev *et al* (1951) are as follows: length of males 410–435 mm (5 measured), that of females 435–460 mm (8 measured), with averages of 421 and 447 mm respectively. The wing span of males was 910–950 mm (5 measured) and that of females 940–1050 mm (8 measured), their respective averages being 940 and 1008 mm. The wing of males varies between 268–295 mm, the average being 283.2 (for 53 birds) and that of females 277–311 mm, averaging 296.4 mm (for 66 birds). Males average a shorter wing length than females.

In Finland (v. Haartman *et al* 1967) and in the European part of the USSR (Dement'ev *et al* 1951), the weight of the nominate race males varies between 410–550 g (average 474 g for 13 birds) and that of females 410–800 g (average 583 g for 22 birds).

There seems to be not only a noticeable size difference between females and males but also between the races *S. a. aluco* and *S. a. sylvatica*. Southern (1970) has weight measurements for *S. a. sylvatica* in England. Five males weighed 390–556 g (average 454 g), and 15 females 345–600 g (average 478 g). Thus *sylvatica* males would seem to be 20 g lighter and females even 100 g lighter than those of the nominate race.

There are also clear differences in the weight of southern and northern *aluco* populations in Europe as shown below:

Weight in g

	Females	Males	Source
West USSR	642 (4)	472 (3)	Dement'ev *et al* (1951)
Finland	570 (18)	475 (10)	v. Haartman *et al* 1967)
East Germany	561 (65)	441 (45)	Piechocki (1980)
Belgium	553 (58)	440 (12)	Delmée *et al* (1978)
Italy	517 (19)	425 (21)	Moltoni (1949)

It is possible that there is too little information here to prove that the weight of the nominate race decreases not only from north to south but also from east to west.

Wing length measurements are more readily available than body weights for all west Eurasian races of the Tawny Owl. Due to the strong sexual dimorphism it is advisable to separate the sexes in all comparisons. Table 25 shows that wing lengths are shortest in the English owls and longest in owls of the Ural region of the USSR, i.e. in the north-eastern part of the species' range.

Vaurie, in his summary of wing lengths from birds in what he termed the *aluco* group of Tawny Owls of western Eurasia, stated that wing length increases from west to east and decreases from north to south. Generally, his claim seems to accord with measurements in Table 25 but they do not fully support the second part of his statement. In fact, they seem to show an increase from north to south in countries along the Atlantic seaboard and a decrease southwards from the Urals. Unfortunately, the birds measured in Morocco were not sexed, but even if all were females they were much larger than owls in England, or even those in Sweden.

IN THE FIELD

The Tawny Owl is seldom seen, but its familiar wavering hoot is so often heard (even in the parks and gardens of suburbia) that, in Britain at least, it is one of the more widely known wildlife sounds. The owl may sometimes be located at dusk, or later, on a bare branch or even a chimney-pot in towns, silhouetted against a moonlit sky or in the glow of street lighting, when the chunky, large-headed, short-tailed proportions can be noted. It shares this portly, broad-headed shape with Tengmalm's Owl, though the Tawny is larger and has quite different calls.

When seen by day, whether flushed from a roost, or close against a tree-trunk, or among masses of twigs or leaves in a thicket or tree-top, the Tawny Owl's large all-dark eyes set in a generous, well-rounded facial disc, along with its compact, broad-headed shape are enough to distinguish it from all other European owls. Its brown, grey-brown or pale grey plumage is well-streaked, mottled and vermiculated.

Ornithologists have yet to discover an overlap in the ranges of Tawny and Hume's Owl, though their close proximity in Israel/Lebanon, along with their similarity in size, shape and call should warrant caution when identifying single, calling birds in darkness or semi-darkness in the desert areas of the Middle East. Both Tengmalm's and Hume's Owls are quite different from the Tawny when seen in daylight, Tengmalm's being noticeably smaller and with a 'surprised' expression on its yellow-eyed face, unlike the 'worldly-wise' look of the dark-eyed Tawny Owl. Hume's Owl is slightly smaller than the Tawny Owl with sandy-buff coloration, no dark markings, and orange eyes. It also seems to perch more at an angle, or even horizontally, rather than upright.

The Ural Owl is superficially similar to the Tawny Owl because of its dark eyes but these are smaller than the Tawny's and, being set in a pale face, give the bird a 'bland' expression. It is also a larger bird than the Tawny with a proportionately smaller head but longish tail, and is paler and much more neatly streaked.

The short, broad wings and short tail of the Tawny Owl enable it to manoeuvre easily among the branches and thick foliage of the mature wooded areas it prefers. However, it is one of the most nocturnal of all European owls and to see it flying by day is an extremely rare event. In over 20 years of birdwatching in Britain and all over

Europe, including two long spells living within Tawny Owl territories, Ian Willis has only seen it flying in daylight on two occasions, each time a bird that had been inadvertently flushed from a roost. In that time he heard perhaps scores, if not hundreds, of separate birds. Considering how common they are, at least in large parts of their range, it is quite extraordinary how excellent camouflage plus the habit of 'freezing' in thick foliage or masses of small branches, or against a tree-trunk, enables most birds to escape notice by human beings.

VOICE

The Tawny Owl has been described as the most musical of all the European owls. Muir (1954), Arvola (1959), Andersen (1961), Wendland (1963) and Southern (1970) have described ten different basic 'calls' of adults in the breeding season, and five of the young. The normal 'song' – the familiar hooting of the male – has several functions; first, as a territorial call; second, a courtship call; and third, an announcing call used by the male when bringing food to the female. This well-known hoot consists of a long drawn out *hoōo*, a pause of two or three seconds (a pause of 4–6 seconds, according to Andersen 1961), an abrupt and subdued *hū*, followed at once by a prolonged and resonant final phrase *huhuhuhooo* (Southern 1970). This song has a beautiful, pure ocarina-like tone, the two series having a distinct vibrato and a fall of pitch in their extended last note. Sometimes, the female makes a similar hooting sound to the mating male. Southern (1970) writes that hooting females are often heard, especially in autumn. However, the female's hooting is less clearly phrased than the male's, the last phrase having a more wailing quality, approximately *wow-wow-hooo*. Andersen (1961) calls these particular sounds the incomplete song, stating that they are commonly uttered by either sex. He described it as a grating, hoarse version of the normal song. With this the male generally announces his arrival with prey. Goodwin (1956) has heard a Jay *Garrulus glandarius*, give a very passable imitation of this incomplete song on seeing a Tawny Owl in the daytime.

The contact call *kewick* and its variants is the most frequent utterance of the female, but it is also used by the male. In spring the female may answer the male's hoot with *kewick* as a kind of duet. When the female gives this call from the nest the male generally responds soon afterwards by bringing prey to her, loudly announcing his arrival. A similar call is also made by the parents as a contact call when bringing prey to the fledged young. The young will answer with their cheeping call. The *oo*-trill of the male, given immediately after delivering prey is also a territorial conflict call (Wendland 1963). According to Southern (1970), the noises made by two males disputing are highly diagnostic, and very valuable as an aid to discovering territorial boundaries. This call has been described as a loud discordant 'caterwauling' which is quite spine-chilling if heard unexpectedly at close quarters.

Many other calls have been heard during courtship and in territorial disputes. Sometimes, for instance, a hissing trill *co-co-co-co-co-co-co* is uttered during courtship and territorial fights. A low-pitched, soft *oo*-trill (similar to the drumming of Common Snipe *Gallinago gallinago*) is given during courtship. Creaking high-pitched sounds by the female (*ooaoo*) with an accentuated squeaking *a*-sound have been heard usually at times of courtship or 'sham-courtship' (Wendland 1963). The *ee*-trill of the female, *ee-ee-ee-ee* . . . expresses sexual excitement and has been heard as an accompaniment to copulation. A low-pitched, soft *ooi* is generally an expression of tenderness. After copulation the female uses this sound repeatedly for quite a long time.

Wendland (1963) has described two typical warning calls; one being *wett-wett* and the other an *ee*-trill followed by a sort of twittering. Bill-snapping is used to express anger. In the event of moderate danger the Tawny Owl calls *koo-ik*, *koo-ik* or *koo-i*, *koo-i*, but if there is imminent danger to the young, these alarm-notes are changed to the aggressive call (Andersen 1961). This call is a harsh, rapidly-repeated *wick-wick-wick*, frequently given by the female when she is with her chicks in the presence of a human being. This call also accompanies a real or a sham attack in the form of a dive close above or towards the head of the intruder. Andersen (1961) records this note being used also during an attack on a fox, a dog and a Long-eared Owl. If one comes so close to a Tawny Owl that it is prevented from flying from its nest hole or day roost, it will often utter a sudden hissing sound, like a snake's hiss, as do many other hole-nesting birds such as the Wryneck *Jynx torquilla*. In the same situation, and in many others, when a predator or a congener comes close, the so-called bill-snapping is often used.

From the first days of their life the nestlings are capable of a fine, piping series of notes, *bi-bi-bi-bi-bi*. The tiny owlets produce this sound as soon as the brooding female departs from the nest on one of her rare and brief excursions. Older owlets will still use this call in response to mutual pushing and touching, sometimes with bill-snapping as a sequel (Andersen 1961). By the time a young owl is able to swallow prey items whole, its calling note *psji-ii* or *sjiii-ii*, repeated with increasing intensity, changes to long-drawn, high, hissing, squeaky sounds *siii-siii-siii*. The young owl then adopts the begging posture with the body bent forward, wings quivering like an adult female receiving prey from the male. If surprised by an enemy the young owlets often emit a series of bill-snapping sounds.

The fledged young have typical calls which may be rendered *ti-sweep* and *ti-swerp*, individual owlets often using only one version, making it possible to distinguish them within a brood. This call guides the parents to the young after they have left the nest and helps ensure an adequate distribution of food among them (Muir 1954), but it also acts as a kind of social call within the brood and helps to prevent intermixing with neighbouring clutches (Southern *et al* 1954). Fledged owlets usually begin to call at dusk and will call throughout the night during June and into July after which calling begins to diminish (Muir 1954).

A Danish nightwatchman, Hansen (1952), profitting from his occupation, made an excellent study of Tawny Owl calls throughout the year. His study is one of the first of its kind on owls and without doubt one of the best non-academic studies to date. Hansen has shown that the calls can be heard throughout the year, though they are not of equal intensity in all seasons. In his study area in Denmark, calling reached maximum intensity from mid-February to early May, followed by a minimum level in June–July, then another maximum from August to October, and a secondary minimum in December–January. These fluctuations reflect the reproduction cycle, moulting, territorial disputes, etc. (cf. Southern 1970).

Weather has a distinct influence on the owls' calling activity. Strong winds have an adverse effect, and wind and cold together bring a particularly pronounced reduction in calling. Owls also call less frequently in rainy weather, and Hansen (1952) established that owls called less when the moon was up than when the night was overcast. It had been generally held in Finland that the best nights for owl-listening were at the period of the full moon. In the light of Hansen's findings, I suggest that

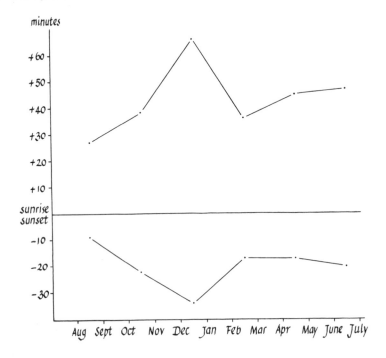

Fig. 16 *Starting and ending of Tawny Owl vocal periods in relation to sunrise and sunset, as recorded by Hansen in Denmark 1950–51 (after Hansen 1952, Table A)*

small mammals and even some small birds are more active on moonlit nights with the result that owls hunt more and call less.

Tawny Owls in Denmark begin calling shortly after sunset and continue steadily till shortly before sunrise. On average, calling started 20 minutes after sunset and ended 43 minutes before sunrise (Fig. 16). This Figure also shows that calling activity is less during December and January when calling begins on average 34 minutes after sunset and ends 66 minutes before sunrise. Hansen had to sleep after his work at night and so his findings do not cover the daylight hours. However, Tawny Owls rarely call during the day. In my data from Finland there was only one instance of a Tawny Owl calling by day (on 19th April at 15.00 hours.) and all the other calls recorded were between 21.35 and 02.30 hours. (Mikkola 1971). This is further confirmed by Ian Willis's own experiences over several years in two different parts of Britain. Calling during the day was only heard once in two years from a pair of Tawny Owls in Kirkcudbrightshire in south-west Scotland (July, 16.30 hours – the brief hooting typical of the male).

BEHAVIOUR

The differences between Tawny Owl and Ural Owl are more distinct in morphological aspects than in behaviour. Each species remains within its nesting territory all the year round and the pair-bond lasts for life. The courtship display largely corresponds in each species but the break in territorial behaviour between the autumn and spring periods is more pronounced in the 'northern' Ural Owl than in the Tawny Owl (Scherzinger 1980). Established Tawny Owl pairs are often seen together, even in the same tree, throughout the year. In late August and early September they are completing their moult and are silent.

The first territorial fights will occur as early as October and November, when territories are asserted by newcomers or re-asserted by established birds. The male determines the territory, the female the nesting hole (Wendland 1963). The predominant calls at this time are territorial hooting, the *kewick* contact call and mingled wails and screams when owners meet on their boundaries (Southern 1970). The transition from autumn to winter is marked by a final establishment of territories and the appearance of pre-breeding behaviour. Territorial challenges and boundary disputes continue but on a diminishing scale. The female and male tend more and more to roost together.

According to Southern (1970), courtship feeding begins in the winter period (December to February), becoming progressively centred on the future nest site. There is an exchange of disjointed hooting from the male and a mixture of contact and soft calls by the female. In courtship, which Beven (1969) has described, the male may indulge in wing-clapping and when pursuing the female will utter screeches, mewings, groans and rattles which have often given rise to tales of ghosts. During courtship the male perches near the female and sways from side to side, then up and down, raising first one wing then the other and finally both together. The male's plumage is puffed out, making the bird almost round, then tightly compressed. Meanwhile he grunts softly, sometimes sidling a foot or so along the branch and back again. The female may puff out and quiver her feathers. During copulation the female utters the *ee*-trill, or the male the *oo*-trill, as described by Wendland (1963). He also noted sham-courtship by pairs that do not breed.

Wendland (1972) knew, and could identify by their individual colour or behaviour, two separate Tawny Owls which stayed in their territories during the 13 years he studied them, and Dement'ev *et al* (1951) stated that one Tawny Owl was faithful to the same nest hole for ten years. Tawny Owls are generally monogamous but some males are known to be polygynous. Scherzinger (1968) found two Tawny Owl females nesting about 50 m apart and sharing the same male.

Occasionally a Tawny Owl female with nestlings may attack a human approaching the nest, even in daylight, and may even draw blood with its talons. In Britain at least two people are known to have lost an eye from attacks (Beven 1969). Eric Hosking, the celebrated bird photographer, suffered in this way quite early in his career. Such aggressive behaviour is, however, exceptional. Wendland (1972) has studied about 50 Tawny Owl nests with young in Grünewald, near Berlin, without any owl attacking him. On the other hand, when studying one Tawny Owl in a Berlin park, he was vigorously attacked. He concluded that Tawny Owls become aggressive to humans in populated areas. My observations support this conclusion, and in sparsely populated central Finland I have never met an aggressive Tawny Owl female although such behaviour is well known amongst the more urban owls in southern Finland. It may be that the owl becomes more aggressive at nests which are visited more often.

Despite its sometimes aggressive behaviour the Tawny Owl can also be quite tame. A recent radio programme in Britain gave an example. Mr and Mrs Lewcock had a Tawny Owl which had been deserted by parents when young two years earlier. They kept the owl in an aviary and released it when it was adult. The owl kept returning to the house, particularly during the severe winter of 1978/79, and tapping on the window at night. In the following spring (1979) the owl became more and more unwilling to leave the house and seemed particularly attached to the sideboard in the living room. A box and some grass were provided and she stayed in the sideboard for 30 days, laying and incubating four eggs, two of which hatched. Her mate would come to the garden with food, hooting the familiar wavering *hoo-ooo-ooo*, whereupon the female would fly out to join him with a *kee-wick* in reply. The food pass always took place away from the aviary where the female had once been kept.

The territorial behaviour of the Tawny Owl in mature woodland has apparently evolved to enable it to locate and secure sufficient food for its daily requirements. At Wytham Wood, Oxford, the average territory was 12 ha in closed woodland and 20 ha in mixed woodland and open land (Southern 1970). Territories were sometimes much smaller, but according to Southern and Lowe (1968), territories of less than about 8 ha were too small to be viable for breeding. Tawny Owls studied in Belgium had territories of about 65–75 ha when living in beechwood with little lesser vegetation (Delmée et al 1978). And in Norway, where the prey density is far less than in England or in Belgium, the mean territory size was about 102 ha per pair (Hagen 1948).

The Tawny Owl defends its territory vigorously against neighbours with 'song', with threatening behaviour or in flying skirmishes. Andersen (1961) has witnessed how a Tawny Owl on several occasions attempted to expel a Long-eared Owl from its territory, although the male Tawny Owl's numerous flight skirmishes did not result in any effective territorial isolation between the two species. Predatory mammals, too, such as cats, foxes and dogs, are driven from the vicinity of the nest (Wendland 1972). In England, there is a record of a Tawny Owl that attacked a fox in winter (Paterson 1964). The fox was drinking at a pond, when, without warning, a Tawny Owl swooped and attacked it. The attack was unprovoked and it was unlikely that the owl would have had a nest in January when this incident took place.

The Tawny Owl is often mobbed at its daytime roost by other birds such as Robins, Blackbirds, tits and Jays. If the owl remains still, as it usually does, the birds soon tire of mobbing and leave it in peace. If, however, the owl tries to escape by flying, it is followed by a crowd of angry birds and their noisy alarms are intensified. Birds of prey such as Kestrels and Sparrowhawks will sometimes mob the Tawny Owl, and although it may kill and eat birds, including the smaller birds of prey, it never attacks them in such circumstances. No doubt this is because it prefers the silent surprise approach in darkness, snatching a bird from its perch (Beven 1969).

Most authors agree that the Tawny Owl usually hunts by waiting quietly on a perch, watching and listening. After detecting a prey animal, such as a mouse moving in the grass, the owl glides down or drops onto it and, at the moment of impact, extends its wings to cover the victim, which is usually killed immediately by the powerful feet and claws. Sometimes a blow from the beak at the base of the victim's skull is also used (Beven 1969). Tawny Owl territories studied in Britain have been almost always in woodland, which explains why the owl so frequently hunts from perches as as described by Beven (1969), Southern (1954) and Southern and Lowe (1968). Two radio-tracked owls in much more open habitats in southern Sweden (Nilsson 1978) devoted about one third of their active time to hunting on the wing. Nilsson watched them fly on moonlight nights 2–3 m above marsh and grassland between small clumps of bushes. Their flight was slow, frequently interrupted with glides. Nevertheless, hunting on the wing alternating with hunting from a perch has also been recorded in Sweden.

The widely varied diet of the Tawny Owl is due largely to the range of its hunting techniques. Burton (1950) suggested that Tawny Owls may sometimes dig for burrowing beetles, *Ceratophylus typhaeus*, and in the process of eating the beetle it swallows the earth and loose roots which are later found in the pellets. Recently, MacDonald (1976) has described the methods used by the owl when preying on earth-worms. The owl, after perching for some time on a post, drops to the grass below. It then sits motionless until it seems to hear a sound, whereupon it turns its head and cranes its neck, apparently trying to locate the source. It may then take a few hops and repeat the head and neck movements until, finally, it bounds forward, the wings partially outspread, to take the worm in its bill. According to MacDonald (1976), the owl may sit motionless for up to ten minutes before pouncing on another worm. The Tawny Owl will also prey on water animals such as water voles, water shrews, fish and frogs, should there be a stream or pond nearby. Whilst hunting it may hover and is also reported to beat its wings on bushes to startle birds into flight. As mentioned, another hunting method is to snatch birds, and occasionally bats, from their roosting perches. Incubating birds, such as Blackbirds, Woodcocks and pigeons, have been picked off their nests (Beven 1969).

The Tawny Owl has evolved various physiological properties to help its hunting abilities, amongst them good vision and hearing, and a good memory. The Tawny Owl's memory has been tested, in Poland, in an experiment in which several identical boxes were placed on the floor of the owl's cage (Macura 1959). Bait such as horsemeat or a mouse was placed under one of the boxes, in full view of the owl. It was found that the owls in the several tests were able to find the right box from among the identical boxes. They retained this ability for 15–20 minutes when there were three boxes to select, but an especially tempting bait, such as a mouse, lengthened the recall to 30 minutes or more. Macura (1959) demonstrated that Tawny Owls are endowed with a considerably better memory than other birds tested by other authors, and a better memory than cats, dogs and racoons, though markedly poorer than that of apes and young children.

The Tawny Owl's threshold of visual acuity has been shown to be generally higher than that of other nocturnal vertebrates (Martin and Gordon 1974). A cat's visual acuity is 5.5', an owl monkey's 8.0' and a rat's 20–52' compared with the Tawny Owl's 3.7'. Under comparable stimulus conditions the visual acuity of the Tawny Owl is, however, lower than man's, but similar to that of a pigeon. So although the Tawny Owl's eye is well adapted to its nocturnal habits, it has not lost its acuity when compared to that of the diurnal pigeon's pure-cone fovea.

Experimental work at the Free University of Amsterdam by van Dijk has shown that Tawny and Long-eared Owls (both species with large external ear openings) can hear low (2 kH) and medium (6 kH) frequency notes about ten times better than humans. For the Tawny Owl the range of maximum sensitivity is 3–6 kH. By comparison, human sensitivity is greatest with lower-pitched sounds of about 1 kH. The Tawny Owl's upper limit of hearing is probably similar to our own, but it may be less sensitive to low frequencies than we are, 100 cps (0.1 kH) seems to be its lower limit (Sparks and Soper 1970).

The hunting activity of Tawny Owls has been studied by automatic registration of nest visits at three places in Finland (Grönlund and Mikkola 1979) and in one place in

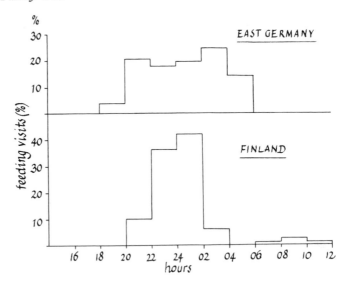

Fig. 17   Tawny Owl hunting and feeding activity from automatic registrations at single nests in Finland (Grönlund and Mikkola 1979) and in East Germany (Ritter 1972). The latter site was studied between 8th April and 18th May 1968, and the former between 13th and 31st May 1976. The feeding visits shown are a percentage of all registered visits

East Germany (Ritter 1972). The Finnish and German results each reveal that the Tawny Owl hunts almost entirely at night. However, in Finland the length of a summer night is only about four hours, which explains why the Tawny Owl continues hunting into the daylight morning hours, especially when feeding hungry owlets. In East Germany the summer night is about nine hours and this seems long enough to enable the Tawny Owls to confine their hunting to the hours of darkness and near-darkness. In East Germany their hunting activity is clearly biphasic, showing peaks immediately after sunset and shortly before sunrise. In Finland, on the other hand, the evening and morning peaks merge into one, just after midnight (Fig. 17). Wendland (1963), studying the Tawny Owl's nocturnal activity in West Berlin, found that it began 18 to 20 minutes after sunset. This was about 10 minutes earlier than his Long-eared Owls. The Tawny Owls' hunting area in the Grünewald was fairly small, its normal hunting radius being about 200–700 m from the nest site, and at most 1000 m.

FOOD

Like all other owls, the Tawny Owl casts up indigestible parts of its prey as pellets. However, V. P. W. Lowe (cf. Southern 1969) and Ruprecht and Raczynski (1974) have shown that when captive Tawny Owls were fed weighed rations of prey and the pellets analysed, a considerable proportion of small rodent prey items, depending on species, does not turn up in the pellets. This means that some small rodents are digested sufficiently to be passed through the intestines. In the experiments by Lowe, out of 158 wood mice *Apodemus sylvaticus* fed to the owls, 40% were not recovered from the pellets, the respective figures for bank voles *Clethrionomys glareolus*, short-tailed voles *Microtus agrestis* and house mice *Mus musculus* being 33%, 15% and 60%. On the other hand, Ruprecht and Raczynski (1974) noted that the greatest non-recovery (up to 50.8%) was found in young Tawny Owls. In adult owl pellets the losses were not more than 16% in the number of prey items identified. Guérin (1932) has recorded the first pellet from a young Tawny Owl at about eight days, but according to Gilliard (1958), nestlings less than a month old are able to decalcify most of the bones they eat.

Despite such methodological drawbacks, Southern (1969) has concluded that pellet analysis remains the easiest way of accumulating sufficient data on the Tawny Owl's prey. But collecting Tawny Owl pellets in quantity is a time-consuming business because the nocturnal roosts and feeding stations where pellets can be found are often well scattered, added to which the pellets quickly break down in moist undergrowth. Observations made on Long-eared Owls in conifer woods suggested that their pellets disintegrated in about eight weeks (Fairley 1967) and it seems probable that Tawny Owl pellets would not last any longer in oakwoods (cf. Beven 1967).

The Tawny Owl produces one or two pellets daily and usually casts them before going to roost, which explains why relatively few pellets are found below the roosting sites. Pellets are found mainly under trees used by the owl as pellet-dropping stations. These stations are often changed at different seasons, rendering pellet collection difficult. However, useful collections of pellets and other prey remains can be made by regular visits to the nest and by locating nearby tree roosts.

According to Glue (1971) it is relatively easy to distinguish between Tawny and Barn Owl pellets, although both normally range from 30 to 70 mm in length and 18–26 mm in width. Barn Owl pellets are hard, compact and black with a characteristic varnished appearance, whereas Tawny Owl pellets are usually of a looser texture and grey when dry. Southern (1954) has shown that the appearance and even the size of a pellet largely depends on the owl's diet. Large prey such as rabbit *Oryctolagus cuniculus* and moles *Talpa europaea* cause large and loose pellets with a characteristic pale grey or black colour according to the species. Shrews usually mingle with other rodent prey but if they are the staple diet they produce a small black pellet. Tawny Owls often cast small, brown, hard pellets largely composed of earth and vegetable fibres, and Southern (1954) maintains that such pellets are composed of numerous earthworm bristles (chaetae) and the remains of insects, beetles especially. After gastropod molluscs have been eaten, the pellet may set hard, as if with glue (Southern 1954), but unfortunately, there seems to be no practical way of quantifying the number of earthworms or molluscs eaten to produce such pellets.

Fortunately, the Tawny Owl will readily use nest boxes in and around which prey remains can be found once breeding is over. In Finland (e.g. Leppänen 1970, Mikkola 1968, Kuhlman and Koskela 1980) and in Sweden (Holmberg 1976) all the main food studies of this species are based on nest box contents collected and analysed after the breeding season is over. My observations in Vilppula, Finland (Mikkola 1977) have shown that an analysis of nest contents alone probably does not give an accurate picture of prey categories in the diet. The hunting male (sometimes the female) brings larger prey for the nestlings than it would normally require for itself. Similarly, the proportion of bird remains is much higher (26% against 3%) on the nest bottom than in the pellets (Table 26). This is partly due to the fact that the nest contains remains from the entire breeding season, whereas the pellets analysed were all cast before the owlets left the nest, i.e. during the spring. Also, nestlings and juvenile birds are more readily available as prey during the summer months.

The Tawny Owl's diet has been much studied in central Europe. Dr Otto Uttendörfer summarised (1939, 1952) about 72,000 prey items from all over Germany. The breakdown of his material was as follows: 62.5% mammals, 11.8% birds, 10.2% frogs, 0.6% fish, 0.06% lizards, 0.07% molluscs, 0.01% crustaceans and about 14.8% insects. In addition the owls had taken an unknown quantity of earthworms. Uttendörfer's work has since been continued in West and East Germany. In West Berlin, Wendland (1972) has identified 31,986 vertebrate prey between 1952 and 1971. The Tawny Owl's diet has also been well documented in the USSR (Gruzdev and Likhachev 1960), in Poland (Skuratowicz 1950, Cais 1963, Bogucki 1967), Bulgaria (Simeonow 1963), France (Guérin 1932, Thiollay 1968), Holland (Smeenk 1972) and in Spain (Lopez Gordo 1973).

In Table 27 I have compared the Tawny Owl's diet in Fenno-Scandia and at Wytham, England. In Fenno-Scandia it would appear that *Microtus* and *Clethrionomys* voles together form 38.7%, and in England 39.7%, of prey animals. In Wytham, *Clethrionomys* voles dominated with 27.7%, and in Fenno-Scandia *Microtus* voles comprised 27.1%. This is clearly due to the fact that in Wytham the Tawny Owl hunts entirely in woodland where *Clethrionomys* voles are most numerous. In Fenno-Scandia the Tawny Owl often breeds near farmhouses and fields where *Microtus* voles are common. In England, mice, moles, rabbits and insects are all far more common prey than in Fenno-Scandia. In addition, there were numerous earthworm pellets in Southern's material, but very few, if any, in the Fenno-Scandian studies, and these contrasts reflect the different abundance and availability of prey species in the two areas. A somewhat puzzling difference was that many more birds and frogs were eaten in Fenno-Scandia, but Southern (1954) has pointed out that the lack of frogs in Wytham is due to the absence of any suitable standing water, and this would also explain why he had no fish and only very few water voles *Arvicola amphibius* in his material.

One has to remember that the Wytham owls were only a small sample of Tawny Owls in Britain, which elsewhere in the country may add more birds and frogs to their diet. Indeed, the small pellet samples I collected in the New Forest and at Sunbury gave a quite different picture of the owls' diet (Table 28), with 23 frogs and 20 birds among the 93 prey items. I identified two common frogs *Rana temporaria* from the New Forest, and one from Sunbury, where the owl had also eaten 17 marsh or lake frogs *Rana ridibunda*. Three more frogs I thought were hybrids between *Rana ridibunda* and *R. esculenta* (edible frog) but this identification needs confirmation. The birds identified were Jay *Garrulus glandarius*, Blackbird *Turdus merula*, Mistle Thrush *Turdus viscivorus*, Robin *Erithacus rubecula*, Pied Wagtail *Motacilla alba*, House Sparrow *Passer domesticus*, Chaffinch *Fringilla coelebs*, Great Tit *Parus major*, Coal Tit *Parus ater* and Wren *Troglodytes troglodytes*.

Southern (1969) has demonstrated that there are seasonal trends in the Tawny Owl's diet. In Wytham Woods the proportion of moles and beetles (mainly cockchafers) increased markedly after the first week of May when the young owls were about half-grown. At the same time the proportion of mice and voles decreased. This decline in the volume of small rodents coincides with the growth of ground cover. Southern and Lowe (1968) had earlier shown that the denseness of vegetation affected the hunting pattern and success of Tawny Owls. There are some good examples of how single owls or pairs may specialise in the prey they hunt. Schaefer (1975) studied the pellets of a Tawny Owl pair in Bussau, West Germany, in 1970 and 1971, and identified 726 prey items, of which 261 were frogs (36%), small mammals made up 44.5%, birds 6.3% and insects 13.2%. There are many records of such specialists in Finland with diets which may comprise 70–80% birds (Leppänen 1970), but moles, cockchafers and earthworms are less numerous in Finland than in England, and Tawny Owls generally consume more birds (25.5% out of 2,800 prey items).

In some areas of Britain there are three different woodland owl species that co-exist and it is therefore interesting to compare their respective diets in such a situation. Table 29 shows the vertebrate diet of Barn, Tawny and Long-eared Owls in Britain in numerical percentages. The Barn and Long-eared Owls offer an interesting contrast with the Tawny Owls because they take a large proportion of short-tailed voles (45.8 and 49.4%) which live mainly in open terrain. On the other hand the Tawny Owl takes more than 55% of small woodland mammals, i.e. bank voles and wood mice. Thus where diet is concerned the Tawny Owl seems to be the true woodland owl. This strengthens the view that the choice of hunting terrain is responsible for the main differences in diet between the three woodland owls. Other important differences are that the Barn Owl eats twice as many shrews as the Tawny Owl and as many as seven times more than the Long-eared Owl, which in turn takes small birds much more frequently than the other two species. The similarity index between Long-eared and Barn Owl diets is 0.71, whilst that between them and the Tawny Owl is 0.65 and 0.46 respectively. This could indicate that there is more food competition between Barn and Long-eared Owls and between Tawny and Long-eared Owls, and less between Tawny and Barn Owls. However, short-tailed voles are so plentiful for much of the time that competition between Barn and Long-eared Owls may be at a low level.

All three owls seem to have a different strategy when reacting to a scarcity of small rodents. The Barn Owl will alternate its diet with shrews and the Long-eared Owl with small birds, whereas the Tawny Owl uses all available alternatives, such as moles, frogs, insects and earthworms, but also shrews and birds. At such times competition may be mainly between Tawny and Long-eared Owls.

BREEDING BIOLOGY

Tawny Owls in Europe usually breed in broadleaved woodland and forests and open parklands although occasionally they inhabit coniferous forests, particularly in Spain. In parts of Asia, Tawny Owls breed in tall coniferous forests in the mountains up to about 3000 m (Voous 1960). Though woodland is the Tawny Owl's preferred habitat, it is adaptable and has even taken up residence in cities such as London and Berlin where there are large wooded parks and gardens. The breeding Tawny Owl chooses a natural hole or a nest box in a tree, but occasionally nests have been found on ledges of old buildings and in chimneys. Tawny Owls will also use (in order of frequency) the old nest of a crow, Magpie, Sparrowhawk or Buzzard, and sometimes a squirrel's drey. It will also use a Raven or Buzzard nest on a cliff or simply a bare ledge. Occasionally it has bred in the shelter of old tree roots, on the ground beside a rock, or in a rabbit hole. According to Donald Watson (*in litt.*), ground nests are quite common in Galloway, in south-west Scotland, in fact in the absence of mature timber, ground nests are typical, especially in conifer plantations. Elsewhere in Scotland

Andrew Dowell (1979) discovered a Tawny Owl's nest in an abandoned car. The nest was under the back seat of an old Morris which was left without windows on a rubbish dump. This is a most curious choice of nest site for such a traditionally tree-based species.

I have examined records of 242 Tawny Owl nests in Finland from 1940 to 1975. The following sites were used: man-made nest boxes, natural holes in trees, buildings (mainly barns), tree-stumps and disused stick nests of other birds, and also squirrel dreys (Table 30). The table shows that over the decades some basic changes have taken place in the owl's choice of nest sites. Until the end of the 1960s, natural holes in trees were used most frequently, but nesting in buildings seems to have been fairly common at that time. Since 1960, nest boxes have been widely provided (especially in southern Finland, the source of most of my material) and Tawny Owls used them more often than any other type of nest site. Professor Merikallio listed 23 tree-hole nests in Finland; eight of them were in aspen, five in birch, four in pine, two in spruce and two in lime. It would seem from this that the Tawny Owl prefers sites in broadleaved trees. In Germany (Wendland 1972) Tawny Owls also preferred nest sites in mature oaks even though pines, with suitable holes, were the most numerous tree species in the study area. In Finland, nest boxes are often in damp heath forests or by the side of rivers and lakes, which is the reason why these habitats comprised most of my material. Spruce forest made up 64% of the biotopes used, but only one nest was found in natural forest far from human habitation, 34% of nests being in parks and large gardens in built-up areas (cf. Lahti and Mikkola 1974). In Finland it seems that availability of a suitable nest site is more important than the biotope.

The habitat selection of Tawny Owls has been tested in Switzerland by providing a generous supply of nest boxes in different biotopes (Eiberle 1970). The main conclusions were that Tawny Owls clearly preferred moist, vegetated forests, and 54% of the nest boxes offered in such a habitat were occupied. In drier habitats in deciduous forest etc, only one third of the boxes was used. In moist deciduous forests all the boxes were used at least once during the five-year study, whereas in drier forests 37.5% of the boxes were never occupied. According to Eiberle (1970), it is likely that small mammal prey is more common in moist forests than in dry habitats. It is also possible there are snow-free places near areas of water in early spring where the owls can more easily catch their prey. It would seem, therefore, that when suitable nest sites are widely available, the accessibility of food at the beginning of the breeding season may affect the final choice of habitat.

The Tawny Owl does not usually bring material to its nest, but there is one British report of an owl making a rudimentary nest (Witherby *et al* 1940). In Europe the Tawny Owl usually begins breeding in mid-March. In England, Southern (1970) found a significant correlation between late winter temperatures and the start of breeding. His results also suggested that later breeding is associated with lower numbers of available prey, but statistically this correlation was not significant. Linkola and Myllymäki (1969), from a large amount of Finnish data, concluded that the onset of breeding is delayed in poor mouse years, and that prey availability governs the timing of breeding. It has long been known that climatic differences can, to some extent, cause small rodent fluctuations (Siivonen 1943). Wendland (1972) in Berlin, noted that egg-laying by Tawny Owls breeding in parks and other built-up areas frequently occurred one, or even two months earlier (February as against March/April) than the egg-laying by owls in woods and forests. He postulated that the explanation for the earlier breeding in parks could be the higher temperature in built-up areas, or the greater availability of food at the beginning of the breeding season.

Tawny Owls' eggs are almost round and pure white. The average measurements for 100 British eggs are almost the same as those for 142 eggs from the USSR (Dement'ev *et al* 1950) and Finland (Merikallio 1955):

	Average size of eggs
Britain	46.69 × 39.06 mm
Finland and USSR	47.27 × 38.98 mm

However, eggs in Finland and Russia seem to be slightly longer than those in Britain where breeding females are more than 100 g lighter than Russian and Finnish birds (478 g as against 583 g). The average weight difference of females has more significance if we compare the average weight of eggs: in Britain 31.1 g, but 39.1 g in Russia and Finland. The figures seem to indicate that the larger females lay more than proportionately heavier eggs. This again may be one explanation for reversed sexual dimorphism in owls (discussed in a later chapter).

In Finland the Tawny Owl lays from two to six eggs (19 × 2; 68 × 3; 91 × 4; 46 × 5 and 13 × 6), but sometimes only one (5 × 1) and once, exceptionally, eight, which might imply two females laying in the same nest. The average clutch size from the above data is 3.8 eggs. Like the Great Grey Owl, the Tawny Owl varies its clutch size according to vole abundance. In peak vole years the average clutch size was 4.2 (70 nests); one year before the peak it was 3.6 (52 nests), and one year afterwards 3.1 eggs (18 nests). In intermediate years, 28 nests averaged 3.0 eggs (Linkola and Myllymäki 1969). Clutch sizes also vary according to geographical location, decreasing from north to south and from east to west (Table 31). In central Europe the clutch size is lower (3.3) than in Finland (3.8) but correspondingly higher than that in England (2.7). Also Dement'ev *et al* (1950) have stated, but without full details, that Tawny Owl clutch sizes are larger in eastern Europe (i.e. Russia) than in western Europe. Dement'ev maintains that nests with seven or eight eggs occur more frequently in Russia, though in western Europe this would imply two females laying in one nest (cf. Glutz von Blotzheim and Bauer 1980).

Although the brood size in Finland is larger than in Britain (3.05 as against 2.27), it is clear that a greater percentage of Finnish eggs fail to hatch for one reason or another (Table 31). In Finland the brood size is 0.8 lower than the average clutch size, whereas the corresponding difference for Britain is only 0.4. In this context we should remember that the average brood size represents only those nests in which at least some eggs have hatched. According to Linkola and Myllymäki (1969), the proportion of whole clutch failures in the Finnish results is no more than moderate and no obvious tendencies were detected between different phases of vole fluctuation, i.e. nests do not fail completely during poor vole years. In Finland the Tawny Owl lives at the northern extremity of its range where climatic conditions are particularly stringent. From this it would appear that larger clutches may be laid in order to compensate for the higher losses of eggs and young.

In Wytham Woods, Southern (1970) found an interval of three or four days to be usual between the laying of the first and second eggs. Normally, eggs are laid at intervals of 48 hours, and are incubated for 28–29 days by the female alone. It is always stated that incubation starts with the first egg, but Southern (1970) observed no incubation before the second egg was laid, and he calculated the average incubation time to be 29.7 days for a single egg. The first egg laid was not always the one to hatch first, proving also that incubation may not take place before the second egg is laid.

When the young have hatched, the male brings more food, either to the nest or to the female waiting nearby. Once the chicks are 6–7 days old the female may leave the nest to hunt, but when not hunting, and especially during the day, the female always remains near the young. Fledging occurs after 28 to 37 days, the average at Wytham being 31.2 days (Southern 1970). Earlier, Southern *et al* (1954) noted that if deep nest holes are scarce and shallow ones or open nest sites have to be used instead, the young birds often fledge prematurely before they can fly. But even so, by then they are adept at climbing bushes and young trees, usually trying to reach the highest point (cf. Wendland 1963). Southern *et al* (1954) found that young Tawny Owls are dependent on their parents for food up to three months after leaving the nest. As the young owls gradually learn to fend for themselves they also establish territories. It is during this period that the mortality rate of young owls is high. Those young that cannot secure a territory inside the parental one must either starve or move out, and this process helps achieve equilibrium in the adult population of the following spring (Southern 1970).

The winter mortality among young Tawny Owls in Finland depends on available food levels and weather conditions. When both are adverse, high mortality rates result. On the other hand, with an adequate food supply many young owls will survive even in extremely unfavourable weather conditions (cf. Linkola and Myllymäki 1969). Saurola (1979) has given details of recoveries of Tawny Owls during their first year, after being ringed as nestlings in Finland from 1968 to 1977. His figures are relative numbers of recoveries per 1000 birds ringed ($+$ = more than 0, but less than 0.5).

Collided with car	15	Trapped in building	13
Collided with train	2	Caught in a trap	+
Collided with window	2	Accidentally poisoned	+
Collided with wires	4	Naturally drowned	3
Collided with other objects	1	Naturally preyed upon	4
Entangled in net	1	Naturally starved	1
Entangled in barbed wire	+	Found dead, reason unknown	26
Entangled by foot	1	*Total number of recoveries*	579

These data show that Tawny Owls are often hit by cars or trains, and that several are trapped in chimneys, ventilators, etc, in buildings. The number of starved owls seems exceptionally low compared with unnatural causes of death. One reason might be that most starved owls are eaten by other animals and their remains found less often than, say, owls hit by vehicles.

The Tawny Owl reaches sexual maturity within a year and can, therefore, breed during the first year of its life (cf. Wendland 1963). In central Europe, one ringed Tawny Owl lived 18 years and 7 months and in Britain one caged Tawny Owl survived 27 years (Glutz von Blotzheim and Bauer 1980).

DISTRIBUTION

Tawny Owls belong to the palearctic faunal type in which the western group of owls

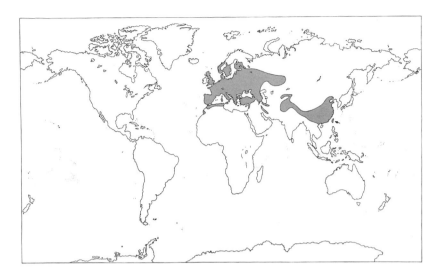

TAWNY OWL – mainly resident – shaded area indicates breeding distribution

is the European distribution element, and the eastern group is the Chinese-Himalayan element (Voous 1960). The Tawny Owl's distribution is, therefore, discontinuously palearctic and oriental, in temporal, boreal, Mediterranean and steppe climatic zones and mountains. According to Voous (1960), it is not known if Tawny Owls in Asia are already geographically separate from European owls or whether ecological isolation may be leading towards the evolution of two different species. However, Dement'ev *et al* (1950) have stated that owls from Central and eastern Russia intergrade with the Siberian subspecies *Strix aluco siberiae* and *S. a. härmsi*. Eck and Busse (1973) listed 15 subspecies of the Tawny Owl, but Dement'ev *et al* (1950) recognised only 11 subspecies, of which six inhabit the western sector of the world distribution (also Vaurie 1965). These six races are: *Strix aluco aluco, S. a. sylvatica, S. a. mauritanica, S. a. siberiae, S. a. willkonskii* and *S. a. sancti-nicolae*. (For a comparative account of these races see under *Description* at the beginning of this chapter.)

The world distribution of Tawny Owls extends throughout Europe and North Africa (Morocco, Tunisia and Algeria) eastwards to Iran and western Siberia. The Asiatic range covers north-western India, the Himalayas, southern China, Korea and Taiwan (Dement'ev *et al* 1950, Voous 1960 and Vaurie 1965).

In Europe the Tawny Owl is the commonest and most widespread owl, being absent only in Ireland, the extreme north of Scotland, northern Russia, northern Scandinavia, Iceland and some of the Mediterranean islands (Everett and Sharrock 1980). In Finland the Tawny Owl is a relatively new arrival although it is now one of the more common owls in south-west and south-east Finland. The first Finnish record was a Tawny Owl shot in Helsinki on 14th December 1875, and the first nest was found at Ruissalo, Turku in 1878 (cf. Collin 1886). The next records of nesting are from Lohja 1880 and from Taivassalo 1883 (Merikallio 1958). The real expansion to the north began in the 1920s and particularly during the warmer years of the 1930s. By then the Tawny Owl had achieved its present distribution with its somewhat easterly concentration (cf. Merikallio 1958). In Norway and Sweden the Tawny Owl has extended its northern range far less than in Finland, but overall populations are clearly larger and more stable. For instance, Ulfstrand and Högstedt (1976) estimated the Swedish Tawny Owl population to be around 10,000 pairs, whereas Merikallio's estimate for Finland in 1958 was only 2,000 pairs. Owlwatchers in Finland have tried to collect all owl nest records in recent years, resulting in 249 Tawny Owl nests records for 1979 (Forsman *et al* 1980) and 221 for 1980 (Jokinen *et al* 1982). The owlwatchers perhaps know of no more than 10% of the total number of nests, in which case Merikallio's estimate of the 1958 Tawny Owl population would still hold true today.

In Britain, Parslow's (1973) historical survey has shown that there was a decline in numbers of breeding Tawny Owls in the 19th century on account of human persecution. This was followed by an increase in the 20th century, particularly in southern Scotland. This general increase continued until 1950. Parslow found no evidence of marked changes in recent years in most parts of Britain. Tawny Owl numbers have largely remained unchanged. He estimated that there were more than 10,000 but less than 100,000 Tawny Owl pairs in Britain. According to the British Trust for Ornithology's more recent *The Atlas of Breeding Birds in Britain and Ireland* (comp. Sharrock 1976), it is suggested that it would be surprising if the number was not nearer 100,000 rather than 10,000 pairs.

In most of the central European countries, distribution correspondents report that Tawny Owls are evenly distributed and common in their countries; this is true of Poland, Hungary, Czechoslovakia, Yugoslavia and Austria; and also of Switzerland where this owl, of course, does not breed in the higher Alps. In Germany Wendland (*in litt.*) has found that the Tawny Owl nests only below 1,200 m in the Alps. Elsewhere in Germany (East and West) the Tawny Owl is common even in large towns and cities. In West Berlin there are 120 or more Tawny Owl pairs in an area of 469 km² (Wendland, *in litt.*). In East Germany there are about 25,000 Tawny Owl pairs (Melde, *in litt.*).

In Holland the Tawny Owl is fairly rare in northern areas but common elsewhere (Texeira, *in litt.*), and in Belgium it occurs throughout the country and has most likely increased its numbers recently due to the provision of nest boxes. Huyskens (*in litt.*) estimated that there are about 3,000–4,000 pairs. In France the Atlas survey results suggested that the Tawny Owl is certainly as abundant as the Barn Owl, but that the population is less than 100,000 pairs (Yeatman 1976).

In Spain the Tawny Owl's distribution is more patchy than in France because Spanish forests and woods have become greatly fragmented in recent times. According to Herrera (*in litt.*) this is particularly true in the Andalusian region. In the Balearic and the Canary islands, Tawny Owls are only accidentals and possible records of breeding need further investigations (Morillo 1976). In Portugal the Tawny Owl is said to be more common in central and southern parts (Vicente, *in litt.*), and in Italy in northern and central areas (Lovari, *in litt.*) but breeding records are known from all parts where suitable habitats exist. In Greece the Tawny Owl is not a rare breeding bird and it has also bred on the island of Rhodes (Bauer *et al* 1969).

In Turkey most Tawny Owl records are from the west, but further research may show that it is more widely distributed and perhaps absent only in the east and south-east of the country (Reports of the Ornithological Society of Turkey). In Cyprus the Tawny Owl is a rare visitor, but one breeding pair has been recorded in 1966 at Lefkonico (Leontiades, *in litt.*). In Morocco, Tawny Owls are local and

TAWNY OWL – shaded area indicates breeding distribution

relatively rare, dependent on a few suitable habitats and, as a result, are more common in the north-west.

In European USSR the Tawny Owl is said to be common in the central zone, but rare in the taiga and the Crimea. Randla (1976) estimated that there are about 500 Tawny Owl pairs in Estonia. In Bulgaria the Tawny Owl is common in mountain forests but less so in forests on the plains (Dontchev, *in litt.*), and in Rumania it is absent in the eastern Delta area and breeds only rarely in the south-east region (Munteanu, *in litt.*).

In the Near East the Tawny Owl breeds in the south to Israel (Etchécopar and Hüe 1970), but at present no overlap in range with Hume's Owl is known. (For more details see under that species.) MacFarlane (*in litt.*) has heard this owl three times in Lebanon and believes it is probably resident in small numbers throughout the coastal mountain range. According to Scott (*in litt.*), the Tawny Owl is a common resident of forests in the south Caspian region and locally common wherever good forest exists in the Zagros oak woodlands in the west, and it probably occurs in northern Azarbaijan in one remnant of Caucasian deciduous woodland. It may occur in isolated patches of riverine woodland in north-west Iran (see map).

Throughout their range adult Tawny Owls are known to be highly sedentary but during their first year of life young owls may wander further afield, especially in areas which have severe winters. Normally, young owls try to establish territories somewhere near where they were born, as most ringed owl recoveries show. Owlets ringed in the nest have been found less than 10 km away. Results from Finnish ringing recoveries of young Tawny Owls reveal that 45% came from less than 10 km, 39% were found between 10–50 km, and 9% between 50–100 km from the nest. Only 7% of the owls were recovered more than 100 km away from their place of ringing and the farthest recorded distance travelled by a Tawny Owl in the course of nomadic wandering was 1960 km, from south Finland to south Russia (v. Haartman *et al* 1967).

17: Hume's Owl *Strix butleri*
(Hume)

DESCRIPTION

The colour of the upperparts varies from dark browny-buff to paler brown-buff with sparse, dark brown, drop-shaped streaks not standing out particularly well from the ground colour. There is a wide golden-buff area on the lower nape and upper mantle in the form of a wide 'collar', broken by dark spotting. The upper wing-coverts are approximately the same colour and pattern as the rest of the upperparts but the spotting or streaking is almost absent. The flight-feathers and tail are heavily barred with black-brown and sandy-buff. The bird captured by Jennings (1977) had a buffish-grey facial disc with delicate brown barring round the disc below the eye. In addition, the central crown feathers were tipped brown and formed a dark line down the forehead to where the discs met.

The under parts are whitish, well-marked with orange-buff, particularly on the upper breast. There are a few dark feather-shafts on the flanks but the legs are feathered whitish, with no marking. The bill is light horn-coloured and the claws bluish-grey, and the feathering on the toes is limited to a few white hairs.

An examination by I.W. of colour photos taken by Y. Leshem of birds in the wild (in a cliff crevice) and in captivity (at a friend's house), of the latest literature (Leshem 1974) and of two skins at the Tring collection, make it clear that there is some variation in tone and colour in this species. Birds may vary from dark to pale browny-buff above and from bright golden-buff to pale sandy-buff below. The plumage of both sexes is said to be similar.

Hume's Owl is generally depicted with dark eyes. However, two females checked by Mendelssohn *et al* (1975), and a specimen photographed in the field (Leshem

1974), had yellow irides. The orange iris was also noticed by Jennings (1977). This has been known since 16th August 1950 when one specimen (now in The British Museum) was collected by W. S. Adams in Saudi Arabia at the Mahd Dhahab gold mine, about 400 km NNE of Jedda. This owl has a note on its label which says that the irides are orange-yellow. Until 1977 this specimen was in the Meinertzhagen collection, and unfortunately Meinertzhagen did not include the eye colour in his description of the birds in his *Birds of Arabia* where the specimen is mentioned.

The wing lengths of four females measured are 310 mm, 315 mm, 322 mm and 340 mm, and of three unsexed birds 247 mm, 285 mm and 295 mm. The recorded weights of two females are 214 g and 220 g, and that of one unsexed bird 225 g (Mendelssohn *et al* 1975 and Jennings 1977). Measurements of this species in the collection at Tel Aviv University give a body length of 300 mm and a wing span of 253 mm (Leshem 1974). The wing lengths of the five owls recorded by Meinertzhagen range from 251 mm to 257 mm.

The wide range of wing lengths (247–340 mm) may indicate that the female is somewhat larger than the male, as is the case with most owls.

IN THE FIELD

The bird looks like a small sandy-brown Tawny Owl, the main difference being the paler and unstreaked underparts and the orange-yellow irides. Hume's Owl perches at an angle, rather than upright like the Tawny Owl. The different perching attitudes may be attributable to the fact that Tawny Owls usually perch on branches, which allows the tail to hang down, whereas Hume's Owl usually perches on rocks, which generally obliges a more horizontal posture.

Its flight is buoyant, even butterfly-like when manoeuvring, but direct and silent from point to point (Jennings 1977). Compared with the Tawny Owl, Hume's Owl appears to have a proportionately longer wing in flight. In its wing formula the first primary falls between the 7th and 8th primaries and the longest is the 4th. The tail has six bars but in flight only five bars show because the bar nearest the body is the least distinct.

Most of the records of this bird are from cliffs and steep-sided wadis with only minimal vegetation (acacia). It is probably a wholly nocturnal owl which lives among rocks and in palm groves close to rocks. Mendelssohn (*in litt.*) states that water, in the form of springs or rock pools, is present at all the known localities in Israel.

VOICE

I.W. and several colleagues on a visit to Israel in late March and early April, 1975, heard a Hume's Owl calling all through the night in a gorge in the Negev desert and it sounded quite different to a Tawny Owl. He writes: 'It was like the sound of *Strix aluco* in quality but in the form of one long note with no quavering, just a light hesitation in the middle.' Jennings (1977) and Aronson (1979) have described the same call as *Hoooo-huhu-huhu* and *Whoo-who-whoo*, i.e. a longish hoot followed quickly by two short double notes. The call is soft compared with the Tawny Owl's and at a distance may even sound superficially like a dove.

The usual call lasts approximately two seconds and may be repeated at between 15 second and one minute intervals, but sometimes as much as half an hour later. Once, in April, Jennings (*in litt.*) time a series of 25 calls from 19.10 hours to 19.25 hours. The shortest interval between calls was 17 seconds and the longest 1 minute 25 seconds.

Calling has been heard at night in January, February, March, April and in September, but Hume's Owl probably calls at other times of the year, too. Calling generally starts about 20 minutes after sunset and may continue all night. On one occasion, in March, it continued until two hours after dawn in bright sunshine (Jennings 1977).

Calling is usually from a perch but hooting birds are continuously on the move and may call whilst in flight. The owl reacts strongly to an imitated call, even if only the first syllable, *hooo*, is imitated or played back to it with a tape recorder. The owl will complete the call with the second syllable, *huhu-huhu*, move closer, circle and follow the mimic.

The only other note ever heard is an excited and agitated *Hu-hu-hu-hu-hu-hu-hu* which lasts for two or three seconds. This call is made when another bird is in the vicinity or when its call is imitated or played back from a tape recorder. Meinertzhagen's (1930) clear and continuous *hoo* and Mendelssohn *et al's* (1975) often-repeated *hooo* are essentially the agitated call, although they each described this as the usual call.

BEHAVIOUR

Very little is known about the behaviour of Hume's Owl, even thought it is mentioned in the Old Testament (Isaiah 34:14) (Leshem 1974). Jennings (*in. litt.*) once heard two birds calling in a duet and one bird will enter into a duet with a mimic, calling alternately. According to Mendelssohn *et al* (1975), the smallest distance between localities for *Strix butleri* and *Strix aluco* has been only about 20 km. Interspecific competition could therefore take place if the species have some ecological similarities in their breeding. Jennings (*in litt.*) has made an interesting suggestion that the absence of the Little Owl *Athene noctua saharae/lilith* on the Tuwaiq escarpment in Saudi Arabia could be due to competition with Hume's Owl.

In a period of five years Aronson (1979) came to know of 15 Hume's Owls which were killed by cars in Israel indicating that this owl often hunts animals crossing roads. Another bird was found with symptoms of poisoning. The person who found this owl treated it and has kept in in his house for over four years (1979). This is probably the first time that this bird has been kept in captivity.

FOOD

The stomach of a Hume's Owl specimen from Sinai contained a Rock Gerbil *Gerbillus dasyurus* and in another stomach of a specimen found dead in the Negev the remains of *Tenebrionidae* were found (Mendelssohn *et al* 1975).

More recently, in Israel, Yossi Leshem collected 52 pellets of this owl from a roosting place in the Negev and these contained remnants of 101 animals (Table 32). The Rock Gerbil and other small mammals formed 48% of the food items. In numbers, the proportion of the *Arthropodes* was almost the same (47%) but, in terms of weight, small mammals are more important prey items. There were also three small birds, three reptiles and an insect in this material.

Richard Porter (*in litt.*) on 30th October 1981 watched in the light of his car head-lamps a Hume's Owl hunting from fence posts at a location by the Dead Sea. The bird was in view for 15 minutes from 1930 hours onwards during which time it made three sallies after flying insects (moths?), wheeling round in the light of the lamps 'like a large, broad and rounded-winged Nightjar *Caprimulgus europaeus*.'

BREEDING BIOLOGY

This species seems to be found mainly in the desert but near water sources which are in steep, cliffed wadis. Presumably rock holes are used for nesting as there are no suitable trees in these areas and the owls are not found near buildings. Ben King (*in litt.*) has, however, heard Hume's Owl on Jebel Souda, Saudi Arabia, in a place covered with quite large juniper trees, wild lavender, oleander, etc. In such a vegetated habitat, nesting in a tree-hole or in an old nest of another bird could take place. However, rocks certainly appear to be an essential medium for its life style as suggested by Jennings (1977).

So far I have seen no description of this owl's breeding biology.

The bird found, in March 1973, in Israel by Yossi Leshem (1974) was young; it would seem therefore that egg-laying could commence early in January or even December. On the other hand Jennings (1977) caught an owl in July in Saudi Arabia and this bird was not very old as it still had traces of down at its neck. Jennings suggested that Hume's Owl could have an extended breeding season as does its near relative the Tawny Owl.

The main breeding season in Israel could be during the months February to April, as most of the reports of calling records are from this period. However, nidification has not yet been described.

DISTRIBUTION

Hume's Owl is a representative of the palaeoxeric-faunal type belonging to the fauna of the deserts of the southern palearctic region. Hume's Owl has been found on the coast of Baluchistan, in Saudi Arabia and from Syria to Sinai in the Middle East (Vaurie 1965), but less than ten specimens exist in collections worldwide and it is said to be extremely rare (Meinertzhagen 1930, Etchécopar and Hüe 1964, 1970 and Ali and Ripley 1969).

In 1973, Yossi Leshem, an ornithologist in Israel, saw and photographed Hume's Owl in the wild. This was probably the first time that this owl had ever been photographed. This encounter established that the owl existed in the Judean desert and in recent years more and more observations have been made not only in Israel but also in Saudi Arabia. Since 1978 Hume's Owl has been sighted in 31 different locations in the Judaen desert, the Negev and Arava and in Sinai (Aronson 1979). In addition, Michael Jennings (*in litt.*) has heard and seen this owl numerous times in Saudi Arabia, near Medina and Riyadh, whilst in late 1982 Robert Fryer (*in litt.*) disturbed one from a hole in granite 176 miles south of Ha'il, a newly realised locality for the species. It has also been recorded recently in Oman (Jennings, *in litt.*).

It therefore appears that, in suitable habitats, Hume's Owls are far from rare but that they are likely to be found only after a careful search. In the Judean desert they can be located in most of the large wadis that spill into the Dead Sea Valley (Aronson

1979). In the Arabian Peninsula Hume's Owl is probably resident throughout the Tuwaiq escarpment, Hejaz and Asir provinces of Saudi Arabia, possibly in the Hadramaut and certainly in the mountains of Oman (Jennings 1977 and *in litt.*).

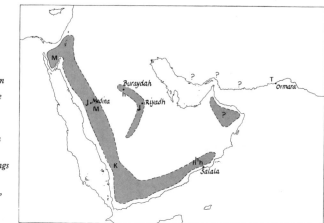

<table>
<tr><td>🌣</td><td>range fairly well known</td></tr>
<tr><td>🌣</td><td>limit of suggested range</td></tr>
<tr><td>T</td><td>type specimen collected</td></tr>
<tr><td>M</td><td>location of specimens noted by Meinertzhagen in Birds of Arabia</td></tr>
<tr><td>J</td><td>heard by M. C. Jennings</td></tr>
<tr><td>K</td><td>heard by Ben King</td></tr>
<tr><td>h</td><td>reports of owls 'hooting' and thought to be Strix (butleri)</td></tr>
</table>

HUME'S OWL – world distribution – conjectural range for Arabian Peninsular as compiled by M. C. Jennings – range for Israel and Sinai after Meinertzhagen, Mendelssohn, Yom-Tov, Safriel and Leshem

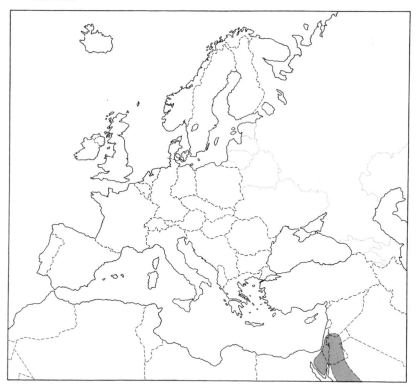

~~~ *boundary of known range in Israel and Sinai*

~-~- *conjectural range eastwards and southwards (after M. C. Jennings)*

18: Ural Owl *Strix uralensis*
(Pallas)

The adult plumage of Ural Owls of both sexes is greyish- to brownish-white streaked with dark brown, the streaks being most clearly seen on the underparts. The flight-feathers and the long tail have broad transverse dark brown bars on a buff or buff-white ground colour, and are tipped with white. The facial disc is almost circular and greyish-white without any markings, a ready distinction from the lined face of the Great Grey Owl. The head is round, the iris is dark brown and the eyes are smaller than those of many other members of the *Strix* genus. The bill is yellow and the claws are horn-brown or yellow with horn-brown tips, and as with other owls the colour of the claws tends to be lightest in young birds.

The nestlings are initially covered with ochre-tinged white down. The mesoptiles are ochre with brown bars and broad white feather edgings on head, neck, back, breast, belly and flanks. Immediately after shedding their natal down (a period when the white feather-tips become particularly prominent) young birds appear whitish, but during the subsequent growth of feathers they become brown with whitish bars. During this phase it seems to be almost impossible to distinguish the young Ural Owl from the young Tawny Owl unless parent birds are present. This difficulty has led to a number of unfortunate ringing recoveries, concerning birds ringed incorrectly as Tawny Owls merely because they were found near human dwellings. As with the ringing of all young birds, much misunderstanding can be prevented if the identity of the parent birds is first established. Recently, Scherzinger (1980) has shown with photos taken in captivity that there are some minor differences between Ural and Tawny Owl nestlings already at the age of a few days (cf. also Tawny Owl). At the ringing age (four weeks) the Ural Owl chick has a much more developed facial disc and its strong bill is clearly more prominent and longer than that of the Tawny Owl. Unfortunately, Scherzinger gave no exact measurements to aid bird ringers.

Some nine to eleven subspecies are recognised in Eurasia, having morphological variations in size and colour.

Western and central Europe is inhabited by *Strix uralensis liturata*, to which the above description applies. The nominate race *S. u. uralensis*, living in W. Siberia, is paler throughout than *liturata* and less heavily and darkly streaked. The scapulars and upper wing-coverts are much whiter and the ground colour of the entire plumage is whitish. Birds from the Ural region are the whitest, whilst in the central zone of the European part of the USSR occur birds combining the characters of darker *liturata* and whiter *uralensis*, clearly belonging to hybrid populations.

Colour is not, however, the only difference between the two European subspecies. The wing of the nominate form is a little shorter than that of *liturata* as shown below:

Wing-length (mm)	Females				Males				Author
	Min	Max	Aver.	N	Min	Max	Aver.	N.	
S. u. liturata	357	382	366.5	26	342	368	354.0	21	Dement'ev
S. u. uralensis	348	368	357.7	40	338	354	347.4	18	et al (1951)

Unfortunately only the weights of four birds of the nominate form have so far been published. One female was 950 g and the weight of three males was 560–712 g, the average being 657 g (Dement'ev *et al* 1951).

In Finland (v. Haartman *et al* 1967) and in the European part of the USSR (Dement'ev *et al* 1951) the weight of *liturata* males is 650–800 g (average 720 g for 11 birds), and that of females 630–1,020 g (average 871 g for 19 birds). There would seem to be a noticeable size difference not only between females and males, but also between the *liturata* and *uralensis* forms.

IN THE FIELD

This large, pale, small-eyed, long-tailed owl is not likely to be confused with an adult grey-phase Tawny Owl, although the young of these two species are closely similar. Its long tail often hangs down in flight. The relatively small eyes suggest that the Ural Owl is less nocturnal than the Tawny Owl. An adult Ural Owl is only a little smaller than a Great Grey Owl, from which it differs chiefly in its light colour, dark eyes, unlined facial disc and no black patch on its chin.

As the Ural Owl flies it appears almost white, ghost-like, and (the nominate form especially) could be mistaken for a female Snowy Owl, despite the fact that the latter species is a little larger. However, the shorter tail, whiter back, large yellow eyes and transverse bands on the underparts should serve to distinguish the Snowy Owl.

Although one tends to think of the Ural Owl as an inhabitant of the wilds, many of them hunt near farmhouses, particularly outside the breeding season. The flight is like that of a Buzzard *Buteo buteo* but with much deeper wing strokes.

VOICE

During the period of courtship the usual call of the male Ural Owl is a deep hooting *wóhu . . . wohu-huwóhu*, with a pause of about four seconds after the first two syllables. This call is used territorially and, more frequently, as a means of communication with the female (Holmberg 1974). The male's hooting song has a barking quality *huow-huow-huow*. He also utters a single *huu* in excitement. The female has a variety of calls at the nest, including barking, gobbling, chuckling and hissing. The female's hooting is much harsher and somewhat lower-pitched than the male's. During copulation she utters a weak twittering. Both sexes snap their bills when angry.

Like other members of the *Strix* genus, this species has a sharp cry *korrwick* which is harsher and longer than the similar notes of the Tawny and Great Grey Owls (Ferguson-Lees 1969).

The food-begging call of the young is slightly hoarser and lower-pitched than that of young Tawny Owls. On the whole, adults and young are relatively silent and several hours can be spent in a Ural Owl territory without hearing anything, even if weather conditions seem ideal (cf. Holmberg 1974).

BEHAVIOUR

The Ural Owl is similar to the closely-related Tawny Owl in that both are sedentary, the adults remaining in their territories even during poor rodent years. It seems likely that Ural Owls remain paired for life. One natural hole in a birch near a farmhouse in Finland was occupied by Ural Owls, perhaps the same pair, for a period of 18 years between 1953 and 1970 (Mikkola and Mikkola 1974).

Within its territory the Ural Owl does not always use the same nest site during consecutive years if other suitable nests are available (Pukinskii 1977). When nesting in old Goshawk *Accipiter gentilis* nests, the Ural Owl may be obliged to change its nest, depending on the Goshawk's choice of nest, if holes in trees or nest boxes are not available inside its territory. Even if the female Ural Owl has already laid her eggs in her chosen nest she remains highly vulnerable to the attentions of a nest-hunting Goshawk. On 17th May 1971 Kauko Huhtala (*in litt.*) visited a raptor's old nest, which contained three characteristically bluish-white eggs of a Goshawk and one smaller, white egg of a Ural Owl. The Goshawk female incubated all four eggs, and it was the owl's egg which hatched first. On 23rd May the nest contained a newly-hatched Ural Owl chick (37 g) and three eggs of the real owner. But the Goshawks were not good step-parents, because the owlet soon disappeared and on 8th June the nest contained only three Goshawk nestlings about one week old.

The territory of a pair of Ural Owls is much larger than that of a Tawny Owl pair and, at least in Finland, two occupied nests during the same year are rarely less than two (often four) kilometres apart (Lammin-Soila and Uusivuori 1975). By contrast, some suitable forest areas contain quite high densities of Ural Owl pairs. For example, 15 pairs in an area of 70 km^2 in Sweden (Lundberg 1974) and 6 pairs in another forest of 25 km^2 in Leningrad District, USSR (Pukinskii 1977), from which one can estimate that the average size of a Ural Owl's territory is about 450 ha.

The Ural Owl frequently appears to mark its eventual nest-site with feathers as early as the autumnal display, but the courtship display is most intense at the end of March and the beginning of April. Courtship feeding commences during the pre-copulation period, in March. The male announces its intention to deliver a prey item with a deep hooting territorial call and the female answers with a harsh barking from the neighbourhood of the selected nest-site. In the course of presenting the food to his mate, the deep hootings of the male change to a low-voiced barking while the female continues her harsh barking. A similar vocal duet also occurs at copulation. In Sweden the date for nine witnessed copulations has varied from 14th March to 13th April, the mean date being 31st March (Lundberg 1976). Egg-laying follows closely upon copulation but copulation does not necessarily mean that breeding will occur. During poor rodent years Ural Owls will stay in their territory but will not breed (cf. Lundberg 1976).

Throughout the breeding period the female remains in the close neighbourhood of the nest by day and night. If an intruder (four- or two-legged) threatens the nestlings, she will attempt to divert attention from the nest by flying off in a conspicuous fashion. If unsuccessful, she will utter a short, forceful barking, or the harsh hooting mentioned above in connection with copulation (Holmberg 1974). Either sex, but especially the female, snaps its bill when angry and, like most of the *Strix* genus, the Ural Owl will defend its nest fiercely against intruders. The habit has earned this species the name 'slaguggla', which means 'attacking owl', in Swedish. Sleeping has sometimes been observed as a displacement activity after the female has consistently but unsuccessfully attacked a person near its nest (Otto-Sprunck 1967).

The Ural Owl, like the Tawny Owl, is aggressive towards smaller birds of prey in its territory. It is also known that where the Ural Owl and Tawny Owl overlap in range, competition for nest-sites (in hollow trees) occurs (v. Haartman *et al* 1967). This problem is normally solved by the Ural Owl killing or at least driving away any Tawny Owl which comes into its territory. On the other hand there are two Finnish records of Tawny and Ural Owls nesting peaceably near each other; once in the same garden of an estate (Lammin-Soila and Uusivuori 1975), and, on the other occasion, only 300 m apart (Pihlainen 1977). These two exceptions suggest that it is only a lack of suitable nest-sites which caused the many known killings and aggressive behaviour between Ural and Tawny Owls, not a lack of other resources such as food. In some good vole years, when almost all owl pairs are stimulated to breed, the lack of suitable nest-holes seems to be desperate. The year 1973 was such a season in Häme, Finland, when a pair of Tengmalm's Owls and a pair of Ural Owls tried to use a nest box for breeding simultaneously (Lagerström 1978). The female Tengalm's Owl laid first, on 21st March. On 14th April everything was still normal and the Tengmalm's Owl female was incubating her five eggs in the nest box, but on 5th May a female Ural Owl was squatting on the half-broken roof of the nest box, which by then contained three young Tengmalm's Owls and one egg of the Ural Owl. The nest box entrance was too small for the Ural Owl, so it had tried to open the roof, but with only partial success, although one egg had, presumably, fallen through to the interior. Without any direct contact with the egg, the Ural Owl female started to incubate it, so strong were her instincts. The Tengmalm's Owl female had not been seen near the nest since 14th April and it is possible that the Ural Owl had killed her. The male Tengmalm's Owl was still alive but showed great anxiety when seen near the nest box and the female Ural Owl.

When Lagerström next visited the site about two weeks later, the Ural Owl female was still 'incubating' on the roof, and the nest box contained her own egg along with one live and two dead Tengmalm's Owl chicks. The presence of food remains (water voles, etc) persuaded Lagerström that both males (Ural and Tengmalm's) had fed the nestlings of the Tengmalm's Owl, but only occasionally, because the largest chick alone survived and fledged.

The Ural Owl's usurpation of smaller nest boxes intended for Tawny, and even

Tengmalm's Owls, reflects its strong instinct to nest in holes, and also the present lack of suitable nest sites.

The activity of the Ural Owl has been studied by automatic registration of nest visits at three breeding places in Finland, two in 1971 (Huhtala and Mikkola) and one in 1976 (Korpimäki). The results reveal that although the Ural Owl hunts mainly at night, it is also active during the day (Fig. 18). Activity in the morning, between 08.00 and 10.00 hours, was very low in all three cases, but otherwise some individual variations can be seen in the activity patterns of the different nests. In nest number one, 69.2% of all registered nest visits took place between 20.00 and 04.00 hours, and in the nest number three 68.6%, but in nest number two the corresponding figure was as low as 45.1%.

During the period when the young were being fed, the mean number of nest visits per day were 7.1 (one young), 13.1 (two young) and 15.7 (three young), showing a positive correlation between the number of visits and the number of owlets. Only nest number one was studied during the incubation period, when the mean number of visits was 8.9, which is much lower than that during the feeding period (13.1, as shown above).

For most of the breeding period prey is brought by the male alone, and generally given to the female. When the young owls have left the nest, the male delivers the prey directly to them, and it is at this time that the hooting and barking duets of the adults cease (Holmberg 1974).

Although the Ural Owl very often breeds in large coniferous woods, it prefers the more open sections and the forest edges for hunting. This is why modern forest habitats characterised by large clearings of felled trees have proved attractive to it. The Ural Owl often relies on 'still-hunting' from a suitable perch where it waits for prey to move, but I have also seen it flying low over an open area searching for its prey from the air. During autumn nights one can sometimes see Ural Owls in the beams of car headlights, as they watch at the kerb for rodents crossing the road. Unfortunately, many owls are killed as a result.

FOOD

Although the Ural Owl is strongly territorial and highly sedentary, the nocturnal roosts and feeding stations where it deposits its pellets are usually so well scattered throughout its territory (400–500 ha) that collecting any useful quantities of pellets is no easy task. As a result its food has been less well studied than that of any other northern owl. However, the Ural Owl will take fairly readily to nest boxes, and, by regularly visiting these and finding nearby tree roosts, useful collections of pellets and prey remains have been made recently in Finland as well as in Sweden. One hundred Finnish pellets collected in this way averaged in size 6.2 × 2.5 × 2.2 cm, the largest measurement being 9.4 × 2.5 × 2.0 cm and the smallest 3.5 × 1.9 × 1.3 cm. Pukinskii (1977) claims that Ural Owl pellets in the USSR reach a maximum of 15.5 × 3.0 cm, the minimum size being 10.0 × 2.0 cm. Either there are huge differences between Ural Owl pellet dimensions in Finland and the USSR or, perhaps, Dr Pukinskii may have measured some Eagle Owl pellets in error.

In addition to pellets, prey remains in the nest have been analysed during breeding season studies in Finland (31 nests scattered throughout the country up to the Arctic Circle) and in Sweden (13 studied by Lundberg near Uppsala, about 60°N). These

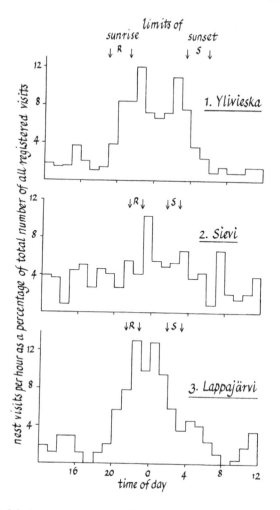

Fig. 18 Ural Owl activity during the breeding season at three different nest sites in Finland (Huhtala, Korpimäki and Mikkola 1979). Registrations were at: 1, Ylivieska (2 young) 19th April to 5th May 1971; 2, Sievi (3 young) 14th May to 10th June 1971; 3, Lappajärvi (1 young) 15th May to 13th June 1976)

two studies have been compared in Table 33 along with a lesser number of analyses from Norway (Mysterud and Hagen 1969) and from Germany (Schäfer and Fincken-stein 1935, Uttendörfer 1952). The number of Ural Owl's prey animals listed in Table 33 totals some 3,433 specimens.

Like other *Strix* owls, the Ural Owl feeds mainly on small mammals in the breeding season, but *Microtus* and *Clethrionomys* voles are a less important part of its diet than is the case with most northern owls, constituting only 29.9% and 16.9% respectively. The Swedish results demonstrate the importance of water voles to the Ural Owl, but many shrews, mice, rats, squirrels, and even hares, are also taken. The total number of mammals in the owl's diet was greatest in Sweden (86.2%) and smallest in Finland (74.8%).

Birds form less than 15% of the Ural Owl's diet, but the variety is remarkable. In the Finnish analysis alone there were 333 birds of at least 35 different species, ranging from Goldcrest *Regulus regulus*, through species such as Cuckoo *Cuculus canorus* and Nightjar *Caprimulgus europaeus*, to Black Grouse *Tetrao tetrix*. Some of the birds taken were other owls, and these formed 3.3% of birds consumed. They included ten Tengmalm's Owls, one Long-eared Owl and two Ural Owl chicks, the latter providing some evidence of cannibalism.

The remainder of the Ural Owl's diet comprises frogs (4.4%), which are fairly frequently taken, and insects (1.7%). Most of the insects are beetles (*Coleoptera*). Fish and lizards are only occasional food items; both were found once in the study (Table 33).

It would be tempting to suggest that there are differences in the Ural Owl's diet in various countries (in Finland birds are most commonly taken, in Sweden water voles, in Norway shrews and in Germany mice and rats) but it is unlikely that these differences are stable. The composition of the Ural Owl's food fluctuates widely, even at the same nest site, depending on variations in small mammal populations in different years. In Finland, for example, during the vole-plague years of 1965–66 at one nest in Virrat the proportion of Short-tailed Voles *Microtus agrestis* consumed was 50%, the total of all voles being 82%. In 1970, voles were almost absent in the vicinity of the same nest and the proportion of Short-tailed Voles was then only 5% (total voles 17%). In the same year the Ural Owls consumed a high percentage of birds (48%), and also insects (12%), frogs (10%), shrews (9%), squirrels (2%) and hares (2%) (Mikkola and Mikkola 1974).

In his 'Birds of Ussutain Country' (1954) Vorobiev pointed out that in the summer of 1949, when small rodents became scarce in Primorie, USSR, Ural Owls lived on birds, frogs and, in the autumn, even grasshoppers. This habit of changing to other prey when small rodent populations crash has also been documented in the USSR by Kislenko (1967). He relates how in the summer of 1963, in the vicinity of Veniukovo, Khabarovsk district, many owls and raptors reflected this adaptation in their breeding biology. Black Kites *Milvus migrans* laid only one egg per nest, while the Pied Harrier *Circus melanoleucus* and the Ural Owl did not nest at all. During that summer Kislenko examined three Ural Owls' stomachs. On 20th May a male was collected which had some remains of a Jackdaw *Corvus monedula davuricus*, in its stomach. In the stomach of a female, on 21st May, some remnants of a common lizard *Lacerta vivipara*, 8 dung beetles *Pentodon idiota* and 17 carabids (10 *Carabus smaragdinus* and 3 *Sabrus sp.*) were found. In another female, on 25th June, some remains (feathers and bones) of two Black-faced Buntings *Emberiza spodocephala*, one female Red-backed Shrike *Lanius cristatus* and a few chitinous remnants of one or two insects were found (Kislenko 1967). The Ural Owl seems to be more able to change its diet than the Great Grey Owl, for instance, a factor which enables it to remain in its territory all the time.

It seems worthwhile to mention a Ural Owl pellet analysis made in Japan (Imaizumi 1968), even though it is far outside our area. The examination of 180 pellets of Ural Owls *Strix uralensis hondoensis* again indicated a predominance of small mammals in the food. Pellets were collected in June and July 1967–68 at three locations in Niigata, Honsu, containing on average 2.3 prey animals per pellet. The local *Microtus* vole *Microtus montebelli* formed 68.2% of the 419 prey animals, mice and rats 13.8%, other

small mammals (shrews, moles, etc) 5.8% and birds 12.2%. The Ural Owls' captures
were different from those caught in traps nearby:

	In pellets (%)	In traps (%)	
Apodemus speciosus	6.7	29.8	(n = 246)
Urotrichus talpoides	2.4	50.5	(n = 417)
Microtus montebelli	68.2	5.2	(n = 43)
Crocidura dsinezumi	1.2	10.4	(n = 86)

The *Crocidura* shrew, the *Urotrichus* Japanese shrew-mole and the *Apodemus* mouse
were caught in less quantities by the owls, which seemed to capture many more
Microtus voles than the traps (Imaizumi 1968).

The diet of Ural Owls in autumn and winter has been studied in the Carpathians
(Sládek 1961–62), in Norway (Mysterud and Hagen 1969) and in Finland
(H. Mikkola, this study). Figures based on the contents of 208 Ural Owl stomachs
are presented in Table 34.

In a Finnish examination of 45 Ural Owls, seven stomachs were empty and the rest
contained an average of 3.1 prey animals per stomach. One stomach held the remains
of 15 prey animals (13 frogs *Rana sp.* and 2 Common Shrew *Sorex araneus*), while
another contained 11 prey items (8 Common Shrews and 3 large frogs).

If we compare the Ural Owl's food at different seasons (Tables 33 and 34), it
appears that outside the breeding season the proportion of water voles dropped to
0.8%, while shrews increased to 17.8%. One would expect that the percentage of birds
eaten would increase during the winter, when the snow cover is often so thick that
small mammals are less accessible to predation. However, according to the evidence,
the percentage of birds taken is no more than 10.6%. Outside the breeding season,
two Capercaillie *Tetrao urogallus* (females, which were possibly carrion or injured
birds), three Hazel Hens *Bonasia bonasia*, one Magpie *Pica pica*, one Waxwing
Bombycilla garrulus and five Tree Sparrows *Passer montanus* have been recorded.
Frogs are taken more often during the autumn (9.7%) than in spring and summer
months. In the Finnish results, for example, the percentage in autumn was as high as
27.4 (Table 34). One can imagine that frogs are vulnerable at this time of year when
gathering in groups in their wintering ponds and wells (cf. Koskela 1975). Even so,
despite the wide range of food eaten, the Ural Owl's diet consists principally of small
mammals (63.2% to 80%).

BREEDING BIOLOGY

In the southern parts of its extensive range, the Ural Owl usually breeds in montane
forests, including beech woods (Voous 1960), but elsewhere it prefers dense mixed
forests and high, though not too dense, coniferous forests. Until recently, a typical
nesting place would be a cavity in the stump of a pine or a spruce, such sites being
common in natural forests where old trees tend to break off 3–6 m above ground
(Ferguson-Lees 1969). With changing conditions in the forests of northern Europe
and Asia, the Ural Owl has had to adapt to a variety of nesting sites in order to survive
(Mikkola 1974). These changes have been studied in Finland by Lahti (1972) and
Lahti and Mikkola (1974), and in Sweden by Ingritz (1969) and Ahlén and Larsson
(1972).

In Finland, 250 nests were examined and sites found to be used were tree-stumps, holes in trees, nests made of twigs, nest boxes, buildings, rock faces and flat ground.

Tree-stumps used as nest-sites were 1.2–10 m high, the average being about 4.5 m (46 stumps). The depth of the nest-hole varied from a shallow depression of about 2 cm to more than 1 m, and the diameter varied 25–50 cm. Holes in trees usually form where the trunk is fractured or a branch has broken off. A cavity large enough for a Ural Owl's nest is sometimes formed when an old hole made by a Black Woodpecker *Dryocopus martius* decays. The majority of the twig nests used by Ural Owls had been built by hawks, as shown below:

Builder	No. of nests	%
Goshawk *Accipiter gentilis*	23	33
Buzzard *Buteo buteo*	14	20
Honey Buzzard *Pernis apivorus*	8	12
Sparrowhawk *Accipiter nisus*	2	3
Hawk sp.	6	9
Hawks total	53	77
Raven *Corvus corax*	2	3
Hooded Crow *Corvus corone cornix*	2	3
Red Squirrel *Sciurus vulgaris*	3	4
Man-made twig nest (artificial)	3	4
Builder unknown	6	9
Total	69	100

Nest boxes for Ural Owls have been provided in Finland for about 20 years. They are best made from a hollowed-out log, 50–80 cm deep and 30–40 cm in diameter, and have often been left open at the top, as in natural nesting sites in open tree-cavities (Mikkola 1974). They may also be made of board, in which case they should be wholly or partly covered to protect them from the weather (Lahti 1972). In Norway, cylindrical boxes have been built with an uneven upper edge, thus resembling the top of a natural stump (Hagen 1968). Occasionally, buildings, flat ground and rock faces are used for nest-sites.

Over the decades considerable changes have taken place in the Ural Owl's choice of nest sites in Finland (Table 35). Until the end of the 1950s, stumps and holes in trees were the preferred nesting sites, then the use of old twig nests of other large birds became more and more common. In 1960 the widespread use of nest boxes began, and since the mid-1960s nest boxes have been used more often than any other type of nest-site. There is a remarkable difference between nest-sites utilised in southern Finland (up to 63°N) and in northern Finland (63°–67°N), apparently due to local variations in the Ural Owl population density. In southern Finland nesting in nest boxes make up 42% of all recorded nest-sites, whilst 30% are in natural holes and fissures in trees, including shattered stumps. The reverse applies in the northern half of the country, where Ural Owl numbers are low, and nest box sites comprise only 13% of the total as against 57% for natural tree-holes and stumps. In central and northern Finland, where Ural Owl numbers are low, the proportion of tree-stump sites is as high as 51%. The same is true in Sweden, where the Ural Owl population is not too numerous for the existing tree holes and stumps to provide adequate numbers of nest-sites (Table 35).

Population density is not the only reason for changes in nest-sites of the Ural Owl.

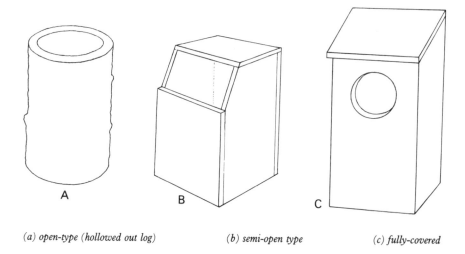

(a) open-type (hollowed out log)   (b) semi-open type   (c) fully-covered

In order to reduce the spread of pests and fungal diseases, modern forest management removes rotten stumps and holed trees. Meanwhile, the Ural Owl population has gradually increased, so the few stumps and tree-holes available fail to meet the demand, and the owls have had to adapt to twig nests, or even move to new habitats. Although twig nests were more common in the 1960s than stump and tree-hole nests, the hole-nesting preference of the Ural Owl is borne out by the wide use of boxes during that period. Many examples show that a nest box is preferred to a nest of twigs. If a box is put up in the neighbourhood of an inhabited twig nest the owl moves into the box, but no transfers in the reverse direction have been observed (Lahti 1972).

In former times the breeding habitat of the Ural Owl in Finland was reported, without exception, to be old coniferous or mixed forest far from human habitation (e.g. Collin 1886, Hortling 1929, Kivirikko 1947), but in the last 25 years its nesting habitat has been more varied. Damp heath forest is still its favoured habitat (67% of 87 nests studied), but it now regularly nests in dry heath forests (21%) and spruce bogs (10%). The variety of nesting habitat is further indicated by additional records of nests in pine bogs and herb-rich forests (Lahti and Mikkola 1974).

Six nests found in the middle of felled areas and one in the middle of an open bog support the view that the availability of a suitable nest-site is more important than the biotope. Similar evidence is provided by birds that breed near centres of human activity. In these cases the nest has usually been sited less than a hundred metres from a house, typically in a hole in a garden tree. In Finland the first such nest, near a farmhouse, was found in 1953 at Virrat, where later, in 1961, the first nesting in a building (an old barn) was discovered (Kellomäki *et al* 1967). At the time of writing about 40 nests in the vicinity of human dwellings are known to the author. The Ural Owl has continued to adjust well to new circumstances, and such adaptability should give it a good chance of success in the future.

Having decided upon a suitable location for its nest, the Ural Owl, like the Great Grey Owl, does not normally add any new material but merely rearranges whatever is present in order to deepen the cup. Recently, however, Helo (1974) found a Ural Owl's nest in a disused Red Squirrel's drey (*Sciurus vulgaris*) with a ring of fresh twigs around it. Helo could not imagine that any bird other than the Ural Owl would have brought the twigs. If his belief is correct, the Ural Owl seems to be capable of repairing its nest to some extent.

An assertion by Ferguson-Lees (1969) that the breeding season of the Ural Owl is rather variable, being largely controlled by the severity of the weather, and tends to start as soon as the snow melts, is not generally true in Finland, where this hardy bird begins breeding while the nest remains covered in snow, a month or two before the forest thaws. The female usually digs and melts the snow from the nest by 'incubating' it before egg-laying, as was observed in Ylivieska between 12th and 18th March, and in nearby Sievi between 20th and 30th March 1971 (Huhtala *et al* 1979).

The commencement of breeding activities is apparently influenced by the quantity of available food, and in good vole years the owls lay eggs much earlier than during poor years (e.g. Linkola and Myllymäki 1969). Lundberg (1976) has put forward an interesting hypothesis of how such regulation might work in Ural Owl populations. During lean vole years, and often in years of multiplying vole populations, the winter density of voles is so low that the male cannot provide the female with the requisite quantities of food prior to nesting. Undernourishment of the female in poor vole years would prevent her from laying, whilst in other years breeding success would be regulated by the nutritional condition of the female. This hypothesis would be strengthened if it could be demonstrated that the act of food presentation is in some way associated with oviduct development and ovulation in the female.

The clutch size of the Ural Owl has been studied in southern Finland by Linkola and Myllymäki (1969), northern Finland by Helo (1974) and in central Sweden by Johansson (1978). Their findings are as follows:

	Eggs per clutch						
Number of clutches:	1	2	3	4	5	6	*Average*
South Finland	3	13	28	12	2	1	3.0
North Finland	1	—	4	2	2	2	3.9
Central Sweden	4	5	8	9	2	—	3.0
Total	8	18	40	23	6	3	3.1

The number of eggs recorded in Finland has varied between one and six per clutch, but there is one record relating to a nest containing seven young at Vilppula in 1973 (R. Laskujärvi). The average clutch size in northern Finland is 3.9, whilst that in southern Finland and in central Sweden is only 3.0. Surprisingly, Linkola and Myllymäki (1969) found no good correlation between clutch size and fluctuations in vole numbers. A higher reproduction rate occurs in peak vole years but frequently in subsequent years, too, when vole numbers are less (also Lundberg 1976).

The rounded white eggs are usually laid between late March and mid-April. Incubation, by the female, lasts 27 to 29 days in the milder regions, but in Finland, because of the cold climate, it often exceeds 30 days (cf. Helo 1974). At Sievi, Finland, young at one nest hatched every other night and their weights varied 40–42 g (Fig. 19). The feeding activity of the parents was at its peak when the oldest youngster was two weeks' old and the female had ceased to brood the young. The oldest chick climbed from the nest when 26 days old. Its weight was then 574 g. It was unable to fly. The parents clearly had difficulties in obtaining enough food, especially during cold

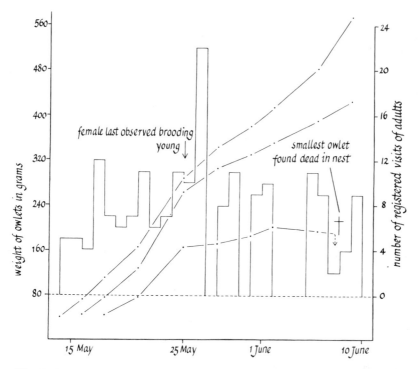

Fig. 19 Weight increase of young Ural Owls compared with feeding visits of their parents, at Sievi, Finland, in 1971 (Huhtala, Korpimäki and Mikkola 1979). The dots indicate the dates when the owlets were weighed. The columns indicate the number of night visits to the nest, automatically registered

nights, such as that of 8th June, when the smallest owlet died. There had been only two feeding visits during the previous night (Fig. 19).

In the summer of 1972 I kept a young Ural Owl at home between 28th May and 22nd July. When it came to me its weight was 340 g, from which I deduced it to be about 20 days old. The daily food intake for an adult Ural Owl is about 125 g (Uttendörfer 1952), but this young owl consumed only 3,022 g in 45 days, i.e. 67 g per day. It was fed on voles, shrews and mice, as it would have been in the wild, and it was free to move around in our rooms. By July it was able to fly and hunt independently and on 19th July it weighed 735 g. A few days later it was released near the forest where it had hatched.

The behaviour and even the voices of this young Ural Owl were more or less the same as those of the young Great Grey Owl I had kept earlier (see Great Grey Owl chapter). The young Ural Owl was most active at night between 22.00 and 23.00 hours, and 02.00 and 03.00 hours, and least active during the afternoons. During the day, it would often be found lying on its belly like a dog, its bill touching the ground. At other times it would drowse while upright on its perch. Upon waking it would begin the typical owl exercise of raising both wings above its head, carpals almost touching, outer halves of the wings stretched outwards like the drooping cross-piece of a 'T' (see drawing below).

Stretching exercise of young Ural Owl upon waking

Ural Owls manifest early sexual maturity. A Ural Owl ringed in Finland as a nestling laid eggs the following spring when only eleven months old (Lagerström 1969); and in Japan a young captive bird laid two eggs at the age of ten months (Kazama 1974).

In Finland, in the period 1961–1976, Valkeila (1976) ringed all the Ural Owl females and young from 120 nest boxes. During the course of this extensive project he found that only 5% of the females ringed as nestlings began breeding in the following spring. By the second spring the proportion had risen to 10%, the third spring 35%, the fourth spring 30%, and by the fifth season 20% were breeding for the first time. In these results the average breeding age for females was 3.5 years, although it would be wrong to take these figures as conclusive. It is quite possible that the older females breeding, apparently, for the first time had already nested elsewhere, or had nested in Valkeila's study area, but had not used the nest boxes provided. More probably, Valkeila's study area had been overstocked with Ural Owls, and this led to the unexpected result. The area where Lagerström (1969) found the Ural Owl breeding at eleven months had a much lower Ural Owl population.

DISTRIBUTION

Like the Great Grey Owl, the Ural Owl belongs to the Siberian faunal type (Voous 1960). It has a trans-palearctic distribution: central, south-eastern, northern, and eastern Europe, eastwards across Siberia in the taiga, north to about 64° to 66°, south to the southern borders of the taiga in western Siberia, the Altai, northern Mongolia, Manchuria, Ussuriland, Korea, Sakhalin, and the main islands of Japan, with a very isolated population in the mountains of western China (Vaurie 1965).

Voous (1960) considered the Ural Owl to be the original geographical representative of the Tawny Owl, which was restricted at first to the boreal coniferous forest belt. Finn Salomonsen believes that its geographical isolation and subsequent species formation took place during the Pleistocene glacial periods. It is probable that the populations at present inhabiting the central European mountain forests (the Bohemian Forest, Austrian Alps, Yugoslavian Mountains, Carpathian Mountains), are relics from that particular period of the post-glacial era when coniferous forests were much more widely distributed throughout Europe than they are today. On the other hand, the isolated population in the mountains of western China has to be regarded as a true glacial relic (Voous 1960, Vaurie 1965).

Nine subspecies of the Ural Owl are recognised in Eurasia (Vaurie 1965). In general, the populations in Europe and Asia are darker in appearance than those in the middle of the range. This accords with the so-called Bergmann and Gloget Laws advancing the idea that races in cold, harsh climates have lighter and more contrasting coloration with blackish markings, and are of a larger size, than those in more temperate climates (Dement'ev *et al* 1951). Three subspecies in Japan also show an increasing darkness of coloration from north to south (Vaurie 1965).

The isolated population of China (*davidi*) is strongly differentiated and is the darkest race of all, with blackish-brown markings, but Ural Owls of central and south-eastern Europe do not differ taxonomically from those of north-western Europe. Only two sub-species are separated in Europe: *Strix uralensis liturata* in western Europe and *Strix uralensis uralensis* in Russia near the Ural Mountains, east of *liturata* with which it intergrades (Vaurie 1965). However, Eck and Busse (1973) have recently shown that Ural Owls living in the mountains of central Europe have a much longer tail (higher wing-length/tail-length index) than the *liturata* and *uralensis* subspecies. Clearly this population has been isolated long enough to form some local characteristics, and they could be distinguished as the form *S. u. macroura* Wolf 1810, or *S. u. carpathica* as suggested by A. Dunaevskii in 1940 (cf. Dement'ev *et al* 1951). *S. u. carpathica* has an interesting variation in its coloration, a large number of Carpathian owls being dark brown, apparently existing alongside the common grey forms also inhabiting this area. Dement'ev *et al* (1951) described this variation (analogous to the '*wilkonskii*' form among Tawny Owls) as not occurring in other parts of the Ural Owl's range.

One has the impression that the Ural Owl's population and even its range have decreased drastically in Central Europe in recent times. In the Bayerischer Wald in

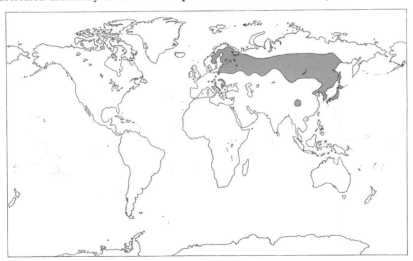

URAL OWL – mainly resident but some individuals wander south in winter through most of north Asiatic range

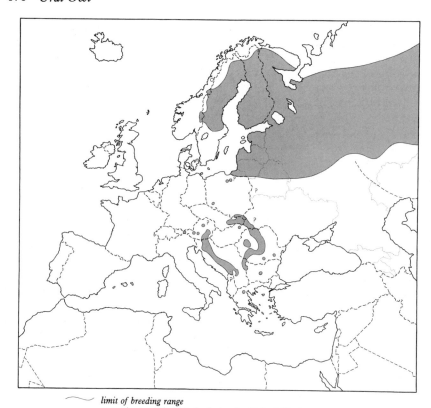

~~~~~~   limit of breeding range
~~~~~~   approximate southerly limit of wintering birds of Siberian race *S. u. uralensis*

URAL OWL

West Germany the Ural Owl was breeding quite commonly until the 1920s, but by the 1960s Kučera (1970) could find none at all. To help this desperate situation Scherzinger (1974) began to breed Ural Owls is captive conditions, and some of his young owls have been re-introduced into the forest.

On a more optimistic note, the Ural Owl is said to be a comparatively 'common' breeder in the Carpathians, which is admittedly a very tiny area in southern Poland. In addition, Tomialojć (1972) documented three nest records of 1909, 1924 and 1950 outside the Carpathian region (indicated by dots on the map). Recently, Jabloński (1976) has published records of 19 Ural Owl nests found between 1966 and 1971 in northern Poland. These nests are indicated by a question mark on the distribution map, because it is not known how critical Jabloński was when compiling his paper (Dr Tomialojć, *in litt.*).

Until 1960 the Ural Owl (*S. u. carpathica*) was known to have bred in Hungary only once, in 1906 (Keve 1960), but since then one more nest has been found in the mountains of Zemplin (Fedor and Babay 1962–63). In eastern Slovakia the Ural Owl has been much more common during the last few years, Dr Šimák knowing of eight to twelve pairs annually, whereas between 1964 and 1968 Danko and Švehlik (1971) knew of no more than four nest records. As elsewhere in its range, in Rumania the

Ural Owl breeds in the mountain forests (beech, spruce, and mixed woodland), but it also nests in woodland in the plains (D. Munteanu, *in litt.*). Recently, breeding has been discovered in the Danube Valley near the Yugoslavian border. In Bulgaria the Ural Owl is extremely rare, having been observed on only two occasions during the breeding season, both sightings being in a forest near the town of Plovdiv in 1905 and 1923 (S. Simeonov and S. Dontchev, *in litt.*). The most southerly record of any Ural Owl in Europe comes from Greece, where a bird was heard calling in June 1956 (Peus 1957, but cit. after Bauer *et al* 1969).

Although the Ural Owl breeds sparsely in Central Europe, this is not true of the northern part of its range. During the last few decades the Ural Owl population has noticeably increased in western Russia (Pukinskii 1977), in Finland (v. Haartman *et al* 1967), in Sweden (Ahlén and Larsson 1972, Lundberg 1974), and very likely in Norway (cf. Mysterud 1969). The cause of the increase in Ural Owl and other owl populations of the Siberian faunal group is, in Siivonen's view (1943), the cooling of the climate which followed the warm period of the 1930s. At the same time, the preferred hunting grounds, such as large clearings and recently abandoned agricultural land, have increased markedly, explaining at least partially the increase in owls numbers (also Lundberg 1974).

Unfortunately, the exact numbers of Ural Owls in Fenno-Scandia and Russia are not known, but there are some rough estimates. Professor Merikallio (1955) estimated that there were about 1,400 breeding pairs of Ural Owls in Finland – although it is reckoned that this figure is about half the present number of pairs. Ulfstrand and Högstedt (1976) calculated that there were perhaps 3,000 pairs in Sweden. In Estonia, USSR, the population density of the Ural Owl in suitable forests is between 0.2 and 0.3 pairs per 1,000 hectares, from which Randla (1976) obtained the figure of 200 or 300 Ural Owl pairs in the whole of the country. The population status in Norway is little known, but its range appears to be very restricted, and in Denmark this owl has never been observed (Rosendahl 1973), even though it nests in nearby Norway and Sweden.

Indeed, Ural Owls are extremely sedentary and very rarely wander outside their breeding range, as shown by the Finnish ringing results. Until 1977, a total of 4,244 Ural Owls had been ringed in Finland (Saurola 1978), but few recoveries were made further than 20 or 30 km from the original nest. Adults and settled birds do not usually move more than 2–3 km from their nesting places. However, young owls sometimes wander up to 200 km in their first autumn before breeding, resembling young Tawny Owls in this respect (P. Saurola, *in litt.*). It appears very likely that the nominate race *S. u. uralensis*, is rather less sedentary, as its winter movements have taken it to the Caspian Sea, and in Western Siberia it is known to be a far-ranging wanderer (Dement'ev *et al* 1951).

19: Great Grey Owl *Strix nebulosa*
(Forster)

DESCRIPTION

The plumage is a combination of whites, greys and browns. The upperparts are irregularly marked with dark and white, and the underparts are boldly streaked over fine barring. The large, circular facial disc is emphasised by the facial barring which forms six or more concentric circles of brown on a white background. The back of the head is very evenly barred. Its massive head may be as much as 510 mm in circumference.

The noticeably small eyes are yellow, edged on the inside with a touch of black and two large outward-facing commas of white. The colour of the bill of adult birds varies from ivory, pale olive green to bright yellow. The bill is surrounded by a black beard. In addition the Great Grey Owl has white moustaches and very prominent white patches in the middle of the fore-neck. It has been thought that these white patches are larger in females than in males but the supposed differences may partly be related to the bird's behaviour, i.e. the extent to which the white patches are exposed.

The white margin on the outer scapulars or shoulder feathers and light ocherish bars on the remiges seem to be more prominent in males than in females, which may explain why females often look darker.

The flight-feathers are dusky grey-brown, barred blackish-brown (four bars on secondaries, six on primaries). Basal two-thirds of outer primaries with pale yellow-buff and white ground colour forming a bright pale patch in the spread wing, much duller on the inner primaries. Wing-coverts much as mantle and scapulars but mottled rather than streaked, darker on lesser coverts. Primary coverts grey-brown broadly banded darker. The underwing is a grey, pale version of the nominate race of Eagle Owl with the same dark barring towards rear edge and black-brown carpal semi-circle (see flight plate).

The tail is wedge-shaped, consisting of twelve feathers of which the outer ones are 5 cm shorter than the middle ones. Like the uppertail-coverts the tail is pale grey-brown, densely speckled and vermiculated black-brown and shading into darker distal half. A number of ill-developed darkish bars on middle feathers.

Its fully-feathered legs look as thick as a human wrist. The relatively weak and only slightly curved claws are blackish.

The nestlings have greyish down above and pure white below, with yellowish legs and yellowish-grey iris. Juveniles are olive-brown, darkly barred as well as spotted with white above and completely barred below; broad black face markings extend from the eyes to the ear coverts. Remiges and rectrices as in definitive plumage which the owlets attain in less than five months. Young birds generally have greyer or darker plumage, although varying individually, making it possible to recognise sub-adult owls from older birds from late summer through to April (also Nero 1980).

Only two sub-species are recognised in the world and they manifest morphological differences in coloration but no size differences. Great Grey Owls of northern Europe and Asia *Strix nebulosa lapponica* tend to be lighter and greyer and more finely marked below than the North American ones *Strix nebulosa nebulosa*. In summary the former are white with grey-brown markings whereas the latter are brown with white markings.

In Finland (Mikkola 1981) and in the USSR (Dement'ev *et al* 1951) the weight of *Strix nebulosa lapponica* females varies from 977 g–1,900 g (average 1,182 g for 46 birds) and that of males 660 g–1,110 g (average 878 g for 36 birds). The wing length of males varies from 405 mm–477 mm (average 440 mm for 38 birds) and that of females 438 mm–483 mm (average 464 mm for 83 birds). Females are clearly larger, the size difference between the sexes being readily apparent when a pair is seen together. However, the size difference is not enough to differentiate the sex of single birds.

Young Great Grey Owl, just able to fly

IN THE FIELD

Heavy-headed and long-tailed, the Great Grey Owl has a shape unlike that of any other bird. Due to its fluffed-out feathers it would seem to be the largest of all owls, although its weight is only half that of the Eagle Owl. The Great Grey Owl has the largest and most perfectly circular facial disc of any owl, possibly indicating an advanced sense of hearing, which it shares with other *Strix* owls.

In the *Strix* genus it is the only owl with pure yellow eyes, which are small (12.5 mm in diameter) compared with, for example, those of the Tawny Owl, which are 16–17 mm. It flies easily with slow, airy wing beats and is very agile in passing between trees. With wings only partly spread it can move its wing tips in a rapid, shallow manner like a falcon, quickly attaining high speed. The most noticeable aspect of the flight behaviour is its low-speed, silent, manoeuvrable glide with which it moves from one perch to another. In flight a distinctive white and buff patch shows across the base of the primaries as well as white areas on the scapulars. At close quarters conspicuous white crescents and chin stripes are a distinctive part of the facial plumage. Because these glossy white feathers reflect so much light on a dark day, or late in the evening, they often may be an aid to identifying this species. The white patches may also function as a species recognition signal (e.g. Wahlstedt 1969).

Especially during the winter this owl will often be seen within built-up areas and near farmhouses. The Great Grey Owl will show very little fear of man and it is quite easy to approach trees where they are perched. Tameness or docility appears to be one of its notable characteristics, although marked aggression can be shown when protecting its young.

VOICE

In Finland I have heard Great Grey Owls calling as early as mid-February, but in Sweden typical territorial calling has been recorded in the first mild weather of January. As Berggren and Wahlstedt (1977) noted, the male's territorial call may be given not only in early spring but also late in the breeding season in June and July and sometimes in autumn. During the winter of 1973–74 Great Grey Owls remained in Sweden in their winter territories because it was a good vole year, and these owls were calling during the season. A recent study by Jon Winter (1981) in the Sierra Nevada, California, USA, also indicates that Great Grey Owls are vocally active all year. The pair studied by him responded readily to tape-recorded calls in all months so far tested (April to December). However, the main period for territory announcement is March to mid-May.

The primary territorial song is a series of regularly spaced *ho* notes of equal duration and interval, and up to eight or twelve in succession. According to Winter (1981), the whole call lasts about 6–8 seconds with a mean interval of 33 seconds between calls. The normal speed of hooting is about 1.5 notes per second but can also be slower. Echograms of these two types of song are given in Fig. 20. Berggren and Wahlstedt (1977) maintain that the difference between normal and slow calls can be easily recognised in the field.

The territory call is reported to be audible under ideal conditions up to 800 m (Höglund and Lansgren 1968), but normally its carrying power is only about 500 m (Mikkola 1976). Thus, the song is very weak compared to other species of owls, which explains why so few people know this call.

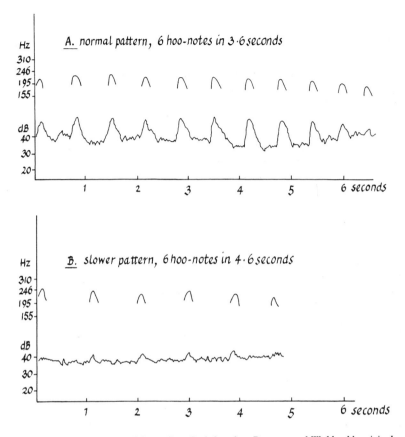

Fig. 20   *Territorial hooting of Great Grey Owl, based on Berggren and Wahlstedt's original echograms (1977)*

As a rule, the male starts calling at sunset and stops at sunrise, sometimes slightly later. Calling in the daytime has not been reported thus far, even though this owl is said to be the only truly diurnal member of the *Strix* genus (e.g. Grossman and Hamlet 1965).

At the beginning of May, 1972, Berggren and Wahlstedt (1977) had an opportunity to follow the calling activity of an obviously unpaired male. Fig. 21 shows that this owl started its territory announcements at 21.10 hours (sunset 20.30) and the last call was heard at 00.50 hours (sunrise 03.00). Thus, the territory calling lasted 3 hours and 40 minutes, during which not less than 310 series of calls were recorded.

Winter (1981) studied the Great Grey Owl's calling activity in California between 25th May and 23rd September 1980. A frequency distribution of unprompted calling activity (Fig. 21) shows that the owls in Sierra Nevada were most vocally active at 01.00 hours, when 18% of all calls were recorded. Between 01.00 and 04.00 hours, 56% of the calls were recorded with a pre-midnight peak of 12% of the sample at 22.00 hours. In California, calling frequency declines conspicuously around midnight making the distribution bimodal. A similar pattern can be seen in the material of

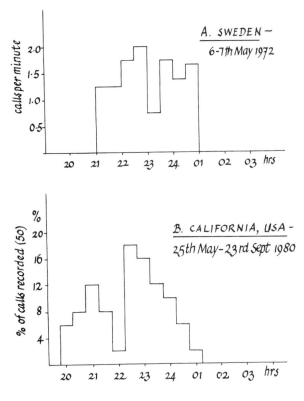

Fig. 21   Vocal activity of male Great Grey Owls in Sweden and California, USA. Swedish data is Berggren and Wahlstedt (1977); California data is Winter (1981)

Berggren and Wahlstedt (1977) from Sweden (Fig. 21) where a drop in calling activity was also noted near midnight.

The female has also been heard to use this territorial hooting at the nest in spring, before the egg-laying period. However, the most common call given by the female is a soft mellow hoot serving as communication with the male at the nest. Höglund and Lansgren (1968) described this call as *vee-vee*, and thought that Wahlstedt (1959) meant the same with his *niéh-niéh*. Nero (1980) wrote the same call as *whoop*, which is the best English spelling of it, thought it demonstrates how impossible it is to describe songs and calls in this way. The male also announces his presence at the nest with a low mellow hooting. This note is weak and can be heard over a distance of 300 m at most.

Another call used by both sexes, and heard less often, consists of a series of double notes given very rapidly (even three times a second and up to a hundred times in one sequence) (Wahlstedt 1969). It is evidently a defensive or warning cry uttered with great vigour but carrying only about 50 m.

The hungry chicks give rapid, chattering or chirping notes *che-a* (Höglund and Lansgren 1968) or *sher-richt* (Nero 1980) growing stronger and more raucous with age.

Berggren and Wahlstedt (1977) have shown with echograms that the female's call is reminiscent of the begging calls of the chicks and juveniles and that it signals the female's willingness to be approached by the male.

When the nestlings are small the female has sometimes uttered purring notes *korr-korr-krrr-krrr*, after the male has left prey for the nest. Höglund and Lansgren (1968) have heard similar notes when the female has been brooding the young.

The female's normal alarm note is a deep growling preceded or followed by bill-snapping. On hearing the alarm note the small young become silent. When bigger, the chicks also snap their mandibles together to produce a loud noise – probably a stylised biting movement given as a warning, as it seems to occur especially in situations where the young have been handled.

A loud heron-like squawk or bark climaxes a series of notes, ranging from vigorous hooting to high-pitched wails and squeals, uttered by the female in alarm situations, especially during injury-feigning or distraction display. The greater the distress the more extreme are the calls (also Nero 1980).

There are many more rasping, screeching, cooing or whistling calls ascribed in the literature to male and female Great Grey Owls. As well as those given by Nero (1980), these vocalisations carry meaning not only in terms of specific syllables but also in intonation and strength. But our written descriptions can never properly illustrate the vocal capability of this species, and the more we know about any owl the more numerous the various calls will be.

BEHAVIOUR

The aggressiveness of Great Grey Owls at the nest is probably the best-known feature of their behaviour (cf. Aarnio and Häyrinen 1967, Höglund and Lansgren 1968, Mikkola 1974, etc). As a rule the female is the more savage and defends her nest and young so persistently and frantically that it is difficult to make a close examination of the nest. In most cases it is necessary to mask the face to protect the eyes from serious injury. I know of two people who have lost an eye because of the Great Grey Owl, and there is at least one report of a man breaking a leg as a result of being knocked out of a tree, and most other people who have dealt with an angry female come away with bruises and gashes.

Whilst incubating, the female Great Grey Owl is quite fearless but not yet aggressive. During this period it is quite easy to approach the nest-tree. She will peer over the side of the nest, although this in itself can be quite disconcerting as one climbs the tree, her head being as big as a child's. When thus disturbed she snaps her bill continually and assumes a defensive posture.

Once the eggs are hatched the female becomes more aggressive and, particularly when the chicks grow larger, she frequently attacks intruders. However, certain differences in behaviour have been noted in individual birds. Some females have shown no aggression when the young are still in the nest but of an age when the female no longer tears the prey to pieces for them (Höglund and Lansgren 1968).

According to my observations, owls nesting on the ground or on a low stump have been more aggressive than those nesting in a raptor's old nest high up in a tree. It has been mentioned in the literature that the degree of aggressiveness may have a connection with the food supply. Sandman (1897) relates that Great Grey Owls were very irascible at the nest during the rodent year of 1888. In the following summer only one pair was found with young in the nest, the supply of rodents was poor and the owls were tractable. Similarly, Höglund and Lansgren (1968) met with their least aggressive females during a poor vole year (1963).

Usually when one is in the neighbourhood of a nest or of any young out of the nest, the female warns by a growling sound. If one approaches too closely to a chick the female attacks after momentarily unfolding her wings. The Great Grey Owl is very ready to use its talons and it is likely that it is capable of chasing away most intruders which intentionally (predators), or casually, come close to the young.

I have never met an attacking male but, according to Höglund and Lansgren (1968), in some cases the male will help its mate to protect the nest. In such cases, if one has to go near the nest it is essential to wear suitable protective clothing, as both birds will attack, most probably from different directions. A motorcycle crash helmet with visor is required wear in such circumstances.

Pair-formation, courtship, mating and territoriality are among the least-documented aspects of Great Grey Owl behaviour. However, aerial displays, mutual preening and courtship feeding are known to occur in this species.

Nero (1980) has given an excellent description of courtship feeding in his book. He writes: 'Despite the low temperatures (on cold February mornings), the owls unknowingly respond to changing day-length, and certain behaviour gradually changes, too. The male, instead of immediately swallowing a captured mouse, carries it to a nearby perch and sits motionless, staring quietly, prey hanging from its bill. . . . The sight of the dangling mouse releases in the female an ancient pattern – a curious mimicry of a hungry, young owl – shifting her weight deliberately from one foot to the other, bobbing her head and hooting softly, she begins chirping like an owlet. . . . He sits, watching closely as she flies toward him and lands on a nearby perch. After some hesitation, for she is larger than he is, stimulated by the female's continued display, the male flies to perch beside her, closing his eyes as he leans toward her, holding out the mouse. With closed eyes and a slight mewing sound the female seizes the mouse. At the moment the female takes the mouse from the male the pair bond is formed or renewed. The ritual of courtship feeding will be repeated again and again, strengthening the social bond.'

Courtship feeding has an important nutritive value for during the period in which the eggs are developing, the female's energy requirements are greater than the male's.

Nero (1980) maintains that for the Great Grey Owl preening is one of the strongest patterns evident in pair bonding behaviour.

In his thesis Oeming (1955) has briefly described the preening of two captive birds: 'During courtship the male would fly to the female's stump and face her. Standing face to face with breasts touching he would commence rubbing his beak over hers, at the same time uttering a faint droning or humming sound. Often he would circle her face with his beak in a similar manner. This kind of pre-copulation behaviour was observed regularly during eight days and would occur at any time during the day or night.' Unfortunately the female died soon afterwards. A similar preening has been recorded for Barred Owls *Strix varia* (Bent 1938) as well as for Ural Owls (A. Leinonen, *in litt*).

Fitzpatrick (1972) suggests that allopreening in birds may function as a means of sex recognition in some monomorphic species, and it may, in addition, provide a ritualised mechanism for pair bond maintenance in species that pair for extended periods.

Threat posture of Great Grey Owl – wings are dropped and bill is snapped –
such behaviour often precedes flying attack on intruder

The act of mating has been described by Nero (1980) as follows: 'The male flew into a tree, where shortly he was joined by the female. At that point the birds were about 3 m (20 feet) apart on the same branch. When the female flew, the male followed and, like a Raven (*Corvus corax*), cupped his wings, braking and falling upon her in mid-air. He dropped onto the female for a second, then they separated and flew off together.' This incident happened on 28th February 1978 between 18.00 and 18.30 hours. Presumably this was an established pair, the aerial contact indicating a strong sexual motivation in the male.

Great Grey Owls seem to appear in their territories a few weeks before breeding starts (Wahlstedt 1969). How they select a nest site has not been much studied, but either the male visits various nests, finally deciding upon one of them, from which he will call to his mate, or it is the female who determines which nest is used (Höglund and Lansgren 1968).

The Great Grey Owl nesting on a stump at Konnevesi in 1972 first tried to use a nearby stump 30 m away. The female had started to excavate the soft outer layers but she was unable to remove the hard central core. This raised centre prevented her from laying and she chose the other nearby (and more rotted) stump.

Practically nothing is known of why some owls choose to nest on the ground, on tree stumps or in raptors' old nests in preference to one of the alternative sites. It would seem that a suitable nest is often more important than the biotope in which it is situated, but why don't all owls nest on the ground and in an ideal biotope? I would like to suggest that a Great Grey Owl which nests on the ground one year will very probably do so again the following year. The same fixed behaviour should be true for the users of other types of nests. If so, the stump-nesting owls could be identified, as could other nest-site users. Wahlstedt (1976) has an interesting observation from Sweden which seems to illustrate my hypothesis.

In 1973 a Great Grey Owl pair nested on a stump and the following year a pair also nested on a stump only 1 km away. Unfortunately, Wahlstedt was unable to prove that it was the same pair but he thought it very likely. It would appear that a class of stump-nesting Great Grey Owls exists. Naturally, things are never quite so simple and straightforward in nature but some kind of preferences may, of course, exist. This maintains the heterogenity of the population which is necessary on the long road of evolution.

In Finland, two Great Grey Owl females which had been using the same nest were shot (Sorsakoski/Merikallio), and this may be the explanation also for the two nests, each containing nine eggs, found in Sweden (Merikallio). But it may also be an indication of bigamy, two females with one male. Snowy Owl (Portenko 1972), Eagle Owl and Short-eared Owl (unpublished Finnish observations) males are known to be polygynous on occasions and there is no reason to doubt that the Great Grey Owl may be also. I have suspected bigamy on two occasions (Oulu, 1970, two nests; and Konnevesi, 1972, three nests). In each case two nests were close together and during nest visits only one male was ever seen.

In North America it has been calculated that the territory of the nominate subspecies *S. n. nebulosa* is about 2.6 km². The maximum diameter of the territory is about 2.3 km (Craighead and Craighead 1969). This example demonstrates that the Great Grey Owl's territory is much larger than either the Tawny Owl's or the Ural Owl's. Nevertheless, territorialism is not a fixed and stereotyped trait of behaviour and this means that its characteristics and mode of action are directly conditioned by the availability of food. Territorialism must be considered as the means which permits predators to adjust their density to the food resources of the area (Blondel 1966). For example, Pitelka *et al* (1955) and Lockie (1955) have shown that the size of an owl's territory diminishes with an increase in the density of prey animals.

In Finland and Sweden some Great Grey Owl territories have probably been very small, since two nests have often been found close together – in Sweden as little as 100 m apart (Höglund and Lansgren 1968). In Konnevesi, Finland, three nests were known within 400 m of one another (Mikkola 1976). Although these nests were in such close proximity, no aggressive encounters between the inhabitants of the different nests were observed. This would suggest that the Great Grey Owl is tolerant towards others of its own species and is not much averse to living side by side with another pair.

There are some indications that nomadic Great Grey Owls move with other owls or pairs of owls when searching for new breeding areas after a crash in the vole population. When these invading birds find a suitable new area with plenty of voles, they may nest in loose colonies, like Short-eared Owls (e.g. Grönlund and Mikkola 1969). Wahlstedt (1974) has reported an observation of Great Grey Owl, probably migrating, in the Övertorneå region of Sweden. Three Great Grey Owls were seen in May, two flying in daylight at a considerable height to the west whilst the third was perched in a tree-top below. One example of colonial behaviour and nomadism is another observation made by Wahlstedt (1974) in the Boden-Luleå district in 1973. Between 16th and 29th March two pairs were calling from fixed territories within a small area, and on 1st April seven pairs were counted in the same area. Four or five new pairs were spread over a distance of 3 km and remained there during the rest of the breeding season.

In addition, during the winter Great Grey Owls seem to establish a definite home range. In one case studied in Canada the size of a home range was approximately 45 ha (Brunton and Pittaway 1971). Inside this winter territory individual birds have been observed to show great interest in other Great Grey Owls hunting nearby. However, real clashes in the winter range are rare. Brunton and Pittaway (1971) described one incident as follows: 'As we observed on February 26, 1966, a sitting Great Grey Owl from a distance of 100 feet, we saw another flying directly towards it. When the flying bird was approximately 250 feet from the perched bird, the latter (which appeared to be giving the other its complete attention) gave a short, rasping call, followed by a drawn-out *who-oo-oo-oo-oo*. The rasp was given once and the *who-oo-oo* three times, each call being separated by a pause of approximately two seconds. It seemed that the perched bird was directing these calls towards the flying bird. Immediately after the last call, the approaching bird changed its course and flew away, at right angles to the sitting bird. Throughout this episode, a third bird (appearing approximately 30 minutes before either of the other two) was perched on a telephone pole 200 yards away. It remained silent and did not fly from that perch. The other two Great Grey Owls seemed to take no notice of this bird. The bird which called had been followed by Pittaway for an hour, during which time it had been actively hunting. It took the perch only a few minutes before the above encounter ensued.'

It is difficult to tell if this is the normal way territorial disputes are resolved, as it is the only incident of its kind so far described.

There is also an observation relating to possible intraspecific killing by a Great Grey Owl. Fisher (1975) saw a Great Grey Owl standing on top of a dead one, but when he examined the site he found no signs of a significant struggle. The thin body of the dead owl was still warm. No blood was found nor were broken bones or external haemorrhages present, although a small area of skin had been opened on its breast and there was a hole approximately 4 cm in diameter in the ear region. From these facts Fisher suggested that the Great Grey Owl had attacked and killed one of its own kind, but possibly an individual so diseased or starved that the live bird had responded to its abnormal behaviour.

Like most nomadic owls, the Great Grey Owl seems to be tolerant of other birds of prey nesting in its territory. Ural Owls, Hawk Owls and Tengmalm's Owls have all nested undisturbed near Great Grey Owls, though all compete with the Great Grey for voles. Short-eared Owl, Pygmy Owl, Kestrel *Falco tinnunculus*, and Spotted Eagle *Aquila clanga* have shared hunting grounds in Finland and Sweden (cf. Wahlstedt 1969), but Hobby *Falco subbuteo* and Long-eared Owl have been seen to attack Great Grey Owls which used the same range (Pekka Helo, *in litt.*).

In addition, there are some interesting observations on the aggressive interactions between Great Grey Owls and other owl species. In Sweden a Great Grey Owl resorted to bill-snapping at a Ural Owl which came within 50 m of its nest (Wahlstedt 1969), but in Finland a pair of Great Grey Owls allowed a Tengmalm's Owl free passage to within 30 m of their nest. On the other hand a Great Grey Owl once ate an adult Tengmalm's Owl in Haapavesi, Finland, as analysis of pellets revealed (Mikkola and Sulkava 1970). On another occasion a Great Grey Owl took and ate a nestling Ural Owl that was no more than 500 m from the Great Grey Owl's nest (Kauko Huhtala, *in litt*). In Canada a dead Barred Owl was found about 15 m from the base of a large black poplar which contained a Great Grey Owl's nest. Unfortunately this adult owl was too badly decomposed to enable the exact cause of death to be determined (Oeming 1955).

The Great Grey Owl can and often will take possession of a nest which a Goshawk *Accipiter gentilis* had already begun to repair and embellish (e.g. Höglund and Lansgren 1968), showing these two species to be highly competitive. Pulliainen and Loisa (1977) described how a male Great Grey Owl defended its nest against an attacking Goshawk by spreading its wings and ruffling its plumage. Similarly, Law (1960) observed a Goshawk make several dives at a Great Grey Owl but the owl merely ruffled its feathers and ducked its head until the Goshawk moved on.

In Canada a Red-tailed Hawk was seen diving at a female Great Grey Owl (Oeming 1955). The owl immediately adopted a defensive attitude, hunching its shoulders and fluffing out its feathers. She made no attempt to fly at the hawk which in turn made no further assaults. Ravens have been seen flying with this owl but never diving at it (Law 1960).

In 1974 a Great Grey Owl nested near a Peregrine *Falco peregrinus* in Finnish Lappland. The owl must have approached too closely to the falcon's nest on one occasion because many Great Grey Owl back feathers were discovered nearby, an indication that fighting had taken place (Seppo Saari, *in litt.*).

The evidence seems clear that the Great Grey Owl, despite its large size, seems to regard large and hawk-shaped birds flying in the vicinity of its nest as potential threats (cf. Pulliainen and Loisa 1977). Even the Hooded Crow *Corvus cornix* is not welcome to nesting Great Grey Owls.

Calls from these species are not necessarily made in order to release a defence reaction in the owls but they might provoke one. Pulliainen and Loisa (1977) observed that when the above-mentioned intruders were within sight of the owls, the male Great Grey immediately flew in from his own position to perch on a branch of the nest tree. The female may also bring the male to the nest by shrill calls.

The Great Grey Owl's diurnal activity in winter has been studied both in Finland and Canada. Leinonen (*in litt.*) discovered that in Central Finland in January the Great Grey Owl would regularly hunt during daylight, five hours at most. During

February the daylight hours have increased to seven or eight and the owls were rarely seen at midday but hunted more often just before or after sunset. In March even the nights are growing light and the owls did not hunt at all in the day-time and there were two sightings only. It seems that the owls prefer to hunt at dusk but will adjust their crepuscular habits in the depths of winter when the day length is so short.

Brunton and Pittaway (1971) have also studied the Great Grey Owl's winter activity but in their study area in Canada the winter day is much longer than in Leinonen's Finnish study area. The peak hunting hours of the Canadian birds were in the early morning, then from late afternoon to dusk. Only after winter storms when the owls were undoubtedly having difficulty in obtaining food was hunting continued throughout the daylight hours. Normally, however, the owls had a 'rest period' about midday, spending much time dozing with perhaps some preening. On several occasions in 1969, Brunton and Pittaway watched the owls from noon until dark (when activity decreased drastically). They checked again after dark (as late as midnight), but reported that the owls had rarely moved and were no longer active.

It would seem therefore that Great Grey Owls tend to be primarily crepuscular or diurnal in their winter hunting behaviour.

The activity of the Great Grey Owl during the incubation period has been thoroughly studied by Pulliainen and Loisa (1977) at a nest in Finnish Lapland. The incubation intensity was most closely recorded during nine 24-hour periods between 6th and 25th May. During this time the female was absent from the nest 0.63% of the time (= 82 minutes). Figure 22 shows the percentages of time spent by the female away from the nest at different times of the day. Between 06.00 and 17.00 hours the female was absent from the nest only once (on 21st May at 13.20–13.23 hours). Usually the female left the nest around midnight (21.00–01.00 hours). Thus the longest incubation period was before and after noon. The duration of four long incubation periods was recorded. They were 651, 868, 1,142 and 1,329 minutes, the average being 997.5 minutes. The duration of other, shorter incubation periods varied between 43 and 487 minutes, the average being 181.2 minutes (number of incubation periods = 21). During these nine days the female left the nest on average 3.1 times per day (night) the range being 1–5. The longest spell of absence was only five minutes and the mean length of 31 spells was 2.8 minutes.

During her absences the female usually moved at a radius of 100–200 m around the nest. She would fly from the nest and perch on a stump where she ejected a pellet and/or evacuated. The female was never observed to evacuate at the nest. Sometimes the female would leave the nest and do nothing in particular, but she was never seen to catch any prey animals during the incubation period.

The female would spend the major part of the incubation sitting quietly on her eggs. She would also shift the eggs, improve her posture by swaying backwards and forwards and from side to side whilst settled, rise up then resettle to face a different direction and ruffle and preen her plumage. The settling movements often followed the other activities. During 120 hours of continuous observation (Pulliainen and Loisa 1977) the female moved her eggs a total of 11 times between 18.00 and 06.00 hours. The female turned the eggs four to five times daily (average 4.4) and ate three times per day.

The fact that the female is larger than the male seems to have some connection with her incubation habits. When compared with other northern bird species, the Great Grey Owl female is an extremely intensive incubator, leaving the nest only 0.63% of

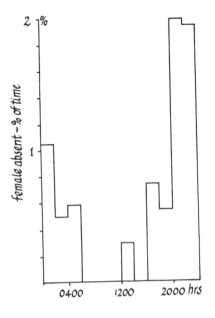

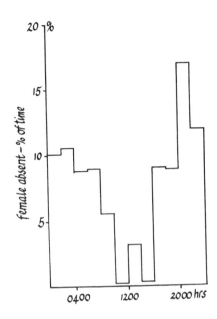

Fig. 22   Absences from nest of a female Great Grey Owl during the incubation period. Material collected by Pulliainen and Loisa (1977, Table 2) during nine 24-hour study periods, between 6th and 25th May 1974 at a nest in Finnish Lapland

Fig. 23   A female Great Grey Owl's absences from the nest during the nestling period. Material collected by Pulliainen and Loisa (1977, Table 2) during twelve days between 27th May and 21st June 1974 at a nest in Finnish Lapland

the time. Rough-legged Buzzard *Buteo lagopus* and Capercaillie *Tetrao urogallus*, for example, studied by Pulliainen (1974, 1971) left their nests unattended 5.0% and 3.9% of the time. Incubation frequently takes place at very low ambient temperatures when the temperature at night regularly drops to −20°C. The female therefore needs a relatively large body to produce heat for incubation and to compensate for heat loss. This in itself does not explain why the male is smaller; the answer lies in its hunting habits. The male Great Grey Owl hunts alone during the incubation period and feeds the female at the nest, and during the first two weeks of the nestling period the male continues to offer prey to the female who then feeds the young. He does not directly offer the food to the young which is more common among altricial birds. The smaller male can hunt more agilely and more deftly than the female, attributes necessary for capturing the small rodents needed by the young chicks. In addition, he can locate and carry food less expensively and is thus capable of fetching it from a greater distance. Even so, the male's size still creates difficulties in hunting in the enclosed forests and it tends to hunt in open country over fields, marshes, clear-cut areas and similar places, especially those where *Microtus* species are available (cf. Mikkola 1976 and Pulliainen and Loisa 1977).

Pulliainen and Loisa (1977) also studied the daily activity throughout the nestling period at a nest in Finnish Lapland in 1974. During the two weeks after the first chick hatched the female warmed her young very intensively, spending 99% of her time at the nest. When the oldest chick was 14 days old the female began leaving the nest for 13% of the time, mostly perching close by.

During the chick-warming period the female was off the nest 1–6 times a day (average 3.7), but when the oldest chick was 15–24 days old the corresponding range was 3–11 (average 5.6). However, during the first period the mean length of 26 absences was 4.0 minutes (range 2–10) and during the latter period the mean length of 28 absences was 33.7 minutes (range 7–105). Figure 23 shows the times spent by the female off the nest at different times of the day during twelve days between 27th May and 21st June. Between 18.00 and 06.00 hours the number of absences was 35, and between 06.00 and 18.00 hours the number was 19. Thus 52% of the absences took place during the eight hours around midnight (20.00–04.00 hours). During these twelve days the female was off the nest a total of 738 minutes between 18.00 and 06.00 hours; and correspondingly 310 minutes between 06.00 and 18.00 hours. The mean length of 19 absences at 06.00–18.00 hours was 17.5 minutes, and that of 35 absences at 18.00–06.00 hours was 20.4 minutes.

In addition to warming the young with her body the female preened and fed them, and also ate the pellets they produced. In rainy weather she formed a protective umbrella for the chicks with her spread wings. The young were also observed preening their mother. In hot weather they panted (Pulliainen and Loisa 1977). The nest was kept clean because the chicks, when defecating, would back to the edge of the nest and discharge over the side (also Oeming 1955).

Pulliainen and Loisa (1977) concluded that during the incubation period, activities at the nest were concentrated in the darker half of the diel cycle, whereas in the nestling period the great need for food forced the male to be active throughout the day. However, it should be remembered that these studies were carried out mainly in continuous daylight, a phenomenon occurring at this latitude for about one month during the summer. This might explain why the Great Grey Owls' activity showed no biphasic rhythm as it did in Central Sweden, which is at a lower latitude and has a distinct, if short, night in midsummer (cf. Wahlstedt 1969).

Grossman and Hamlet (1965) have claimed that the Great Grey Owl is the only truly diurnal member of the *Strix* genus, though becoming more nocturnal in the southern part of its range. This is patently incorrect because in the far north the short nights of summer oblige most of the owls, including the present species, to concentrate their activities around midnight (cf. Mikkola 1970 for Pygmy Owl and Klaus *et al* 1975 for Tengmalm's Owl).

The Great Grey Owl's relatively small eyes would seem to be linked to daytime hunting, presumably another trait associated with long day length in far northern latitudes. Great Grey Owls can see surprisingly well, even in bright sunlight over snow, and it appears that they have good visual acuity. Nero (1980) reported seeing a Great Grey Owl at midday in early February fly at least 200 m to pounce on a vole on top of the snow, apparently having seen the prey from that distance.

Good visual acuity in Great Grey Owls has also been reported by Pittaway and Brunton (1969) who observed that owls responded immediately to a mouse appearing on top of the snow at a distance of 200 m. But my own observations of hunting behaviour support the belief expressed by many others that this owl can find its prey by sound alone (Law 1960, Höglund and Lansgren 1968, Nero 1969), thus enabling it to locate and successfully capture prey beneath snow cover. Within the *Strigidae* family there is a more or less pronounced morphological asymmetry in ear structure. In most species with asymmetrical external ears the asymmetry is confined to the soft anatomy structures. However, the bilateral ear asymmetry also extends to the temporal parts of the skull in Great Grey, Ural and Tengmalm's Owls (Norberg 1977, 1978).

Available evidence suggests that bilateral ear asymmetry in owls serves to make the vertical directional sensitivity patterns differ between the two ears for high frequencies, thus making possible vertical localisation of prey based on binaural comparison of the intensity and spectral composition of sound (Norberg 1977).

The first direct observations of a Great Grey Owl hunting were described by Tryon (1943) who saw an owl making repeated pounces from an elevated position to a certain spot where it finally managed to catch a Pocket Gopher *Thomomys talpoides*. He writes, 'I was astonished to find the same owl, to all appearances, sitting in the same position on the same perch. The owl caught from this perch in a very short time four Pocket Gophers and one mouse.' On examining the spot where a Pocket Gopher was seized, Tryon found that the owl had apparently broken through the thin roof of one of the feeding runways of the gopher's burrow. Thus the position of the prey had been determined by means of auditory stimuli only. With its relatively long toes and talons the Great Grey Owl can grasp over a comparatively large surface and catch a prey animal which may be hiding in moss, or the like, revealing its position by the sound of its movements alone.

The Great Grey Owl's winter hunting methods have been well described in Canada (Law 1960, Godfrey 1967, Nero 1969, Brunton and Pittaway 1971), and in Finland (Kemilä, *in litt.*, Leinonen 1980).

A friend of mine, Eero Kemilä, has managed to take an excellent series of photographs of a Great Grey Owl hunting in the middle part of the day over a snow-covered field in Finland. The snow, which was new and soft on the surface, was more than 50 cm deep but there was a layer of ice about 1 cm thick just below the surface. Small mammals were moving about under this hard layer and none were seen on the surface. The bird must have relied entirely upon its hearing to pin-point the movements of the invisible rodents. (See photos 57–61.)

The usual hunting method of the Great Grey Owl can be described thus. When looking out for prey, the owl most frequently perches on a bush, on a post or part way up a tree. As it watches and listens it turns its head from side to side, occasionally peering intently towards the ground. When listening to a prey animal it may occasionally seem completely unaware of an approaching observer, so much is it concentrating on its intended victim. Pittaway and Brunton (1969) wrote that 'it seems almost hypnotized by the prey activity below.'

When the prey animal is located, the owl flies directly towards and above its target, which is normally not more than 20 m from the vantage point. Often the owl hovers briefly before dropping to the ground.

As it dives downwards its head is suddenly directed towards the prey and it almost seems that the head hits the surface of the snow first. However, both Eero Kemilä and Leinonen (1980) believe that in the instant before hitting the snow the owl will draw back its head, extend its legs and stretch its feet forwards with the talons fully spread. However, the high speed of the dive renders it impossible to prove precisely what does happen by direct observation.

A study of films taken by Veikko Korkolainen in Finland revealed that, usually, the

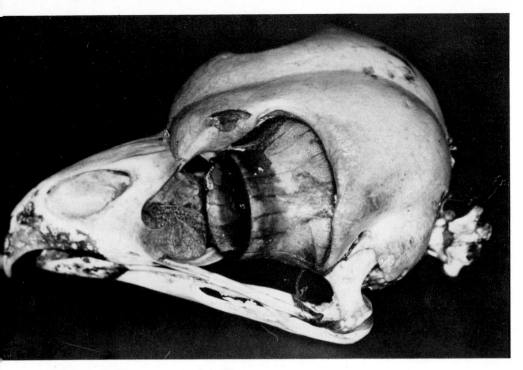

1 Skull of Eagle Owl, with hard parts of the eye in place. *(Pekka Kuhmonen)*

2 Flight feather of Ural Owl. The scanning microscope enlargement shows the superfine edges of the feather webs which, as well as being a reason for the extreme softness of an owl's plumage, are an aid to silent flight. *(Juhani Koivusaari and Alpo Pelttari)*

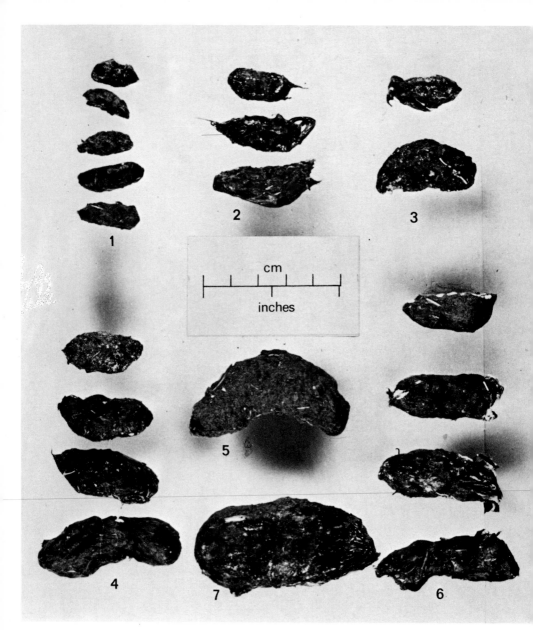

3   A selection of typical pellets from seven owl species: (1) Pygmy Owl, (2) Tengmalm's Owl, (3) Hawk Owl, (4) Short-eared Owl, (5) Great Grey Owl, (6) Long-eared Owl, (7) Eagle Owl. *(Heimo Mikkola)*

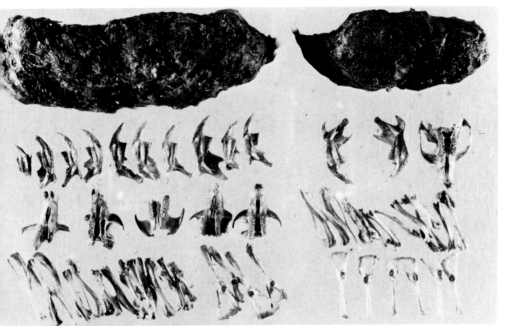

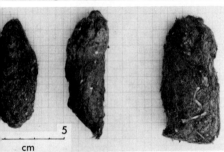

4   Two Great Grey Owl pellets and their contents (small bones, such as ribs, not shown): five Field Voles *Microtus agrestis*, one Bank Vole *Clethrionomys glareolus* and one Wood Lemming *Myopus schisticolor*. (*Heimo Mikkola*)

5   Typical Ural Owl pellets. (*Juhani Koivusaari*)

6   Remains of three Ground Voles *Arvicola terrestris*, the contents of a Ural Owl pellet (100×42×36mm). Note that there is only one skull. (*Juhani Koivusaari*)

7   Barn Owl about to alight, showing the spread of talons. Scotland. *(Donald A. Smith)*

8   Barn Owl that has been hunting in wet herbage. The prey is a vole. Scotland. *(Donald A. Smith)*

9 Male Barn Owl with Field Vole *Microtus agrestis* at nest in disused water tower, 11m above ground level. Wales. *(Graham F. Date)*

10 Barn Owl and young. The oldest and strongest is foremost in this brood about to receive an *Apodemus* mouse. The nest is the same as in Photo 9. *(Graham F. Date)*

11　Striated Scops Owl at its nest in a tree. The 'ear-tufts' are laid flat when the owl is active but not on the alert. USSR. (*E. N. Gojovanovoj*)

12　Whilst brooding her young this female Stria Scops Owl raises its 'ear-tufts' and almost closes eyes to help break its outline and to hide the c spicuous yellow irides. USSR. (*E. N. Gojovano*

13, 14 Two photographs of a migrant Striated Scops Owl caught in a mist net by Israeli ringers at Eilat. A rare item of evidence of the species' continued occurrence in the Middle East. (*Hans Wolhmuth and Morten Müller*)

15 Adult Scops Owl returning to nest site in cherry tree *Prunus sp.* Austria. (*Jakob Zmölnig*)

16 Insects form the bulk of the Scops Owl's food. This bird, nesting in an almond grove *(Prunus amyg dalus)* in southern France, is carrying a bush-cricket *(Tettigoniidae sp.)*. *(Jacques Blondel)*

17 The Scops Owl is one of the smallest European Owls. If seen by day the 'ear-tufts' are generally conspicuous. USSR. *(J. B. Pukinskii)*

18 A brood of young Scops Owls aged three to nine days. Austria. *(Lilli Koenig)*

19　A classic breeding site for an Eagle Owl, high above a river valley, in eastern Czechoslovakia. (*Ladislav Šimák and Jan Švehlík*)

20　Female Eagle Owl with young at a nest in Finnish Lappland, one of the most northerly nests known in its world distribution. (*Seppo Saari*)

21　Female Eagle Owl with two large young. Note the infertile egg on the left. USSR. (*E. N. Gojovanovoj*)

22 The large, white Eagle Owl of western Siberia *Bubo b. sibiricus*, confirms the rules of Bergmann and Gloger that races of cold, harsh climates have lighter and more contrasting coloration, with blackish markings, and are larger than those living in more temperate climes. USSR. (*J. B. Pukinskii*)

23 When danger threatens, the huge Eagle Owl rarely attacks but adopts an impressive threat display. USSR. (*J. B. Pukinskii*)

24   Brown Fish Owl at a daytime roost in eucalyptus tree. Spring 1980, Israel. *(Ami Boldo)*

25–32 Photographs taken at a Snowy Owl nest site in the Hardangervidda, southern Norway. Until Snowy Owls nested in the Shetlands, in the late 1960s, the Hardangervidda was the most southerly breeding area for this predominantly arctic species.

25 Male Snowy Owl near nest. (*Edvard Barth*)

26 Female Snowy Owl alighting near nest. (*Edvard Barth*)

27 Female Snowy Owl on nest. (*Edvard Barth*)

28 Snowy Owl nest site (nest in foreground) on a barren upland plateau. (*Edvard Barth*)

29 Snowy Owl nest scrape with four eggs and three recently-hatched young, surrounded with prey items. (*Edvard Barth*)

30 Snowy Owl female feeding and brooding young. (*Edvard Barth*)

31 Six young Snowy Owls show their asynchronous hatching; there is also an unhatched egg and a pellet from a parent bird. (*Edvard Barth*)

32 Female feeding young Snowy Owls. (*Edward Barth*)

33 *(top left)* Female Hawk Owl brooding at a typical nest site, a hole in a dead tree. Usually, such a nest hole is too deep to expose the sitting bird. Finland. *(Pekka Helo)*

34 *(top right)* Adult female Hawk Owl in injury-feigning display below nest. Finland. *(Pekka Helo)*

35 Hawk Owl photographed during a winter invasion of the species into Finland. *(Hannu Hautala)*

36 (*top left*) Male Pygmy Owl. Finland. (*Hannu Hautala*)

37 (*top right*) Female Pygmy Owl alighting at nest, wings and tail spread for maximum braking. Finland. (*Eero Jussila*)

38 The Pygmy Owl's small size is manifested by the fledgling Redwing *Turdus iliacus* it has caught. The female is able to tackle species as large as itself, but the male usually takes smaller prey. Finland. (*Hannu Hautala*)

39 Adult Little Owl at nest in Wales. Food brought to the nest was mainly earthworms, and caterpillars of Common Wainscot Moth *Leucania pallens* and Ghost Moth *Hepialus humuli*. *(Graham F. Date)*

40 The Little Owl regularly hunts on foot, having legs almost as long as its close relative the ground-dwelling Burrowing Owl *Athene* (formerly *Speotyto*) *cunicularia* of North and Central America. The bird depicted here is one of the pale races of Central Asia, probably *bactriana* or *orientalis*. USSR. *(E. J. Gojovanovoj)*

41 In some parts of their range Little Owls are quite at home in villages and suburban areas. The bird shown is finding shade in the chimney stack of a house in an outer suburb of Istanbul. *(Ian Willis)*

42 Tawny Owl. Wet, windy conditions prevailing at the time almost certainly accounted for the preponderance of earthworms in food brought to this nest in Wales. (*Graham F. Date*)

43 The Tawny Owl's relatively short, broad wings, typical of woodland birds of prey, are well shown in this photograph. Scotland. (*Donald A. Smith*)

44 This Hume's Owl was found near En Gedi by the Dead Sea, apparently suffering from secondary poisoning, and nursed back to health. (*Yossi Leshem*)

45 Hume's Owl roosting during the day in a cave in a wadi of the Tuwaiq Escarpment, Central Saudi Arabia, July. (*M. C. Jennings*)

46 *(top left)* Ural Owls begin breeding early in the year; as shown by the unusually large number of six eggs in this nest in the Slanske Mountains of eastern Czechoslovakia, photographed on 19th March 1977. *(Ladislav Šimák and Jan Švehlík)*

47 *(top right)* Female Ural Owl on eggs after a heavy snowfall. Sweden. *(Carl-Erik Ekman)*

48 Ural Owls once nested almost exclusively in the stumps of dead trees, as is the case with this Finnish bird. *(Pekka Helo)*

49 *(above)* A female Ural Owl reluctant to leave her five- to seven-days old young. Sites such as this raptor's old nest are becoming more commonly used in Europe. The long tail is clearly shown. Czechoslovakia. *(Ladislav Šimák and Jan Švehlík)*

50 *(left)* When brooding a full clutch of young, the female Ural Owl often has a hunch-backed appearance due to its erected back feathers and drooping wings. Czechoslovakia. *(Ladislav Šimák and Jan Švehlík)*

51 *(below)* Ural Owl. The same nest as in Photo 50. *(Ladislav Šimák and Jan Švehlík)*

52 Female Ural Owl attacking visitor to the nest site. Her talons are forward, ready to rake at the intruder's eyes should he be unwary enough to expose his face at this moment. Czechoslovakia. (*Ladislav Šimák*)

53 A male Ural Owl bringing a Field Vole *Microtus agrestis* to the brooding female at a nest site on the upper floor of a grain drying barn in Finland. In recent years outbuildings have occasionally been used as nest sites. (*Hannu Hautala*)

54 A pair of Great Grey Owls at a tree-stump nest in Finland. The female (left) is protecting the young; the male has just arrived with prey, which is concealed by his drooping wing. *(Eero Kemilä)*

55 *(centre)* Great Grey Owl owlet swallowing a Field Vole *Microtus agrestis* which the female has just presented to it. Young Great Grey Owls leave the nest long before they are able to fly. Finland. *(Eero Kemilä)*

56 *(bottom)* Female Great Grey Owl about to attack the photographer. This owl will readily strike a human intruder near the nest, sometimes so vigorously that it injures itself. Finland. *(Antti Leinonen)*

57–61   A remarkable sequence of photographs showing a Great Grey Owl hunting in snow (see text for this species). Finland. (*Eero Kemilä*)

62 A Long-eared Owl erects its 'ear-tufts' in the presence of the photographer. USSR. (*J. B. Pukinskii*)

63 Female Long-eared Owl about to fly at an intruder near the nest. The fluffed-up plumage and loosely-held wings are an intimidation posture. Czechoslovakia. (*Ladislav Šimák and Jan Švehlík*)

64 Adult Long-eared Owl making a feint at the photographer near the nest site. This species, unlike the *Strix* genus, rarely strikes an intruder. Czechoslovakia. (*Ladislav Šimák and Jan Švehlík*)

65 Long-eared Owl's nest with six eggs, a fairly common clutch size for this species in a good vole year. April, Czechoslovakia. (*Ladislav Šimák and Jan Švehlík*)

66 Long-eared Owl parents showing signs of anxiety near the nest; the female is the larger bird at the top, the male below. May, Czechoslovakia. (*Ladislav Šimák and Jan Švehlík*)

67   Adult male Short-eared Owl. Finland. (*Hannu Hautala*)

68　Nest site of Short-eared Owl in a young forestry plantation. Scotland. (*Donald A. Smith*)

69　Female Short-eared Owl brooding young. Finland. (*Hannu Hautala*)

70 African Marsh Owls, like other *Asio* owls covered by this book, can raise or lower their 'eartufts' at will. Kenya. (*J. F. Reynolds*)

71 African Marsh Owl hunting, about an hour after sunrise. Kenya. (*J. F. Reynolds*)

72 Tengmalm's Owl carrying prey to the nest hole. Finland. (*Hannu Hautala*)

73 Tengmalm's Owl about to alight at the nest hole with a vole. Finland. (*Eero Jussila*)

74 Tengmalm's Owl young in nest box showing the pale face markings which act as a guide for the parent birds in the darkness of the nest cavity when feeding the brood. Finland. (*Pekka Helo*)

75 Adult Tengmalm's Owl in winter in Finland. The species is more active by day during the northern winter. (*Pekka Helo*)

feet were brought forward beneath the chin at the last moment. As the owl makes its plunge, the wings are partly closed before the strike so that for the final metre or so there is a rapid acceleration. However, Nero (1980) has several observations, films and photographs showing that the plunge is often made with the feet well back under the tail, the owl entering the snow face foremost. He reported that at five holes an impression of an owl's face was visible, including in one case even the outline of the bill. The heavy facial disc feathers might serve as protection when plunging into snow.

With one exception, all the reported observations I have found refer to capture of the prey by means of the feet, as would be expected if the owl has to capture its prey under snow. Nero's earlier (1971) statement that the prey animals are captured with the feet, and later transferred to the bill, is well supported by the literature. However, Nicholl and Scott (1973) saw a Great Grey Owl capturing a vole with its bill. In this case the vole was above the snow cover for some time, which fact may explain the owl's apparent deviation from the more usual method of capture. Prey animals which come to the surface of their ventilation shafts may also be taken in the same manner.

After capture the prey is usually killed by bites to the head or back of the neck while the owl still has its head under the snow. Usually the owl swallows its prey whole, an act which takes only two or three seconds – it is done so quickly that an observer may easily miss it and conclude that the owl has caught nothing. Great Greys have been regularly observed spending considerable time on the surface of the snow after the prey animal has been eaten, up to five minutes or more. Hunting may continue for hours, for at least two-thirds of the owl's intended victims escape for various reasons, such as deep snow, a protecting twig or other matter covering the prey, or the frozen snow crust. The owl must continue to hunt until its hunger is satisfied.

Craighead and Craighead (1956) reported, on the basis of a feeding experiment, that an adult female Great Grey Owl's maximal daily consumption of food was 162 g. This is in agreement with my own estimate that a single Great Grey Owl would need approximately 150 g of food per day (Mikkola 1970).

Throughout the breeding season the hunting duties are mostly performed by the male alone, the incubating female making no attempt to hunt even though a possible prey victim may approach very closely, such as a squirrel to the rim of the nest (Pulliainen and Loisa 1977). The prime hunting ground is typically an open bog, a clear-cut area or a field not more than a few hundred metres from the nest. The prey is located, mainly by hearing, from a suitable vantage point, usually a small tree, and will be carried from the hunting area through the forest in the talons. When about 50 m from the nest the male will alight and transfer the prey to its bill before flying on to the nest (cf. Wahlstedt 1969), where the female is the constant guardian, either remaining in the nest or very near it. The female receives the prey from her mate with her bill and then either consumes it herself, or, depending on the age of the young, passes the whole animal to them or tears it to pieces for them. The prey is only dealt with in this way whilst the young are unable to devour the animal whole, which they are usually able to manage at about 14 days, sometimes younger, depending on the size of the prey. When the young have reached this stage the male will deliver the prey directly to the nest, especially if the female is absent when he arrives with food (Höglund and Lansgren 1968). Normally, if the female is near the nest when the male arrives, he will carry the prey to the female's perch and the female will then take it to the nest. The female may also keep prey animals for some time at the nest before eating them or feeding them to the young.

When the eggs are hatching and at the beginning of the nestling period, the female does not always accept the prey brought in by the male (Pulliainen and Loisa 1977). If this occurs the male will wait a while before re-submitting his catch to the female. If she remains disinterested in the offer, the male will either leave the prey at the nest or carry it away. Sometimes, when the young are strong enough to devour entire prey animals, the female will take no part in feeding them. Then the male alone delivers prey to them, and also to the female as she sits near the nest (Höglund and Lansgren 1968).

FOOD

For hunting, Great Grey Owls favour open country such as marsh and cleared forest. They release their pellets mainly during hunting while sitting in a suitable vantage point, which may be a prominent tree with thick branches or a birch or alder bent over into an arc by the weight of snow.

Because of their large size Great Grey Owl pellets are easy to find under these watching places. During the breeding season a good number of pellets can be found at varying distances from the nest, but usually within a radius of 50–100 m (Mikkola and Sulkava 1970). The female sometimes eats the owlets' pellets or carries them away from the nest. When the owlets are growing their pellets may remain on the rim of the nest or fall beneath the nest tree.

Pellet measurements have been made in Finland (Mikkola 1971), Sweden (Höglund and Lansgren 1968) and in California, USA (Winter 1981), the results being as follows:

	length (mm)			width (mm)			no. of
	min.	max.	average	min.	max.	average	pellets
Finland	35	110	63	18	44	29	100
Sweden	38	101	66	21	35	26	51
California	29	89	57	20	43	32	32

Although this body of information is relatively small there are only minor differences in average lengths and widths.

The food composition is known to affect the overall size of pellets, and I have also noted that the size of pellets clearly depends of the age of the owlets (Mikkola 1981). When I had two young Great Grey Owls in captivity at the age of two weeks they produced pellets between 30×10 mm and 36×16 mm in size. When the young were three weeks old the pellets were about 48×25 mm and 46×28 mm, and at the age of one month the pellets were around 72×26 mm, which is already more or less the average for adult owls.

Höglund and Lansgren (1968) have measured the dry weight of Great Grey Owl pellets in Sweden. The maximum weight they recorded was 21.7 g and the minimum 4.2 g, the average being 9.4 g for 51 pellets. They also weighed the skeletal remains in these pellets, the maximum being 6.2 g and the minimum 1.2 g, with an average of 2.7 g. The ratio of the weight of a pellet to the weight of the skeletal remains in it is of particular interest. In this material the proportion of bone fragments amounted to only about 30% of the total, whereas the corresponding values for the Eagle Owl (Höglund 1966) and for the Long-eared Owl (Mikkola 1971) are 50% and

40–50%. This seems to indicate that the Great Grey Owl has less bone in its pellets compared with the other two, which could mean that the bone digestion ability of the Great Grey Owl is greater than that of the Eagle and Long-eared Owls. However, it is more likely that this signifies only that the pellets of the Great Grey Owl contain a considerable amount of hair from small rodents and shrews. At least in the Eagle Owl, which feeds on larger animals, the pellets will contain relatively small amounts of hair but more indigestible bones, because muscles and other soft parts, which are entirely digested, make up a greater proportion of the food consumed (cf. Höglund and Lansgren 1968). Therefore, I conclude that the pellets of the Great Grey Owl can give us a comprehensive picture of food items eaten.

Great Grey Owl pellets have been studied during the breeding season between 1955 and 1974 at 37 nests in South and Central Finland (Alaja and Lyytikäinen 1972, Eskelinen and Mikkola 1972 and Mikkola 1971, 1973, 1974 and 1976), 19 nests in Swedish Lapland (Höglund and Lansgren 1968), 4 nests in Finnish Lapland (Pulliainen and Loisa 1977) and at one nest in Kola Halbinsel, USSR (Mikkola 1972). Figure 24 shows the location of the above listed 61 nests in Fenno-Scandia.

A total of 5,177 prey animals has been identified (Table 37). This summarised material shows that Great Grey Owls feed primarily on small mammals, 19 species of which are presented in the Table.

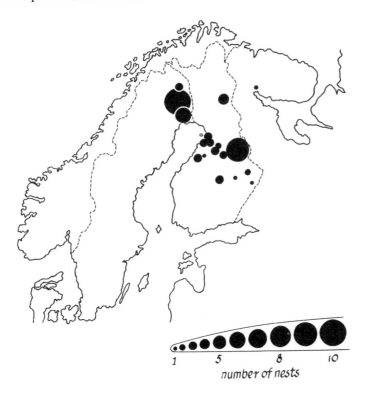

Fig. 24   Localities of 61 nests of Great Grey Owls in Fenno-Scandia where pellets have been studied

The majority of the prey (90%) come from two families of voles, *Microtus* and *Clethrionomys*. Of these, Short-tailed Voles *Microtus agrestis* were easily the most numerous, accounting for 66.2% of the total. Ground Voles *Arvicola terrestris* and Wood Lemmings *Myopus schisticolor* were also present in many samples but only in small numbers, percentages being 1.7 and 1.8 respectively.

Six species of shrews (*Soricidae*) formed 4.5% of the food animals, the great majority (2.8%) of them being Common Shrews *Sorex araneus*.

Mammals other than voles and shrews made up only 0.5%. These consisted of one Mole *Talpa europaea*, one Muskrat *Ondatra zibethicus*, four Red Squirrels *Sciurus vulgaris*, 15 Harvest Mice *Micromys minutus*, one Brown Rat *Rattus norvegicus* and four Pygmy Weasels *Mustela rixosa*.

Of the 82 other animals found in the pellets, 53 (1%) were birds, 26 (0.5%) were frogs *Rana spp.* and 3 (0.06%) invertebrates. Two of these were terrestrial snails (*Gastropode*) and one beetle (*Coleoptera*), all of which were identified at the nest in the Lapland Reserve, USSR by Dr Semenow-Tian-Shanski.

The following 14 bird species or groups were identified: three grouse *Tetraonidae sp.*, two Hazel Hen *Bonasia bonasia*, one Tengmalm's Owl *Aegolius funereus*, one Crossbill *Loxia curvirostra*, three plovers *Charadriidae sp.*, three Fieldfares *Turdus pilaris*, five Redwings *Turdus iliacus*, eight thrushes *Turdus sp.*, two Great Tits *Parus major*, one tit *Parus sp.*, two Redpolls *Carduelis flammea*, ten Chaffinches *Fringilla coelebs*, one Rustic Bunting *Emberiza rustica*, two Jays *Garrulus glandarius* and two unknown birds. In addition, I have included seven young Great Grey Owls consumed by older owlets or adults. These seven victims show that cannibalism is not rare with this owl.

The material demonstrates that despite its varied intake the Great Grey Owl eats small voles and shrews almost exclusively. If one takes the average weights of its prey, it can be seen that animals in the weight group of 10.0–49.9 g constituted 95.2% of the total and 87.7% of the biomass of the prey (Table 37), the next largest but clearly less important group being 100.0–499.9 g. The weight groups of the smallest (less than 10 g) and largest animals (more than 500 g) were of slight importance. The heaviest prey animals in this material were Muskrat, Brown Rat and Red Squirrel. I estimated that 5,177 identified prey animals weighed 169,170 g resulting in the average of 32.7 g per prey animal (Mikkola 1981).

Recently, in California, USA, Winter (1981) estimated that the mean prey weight of the Great Grey Owl was as high as 87.3 g, nearly three times the Fenno-Scandia figure. In California the most abundant prey was the Botta Pocket Gopher *Thomomys bottae mewa*, accounting for 67% of the sample of 150 prey items. By assuming an average weight of 104 g for the Pocket Gopher, Winter estimated that this species alone comprised 84.5% of the prey biomass, when the local *Microtus* vole *Microtus montanus* made only 21% in his material and 10% of the total biomass. However, it is clear that during a good vole year in California *Microtus* voles would form the majority of the sample as well as of the prey biomass. Winter's study year (1980) was clearly a poor vole year in California with a consequent effect on his findings, but they demonstrate that in California the Great Grey Owl is able to compensate for the lack of *Microtus* voles by consuming more Pocket Gophers.

Large mammalian prey such as the Blue Hare *Lepus timidus* have been regularly reported in the literature as a staple food of the Great Grey Owl, but such large prey animals have never been found in pellets. However, on 25th June 1974, Pulliainen and Loisa (1977) witnessed one young Blue Hare being brought to a nest in Finnish Lapland. The female was seen feeding herself and her young with it for 20 minutes, in the evening between 20.35 and 20.55 hours. Also, Blair (1962) found remnants of a hare in the stomach of a female he dissected during a vole plague year in Norway, but he adds that such captures do not appear to be common. In North America, Bent (1938) includes young rabbits *Sylvilagus* and hares *Lepus* in the diet of the nominate race.

In order to obtain a picture of the availability of different small mammals at the nest of Great Grey Owls, two samplings were made in Finland using snap-traps. I did this first between 14th April and 30th July 1972 at two nearby nests in Konnevesi, Finland (Mikkola 1976), and Pulliainen and Loisa (1977) repeated the experiment at a nest in Finnish Lapland between 21st July and 1st August 1974. These results have been summarised in Table 38. A comparison of the trapping results and food composition of the Great Grey Owl shows that in Finnish Lapland the overall percentages of *Microtus* voles (86.0 and 87.6), *Sorex* shrews (5.3 and 2.5) and *Clethrionomys glareolus* voles (8.8 and 9.9) correspond reasonably well with each other. On the other hand among *Microtus* voles the relative proportion of Short-tailed Voles in the food was greater than its general availability in open country habitats had indicated. Also, at Konnevesi, Short-tailed Voles occurred marginally more often in the pellets than in the traps (71.2 vs 15.2%), the case of the Bank Vole being exactly the opposite (12.9% in the food as against 65.2% in the traps). This would seem to indicate that the Great Grey Owl favours Short-tailed Voles in preference to other small mammals and/or that it hunts mainly in microhabitats where the Short-tailed Vole is more numerous than in our trapping results. In Konnevesi the small shrews were present in the Great Grey Owl's pellets although they were not found in the snap-traps. This shows the selectivity of our trapping method and makes the owl's food a better source of information on the existing small mammal fauna in its territory than the trapping results.

In winter it is not easy to find pellets if the owls keep to the woods. However, during large invasions a number of owls often hunt in open fields where there are still plenty of voles available. Their pellets can be found under fence posts or telegraph poles, or under trees surrounding the fields. During the winter of 1981 a large invasion of Great Grey Owls took place in Finland, and winter pellets were collected in three different fields in central and southern Finland (Mikkola 1981).

From these pellets I identified a total of 207 prey animals (Table 39). In this material *Microtus* voles made up about 80% of the food and the remaining 20% consisted of 10 other small mammals. The Red Squirrel *Sciurus vulgaris* was the heaviest prey animal taken by the owls. The winter food does not seem to differ from that of the breeding season.

Many hunters have claimed that the Great Grey Owl regularly feeds in winter on larger animals such as hares and big game birds. And, indeed, it will do so at times. There is a sight observation at Vehkalahti, Finland in 1981 of two Great Grey Owls killing and eating a hare *Lepus sp* and of one of the invading owls taking a Pheasant *Phasianus colchicus* during the same winter. At Porvoo another owl was said to have caught a small cat but unfortunately it left no remains in the pellets I later studied (Mikkola 1981). In Canada a Great Grey Owl has been observed flying with a Snow-shoe Hare *Lepus americanus* in its claws. According to Brunton and Pittaway (1971), the owl was first seen with the hare in a tree about 3 m above the ground.

When flushed, it flew about 200 m with great effort, though steadily losing height, until finally landing with the hare on the snow. A Snow-shoe Hare weighs between 1,362 g and 2,270 g (Peterson 1966), and this observation is truly astonishing when one remembers that the Great Grey Owl typically weighs between 884 (male) and 1,186 g (female). Even so, feeding on hares, house cats and pheasants is definitely rare and some of these records may represent feeding on carrion. The owls may not have killed the animals themselves.

On the basis of all the pellet analyses we can safely conclude that small mammals make up the largest proportion of food for the Great Grey Owl. They do, in fact, seem to be reluctant to change from small voles and shrews to other food and, for this reason, do not normally remain in their territory all winter unless voles are numerous. As soon as the supply of small rodents and shrews falls to a certain minimum, the scarcity will cause, or release, a starvation migration. This would not be the case should the Great Grey Owl be able to stay alive by taking prey such as hares, squirrels, tetraonids, corvids, tits, and several other birds which occur in these areas even in winter.

BREEDING BIOLOGY

It was Sandman (1897) who first suggested that usually the Great Grey Owl would build a nest of its own, very similar to that of the Goshawk. Also, Olofsson (1910) believed that a nest he found was made by Great Grey Owls. Schaaning (1916) believed one Great Grey Owl's nest he saw to be the work of the birds – a loose, artless platform of dry twigs, through which the owlets could be seen from below. Curry-Lindahl (1961) referred to a similar nest and there are other, less trustworthy records of these owls building nests for themselves. Curry-Lindahl maintains that the Great Grey Owl may also enlarge the nest with a wreath of dry sticks and with spruce and pine twigs still carrying their needles.

However, most observations in modern times speak in favour of the idea that the Great Grey Owl does not build or enlarge the twig nest (e.g. Hagen 1952, Höglund and Lansgren 1968, Mikkola 1973, Wahlstedt 1974). Lately, Pulliainen and Loisa (1977) have suggested that the Great Grey Owl completely lacks any instinctive nest-building movements in its behaviour (also Schuster 1930). As this must be a result of a long evolutionary process, it is hard to believe that the situation was very different less than 100 years ago when Sandman (1897) made his observations, but one will probably never know.

Pulliainen and Loisa (1977) point out that many other birds not only build up a new nest every year but continue some kind of nest-building movements throughout the nesting period. The Capercaillie *Tetrao urogallus* and the Dotterel *Charadrius morinellus*, for instance, whose nests are only shallow hollows in the ground, remove small particles (sticks, feathers, etc) throughout the incubation period, and thus perform nest-building movements (Pulliainen 1971). The Great Grey Owl, however, does not perform any nest-building activities, it only scratches the bottom of the nest site.

In old stick nests such scratching of the centre brings some twigs to the edge of the nest. The twigs accumulate at the rim and these may be misinterpreted as additions made by the owl. Sometimes the owl may excavate a thin hawk's nest too thoroughly and the bottom may drop out (cf. Höglund and Lansgren 1968).

In conclusion one may say that, like most owls, the Great Grey Owl never provides new material but only deepens the bottom of the nest. Goshawks start to enlarge or build their nests at the same time that the Great Grey Owls are looking for suitable nests. Thus, all fresh twigs seen on an owl's nest could have been brought by a Goshawk nesting nearby, and it frequently happens that the Great Grey Owl will take possession of a nest which a Goshawk has already begun to repair and refurbish.

In Finland, 185 nests of the Great Grey Owl have been studied closely enough in the years 1890–1981 to say that 82.7% (153) of them have been twig nests, 13% stump nests, 2.7% on flat ground, 0.5% on cliffs (rock face), 0.5% on a large stone and 0.5% on a barn roof (Table 40). Instances of nesting in buildings have never been recorded before 1976, as far as I know, when one took place at Kaavi, Finland. Tree stumps (21) used as nest sites in Finland were 0.7 to 5.0 m high, the average being 1.8 m. I have included in this category of nests two special ones on an upturned rootstock of a fallen spruce (Vesanto 1972 and Sievi 1973).

The original builders of the stick nests used by Great Grey Owls in Finland are listed below:

Builder	%
Goshawk *Accipiter gentilis*	56.6
Buzzard *Buteo buteo*	17.9
Goshawk or Buzzard	2.8
Honey Buzzard *Pernis apivorus*	4.1
Rough-legged Buzzard *Buteo lagopus*	4.1
Golden Eagle *Aquila chrysaetos*	2.1
Osprey *Pandion haliaetus*	0.7
Sparrowhawk *Accipiter nisus*	0.7
Unknown raptor	2.7
Raptors total	91.7
Magpie *Pica pica*	2.1
Hooded Crow *Corvus cornix*	2.1
Raven *Corvus corax*	0.7
Man-made artificial stick nests	3.4
	100.0
Number of nests studied	145

Together, Goshawks and Buzzards are the original builders of over 77% of all stick nests used by Great Grey Owls. Near Kemi in Finland, in 1977, Rauhala (1980) with the help of friends made 20 artificial stick nests for Great Grey Owls. Five of these nests were already occupied by the owls during the next summer of 1978.

In Finland, the Great Grey Owl has never been known to nest in a nest box or in a real hole, although holes and crevices are typical nest sites for other *Strix* owls. This is true even when the boxes are large enough for Great Grey Owls. Two friends of mine, Pekka Helo and Antti Leinonen, have made a new type of box specifically for Great Grey Owls, in Kainuu, Finland. These boxes are about 40 × 30 cm in size with a height of only 15 cm, and they are left open at the top. So far only one of the boxes has been accepted by a Great Grey Owl. It marked the box with its feathers and started to excavate the soft material in the bottom, but nothing more happened, and later the owl was found dead near the box. Antti Leinonen believed that a Goshawk nesting nearby had killed the owl.

Tree stumps used by the Great Grey Owl differ distinctively from those of the Ural Owl. Great Grey Owls do not use hollow stumps with a deep cavity, instead the eggs are laid in a shallow depression (from 2 to 15 cm) dug by the female on top of the stump. Thus, the Great Grey Owl would seem to be thoroughly adapted to so-called open nesting. Even the shape of the eggs is more oval than those of the Ural and Tawny Owls.

The number of Great Grey Owls with a preference for stump nests varies in different parts of Finland (Table 40). Nesting on stumps seems to be almost three times more common in southern parts of the country compared with the central and northern areas, though the reason is not known. With its dense plumage the Great Grey Owl, even when young, is well adapted to the cold climate. It is known that sunshine often forces the young to leave the nest when they are still very small and quite unable to fly. Nests on a low stump instead of in a hawk's old nest are obviously better protected from excessive sunshine – and at least it is easier to jump down from the stump. As a result, nests on stumps should be more common in mild springs, and in cold summers the owls will not be troubled high up in a hawk's old nest even in the south. The summer of 1972 was very warm and all four nests found in my southern study area (Vesanto and Konnevesi) were on stumps, which adds support to my hypothesis.

In California, USA, the Great Grey Owl breeds at the most southerly point of its world distribution range. Only five confirmed nests have ever been found, but all have been on the top of large stumps (Winter 1980). This information seems to be further confirmation that nesting on stumps is more common in the southern parts of its breeding range. In Canada, Oeming (1955) had a larger incidence of nesting by Great Grey Owls and only two records of nesting on old spruce stumps. The other nests were formerly those of Red-tailed Hawk *Buteo jamaicensis*, Goshawk, the Great Horned Owl *Bubo virginianus* or, occasionally, crows.

In Finland the location of nest sites has varied from birch forest to an old spruce wood; the biotopes of 106 nests studied were as follows (Mikkola 1981):

	%
Damp heath coniferous forest	45
Dry heath coniferous forest	11
Spruce bog	35
Pine peat bog	6
Herb-rich forest	3
	100

It seems that a suitable nest is often more important than the immediate habitat in which it is found.

The Great Grey Owl, earlier known as an inhabitant of the wilds in Finland, has nowadays been found breeding near farmhouses (on two occasions within 300 m) in two different localities (e.g. Aarnio and Häyrinen 1967). On one occasion the nest was only 40 m from a small cottage which was used occasionally by foresters (Oulu 1970).

The only true nesting near civilisation, however, took place at Kaavi in 1976 when the owl nested on a barn roof in the middle of fields, less than 200 m from houses.

A marsh and an area cleared by felling were within 150 m of some of the nests, and a stream, cultivated land, a lake and a house were at varying distances as shown below:

	Min.	Max.	Average	Nests
Marsh	5	1,000	147	52
Area cleared by felling	0	500	142	44
Stream	20	1,000	339	27
Lake	10	10,000	1,151	45
Cultivated land	0	10,000	1,240	51
House	200	10,000	1,967	51

Min. = shortest distance in metres.
Max. = longest distance in metres.

The proximity to the nests of marsh and cleared forest is indicative of the owl's hunting technique and requirements because this species favours open terrain.

The choice of the nest biotope is determined in part by the location of the available nests of other birds of prey. In Finland almost 60% of the Great Grey Owls nested in old nests of Goshawks, and the Goshawk habitually breeds in desolate old spruce forests and on pine moors. It is also common for Goshawks to nest near marshes, clearings, small fields and riversides (v. Haartman *et al* 1967–72).

As in Finland, stick nests are the most common nest types of Great Grey Owls in Sweden. Höglund and Lansgren (1968) and Wahlstedt (1969) knew of no other nest types for this owl and the original builders of the 23 nests they recorded were: Goshawk (8 times), Buzzard (5), Honey Buzzard (5), Rough-legged Buzzard (2), man-made (2) and Raven (1). As noted, the Swedish ornithologists were successful with artificial stick-nests on two occasions, and since the publication of the above details, two more man-made stick-nests have been used by Great Grey Owls in Sweden. The details of all four are as follows:

Place	Year	Author
Övertorneå	1961	Höglund and Lansgren 1968
Pajala	1964	Höglund and Lansgren 1968
Boden-Luleå	1973	Wahlstedt 1974
Boden-Luleå	1977	Stefansson 1978

The first record in Sweden of Great Grey Owls nesting on a tree stump was in 1973 (Wahlstedt 1974). The nest was on top of a thin (diameter 20–25 cm) birch stump at a height of 8–9 m. Later, three more stump nests were found by Wahlstedt (*in litt.*) in 1973 and 1974. And recently, Stefansson (1978) found a Great Grey Owl nesting on a stump which was only 60 cm high. In addition to these typical nest sites there is a Swedish record of a Great Grey Owl nesting in a nest box. Nest boxes are clearly the most common nest sites for all other *Strix* species (Tawny and Ural Owl) in Fenno-Scandia (cf. Lahti and Mikkola 1974) but the Great Grey Owl has never been recorded using them before. Unfortunately, Wahlstedt (1974) gives no further information about this observation, so it is not known what type of nest box it was or its dimensions.

In Canada, Dr Nero has specialised in making artificial twig nests for the owls and his efforts have been well rewarded. He wrote to me in 1978: 'Good response to our man-made nests, e.g. of five nests built last December (1976) along a three-mile stretch of a road, three nests were occupied by pairs of Great Grey Owl the following April. Preferred habitat hereabouts seems to be Tamarack *Larex laricina* – even stunted stands of Tamarack, and even fairly dense. Great Greys fly through that stuff like grouse.'

Recently, in his book, Nero (1980) tells that the total number of nests built by him and his colleagues is about a hundred. To date, of 32 recent Great Grey Owl nestings, 16 were in man-made nests, six in rebuilt nests and ten in completely artificial nests. In addition, their man-made structures were used by Great Horned Owls twice, Long-eared Owls twice and Red-tailed Hawks five times. The best response has been obtained from nests built in spruce-tamarack or tamarack bogs, often over water. In such areas where natural nests are scarce, man-made nests seem to be a useful management technique.

The Great Grey Owl male may begin seeking nest sites as early as mid-February. The male plays an important role in finding a suitable nest but the female probably makes the final choice. Prior to egg-laying a female may visit more than one nest, accidentally losing several feathers in the process. This is why one often finds fresh feathers in nests visited by the owls from mid-February into May. Selection of a nest site seems to be based in part on the presence of high prey population (Nero 1980).

In Finland and Sweden, dates of egg-laying usually range from mid-April to mid-May. According to Helo *et al* (1980), in 1977 the first eggs were laid at Kainuu, Finland, on 24th April and the latest nest was started on 10th May, and on average the first egg was laid in 16 nests on 1st May. In the following year (1978) the earliest egg-laying was 6th April and the latest 28th April, the average for the first egg laid, in nine nests, was 18th April. This difference between the years possibly depends on rodent abundance. Egg-laying clearly starts later if prey is scarce.

In Professor Merikallio's large amount of information the earliest nest ever recorded in Finnish Lapland was one containing six eggs found on 16th April 1904 at Muonio. With an egg-laying interval of three days, this clutch would have been begun by end of March. 1904 was an exceptionally good vole year, explaining this early timing. The latest nest to be found was on 19th June 1916, at Kittilä, containing five eggs. It is always possible that such a late nest is a replacement of an earlier one or even a second one.

An old egg-collector, Sandman (1897), wrote that it was easy to collect a large number of Great Grey Owl eggs because a second clutch was laid if the first one was removed. During good vole years the owl may lay as many as three clutches, but I hope that egg-collectors are now approaching extinction (before the Great Grey Owl) so that no one will test this habit any more.

There is an observed instance of replacement breeding in Sweden, where Höglund and Lansgren (1968) found a nest with eggs at the beginning of May. Later, on 28th May the nest was surprisingly empty but on 4th June there were two eggs in it and by 19th June the clutch numbered four.

Schaaning (1916) maintains that, as a rule, as much as 6–12 days elapse between the appearance of the third or fourth egg and its successor in larger clutches, whereas smaller clutches are laid at the rate of an egg a day. One female he kept under observation nevertheless laid her last two eggs in the course of 24 hours. Recently, in

Finland (1978), Antti Leinonen (*in litt.*) discovered that in a nest of five eggs, four were laid with 24-hour intervals, and only three days elapsed between the fourth and fifth eggs. This may be a normal case, the twelve-day interval being the extreme.

Among 241 clutches recorded in northern Europe between 1864 and 1977, the clutch size varied from 1–9, with an average of 4.4 (Mikkola 1981). The clutch size in Finland in 1966 was 4.6 ± 0.37 (7 nests) but in the following summer it was only 3.3 ± 0.29 (7 nests) due to the lower prey density. Clutch size seems to become larger from south to north, as is usual with birds. According to Mikkola (1981), the average clutch size in south Finland (60°–64°N) is 3.9 (12 nests), in north Finland (64°–68°N) it is 4.4 (58 nests) and in north Norway (70°N) it has been as large as 4.8 (8 nests) (Schaaning 1916).

Average clutch sizes as well as variations in egg numbers of the Great Grey Owl are much higher than those of other *Strix* owls in Europe. In Finland, the clutch size of the Ural Owl averaged 3.0 in 59 nests studied by Linkola and Myllymäki in 1969, with minimal influence on egg-laying by vole numbers. This is close to the Tawny Owl which, in Finland, lays on average 3.3 eggs (188 nests, Linkola and Myllymäki 1969). The clutch size of the Tawny Owl fluctuates like the Great Grey Owl's in accordance with vole populations. An explanation for this difference among the *Strix* owls can be found in their food habits. The Ural Owl, which has the most varied diet, has less variable egg numbers and a lower clutch size. The clutch size and the variations in egg numbers are greatest in Great Grey Owls, which have the most restricted prey species, mainly voles and shrews. In this context the Great Grey Owl resembles more the Snowy and Hawk Owls and both *Asio* owls than its close relatives the Tawny and Ural Owls. Under certain circumstances no breeding takes place among the rodent-feeding owls.

Even though the average clutch sizes of the three *Strix* species are so noticeably different (Ural 3.0, Tawny 3.3 and Great Grey Owl 4.4), there are not such clear differences in percentage terms between the clutch weight and the female's weight, these being Ural 17%, Tawny 20% and Great Grey Owl 19% (Mikkola 1981). It is known that smaller owl species lay much heavier clutches relative to body weight, the corresponding figure for Pygmy Owl being about 67% (Heinroth 1922).

Although most owl eggs are round, those of the Great Grey Owl are ovoid or conical, which has been seen as an adaptation to the open nest site (Mikkola 1973). The female alone incubates the eggs and, depending on weather and temperature, may sit on the nest for 24 hours daily, despite snow and cold, wind and rain.

According to Pukinsky (1977), the incubation period for a Great Grey Owl egg is about 28 days. Antti Leinonen found one Great Grey Owl's nest in 1978, at Hyrynsalmi, before all the eggs were laid, and calculated that the fourth egg had been incubated 29–30 days before hatching. However, there is one record showing that incubation may last much longer. At a nest studied by Pulliainen and Loisa (1977) in Finnish Lapland the incubating female was seen on 21st April. The first chick hatched on 27th–28th May, so that the length of this particular incubation period was at least 36 days.

Chicks hatch at intervals of one to three days. At Konnevesi in 1972 the first chick hatched on 20th May, the second on 21st May and the third the following day. However, the fourth chick hatched either on 24th or early on 25th May, two or three days after the third (Mikkola 1981). The newly-hatched young weigh 37–38 g (Höglund and Lansgren). In Finland, only one owlet has been weighed at hatching, on 2nd June 1970 at Oulu, and its weight was 40 g. The growth rate of the chicks is rapid, particularly during their first days of life. The fact that they can almost treble their weight in five days and attain a weight of about 500 g by 14 days demonstrates the importance of an ample supply of food items. It is also evident how susceptible this 'specialist' species is to variations in the rodent supply.

An assured abundance of food is necessary for the normal development of a brood. In Konnevesi (1972) the weight of the oldest chick increased from 40 g to 225 g in one week whereas the corresponding figures for the youngest chick were only from 40 g to 90 g. This smallest owlet was eaten by the older ones when 14 days old. A few days earlier I had already seen the oldest and strongest chick trying to swallow the youngest because it was too weak to defend itself (Mikkola 1976).

It seems to be fairly common that owlets left behind in their development because of the scarcity of food will succumb sooner or later to juvenile cannibalism or starvation.

In Finland, from 42 nests whose clutch sizes were known, 80.5% of the eggs hatched and 72.1% of the chicks left the nest. Thus, only 58% of the eggs survived and the average number of young leaving the nest was 2.4 (Mikkola 1981). Man was responsible for the disappearance of 12 eggs and 9 owlets, and is clearly the owl's main enemy.

Great Grey Owl young are incapable of flight when they leave the nest. They leave the nest at from 20–29 days, the weights varying between 425 and 630 g (Höglund and Lansgren 1968, Mikkola 1976). Even though they cannot fly, they are surprisingly agile, climbing and flapping their way up trunks and limbs. After 6–8 weeks they are usually still near the nest and stay together and may remain within the territory for some months while the female keeps guard.

Recently, in 1974, Pulliainen and Loisa (1977) studied the feeding activities of Great Grey Owls in Finnish Lapland. During the period 6th May to 21st June they recorded that the male brought 137 prey animals to the nest, but the female only 6, during 504 observation hours. Throughout the incubation period only the male brought prey animals to the nest, the numbers varying between 3 and 5 (mean 3.7) per day. All these animals were vole-sized, and the female devoured 3 or 4 entire animals per day. She clearly regulated her food consumption and when, on 24th/25th May, the male brought in five animals, the female accepted only four; the fifth was carried away by the male. If one takes 50 g as the mean weight of prey animals, then the female consumed 150–200 g of food daily (Pulliainen and Loisa 1977). During the hatching period (27th to 31st May) the male brought her 4–7 animals (mean 5.7) daily (Fig. 25), and in three days of the four day period the female accepted only 11 of 17 prey animals offered; the remaining six were carried away by the male. On 30th/31st May the female ate two entire animals herself and tore three apart for the young.

At the beginning of the nestling period (3rd to 12th June) only the male brought prey animals to the nest (Fig. 25), but after 14th June the female was observed to bring in a few prey animals. The number of vole-sized animals brought by the male varied between 7 and 14 (mean 9.7) daily, while the female brought at most two such animals daily. During nine days of an 18-day period, 93 vole-sized animals were brought in, four of which were eaten exclusively by the female. She tore 48 prey animals to pieces for her young, eating parts of 26 at the same time for herself. The young consumed 37 entire animals and three animals were carried away by the male and one by the female.

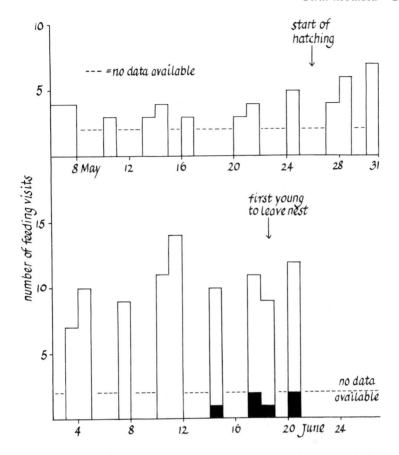

Fig. 25 *Daily feeding visits of Great Grey Owl at a nest in Finnish Lapland (Pulliainen and Loisa 1977). Black columns represent females, white columns males*

When the oldest chick was 11 days old it was seen for the first time swallowing whole a vole-sized prey animal, and a second about four hours later. During 24 hours on 20th/21st June when the owlets were 20–24 days old they ate 11 vole-sized animals. At that time the oldest chick was outside the nest and the female did not herself feed at the nest (Pulliainen and Loisa 1977).

In the summer of 1970 I had two young Great Grey Owls at home between 13th June and 30th August. Both of them were brought to me because they had been found lying under different nest trees. It is probable that the largest owlet in each nest had driven out the youngest, and this was why they were not put back in the nests but brought to me.

Whilst in my possession the owls were free to move around for most of the time, either inside our house or in the garden, but at night they were kept outside in a large cage (2.5 × 2 × 3 m). The owls were fed with voles, shrews and mice as in the wild. Sometimes as an experiment I gave them fish, birds and earthworms, all of which

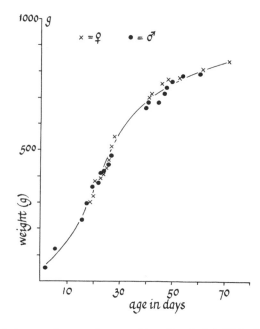

Fig. 26   *Weight increase of two captive young Great Grey Owls in Finland (Mikkola 1981)*

were accepted without hesitation. At the end of that summer our house was becoming too small for these full-grown owls (which had become quite tame) and so I gave them to the Korkeasaari Zoo in Helsinki, Finland, where Dr Ilkka Koivisto promised to take special care of them. Next spring the zoo established that one of my owls was a male and the other a female, as I had suspected at the beginning, and in the following text I will separate male and female where relevant.

It was known that the male had hatched on 28th May as so was 16 days old when brought to me on 13th June. The young female's original nest had not been so well studied, but most likely she was 19 days old when I received her (15th June). The young male was 23 days when I first noticed him making typical owl-like head-bobbing movements, waving his head up and down and from side to side. This kind of head-bobbing may seem amusing to the observer but it is only the owl attempting to assess what it sees as fully as possible before deciding what action to take. They improve their three-dimensional vision by constantly moving and bobbing their heads so that both eyes view the object under scrutiny from a variety of slightly different angles (cf. Everett 1977).

When less than 21 days old the young owls were sleeping on their bellies, rather like a dog, their bills touching the ground, and until 24 days old they would lean against each other when sleeping. Later they would drowse in an upright position, separately on their perch. At 40 days the owls started to tear prey animals to pieces, holding them firmly with both feet. At the same time they manifested various hunting movements, especially when at large in the garden, where they usually tried to catch everything which moved. At 55 days my young owls were able to fly quite well but probably in the wild they would have learnt to fly a little earlier (cf. Portenko 1972).

At night the young owls were often extremely alarmed if a cat, hedgehog or dog was close to the cage but during the day the young female easily managed to terrify a large dog by jumping onto a fence, snapping her bill loudly and taking up her defensive posture. In this position the spread wings hang far behind and the owl ruffles its feathers to try to look as large as possible.

Whenever an aeroplane flew over the house they were very afraid and took up a typical defensive position and used a special quivering voice which clearly expressed great anxiety, and an eagle-like kite caused this same reaction.

The daily food intake for an adult Great Grey Owl is about 150 g per day (Mikkola 1970), 150–200 g (Pulliainen and Loisa 1977) or even 180–320 g (Eck and Busse 1973). All of these estimates seem to be far higher that the average requirements of the young owls in my study. During a 50-day experiment the male ate on average 76.4 g per day, and the corresponding figure for the young female was 80.6 g per day.

Figure 26 shows the weight increase of my owls including three first weighing values which were obtained in the field. The weights of the young male and female are, perhaps surprisingly, equal at the beginning of life (60 days at least), when one remembers that the adult female is approximately 300 g heavier than the male.

DISTRIBUTION

The Great Grey Owl belongs, like the Ural Owl, to the Siberian faunal type, but occupies a vast circumpolar range in boreal climatic zones and boreal mountain regions (Voous 1960). It is, incidentally, the only species of the *Strix* genus that occurs both in Eurasia and North America.

GREAT GREY OWL

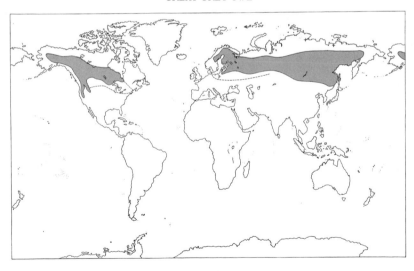

◗ breeding distribution

------ southern limit of occasional winter wanderers

+ records of autumn wanderers in northern Siberia

In the Old World this owl is found in northern Norway, Sweden, Finland, perhaps Poland, and in the Soviet Union.

In Norway the Great Grey Owl breeds in Nord-Trondelag, in the upper part of Anarjokka, in the inner part of Finmarksvidda and in Øver Pasvik. However, breeding has been proved in these areas only when this owl has been very numerous elsewhere in Fenno-Scandia. Schaaning (1916) found 14 nests of this owl in Pasvik in 1904 and this is still the highest number ever found in Norway. Between 1905 and 1962 there are only five published records of nests from Norway: one in 1921, one in 1934 and three in 1937 (Haftorn 1971). After that the Norwegians have some reports in summer in 1962, 1963, 1966, 1969 and 1972 indicating breeding, but no one has made a serious search for a nest (cf. Mikkola 1981).

This owl breeds in Sweden in the northern coniferous forests of Lapland and Norrbotten, but some nests have been found as far south as Jämtland and in Ångermanland (Höglund and Lansgren 1968). In the 1960s the main breeding area in Sweden was around and to the north of the Arctic Circle, towards 68°N. But in the 1970s the highest concentration of breeding Great Grey Owls was found in the coastal district of Norrbotten between 65° and 66°N (Wahlstedt 1974 and 1976).

For security reasons Swedish ornithologists have ceased publishing distribution maps for this owl (cf. Everett and Sharrock 1980), though I feel that this overestimates the risk. I do not believe anyone could find any of my Great Grey Owl nests if I were to give him a dot covering at least an area of 100 km². The situation might be different in Great Britain where a dot may include a certain island or a small forest which can be searched thoroughly.

There are several Swedish reports listing the nest records of the Great Grey Owl between 1954 and 1978 (Höglund and Lansgren 1968, Stefansson 1978 and Wahlstedt 1974 and 1976). As shown in Fig. 27, breeding records have been more common in the last few years. For instance, in 1977 no less than 40 nests were found in Sweden, and during the previous vole year, 1974, Wahlstedt (1976) knew of 32 nests. In the 1960s the maximum annual number of known nests in his area was eight (in 1966).

In Finland between 1954 and 1981 the Great Grey Owl has bred in all parts of the country, not just in the treeless regions in Lapland and in a narrow coastal belt in the most south-westerly part of Finland.It has also bred on Hailuoto Island near Oulu, but not on the Åland archipelago between Finland and Sweden. But it is only in extremely good vole years that nests are spread all over this area. More often nests are found only in northern Finland or in some years (such as 1973) in south-west and central Finland. In 1981 all the nests were in the south-eastern parts of the country, mostly near the Russian border.

Figure 27 shows the number of nests I know to have been found in Finland between 1954 and 1981. I have to remind the reader that this does not mean that all nests have been reported to me, or that we find more than a small proportion of the existing nests each year. Naturally, we have tried to locate as many nests as possible every year, but in our forests, and with this owl, the task is a huge one.

However, Fig. 27 demonstrates how the three or four year vole cycle clearly governs the numbers of breeding Great Grey Owls. Breeding peaks are all during the best vole years. After one or two peak years there is always a drastic decline and for some years almost no nests are found, then the numbers slowly begin to increase again. This same Fig. 27 also shows the increase of owl-watching in Finland since the 1960s. It is believed, however, that more intensive owl-watching is not the only reason

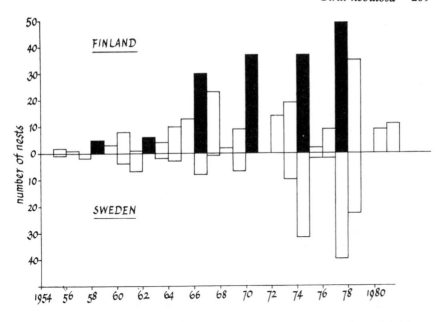

Fig. 27   Great Grey Owl nests recorded in Finland 1954–81, and Sweden 1954–78 (Mikkola 1981 and this study). Black columns are good voles years in Finland

why so many more Great Grey Owls have been found breeding in peak years in the 1960s and 1970s compared with those of the 1950s.

The fact that the Great Grey Owl has become more common in Finland from 1954 to 1981 may be connected with the climate which has become colder (cf. Mikkola and Sulkava 1969). A friend of mine, Kauko Huhtala, in his unpublished PhD thesis shows that climatic changes have produced a similar increase for several northern and eastern bird species in Finland, as well as for the Great Grey Owl.

There is far less available information on the distribution and numbers of the Great Grey Owl in the Soviet Union than in Fenno-Scandia. However, we have some recent data for the European areas of the USSR. According to Dr Semenov Tian Shanski (*in litt.*), two nests of the Great Grey Owl were located in 1964 in the Murmansk district but apart from these he knows of only three single sight observations between 1941 and 1973. More recently, Dr Pukinsky (1977) wrote that there is one Great Grey Owl pair every 30 km in the Archangel area. Some observations made by Finns during the Second World War suggest that there may be an even higher density of Great Grey Owls just behind the Finnish-Russian border. Taxidermist Aug. Artimo wrote to Professor Merikallio that during the war he saw 72 Great Grey Owls in 1942–43 in eastern Karelia, now in the USSR, and that people sent him about 300 Great Grey Owls killed in that period from the area between Lake Ladoga and Lake Ruka (Kuusamo, Finland). Which is why Mr Artimo suggested that the owl should be named the East Karelian Owl instead of the Lapland Owl as it is called in Finland and in most European countries (cf. Mikkola 1981).

Pukinsky (1977) knows of only six nest records ever in the Leningrad district; and in Estonia the owl has bred only during the first half of this century and not since according to Randla (1976).

In Poland the Great Grey Owl has officially nested only twice, in the Bialowieza forest in the 1930s, these nests being the most southern ones in Europe (Grote 1949). The last Great Grey Owl record was in this same forest in June 1953 (Borowski 1961). However, between 1966 and 1971 Dr Jablonski found many Great Grey Owl nests in Masovia (Mazowiecka) district in Central Poland according to his paper published in 1976. Although I have been warned from Poland not to cite Dr Jablonski's records because of their possibly uncritical nature, I wish to do so as it is almost impossible to prove or disprove observations made at least ten years ago. Similar circumstances have occurred in Finland where two Great Grey Owl pairs bred in 1958 at Loimaa, south-west Finland. A friend of mine, Heikki Kangasperko, published his records and even sent two young from these nests to the national zoo in Helsinki. Professor E. Merikallio, however, discounted the records on the grounds that the Great Grey Owl had never earlier been found so far south in Finland. When publishing their Finnish book *Pohjolan Linnut* (Nordic Birds), v. Haartman *et al* (1967) also ignored some southern nests, regarding them as unsubstantiated, and showing themselves to be influenced by the Finnish name for the species, Lapland Owl. Generally, I am inclined to believe that the Great Grey Owl is much more common in Poland and in the European parts of USSR, especially in the district of Leningrad and in Estonia, than previously stated, and so I prefer to believe Dr Jablonski's reports. He maintains that the Great Grey Owl bred in 1966 and 1967 near Antonowo, in 1966, 1967 and 1970 near Garnek, and in 1971 in the nearby village of Brok. Also, Pukinsky (1977) believes that the Great Grey Owl still breeds quite near to Poland in Lithuania and in Belorussia, although it was clearly more common in Belorussia only, at the beginning of this century, around 1902 and 1903.

It is interesting to note that during the Pleistocene Period (3 million to 10,000 years ago) the Great Grey Owl also inhabited Romania according to fossil findings (cf. Burton ed. 1973).

In Siberia this owl breeds south to Tuyraen, Tara, Altai, Transbaikalia, Amur River region and to the north on Obdorsk, Taz river to 65°N, Yakutia to 68°N and in the east to the forested parts of the Anadyr River basin and Koryak Land (Peuzhina River), the Okhots coast and Sakhalin Island (cf. Dement'ev *et al* 1951).

In the New World its known breeding range runs from central Alaska and Canada south in the western mountains to central California (e.g. Sierra Nevada 37°N), northern Idaho, western Wyoming and Montana, extreme north-western Minnesota and south-central Ontario (Godfrey 1966). In Canada, the heart of its North American range, it breeds in most of British Columbia, northern and central Alberta, northern Saskatchewan, in Manitoba, Ontario and in Quebec (Nero 1980). Though divided into two separate populations, North American *S. n. nebulosa* and Eurasian *S. n. lapponica* both have almost all features in common, and for the most part can be treated as one. The Eurasian subspecies is, however, slightly paler and more strongly streaked than its North American counterpart.

The status and distribution of the Great Grey Owl in North America is poorly known but Nero (1980) has estimated that there may be upwards of 50,000 birds.

Practically nothing is known about the density of Great Grey Owl populations in the Soviet Union but in eastern Siberia (Yakutia) it is said to be common (Dement'ev *et al* 1951).

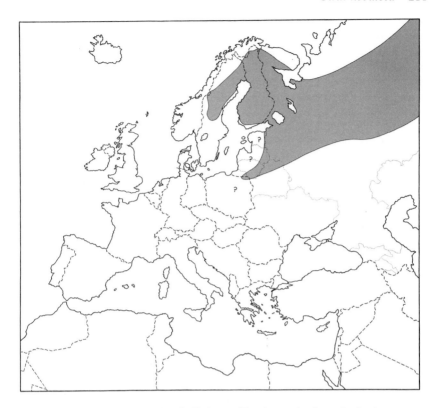

GREAT GREY OWL – breeding distribution – resident, but occasionally wanders in winter to Germany, northern Ukraine and southern Urals

In Sweden there are more than a hundred breeding pairs in good vole years (Ulfstrand and Högstedt 1976); and in Finland, from my own observations in central and southern regions, I believe that there may be more than a thousand nests in good years. This figure may sound too high when recalling that a maximum of 49 nests were known in 1977, one of the best vole years, but one has to remember how vast the forests are in Finland and how secretive this owl can be when nesting, and how seldom they are to be seen away from nest sites.

I have long believed that the Great Grey Owl leads an essentially nomadic life, erupting through the coniferous zone westwards as well as southwards in response to food availability and thus to climatic conditions, but too few owls have been ringed and recovered to date to establish this hypothesis as to its movements. On the contrary, there are several examples of pairs that have bred (or at least have stayed) for two or even more consecutive years at the same nest site, although the voles have clearly been scarce for some of these years (e.g. Siipyy and Hyrynsalmi, Finland). And according to Wahlstedt (1976), four recoveries of ringed adult females were made in Sweden in 1974 at places where they had earlier been ringed. Three of them had been ringed as adult owls at the nest in 1973 and the other as an adult in 1970 only 1.5 km from the place of recovery in 1974. These cases could mean that some adult birds manifest similar nest site tenacity to the other two *Strix* owls – Tawny and Ural Owl. However, according to my food studies, the Great Grey Owl does not show any adaptability to declining prey species, which would facilitate a sedentary existence, and allow it to remain on the breeding grounds in years of poor food supply without breeding. Therefore, it is more likely that most of the population leads some sort of nomadic life. Young owls at least have been found far from their ringing sites. One young Great Grey Owl ringed by Nero (1980) in Winnipeg, Canada, was found during its first winter in Minnesota, USA, about 753 km (468 miles) away. In Finland, 17 recoveries to date reveal that young Great Grey Owls have usually been killed during their first autumn whilst between 0 and 226 km from their nest (P.Saurola, *in litt.*). Two nestlings of the pair studied at Boden, Sweden, were recovered more than a year afterwards, one 20 km ENE and the other 220 km NE of the ringing place (Wahlstedt 1969).

An owlet ringed at Luleå, central Sweden, in June 1974 was controlled four years later as a female in a nest at Pajala, north Sweden (Stefansson 1979). An adult female ringed in Sweden on 19th June 1961 was found four years later in Finland, 110 km north of the ringing place. Another recovery from Finland which indicates post-breeding movements is an adult ringed on 4th June at a nest and found 22 km to the south on 15th October of the same year (P. Saurola, *in litt.*).

Great Grey Owl eruptions follow the same pattern as those of the Hawk Owl. When the population of voles is at a normal level most of the owls winter in the nesting area, but after peak vole years remarkable invasions may occur, with birds penetrating south Sweden, south Finland, Poland and the Ukraine. These wanderers can also move northwards. For example, in Siberia there are observations on the Lower Khatanga and Yana Rivers (Dement'ev *et al* 1951).

In Finland Professor E. Merkallio listed the following major invasion years: 1895/96, 1907/08, 1908/09, *1911/12, 1912/13, 1928/29,* 1930/31, *1935/36, 1939/40* and *1942/43*. In the invasion years (italics), according to Merikallio, the owls did not originate in Finland but came from the east, and in 1942/43 especially from Eastern Karelia.

More recently, there have been noticeable invasions in 1955/56, 1962/63, *1963/64*, 1964/65, *1968/69*, 1970/71, 1974/75, 1976/77 and *1980/81*. In the italicized years the invasions must have come from Russia because during the previous summers only four, two and nine nests respectively were found in Finland (Fig. 27). The invasion during the winter 1980/81 is said to be the largest ever seen in Finland, hundreds of Great Grey Owls being seen in south and central Finland (cf. Mikkola 1981).

Large invasions of Great Grey Owls also occur in North America following a vole crash in the northern forests. In such years this owl is a rare winter visitor as far south as the fortieth parallel, the limit of its wanderings being reached in southern New England, New York, New Jersey, Ohio and Illinois in the east and California in the west (Fisher 1893).

Sizeable invasions by Great Grey Owls have occurred in North America during 1965/66, 1968/69, 1973/74, 1977/78 and 1978/79 (Green 1969, Nero and Taylor 1969, Godfrey 1967 and Nero 1980). After some of these invasions the owl has bred near the USA/Canadian border in areas where it is normally considered a winter visitor only (Nero 1970).

20: Long-eared Owl *Asio otus*
(Linné)

The basic tone of the adult Long-eared Owl (male and female) is rich buff-brown with dark brown streaks. The back has dark brown vermiculations and small brownish streaks forming a marbled pattern, and the wings are marbled by white or buff fringes to the coverts. The upper tail is closely barred with dark brown on rich buff (six to eight bars), giving a dark, uniform effect at long range. The under parts are usually buffish in ground colour with broad, longitudinal stripes (more noticeable on breast and belly), and with narrow cross-bars on the crop. A few dark streaks are the only markings on the buffish under tail coverts. The face is cat-like, being slightly elongated with a rather angular pattern. The facial disc is ochreous-buff with black patches around the deep orange eyes. The 'ear-tufts' of the Long-eared Owl are usually conspicuous but are sometimes held flat, almost always so when the bird is in flight. The bill and claws are black, the cere grey.

The natal down is fairly thick, short and soft (white, according to Harrison (1975), and ochre, according to Dement'ev *et al* 1951) and at this stage the elongation of the 'ear-tufts' is already noticeable. In the mesoptile plumage the feathers of the back, wings and breast have dark brown bars and russet-ish tips, giving the birds a reddish appearance. The face is almost black and the remiges and rectrices are the same as the adults'.

Over its considerable world range and within localised populations the Long-eared Owl shows tremendous colour variation, ranging from a deep chestnut brown nearing black to a fairly pale fawn. Dement'ev *et al* (1951) consider these variations to be of an individual nature with no regard to geographical locations, but more probably related to age and sex. Godfrey (1966). for instance, states that females are darker than males. Long-eared Owls of the North American race *wilsonianus* have a distinctly red-brown facial disc.

No geographical colour variation appears to exist among Long-eared Owls in Europe and Asia, but the island forms from Madagascar and the Canaries are darker than Eurasian birds, as is the Stygian Owl *Asio stygius* of South America (Flegg 1969).

The total length of males ranges 350–375 mm (average 362 mm from 11 birds) and that of females 371–401 mm (average 380 mm from 15 birds). The wing length of males is 276–309 mm (average 295 mm from 125 birds) and that of females 282–320 mm (average 299 mm from 150 birds) (Dement'ev *et al* 1951). The weight of males is 200–360 g (average 288 g from 22 birds) and that of females 280–390 g (average 327 g from 20 birds) (Dement'ev *et al* 1951 and v. Haartman *et al* 1967). Thus, the female is clearly heavier, and sexual dimorphism is similarly exhibited in the most important skeletal elements of both sexes, which show an almost identical degree of dimorphism in the different bones (Winde 1977).

IN THE FIELD

This medium-sized owl has highly effective cryptic plumage which renders it almost invisible as it perches motionless, often close to the rough, lichen-covered bark of a tree or in dense foliage during daylight hours. In addition, its nocturnal rather than crepuscular habits explain why this common owl is so seldom seen and relatively little studied (Flegg 1969).

The Long-eared Owl usually perches in an upright position and can look surprisingly thin, especially when adopting its typical, camouflage posture, and many must be overlooked at such times. However, Ray Hawley's long experience of this species on moorland near Sheffield, England (Hawley 1966), showed that birds usually perched at an angle of about 45° when on a point of vantage on open moorland near the nesting wood. In a strong wind the body was held almost horizontal. Roosting birds can often be approached to within one or two metres before they will fly. Although Long-eared Owls prefer to roost in trees or bushes, often in deep cover, they may roost on the ground. When hunting over open country they will settle in trees, sometimes isolated ones, bushes, posts and even on the ground. The Long-eared Owl is essentially nocturnal and arboreal like the Tawny Owl but confusion with this species should not arise. The Tawny Owl is much bulkier with a relatively massive head and dark eyes.

Hunting or passage birds encountered in open areas of heath or marsh may present problems of identification, particularly if the long 'ear-tufts' and orange eyes cannot be seen well, and confusion may arise with its close relative, the Short-eared Owl. Three Long-eared Owls on Holy Island, north-east England, in September 1974, possibly passage migrants, exemplify a situation often met with by birdwatchers on the east coast of Britain, where tired or unwary immigrants occur each autumn. These particular birds were often seen flying about in the middle of the day by Ian Willis, several colleagues and other bird-watchers. In the three days that the owls were observed, one of them showed a fondness for perching in a relaxed manner on fence posts in bright sunlight, quite oblivious of up to ten birdwatchers peering at it. Late one afternoon in the same locality a single Long-eared Owl was seen in silhouette on

the low branch of a gnarled hawthorn, while a Short-eared Owl quartered the fields beyond. The foregoing incidents highlight the possibility of finding both of these *Asio* owls in the same habitat by day.

In flight, when the 'ear-tufts' are flattened and the eyes are difficult to see (or they may even appear yellow in certain lights), the Long-eared Owl's greyer, less buffish coloration and more compact proportions should be looked for. The wings are shorter and broader than the Short-eared Owl's and this, together with the shorter, squarer tail, produces wing proportions reminiscent of a Buzzard *Buteo buteo*. (Fuller details of the Long-eared Owl's flight appearance are given in Chapter 21: Short-eared Owl.) With good views of a Long-eared Owl on the ground or perched, identification should be easier. It is more slightly built than the Short-eared Owl and generally darker and more uniform in appearance. The buff face usually appears elongated because of the pale area down the centre, edged with dark stripes extending to the prominent 'ear-tufts' (Davis and Prytherch 1976). It must be remembered, however, that, like the smaller but equally nocturnal and 'eared' Scops Owl, the present species may change its facial shape dramatically as part of its camouflage posture, and when relaxed its facial disc may appear quite round as shown in the drawing overleaf.

VOICE

Hawley (1966) summarised the Long-eared Owl's vocabulary as 'remarkable' and concluded, after studying the calls of this owl over thirteen years, that the existing

Facial expressions – (left) relaxed, (right) alarmed

reference books did not adequately reflect the sheer range and even individual variation of calls employed by the species. Individual birds seemed to adopt their own versions of the more typical calls, particularly during aggressive displays.

The territorial 'song' of the male is a quiet but penetrating *hoo-hoo-hoo-hoo*, audible for up to a kilometre away (Witherby *et al* 1940). The notes may be spaced at regular intervals, as stated in *The Handbook of British Birds*, or at varying intervals between two and eight seconds (see, for example, Wendland 1957). Between ten and more than two hundred 'song hoots' may be given prior to a display flight, but usually about thirty are delivered (Hawley 1966). This simple call can be imitated by blowing across the neck of a suitable bottle, which may cause the owl to answer and to move closer (Flegg 1969). Fitzpatrick (1973) was puzzled by a Long-eared Owl coming to look at him when he was imitating the typical eight-hoot call of the Barred Owl *Strix varia*, but the two species have similar voices and perhaps the puzzled Long-eared Owl may have felt compelled to discover the source of the sound.

The territorial call is typically uttered whilst the bird is perched, though sometimes during flight and, exceptionally, from the ground. In Hawley's Sheffield study areas it was strongly suspected (and indeed proved on three occasions) that the song branch was high in a tree. It may sometimes have been the case that the male sang from the very apex of a conifer. Males would usually begin calling in the evening half-light. In Sweden a male began calling in April at about 20.00 hours and continued calling for the next four hours, then became silent until a much shorter burst of vocal activity a little before sunrise, between 03.00 and 04.00 hours (Wahlstedt 1959).

The female's principal call is a quiet *shoo-oogh* which does not end abruptly like the male's lower-pitched note, but dies away softly like a heavy sigh. It has the quality of the sound produced by blowing through a comb and paper. It is audible for up to 60 m (Wendland 1957) and can sound rather like a lamb or a slightly high-pitched sheep call (Hawley 1966). It lasts for about a second, being repeated sometimes for long periods at approximately twelve second intervals. The call is more regularly uttered just prior to nest selection, which is in late February in the Sheffield area in England, and may be given from any part of the breeding wood. Once the nest has been selected the female spends most of her time in its vicinity. During the subsequent month or so, until the eggs are laid, she calls for much of the period at about eight second intervals, increasing to approximately five second intervals, and even more rapidly on detecting the approach of the male in display flight (Hawley 1966).

The female almost always calls from a perch, and slightly different variations of the call are produced by different individuals. The male, and more rarely the female, uses a cat-like hissing *chwau* when exchanging prey, or immediately afterwards. If an intruder approaches the nest the occupying birds call *oo-ack, oo-ack*, prefaced sometimes by a barking *woof-woof*.

Anger and agitation are expressed by bill-snapping or various types of squealing, growling and wailing noises (cf. Witherby *et al* 1940, Hawley 1966, and Wendland 1957). Flying birds utter a high-pitched *yip-yip-yip* call, which is virtually indistinguishable from the typical flight call of the Barn Owl. Normally, it is given as a three note call, and is presumed to be a contact note. The same call, but repeated in a series of about ten notes, has been heard from an agitated bird during aggressive display, the notes gradually falling in pitch to the end as rather dog-like *yerk yerk* or *yak yak* calls. The latter noises have also been described coming from flying birds in March, uttered in a fairly rapidly repeated six or ten note sequence (Hawley 1966).

The food-begging call of the young is a characteristic high-pitched piping *pzeei*, which is often repeated at intervals of about five seconds (v. Haartman *et al* 1967). Hawley has described a whole brood of small young calling together, as they usually do, as sounding rather like the jingling of small coins. The smallest young's call is the highest pitched and the most frequent. When older, the young have a discordant hunger cry resembling the noise of a gate with squeaky hinges. This distinctive cry is very far-carrying and in settled weather may be heard a kilometre or more away. It has been used as an aid when estimating the population size of this owl in Finland (Joutsamo 1969, Grönlund and Mikkola 1978). Very curious fledged juveniles investigating human intruders near the nest may utter a weak, high-pitched, slightly hollow-sounding *eewick*, audible up to 15 m (Hawley 1966).

Outside the breeding season the Long-eared Owl is generally silent. Sometimes, however, late in October and early November males begin calling to mark out their territories (Glue 1977).

BEHAVIOUR

The Long-eared Owl is principally a sedentary species, although the northernmost breeding birds will normally winter in southern temperate regions. When an ample food supply is available, it demonstrates its hardiness by wintering as far as 64°N in Finland. Its migratory movements are consequently irregular and dependent to a large extent on the food supply available.

The size of a Finnish Long-eared Owl territory is between 50 and 100 ha (Koskimies 1979) in a good vole year, but in Denmark Trap-Lind (1965) found three pairs nesting inside a small patch of forest of hardly more than 2 ha. Normally, the population density of Long-eared Owls, where studied, has varied between 10 and 50 pairs per 100 km² (see, for example, Mebs 1966, Korpimäki *et al* 1977). Five nests studied by Wendland (1957) were 600, 900, 1,500 and 2,000 m apart. Resident owls occupy their territories throughout the year but do not normally use the same nest in consecutive years. A new nest may be no more than 100 m from the old one, which may then be re-used the following year. In northern areas, and often in the south, the abundance of food alters so greatly over a four-year period that males are compelled to find a new territory with a better food supply. In Britain and Central Europe such individuals begin defining their territories in March or April, at the earliest, when most residents are already incubating full clutches (Glue 1977).

In the breeding season the Long-eared Owl performs a zig-zag flight among the tree-trunks, or flies above the tree-tops, clapping its wings beneath its body at the end of each slow beat, but losing little height, unlike the Short-eared Owl during its similar display flight, when it claps its wings together rapidly a number of times, losing height in consequence. The Long-eared Owl only claps its wings once each time, though perhaps six to twenty such claps will be made during a display flight, sometimes even more when excitement intensifies (Hawley 1966). This aerial performance is part of courtship, and mostly the male will fly directly from the song post to the female. Both sexes are known to clap their wings, though the female much less frequently. In Germany Fritz *et al* (1977) witnessed 13 copulations by a pair at one nest. The male prepared the female for the act with calls and display flights, followed

Copulation of Long-eared Owls (based on sketches by R. Fritz)

Pre-copulatory postures by male Long-eared Owl in presence of female (after R. Fritz) – upper drawings show signalling with wings, (A) highest point reached by wings, (B) lowest point reached by wings – lower drawings show 'bucking'. (C) highest point, (D) lowest point

by dramatic movements of the body and wings whilst perched near the female or on the nest. These actions, apparently stimulated by the sight of the submissive female, consisted of bucking movements of the horizontally-held body, like a human being performing press-ups, and wing-signalling in which the wings were waved up and down, as the drawings above illustrate (after Fritz *et al* 1977). The female, lying flat across her perch, wings slightly drooped, only once failed to allow the male to mount her. Copulation lasted three seconds, and on eleven of the thirteen witnessed occasions it took place on a branch. Twice, when the male was performing his display on the nest, the female flew in to join him before the end of his 15 to 20 seconds-long display.

Nesting Long-eared Owls are rarely so aggressive towards a birdwatcher in the immediate vicinity of a nesting tree that some form of head protection, such as a motorcycle crash helmet, becomes necessary. I know of only one case where this was so. Nevertheless, zig-zagging flights in and out of the nest tree and wing-clapping are performed as an expression of agitation when the nest is threatened, and the owls may also feign injury. The latter tactic can be quite spectacular. The bird flies directly at the intruder and, when only three to four metres away, tumbles to the foot of the nest tree and beats its wings and legs feebly before dragging itself a metre or so, then flying off (Hawley 1966). Sometimes the Long-eared Owl attempts to frighten away its enemies by making itself appear as large and fearsome as possible. In this dramatic posture the feathers are ruffled, the primaries are spread and drooped and the secondaries arched over the back, so that the wings form a huge frame around the head. The glaring orange eyes add to the illusion that the owl has suddenly inflated to twice its original size. Owlets in or near the nest will employ the same tactics and no doubt may manage to deter a number of predators by themselves.

Holland (1974) reported on the behaviour of Long-eared Owls in the presence of his dog. Soon after sunset the majority of owls roosting in the area were attracted by the dog. The owls descended as low as half a metre above the dog's back, sometimes steeply, sometimes making a gentle descent. The maximum number of owls seen performing simultaneously was 16 (average 6 in 19 visits). Holland (1974) concluded his interesting report by commenting that 'this method of observation can be recommended to anyone who wishes to see Long-eared Owls at close range; their behaviour was like an air display'.

Like its very close relative, the Short-eared Owl, this species often roosts communally in winter, although it chooses to do so in bushes and trees rather than on the ground. In Britain roosts of up to 29 birds have been recorded in recent years, though usually they contain between six and twelve birds (Glue and Hammond 1974, Glue 1976). In Ost Friesland, West Germany, approximately fifty Long-eared Owls congregated in a small pine plantation each winter for four years (Holland 1974). A collection of wintering owls was counted in Spain by Araujo *et al* (1973), who found a maximum of 23 in November, the number decreasing thereafter. Winter gatherings evidently occur further east also, twelve being noted by U. Hirsch at Birecik in southern Turkey in January and February 1973, and a roost of up to eleven was discovered by J. R. Taylor in a coniferous plantation at Ankara in August 1975 and observed until November (Ornithological Society of Turkey Bird Reports 1970–1975).

It is well known that the Long-eared Owl is a nocturnal hunter, spending the day in a thickly-foliaged tree, often close to the trunk. Wendland (1957) noted that between 10th March and 21st May the male left his daytime roost tree between 2 and 44 minutes after sunset (average 29 minutes from ten observations). This first hunting phase began between 18.24 and 20.15 hours and lasted until 22.30 hours. Around midnight hardly any activity was seen at the nest. The second phase of hunting activity began at 01.30 hours and ended between 15 and 30 minutes before sunrise. The male's last food visits to the nest were seen by Wendland (1957) between 03.04 and 03.40 hours.

However, it would be a mistake to believe that in all circumstances the Long-eared Owl hunts only in darkness. For instance, in Finland the extremely short summer nights oblige Long-eared Owls to hunt in bright sunlight. This owl has even bred successfully above the Arctic Circle where there is no night at all during midsummer. Daylight hunting by Long-eared Owls has recently been observed in lower latitudes. Bayldon (1978) saw Long-eared Owls hunting from the late afternoon (16.00 hours)

Young Long-eared Owl in threat display

onwards in southern Bavaria in the second week of June and considered this not unusual behaviour.

The hunting method most commonly observed involves quartering open ground over a regular hunting territory at a height of 50–150 cm. The wing beats, which are quite fast and not normally raised above the line of the body, are interspersed with short intervals of gliding. During glides the wings are usually held level and only occasionally raised in a shallow 'V'. Prey is captured from quartering flight by a deliberate stall, which brings the owl to the ground feet foremost, talons at maximum spread, pinning the small mammal and absorbing the impact of landing. Occasionally, Long-eared Owls disturb roosting birds or hover effectively over low herbage and bushes before plunging to kill small mammals (Glue and Hammond 1974). Flegg (1969) mentions observations of pairs of owls working along a hedgerow, one on each side, one creating a disturbance, the other taking the alarmed bird in flight.

FOOD

As with the Barn Owl, pellets are generally ejected at the roost and while the bird hunts. Hagen (1965) showed that on 21 of the 30 days he studied a Long-eared Owl it produced one pellet per day. On two of the remaining nine days, no pellets at all were ejected and on the other seven days two pellets per day were produced. The number of pellets ejected was consequent upon the amount of food eaten, so that pelletless days were preceded by days in which none or a mere 27 g of food had been consumed. In the 21 cases when a pellet was produced daily, the amount of food consumed on each preceding day was approximately 63 g, and the corresponding figure for the seven days producing two pellets per day was 91 g. The average interval between night feeding and the ejection of a pellet was 18 hours, though varying between 10 and 22 hours (Hagen 1965). In the wild bird the undigested remains of prey eaten during the first phase of night hunting will be produced as a pellet the following day. The undigested remains of prey consumed during the second hunting phase before sunrise will be ejected while the bird hunts the following night (cf. Guérin 1928). Thus, it would be a mistake to expect that all of the pellets produced by a Long-eared Owl in a given period will be found under the owl's day-time perch.

Long-eared Owl pellets are normally elongated, pale or dark grey masses of fur and feathers, enveloping a core of small mammal and bird bones. As shown below, the size of the pellets is, on average, more or less the same in all European countries studied:

Season	Av. size of pellets	Number	Author	Country
Breeding	4.0 × 2.1 × 1.8 cm	59	Mikkola	Finland
Breeding	4.6 × 2.25 × 1.95 cm	363	Hagen (1965)	Norway
Breeding	4.9 × 2.1 × 1.8 cm	100	Rörig (1910)	Germany
Winter	3.7 × 2.0 × 1.5 cm	221	Heitkamp (1967)	Germany
Breeding	3.8 × 2.0 cm	220	South (1966)	England
Winter/breeding	3.3 × 1.9 cm	2,484	Glue and Hammond (1974)	Britain and Ireland
Breeding	4.6 × 2.1 cm	148	Araujo et al (1973)	Spain

It will be noticed that the list shows slight seasonal variations in that winter pellets are smaller than those formed in the breeding season. Seasonal variations have also been recorded in the pellets of Tengmalm's and Short-eared Owls (Erkinaro 1973). Glue (1969) asserts that it is often difficult to distinguish between the pellets of Long-eared and Tawny Owls, because both produce pellets which are friable in texture. This is true if one has only a few pellets to study but a large sample would reveal that Tawny Owl pellets are, on average, much larger (5.5 × 2.4 × 2.0 cm). Especial care is needed for Short-eared Owl pellets, which are only slightly larger than those of the Long-eared Owl (cf. Table 4).

Raczyński and Ruprecht (1974) demonstrated that the pellets of the Long-eared Owl give only a partial picture of the bird's diet. Their experiments showed that 14 (21%) of 67 individual prey items given to the owl could not be identified when the pellets were later analysed because some of the bones had dissolved in the owl's stomach (Mikkola 1971), however, seem to indicate a different situation. In 1969 I ran a short test using a tame young Long-eared Owl. In June and July it was given seven laboratory mice, three rats, four Common Shrews *Sorex araneus*, two Bank Voles *Clethrionomys glareolus* and one Yellowhammer *Emberiza citrinella*. Its pellets were collected and later dissected, whereupon all the larger bones and skulls of the above-mentioned prey animals were located with ease. In this experiment no bone was digested in the stomach of the one month old owlet. It may be concluded that pellet analysis probably provides fairly reliable information on the Long-eared Owl's diet.

The most remarkable studies on the food of the Long-eared Owl were made in Central Europe earlier this century. Czarnecki (1956) summarised a list of no fewer than 122,000 prey items. Most of the list, 73,600 prey items, originated from Germany from Uttendörfer and his colleagues (cf. Uttendörfer 1939 and 1952), the rest was composed of the following: Holland 24,000 prey items (Tinbergen 1933); Poland 11,700 (Czarnecki 1956); Denmark 9,700 (Skovgaard 1920); and Hungary 3,065 (Greschik 1910 and Viscian 1932). By far the most important prey species was the Common Vole *Microtus arvalis*, forming 66% of the 121,708 vertebrates. Other small mammals made up 25.8%, birds 8.1% and frogs, lizards and fish the remaining 0.1%. In addition, there were at least 400 insects and some other invertebrates but, strangely, none of the authors remarked on these.

The above-mentioned information is widely known and appears in all the standard handbooks, and it seems unnecessary to present it in detail here. Instead, Table 41 shows what has been learned from more recent studies in Britain and Ireland (Glue and Hammond 1974), Finland (Soikkeli 1964, Sulkava 1965, Mikkola 1977 and Grönlund and Mikkola 1977, 1978), France (Thiollay 1968 and Chaline *et al* 1974), East Germany (Haensel and Walther 1966), Sweden (Källander 1977), Spain (Araujo *et al* 1973) and Rumania (Catuneanu *et al* 1970).

This new data indicates that Long-eared Owls feed not only upon Common Voles but also on a wide variety of small and medium-sized mammals. Nevertheless, the Common Vole was numerically by far the commonest prey animal in France and East Germany, accounting for 84% and 78% respectively of the total prey examined. The Short-tailed Vole *Microtus agrestis* was the most numerous prey animal in Britain (47%), Finland (47%) and Sweden (65%). In Spain pine voles *Pitymys spp* altogether formed 42% of the diet and in Rumania various species of mice were taken more frequently (57%) than voles. In all the countries where food was studied small mammals formed 85–98% of the total prey. Birds were commonly eaten only in Britain (15%) and Rumania (12%), and only very occasionally did this owl take frogs, fish or insects (mainly beetles). There is little doubt that differences in regional faunas were the primary reasons for the differences found in the diet of Long-eared Owl populations in widely scattered parts of Europe (also Hagen 1965).

It is clear that the prey of the Long-eared Owl also varies according to the season. At 20 sites in Britain pellets were collected methodically over the year and Glue and Hammond (1974) were able to compare the range of vertebrate prey taken during the breeding season (March to July) with that taken during the rest of the year. The results (expressed as percentages of prey numbers) were as follows:

	Breeding season %	Non-breeding season %	Change ±%
Short-tailed Vole *Microtus agrestis*	50	45	−5
Wood Mouse *Apodemus sylvaticus*	21	16	−5
Bank Vole *Clethrionomys glareolus*	14	9	−5
Brown Rat *Rattus norvegicus*	3	3	0
Common Shrew *Sorex araneus*	3	2	−1
Other mammals	1	2	+1
Birds	8	23	+15
Total numbers	3,578	2,577	

The most striking change in the non-breeding season is the threefold increase in number of birds in the diet. Glue and Hammond (1974) suggested that this was due to a greater dependence on communally roosting House Sparrows *Passer domesticus* in the autumn and winter months when they comprised numerically 14% of the whole diet, compared with the much smaller number, though wider variety, of young woodland birds caught in the summer.

This shifting of emphasis to birds as food during the non-breeding season has not been noted in Fenno-Scandia (cf. Hagen 1965, Sulkava 1965 and Källander 1977), as shown below:

| | Norway | | Finland | | Sweden | |
	Summer %	Winter %	Summer %	Winter %	Summer %	Winter %
Small rodents	91.3	95.5	94.0	99.6	94.7	96.5
Shrews	5.8	2.8	4.6	0.4	2.5	2.1
Birds	2.9	1.7	1.4	—	2.8	1.4
Total numbers	2,315	1,314	703	233	5,148	8,769

The Long-eared Owl is able to winter in Fenno-Scandia only when *Microtus* voles are plentiful. It cannot survive there by attempting to exploit secondary sources of food such as shrews or small birds. Bird life in the countries of northern Europe is extremely sparse in winter, unlike conditions in Britain, some Central European countries and the whole of southern and south-western Europe. From this example, it seems reasonable to conclude that despite its wide-ranging diet the Long-eared Owl relies heavily on mice and voles, especially *Microtus*, which explains why its breeding density is so largely determined by the abundance of these rodents.

BREEDING BIOLOGY

Long-eared Owls are found in forest, woodland and scrub of all kinds, but only on the very edges of larger woods and forests. Most breed in small patches of woodland amongst open meadows and fields. In Finland all 91 Long-eared Owls' nests examined in a number of studies were no more than 500 m from the nearest cultivated land (cf. Grönlund and Mikkola 1977, 1978, Juvonen 1976 and Korpimäki *et al* 1977). Most of the 200 nests similarly inspected in Britain were in isolated plantations, shelter-belts, copses, thickets or overgrown hedges surrounded by open country, which often embraced moorland, heath, marsh, rough grassland or farmland (Glue 1977). The proximity of the nests to marshland and fields is indicative of the owl's hunting techniques and requirements, because this species favours open terrain in its quest for prey.

Nonetheless, the choice of nest-biotope might be determined in part by the situation of the available nests of other birds, because the Long-eared Owl usually lays its eggs in the large old nest of another bird or a squirrel's drey. The nests most frequently used in Britain (Glue 1977) and in Finland are those of the Carrion/Hooded Crow *Corvus corone* and Magpie *Pica pica*, although other original occupants vary considerably in size from Jay *Garrulus glandarius* and Woodpigeon *Columba palumbus* to Grey Heron *Ardea cinerea* (Table 42). A squirrel's drey is used much more frequently in Finland than in Britain, and 17 (i.e. 7%) of 256 nests studied in Britain were neither old nests of other birds nor squirrel's dreys:

Natural tree growths (witches' brooms)	3
Large open-fronted nest box	1
Man-made nest of sticks	2

Natural cavity in willow	1
On ground beneath dead bracken or bramble	8
On ground among heather	2

Such nests did not feature in the Finnish study material (Table 42) but v. Haartman *et al* (1967) reported two ground nests in Finland, one in 1955 and the other in 1958. Glue (1977) considered that ground nests are usual where suitable platforms are lacking. Recently, Hautala (1977) photographed a Finnish Long-eared Owl breeding in a nest-box originally built for Tengmalm's Owls, though used by Kestrels *Falco tinnunculus* in the previous two summers. In Britain and on the Continent Long-eared Owls have, until now, used only open-fronted nest-boxes, some pairs occupying them quite regularly (cf. Cave 1968). Occasionally, Long-eared Owls utilise duck nesting-baskets in Holland (Haverschmidt 1946). These examples suggest that it might prove fruitful to make artificial twig nests and/or open nest-boxes for Long-eared Owls in areas where suitable platforms are scarce or non-existent. An interesting new development has been the utilisation by nesting Long-eared Owls of a specially provided willow basket of a type normally used by apple or potato pickers. Several baskets, variously constructed of wire-netting or willow, were fixed to trees in a mixed wood in Cambridgeshire, England, where owls were known to overwinter, and in 1981 one was adopted (Garner 1982).

Although the Long-eared Owl prefers to raise its young at ready-made sites, twigs are sometimes used to construct a distinct nest cup. Glue (1977) tells of a male Long-eared Owl that was seen to carry a larch twig to an occupied but empty tree nest which contained eggs a few days later. Fresh material found in four other nests may have been involved originally in the complicated courtship display.

Conifers comprised 74% of the 194 nest trees listed in a British inquiry (Glue 1977), while pine supplied 66% of nest sites in a Finnish sample (Table 43). The average height of nests in trees was 6.7 m in Britain and 8.2 m in Finland. Of course, the heights quoted in Table 43 depend largely on the original nest builders and the sizes of the available trees.

The breeding season begins much earlier in Britain than in Denmark and Finland, as the dates for first eggs show:

	March			*April*			*May/June*		
	2–11	*12–21*	*22–31*	*1–10*	*11–20*	*21–30*	*1–10*	*11–20*	*21–30*	*31–9*
	%			%				%		
Britain 140 nests	5	11	24	26	14	11	6	1	1	1
Denmark 103 nests	–	–	11	27	31	19	8	–	4	–
Finland 62 nests	–	–	8	11	3	34	34	8	2	–

In Britain data from 140 nests (Glue 1977) showed that most clutches were laid from late March to early April, with a mean date of 4th April, although the laying season extended from 4th March to 7th June. Egg-laying usually commences at the end of March in Denmark (Trap-Lind 1965) but most clutches are laid in the middle of April. In Finland the majority of clutches (68%) are complete by the end of April or beginning of May (Juvonen 1976, Korpimäki *et al* 1977). In Britain clutches in February are not unknown. Whittaker (cited by Glue 1977) discovered one definite and one probable case of eggs laid in the last few days of that month. Scott, writing of

Ireland, describes February eggs as exceptional, the earliest clutches being 13th and 23rd February.

The female Long-eared Owl is very sensitive to intrusion whilst egg-laying is in progress, and may abandon her nest if it is visited at this stage (Juvonen 1976). Fortunately, records indicate a frequent replacement of lost clutches. Already, early in this century Barrows (1912) had remarked how, like most other birds of prey, the Long-eared Owl, when robbed of its eggs, will lay a second set in the same nest or renest in the same locality. Recently, Glue (1977) had 22 replacement clutches in his material for Britain; four of the replacements were laid in the same nest as the original clutch.

There is no evidence of second broods in Finland but in Britain two successful clutches are occasionally laid (Glue 1977). At one site a second clutch of two eggs was laid in the original nest and, at another, a second nest 10 m from the first was adopted.

The eggs are short, elliptical, white and slightly glossy, and are normally laid on alternate days. However, in some cases, the female may increase the interval between layings (Wallace 1955). As a rule, incubation commences with the first egg but may, at times, be delayed. Incubation ranges from 25–30 days (Witherby *et al* 1940) and is by the female, although the male has been known to incubate for short periods and brood tiny young (Glue 1977). Many females are tight sitters, not flying until the tree is climbed, others will leave when the tree trunk is rapped. In the early stages of incubation the female leaves the nest for short periods during the day. Later, she is absent only in the evenings, hunting near the nest for some eight to ten minutes (Armstrong 1958).

Clutches of one to nine eggs have been noted from 413 European nests, with an average of 4.9 eggs per clutch:

	Clutch size		
	Variation	*Average*	*N*
Finland (Mikkola, this study)	2–9	5.3	142
Denmark (Trap-Lind 1965)	3–7	5.1	108
Germany (Ziesemer 1973, Rockenbauch 1978)	2–8	4.8	60
Spain (Araujo *et al* 1973)	3–6	4.7	16
Britain (Glue 1977)	1–6	4.0	87
Total	1–9	4.9	413

The clutch size of the Long-eared Owl decreases from north to south as it does for most European owls. Moreover, the mean clutch size from British records (4.0) is significantly lower than that of continental birds (Germany 4.8 and Spain 4.7). This fact appears to contradict the hypothesis of Murray (1976) that the clutch size of Long-eared Owls increases to the west as well as to the north. Working in North America, he found the average clutch size between latitudes 25°N and 54°N to be 4.5 eggs (393 nests).

The largest clutch ever reported is ten (Dement'ev *et al* 1951), which was laid during a vole plague year in the region of Kazan, western Russia, in 1891. If not laid by two females, this record indicates that the Long-eared Owl is able to produce much larger than normal clutches provided that there is an abundant food supply. More intensive studies are needed, however, to demonstrate more fully the links between the breeding season, clutch size and food supply.

Some work has already been carried out in this direction and Hagen (1965), Linkola and Myllymäki (1969) and Ziesemer (1973) have demonstrated the effect of a four-year vole cycle on the brood size of the Long-eared Owl in Norway, Finland and Germany (Table 44). Brood sizes are at their highest during the two peak years of vole populations and are very low in the other two years of the cycle. The mean brood size of the Long-eared Owl in five European countries varies from 2.4 to 3.7, as shown below:

| | Brood size | | |
	Variation	Average	N
Norway (Hagen 1965)	1–?	3.1	21
Finland (Mikkola, this study)	1–7	3.1	132
Germany (Ziesemer 1973, Rockenbauch 1978)	1–7	3.7	77
Spain (Araujo *et al* 1973)	1–6	3.5	10
Britain (Glue 1977)	1–5	2.4	89
Total	1–7	3.0	329

It can be seen that the average brood size in 329 successful nests (where at least one young reached the flying stage) was three, a deviation of only 61% from the mean clutch size (4.9). In Finland the brood size deviated by 58% from the average clutch size, in Germany 77%, in Spain 75% and in Britain 60%. This seems to indicate that breeding success is lower in northern parts of Europe, as well as in Britain, compared to Germany or Spain. The following account illustrates more fully this difference in breeding success.

Glue (1977) wrote that 78 nests were found in Britain during incubation and followed through to the fledging period, and no less than 46 of these (i.e. 59%) failed totally, 39 being losses of complete clutches and seven of complete broods. Where known, failures were caused by: robbery by man (13 nests), infertile or addled eggs (4 nests), and single clutches destroyed by rain, or taken by Hooded Crow or Jay. Conversely, of 73 nests studied by Rockenbauch (1978) in Germany, 51 (i.e. 70%) were successful. Losses of complete clutches occurred in 19 cases and three nests with young were lost. The causes were, for the most part, unknown but Pine Martens *Martes martes* robbed two of the nests, one containing six eggs and the other six young. Once, a Long-eared Owl was seen fighting with a Kestrel and the owl lost her nest, and three owls were killed by hunters while doing battle with Hooded Crows.

It is difficult to explain why breeding success is so low in Finland and Britain compared with Germany and Spain, but it would seem to indicate that this owl is better adapted to conditions prevailing in Continental Europe.

The male owl not only deposits prey at the nest before egg-laying commences but also delivers food to the female throughout the incubation period and provides most of the food for the fledglings.

Shortly after hatching the young weigh about 16–20 g (Mebs 1966, Araujo *et al* 1973). The body, head and tarsus are covered with white down and the eyes, closed at hatching, are open after five days to reveal brilliant yellow irides. Depending on the availability of food, the discrepancies in size of the owlets (which will have hatched at one- or two-day intervals) may lead to cannibalism in some instances and to a further size increase of the oldest chick.

By seven days of age black feathers will have developed at the base of the orbital region at each side of the bill, and the bird can hold its head erect for a few minutes. At this stage the owlet may snap its bill if approached or handled. After a further five days the dark feathers around the eyes will have developed more extensively until the whole face is a black mask with glaring yellow eyes. The breast is light grey and the belly has nine dark horizontal stripes. Two grey tufts on the forehead are the first infantile suggestion of the 'ear-tufts' of adulthood. By this time the young owl will respond when handled by erecting its feathers and throwing its wings outwards and forwards in a defensive posture, accompanied by hissing and bill snapping. The female now leaves the young alone on the nest though continuing to visit them with prey. When the owlets are three weeks old they leave the nest by climbing or jumping, but will be unable to fly until they are at least four weeks old, when the primary, secondary and tail feathers will be well developed, although the coverts, breast and head will be still downy.

During the fledgling stage both adults go hunting and join in care of the young. Fledglings do not attempt to return to the nest after they have extended their explorations into the surrounding area. Young owls appear to be dependent upon the adults until they are at least 60 days old. A tame young Long-eared Owl that I reared in 1969 first showed signs of wanting to hunt independently at the end of July.

The daily food intake for an adult Long-eared Owl is about 80 g (Mebs 1966), or even as much as 90–120 g (Eck and Busse 1973). These estimates are much higher than the average food requirement of the young owl that I kept. Its diet was carefully registered over a period of 20 days between 25th June and 2nd August, when the average amount of food consumed per day was 39.2 g (min. 10 g and max. 100 g). If the same is also true in the wild, a daily Short-tailed Vole should satisfy the hunger of a young owl.

DISTRIBUTION

The Long-eared Owl belongs to the holarctic faunal type. It has a circumpolar, holarctic distribution in boreal, temperate, Mediterranean and steppe climatic zones. The northern limit of its range approaches the July isotherm of 59°F, this boundary being located noticeably to the south of those owl species with an exclusively boreal distribution, e.g. Hawk Owl (Voous 1960).

The Long-eared Owl forms one part of a species group with an almost cosmopolitan distribution. The Stygian Owl, a New World species ranging from Mexico to northern Argentina, is a large, dark relative of the Long-eared Owl. Recently, the Striped Owl *Asio clamator*, distributed from Mexico to Bolivia, has been recognised by Eck and Busse (1973) as an *Asio* owl rather than a *Rhinoptynx*, the latter relationship being the one favoured by previous authors. Finally, Africa is the home of three long-eared owls. Full specific status is usually given to the Madagascar Long-eared Owl *Asio madagascariensis*, a species restricted to that island. The Abyssinian Long-eared Owl is usually described as a race of *Asio otus* with the trinomial *A. o. abyssinicus*. It occurs only in the high mountains of the Eastern Congo and on Mount Kenya and in the highlands of Ethiopia (Brown 1970). Long-eared Owls living on the Canaries (*A. o. canariensis*) are no more than an island race, though they are smaller in size.

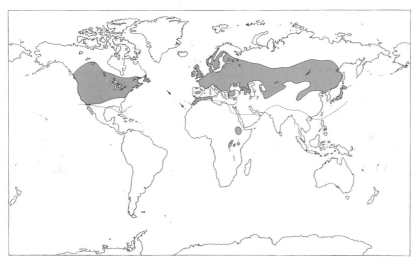

LONG-EARED OWL – *the East African subspecies is sometimes treated as a separate species*
A. abyssinicus

approximate southerly limit of more or less regular wintering movements of northern populations,
involving irregular numbers

breeding distribution

Only two more subspecies are recognised. Together they form a band around the
northern hemisphere; the Eurasian race is the nominate form *A. o. otus* and the North
American form is *A. o. wilsonianus*. The Old World birds are generally paler and more
finely barred on the belly and seem to be more completely streaked below. They are
mainly sedentary but, in general, the northern populations move south or west in
winter. In Britain, for instance, the birds are often faithful to one locality, returning
annually to breed or winter in the same wood or clump of trees (Glue and Hammond
1974). Circumstances are rather different in Fenno-Scandia where the Long-eared
Owl is a migratory bird, wintering in favourable years only and showing marked
oscillations in density of breeding population and average clutch size, depending on
the population density of *Microtus* voles. By adopting a degree of nomadic behaviour
the Long-eared Owl quickly builds its numbers in areas rich in *Microtus* voles. It has
been estimated that about 80% of the Long-eared Owls in Finland are nomadic birds
which breed only when and where food is sufficiently abundant (Juvonen 1976).
Parallels to the Fenno-Scandian observations have lately come from Germany
(Rockenbauch 1978). He noted that in the high regions of the Schwäbische Alb
(600–850 m) Long-eared Owl invasions create very marked fluctuations in the
population.

Migration may be in groups, and flocks have been recorded arriving from the sea in
the Orkneys and Shetlands and on the north-east English coast. Passage is also
well-defined at high Swiss mountain passes such as the Col de Bretolet (Flegg 1969).
Spring and autumn migrations have been studied on the Courland Spit, on the
Russian Baltic coast where 392 Long-eared Owls were ringed between 1957 and 1968
(Belopolsky 1975). Each spring the first Long-eared Owls appeared on the spit at the
end of March and the bulk of the passage took place in April and early May, the

LONG-EARED OWL – breeding range – regular winter movements south of breeding areas

migration thus extending over a considerably long period. The return movements in autumn began about the middle of September, gradually strengthening during October, reaching its peak at the beginning of November, and probably dwindling away altogether before the beginning of December.

The number of owls caught on the Courland Spit varied greatly from year to year (Fig. 28). Belopolsky's figures (1975) show a decreasing trend from 1957 to 1968, which might indicate a more general decrease of Long-eared Owl populations in the northern part of the bird's range. So far, there have been 20 recoveries from the 392 owls ringed in the eleven-year period noted above. Five recoveries were from the USSR, three from Poland, four from East Germany, two from France and one each from Finland, West Germany, Belgium, England, Czechoslovakia and Italy. The results reveal that the flights to wintering sites in Western Europe fan out over a broad front, extending from SSW to W, and attain distances ranging 40 km to 1,630 km (average 741 km, 17 birds) from the place of ringing. Only a few owls were trapped in their breeding haunts in regions E to NNE of the ringing station at distances of 550–1,750 km (average 980 km, 3 birds). One of these was in Finland and the other two were re-trapped in more easterly regions of the USSR.

On the strength of his questionable line survey results, Merikallio (1958) suggested that the Finnish Long-eared Owl population was 2,500 pairs. He also mentioned the discovery of a nest at Ivalo in 1931 which, at latitude 69°N, is undoubtedly the most northerly nest ever found. At a similar latitude, in Iceland, the Long-eared Owl is known only as a rare straggler and has never been known to breed (Gudmundsson, *in litt.*).

In Britain the species is widespread but rather scarce in central and south-west England, Wales and West Scotland. This somewhat irregular distribution has developed since about 1900, reflecting a substantial decline that coincides with the timing of the Tawny Owl's increase. As Long-eared and Tawny Owls have similar ecological requirements, competition between the two owls is probable.

There is no evidence of a general reduction of breeding numbers in Ireland. It would be tempting to suggest that this is due to the absence of Tawny Owls in Ireland, but recent local increases can also be attributed to additional habitat provided by maturing forestry plantations (cf. Sharrock 1976).

Araujo *et al* (1973) believe the Long-eared Owl to be a much more regular breeding bird in Spain than was earlier suspected, nesting probably occurring, in favourable years, in all Spanish provinces. On the other hand, according to my correspondents, it is absent as a breeding species in Portugal, Corsica, Sardinia, Italy, Greece and Crete. However, it is most likely that this owl does breed in all these Mediterranean countries during an abundance of small rodents. Indeed, Vaurie (1965) writes that the Long-eared Owl has bred in Italy, Sicily and northern Greece, though this was not noted by my local correspondents. It has also bred in Majorca in 1970 and 1973 (Mayol 1971, 1973) and in 1968 and 1969 two pairs were found at Salamis in Cyprus (Leontiades, *in litt.*). Vaurie, in his *Birds of the Palearctic Fauna* (1965), wrote that it breeds in Morocco, Algeria and Tunisia, a situation confirmed in Etchécopar and Hüe (1967). The situation in Turkey needs clarification, though the few breeding records marked on our map currently suggest a fairly wide distribution in the western half of the country. Long-eared Owls are much more widely reported in Turkey in winter, which may indicate an influx of wintering birds. Some birds from Europe winter from

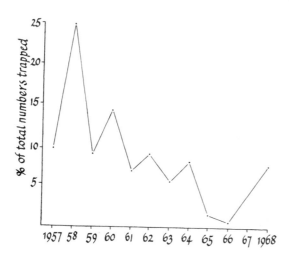

Fig. 28 Long-eared Owl yearly ringing totals as percentages of 358 owls trapped between 1957 and 1968 on autumn migration along the Courland Spit, Baltic coast, USSR (Belopolsky 1975)

Palestine to Egypt and from Iraq to southern Iran (Ethcécopar and Hüe 1967 and 1970).

Throughout its European range the Long-eared Owl is less numerous than the Tawny Owl, its most effective competitor. Sharrock (comp. 1976), basing his figures on the British and Irish atlas records, estimated the Long-eared Owl population of the British Isles at over 3,000 pairs but most unlikely to exceed 10,000 pairs. The corresponding figure for Sweden is 10,000 pairs (Ulfstrand the Högstedt 1976) and not more than 10,000 pairs for France (Yeatman 1976). However, one should remember that irregular movements of this owl can change these numbers considerably. In the winter of 1975–76 exceptional numbers of Long-eared Owls invaded Britain. Glue (1976) suspected them to be of Continental origin, although the explanation for the movement is unknown. The reason may have been a failure of rodent supply on the Continental breeding grounds. After the sudden collapse of a vole population many Long-eared Owls are found dead, having failed to reach areas where prey is more abundant (Smeenk 1972).

21: Short-eared Owl *Asio flammeus*
(Pontoppidan)

DESCRIPTION

The back of adult birds of either sex is generally pale buff and dark brown, more blotched than streaked, giving a distinctly mottled effect. Unlike that of the Long-eared Owl, the dark carpal patch is conspicuous, since there is more contrast with the rest of the wing, which is usually paler than that of the Long-eared Owl, the primary patches being sandy-buff to white. The longish wing is tipped with black above and there are some dark bars across the outermost part of the unmarked primary patch; these bars continue across the whole of the otherwise pale grey-buff secondaries. The tail is shortish and slightly wedge-shaped with dark barring, like shallow arrows, on a buff ground colour, darker above than the pale off-white basic tone below. The underparts are pale buff, with dark streaks confined mainly to the upper breast and neck. Also, the under wing coverts are pale buff to white, giving a very pale appearance, and the under tail coverts are whitish with a few fine, dark streaks. The primaries and secondaries below are off-white, noticeably barred dark at the tip of the wing, and finely so along the outer half of the secondaries. The two innermost secondaries are much more boldly marked underneath than the rest and may show as a small dark patch in flight. The greater primary coverts are tipped dark grey, appearing as a black half-moon-shape carpal patch in flight. The face looks bulbous, pale whitish with dark areas around the lemon-yellow eyes. The short ear-tufts are rarely prominent in the field. The claws are black and the bill a dark horn-colour with a much lighter tip.

The owlet is initially protected by a thick, soft, short pile of down which is light buff on the upperparts, darker on either side of the mantle, and whiter beneath. It extends fully to the claws with the exception of a bare patch at the back of the leg joint. The subsequent or mesoptile plumage is creamy and russet-ish below, brown with russet-ish patches and edgings above; the remiges and rectrices are patterned as

Juvenile Short-eared Owl

in the adults. The face is black-brown with unusual white, downy 'moustache' and 'beard' patches. Hortling (1952) maintains that the exact pattern of these pale facial patches is unique to the young Short-eared Owl.

The sexes differ in that males are generally paler than females (Lockie 1955, Clark 1975), but extremely wide individual variations occur, with certain males exhibiting as much yellow ground colour as females, and certain females displaying almost pure white background tones. Such differences can also be due to age, for old birds are often much whiter than younger ones; for example, a three-year-old female can be lighter than a one-year-old male. From this it must be clear that sexing birds by colour, in the field, is not recommended.

Over the major part of its European, Asian and North American range, no geographical variations of colour or form have been found, these populations constituting only one subspecies *Asio flammeus flammeus*, but seven other subspecies have been described from the rest of the world.

The total length of males varies 340–415 mm (average 373 mm from 36 birds) and that of females 340–423 mm (average 382 mm from 28 birds). The wing-length of male is 281–329 mm, the average being 308 mm from 90 birds, and that of females 285–335 mm, with an average of 310 mm from 88 birds (Dement'ev *et al* 1951). Thus, females are only slightly larger even though they are much heavier, their weight being 400–430 g (average 411 g from 4 birds) and males 320–385 g (average 350 g from 10 birds).

IN THE FIELD

The Short-eared Owl is one of the few European owls encountered frequently by day in very open habitats. Ordinarily, it settles on the ground in rough grass or vegetation which provides some cover, but in the breeding season it will also perch fairly freely when trees are present near its nest (Witherby *et al* 1940), or even roost in woods (Donald Smith, pers. comm. See under 'Behaviour'). It is often seen in parties, especially during the winter, perching on walls, posts or isolated trees or bushes while hunting. Normal carriage is less upright, the body more slanting than in most owls. Short-eared Owls have longer wings and a relatively small head compared with the other medium-sized owls described in this book.

Though similar in size to its close relative the Long-eared Owl, the Short-eared Owl may be identified by the following aspects, summarised by Davis and Prytherch (1976):

'The Short-eared Owl is slightly more heavily built than the Long-eared, generally less dark and less uniform in appearance. The Short-eared Owl has lemon-yellow, rather than orange, eyes, which are surrounded by dark-tipped feathers, in a pale facial disc. The upperparts are generally pale buff and brown, more blotched than streaked, giving a less uniform and distinctly more mottled effect than the Long-eared Owl above. The Short-eared Owl has a more prominent dark carpal patch at the 'wrist' on both the upper and lower surface of the wings. The wings are broad at the base but taper slightly to give a narrower, more pointed appearance to the outer part, and this effect is intensified since the wings are usually also held forward. The tail of the Short-eared Owl is somewhat longer than that of the Long-eared, with fewer, more prominent bars (four to five), enhanced by the paler ground colour. It is also slightly wedge-shaped, and the bars form a series of shallow arrows rather than smooth curves. The Short-eared Owl has heavy streaking on the upper breast and around the neck extending faintly onto the flanks and belly, but the ground colour is a much paler buff over the remaining underparts, so that they are well demarcated from the breast. The under tail coverts are whitish with perhaps a few fine, dark streaks' (Davis and Prytherch 1976).

All Short-eared Owls display much smaller ear-tufts than Long-eared Owls. It seems likely that Short-eared Owls, active by day over open country, do not need special 'outline' recognition signals as much as their woodland relatives (Mikkola 1973). These tufts, however, are regularly erected when the owl is agitated or enquiring (D. Watson and D. Smith, pers. comm.).

The flight of the Short-eared Owl is powerful and direct, for although the wing-beats are slow, they give an impression of great power, due to the conspicuously long wings. The hunting flight is more wavering than that of the Long-eared Owl, accentuated by more frequent and slightly shallower wing-beats. During glides the wings are often held in a shallow vee with the outer parts forward, but it also glides on level wings like the Long-eared Owl (Davis and Prytherch 1976).

VOICE

The Short-eared Owl has a fairly restricted repertoire and a voice which is not particularly powerful, in keeping with its liking for an open habitat and its often diurnal habits. This has led to the generalisation that open country owls are less vocal than those of thickly wooded areas (Sparks and Soper 1970). This may be true when one compares the noisy Tawny Owl with the more silent Short-eared Owl, but the supposition loses weight if, for example, the Long-eared Owl, which is fairly silent and very much a woodland dweller, is compared with the Little Owl, a relatively noisy species living in open or fairly open country.

The territorial song of the Short-eared Owl is a low-pitched, hollow *boo-boo-boo-boo* resembling the distant, slow puffing of an old steam engine. On 14th May 1967, I watched a male calling from the top of a spruce near a bog, and noted that the bird repeated his song five to six times per hour, each song consisting of 16 to 20 *boo* notes at a speed of two per second. More typically, the male sings only during his special display flight, and the responsive female usually answers from the ground with her low, ugly, harsh *ree-yow* call.

When the nest is threatened the Short-eared Owl has a whole repertoire of shrill notes *keaw-keaw*; *tyak*; *tyarrp*; a hoarse, barking *kwowk* and raucous, nasal noises, but it may simply snap its bill, expressing anger or agitation. A chirruping call from the male and a moaning note uttered by the female have also been noted near the nest (Witherby *et al* 1940).

Young birds beg with a long wheezing *psssss-sip*, rising at the end, but the owlets are, on the whole, very silent compared to the young of the 'wood owls'. Donald Smith (pers. comm.) describes a female with a Short-tailed Vole *Microtus agrestis* uttering 'some guttural croaks, which elicited a squeaking response from the two owlets which had left the nest and were secreted in the surrounding grass'.

Outside the breeding season the most commonly heard vocalisation of this species is, according to Clark (1975), the *reee-ow* or modifications of it. It is given, presumably, as a threat during territorial skirmishes in the winter. In this context it is heard more frequently earlier in the winter, suggesting that the number of aggressive encounters diminishes as winter progresses. The female's *reee-ow* or *kee-ow* is consistently higher in pitch and tends to be more monosyllabic than the male's. Conversely, the male's call seems to be disyllabic, with the first syllable low and rasping. This detectable difference in pitch is in accordance with Miller's report (1934) that in this species there are sexual differences in the syrinx.

Birds found injured and kept by Donald Watson (pers. comm.) at his home in south-west Scotland for some years have given a variety of calls, the most important of which is an explosive *kook-ook-a-rook!*, reminiscent of a Red Squirrel *Sciurus vulgaris*. Other calls have been a long, drawn-out *sku-r-r-t* or *whu-r-r-t*, beginning with a whistling element and running into a hoarse sound, 'like that made by water in a tap half-turned on'; *wee-ow*, which is perhaps a version of the *kee-ow* call, uttered when the bird is standing on food, especially on a carcase such as a Rabbit *Oryctolagus cuniculus*; and a whistling piping, rapidly repeated. Hissing is uttered when a bird feels threatened, and a soft, grunted note *whu* (the 'u' being pronounced as in 'bun') has been heard immediately prior to the hissing.

BEHAVIOUR

In Europe the Short-eared Owl is essentially a migratory species, only in the tropics is it sedentary. In addition, it is a veritable nomad, which helps to explain why its populations are very unstable in the region dealt with in this book. Only during the short breeding season are the owls tied to an area by their nest; outside the breeding season they will travel far and wide in search of food.

Lockie (1955) found that Short-eared Owls are strongly territorial in the breeding season and, even when hunting, are always on the look-out for and vigorously responsive towards trespassing owls. An owl would often cease hunting, chase an intruding bird and then return to its hunting. However, their territories are sometimes remarkably small, as the following examples indicate. In Germany, in a 1971 study, territories were believed to vary between a mere 9 ha and 22 ha (average 15 h, 7 nests found) (Hölzinger *et al* 1973). In Finland Rikkonen *et al* (1976) reported a mean territory size of 25.5 ha (9 nests found), Grönlund and Mikkola (1969) recorded 50 ha (40 nests found) and Korpimäki *et al* (1977) 200 ha (33 nests found). In Scotland

Lockie (1955) found the mean territory size to vary between 17.8 ha (7 nests found) and 137.2 ha (2 nests found) in an apparent response to a diminishing food supply. Likewise, Pitelka *et al* (1955) showed that the size of Short-eared Owls' territories diminishes with an increase in the density of prey animals (*Microtidae*). Thus, we can conclude that territorialism in this species is not a fixed and stereotyped trait of behaviour, but its characteristics and mode of action are directly conditioned by the availability of food.

Lockie (1955) noted three displays performed by this owl which were defensive in nature: exaggerated wing-beats (in which the wings are brought high over the back), wing-clapping below the body, and the skirmish in which one owl hovers in front of a second owl, frequently presenting its talons. Exaggerated wing-beats and the skirmish are the major aerial displays used in establishing and maintaining territories, both in winter hunting and spring breeding (Clark 1975).

Courtship displays are made in response to sexual tendency and in the Short-eared Owl are performed predominantly by the male. A major display of this type is the high-altitude wing-clap, in which the wings are suddenly held below the body and clapped vigorously, while the bird drops like a stone. It is repeated after the bird has once more gained height and has circled. Each burst of clapping commonly consists of between 2–6 claps, and is extremely short, usually lasting from 0.5 to 1 second. A typical display is terminated after 15–20 claps have been given. Clark (1975) reported 13 bursts lasting an average of 0.8 seconds each.

Simson (1966) wrote that occasionally the owl hovers into wind and hoots its courtship song, a pulsating *voo-hoo-hoo-hoo-hoo* which generally lasts about 3 seconds. If the female is present in the male's territory, she may be hunting or she may perch and observe the male, occasionally calling *keeee-yow*. At Lapua, in Finland, Short-eared Owl males started their display at 17.00 or 18.00 hours, continuing until 02.00 or 03.00 hours, but display was observed or heard almost every hour of the day, especially on cloudy days. During cold weather the males did not display at all (Grönlund and Mikkola 1969).

Courtship feeding precedes copulation, which takes place on the ground. The male flies in with prey and lands in the territory within sight of the female. The female repeatedly utters her harsh call and the male hoots three or four times as he comes in to land. In all cases it is the female that flies to the male, who still holds the recently caught prey in his bill. On being joined by his mate, the male partially opens his wings and the female takes the prey. After turning into position alongside the female, the male mounts her and opens his wings fully, in order to maintain his balance. During copulation the male holds his body horizontally and dismounts after about four seconds (Clark 1975). After copulation the female flies to the nest scrape and settles on it as if eggs were already present.

Female Short-eared Owls, whilst brooding eggs or young, half close their eyes and deliberately hide the glaring yellow iris, though without occluding the pupil. It has been suggested that this tactic removes the only obvious feature of a sitting bird, the yellow iris, making her virtually invisible to a potential enemy (D. Smith, pers. comm.). D. Watson (1972) has described a dramatic facial transformation in a sitting owl closely approached by him: 'Her round face, in fear or anger, shrank visibly, the pupils enormously dilated and the 'ear-tufts' raised till she looked almost like a Long-eared Owl.' It is difficult to disagree with him that this facial expression might act as a deterrent to an approaching enemy.

Behaviour towards a human observer at the nest varies greatly between pairs, and even in the same individual on successive occasions. Some birds sit very close, almost allowing themselves to be touched, while others leave the nest when the observer is still some metres away. Usually the male, however, appears high above when one is still a few hundred metres from the nest. As one approaches the hidden female, the male will come lower and lower, circling and barking. When the nest is only a few steps away, the male crash-dives to the ground – crash is not an exaggeration. He dives groundwards away from the nest with a force that would seem injurious, rolling over and then, looking back with wings outspread, gives the appearance of being severely damaged. To the experienced owl-watcher this type of behaviour is the surest clue that a Short-eared Owl's nest is close by (also Trann 1974).

When a number of pairs are breeding near each other, they may sometimes defend their nests as a group of perhaps five or more, by circling together over the observer. But a close approach to a particular nest, may cause a contradictory response from its owner, and the observer may be left in peace if the owner feels that the other males are now too near his nesting territory. He now defends his territory against them rather than the intruder, the initial cause of the disturbance (Grönlund and Mikkola 1969).

Short-eared Owls are often more aggressive towards human intruders than is generally realized, and at times their belligerency recalls the behaviour of nesting *Strix* owls. It seems worth adding a warning to take care in the vicinity of nests containing young birds, because on occasions an adult owl will attack. A friend of mine was rapped on the head by the females at almost every one of the 23 nests that he studied in 1969. At one nest the female and male birds each struck him on the head during every visit to weigh the young, and later whilst ringing them (Grönlund and Mikkola 1969). However, Donald Smith (pers. comm.) writes that when photographing pairs of Short-eared Owls in south-west Scotland he has 'rarely come across aggressive Short-eared Owls which were prepared to "bounce" me'.

The owl itself dislikes being mobbed. In the Outer Hebrides Meinertzhagen (1959) saw some Black-headed Gulls *Larus ridibundus* mobbing three Short-eared Owls sitting on tussocks; the gulls becoming bolder and bolder until three angry owls rose and for some fifteen minutes chased the gulls and with their superior strength clawed more than one of them. Similarly, Brewster (1925) records cases of Short-eared Owls mobbing large birds – Black Ducks *Anas rubripes* and Great Blue Herons *Ardea herodias* – possibly for amusement. On the other hand, K. D. Smith (1965) watched a migrant Short-eared Owl forced to the ground by 90 corvids in Morocco, the Brown-necked Ravens *Corvus ruficollis* and Ravens *C. corax* encircling the unfortunate bird, while the Ravens even began pulling its wings. Smith drove them off, but the owl, which also flew off, was again forced to the ground further on. Unfortunately, the outcome of this episode was not observed.

Crows also plunder Short-eared Owls' nests, and Donald Smith (pers. comm.), whose experience of this owl in south-west Scotland extends over a number of years, has written: 'I consider that one of the major predators is the Carrion Crow *Corvus corone*, and I once had the misfortune to observe a flock of Carrion Crows quartering the moor. There were 29 crows in the pack and they flew in line abreast. When a male Short-eared Owl flew up to do battle, he would be sorely pressed and the female would join him. Some of the pack who were waiting and watching would observe where she rose from and would immediately descend and take the eggs.'

Meinertzhagen (1959) remarks that the Short-eared Owl is largely an afternoon hunter. Certainly, this is the case in Finland where 483 observations of hunting owls were timed as follows: 13% were between 21.00 and 03.00 hours, 13% between 03.00 and 09.00 hours, 8% between 09.00 and 15.00 hours, but 66% were between 15.00 and 21.00 hours (Mikkola 1968, Korpimäki 1978). These results show quite clearly that Short-eared Owls are less nocturnal than most other species of owls. In fact, they hunt far more by day than any other European owl. However, Clark (1975) has suggested that Short-eared Owls are obliged to hunt during the day only when there is insufficient prey available at night.

The majority of hunting Short-eared Owls has been observed to adopt the coursing (alternate flapping and gliding) flight technique. Coursing flights are usually made between 0.3 m and 2 m above the vegetation and rarely exceeds 3 m (Clark 1975). A second hunting technique frequently adopted is that of Kestrel-like (*Falco tinnunculus*) hovering, with descent towards the prey on wings raised in a deep dihedral. The velocity of the descent is controlled by the amount that the wings are raised. Hunting from a perch is usually resorted to only when weather conditions are unfavourable for other methods. The owl watches the ground near the perch and swoops down on its prey.

Although essentially a specialist at catching small mammals by quartering the ground, the Short-eared Owl will use other methods. Glue (1977) describes how the owl will sometimes use fence posts as vantage points, flying from post to post along a fence until a small mammal is spotted and pounced upon. Occasionally, Short-eared Owls will pounce on small birds from higher perches (Johnston 1956), but such attempts are rarely successful.

In his Stirlingshire forest, Lockie (1955) found that hunting seemed to be confined within the territory while the female incubated, and also, later, whilst the nestlings were being fed. Territorial skirmishes were so violent and the owners so alert, that no intruder hunted unmolested for long. However, hunting is confined to a territory only when there is enough food. The year 1967 was not a particularly good vole year in Oulu, west central Finland, and the few nesting Short-eared Owls present were obliged to hunt up to 1.5 km from their nests (Mikkola 1968).

One male, watched closely by me at Oulu in 1967, had a very special method of food delivery when returning to the nest after the long hunting trip. He flew in with a vole to a height of about one metre above the female on the nest, made a turn over her and dropped the prey animal by the nest without landing. The male immediately returned to his hunting area, which was over a kilometre from the nest. On 25th May I obtained only one Short-tailed Vole from 250 traps set in the owls' territory, so the male was, indeed, compelled to hunt far from his sitting mate, and the prey-dropping was, presumably, a way to save time.

There is little in the literature concerning the efficiency of an owl at catching vertebrate prey. However, Lockie (1955) has noted that a 'presumed female' Short-eared Owl succeeded in 18% of the 28 pounces noted, while the 'presumed male' of a pair succeeded in 13% of its 45 observed pounces. The hunting results for a single male parent owl, according to Clark (1975), were as follows: successful 22%, unsuccessful 68% and unknown 10%, out of 192 hunting observations. The Short-eared Owl, upon making a successful pounce, nearly always flies to another location to eat its prey, exposing itself to piracy either by other owls or by other avian predators. For example, the piratical behaviour of Kestrels and Hen Harriers *Circus cyaneus* towards Short-eared Owls is well known (cf. Clegg and Henderson 1971; Clark 1975;

Watson 1977). On the other hand, the Short-eared Owl can in turn be piratical. Wood (1976) saw one of them rob a Stoat *Mustela erminea* which was carrying a small mammal, and Gordon Riddell (cited by D. Smith, pers. comm.) has seen them robbing Kestrels.

Roosting sites are usually on the ground among tall grass, sedges or heather, but Donald Smith has described to Ian Willis how, contrary to common opinion, they frequently roost in woods, at least in south-west Scotland; a circumstance which would make it 'very easy to mistake them for Long-eared Owls'. Communal roosts are normally formed during the winter and there is some evidence that Hen Harrier roosts are occupied by Short-eared Owls by day, possibly in Britain and certainly in North America (Watson 1977; Craighead and Craighead 1956). Winter roosts may often contain between 6 and 12 owls, but others of 30 to 40 occur from time to time (Glue 1977).

FOOD

A captive Short-eared Owl consumed a mean daily diet of 78 g (15–165 g) in a period of 34 days (Clark 1975).

Food pellets regurgitated by Short-eared Owls vary considerably in shape and size, and in a laboratory study Chitty (1938) was able to show that the determining factors include the size of the meal, the state of hunger, the nature of the prey and the time of day. More recently Erkinaro (1973) has shown that there is a great seasonal variation in the average dimensions of Short-eared Owl pellets, the pellets being twice as large in spring and autumn as in summer and winter. In spring and autumn when the pellets are at their largest, the owls maintain a long, almost uninterrupted rest phase by day, while in summer and winter their activity is spread almost evenly throughout the 24-hour period.

I have measured 200 pellets collected in the breeding season in Finland and their average size was $4.8 \times 2.2 \times 1.8$ cm, which is similar to that obtained by Glue (1977) from 740 pellets in Great Britain (4.5×2.2 cm). Typically, fresh pellets are elongated, roughly cylindrical, dark grey and formed from a tightly-massed conglomeration of fur or feathers with a central core of mammal and bird bones. Short-eared Owl pellets resemble quite closely those of the Barn Owl, which also hunts primarily over open country and deposits some of its castings on grassland. However, Barn Owl pellets are larger on average ($5.0 \times 2.7 \times 2.2$ cm), virtually black in colour when fresh, and later assume a characteristic varnished appearance (cf. Glue 1967).

It has been suggested that the Short-eared Owl produces pellets that are unreliable for quantative data (Kirkpatrick and Conway 1947) while others have claimed the contrary (Craighead and Craighead 1969, Errington 1932, Munyer 1966). In order to check this, Clark (1975) ran a test using a captive Short-eared Owl. His test results showed that examination of the 38 pellets produced (one per day in this case) would have underestimated mammalian prey by 2.4%, the equivalent of one Meadow Vole *Microtus pennsylvanicus* and one House Mouse *Mus musculus* out of the 83 prey animals. It seems, after all, that the analysis of pellets gives a reasonably accurate picture of the food consumed by this owl.

Relatively little work has been reported in the literature on the summer food habits of Short-eared Owls, and for a very good reason. It is usually difficult to locate the pellets which are scattered throughout the hunting grounds and not deposited at the nest like those of many other owls. The owlets do not cast their first pellets until they are 8 or 9 days old and, as they usually leave the nest at about 12 to 16 days old, few of their pellets are to be found at the nest. In addition, it appears that the parents remove the pellets as a part of nest sanitation (Clark 1975), the female even swallowing them as they are produced (Donald Smith, pers. comm.). Nevertheless, by regular systematic searches over suitable open terrain one can sometimes collect quite good samples of pellets and so assess the diet of the breeding owls. In Finland, I noted that pellets are to be found in greatest numbers at the foot of fence-posts, beside barn walls and on hummocks 20–200 m from the nest. In a few instances the male's resting site was also found, with tens of pellets, perhaps 300–500 m from the nest (Mikkola and Sulkava 1969).

The food of Short-eared Owls at nest-sites has been studied in Finland (Grönlund and Mikkola 1969; Mikkola and Sulkava 1969; and Mikkola, this study), in Norway (Hagen 1952 and Klemetsen 1967), in Germany (Hölzinger *et al* 1973 and Kumerloeve 1968), in Britain (Jeal 1976 and Glue 1977) and in Hungary (Kulczycki 1966). Some comparable results have been summarized in Table 45, which gives the proportions of different prey groups by numbers. In Finland I have identified 2,520 prey animals eaten by Short-eared Owls at 60 nests. Voles formed by far the most abundant prey group (85%), including the Short-tailed Vole (50%), the Common Vole *Microtus arvalis* (27%), *Microtus sp.* (1.9%) and the Ground Vole *Arvicola terrestris* (0.8%). Five species of shrews made up 6.5% of prey items and three species of mice 4.0%. The 45 birds consumed were 1 Cuckoo *Cuculus canorus*, 4 young Short-eared Owls (cannibalism), 1 Wryneck *Jynx torquilla*, 1 Yellowhammer *Emberiza citrinella*, 7 thrushes *Turdus sp.*, and 31 not specifically identified small birds, such as pipits, larks, warblers and finches. Insects (all of them *Coleoptera*) formed 2.5% of the food of the Finnish Short-eared Owls. Other prey groups, including frogs (*Rana sp.*), lizards *Lacerta vivipara*, one Stoat and one Weasel *Mustela rixosa*, were known to have been consumed, but their proportions in the diet were not more than 0.1% (Table 45).

Results from Norway (Hagen 1952) and Germany (Hölzinger *et al* 1973) give a picture of the food of the Short-eared Owl almost identical to that from Finland. However, Table 45 does not show that other *Microtus* species may also constitute the principal food of the owls. On the fells in Norway Short-tailed Voles formed no more than 20% of the total prey, but another *Microtus* species common on those wild uplands featured largely among the prey animals, namely, the Root Vole *Microtus ratticeps*. Hagen (1952) claims its contribution was 47%, but, in reality, there were probably many more caught and consumed, as he was unable to identify 102 voles. In the studies of Hölzinger *et al* (1973) from Germany, Common Voles were dominant (84%) as against 10% for the Short-tailed Vole.

In Britain Short-tailed Voles are the principal food of the Short-eared Owl, being 83% of 1,857 prey items from 11 breeding sites analysed by Glue (1977). The remainder was made up of mice 5.1%, Common Shrews *Sorex araneus* 3.9%, birds 3.8% and others (no details) 3.8%.

Thus, all the above-quoted studies show the diet of most Short-eared Owls to consist of at least 95% small mammals. They also show that populations do specialise to a remarkable extent in *Microtus* voles. But what happens if *Microtus* voles are scarce or unavailable?

The small sample from Hungary in Table 45 shows that the Short-eared Owl will take shrews if *Microtus* voles are scarce. Glue (1977) described how, in the absence of

Microtus voles on the island of Rhum, Inner Hebrides, Pygmy Shrews *Sorex minutus*, Wood Mice *Apodemus sylvaticus* and Brown Rats *Rattus norvegicus* were the chief foods, while on coastal marshes bordering farmland in Norfolk, England, the owls were feeding their young primarily on immature Brown Rats, plus a few small birds.

The diets of five pairs of Short-eared Owls breeding on the island of Skomer, off the Welsh coast, were examined by Glue (1977). He discovered that Skomer Voles *Clethrionomys glareolus skomerensis* and Rabbits *Oryctolagus cuniculus* comprised 44% and 42% respectively of the total prey weight. Wood Mice and birds were items of secondary importance, the latter including Rock Pipit *Anthus spinoletta*, Wheatear *Oenanthe oenanthe* and Storm Petrel *Hydrobates pelagicus*.

On Amrum, an island off the German coast, where *Microtus* voles are absent, there is a thriving population of breeding Short-eared Owls. Here the Ground Vole formed 60% of the 249 prey items examined by Kumerloeve (1968). Wood Mice and Rabbits were eaten in some numbers (15.7% and 3.2% respectively), but the most interesting discovery was the relatively high proportion of birds (20%) as prey. The birds taken were: 1 Partridge *Perdix perdix*, 1 Quail *Coturnix coturnix*, 1 Ringed Plover *Charadrius hiaticula*, 1 Lapwing *Vanellus vanellus*, 1 Turnstone *Arenaria interpres*, 4 Dunlin *Calidris alpina*, 2 Redshank *Tringa totanus*, 5 Snipe *Gallinago gallinago*, 2 Black-headed Gulls, 6 Common Terns *Sterna hirundo*, 1 Turtle Dove *Streptopelia turtur*, 8 Skylarks *Alauda arvensis*, 4 Starlings *Sturnus vulgaris* and 12 unidentified small birds. Caches of bird prey are hidden and returned to by migrants on the Isle of May, off the Scottish coast (Watson 1972).

It is clear that when *Microtus* voles are scarce or unavailable, Short-eared Owls will turn to birds or alternative mammalian prey. This demonstrates that the Short-eared Owl is polyphagous, pursuing a large number of prey species.

The preponderance of small rodents (especially voles) in the diet of Short-eared Owls in Europe as well as in North America (cf. Clark 1975) has suggested to me and many others that the owls will actively seek these rodents because they prefer them as food. But recently, Clark (1975) has put forward an interesting hypothesis by suggesting that this dominance is probably only a result of the affinity of this owl for an open country habitat. His evidence from Manitoba suggests that, like many other predators, the Short-eared Owl takes whatever prey is most available and vulnerable to them. The fact that voles, at least at times, dominate a variety of open habitats in terms of relative numbers, perhaps with peak activity periods common to predator and prey, suggests why they often form the bulk of the Short-eared Owl's diet.

Although food in the breeding season has not been studied very thoroughly in Europe, there are many references in the literature to the autumn and winter food of Short-eared Owls. The reason for this is that whereas few breeding places in Central Europe are occupied every year, it does serve as a wintering ground for the northern owls. The owls generally roost communally and return to the same localities in varying numbers each year.

Short-eared Owls are frequently shot at the beginning of the hunting season in Finland, because the duck-hunters shoot at anything flying over the lakes and marshes. Some of these illegally killed owls have been brought to the taxidermists Pentti Alaja and Heikki Kangasperko, and I have been able to analyse the stomach contents of 36 Short-eared Owls killed during the autumn (July to October). The results have been compared with the autumn pellet analysis of Aho (1964), also from Finland. Table 46 shows that the two sets of remains differ greatly in many respects.

The occurrence of *Microtus* species in the autumn pellet material is equal to that found during the breeding season, but in the stomach analysis *Microtus* voles formed only 31% of the total prey items. Shrews comprised as much as 25% and insects (all of them *Geotrupes sp.*) 14% (Table 46). Other small rodents made up 29%, including Harvest Mice *Micromys minutus* 14%, Bank Voles *Clethrionomys glareolus* 10%, House Mice 4% and Ground Voles 1%.

The food of the Short-eared Owl in its wintering areas has been studied in Britain (Glue 1977), in France (Martin and Saint Girons 1973), in Germany (Uttendörfer 1952), in Ireland (Fairley 1966 and Glue 1977) and in Yugoslavia (Schmidt and Szlivka 1968). The percentages for some main prey species have been presented in Table 47. Short-tailed Voles were the chief food only in Britain, whilst Common Voles formed 67% to 98% of the total prey in France, Germany and Yugoslavia. Both *Microtus* voles are absent from Ireland, where the results showed that the Brown Rat is the principal prey animal for the Short-eared Owl when wintering on coastal saltmarshes and bogs (Glue 1976). Table 47 shows that birds are clearly much more important as winter food (14% in Britain, 17% in Ireland and 16% in Yugoslavia) than as summer food (4% in Britain, see also Table 45).

Throughout the year some individuals, or even small populations, may specialise in their food habits to a remarkable extent. Birds, for example, were found by Glue (1977) to be the owl's main food at five winter sites. Rabbits were the principal prey for six to eight owls wintering on chalk downland in Wiltshire, England, while Wood Mice dominated the diets of four or five owls, and Brown Rats were the main food eaten at four coastal saltmarsh and agricultural roosts in Norfolk and Cambridgeshire, England (Glue 1977). Thus, Short-eared Owls will turn to avian or alternative mammalian prey in winter if *Microtus* voles are scarce due to frost and snow cover.

In conclusion, we can say that the Short-eared Owl is often monophagous, only eating voles, but it can adapt itself locally and manifest an individually developed specialisation, depending on the prevailing conditions. This is an opportunistic species which will, if necessary, take a wide variety of prey animals.

The Short-eared Owl is one of the few birds of prey for which there is evidence of a sense of smell. The information is slight but it seems worth recounting here. Donald Watson related to Ian Willis (May 1979) how one of the broken-winged Short-eared Owls he had been caring for showed signs of having a sense of smell. The owl would reject liver if it was slightly 'off', without taking it in its mouth, or even touching it with its bill. On being presented with liver in this state, the owl's reaction would be to move to take it in its bill, but at the last moment it would quickly withdraw, having made no contact with the food. On the other hand, it would always unhesitatingly accept fresh liver.

BREEDING BIOLOGY

The Short-eared Owl breeds in open country, on moorland, marshland, bogs or dunes. In Finland, nests have also been found in forest areas cleared by felling. At Lapua, in 1969, a total of 23 nests were found; 21 of them were sited by drainage ditches between fields and two by a marsh. The survival value of positioning a nest by a ditch is obvious when one remembers that agricultural activities would otherwise destroy the nest later in the spring (Grönlund and Mikkola 1969). It is true that flooding might also sweep away the owl's nest, and there is a definite tendency to pick drier sites for laying eggs and rearing young (also Clark 1975). All in all, it appears that open conditions and a suitable food supply are the prime requisites for nesting.

As long ago as 1930, Schuster had pointed out that the Short-eared Owl is the only Palearctic owl which almost regularly builds a nest. It shares, along with its close relative the African Marsh Owl, and with the Snowy Owl, the distinction of being one of the few owls in our area that regularly nests on the ground. The nest is usually a shallow depression sheltered by heather, tall grass, reeds, bushes or fallen trees. During his studies Clark (1975) watched a female constructing a nest, and saw her make a scrape before lining the nest with stalks of stubble.

Some nests have been reported to be in old nests in trees but, unfortunately, too many of the observers lacked the expertise to distinguish Short-eared from Long-eared Owl nests. However, one nest in a tree reported by Böhme (1971) seems genuine. Hagen (1952) described how Olstad found a Short-eared Owl nest on a ledge, and once, in Finland, this owl nested on the top of a broken stump at a height of three metres (v. Haartman *et al* 1967). All the above instances, however, are exceptions to the general rule.

The breeding season of this species and its fecundity varies a great deal in direct relationship to the population of its prey. In times of exceptionally large rodent populations, breeding in Finland may commence at the beginning of April, although the month of May is more usual. Two broods are sometimes raised, which explains why nests with eggs have been found as late as the end of July. At lower latitudes, such as in Great Britain, breeding begins earlier with many clutches being completed in March.

It has been demonstrated elsewhere in Europe that certain conditions, perhaps an abundant food supply and warm temperatures, will encourage reproduction in this species at a time when the urge is usually quiescent. In southern Russia during the winter of 1906/7, a plague of voles and mice induced breeding in December and January (Mead 1969). Brauner (1908) related finding owl eggs and young in a field in Rumania in the autumn and winter of 1907. Bakker (1957) wrote of Short-eared Owls breeding in December 1951 in the Netherlands (also Eriks 1952). Many of the young of these winter clutches died because of frosts. In Rumania (Brauner 1908) and in Holland (Bakker 1957) autumn temperatures had been unusually mild and mice had been very abundant.

Thirty eggs at four nests studied by Grönlund and Mikkola (1969) were laid at intervals of about 26 hours (minimum 21 hours and maximum 32 hours). However, Witherby *et al* (1940) stated that, normally, eggs are laid at about 48-hour intervals, although sometimes with a pause of up to a week or two. There is a reasonable explanation for this difference. The egg-laying time as well as the clutch size of the Short-eared Owl is determined by the availability of prey animals (mainly voles) before egg-laying (cf. Mikkola and Sulkava 1969). The clutch size of the Short-eared Owl varies from 2 to 13, according to 121 European records, tabulated as follows:

Eggs per clutch	2	3	4	5	6	7	8	9	10	11	12	13	Av.
Finland	–	–	5	4	12	12	12	12	5	1	1	1	7.4
Norway	2	–	–	1	2	4	4	2	2	1	–	–	7.2
Denmark/Germany	–	–	5	3	5	9	11	4	1	–	–	–	6.9
Completed clutches	2	–	10	8	19	25	27	18	8	2	1	1	7.3

In Finland the mean clutch size was 7.4 (Mikkola, this study), in Norway 7.2 (Hagen 1952) and in Denmark and Germany it was 6.9 (Rosendahl 1973, Hölzinger *et al* 1973), thus increasing towards the north of its range, like many other owls. The same trend is also found in North America (Murray 1976), where the average clutch size for the Short-eared Owl was calculated to be only 5.6 (186 nests found). Of the North American eggs about 70% were between latitudes 25°–50°N (i.e. south of the European clutches tabulated above), this showing quite clearly that clutch size decreases the further south that the birds nest. Schmidt (1960), writing of the Carpathian Basin, gave the average number of eggs as 5.68 but, unfortunately, he published no further details.

Rendall (1925) realised that Short-eared Owls are capable of laying larger than normal clutches when food is abundant. Indeed, the exceptionally large clutches of 14 from Scotland (Adair 1892) and 13 from Finland (Mikkola and Sulkava 1969) were laid during so-called 'vole plague' years. The largest clutch ever reported in the literature was 16 (12 eggs and 4 small young). This nest was also found during a peak vole year (1911) and found by E. W. Suomalainen at Maaninka, Finland (v. Haartman *et al* 1967). Besides the abundance of prey, in this case polygamy could explain this huge clutch, two females mated to one male laying their eggs in the same nest. I once suspected polygamy at Liminka, on the Finnish Bothnian coast, when two females nested about 300 m apart and never more than one male was seen in the vicinity of the two nests. More substantial evidence of polygamy is an early observation from Nilsiä, Finland, where two females were discovered incubating eight eggs at one nest (v. Haartman *et al* 1967).

Forster (1955), working in Canada, stated that both sexes incubate and care for the young. However, in Europe, it is usually the female alone that incubates, beginning with the first egg. If an egg becomes displaced beyond the perimeter of the nest, the owl will try to recover it by hooking it beneath its bill and pulling it back into the nest. The male brings food to the brooding female on the nest, or the female flies to take it from the waiting male a little way from the nest. In four nests containing 30 eggs, examined by Grönlund and myself (1969), incubation of the first and last eggs took the same time, the average incubation time for each being 25.7 days (minimum 24 days and maximum 29 days). This agrees with Witherby *et al* (1940). In the first-mentioned study about 25 hours (minimum 21 hours and maximum 32 hours) elapsed between eggs hatching. The interval between laying was 26 hours, and one can conclude that all eggs are incubated more or less equally (Grönlund and Mikkola 1969). One should also bear in mind that food supply has an effect on the process of incubation, which may explain why results as reported often differ. Mead (1969) writes, for example, 'incubation for the first eggs takes about three or four days longer than the later ones, as it is usually not continuous for the first few days'.

The Short-eared Owl's preference for ground nesting puts it much at risk in the breeding season, especially where agricultural practices make nests vulnerable. In Finland, 12(30%) out of 40 nests studied were totally destroyed during the breeding season (Grönlund and Mikkola 1969, Korpimäki *et al* 1977). The reasons were as follows:

	Nests
Female taken by a Peregrine *Falco peregrinus*	2
Eggs eaten by Hooded Crow *Corvus corone cornix*	2
Eggs crushed by tractor	2

Eggs burnt by grass-fire	1
Eggs unhatched	1
Young eaten by American Mink *Mustela vison*	2
Unknown reasons	2

Human beings were the cause of these failures on three occasions, by driving tractors and by setting fire to grass at the nest-sites.

In Scotland Lockie (1955) found that breeding success was even lower; of 24 nests found with eggs in 1954 only five clutches survived to hatch, and of these only two broods reached fledging, the chief predators here were Carrion Crows and Foxes *Vulpes vulpes*.

Grönlund and Mikkola (1969) found that on hatching the young weigh 14–17 g (average 15.4 g from 5 owls). As soon as they can support themselves in an upright position, after three to four days, they start to beg for food by flapping their wings and giving the *psssss-sip* call, followed by gaping. The eyelids open on the eighth or ninth day, when the young also begin casting pellets (Clark 1975). To counter the exposed nature of their ground nest-site and its vulnerability to predators, the owlets develop quickly, increasing their weight by 300% during the first five days, and by the same amount during the next five days (Fig. 29). If the parents cannot find enough food for their youngsters during this period, the strongest owlet will often eat the weakest, which helps ensure that at least some of the brood will survive. When food is abundant the parent owls control juvenile cannibalism by laying a cache of surplus food a few centimetres from the nest (cf. Ingram 1959). This practice has also developed in other species, for example, Great Grey and Snowy Owls.

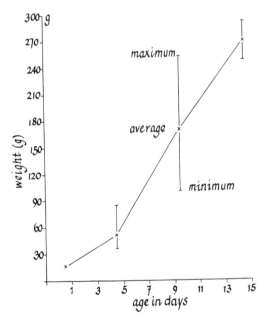

Fig. 29   *Weight increase of young Short-eared Owls at Lapua, Finland, in 1969. A total of 48 measurements obtained from 11 nests (Grönlund and Mikkola 1969)*

Young Short-eared Owls normally leave the nest before completion of fledging (Grönlund and Mikkola 1969), usually when about 15 days old (minimum 14 days and maximum 18 days from 20 young). At that time each youngster weighed about 270 g (Fig. 29). In south-west Scotland, D. Watson (1972) has noted that the owlets begin to scatter from the nest at about 12 days. Runs are made through the grass or other herbage surrounding the nest by the young owls, who are fed by the parents dropping prey to them, or by the female bringing prey, brought in by the male, through the grass a metre or so to the hidden owlets (D. Watson 1972; D. Smith, pers. comm.).

The begging display of the young after leaving the nest has been described by Clark (1975): 'the owlet, upon seeing the parent carrying prey in its beak, begins calling, ruffles the body feathers, vibrates its wings close to the body.' The young owl has conspicuous white patches of feathers on either side of the bill, their function clearly being to facilitate and stimulate the parent's transfer of prey from its own bill to the owlet's.

Once they have left the nest the young do a considerable amount of walking before they can fly, which is usually when they are 24–27 days old (Witherby *et al* 1940). Sexual maturity is attained at a year or less, and some owls are known to have lived for at least twelve and a half years (Mebs 1966).

DISTRIBUTION

The Short-eared Owl belongs to the holarctic faunal type having circumpolar holarctic and discontinuous South American distribution. The colonies on noticeably isolated island groups such as the Hawaiian, Galapagos and the Caroline Islands probably resulted from the enormous migrations and dispersal movements which this species exhibits everywhere (Voous 1960).

Throughout the main European, Asian and North American parts of its range there is only one subspecies *Asio flammeus flammeus*, but at least seven others are known from other areas. For instance, the Galapagos race is lava-coloured, streaked and barred below like a Long-eared Owl; the Colombian race *Asio flammeus bogotensis* is also darker than the nominate form and a little smaller (Borrero 1962).

In northern parts of Europe the Short-eared Owl breeds regularly every summer, although fluctuating markedly in numbers in accordance with the numbers of voles present, but there is no other evidence of widespread change in its distribution or numbers.

Merikallio (1958) stated that the Short-eared Owl was the commonest owl in Finland, the results of his line surveys revealing 9,000 breeding pairs and this estimate for 20 years ago seems sound, at least for good vole years. In Sweden, Ulfstand and Högstedt (1976) estimated that the overall Short-eared Owl population was about 8,000 pairs, increasing in peak vole years to over 10,000 pairs. Randla's estimation (*in litt.*) for Estonia, is about 100 pairs but, as in northern regions, their numbers greatly depend upon the abundance of small rodents.

In Iceland the Short-eared Owl breeds sparsely in most lowlands areas (Gudmundsson, *in litt.*). Professor Bengtson (*in litt.*) estimated the size of the breeding population as something like 150–300 pairs.

The Short-eared Owl breeds throughout Britain apart from south-west and most of southern England, the Midlands, parts of the western Highlands, the Isle of Lewis and in Shetland. When there is a vole plague the number of breeding owls may increase dramatically, especially in northern areas (Adair 1892, Goddard 1935, Lockie 1955, Picozzi and Hewson 1970). The continued spread of coniferous plantations has led to a general increase in the numbers of Short-eared Owls, which find a perfect breeding habitat among the young trees. Grazing animals are excluded from the plantations, resulting in huge tracts of long, tangled grass that encourages the moorland vole populations to expand rapidly. During poor vole years the population of Short-eared Owls in Britain is probably little more than 1,000 pairs (Sharrock 1976), although Parslow (1973) suggested that its number might reach 10,000 pairs in peak years. The Isle of Man holds a small breeding population and the Short-eared Owl has bred successfully at least once in Ireland in 1959 (Glue 1977). The lack of regular breeding in Ireland probably reflects the absence of voles there (Sharrock 1976, among others). Dr Sharrock stated that 'Short-eared Owls are probably more firmly established in Britain than at any time for at least a hundred years'.

In continental Europe, unfortunately, this owl has not been so successful. As a result of cultivation and the regulation of water-levels on its breeding grounds, it has vanished as a breeding bird in many parts of Central Europe, for example, in the Rhineland (Voous 1960). There is only one breeding site in Switzerland, used for the last time in 1953 (Schifferli, *in litt.*). In Hungary there are no more than two or three breeding pairs, and nesting is irregular (Horváth, *in litt.*). In Czechoslovakia five confirmed breeding records were obtained between 1973 and 1975 (Kučera, *in litt.*), the same number as in Austria (Scherzinger, *in litt.*). In Greece one pair bred in 1962 (Bauer *et al* 1969) and another in 1971 (Bauer *et al* 1973). There are no recent breeding records from Yugoslavia (Vasić, *in litt.*), and the breeding area shown on the distribution map must therefore be treated with reserve. There has not been a single breeding record from Rumania since the 1930s (Munteanu, *in litt.*), and Dontchev (*in litt.*) knows of no reliable breeding records from Bulgaria. It seems that in eastern Europe the Short-eared Owl is now a scarce breeding bird.

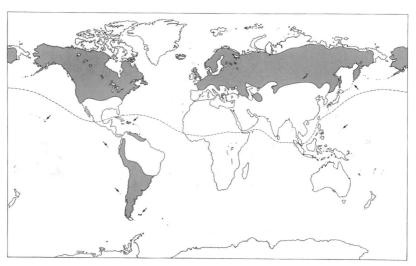

SHORT-EARED OWL

----- *approximate southerly limit of wintering range of northern populations*

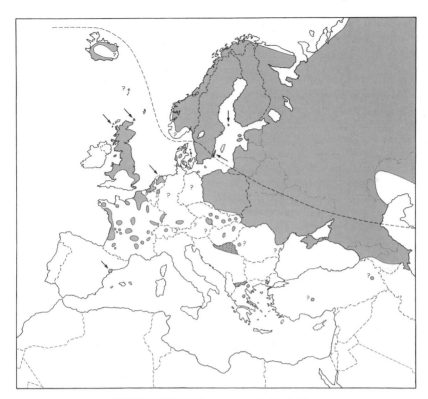

SHORT-EARED OWL – winters south of dashed line

no recent breeding records

On a brighter note, the situation has improved somewhat within the last decade in some western European countries. For instance, up to four pairs have bred regularly within the last six to seven years near the Dutch–Belgian border at Zandvliet (Huyskens, *in litt.*). Hölzinger *et al* (1973) have studied the breeding history of Short-eared Owls on a south German nesting ground. Over a period of 18 years, pairs breeding on moorland near Ulm were documented as follows:

1956	3 pairs	1965	1 pair	1971	14 pairs
1960	2 pairs	1967	17 pairs		
1964	8 pairs	1968	1 pair		

The Short-eared Owl appeared there as a breeding bird to an increasing extent every three to four years, its peak numbers always coinciding with the highest populations of the *Microtus* voles which formed its main food supply. Nevertheless, not every good vole year proved an equally successful breeding year for the Short-eared Owls in that area. Such evidence strongly suggested to Hölzinger *et al* (1973) that the Short-eared Owl leaves its regular breeding quarters in northern Europe when its food supply is scarce, moving into areas in West and Central Europe with good vole populations, and returning northwards within the breeding year. For this reason only a few regular breeding places exist in Central Europe. Besides this irregular ebb and flow of sections of the populations, the northernmost owls migrate southwards each autumn and it is then that Central Europe becomes their wintering ground. In general, *Microtus* voles in arctic and sub-arctic areas show population peaks every third or fourth year (cf. Hörnfeldt 1978), which accounts for the periodic invasions of Short-eared Owls over the same time span, with breeding taking place in Central European habitats that are not occupied annually.

The nomadic Short-eared Owl has a patchy distribution, as available ringing results show. Continental birds frequently move to Britain and vice versa. British-ringed owls have been recovered in Belgium (1), France (2), Spain (3), Gozo, Malta (1), while birds ringed in Finland (3), Iceland (1), Norway (1), Sweden (1), The Netherlands (1) and Belgium (1) have been recovered in the British Isles (Glue 1977). In short, 'they are nomads who camp where the table is laid' (Géroudet 1965). They have not entirely abandoned a settled existence and are able to regulate their clutch size to a certain extent to meet their prospective food supply; and, if too many eggs are laid, the food supply dictates the extent of cannibalism. These facts suggest that the species is opportunistic in its breeding habits, and it is not surprising to find such an owl inhabiting, if only for part of the year, every continent, with the exception of Australia.

22: African Marsh Owl *Asio capensis*
(A. Smith)

DESCRIPTION

The sexes are similar. The upper parts are a uniform earthy brown, covered with a fine, though faint, overall pattern of darker wavy barring, only noticeable at close range. There are some pale buff or rufous-buff spots or mottlings on the greater and median coverts. The bold, golden-rufous colour on the primaries, which on the open wing is crossed with wide black bars on the distal half, shows on the closed wing as a rufous-orange and black chequer-board pattern. The ends of the primaries are solid black, though the inner five are broadly tipped a dusky buff. The secondaries are broadly barred black and light rufous with a wide whitish-buff rear edge. The upper tail has four clear black bars on a pale rufous ground – colour suffusing to creamy outer feathers. The tail is tipped creamy-white except for the middle three feathers which are completely rufous.

The underparts are buff or buffish-white with faint dark barring. The earthy brown colour of the upperparts spreads broadly across the upper breast. The feathering of thighs and tarsi is rich buff.

A black narrow border surrounds the pale buffish-white facial disc, in which the all-dark eyes, each surrounded by a small area of black, stand out distinctly.

The African Marsh Owl has short ear-tufts which are hardly visible; these are more sharply pointed and smaller than those of the Short-eared Owl. The bill and claws are blackish. Young birds are more deeply coloured than the adults.

The total length varies 305–370 mm for the whole of the African population, though *tingitanus* seems to be the smallest race. The wing length in South African birds is 270–300 mm (average 285 mm from 23 birds) (Makatsch 1969, and McLachlan and

Liversidge 1970). These measurements show that this is a smaller species than the Short-eared Owl.

IN THE FIELD

A combination of dark, uniform, earth-brown upperparts (unique in the owls of our region) and noticeably contrasting pale orange patches at the base of the primaries, readily distinguishes this species in flight. Also, in flight, the body is pale underneath with a dark forepart. The perched bird can be recognised by dark brown unstreaked upperparts with an orange-and-black-patterned primary patch, and pale, only faintly marked underparts with a uniformly dark upper breast, and a pale face with dark eyes.

VOICE

The normal call of the African Marsh Owl is a deep *kaaa*, rather like a frog's croak (see McLachlan and Liversidge 1970). The call sounds like a distant Greylag Goose *Anser anser* in the recording of the African Marsh Owl in the set of discs 'A Field Guide to the Bird Songs of Britain and Europe' (Palmer and Boswall 1974). It is given from the ground, or in flight. During display it may be repeated several times in quick succession *kaa-kaa-kaaa-aa-aa* (with variations). The adults also grunt softly in flight.

The young have two rather similar calls: in the nest a husky *queeeep*, but out of it the hunger call is more a soft, rather musical *too-eeee* with rising inflection, which can be heard over 100 m away. A third call has only been heard from hand-reared birds, *wheee-o*, uttered on seeing a cat or a dog. It appears to be a cry of apprehension or alarm (Smith and Killick-Kendrick 1964).

BEHAVIOUR

Display flights may be seen at dusk and on moonlit nights, and take the form of long flights in wide circles, with deliberate wing beats and periodic wing-clapping. Aerial chases occur and, occasionally, pairs come together, flying up to meet each other feet to feet. Food has not been seen to pass from one bird to the other on such occasions.

Normally, the occupants of a territory will chase away intruding owls, but on one occasion, when visiting a nest of newly-hatched young, the two adults flew around anxiously, and adults from neighbouring territories appeared, so that finally there were five owls flying closely round the nest with no sign of fighting (Smith and Killick-Kendrick 1964).

At two nests containing well-incubated eggs or newly-hatched young, the adults, when disturbed, gave a vigorous distraction display. They would fly around in tight circles and then crash to the ground, flapping in the grass and uttering a noise that is best described as a squeal. This noise was only heard when feigning injury (Smith and Killick-Kendrick 1964). It is probable that such a display would serve to lure a dog or similar predator away from the vulnerable young or eggs in a ground nest (Brown 1970). Such displays are also seen, however, in some other owls but their purpose is more conjectural. Such behaviour may have evolved in ground-breeding owls and then persisted in some that now nest in trees.

Like the Short-eared Owl, the African Marsh Owl seems to have a very small territory, depending on the biotope and the availability of prey species. Small boggy areas probably hold only one pair, but larger swamps may have several well-defined territories. The African Marsh Owl shows itself during the day but like the Long-eared Owl it prefers hunting at night, from some vantage point, such as roadside kerbs, where the bird no doubt watches for rodents crossing the road. As a result many hunting owls are killed by cars at night.

There is at least one recent observation of a roost in Morocco, where on 15th November 1976 M. Mallalieu and T. Hodge (*in litt.*) came across at least five African Marsh Owls roosting together in an orange grove between Tangier and Rabat.

FOOD

Mackworth-Praed and Grant (1952) believed that the African Marsh Owl fed largely on insects, scorpions, etc. In Nigeria, however, food carried to the nest was observed to be almost exclusively rodents, ranging in body length 2.5–15 cm; on only one occasion was an insect, a locust, carried to the nest (Smith and Killick-Kendrick 1964). Vernon (1971) has studied the owl's food outside the breeding season in South West Africa. Several pellets were collected, which indicated that the owls were preying mainly upon birds. In all, there were 17 bird skulls, 2 skulls of Short-eared Gerbil *Desmodillus auricularis*, and 1 skull each of Pygmy Gerbil *Gerbillus paeba* and Gerbil Mouse *Malacothrix typica* in the pellets. All the birds were thought to be small seed-eaters.

During the breeding season it would seem that this owl eats mainly rodents, but at other times it will also take birds. Insects, too, may form part of the diet at any time of the year, especially when rodents or birds are unavailable.

BREEDING BIOLOGY

In ecological terms the African Marsh Owl is very like the Short-eared Owl, living in similar open, grassy or marshy habitats and differing only in being more nocturnal.

The African Marsh Owl nests on the ground in a tunnel, which it forces through the vegetation, or in a well-sheltered hollow under a large tuft. Occasionally, it uses an old crow's nest in a tree. Like the Short-eared Owl, it has some instinct for nest-building and usually brings dry straw and hay to its nest.

In Morocco breeding usually starts in April, when it lays a clutch of two to four white eggs, sometimes up to six. When incubating, the adults sit closely and soon return to the nest after disturbance. Eggs hatch at intervals of two days. When newly-hatched, the young are covered with a pale fawn down. The eyes remain closed for six to eight days. The young spend two or three weeks in the nest, then leave and are probably fed nearby for another two or three weeks. At three or four weeks the primaries are well-grown, but the tail-feathers are only about one centimetre long. By the eighth week the facial disc is fully developed, and by the tenth week traces of down show only on the breast (Smith and Killick-Kendrick 1964).

DISTRIBUTION

The African Marsh Owl is a representative of the Ethiopian fauna. It replaces the

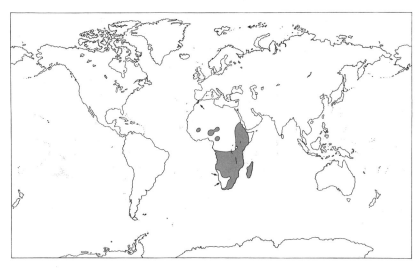

AFRICAN MARSH OWL – shaded area indicates breeding distribution

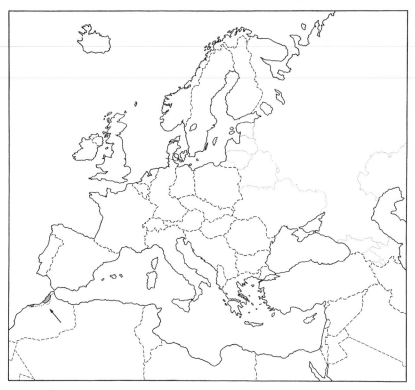

AFRICAN MARSH OWL

- present breeding distribution
- ----- limit of previously known breeding range, excluding Algeria where it bred in the past

Short-eared Owl in Africa, especially south of the Equator, where the Short-eared Owl does not occur. The African Marsh Owl, sometimes called the Algerian Marsh Owl, breeds from North Africa to the Cape, and is common locally (Brown 1970).

Chapin (1939) states that *Asio capensis capensis* is found in southern Africa north to the southern Congo and Abyssinia, and possibly Bahr el Ghazal, though the Sudanese subspecies more closely resembles the redder *Asio capensis tingitanus* of North Africa and southern Spain. However, according to Purroy (*in litt.*) there are no breeding records of this owl from southern Spain during the last 20 years, and he leaves open the question of whether it has recently bred in Europe. As a result, the African Marsh Owl has lately been considered as only an accidental bird in southern Spain and Portugal (Vicente *in litt.*). Perhaps *Asio c. tingitanus* is declining in North Africa, because Smith (1965) saw only two birds in Morocco during 15 months spent entirely in the field. Certainly, its breeding range in Morocco has contracted sharply in recent decades (see map), and even before then it had disappeared from Algeria, where it bred in the north.

The only information of recent numbers is at a very local level and concerns the roost cited under *Behaviour* (see above).

Mirage, Sahara

23: Tengmalm's Owl *Aegolius funereus*
(Linné)

DESCRIPTION

A smallish owl with a relatively large head, its upperparts are a fairly dark chocolate brown with bold white spotting, the attractive appearance of which is responsible for the Finnish name of helmipöllö (Pearl Owl). Individual colour variation is considerable among adult birds, with some having somewhat russet hues in the overall brownish coloration, while others are more greyish. The underparts are off-white, broadly streaked darkish brown, this streaking being particularly dense on the breast and trailing off on the lower belly. The facial disc is greyish-white, clearly framed with a blackish border, the pale areas continuing above the eyes in the form of arches.

The tail is short and brown above with narrow white cross-bars. As in other northern species of owl, the legs and feet are well-covered in feathers, which are unstreaked white. The claws are blackish-brown, the eyes bright yellow, and the bill wax-yellow.

Juvenile birds are distinctly different in coloration from adults and from all other owls in our area, being dark chocolate brown overall, and even darker and sootier on the facial disc, with whitish marks above and below the bill, and some white spots on the scapulars and greater wing-coverts. The flight feathers and tail are grey-black crossed by rows of small white spots.

The total length of Tengmalm's Owl ranges 233–282 mm (Haartman *et al* 1967); according to Dement'ev *et al* (1951), the wing length of males is 154–170 mm (average 163.0 mm from 21 birds) and that of females 163–181.4 mm (average 174.7 mm from 34 birds).

Géroudet (1965) gave the weight of males as 116–133 g (89 birds weighed) and that of females 150–197 g (100 birds weighed). He did not list exact averages for his weights, but the average for females is usually between 165–170 g and that for males 120–125 g, thus showing that Tengmalm's Owl is extremely dimorphic, the female being much larger and heavier.

IN THE FIELD

Although Tengmalm's Owl is similar in size to the Little Owl, though slightly larger, it is more reminiscent of a small Tawny Owl in build, having a disproportionately large head and a very distinct facial disc. It could possibly be confused with the Little Owl but the shape of its facial disc is quite different, the pale, dark-bordered arch-shapes above each eye giving the bird a surprised expression, unlike the scowling or frowning expression of the Little Owl. Other points of difference from the Little Owl, which are apparent at close range, are the much thicker (rather than bristly) feathering on its toes, and the white spots instead of narrow white streaking on the crown. Although lacking the ear-tufts of some other owls, it will occasionally raise the feathers of the front of he crown, giving the appearance of two short horns, whereupon the bird looks even more 'surprised' than usual.

Tengmalm's Owl commonly roosts on the branch of a conifer, perched in an upright stance close to the trunk like a Long-eared Owl. In flight Tengmalm's Owl again recalls the Long-eared Owl, for it flies with a silent, wavering flight rather than in the bounding manner of the Little Owl.

VOICE

The territorial 'song' of the male, which varies considerably from individual to individual, consists of a rapid Hoopoe-like *Upupa epops* succession of hoots, normally five to seven *poo* syllables (minimum three and maximum nine syllables), rising at first and falling at the end, and lasting approximately two or three seconds. This 'song' can often be heard up to 2 km away.

In early spring, in Finland, von Haartman (1967) once counted a male that hooted 1,559 times between 20.17 and 21.39 hours, the maximum frequency of calls being 227 in one ten minute period. März (1968) estimated that during one night a male may call 4,000 times, which must be really hard work for the owl! However, König (1968) noted that the territorial song is only uttered as intensively as this by unpaired males. As soon as they are paired they do not hoot regularly and soon become quite silent. The male's hooting activity is also clearly affected by strong wind, low temperature and, even, cloud cover as shown in Table 48. König considered that approaching bad weather and low atmospheric pressure was likely to inhibit the owl's hooting. He offered no detailed observations, but my own seem to fit with his suggestion (cf. Mikkola 1971).

In Finland the territorial hooting of Tengmalm's Owl may begin as early as 19.15 hours and continue until 06.00 hours. However, I have twice heard this owl hooting by day, even in bright sunlight, and Norberg (1964) has noted similar behaviour on three occasions. Territorial hooting takes place in March, April and May in Finland, whereas in Germany, Kuhk (1953) reported the owl calling throughout the year except in July and August.

Sometimes the female also utters a weak 'song' which is similar to the male's territorial hooting. König (1968) suggests that this is perhaps uttered when the female is bored or in conflict.

In addition to the snapping *zjuck*, Tengmalm's Owl has screeching and yelping excitation calls. They can be described as *ooh-vack*, *kuwack* and *waihk*. A modulated *muid* and a hollow *hooh* are used as contact calls.

When the male announces his arrival at the nest-hole by 'singing', or with contact calls, the brooding female answers with a high-pitched *seeh*. Jingling sounds are uttered by either sex when agitated, and during copulation the female *chirks*. Nestlings have high and hoarse calls, which become lower in tone after they have left the nest-hole. When disturbed, they utter a hard *bibber* or snap their bills and hiss (König 1968).

BEHAVIOUR

The territorial hooting or 'song' of Tengmalm's Owl is usually given only in the immediate neighbourhood of the intended nest-hole. If a female approaches the 'singing' male, his 'song' becomes irregular and stuttering, which König (1968) calls 'engagement-song'. As the pairing excitement increases, the male utters a long, soft trill, which may also be used as a demonstration-song when showing the nest-hole to the female.

Copulation takes place outside the nest-hole, the initial acts occurring two weeks before egg-laying. The female is commonly in the nest a few days before the first egg is laid and the male brings her one to three prey animals per night. In some circumstances an unpaired male will carry food to a nest-hole.

Unlike many other owls, Tengmalm's Owl does not seem to pair for life, or even for several consecutive years, and the female seeks a new nest-hole after each breeding season. In Finland, for example, J. Tanila ringed a female at the same nest-hole each year from 1956 to 1961 (except in 1960 when there was no nest) and each year it was a different female (cf. v. Haartman *et al* 1967).

The size of a Tengmalm's Owl's territory is unknown, but two nests were once found as close as 100 m apart, and the spacing is often no more than 200–300 m (cf. v. Haartman *et al* 1967 and Mebs 1966). Conversely, the hunting range can be quite extensive; in Germany the remains of a House Sparrow *Passer domesticus* were found at a Tengmalm's Owl nest more than 2 km from the nearest villages where this prey species occurred (König 1969).

An owl in residence at a nest always comes to the entrance hole when an observer approaches the nest tree or knocks against it. I have visited nests over a hundred times during the incubation period, or when the female was in the nest with the young during the day, and on none of these occasions did the owl leave the nest directly without first staying in the entrance hole. Usually it did not fly until I came to within three or four metres. Sometimes it simply withdrew into the cavity when I approached even nearer, and it was then difficult to persuade the owl to leave the nest. When it finally did leave, it usually flew to a nearby tree, 10–20 m away, and returned as soon as I had left the vicinity of the nesting tree.

Tengmalm's Owl has never attacked me on my visits to its nests. The habit of coming to the entrance hole when disturbed is typical behaviour in this species. It may have survival value since it helps to prevent the owl being taken in the nest by a predator. In addition, because the owl has the same general colour as the pine trunks in which it breeds, blocking the opening conceals the nest-hole, which would otherwise be easily detected and invite inspection, possibly by a Pine Marten *Martes martes*. However, the incubating female is always in danger of being surprised on the nest and killed by a Pine Marten, its principal enemy. In addition, Tengmalm's Owls are preyed upon at all times by larger raptors, particularly by larger owls and Goshawks *Accipiter gentilis*.

From 1970 to 1974 I studied the activity of Tengmalm's Owl, with Drs Klaus and Wiesner (1975), by automatic registration of nest visits at five breeding places in Finland and in East Germany. The mean numbers of nest visits per day ('actions') were found to be 2.4; 4.1; 3.2 during the incubation period, and 13.1; 13.0; 4.7; 5.3 and 8.6 during the rest of the breeding season. The number of feeding actions per day was correlated positively with the numbers of young owls and negatively with the amount of rainfall, although some individual variations were noticed (cf. Klaus *et al* 1975).

Tengmalm's Owl is a mainly nocturnal species and birds finding themselves unexpectedly exposed to the mid-day sun show signs of being completely dazzled. From Fig. 30 it can be seen that the length of time that birds were active more or less equals the hours of darkness, and this latter period alternating with the daylight hours is the basis of the owl's circadian rhythms. There is little variation in the evening at

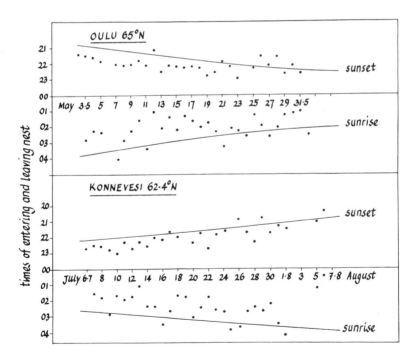

Fig. 30   Activity to and from nest of Tengmalm's Owls during breeding season, at Oulu and Konnevesi, Finland

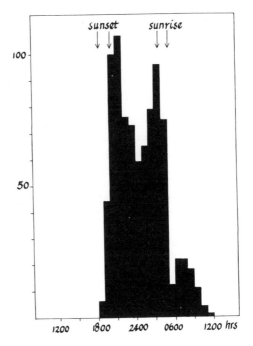

Fig. 31   *Tengmalm's Owl activity at Jena, East Germany*

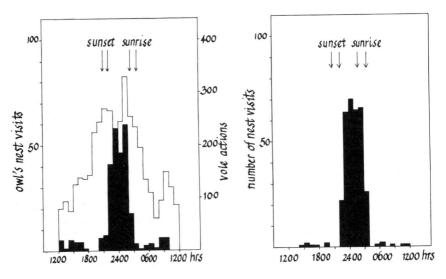

Fig. 32   *Tengmalm's Owl activity of Konnevesi*
and Bank Vole activity at Valtimo

Fig. 33   *Tengmalm's Owl activity at Oulu*

the beginning of the night's activity, unlike the morning finishing time which varies much more from day to day.

The circadian rhythm of Tengmalm's Owl is biphasic and dependent on the length of night, and therefore on the latitude of the breeding area. At Jena, East Germany, the first peak of activity was between 20.00 and 22.00 hours, the second peak being between 02.00 and 05.00 hours (Fig. 31). Around midnight, activity decreased to about half of the maximum level. At Konnevesi, Finland, the peaks were between 23.00 and 24.00 hours, and between 01.00 and 02.00 hours (Fig. 32). At Oulu, in Finland, we noticed a peak of shorter duration between 23.00 and 03.00 hours, corresponding to the short night in this region, only 172 km south of the Arctic Circle (Fig. 33).

Activity in the early morning between 06.00 and 07.00 hours was very low in all three examples. The lengthy interval between the male's hunting periods was perhaps unnoticed by the young, who were fed by the female on prey stored at the nest hole.

It is interesting to compare the activity of Tengmalm's Owl with that of its prey animals. Peaks of activity by Bank Voles *Clethrionomys glareolus* at Valtimo, eastern Finland (Heikura, unpublished material), coincided with those of Tengmalm's Owls at Konnevesi, in south central Finland (Fig. 32). Each species was mainly nocturnal and each had a clear peak before noon. Another similar link between predator and prey activity is found in the Short-tailed Vole *Microtus agrestis*, which in summer is most active at night when Tengmalm's Owl is hunting (Erkinaro 1969).

Norberg (1970) has made a special study of the hunting technique of Tengmalm's Owl including photographic sequences of prey capture. The owls always hunted in forest, particularly the denser areas. They watched for prey from relatively low perches, at a mean height of about 1.7 m (from 154 observations), and waited quite a short time at each perch, on average only 1 minute 48 seconds (132 observations). Between perches they made rapid, short flights, the mean distance being 17 m (153 observations). The owls flew skilfully despite the dense forest and rarely brushed against vegetation. Prey was always located from perches; four strikes at prey were made from a distance of about 4.5 m, and three of them were successful.

Norberg (1970) described the behaviour of Tengmalm's Owl in the act of capturing prey, basing his account on the four strikes referred to above, and on observations and photographs of a female owl striking 31 laboratory mice released near a nest. In general, rustling sounds from the prey moving amongst vegetation were the first clues to direct the owl's attention to the prey. When preparing to strike, the owl faced towards the prey and looked intently at it with an air of total concentration. Because the eyes are not very mobile, the whole facial disc was directed at the prey. Before taking off for the attack, the owl lowered its head then immediately launched itself from the perch. In the initial part of the strike-flight it beat its wings in order to gather speed, and towards the end of the strike it glided for a metre or so with the whole body aimed towards the prey. Not until immediately before impact, less than 25 cm from the prey, did the owl draw its head back, extend its legs and stretch its feet forwards with the talons fully spread, the feet covering an oval area of about 26 cm^2. Its eyes closed just before impact, apparently for protection as it plunged into the ground vegetation. Upon impact the owl spread its wings and tail for additional stability and support on the ground at this crucial moment. The prey was usually killed by bites to the head or back of the neck.

The small size of this owl and its skilful flight in dense vegetation make it well adapted to hunt in forest. The use of low perches and a close-range striking technique enables Tengmalm's Owl to make good use of auditory clues in its search for prey. The remarkable bilateral asymmetry of the ears of this and some other owl species has evolved to aid in locating prey (cf. Norberg 1968), and is related to habitat preferences and hunting methods.

Vertical asymmetry of the external ear openings, or meatuses, makes it possible for the owl to judge the precise direction of prey moving in vegetation or snow, simply by turning its head around the longitudinal axis. This direction-finding ability seems dependent on movements of its head to allow simultaneous comparison of the sounds reaching two ears until the high and low frequency components of the prey noises are heard with equal intensity in both ears (cf. Norberg 1968).

The acute attention paid by the owl during the preparation for the strike and the consequent precision of the strike are of great importance, since the prey is often large in relation to the size of the owl. The precise centering of the impact force maximizes the stunning effect on the prey and helps to give a good grip with the talons.

FOOD

The diet of Tengmalm's Owl during the breeding season has been well documented in six areas of south and central Finland (Fig. 34 and Table 49). Study material, based on 9,698 prey animals, has been collected from 95 nests. The owl's main prey species is the Bank Vole which averages 43.9% of its captures. Six species of shrews (*Soricidae*) totalled 20.6% of the food consumed; two species of *Microtus* voles (*agrestis* and *arvalis*) made up a further 20.5%. Other prey animals identified were 16 Ruddy Voles *Clethrionomys rutilus*, 10 Wood Lemmings *Myopus schisticolor*, 6 Ground Voles *Arvicola terrestris*, and a number of unidentified voles *Microtidae sp.* Voles formed 60.2–97.1% of the prey analysed, and were easily the most numerous genus at every site.

Of the remaining prey, four species of mice (*Muridae*) made up 2.1% and birds 5.4%, the latter's size ranging from thrushes *Turdidae sp.* to Goldcrest *Regulus regulus*, the most common species taken being Chaffinch *Fringilla coelebs*. In addition, the owl caught five Flying Squirrels *Pteromys volans*, four Northern Bats *Vespertilio nilssonii*, one Northern Birch Mouse *Sicista betulina*, one frog *Rana sp.* and five beetles *Coleoptera sp.*

Even in different years, fluctuations in the composition of the owl's food seem to be quite small between study areas, and this may be due to difficulty in adapting to non-mammalian prey. To a certain extent Tengmalm's Owl can compensate for a lack of voles by eating more (in a few cases even 60 or 80% more) shrews or mice, but birds hardly ever form a major part of the owl's diet. When nesting near fields the proportion of *Microtus* voles in its diet is greater than that of *Clethrionomys* voles, which dominate in forest areas (cf. Sulkava and Sulkava 1971). Studies on the diet of Tengmalm's Owl during the breeding season have also been published in Norway (Hagen 1959), Sweden (Eliasson 1958, Fredga 1964, Lindhe 1966 and Norberg 1964) and in Central Europe (Uttendörfer 1952, Plucinski 1966, März 1968, Ritter and Zienert 1972 and Klaus *et al* 975). They are summarized in Table 50.

In the breeding season small mammals comprised 92.1–97.6% of the prey analysed in four different areas of Europe. Bank Voles were the most important prey in Finland

Fig. 34   Natural provinces of Finland as used in Table 49

and Norway, Short-tailed Voles in Sweden, and different mice, including the Dormouse *Muscardinus avellanarius*, in Central Europe.

Outside the breeding season Tengmalm's Owl would seem to feed entirely upon small mammals. I have studied the contents of 29 of their stomachs at the Universities of Oulu and Kuopio; eight of the stomachs were empty, but 21 contained the remains of 28 prey animals (Table 51). Shrews formed 42.9% of the diet, voles 46.4% and the remaining 10.7% were mice. There were no birds in these stomachs which indicates that Tengmalm's Owl kills mostly young birds or those which are breeding.

BREEDING BIOLOGY

The favoured breeding habitat is dense coniferous forest of the taiga belt. Although it shows a special preference for spruce, it often occurs in mixed forests of pine, birch and poplar. Further south, it also frequents subalpine coniferous forests and, in Germany, pine forests on the lower mountain slopes and similar forests on the plains.

Like most other owls, Tengmalm's Owl nests in holes. Disused Black Woodpecker *Dryocopus martius* holes may once have been the owl's first choice, though holes of smaller woodpeckers may also have been used. Nowadays, modern forestry has caused a drastic decline of Black Woodpeckers in Fenno-Scandia, where Tengmalm's Owl first adapted to nest-boxes erected for tree-nesting ducks such as the Goldeneye *Bucephala clangula*. Over the years, large numbers of bird-watchers have distributed thousands of nest-boxes for Tengmalm's Owl. In 1974, for example, in Kainuu, Finland, only 4.4% of the owls nested in natural holes, the others used nest-boxes (cf. Helo 1975, who studied 45 nests).

The shortage of suitable holes is so acute that Tengmalm's Owl will even accept a nest box hanging on the wall of a cowshed, or on a birch tree growing in a farmyard – a box, moreover, that was meant for Starlings *Sturnus vulgaris*. I know of at least five such cases in Finland. This is perhaps not really so remarkable, because during cold winters it has been known to seek shelter in human habitations, cowsheds and barns.

No real nest is made, the eggs being laid directly onto whatever debris may be at the bottom of the nest-hole. However, if there is any soft material in the bottom of the hollow tree or nest-box, the owl usually makes a shallow depression (5 to 6 cm deep). This depression, together with one or more prey animals, often headless, are the first sign that a Tengmalm's Owl intends to nest there.

In good vole years breeding may start, even in the north of Finland, as early as the end of February (Helo 1975), but most eggs are laid in April. The clutch size may vary from three to ten, and the glossy, white eggs are almost spherical in shape (Witherby *et al* 1940). The average clutch size of 110 nests was 5.5 eggs at Häme, Finland, but this number seems to decrease southwards, for in Germany it averaged only 3.8 eggs at 34 nests (König 1969).

There is a significant difference in the number of eggs produced between a peak year for voles and other years. In a peak vole year the average clutch size was 6.2 eggs (37 nests) at Häme, Finland; and during a year when vole numbers had decreased, the average was 4.5 eggs (11 nests) (Linkola and Myllymäki 1969). Similarly, in Germany there was a clear difference between the good vole year of 1964 when the average clutch was 5.7 eggs, and the poor vole year of 1967 when it was only 2.7 eggs.

The eggs are laid at intervals of about two days, resulting in young of varying sizes (see photograph). If all the young were of the same size, competition for food in times of shortage would probably result in fewer fledglings surviving. When the young are of varied sizes, if food is short, the older and stronger owlets are likely to survive at the expense of the younger, weaker siblings. Sometimes the younger ones are eaten by older chicks. I discovered seven young eaten in this way when checking through 1,206 prey animals from Oulu, Finland in 1966 and 1967.

The female alone incubates, and in Finland incubation lasts for about 30 days, whereas in Germany it is usually 25–29 days, depending on the weather. If it is cold the incubation period may take 27–29 days, but during warm weather only 25–27 days (König 1969). Kuhk has stated that incubation commences after the second egg is laid, but Norberg (1964) found that in at least five cases the female remained in the nest by day when there was only one egg.

The newly-hatched young weigh about 7–8 g and are covered with whitish-grey down. After three weeks, juvenile plumage has largely replaced the down and at that stage the weights in Finland varied from 135 to 165 g (cf. Fig. 35). Until this stage is reached the female remains in the nest with the young during the day. Throughout their last week in the nest, the young are dark chocolate brown with light marks above and below the bill on the facial disc. At this time the adult birds do not enter the nest on arrival with food, but stay only briefly at the entrance hole before flying off again. On such visits the adult owl almost blocks the entrance hole, making it dark within the nest and the white marks on the face of the young probably guide the adult in passing the prey to them (cf. Norberg 1964).

A few days before the fledglings leave the nest, they appear at the entrance hole during the day. In Finland, owlets stay in the nest for only 28 to 30 days, but in Germany they remain on average for 31 to 32 days (Kuhk 1969). When they leave the nest the young are able to fly.

Each parent brings food to the young in the nest. However, Holmberg (1974) recorded a female Tengmalm's Owl that reared five nestlings alone. He was studying a breeding pair in 1974 when for some unknown reason the male disappeared during the incubation period. Despite this, the female successfully fed herself and incubated her six eggs, all of which hatched. Rodents were abundant, and the female owl had no

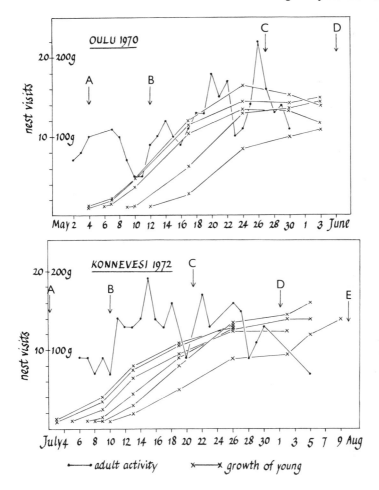

Fig. 35 Tengmalm's Owl nest visits compared with growth of young, at Oulu 1970 and Konnevesi 1972. (A) beginning of hatching period; (B) end of hatching period; (C) end of period when female stayed with young by day; (D) first young leave nest; (E) last young leave nest (?)

difficulty in bringing food to the nestlings. She usually took less than half-an-hour to catch a vole. Five of the nestlings survived to leave the nest at about one month old. Holmberg's observation indicates that it might be possible for a male to have more than one female at the same time. There are no definite observations establishing this, and the male in this case may have been killed, but there is a Finnish record of nine eggs in a nest that were laid by two different females (v. Haartman *et al* 1967).

Another account relating to a nesting Tengmalm's Owl is worth mentioning. In Finland in the summer of 1968, a Tengmalm's Owl ringed as a nestling the previous year, was found breeding in a nest-box 36 km south-east of the original nest-hole where it hatched. In 1969 this same female nested 2.7 km away in a Black Woodpecker hole, and on 28th May it held five fledglings. In that same summer the same female was observed in another nest-box 10.6 km away, looking after her second brood of the season. She was tending four young and one unhatched egg on 8th July. This was the first definite observation of double brooding for this species (cf. Heinonen *et al* 1970), and it demonstrates that Tengmalm's Owl is sexually mature at one year or a little less.

DISTRIBUTION

Tengmalm's Owl belongs to the Siberian-Canadian faunal type. Its general distribution is circumpolarly holarctic, in boreal climatic zones and mountains (Voous 1960). Four main populations occur in the broad transcontinental forest belt, *A. f. richardsoni* in North America, while *A. f. funereus*, *sibiricus* and *magnus* form a large continuum in the taiga of Eurasia. In addition, there is another subspecies, *A. f. caucasicus* in the Caucasus, western China and the western Himalayas (cf. Vaurie 1960).

In a more recent assessment Vaurie (1965) suggested that the variation in this continuous range, from Fenno-Scandia to north-eastern Siberia, is clinal. The birds become paler and greyer, less rufous, more profusely spotted with white, and larger as they range eastwards. Thus, the nominate race *funereus* intergrades with *pallens* (syn. *sibiricus*) somewhere in eastern Europe or western Siberia, while *pallens* intergrades into *magnus* in east Yakutia. Dement'ev *et al* (1951) state that *funereus* is distributed from Fenno-Scandia eastwards to the Urals.

In Northern Europe Tengmalm's Owl is distributed in a more or less regular belt, but there are a number of small, isolated breeding areas in mountains south of the continuous range which are relics from certain periods of the post-glacial epoch.

In many handbooks it is assumed that Tengmalm's Owl is a mainly resident species (Burton 1973, among others). The Boreal Owl *Aegolius funereus richardsoni*, breeding in Alaska and Canada, migrates in winter at irregular intervals in large numbers to the

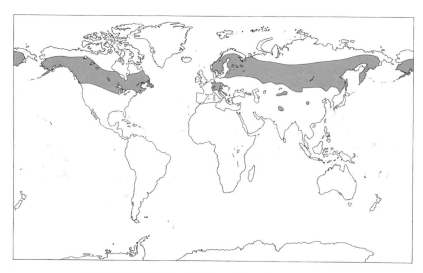

TENGMALM'S OWL – shaded area indicates breeding distribution

TENGMALM'S OWL

breeding distribution

no recent records of breeding

north-central and north-eastern United States (cf. Catling 1972). Occasionally, the nominate race is known to wander during the winter to the lower Volga, the Ukraine, northern Greece, Great Britain and the Pyrenees, which means that the Central European population is not entirely separated from the North European one. It is uncertain whether this also applies to the population living in the Caucasus. It was Mysterud (1970) who first pointed out that the North European population of Tengmalm's Owl is subject to periodic movements, which seem to occur every three or four years, in direct relationship to fluctuations in the breeding rate of small mammals. He assumed the species to be highly mobile, both sexes moving more or less at random between different feeding and breeding areas. Recently, Lundberg (1979) has put forward a new hypothesis concerning characteristics and causes of population movements in Tengmalm's Owl. According to Lundberg, this owl has evolved a strategy of partial migration, adult males being resident and females and young being migratory. This strategy would be as a response to the conflicting selective pressure between the periodical food scarcity, favouring migration, and the urgency of guarding the nest-hole, favouring residency. It was shown earlier, in *Behaviour* and *Breeding biology*, that Tengmalm's Owl females are mobile and not at all faithful to their former territories. Those examples give full support to the

Lundberg hypothesis, but more evidence will be needed to establish beyond doubt that males stay to guard their nest holes and territories in years of low vole abundance as well as in years of plenty.

It is accepted that the density of Tengmalm's Owl populations varies considerably from region to region with the availability of voles, and this may explain the difficulty in obtaining reliable data of the numbers of breeding pairs in different European countries. Merikallio (1958) estimated that there were only 1,500 pairs in Finland, which is surely much too low a figure if Ulfstrand and Högstedt's (1976) estimate of 35,000 for Sweden is a realistic one. Randla (1976) estimated that up to 500 pairs nest in Estonia in years of rich food supplies. Ritter's estimate (*in litt.*) for East Germany was more than 135 pairs, and Bárta's for Czechoslovakia was about 100 pairs.

In a recent study in the Swiss Jura Tengmalm's Owl was found to be a common breeding bird above 1,000 m, the population density being about one pair per square kilometre. It was not, however, evenly distributed, possibly because of competition with Tawny Owls (Pedroli *et al* 1975).

In Hungary, Tengmalm's Owl is known to have nested once only (Horváth *in litt.*), and there are no breeding records from Rumania, although there is one undated egg in the Timisoaka museum from the Carpathian mountains, so the species probably breeds rarely in the Norway Spruce *Picea abies* forests of this range (Munteanu *in litt.*). In Bulgaria the owl bred in the Rila mountains in 1914, 1922 and 1927, but its present status is unknown (Dontchev and Simeonov *in litt.*). Bauer *et al* (1969) suggest that Tengmalm's Owl is a local breeding bird in Greece, though perhaps more intensive bird-watching would increase our knowledge of its distribution in that country.

PART III

ECOLOGICAL RELATIONSHIPS
IN EUROPEAN OWLS

INTRODUCTION

This comparative study of European owls is a summary and discussion of the primary data presented in the opening chapters of this book.

A fundamental question of this book is: Why are there so many or so few owl species in Europe? This problem can be put in a more general way: How is the existing diversity possible in animal communities? The word community is used here to mean all animals living in a known area or in a given place, where there is a fixed number of species having a population of a certain size. An additional question is: Why aren't there more species or larger populations? Does interspecific competition explain their existing diversity?

This general ecological problem has been well documented in the case of plants, animals at lower trophic levels and in the study of the relationships between parasites and their host animals. All owls are high in the predatory chain and, therefore, in this book the problem is studied in relation to high trophic level interactions.

There are two alternative mechanisms of interspecific competition: fights, in which individuals of the losing species are expelled from territories of individuals of the winning species; and resource depletion, meaning that one species harvests resources more efficiently and lowers resource levels to the point where it can still survive but its competitor cannot (cf. Diamond 1978).

In the early days, all field ecologists tended to the view that animal populations were only regulated by competition for food and/or space. More recent research, however, on populations of the Red Grouse *Lagopus l. scoticus*, in Scotland (Watson and Jenkins 1968) and of the Tawny Owl in England (Southern 1970), has paid more attention to the behaviour and social structure of the animals studied and has concluded that territorial and aggressive behaviour regulates their numbers.

The paucity of data relating to interspecific (as well as intraspecific) relationships in species occupying higher trophic levels (cf. Diamond 1978) may give the impression that resources alone play a decisive role in the regulatory functions of a given community (the owls in this case).

269

Part III aims at clarifying the general (as well as some particular) conditions whereby interspecific interactions could affect the community of bird species of high trophic level: it remains a problem for further studies to define the specific conditions that determine when and where a given population (of owls) is either resource-limited or aggression-limited or how these two types of constraints interact. I will approach this problem by describing first the sexual dimorphism in European owls. I have understood the existence of sexual dimorphism as a morphological isolation mechanism reducing potential intraspecific competition.

The second part of this material reviews interspecific aggression among European owls and other birds of prey. Interspecific killing can be seen as the most important indicator of the existence of interspecific competition, especially when a kill is motivated by some reason other than hunger.

The third part describes the relationship of owls with their prey, and the last section deals with the general ecological differences among European owls. This ecological isolation is supposed to reduce the possible interspecific competition contributing to the coexistence of owl species.

24: Sexual dimorphism and differences in diet

In addition to interspecific competition, I think that, particularly in certain owls, a long-term effect is manifested in intraspecific competition: one example is the size differences between the sexes.

Among many birds of prey the female is larger than the male, although in most other bird groups the male is characteristically larger, The direction of size dimorphism among birds of prey is therefore said to be reversed (cf. Hagen 1942, Storer 1952, 1966, Selander 1966 and Newton 1979). Because current generalisations on reversed dimorphism in predatory birds are based for the most part on data from hawks, it is of considerable interest to determine to what extent the data on owls corroborates these findings, especially because, to my knowledge, there has been no detailed examination of the relative degree of sexual dimorphism among the European owls. Also, if not taken into account, the large intraspecific differences in size would make it difficult to compare later any interspecific differences, justifying the importance of the sexual dimorphism comparison at the beginning of this chapter.

Material and methods

The species descriptions in this book give the available measurements, but my analysis of dimorphism is based only upon wing lengths and body weights. This basic material, 1,472 wing length measurements and 644 body weights, is summarised in Tables 52 and 53. Weight would be the best indicator of overall body size, and it is unfortunate that there is not more information on body weights of many species for which adequate samples of wing measurements are available; body weights are not commonly recorded for museum specimens. However, the sources used in Tables 52 and 53 made it possible to arrive at a worthwhile analysis for the 13 'true' European owls dealt with in the book. In my analysis I have used the index that Storer (1966) introduced in his examination of sexual dimorphism in size for three North American Accipiters:

$$\text{Dimorphism Index (D.I.)} = \frac{100 \text{ (av. size of female } - \text{ av. size of male)}}{0.5 \text{ (av. size of female } + \text{ av. size of male)}}$$

This index will be positive if the female is larger or heavier (i.e. reversed sexual dimorphism), and negative if the male is larger. As recommended by Amadon (1943), and Earhart and Johnson (1970), the cube root of body weight, rather than the weight itself, was used, thereby reducing the variability of this measurement to a value comparable to the variability of the linear wing dimension.

Results

The dimorphism indices for wing length and for the cube root of body weight are presented in Table 54. Indices for wing length show that reversed sexual dimorphism is clearly present in Snowy Owl, Great Grey, Eagle, Tengmalm's, Pygmy, Tawny, Ural and Scops Owls in decreasing order of indices, that is to say, the females are larger than the males. Also, all the other owls have a positive index, but so low that we may consider them as monomorphic species (for example, Barn, Short-eared and Hawk Owls, which all have an index lower than 1). The females of Long-eared and Little Owls seem to have slightly longer wings than the males.

In contrast to Storer's findings (1966) for three species of hawks of the *Accipiter* genus, the European owls do not show the same degree of sexual dimorphism in wing length and in body weight. Dimorphism indices of a mean cube root of body weight are actually much larger than the dimorphism indices of wing length for almost every species (Table 54). Surprisingly, this is true even for those species mentioned to be monomorphic in wing length. Pygmy and Little Owls are the only European species

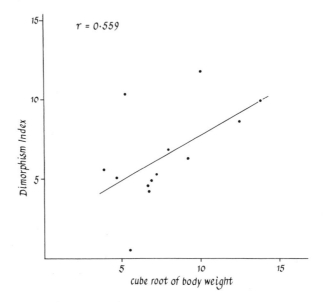

Fig. 36 Correlation between body weight and Dimorphism Index in European owls. Regression equation is y = 0.566x + 2.095. Basic data is presented in Tables 53 and 54

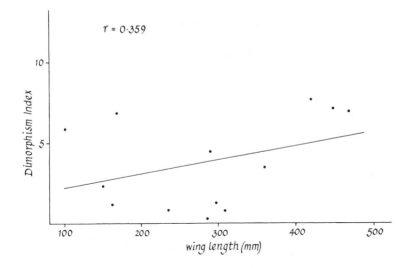

Fig. 37 Relationship of total wing length (both sexes) and Dimorphism Index of wing length. Regression equataion is y = 0.009x + 1.363. Basic data is presented in Tables 52 and 54

in which the relative difference between the mean wing lengths of the sexes is greater than that between the mean cube roots of weight. In addition, the Little Owl is the only species with so low a body weight index value that it is not certain whether the females are at all heavier than the males.

The 13 owls are listed in Table 54 in decreasing order of size (body weight) and there seems often to be a tendency for smaller owls to be less dimorphic than larger owls. However, the correlation coefficient (r) of the dimorphism index of the cube root of body weight, and the mean cube root of body weight for all the species in Table 54 is only 0.559 (Fig. 36), which means that the correlation is statistically not very significant ($p < 0.05$, but >0.01). And correlation between the dimorphism index and the wing length is even less obvious (Fig. 37). This is mainly due to the fact that three of the smallest species, Tengmalm's, Scops and Pygmy Owls, all have relatively large dimorphism indices, which may suggest that the evolution of size dimorphism is more closely related to some other factors than to size *per se*.

SEXUAL DIFFERENCES IN THE DIET OF SOME OWLS

Although many studies have been carried out on the diet of European owls, almost nothing is known about the sexual differences of their predatory habits. Lovari (1978) has published a small amount of material on the sexual differences in the Barn Owl's diet, and his conclusion was that male Barn Owls feed upon a wider range of prey than females, but his findings, based on only 11 males and 13 females cannot provide significant results.

I have examined the stomach contents of 64 Great Grey, 46 Ural and 29 Tengmalm's Owls separated by sex (Table 55). They had all died during the autumn or winter, when each sex hunts only for itself. During the breeding season the female receives most of her food from the male, which is why I felt it necessary to exclude all stomach contents from that time of the year.

It would be tempting to suggest that the female Great Grey and Tengmalm's Owls, both species with a very high dimorphism index, capture larger prey animals on average than the males (Table 55), but, remembering the small number of gizzards studied, no statistically significant conclusion can be drawn. Especially as it was undoubtedly coincidence that the Great Grey Owl which preyed upon Willow Grouse *Lagopus lagopus* from a hunter's trap happened to be a female. With the present material it seems more realistic to assume that, certainly in the broadest sense, both sexes of all the species feed upon food items of more or less the same size. However, with more information it might be possible to prove that female owls have a tendency to take slightly larger prey animals.

Discussion

Several authors have discussed the possible origin and significance of size dimorphism in raptorial birds. Hagen (1942), Storer (1952, 1966) and Selander (1966) believe that the female's greater size permits differential niche utilisation by the sexes; more simply, differences in size allow an increase in the size range of prey species and reduce intersexual competition. This may well be so, but it remains still somewhat obscure why females should consistently be the larger of the sexes.

Usually, it is the smaller male that provides food for the young and for the female while she spends most of her time with them at the nest. Later, when the owlets' food needs have increased considerably, the female hunts too. In general, the average prey weight increases with the greater weight of the predator (cf. Schoener 1968). Thus, the larger female is able to catch bigger prey items than the male to meet the increased food requirements of her rapidly growing family. Indeed, it is known that the larger prey animals (Great Spotted Woodpecker *Dendrocopos major*, Song Thrush *Turdus philomelos* etc), do not appear in the diet of Pygmy Owls studied in Finland until the later half of the nestling period (Kellomäki 1977). This is because the female does not take part in hunting until towards the end of the nestling period and the female is able to kill larger prey items (Jussila and Mikkola 1973). Sparrowhawks *Accipiter nisus* were also observed to take larger prey animals at the end of the breeding season, due to the participation of the female in hunting at that time (Sulkava 1972).

A number of authorities have put forward other explanations for reversed size dimorphism among birds of prey, but relatively little work has been done with regard to owls. Hagen (1942) and Amadon (1959) postulate that such dimorphism may have evolved to protect the young from possible predation by the male parent. Male birds of prey may have weaker parental instincts but stronger predatory instincts than females and thus represent a threat to the young; a larger, dominant female could better protect her young from cannibalism by the male. Cade (1960) believes that the larger size of the female in hawks is related to the difficulty of pair bonding in such birds. These theories do not, however, explain why there are such large differences in size dimorphism between owl species, even if each is efficient in exploiting the range of prey available, thereby minimising competition for the same food resources and improving the likelihood of success in rearing the young.

A more plausible explanation may be that food habits and the degree of size dimorphism have a relationship (cf. Earhart and Johnson 1970): the degree of dimorphism in body weights is greatest among species taking a large percentage of vertebrates and smallest in species concentrating upon arthropods. Species which feed both on arthropods and vertebrates have intermediate dimorphism indices. These findings actually support the theory that sexual dimorphism in size is related to differential niche utilisation. Certainly my low dimorphism index value for the Little Owl can be accounted for by Earhart and Johnson's explanation. They explained reduced dimorphism in insectivorous owls by postulating that such owls ensured less competition by adapting to feed upon a narrow size range of small prey items, for which pronounced sexual divergence in body size would not be advantageous.

Recently Newton (1979) has shown that raptor species preying on agile, fast-moving birds (the more dimorphic raptors) have fewer competitors than those preying on slow-moving invertebrates and mammals. Reduced interspecific competition permits bird-eaters to exploit a wider feeding niche, which provides a greater opportunity for diet division between the sexes through the evolution of sexual dimorphism.

Rensch (1950) concluded that the size differences between sexes are largest among some small birds of prey. This rule holds well among hawks of the Accipter genus, in which small species are preying on agile, fast-moving birds (cf. Newton's view above). Almost the opposite seems to be the case for owls in Europe (this material) and even more so in North America (Earhart and Johnson 1970) where the females of the larger owls have relatively longer wings and are relatively heavier than males compared to the smaller species of either sex.

Even if food habits seem to be the best explanation for this size disparity, I would like to advance another explanation, which may work for at least some northern owls. Let us take two species, the Great Grey and Tengmalm's Owl, which belong to the Siberian faunal type. Each has an extremely large dimorphism index (Great Grey 11.8 and Tengmalm's Owl 10.4). In my feeding studies of the female and male owls (Table 55) there appeared to be no remarkable differences in niche utilisation. Nor do I find any justification for the female being larger in order to protect the young against an 'aggressive' male which, in any case, rarely goes to the nest while the young are most at risk.

There are other reasons which give sexual dimorphism an important biological meaning. The Great Grey Owl and Tengmalm's Owl females are intensive incubators, leaving the nest only when evacuating faeces, and incubating at very low ambient temperatures, often during nights when the temperature drops to 20°C below zero. The female's relatively large body is therefore necessary to produce adequate heat for incubation and to compensate for heat loss (cf. also Pulliainen and Loisa 1977 for Great Grey Owl, and Korpimäki 1981 for Tengmalm's Owl).

An incubating female owl often loses weight quite markedly because the male is unable to feed both the female and the young effectively enough. Korpimäki (1981) has shown that the average weight of several Tengmalm's Owl females decreased from 189 g before egg-laying to 148 g in the second half of the nestling period, and that egg-laying itself caused only an average loss of 11 g. At the same time some males in his study lost only about 2 g. This suggests one reason why females should be heavier than males.

Recently, Snyder and Wiley (1976) also concluded in their extensive review of sexual size dimorphism in hawks and owls of North America, that the reversed nature of size dimorphism in most raptors may be a chance effect but is more likely related to advantages conferred on larger females in terms of copulation, incubation, brooding, and nest defence.

The advantage of the smaller male lies in its hunting habits. The Great Grey and Tengmalm's Owls' hunting of small rodents requires speed and manoeuvrability. Thus, it is reasonable to expect the male, which is responsible for hunting during the breeding season until the young have grown, to be relatively small in size. In addition, the smaller male can locate and carry food from greater distances less expensively.

The two northern owls I have used as an example are not the first predators to which this explanation of size dimorphism has been applied. Balgooyen (1972) has documented this very well with the American Kestrel *Falco sparverius*. The female of this hawk is considerably larger than the male, but field observations and measurements of bills and talons show that they take food of the same size; this excludes the hypothesis that they avoid competition by size. The male helps care for the young, and shows no tendency to eat them. Like the northern owls the female hawk concentrates on incubation, during which time she is fed by the male. When the young are hatched, the male provides most of the food for the young, but at the end of the nestling period the female must join him, for the grown young require a great deal of food. The lighter male is quicker at locating food and can carry it less expensively, and has therefore a larger hunting territory than the heavier female. It would be gratifying it we were able to explain all phenomena of sexual dimorphism in terms of simple energetical rules of thumb. Unfortunately it seems that sexual dimorphism may have a differing biological importance for different owl species, so that there is no one general reason why the female of one species is larger than its mate, when in another species it is not. However, we can study how the existing owls employ their sexual dimorphism to their advantage (or disadvantage) and thus affect future evolution.

25: Interspecific aggression among European owls and other birds of prey

Only rarely can one study interspecific aggression itself, because normally only the final results of interspecific competition are revealed (Diamond 1978). Because of these conceptual difficulties, interspecific interactions have generally been overlooked in birds of prey. A fight, in which an individual of the losing species is killed, is one alternative mechanism of competitive exclusion between species. Non-predatory animals also fight, but then the losing animal may be expelled only from the territory or neighbourhood of the winning species. Interspecific aggression (killings) is the best indirect way of showing that there are overlaps in distribution, hunting periods, habitats and food in European owls (also Herrera and Hiraldo 1976). Ecological isolation is far from complete, explaining why the interspecific competition can sometimes be very strong.

Material and methods

It is well known that owls (*Strigiformes*) and diurnal raptors (*Falconiformes*) sometimes prey on each other, but the records are scattered in the literature (e.g. Lönnberg 1928, Uttendörfer 1952, Craighead and Craighead 1969, Glutz von Blotzheim *et al* 1971, and Mikkola 1976). For this chapter I have checked all the publications available to me (until 1979) as well as certain unpublished sources (e.g. Merikallio archives in Finland), on food items of birds of prey in Europe, and have collated the records of owls as predators or prey of other owls and diurnal raptors. The results are summarised below, but it must be emphasised that owls are the common denominator, and that the records do not include those of diurnal raptors killing other diurnal raptors; nor do they embrace cannibalism, which is a not uncommon habit of many owls and diurnal birds of prey. No attempt has been made to survey records outside Europe, though a few from North America and Africa are mentioned where they seem relevant.

The text deals with the 13 regular breeding owls of Europe in decreasing order of size (maximum total length). There are generally two paragraphs for each species, the first covering the species as predator and the second as victim, but there are no records of the two smallest owls killing other birds of prey and so their treatment is confined to one paragraph. The records for each species are listed in Tables 56, 57 and 58. As, however, there are 2,863 records in all (752 owls killed by raptors, 1,363 owls killed by other owls, and 748 raptors killed by owls), I have had to be highly selective in the text, which should therefore be read throughout in conjunction with the Tables.

Similarly, the bibliography at the end of this work excludes many owl, and especially raptor, food studies which contain no relevant records. At the same time, I have omitted some references in the text in order to prevent confusion and repetition. Finally, many of the records relate to remains found in pellets or at nests. In such cases, of course, there is no absolute certainty that the birds concerned were taken as prey. Many may have been killed during defence of nest sites or as food competitors and, where scavenging raptors were involved, a few may even have been found dead. Alternatively, some may have been taken unfledged from the nest and others may have been sick or injured. On the other hand, some may have been killed but not actually eaten. However, in many cases these various possibilities cannot be distinguished in the records and so for the purpose of this chapter such words as 'predator', 'prey', 'food', 'killing' and 'eating' are used relatively indiscriminately.

EAGLE OWL

Food records include 1,288 owls of 12 species (Table 56) and 705 diurnal raptors of at least 18 species (Table 57). The Eagle Owl is known to kill most of the other birds of prey dealt with in this chapter, but its most numerous victims are Long-eared Owl (768 records), Buzzard *Buteo buteo* (327), Tawny Owl (286) and Kestrel *Falco tinnunculus* (194). Five species with more than 20 records are: Little, Short-eared and Tengmalm's Owls and, more surprisingly, Goshawk *Accipiter gentilis* and Peregrine *Falco peregrinus*. Birds of prey form as much as 3–5% of the total food of the Eagle Owl and 23–36% of its bird food (e.g. März 1958, Emmett *et al* 1972). The number of owls and raptors taken by Eagle Owls is thus considerably greater than their share of bird populations. It is well known that this species does not tolerate other birds of prey in its territory (e.g. Höglund 1966, Sulkava 1966); indeed, in some areas in Norway, Eagle Owls kill almost all the other birds of prey (Hagen 1952). Furthermore, in Norway they are even suspected of taking fairly large young of White-tailed Eagles *Haliaeetus albicilla* from their eyries on occasions (Willgohs 1961). In contrast, Blondel and Badan (1976) have postulated that the Eagle Owl seemingly ignores other inhabitants of rock faces in Provence, France; and, likewise, Jackdaw *Corvus monedula*, Blue Rock Thrush *Monticola solitarius*, Bonelli's Eagle *Hieraaetus fasciatus* and Egyptian Vulture *Neophron percnopterus* appear indifferent to the Eagle Owl's presence and will sometimes nest in close proximity to its eyrie. In the Alps, Richard (1923) remarked that the Eagle Owl co-habited with the Golden Eagle *Aquila chrysaetos*.

On the debit side, only White-tailed and Golden Eagles are known to kill Eagle Owls, there being five records of such attacks, so we may safely conclude that the species has no predators other than man. They do, however, have many tormentors, largely among small- and medium-sized birds, but above all birds of prey and crows. The Eagle Owl attacks them at night when they are practically defenceless and the victim species seeks to pay it back by day. The Eagle Owl is exposed in daylight and its slowness and awkwardness leave it ill-equipped to strike back effectively. The aversion of crows and birds of prey for the Eagle Owl has long been known, and man has made use of it, using an Eagle Owl to lure birds of prey within shooting range. The owl is tied to a low, T-shaped perch and the hunter conceals himself nearby. He watches the Eagle Owl, whose behaviour warns him in good time when a bird of prey is approaching. The owl will ignore small birds, but a large bird of prey elicits a different and dramatic response. The Eagle Owl assumes an aggressive stance, fluffs its feathers, lifts its wings in a characteristic way and snaps with its beak. If the other bird attacks, the Eagle Owl throws itself to the ground and turns, claws directed against the attacking bird. Falcons and buzzards usually attack quite blindly and seem not to notice any shots fired at them. Only Goshawks *Accipiter gentilis* and Sparrow-hawks *Accipiter nisus* show much caution: they attack only once and do not return. Fortunately, this method of hunting, which has contributed to the present sorry state of many birds of prey, is now forbidden in most countries.

GREAT GREY OWL

Despite its large size the Great Grey Owl is highly tolerant of other birds of prey in its territory. My analysis of pellets of this species in Finland disclosed a single adult Tengmalm's Owl as the only victim (Mikkola 1973). In Sweden a Great Grey Owl has once been known to threaten with bill-snapping a Ural Owl that came within 50 m of its nest (Wahlstedt 1969), and more recently, in Finland, a Great Grey Owl took a young Ural Owl from a nest not more than 500 m from its own nest (Kauko Huhtala, *in litt.*). There is a Swedish record of a Great Grey Owl attacking a Rough-legged Buzzard *Buteo lagopus* which strayed into its territory, but the hawk escaped uninjured (Wahlstedt 1969). In Canada, a Great Grey Owl was thought to have killed a Barred Owl *Strix varia* whose corpse was found 15 m from the base of a large black poplar where a Great Grey Owl was nesting (Oeming 1955).

There are seven Finnish records of Great Grey Owls, among the food remains of three other species: Golden Eagles have taken them at least four times (Sulkava 1966, Sulkava and Rajala 1966, and Huhtala *et al* 1976); Eagle Owl once (K. Huhtala, *in litt.*) and Goshawk twice (A. Leinonen and T. Korkolainen, *in litt.*). In addition I once saw a female Goshawk fly at a Great Grey Owl which was diving at me, but the Goshawk saw me and turned away when still a few metres from her intended victim (Mikkola 1981). A Golden Eagle is believed to have killed a Great Grey Owl in Sweden on one occasion (Höglund and Lansgren 1968), and in Canada Lawrence (1926) reported that a taxidermist found the remains of a Great Grey Owl in the stomach of a Golden Eagle. In North America, the Great Horned Owl *Bubo virginianus* appears to be a more than occasional cause of mortality. Oeming (1955) described a case in Alberta where one apparently killed and ate a Great Grey Owl, and three similar cases were reported to him by a trapper. Recently, also in Canada, Nero (1980) has witnessed three other instances of a Great Grey Owl falling victim to this more powerful owl. Proof that close encounters do not inevitably lead to fatal consequences is demonstrated by the case of another North American Great Grey Owl, raised in captivity and released within the nesting territory of a Great Horned Owl, where it established a temporary range and was not molested by the resident birds (Craighead and Craighead 1969).

SNOWY OWL

Portenko (1972) referred to single records of Snowy Owls killing a Short-eared Owl, a Rough-legged Buzzard, and an adult Gyr Falcon *Falco rusticolus*. In North America a Snowy Owl once took a juvenile Peregrine (Portenko 1972), and Levin *et al* (1977) observed a Snowy Owl near a cache of three dead Short-eared Owls and presumed that the Snowy Owl had killed the smaller owls at a time of severe food shortage. From this one could deduce that the species often takes smaller birds of prey, but I know of no other records.

It may be that there are, normally, few other birds of prey on the nesting grounds of Snowy Owls; they and Short-eared Owls sometimes overlap in periods of rodent abundance, but the food of Snowy Owls during the periodic southward extensions of their breeding range has been little studied. In Shetland, a Merlin *Falco columbarius* was the only raptor ever seen in the Snowy Owl's nesting area, but this nimble species would easily outpace the owl and was even watched hovering over the head of the brooding female Snowy Owl (Tulloch 1968).

Perhaps because of lack of opportunity, there are only four records of Snowy Owls being eaten by other owls, the predators, in all cases, having been Eagle Owls. Willgohs (1974) found the remains of one in a pellet in Norway, and Merikallio's archives instance an Eagle Owl seen eating a freshly killed Snowy Owl in Norway in December, and the stomach of another, shot in Finnish Lapland, that contained the remains of two of these birds. Nor are there many records of Snowy Owls as victims of birds of prey. A Gyr Falcon has once, at least, killed a Snowy Owl in Europe (Meinertzhagen 1959) and in North America a female Peregrine killed a Snowy Owl which had already eaten one of the Peregrine's chicks (Portenko 1972).

URAL OWL

The Ural Owl seems to present more of a threat to smaller owls than do Great Grey or Snowy Owls, and the records include 18 victims of five species: at least one immature Hawk Owl in Norway; one adult Tawny Owl in Finland and another in Czechoslovakia; an adult Long-eared Owl; twelve Tengmalm's and two Pygmy Owls in Finland. Unlike some other owls, this species' diet has been little studied which may be why only one diurnal raptor has definitely been recorded amongst its prey. Kauko Huhtala (*in litt.*) has recently found the remains of a Buzzard *Buteo buteo* in the pellets of a Ural Owl in Finland. In addition, there was one possible raptor victim, when Ural Owls and Honey Buzzards *Pernis apivorus* nested 30 m apart in Finland and one of the owls was believed to have killed a Honey Buzzard. There was a broken egg in the Honey Buzzard's nest and many Honey Buzzard's feathers on the ground between the nests (Kellomäki 1971). The size of the Ural Owl and the large size of some of its other prey animals make it very probable that it also takes the smaller falcons and other buzzards. Future pellet analysis should further illuminate this interesting aspect of its diet.

There are 15 records of Ural Owls among the food remains of five other species: White-tailed and Golden Eagle, Goshawk, Eagle Owl, and Great Grey Owl.

HAWK OWL

Like the Great Grey, the Hawk Owl seems to be tolerant of other birds of prey nesting in its territory (Mikkola 1972). In fact, there is no record of it killing any owl or raptor in the breeding season, but Hawk Owls have taken Tengmalm's Owls during the winter on three occasions in Finland.

As victims of other owls and diurnal raptors, Hawk Owls feature 23 times in the records and it is clear that the Eagle Owl, responsible in 17 cases, is their main enemy. The only other owl predator was a Ural Owl, but five raptor predators have been recorded, in each case a single Golden Eagle, Rough-legged Buzzard, Gyr Falcon, Goshawk and Peregrine. This species has a fast, hawk-like flight, which may explain why there are comparatively few records of its being killed by diurnal raptors. There is also a Finnish observation of a Hawk Owl fleeing for shelter in thick spruce on sighting a Goshawk in its territory (Rikkonen, *in litt.*).

TAWNY OWL

The Tawny Owl, like the Ural Owl, is very aggressive towards smaller birds of prey in its territory, and (perhaps because it has been more widely studied) there are records of it eating 38 other owls and 33 diurnal raptors, of six and five species respectively. The owls comprised: one Barn Owl (juvenile), three each of Long-eared and Pygmy Owls, six of Tengmalm's Owls and 23 of Little Owls. In Table 56, 'Owls as Prey', 2+ for Scops Owl means that in Southern Europe the Tawny is listed as a predator of that species on at least two occasions. Apart from single records of Hobby *Falco subbuteo* and Merlin, all the raptors have been Sparrowhawks (15) and Kestrels (15).

In its turn, however, the Tawny Owl frequently falls to other birds of prey, and there are no fewer than 288 records among the food remains of two other species of owls, and 128 records among the prey of seven species of raptors. Almost all the owl predators of this species have been Eagle Owls, but there are two records of a Ural Owl killing a Tawny Owl. It is perhaps surprising that there are not more, because where Ural and Tawny Owls overlap in range, with resulting competition for food and nest sites, the stronger Ural drives away any Tawny that comes into its territory. The diurnal raptor predators of this species are chiefly Goshawks (100 records) but there are also significant numbers of killings recorded for Buzzards (16), Peregrines (5) and Red Kites *Milvus milvus* (4). Surprisingly, there is also one Goshawk listed as a prey of the Tawny Owl (Table 57). The Goshawk attacked a Tawny Owl, but the intended victim managed to sink its own claws into the Goshawk's wingpit. The Goshawk died and the Tawny Owl was so badly injured that the observer decided to end its misery (Saurola 1979).

SHORT-EARED OWL

I know of no records of Short-eared Owls killing or eating any other bird of prey, which is hardly surprising as they feed largely on small mammals and some small birds taken on the ground.

As a victim the species has quite commonly been recorded among the food of other birds of prey, though as a bird of open country it is taken far less often than the Long-eared Owl by predators which hunt mainly in woodlands. Apart from a single instance of a Snowy Owl, the only known owl predator is the Eagle Owl, with 42 records. By far the commonest threat to this species is, however, the Goshawk with at least 66 records. It is also taken by the Peregrine (17 records), Golden Eagle (14), Rough-legged Buzzard (5), Gyr Falcon (4) and two each of Buzzard and Hen Harrier *Circus cyaneus*, while the White-tailed Eagle, Imperial Eagle *Aquila heliaca*, Long-legged Buzzard *Buteo rufinus*, Black Kite *Milvus migrans* and Pallid Harrier *Circus macrourus* have all been known to capture Short-eared Owls on single occasions.

LONG-EARED OWL

Although the Long-eared Owl kills considerable numbers of small birds, there are only four records of its taking other birds of prey: Pygmy Owl (1), Little Owl (2) and Tengmalm's (1). Both Little Owls were in England (Glue 1972, Glue and Hammond 1974).

By contrast, it is the commonest victim of all, and I have been able to find 1,134 records, 772 relating to three other owls and 362 to eight diurnal raptors. The vast majority of records concern two predators: the Goshawk with 317 records and the Eagle Owl with the remarkable total of 768. The only other owls involved (which probably kill this species mainly in territorial attacks) are the Tawny and the Ural Owl, but a considerable range of diurnal raptors prey on Long-eared Owls, with Golden Eagle, Peregrine, Red and Black Kites, Buzzard and Rough-legged Buzzard, and even three Sparrowhawks, proven so far.

BARN OWL

Barn Owls feed chiefly on rodents and although they sometimes catch small birds, there are only eight records of their taking owls or birds of prey. The owl victims were two Little Owls in southern England in 1971 (personal analysis of pellets), an adult Little Owl brought into a nest in Wales which was being photographed in July 1967 (G. F. Date, *in litt.*), three Little Owls in Germany (Jäkkel 1891), and one in France (Thiollay 1968). In Germany and in Spain Barn Owls have eaten three Kestrels (Kiefer 1892, Morillo 1976).

Barn Owls also feature less often as victims than do other medium-sized owls, with Eagle Owls, Golden Eagle, Goshawk, Red Kite, Buzzards, Lanner *Falco biarmicus* and Peregrines having taken them a total of 67 times. In addition, there is an old German record of a Tawny Owl eating a young Barn Owl (Uttendörfer 1952). There are two African records of a Tawny Eagle *Aquila rapax* and an African Hawk Eagle *Hieraaetus spilogaster* eating one Barn Owl each (Steyn 1973 and 1975).

TENGMALM'S OWL

Though not very large itself, there are two instances of it killing the still smaller Pygmy Owl in its territory. In Austria a Tengmalm's Owl attacked a hooting Pygmy Owl, and later Scherzinger (1970) could find no Pygmy Owls in that territory. In Finland the remains of a Pygmy Owl were found in a Tengmalm's Owl's nest (Huhtala, *in litt.*). To demonstrate how unpredictable such behaviour can be there are two Finnish records of Tengmalm's and Pygmy Owls nesting peacefully in the same tree (Kellomäki 1970 and E. Korpimäki, pers. comm.).

The many records at all seasons of a wide variety of predators on Tengmalm's Owl include 59 individuals of six other owl species and 32 of six diurnal raptors. Eagle Owl and Goshawk emerge as the main threats to this species, with 36 and 26 records respectively, the others being Ural, Tawny, Hawk, Great Grey and Long-eared Owls, and Peregrine, Gyr Falcon, Sparrowhawk, White-tailed Eagle and Golden Eagle.

LITTLE OWL

This is the smallest owl recorded feeding on other birds of prey. In southern England, in Kent, a Little Owl was seen eating a freshly killed immature Sparrow-hawk (Davenport, *in litt.*), and Meinertzhagen (1959) writes: 'I know of two cases where this owl has raided Kestrel's nests and taken the young, one case in Hampshire and the other at Tring.' Both localities are also in southern England.

Slightly smaller than Tengmalm's, the Little Owl is a victim at least as often as that species, and to a similar range of predators, with the Eagle Owl and the Goshawk again the most frequent. I have found 80 records of four owl predators, comprising Eagle (48), Tawny (23), Long-eared (2) and Barn Owl (7), and 48 records of nine diurnal raptors, involving Tawny Eagle and Booted Eagle *Hieraaetus pennatus*, Goshawk (32), Red Kite, Rough-legged Buzzard, Buzzard, Peregrine, Lanner and Sparrowhawk. Although the Barn Owl appears to be a fairly real enemy of the Little Owl, the latter often nests and hunts over much the same ground as the Barn Owl, even sharing the same nest tree on occasions and breeding successfully as little as 2 m apart (Glue and Scott 1980).

SCOPS OWL

In southern Europe the Tawny Owl is a predator of the Scops Owl during the breeding season, and it has even been suggested that in some areas it has caused a partial decline in the population of the smaller bird (Everett 1977). They also feature in the prey lists of Eagle Owl (7). Unlike other owls, most Scops Owls leave Europe in winter, but I have no information to show whether they are eaten by birds of prey in the African savannahs, although they are undoubtedly killed on passage through the Mediterranean by Eleonora's Falcon *Falco eleonorae* (2 records, Uttendörfer 1952).

PYGMY OWL

This tiny owl, the smallest bird of prey in Europe, is hardly capable of killing any other raptorial species itself, but it is quite frequently a victim. I have found evidence of eleven birds in the prey remains of five other owl species, these being Eagle, Ural,

Tawny, Long-eared, and Tengmalm's; and 15 records in the food of four diurnal raptors, namely, White-tailed Eagle, Goshawk (10), Gyr Falcon and Sparrowhawk.

PREDATORY INDEX

I have formulated this term for the material considered in this chapter. The primary purpose of the index is to describe the extent of interspecific aggression in species of European owls.

$$\text{Predatory Index} = \frac{P_1 - P_2}{P_1 + P_2},$$

where P_1 = number of other owl species eaten by a particular owl species
P_2 = number of other owl predators of the same owl species

This index is positive (maximum + 1) if the owl is aggressive towards other owls (that is, if it has killed more owl species than are known to prey on it), and negative (maximum −1) if the owl is killed by more species than it has been able to kill.

The Predatory Index of European owls calculated from the material presented in Table 56 is as follows:

	P.I.		P.I.
Eagle Owl	+1.0	Hawk Owl	−0.3
Tawny Owl	+0.5	Barn Owl	−0.3
Ural Owl	+0.4	Tengmalm's Owl	−0.8
Great Grey Owl	+0.3	Little Owl	−1.0
Snowy Owl	0	Scops Owl	−1.0
Long-eared Owl	0	Pygmy Owl	−1.0
		Short-eared Owl	−1.0

It can be seen that the Eagle Owl is the most aggressive towards other owls, with a maximum index of +1, and the Short-eared Owl is the least aggressive with an index of −1. The three smallest owls will inevitably have an index of −1, because of their inability to kill species larger than themselves. For this reason the correlation between the body weight of owls and the predatory index seems to be significant ($p < 0.01$). Nevertheless, size does not seem to be the only important factor affecting the predatory index, but rather the life habits of the various species. It is significant that the three owls most frequently recorded as predators: Eagle, Tawny and Ural Owl, are all highly territorial, sedentary species with a varied diet. They are much more aggressive towards other owls, especially during the breeding season, than are such nomadic species as the Great Grey, Snowy, Hawk and Short-eared Owl which feed primarily on small mammals.

Discussion

Competition among European owls often leads to fatal consequences for the weaker of the two conflicting individuals of different species. When a large owl kills and feeds upon smaller owls and raptors of the same trophic level, as shown in this chapter, the larger raptor in the process of procuring food also annihilates a potential predator. Unfortunately the existing data are too circumstantial to allow an evaluation of the importance of this benefit.

The Eagle Owl and Goshawk emerge (Tables 56 and 58) as being by far the most important predators of owls, together accounting for 89.6% of the records. Buzzard, Tawny Owl, Peregrine, Golden Eagle and Ural Owl, in that order, are the only other species with more than 15 records of owls in their diet. Table 57 does not include the diurnal raptors as predators, but, among owls, the dominance of the Eagle Owl over a wide range of raptors, and the significance of the Tawny Owl in connection with the smaller species are again borne out. Apart from these two, it can be concluded that most owls do not kill diurnal raptors, though they do occasionally take other owls. One reason for this difference is presumably the degree of overlap in activity: as a broad principle, nocturnal and crepuscular hunters will tend to clash with one another, but less so with diurnal species.

The Tables also show, as one would expect, that birds of prey do not generally kill others larger than themselves. However, there are four clear exceptions: Goshawk/ Great Grey Owl, Tawny Owl/Goshawk, Gyr Falcon/Snowy Owl and Little Owl/ Sparrowhawk. Apart from the suspected instances of Eagle Owls taking young White-tailed Eagles from the nest, the two other exceptions (Goshawk/Ural Owl and Sparrowhawk/Tawny Owl) are very marginal in that the raptors may have been large females equal in size to their prey. It is possible that, as records accumulate, instances of smaller species killing larger ones will occur more frequently, particularly where the latter are sick or injured.

As previously stated, the way an owl lives is a more important factor than its size in its relationship with other birds of prey. Generally speaking, the less migratory or nomadic an owl is, the more aggressive it is likely to be towards other birds of prey. Nomadic owls tend to concentrate in areas where there is an abundant food supply, tending naturally to nest near other birds of prey and even forming loose colonies. The territory consists apparently of only the nest site and its immediate surroundings, resulting in a hunting area that may be common to other pairs and other species (cf. Mikkola 1972 and 1973). By contrast, highly resident species guard their hunting ranges as well as the nest site taking pains to prevent other birds of prey from settling within them. In times of sudden food shortage, nomadic species invade new areas in search of a sufficiency of suitable prey. At such times, starving nomadic individuals will attack competitors for reasons which will be different from those of territorial species; for the latter the food value of another predator is probably of secondary importance. When a territorial fight ends in the death of the intruder or weaker individual, sometimes only the head of the loser is eaten.

Among hole-nesting owls, a shortage of suitable breeding places may lead to fights which have nothing to do with food. The records summarised in this chapter include Ural killing Tawny, Barn killing Little and Tengmalm's killing Pygmy Owls. It is difficult to think of any reasons for these conflicts other than competition for nest sites. Nonetheless, it seems likely that Eagle Owls, and probably Tawny Owls, as well as Goshawks and some other diurnal raptors, do take a proportion of smaller birds of prey as food, irrespective of the fact that they may be possible competitors. Hunting owls and raptors when concentrating on finding prey are bold and careless, with the result that they may fall victim to larger birds of prey more often (in proportion to their total numbers) than do other birds. For example, a conspicuous Buzzard, or a Tawny or Long-eared Owl, may be much easier to find and catch than some gamebirds (*Galliformes*). Owls may be easily located by their calling in spring and one can imagine that it would not be difficult for an Eagle Owl to clear its territory of, for example, hooting Tawny Owls (286 records) or Long-eared Owls (768 records).

The drama of the countless and continuous reactions of raptor species on one another does not fall within the scope of this work. It will be sufficient to point out that the cumulative effect on the various nesting species is measurable and significant; is influenced by the timing of nesting activities; and alters predation pressure through the tendency to limit raptor productivity. As stated by Craighead and Craighead (1969) one should not, however, lose sight of the fact that the evolutionary adjustment of a collective raptor population's nesting activities, which reduces intraspecific competition, though perhaps less evident to the observer than is the conflict, is nevertheless very real and significant in permitting numerous species of predatory birds to live and raise their young in apparent harmony and security. Or, to quote from Diamond (1978): 'interspecific competition is more often reflected in peaceful coexistence or in permanent exclusion than in running warfare'.

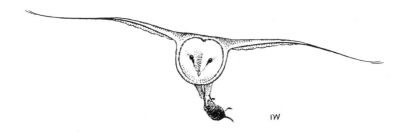

IW

26: Relationship of European owls with their prey

Predation is an ecological factor of almost universal importance for the biologist whose aim is to understand the habits and structure of animals (cf. Curio 1976). Unfortunately the interactions between predators and their prey is complex and no full understanding of this subject is at present possible as regards European owls.

Earlier in this book I have concentrated upon the qualitative relationships which exist between owl predators and their prey (Food sections), but in this chapter I will attempt to quantify these relationships. The following key questions will be considered: what is the importance of predation on the populations of prey? and what role do the populations of prey animals play on the predators?

It must be emphasised that I will limit myself here to owls, leaving aside the predator/prey relationship which exists at other trophic levels. However, it is evident that there is no difference in function between a Pygmy Owl catching a warbler and a warbler catching a mosquito, other than the energy expended in each case.

Before attempting to answer the above-mentioned questions, it is most important to have some notion of the fundamental aspects of owl predation in order to know on the one hand what kinds of prey animals European owls consume and on the other the quantity of food required by the owl predator during a given period of time.

DIET OF EUROPEAN OWLS

Qualitative aspects of the food of European owls have been well documented in Europe, especially in Central Europe (Uttendörfer 1952) and in the British Isles (Glue 1971, 1972, 1976). However, the diet of Europe's owls cannot be fully discussed until recent results from Fenno-Scandia and the Mediterranean region are compared.

Table 59 shows the average diet of ten Fenno-Scandian owls and Table 60 that of the seven owl species studied in the Mediterranean region. The food of Fenno-Scandian owls consists mostly of mammals, *Microtidae* rodents forming between 72% and 97% of the food of six owl species (Table 59). These species, Tengmalm's, Hawk, Long-eared, Short-eared, Great Grey and Snowy Owl, are all clearly 'food specialists'.

Four other owls species: Pygmy, Tawny, Ural and Eagle Owl are more 'food generalists', whose consumption of mammals does not exceed 75%. Birds form between 16% and 44% of their food, the remainder consisting of frogs, lizards, fish and some invertebrates.

In the Mediterranean region the diet of those owls whose feeding habits have been studied appears quite different from that of the northern owls. The main reason for this discrepancy is that insectivorous owls are more prominent in the Mediterranean. The two smallest species of the region, Scops and Little Owl feed almost entirely on invertebrates (mainly insects). The Tawny Owl, as a food generalist, has switched to invertebrates (57%) instead of mammals (29%). The closely-related Hume's Owl *Strix butleri* eats mammals (48%) and invertebrates (46%) in almost equal proportions.

Conversely, the Long-eared Owl, as a food specialist, relies upon *Microtidae* rodents (80%) in the Mediterranean region as it does elsewhere. The Barn Owl is another 'mammal specialist' in this region but instead of scarce *Microtidae* rodents (12%) it feeds on other small mammals (Table 60).

In general *Microtidae* rodents and many insects are a primary food source due to their abundance but they do have dramatic population fluctuations. The abundance of these prey animals waxes and wanes to such an extent that food competition among the owls living on them may be out of the question (cf. Lack 1946). Later, I will approach this problem again and more closely.

Birds, shrews, reptiles and frogs are utilised as supplementary food or as a main food when rodents and insects are scarce. They are mainly a secondary food source, less abundant but much more stable.

The primordial factor determining the individual diet is evidently the list of available prey in the owl's district. In fact, these prey animals must not only be present but available and accessible. The prey species most consumed by owls are evidently those which are the most abundant, therefore a primary food source. Due to the fluctuating character of the phytophagous prey (*Microtidae* rodents and insects in this case) their predators must take the maximum advantage of the prey species when they are most abundant but to be able to replace them when their numbers decrease or collapse. Replacement food is a key factor in the biology of owls and notably for those that consume rodents which have marked fluctuations. It is probable that it can become the limiting factor for many species, especially in the nordic countries, due to the harsh conditions or the small variety of prey animals.

FOOD INTAKE OF OWLS

The quantity of food ingested by an owl in the wild during a given time is difficult to study and we have to resort to information obtained from captive animals. Naturally there is a danger that a captive owl's way of life is not comparable with that of an owl in the wild. Captive birds are often overfed, although birds in the wild may have a greater need for food because of their higher energy usage and so the food intake of a wild and a captive owl may not be too dissimilar.

As most owls are almost exclusively carnivorous, one would expect that the volume of food ingested during a given time would be much smaller than by animals occupying lower trophic levels. The daily food requirements of European owls are indeed modest, the average food intake per day varying between 16% and 48% of the average body weight (Fig. 38). Figure 38 also shows how the relationship between the

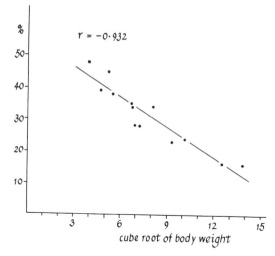

Fig. 38   Relationship of body weight and average daily food intake of European Owls. For basic data see Table 61. Food intake expressed as a percentage of body weight. Regression equation is $y = -3.14x - 55.82$

quantity of prey animals ingested and the size of the owl predator tends to increase with a decrease in the size of the owl, an example of the inverse relationship between body weight and metabolism per unit weight that is found in all animals (cf. Zeuthen 1947, 1953, 1955).

One can, therefore, expect owls to have little influence on prey populations, considering the density of the owl populations and that waste of food is negligible. As it happens, the food wasted by owls is far from negligible. One can often observe numerous prey remains near their nests which the young have not made full use of. However, such food wastage at the nest usually occurs during a 'good vole year' and has no influence on prey populations. This must be borne in mind when the importance of the pressure of predation is studied; it is not just how much food the owl ingests that should be considered.

IMPORTANCE OF PREDATORY PRESSURE ON PREY POPULATIONS

The preceding sub-headings have given some idea of the food requirements of owls, which is necessary if one tries to transpose the question to the level of community, i.e. in a given time how much does an owl population take away from the prey populations? All the European studies deal only with the relationship of one or a few species to their prey animals, and there are none relating to whole community functions. Because of these limitations I can only illustrate the effect which a fraction of the predator community can have on a fraction of the prey population.

PREDATION PRESSURE OF OWLS ON OTHER BIRDS

The predation exercised by diurnal raptors on other birds has frequently been studied, both in Europe and the United States. The work of Tinbergen (1946) gives valuable indications on the pressure that, for instance, the Sparrowhawk *Accipiter nisus* exercises on Passerine populations. Having counted the number of breeding pairs of Sparrowhawks in a given area and the number of individuals of four main prey species (in the diet of the Sparrowhawk), he was able to evaluate the mortality of these four prey species attributable to the breeding Sparrowhawks. He found that, in summer, half the mortality of House Sparrows *Passer domesticus*, a quarter of the mortality of finches and Great Tits *Parus major* and a still smaller proportion of that of Coal Tits *Parus ater* were attributable to the Sparrowhawks. I underline that these proportions refer to the whole of the mortality and not to the total of prey populations (the proportion of Sparrows captured over the total of Sparrows available was of the order of 8%). According to Tinbergen (1946), for 19 other common prey species in his study area, the Sparrowhawk is in all probability an important factor in numerical limitation. He goes so far as to say that for numerous forest birds, at least half of the natural mortality is attributable to predation.

Unfortunately predation by owls on other birds has been less thoroughly studied. This is understandable as this kind of prey has only a supplementary role in the life of owls, especially in Central and Northern Europe.

The best and fullest study so far is that of Erkki Korpimäki (1981) in Kauhava, Finland. He studied Tengmalm's Owls and calcuated the total predation pressure of adult owls and their young on prey populations between 1st February and 30th June. In five years the predation pressures on birds varied between 1.3% and 3.6%, the average being 2.5%. The proportion of birds in the owl's diet was about 14% at the end of the nestling period, explaining why predation pressures on birds are relatively high. At Ilmajoki, Finland, the Sparrowhawk reduced the number of adult and young birds in its hunting area only slightly more than Tengmalm's Owl (3%) (Sulkava 1972), although birds made up to 90% of its food. In the United States three *Buteo* buzzards, Cooper's Hawk *Accipiter cooperii*, the Hen Harrier *Circus cyaneus*, the American Kestrel *Falco sparverius* and several owls consumed 4–11% of the small bird populations (Craighead and Craighead 1969).

After studying the food of the Tawny and Ural Owls in North-Häme, Finland, I made a speculative calculation about the predation pressure of these two *Strix* owls on other birds. According to my calculations, one adult Tawny Owl needs 18 kg of food and one Ural Owl correspondingly 23 kg during a summer (from March to August). As prey, birds form 5.8 kg (32.1%) of the Tawny's and 3.6 kg (15.5%) of the Ural Owl's diet. The average territory size of the Tawny Owl is 118 ha (Nilsson 1977) and the same figure was used for the Ural Owl.

During the summer months one Tawny and one Ural Owl will together eat 9.4 kg of birds in an area 2.36 km², or 4.0 kg per km². According to Järvinen and Väisänen (1978), the total biomass of adult breeding birds in North Häme between May and June is 22 kg/km². Thus, the predation pressures of the Tawny and Ural Owls in that sector would be 18.2% of the total bird biomass of their territories. But this calculation does not take into account the fact that all birds breed during the summer and that not only is the owls' reproductive rate much lower than that of the small birds mainly taken as prey, but *Strix* owls are not the only predators of birds in North Häme.

Numbers given here are static and they do not take into account the flexible interplay that occurs between prey density and territory size. For example, Pitelka *et al* (1955), Lockie (1955) and Southern (1959) have shown that there is a limit to the owl density in a given habitat, this being determined by territorial behaviour. Territorialism must therefore be considered as the mean, permitting the predators to adjust their density to the food resources of the area (also Ratcliffe 1962, Mebs 1964), i.e. territorialism is not a fixed and stereotyped behaviour trait, its characteristics and mode of action are directly conditioned by the availability of food.

The difficulty in all studies of this kind lies in the realm of interpretation. We can cite figures that indicate the extent of predatory pressure on prey animals but one cannot draw a direct inference on the regulatory importance of such figures. In other words despite the existence of birds of prey there certainly is no lack of small passerines.

In reality, there is no general case and predatory pressure is in perpetual change, going hand in hand with the abundance of birds of prey and their prey animals.

PREDATION PRESSURE OF OWLS ON SMALL MAMMALS

Periodic cycles of abundance in numbers of small mammals (especially *Microtidae*) are common in northern and middle latitudes. The causality of these violent fluctuations has been the object of a great number of studies, though it is not the subject of discussion here. However, it is interesting that the numerical status of owls feeding on animals subject to these fluctuations can be correlated to those of their prey animals, and that the abundance of predators does not differ from those of their prey animals, except for a certain time lag and, of course, a change in amplitude (cf. Lack 1954, Hörnfeldt 1978).

Three studies have been carried out on the predation pressure exerted by owls upon small mammals in southern Ostrobothnia, Finland. In 1969 an area of 20 km² supported 40 pairs of Short-eared Owls which laid an average of 7.3 eggs; 4.7 owlets per nest reached fledgling stage (Grönlund and Mikkola 1969). From these territories about 300 pellets were collected and over 600 prey animals identified. On the basis of this material I have calculated the consumption of a population of 40 owl families during the breeding season. The owls remained in the area between 15th April and 31st July; from 5th June onwards 40 pairs fed an average of 4.7 young per nest. One Short-eared Owl ate an average of 80 g per day and produced a pellet for every 30 to 90 g of food taken. The population as a whole required approximately 1,500 kg of food for the period between 15th April through to the end of July. The food items included different groups of prey as follows:

Field and Common Voles	38,255 specimens
Bank Voles	3,733
Shrews	4,241
Mice and rats	2,706
Ground Voles and squirrels	261
Small birds	690
Owlets (cannibalism)	85

The owls therefore consumed over 38,000 *Microtus* voles. Siivonen (1972) has estimated that there can be about 350 *Microtus* voles per hectare during a peak vole year. On the basis of these figures the Short-eared Owls killed about 5% of the total population of voles in the region occupied by the owls.

Having calculated the above-mentioned percentage of predatory pressure I found myself confronted with the puzzling question: just how significant was this 5%? In one sense 5% of the entire *Microtus* vole population is undoubtedly very little, but in another it assumes a greater importance, for Short-eared Owls were not the only predators of small mammals in the area.

In 1977 Korpimäki *et al* studied a larger area and included Tengmalm's, Short-eared and Long-eared Owls as well as Kestrel and Hen Harrier as predators of *Microtus* voles. They found a total of 95 nests of predatory birds in an area of 63 km² occupied by 33 Short-eared, 21 Long-eared and ? Tengmalm's Owl pairs, and 36 Kestrel and 3 Hen Harrier pairs. Their food was analysed and it was calculated that the entire owl and raptor population required 3,252 kg of food. This amount consisted of 83,000 *Microtus* voles, over 13,000 Bank Voles *Clethrionomys glareolus*, 4,500 shrews and 2,500 small birds. According to the trapping results, the density of *Microtus* voles in the study area was about 60 voles per hectare, or a total of 378,000 voles. Thus inroads made into the *Microtus* vole population by owls and raptors seems to be as high as 22%. The present predation percentage seems to be relatively high, because in Canada small mammal predators have been observed to take only 11% of the *Microtus townsendii* population in winter (Boonstra 1977). In the United States the populations of birds of prey were calculated as taking 22–26% of *Microtus pennsylvanicus* and *Peromyscus leucopus* voles during the autumn and winter (Craighead and Craighead 1969), so the effect of birds of prey has been noticed to be relatively high elsewhere. Likewise, it has been estimated that in three months in winter (1st October to 1st January), the predation exerted upon *Apodemus* mice by Kestrels could be held responsible for at least 45% of the mortality of the initial stock of those mammals (Blondel 1967).

Korpimäki (1981) has recently shown that in 1973–79 the Tengmalm's Owls he studied consumed an average of 9.1% of all available small mammals during the breeding season. The predation pressure on *Microtus* voles was clearly highest, but shrews and Bank Voles were consumed in about the same proportions. As the number of owls increased so did their effect on the small mammals, although the density of small mammals increased at the same time.

Lockie (1955) has shown in Scotland that before the breeding season of voles is at its height, Short-eared Owls succeeded, in 15 days, in eliminating 3–13% of the population, whereas later in the season, in July, this percentage was much lower.

The above-mentioned studies apparently indicate that predators are important factors, though not, of course, at all times or in all places, in the regulation of populations of prey animals. One could draw the conclusion that basically many species are regulated by the availability of their food, territory functioning only to space out the total of animals that can be supported.

Moore (1957), on the other hand, had good reasons to doubt that the Buzzard *Buteo buteo* alone could limit the populations of any of its prey animals, but adds that, when these populations diminish greatly (e.g. in the case of Myxomatosis in Rabbits *Oryctolagus cuniculus*), strong inter- and intraspecific competition can result between birds of prey. This competition, moreover, affects birds of prey just as much as the populations of prey animals (Moore 1957). In other words, the fundamental question is: in which way are owl populations either resource-limited or competition-limited?

PREDATION EXERTED BY OWLS ON INVERTEBRATES

For the insectivorous owls, Scops and Little Owls, I have no quantitative indication on the role they play for insect populations, but it seems very doubtful that they could have any remarkable influence upon the numbers of individuals of their prey species.

The predation of owls is exerted in a very limited radius and only touches an infinitesimal part of the population of prey in its entirety. It is difficult to imagine that Scops Owls could have a profound influence on the numbers of moths or locusts in Mediterranean countries, except perhaps in the case of certain local species. As in the case of voles, insects present waves of periodic abundance, but where the populations of *Microtus* voles collapse after having struck against the trophic capacity of the area, the populations of insects are, except in particular cases, reduced by the adverse conditions of autumn. The predation by owls and raptors is quite irrelevant to the falls of density of these populations which occur, anyway, at this season (Blondel 1967).

SELECTIVE ACTION ON THE POPULATIONS OF PREY ANIMALS

This aspect of the effect of predation on prey animals is certainly as difficult to analyse as the quantitative effect previously discussed. In general, one may say that it is the availability of prey that governs the predator's choice. In a recent study by Kellomäki (1977), the Pygmy Owl showed a density-dependent choice of birds and small mammals, their proportions increasing with increasing availability. Also, Korpimäki (1981) has shown that mammals and birds were caught by Tengmalm's Owls more often the more abundant they were in the area, but that the correlations were not significant statistically.

SEARCHING FOR PREY AT SPECIES LEVEL

When the density of a prey population reaches a definite level, the predator forms a specific searching image of the prey and begins to exploit it more frequently and efficiently (Tinbergen 1960). The searching image can be formed because the predator learns to use a certain prey species or a certain hunting habitat or both (Croze 1970).

Korpimäki (1981) noted that Tengmalm's Owl concentrated more and more on particular species (*Microtus* voles among mammals, *Parus sp.*, *Turdus sp.* and Chaffinch *Fringilla coelebs* among birds), when the diversities of small mammal populations and bird fauna increased in the study area.

The Pygmy Owl has on several occasions been observed to have learnt a definite hunting habit. One individual brought, in succession, ten nestlings of Wryneck *Jynx torquilla* to its young (Sonerud *et al* 1972), and in winter a Pygmy Owl stored 20 Redpoll *Carduelis flammea* in a nest box (Kellomäki 1977). Apparently, a searching image had also been formed when 13 Redpolls were found in the stomach of a female Great Grey Owl obtained by Dall on 11th April 1868 from Alaska, as noted by Bent (1938).

Certain Eagle Owl individuals seem to seek the Hedgehog *Erinaceus europaeus* more specifically than the others (e.g. Sulkava 1966, Blondel and Badan 1976) and the Eagle Owl is probably the only natural avian enemy of the Hedgehog; in Britain, Foxes *Vulpes vulpes* and Badgers, *Meles meles* are also known to prey on Hedgehogs.

In Kuopio, Finland, an Eagle Owl learned to feed almost entirely (73% of its diet) on rats living on a waste-tip, which was about 2 km from the owl's breeding site (Mikkola 1974).

Such food specialisation among individuals of the same species is certainly of survival value because intraspecific competition is reduced and the ecological range extended. Specialisation by particular individuals does not mean that they do not change to other food when their favourite species becomes rare or seasonally disappears from the area (Curry-Lindahl 1961).

MacArthur and Pianka (1966) and MacArthur (1972), have observed that a predator living in an environment with little food cannot be a food specialist, because the abundance of prey controls the time spent in search of prey. The same predator can, in a more productive environment, concentrate more on particular species. This is true of Pygmy Owl (Kellomäki 1977) and Tengmalm's Owl (Korpimäki 1981). Occasionally, predators can utilise productive microhabitats and so optimise the use of available resources (Royama 1970). In fact, as Baumgart (1975) remarks, the Eagle Owl's preferred prey animals are not necessarily the most abundant but those that are the most accessible (relative availability, cf. Blondel 1967) and also the most economic. From this fact local variations in the bird's diet can reflect the accessibility of prey animals more than their abundance.

SELECTIVE PREDATION OF PARTICULAR PREY

Another important part of the predation problem concerns the choice of the individual prey. Does a predator attack a particular victim or does it take its prey at random? The quality of the prey individuals (e.g. sex and age) has rarely been examined, although selective predation has been demonstrated to have a clear impact on prey population dynamics (MacArthur 1960, Slobodkin 1968).

Recently, Korpimäki (1981) has found that the small mammal and bird prey of Tengmalm's Owl, in spring, show a clear male predominance. An average of 70.1% of the mammals stored by the owl were males. A slight male predominance had earlier been observed, both among Wood Mice *Apodemus flavicollis* (60.5%) and Bank Voles (56.6%), with Tawny Owls (Southern and Lowe 1968). Thompson (1955) reported that Snowy Owls selectively (65%) preyed upon male Brown Lemmings *Lemmus sibiricus* during early, but not late summer. In general, males are more active and own larger territories than females, so the higher activity and consequent vulnerability of males can explain their predominance in owl prey. Selective predation by owls and other predators on male voles can explain in some cases the known deficiency of males in resident microtine populations (e.g. Myers and Krebs 1971).

Predators may also concentrate upon a certain age group. For instance, Lockie (1955) noticed that in July young inexperienced voles paid a heavier toll than the adults to Short-eared Owls. Beacham (1979) found that avian predators took a higher proportion of smaller and, presumably, young *Microtus townsendii* than did his traps. Pearson and Pearson (1947) reported that the Short-tailed Shrews *Blarina brevicauda* captured by owls were younger than those caught in traps. However, Southern and Lowe (1968) found that there was no size selection of Bank Vole and Wood Mouse populations by Tawny Owls at any time of the year. The previous conclusions could therefore be a result of traps selecting larger animals, or predators selecting smaller animals, or both.

Errington (1956) suggested that predators do not prey randomly upon individuals from a population but, instead, remove those individuals whose social position renders them more vulnerable to predation. In vole populations, smaller animals tend to be subordinate. Roberts and Wolfe (1974) discovered that a Red-tailed Hawk *Buteo jamaicensis* selectively removed subordinate individuals, thus supporting Errington's hypothesis.

For a long time predation has been thought to eliminate odd or otherwise conspicuous individuals from the population and thus to contribute substantially to uniformity. Kaufman (1974) found that Barn and Long-eared Owls depredate conspicuous white mice more than cryptic agouti mice, but that they do so much more in dense than in sparse vegetation.

Dice (1947) records some interesting experiments he has made on the choice of prey animals by Barn and Long-eared Owls. This author has shown that when these owls were presented with a batch of homochromous prey animals and the same number of heterochromous prey animals (all varieties of the same species), they will selectively capture the latter. These experiments prove both the protective role of the homochrome and the capacity, even for nocturnal birds of prey, to choose their prey.

Oddly-marked or coloured animals apparently suffer the attentions of raptorial birds more than those of normal appearance. Müller (1975) has shown that hawks select oddly-coloured prey. Hawks were offered the same colour of mouse for ten consecutive captures and then a choice between that and another colour. The birds usually selected the 'unusual' colour.

There are also many records which indicate that hunting predators react to animals with physical defects, such animals being clearly more vulnerable. Frey (1973) found that 11% of all Pheasants *Phasianus colchicus* caught by Eagle Owls were injured prior to capture, i.e they had broken limbs, etc. According to Kenward (1976), the Goshawk *Accipiter gentilis* will select those Woodpigeons *Columba palumbus* whose nutritional condition is below average. Thus, predators, preying upon the sick and weakly, exert a selective effect through their choice of prey.

Discussion

Despite the paucity of numerical data on the importance of the pressure of predation on prey animals, it seems certain that the regulatory role of owls is not a neutral one. However, the predators' influence is not presumed to initiate a decrease in vole populations, because in theory the growth rates in owl and vole or in owl and insect populations are so fundamentally different, that the growth of the prey population should always be to some extent independent of the pressure of predation (cf. Blondel 1967, White 1978). On the other hand, Oksanen (in press) has strongly criticised the above-mentioned view of a carnivorous population's inability to control a herbivorous one, unless the number of carnivores preying upon that population has the potential to increase more rapidly than the herbivores.

However, it is known that owls as predators benefit from the abundant voles and build up their own stocks, whereupon the impact of the predators grows more and more effective. So, at some point the control exercised by predators alone could be sufficient to maintain the decline (cf. Hörnfeldt 1978).

From the evolutive point of view the selective pressure caused by the predation seems far more important to us. As the few above-mentioned examples show, the predators probably eradicate the weak and otherwise conspicuous (odd) individuals of a prey species. Slobodkin (1968, 1974) has suggested that predators manage their prey so as to ensure its continued availability, the predators taking from their prey those that have the lowest reproductive value. Since predators kill the young and the old and those that are parasitised and have consequently become sterile (cf. Holmes and Bethel 1972), predators indeed appear prudent, but the young and the old are the most easily obtained, thus rendering Slobodkin's (1974) view difficult to prove (also Curio 1976).

27: Ecological isolation mechanisms of European owls

The laboratory experiments of Gause (1934), more recently refined by Hardin (1960) and Levin (1970), led to the formal enunciation of the competitive exclusion principle. This theory predicts that in a given situation one species will be more efficient than another and that by competing for the same limited environmental resources it will eventually replace the other.

Related species often differ, either in habitat or size, and thereby avoid competitive elimination (MacArthur and Levins 1964). The way in which they differ is related to specialised habits in their use of resources, which in turn control the numbers of co-existing species and the evolution of the community in general.

Avian ecologists have often hoped to demonstrate that closely-related species which co-exist in the same area are separated ecologically; Lack (1971) presented an extensive review of this. However, little is known of the isolation mechanisms of owls.

Herrera and Hiraldo (1976) demonstrated (partly using my published materials) that there are food niche differences between Mediterranean and other European owls, but they did not cover other niche dimensions such as habitat selection, nesting habits and hunting methods (cf. Hutchinson 1957, 1959; Whittaker et al 1973).

DIFFERENCES IN MORPHOLOGY

Before comparing functional and behavioural aspects of the biology of owls with respect to ecological isolation and competition, I wish to consider the morphological aspects of these species which may be factors in creating or reducing competition.

One of the ways in which animals are thought to co-exist is by differences in body sizes. Quite simply, different-sized animals eat different-sized foods, or they utilise different resources, until at some point there is no overlap and co-existence is permissible (Wilson 1975).

The limits of similarity among co-existing competitors are unknown, but in many cases it appears that the weight ratio of allied species in competition should be about 2, implying that one species is about twice as heavy as the other (cf. Diamond 1973, Price 1975).

Owls are mostly birds of medium size but the largest species, the Eagle Owl, weighs more than forty times as much as the smallest, the Pygmy Owl (Table 53). Closely-related species should clearly differ in size but this statement seems not to be valid for European owls. The weight ratios of three *Strix* owls are between 1.3 and 2.0 and that of two *Asio* species 1.3 (Table 62). In addition, three large owls (Eagle, Snowy and Great Grey Owl) and five medium-sized owls (Tawny, Short-eared, Long-eared, Barn and Hawk Owl) as well as three small owls (Little, Tengmalm's and Scops Owl) are more or less equal in size within their own group.

Thus, the size similarity between related species, and even with species belonging to a different genus, is high enough to cause or to make possible interspecific competition among co-existing birds.

Larger predators utilise food sizes unavailable to smaller predators, whereas the reverse is only rarely true (Wilson 1975). This gives the large species an absolute advantage as a competitor. The Pygmy Owl cannot eat the optimal food of the Eagle Owl, but the latter can eat the optimal food of the smaller species, though less efficiently.

Though morphology as such is not a niche dimension, differences in external features often serve indirectly as evidence of the ecological segregation in food and feeding habits. For example, three closely-related *Strix* owls have clearly different skeletons and claws (Mikkola 1981). Despite its large size the Great Grey Owl has a remarkably lightly-built skeleton compared with the other two *Strix* owls, explaining why it feeds principally on small prey items.

In addition, the Great Grey Owl has long, slender claws, which are well adapted for capturing fast-moving small mammals on the ground. The short, strongly curved claws of the Tawny Owl, on the other hand, seem well-fitted for grasping birds in the air, and the strong, thick claws of the Ural Owl are appropriate for its role as a predator of larger mammals (Höglund and Lansgren 1968, and Mikkola 1981).

This example shows how, according to Gause's principle (1934), related sympatric species, when forced to evade interspecific competition, may drift apart in structural differences and adjust to their required ecological specialities.

BIOGEOGRAPHICAL DISTRIBUTION

One way of avoiding possible interspecific competition is to have a different biogeographical distribution. There are 13 owl species which regularly breed in Europe but they are not evenly spread all over that continent. Generally speaking, the number of bird species increases towards the south, but in Europe the number of co-existing owls is at its highest at about 57°N latitude (10 species), and from there it decreases both southwards and northwards (Fig. 39). However, Figure 39 shows that the decrease in owl species southwards is restricted to the Mediterranean region (and the Sahara which supports very few owl species); much further south in Kenya the

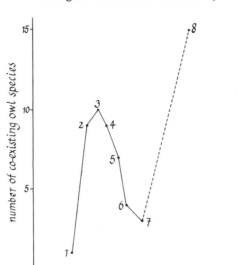

Fig. 39 Latitudinal changes in numbers of co-existing species from Norway to Kenya. Distribution data from Owls of the World *(ed. Burton, 1973). 1, Bear Island, Norway; 2, Central Finland; 3, Estonia, USSR; 4, Poland; 5, Yugoslavia; 6, Greece; 7, Egypt; 8, Kenya*

number of breeding owl species is again 15.

Herrera and Hiraldo (1976) consider that the disappearance of the abundant *Microtidae* voles in the Mediterranean region is followed by the elimination of some owl species. They therefore regard the southern owls to be more resource-limited than competition-limited. However, interspecific competition ought to increase to the south, and the northern species are supposed to be resource-limited (Diamond 1978). This question will be dealt with in the section *Differences in diet*, where it will be shown that interspecific competition can also be very intensive in the north.

In Europe, to judge by the number of co-existing owl species, one can say that the centre of ecological competitive ability seems to be in the middle latitudes.

It is not possible to give a detailed account of the distribution overlap of European owls, but some approximate indications are given in Table 63. Whereas the Snowy Owl occasionally shares a common range only with the northern Short-eared Owls, such species as Eagle, Tawny and Long-eared Owls are likely to encounter almost all other European owls at least in parts of their normal distribution range. The northern species (Great Grey, Hawk and Ural Owl) on the other hand, are well separated from the southern ones (Scops, Little and Barn Owl), even though there are countries in Europe (e.g. Poland) where one can find all the above-mentioned species at the same latitude.

DIFFERENCES IN HABITAT SELECTION

Spatial segregation is a commonly used means of resource partitioning in ecological communities (Schoener 1974). Again it is difficult to give a quantified account of habitat selection among European owls, because most relevant information is either of a general or anecdotal nature. However, Fig. 40 shows the usual habitats of European owls.

Despite its unavoidably tentative nature, Fig. 40 shows that arboreal species undoubtedly predominate among European owls. Great Grey, Ural, Long-eared, Tawny, Hawk, Tengmalm's and Pygmy Owls all overlap considerably in their habitat selection, when living either in mixed forest or in taiga and mountain forests. In addition, the deciduous forests are shared by Long-eared, Tawny, Little, Barn, Scops and Pygmy Owls. The Eagle Owl is a generalist in its habitat selection, being able to live in all other habitats except marshland. The Short-eared Owl specialises in marshy habitats and the Snowy Owl alone inhabits the tundra.

The strongest evidence of species overlap in the same habitats is the presence of an owl species in the diet of another species (cf. Interspecific Aggression, Table 56). The results demonstrate that spatial overlap among all European species (except those having a totally different geographical distribution) is common and horizontal segregation is far from complete (also Herrera and Hiraldo 1976).

The breeding habitat selection of three co-existing *Strix* owls has been studied in Finland during the nesting season by Lahti and Mikkola (1974) and by Mikkola (1981). The main results of these studies have been summarised in Table 64. Firstly, the habitat selection between *Strix* species is not strikingly different, i.e. spatial separation is far from complete. By using the Index of Community Similarity

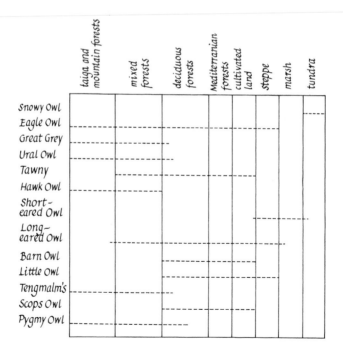

Fig. 40   Habitat selections of European owls (Voous 1960)

(MacNaughton and Wolf 1973) I found that the similarity of the nesting habitats between Ural and Tawny Owl is 0.67 and that between Ural and Great Grey Owl 0.65 (Table 64). The clearest differences in habitats selected is between Tawny and Great Grey Owl (0.47) showing that they only rarely compete for the same breeding habitats.

DIFFERENCES IN NESTING HABITS

In this context I will deal only with the competition for breeding places. Udvardy (1951) stated, in his extensive review, that competition for breeding places is most common amongst hole-nesting birds. This statement also seems to hold true for European owls (see also Interspecific Aggression chapter). A tree-hole or a nest box is a typical breeding place with eight European owls and only Snowy, Eagle and Short-eared Owls have never used holes in trees for breeding (Fig. 41). Figure 41 shows that two co-existing *Asio* species very clearly differ in their nest site selection: the Short-eared Owl nesting exclusively on the ground, whereas the Long-eared Owl frequently uses an old twig nest of another bird or a squirrel's drey. On the other hand, three closely-related *Strix* owls seem to choose highly similar nest sites.

The nest site selection of these three *Strix* owls has been closely studied in Finland (Lahti and Mikkola 1974 and Mikkola 1981). Ural and Tawny Owls are distinctively

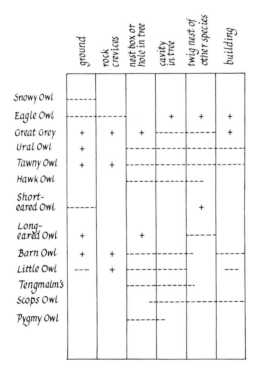

Fig. 41   Nest site selection of European owls (Harrison 1975). Cross indicates occasional breeding place

specialised in hole-nesting, whilst the Great Grey Owl exclusively uses open nests (Table 65). The similarity index has been calculated from the same formula as in Table 64.

The similarity index between the nest sites of Ural and Tawny Owls is 0.47, between those of Ural and Great Grey 0.42 and between Tawny and Great Grey Owls only 0.09 (Table 65). Thus, the overlap values for nest sites of these three *Strix* owls are much lower than those for nesting habitats (Table 64). Competition for breeding habitats and nest sites seems to be most intensive between Tawny and Ural Owls, both of which are tenacious of their chosen nest site, the same territories being inhabited year after year. In contrast, Great Grey Owls seem to change habitat and nest site according to food availability (Mikkola 1973, 1981).

When competing for a nest site the Ural Owl will drive away, or even kill, the weaker Tawny Owl (see Interspecific Aggression). The Great Grey Owl does not compete with the other two species but nests peaceably alongside them (Mikkola 1976).

DIFFERENCES IN HUNTING METHODS

Predators may divide food resources simply by hunting in different ways, at different times and in different places. For the hunting methods I will deal only with time, the daily feeding activity, because hunters of prey animals are more likely to hunt at different times of the day (Schoener 1974). The daily activity of four Central European and six North European owls have been investigated and a comparison of their hunting times can be made. The index values shown in Tables 66 and 67 have been arrived at from the formula:

$$\frac{\Sigma\,(2\,m_h)}{\Sigma\,(a_h + b_h)}$$

where a_h = percentage share of hourly feeding visits in daily activity of owl *a*
  b_h = percentage share of hourly feeding visits in daily activity of owl *b*
  m_h = minimum percentage value of hourly feedings in any of those two daily activities compared

The average similarity of the hunting activity of four Central European owl species studied is only 0.57 and that of the six North European species 0.61. Two entirely nocturnal species, Tengmalm's and Tawny Owl, have been studied both in North and Central Europe and would seem to have the same activity overlap in both places. The similarity index value (0.83) of these two owls is highest in this material and indicates the possibility of vigorous competition and explains why Tengmalm's Owl often falls prey to Tawny Owl (see *Interspecific Aggression* Table 56). In Germany the Tawny Owl is instrumental in thinning the Tengemalm's Owl population as a direct result of interspecific competition (Vieweg 1979).

Some closely-related owl species seem able to avoid heavy competition by hunting, in part, at different times. For instance, in Finland the Tawny Owl is the most nocturnal of the three *Strix* species, as shown in Fig. 42. It hunts almost exclusively at night until the young are well-grown and need large amounts of food, whereupon the adults have also to bring in food during the day. The Great Grey Owl is the most

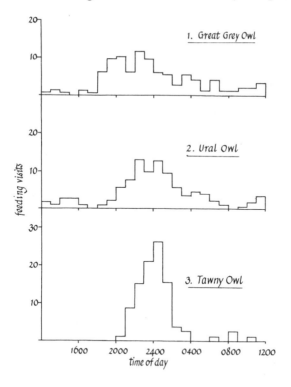

Fig. 42   Feeding activity of three Strix owl species in Finland (Mikkola 1981)

diurnal of the three. It is most active in the early morning and the late evening, only ceasing to feed its young around noon. The Ural Owl fits between the other two, hunting mainly at night but remaining active in the day (Mikkola 1981). Similar isolating mechanisms have been noted between Short-eared and Long-eared Owls (*Asio* species) in Finland. The two species may nest as close as 30 m without disturbance or injury to the other, and may even hunt the same kind of prey (mainly *Microtus*) with no apparent detriment to each other's success. Short-eared Owls are more diurnal, Long-eared Owls more nocturnal and thus neatly exploit the habitat with little competition throughout the twenty-four hours (cf. Mikkola 1973).

A smaller species can sometimes change its normal circadian rhythms to avoid meeting the larger owls. On one occasion when Tengmalm's Owl and Pygmy Owl bred in the same tree, the former was normally active at night and the latter only in the daylight hours (Mikkola 1978). Curio (1976) has also described how, among different species of predators, the higher ranking species may impose a regimen of periodicity upon the biologically inferior. On the islands of the Galapagos Archipelago where the Galapagos Hawk *Buteo galapagoensis* is absent, the Short-eared Owl (*Asio flammeus galapagoensis*) is active both day and night, whereas on other islands it confines its activity to the safer night-time hours. If it dares to take wing in the presence of the hawk during the day, it will be attacked immediately (de Vries 1973;

also Meinertzhagen 1959). It would seem possible that interactions of this kind have contributed to the habitually crepuscular and nocturnal life of *Strigiformes*. About 80 of the 134 owl species in the world hunt by night and many others around dusk (see Sparks and Soper 1970), whereas very few members of about 280 *Falconiformes* are crepuscular or nocturnal (cf. Brown and Amadon 1968).

DIFFERENCES IN DIET

The food-niche characteristics of European owls have been well documented by Herrera and Hiraldo (1976) but because of a lack of appropriate food data they excluded two species (Tawny and Short-eared Owl) from the Scandinavian owl community, and two from the Mediterranean community (Long-eared and Hume's Owl). However, more information is now available and all these species, 14 to be precise, can be included in this analysis. In Tables 68 and 69, only the main prey groups (functional ones) have been used, because this grouping is sufficient for a discussion of interspecific competition (cf. Lack 1946).

It was shown in the chapter *Diet of European Owls* that the average diet of ten owl species in Fenno-Scandia consisted mostly of mammals (85%, mainly *Microtidae*) and that birds made up about 12%. The remaining 3% consisted of frogs, lizards, fish and invertebrate animals, these being only occasional food items.

In the Mediterranean region the seven owl species' average diets proved to be quite different (Tables 59 and 60). Mammals were still the major constituent (47% – *Microtidae* 14%) but the proportion of invertebrate prey rose to 43%. The rest of the diet consisted of birds (7%) and frogs, lizards and fish (3%).

However, the average food of many different owl species tells us nothing about the possible interspecific competition for food which may occur in the two sets of owl communities studied. For this reason I have used the Index of Community Similarity as a measure of food niche overlap in Fenno-Scandian and Mediterranean owl communities.

The index values shown in Tables 68 and 69 have been calculated from the formula (MacNaughton and Wolf 1973):

$$\frac{\Sigma \, (2 \, m_i)}{\Sigma \, (a_i + b_i)}$$

where a_i = percentage share of food category i in the diet of owl *a*

b_i = percentage share of food category i in the diet of owl *b*

m_i = minimum value of food category i in any of those two diet lists compared

The average similarity of the diet of ten Fenno-Scandian owl species is as high as 0.80 (Table 68). Six owl species, Tengmalm's, Hawk, Long-eared, Short-eared, Great Grey and Snowy Owl, appear to have more or less equal food niches, as the information presented in Table 68 seems to indicate. The average similarity of the diet of the seven Mediterranean owl species is much smaller, 0.46, the main reason for this being that insectivorous owls are more prominent in the Mediterranean community.

True mammal eaters, such as the Long-eared Owl, also prey on mammals in the Mediterranean region, but some species show clear changes in their food niche from one region to another. The diet similarity between northern and southern populations of the Tawny Owl is only 0.45, while that of the Long-eared Owl is as high as 0.97.

This material leads to the conclusion that food competition seems to be more prominent among Fenno-Scandian owls than among Mediterranean owls. Herrera and Hiraldo (1976) concluded that high population levels of a particular prey type (*Microtidae*) in Central and North Europe produce a close-packing of owl species, which then prey upon this common resource and overlap extensively in their diets.

Small mammals in the north can be considered as a temporarily superabundant food (superabundant *sensu* Lack 1946), characterised by a periodic, rapid multiplication of a prey species, which becomes the almost exclusive food of a large number of predators, including other birds of prey, many mammals, etc. And it is perhaps a superabundancy of food which seems to explain why interspecific competition is not unduly harmful (cf. Lack 1946).

The difficulty involved in the measurement of overlaps in food niches of different owl species is that the same prey animal may have a different food value to a different species at a different time and place. The 'food value' is not an absolute concept as such, but rather it indicates the relationship between a predator and its environment (see also Ghiselin 1966). To exaggerate a little, a certain food item may have a considerable calorific value for species A, whereas for species B it may represent a source of a certain trace element and for species C the same item may provide mere roughage. Thus, even a one-dimensional food niche overlap may be more apparent than real.

However, this analysis of niche overlap may have some value if one takes into account other kinds of niche parameters which could explain away the apparent importance of food partitioning among owl species. Selection pressure is exerted through the quality of the environment (Lewontin 1976), though in simple terms it is often difficult to discern what is *quality* and what is *quantity* (Lindqvist 1978).

Discussion

In the previous chapters I have tried to describe some basic means of ecological isolation among European owl species. The results reveal that no one owl species is completely separated from all other owl species on account of their size, range, habitat, nest site, hunting-time and diet.

The largest owl, the Eagle Owl, is forty times heavier than the smallest, the Pygmy Owl, but both have other owl species in their own size class. The Snowy Owl is almost separated from the others in range, but sometimes shares its distribution with the Short-eared Owl. The latter usually differs in chosen habitat from the Long-eared Owl but in good vole years the two owls may live alongside each other. There is often an extensive overlap in diet, hunting-times and nest sites between different species.

The ecological isolation mechanisms of the owls studied do not seem to have evolved as completely as one would expect. This explains why interspecific competition does sometimes occur intensively, as shown earlier in the chapter *Interspecific Aggression*. The main reasons for this lack of isolation could be that food is often superabundant and that during meagre vole populations the local sympatry of owls is not constant.

When competition involves species using similar mixtures, selection is said to favour the specialisation of species feeding on the same general resources but living in slightly different habitats. This generalisation may be true for European owls but, unfortunately, so far no detailed, quantified account of their habitat selection exists. Moreover, it is clear that the presence of an owl species in the diet of another species must signify that these two species have coincided in the same area (also Herrera and Hiraldo 1976).

According to the evidence presented thus far, even closely-related owls overlap remarkably in all niche dimensions measured. Most of my examples are from three closely-related *Strix* species, which co-exist in Finland. The four niche dimensions measured (nesting habitats, food, nest sites and hunting time) revealed the following overlap:

	Tawny/Ural	Ural/Great Grey	Tawny/Great Grey
in habitats	0.67	0.65	0.47
in food	0.87	0.76	0.63
in nest sites	0.47	0.39	0.08
in hunting time	0.64	0.74	0.50

The overlap between Tawny and Ural Owls is the widest and these species also have the greatest overlap in body size, biogeographical distribution and hunting methods. Almost as wide an overlap can be found between Ural and Great Grey Owls. The narrowest overlap values are those between Tawny and Great Grey Owls, which also overlap least of all in size, distribution and hunting methods.

The wide overlap in niche dimensions which occurs between the *Strix* owls poses a problem where competitive exclusion is concerned. We are therefore faced with the subject of the limiting similarity among co-existing competitors (Hutchinson 1959) or, in other words, how similar can two species be and still persist together. What are the limits to similarity? (Horn and May 1977).

May and MacArthur (1972) and May (1973, 1974) suggested that there is in fact a theoretical upper limit to the similarity between adjacent species, which is not dependent on the degree of environmental fluctuations, but their model assumes a community in a saturated environment with all resources being fully used and the model does not take into account changes in resource abundance.

Pianka (1972, 1974a, 1974b) discussed the possibility that niche overlap does not necessarily mean that competition is inevitable, and that two organisms can share common resources without detriment to each other if the resources are not in short supply. This means that the maximum tolerable niche overlap is set by resource abundance. I would regard this as a partial explanation for the co-existence of the above owl species in widely overlapping niches.

A resource can become the limiting factor of the populations only when it occurs in abundance. On the other hand, competition may not deplete a resource, but a diminishing resource may increase competition (Diamond 1978). Thus, one can safely answer my introductory question by saying that an owl population is both resource- and predation-limited. Despite intraspecific competition for a limited resource and interspecific aggression, it would seem that several owl species can still continue to co-exist without necessarily eliminating one another.

28: Conservation and legal status of European owls

The status of European owls, their numbers and their ability to survive as healthy, vigorous populations into the future is, to a large measure, affected by man's activities and his attitude towards wildlife and the environment in general. Through the deliberate destruction of individual animals or complete habitats man has always had some effect on the shape of wildlife populations. Recently, other more insidious but nonetheless devastating pressures have been placed upon wild populations of birds in the form of industrial and agricultural chemicals, spread throughout whole eco-systems by means of waste outlets into rivers and oceans, or from the nozzles of crop spraying machines (see Holt *et al* 1979, Jensen *et al* 1969, Odsjö and Olsson 1975, Ratcliffe 1970, Westermark *et al* 1975).

The situation is not a simple one and there is much interaction between the interests of man and wild plants and animals, including owls. For example, over the centuries the Barn Owl has clearly benefitted from man's activities on the land, whereby open hunting areas, in the form of cleared forests, and nesting sites (evident in the owl's English name) are each much to its liking. Given that the tree-hole nesting Tawny Owl will kill Barn Owls competing for such nest-holes (Mikkola 1976), it seems reasonable to conclude that the Barn Owl was not a particularly common bird when Europe was covered with dense woodland. On the other hand, Barn Owls, along with certain other widespread raptors such as Kestrels and Sparrowhawks, suffered a decline in the 1950s throughout Europe, coinciding with the greatly increased use of toxic chemicals in agriculture (cf. ICBP 1977, Murton in Burton *et al* 1973 and Prestt 1965). A further factor in the relationship of the Barn Owl with man is that it preys upon certain small mammals, such as rats and mice, harmful to man's food-growing and storing interests.

Today, the disturbed habitats generated by human activities (fields, forest clearings, etc) are often advantageous to many owl species in terms of greater prey abundance and/or higher prey vulnerability, and owls have shown adaptability to the ever-changing world they inhabit.

In order to make conservation plans for European owls one has to know the main factors regulating the population sizes of the different species. Southern (1970) has shown that a particular habitat will support only a limited number of owls, and that territorial behaviour (intraspecific aggression) will usually ensure that each owl's territory is of sufficient size to provide its food.

Tawny Owl pairs studied by Southern in England had territories of about 13 ha in closed woodland, or 20 ha in mixed woodland and open ground. Fluctuations in food supply did not lead to significant changes in the number of adult Tawny Owls. When food was particularly scarce the owls laid fewer eggs, or did not breed at all, these being important ways of retaining a stable owl population from one year to the next. The level of mortality of young owls in autumn was also density-dependent and served as a further adjustment of population size (Southern 1970).

One can conclude from this that intraspecific aggression (territorial behaviour) will regulate the use of limited nest sites, hunting grounds and food resources. But as we have shown, some owls share their habitats with other owls and raptors, and it is impossible to make suitable management plans or conservation programmes without taking interspecific relationships into account. Up to the present, interspecific aggression has been largely overlooked in conservation, mainly due to our limited knowledge of the subject.

In this book all known interspecific killings between European owls have been documented, and the material has also been used to create the following diagram of the 'pecking order' among owls. Clearly, the existence of interspecific aggression makes it pointless to attract 'weaker' owl species into territories of 'stronger' species, and vice versa. An Eagle Owl's territory will be a dangerous home for all other owl species. Similarly, Ural and Tawny Owls are not good neighbours to smaller owls. In many places in western Europe the Tawny Owl has evicted (and preyed upon) the Little Owl from its nesting places; and the Tawny Owl is also listed as a predator of the Scops Owl in southern Europe, and in some areas it is believed to have caused a partial reduction in the population of the smaller bird (Voous 1960 and Everett 1977). Sharrock (comp. 1976) believed that the marked difference in the fortunes of the Long-eared Owl in Britain, as opposed to Ireland, argues strongly in favour of the success of the Tawny Owl in interspecific competition.

When a large owl kills and feeds upon smaller owls and raptors of the same trophic level (as do Eagle, Ural and Tawny Owls) the larger raptor also removes a potential predator of the common animal food reserve. In the case of the Eagle Owl, at least, the importance of this benefit should not be underestimated. For example, if an Eagle Owl kills a Ural Owl during the spring, the former will have more than 300 suitable prey animals in its territory which would otherwise have been taken by the Ural Owl that summer (cf. Mikkola 1970). By eliminating one owl early in the season it may have destroyed a whole family, making the benefit of its action even more significant. When implementing management programmes one should try to avoid such situations, even though the larger owl may be killing the smaller one in its own best interest.

It has recently been realised that one should never introduce Eagle Owls into a

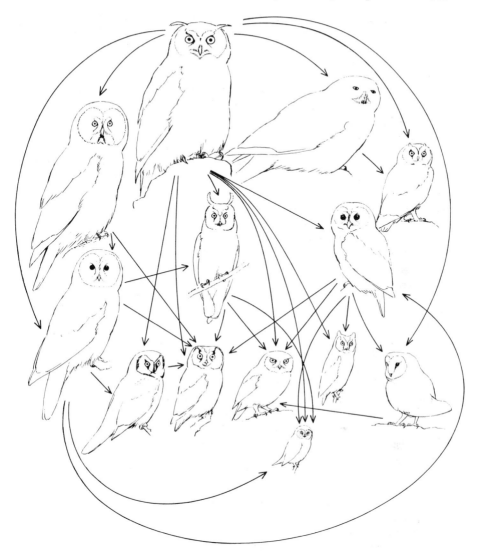

Potential victims of interspecific killing

Peregrine's territory, otherwise the Eagle Owl will eliminate the Peregrines by taking the young falcons, and sometimes the adults, too (cf. Rockenbauch 1978, Olsson 1979). Lindberg (1975), too, has also pointed to the threat posed to the Peregrine by Eagle Owls; and according to Blondel & Badan (1976) the development of a good population of Peregrines in Burgundy in the 1950s was thought to be due to the disappearance of the Eagle Owl. .

On the other hand, in nest site competition the Peregrine seems to be stronger than the Eagle Owl because formerly the Peregrine was able to keep the owl away from some of the best cliff sites. When the Peregrine was eliminated by human disturbance or environmental toxins the Eagle Owl occupied the nesting cliffs (Olsson 1979).

Experience shows how essential it is that all the birds of prey and the owls in a selected area are known if one wishes to maintain the conditions necessary for the continued survival of different owl species. Man is responsible for the need to protect and conserve owls and only man can devise and take the necessary measures to that end.

Habitats are perhaps the single most important factor to be considered by the conservationist intent upon safeguarding a species or community of animals or plants. No living organism is entirely isolated from its environment and from other species of animals and plants with which it co-exists. On the contrary, it fits into a complex web of existence, much as a single gear fits into the total mechanism of a car. Whilst in itself dependent upon other organisms and environmental factors, such as climate and surrounding soil type, that organism in turn influences what happens around it, perhaps marginally, but together it all contributes to a vast interdependence.

The study of all the factors, ecological and environmental, that affect the well-being of a single species, is called autecology and such a study is desirable, if not essential, when wishing to maintain, or create, the correct conditions for the continued survival of that species. The study of habitats and all the organisms contained within them is also necessary, particularly if management, whether limited or extensive, of a particular area is decided upon. This is, for example, one of the reasons why the Royal Society for the Protection of Birds in Britain employs full-time biologists and ecologists who study ecosystems in order to add scientific insight to the management plans of their reserves.

In some instances quick action may be required to protect a rare bird, as happened in 1967 when Snowy Owls were first discovered nesting in the Shetland Islands. An immediate round-the-clock watch on the nesting pair was organised by the RSPB during this first season, as it was for the following eight seasons during which a pair bred. The result of this scheme was a total of 16 young Snowy Owls raised to fledging. A combination of egg-collectors and disturbance from the inevitably large numbers of visiting birdwatchers, eager to see these magnificent and rare birds, might well have seriously affected or even destroyed the owls' breeding chances (cf. Tulloch 1975).

Apart from such isolated cases, in Europe habitats are rarely maintained specifically for owls. At the time of writing (1981) only one reserve designated for birds of prey apparently exists in Europe, at Sabed, near the town of Tirgu Mures in Romania. Enjoying complete protection in this unique reserve are breeding Kestrels, Hobbies, Black Kites, Goshawks, Sparrowhawks, Lesser Spotted Eagles, Long-eared Owls, Scops Owls, Little Owls and Tawny Owls (Puscariu and Filipascu in ICBP 1977).

Plans have also been put to the Spanish government for a huge reserve of 20,000 ha covering the ecologically most important and also the most endangered areas, in which large numbers of Spain's rich raptorial populations live, including representatives of the following owl genera: *Tyto, Bubo, Asio, Athene, Otus* and *Strix* (Garzon in ICBP 1977).

Encouraging moves have been made by the EEC which, in a Directive on the Conservation of Wild Birds, placed Eagle Owl, Snowy Owl and Short-eared Owl on what is known as Annexe 1. This directs member states of the EEC to establish special protection areas for these species. Clearly this will prove difficult in the case of nomadic species such as the Short-eared Owl, but it does reflect the increasing concern felt by Europeans towards owls and their conservation.

With an ever-increasing human population making more and more demands upon the land for food production, housing and industry, it is important that everyone interested in owls should develop a positive attitude towards their preservation. Whilst some species such as the Tawny Owl are still widespread and even common in some areas, others such as the Eagle Owl, heavily persecuted by man in the past, might well fade from the European avifauna if they are not strictly protected. To this end, the breeding of Eagle Owls in captivity, followed by release into suitable wild habitats, is being carried out in Sweden and in Germany. Eagle Owls are also being bred in England so that they may be released into parts of Continental Europe where the species has declined. Norwegian naturalists may well augment the more threatened sectors of their Eagle Owl population by similar captive-breeding and release schemes. The success of such activities will depend to some extent upon whether, when the birds are released, persecution continues.

Buying or leasing areas of woodland, forest and similar tracts of land, either by private conservation organisations or national or local government agencies, is clearly one way to ensure that some living space is provided for owls, especially the rarer or more vulnerable species. Effective wardening of designated areas, fully backed by the law, is a prerequisite for the establishment of such reserves.

But most owls live outside reserves and their fortunes are largely dictated by the activities of landowners, foresters, farmers and planners. If a forest is cut down a whole population of owls may lose their hunting and nesting biotope. However, by leaving little islands of trees in clear-felled areas, as happens in Finland, and by fixing nest boxes to some of the remaining trees, the owls may be persuaded to stay. Not only are nest boxes readily utilised by a number of European owl species (notably Tawny, Ural, Hawk, Tengmalm's, Little, Pygmy and Barn Owls, while experiments are being made with nest boxes for Long-eared and Great Grey Owls), they are also a very convenient way of studying the breeding biology of these owls. Monitoring devices can easily be fastened to the entrance holes in order to record the number of visits made by the parents to the nest, and the top can be opened in order to record what is going on inside an occupied box.

Foresters dislike the rotten stumps and trunks so typical of virgin, naturally regenerating forest, because they harbour the larval stages of insects that are harmful to trees, and so old wood tends to be removed in the name of 'healthy' forestry. Nowadays most forests in Europe are regarded as a crop and the 'weeding out' of dead or dying timber is regarded as good forestry management. But old wood is also full of fissures and holes, the natural nest sites for a number of owl species such as Hawk, Tawny, Ural, Tengmalm's and Pygmy Owls. Its disappearance is therefore detrimental to the breeding success of these owls; even so, the provision of large numbers of nest boxes in Sweden and Finland has brought a noticeable increase in the numbers of Ural Owls.

The existence of interspecific aggression makes it prudent to know which owls are resident in a particular area before nest boxes are introduced (cf. Mikkola 1978). It is usually counter-productive to put a nest box suitable for a Ural Owl or a Tawny Owl within the territory of a Pygmy or Tengmalm's Owl. Even if it is not killed the smaller owl will be seriously disturbed by the larger owl. In East Germany, Schönn has recently (1980) proposed that nest boxes for Tawny Owls should not be nearer than

20 km from Little, Tengmalm's and Pygmy Owl nests. This proposal should also be adopted in Sweden and in Finland, where the rarity of Pygmy Owls in southern parts of these countries may be due to the thousands of Ural, Tawny and Tengmalm's Owl nest boxes that have been provided.

As already mentioned, nest boxes for hole-nesting owls should not be introduced in an Eagle Owl territory, because this species will not tolerate the presence of other, competing birds of prey. The lack of suitable natural holes for breeding for the smaller owls is so great that they will attempt breeding despite the proximity of Eagle Owls if they are attracted to the area by the provision of nest boxes.

Hole-nesting owls will obviously require something approximating to the natural holes in rotten, hollowed trees, disused woodpecker holes, lightning-strike clefts and similar cavities, and the basic design of suitable nest boxes is shown in the Ural Owl chapter.

Appropriately-sized entrance holes are cut for the various species that it is hoped to attract, but the theory does not always work in practice. For instance, in May 1970 Ian Willis and some colleagues were shown a Tengmalm's Owl box put up by Martti Lagerström and some friends near Tampere, Finland, that contained a very cramped, incubating Ural Owl!

Barn Owls may be encouraged to nest in an outhouse or barn by fixing a tea-chest or some other suitably large, fairly durable container, on its side, to the upper level of an inside wall. This species is not a hole-nester, preferring an enclosed space in which to rear its young. Braaksma and De Bruijn (1976), in Holland, have been encouraged by the increasing number of Barn Owls that have tended to use the special breeding boxes provided. Forty-one successful broods have been found in eight years amongst 250 nest boxes.

Other measures aimed at helping the Barn Owl in Holland have included publicity aimed at making the species more popular; a ban on stuffed owls for other than scientific purposes; restrictions on the use of certain pesticides; efforts to raise the numbers of small mammals in nature reserves; conservation and replanting of hedgerows; removal of grilles, etc, that obstructed the bird's access to buildings; continuation of an existing reward scheme whereby 25 Dutch guilders could be paid for instances of successful Barn Owl breeding in buildings; provision of food for the owls during long periods of snow cover; and prevention of disturbance by bird-watchers at the breeding areas. Some of these recommendations may be specific but most are universal and would be valuable everywhere.

It is far less easy to see how help might be given for the nomadic species such as the Short-eared Owl. Fortunately it remains a widespread species and the increased planting of conifers seems to be in its favour, though their attraction as hunting and breeding places lasts only for the first few years whilst the trees are small. Later, the older, taller trees may encourage the spread of the Long-eared Owl, as in Denmark.

Artificial nests other than nest boxes can be helpful in certain cases. Most pairs of Great Grey Owl will readily occupy old nests of raptors, generally those of Goshawks and Buzzards. In forests subject to modern silviculture, old nests of raptors are rare, but artificial nests can do much to improve breeding opportunities for Great Grey Owls. In Canada, Finland and Sweden several of these owls have been reported breeding in man-made nests of branches and sticks in trees. Twenty such nests were provided near the town of Kemi, Finland, in 1977 and five of them were occupied the following year. One nest, built for an Osprey, was at the top of a 16 m high pine (Rauhala 1980).

Great Grey Owls frequently nest on old tree stumps, and a friend of mine, Pekka Helo, found that an artificial substitute for this type of nest could be supplied by nailing an open box filled with sawdust on top of the stump of a tree severed at about 2 m. So far, Pekka Helo has had two successful nests (cf. Hildén and Helo 1981).

Photography at the nest and disturbance by tourists and by birdwatchers is already leading to the demise of the Snowy Owl in southern Norway (Willgohs in ICBP 1977), and it may well contribute to the further decline of the Brown Fish Owl which is only just clinging to the small range it occupies in the eastern Mediterranean. Fortunately, the Israeli wildlife authority is keeping a close watch on a species which has probably suffered significantly from the drainage of wetlands and wide use of pesticides. H. Mendelssohn writes that the Brown Fish Owl 'was, formerly, present in western Galilee and around Lake Tiberias, but is now found only in some valleys on the eastern shore of the lake. The cause of the decline is the use of thallium sulphate as a rodenticide in the 1950s and the drying up of the stream in a valley in western Galilee where it formerly occurred. Water from the stream is now used for human settlements.'

People in general, and birdwatchers and photographers in particular, should be more aware of the susceptibility of the Eagle Owl to disturbance. When breeding, one disturbance at the nest is generally sufficient to cause them to desert their eggs. The early breeding stages should not be studied or photographed, and it is a good sign that photographs of this species at the nest are so rare that we had difficulty in finding one for this book. In Britain recent legislation has made it more difficult for photographers to work at the nests of the more vulnerable owls (see Legal Status, below).

Man's destructive capabilities have been unleashed on predatory birds on a massive scale since the growth of game bird rearing in the 18th and 19th centuries. The zeal and efficiency of game-keepers in many European countries have meant that large numbers of owls have been destroyed as 'vermin'. Many hundreds of Eagle Owls were killed annually in Norway, especially in the earlier years of this century under a state bounty scheme, though fortunately no decline in numbers has been noted there in recent years. The Eagle Owl was on a list of vermin species in France until the early 1960s and, as a consequence, its range and numbers declined markedly (Hudson 1975). Blondel and Badan, writing in 1976, said that although this large owl was widespread and abundant almost everywhere in favoured habitats in south-east France, it still met with persecution. According to one of their correspondents, Besson, 'almost every winter the inhabitants of Nice capture Eagle Owls . . . and in general kill them with sticks!' The same observer noted that a game-rearer killed about a dozen Eagle Owls in two years with a pole trap. Other proven enemies of the Eagle Owl are animal traps and trigger-happy hunters lying in wait to shoot small birds coming in to roost at dusk when Eagle Owls are leaving their day-time roosts in order to hunt.

A favoured method of trapping raptors, diurnal and nocturnal, has been the pole trap. This very unpleasant device, now illegal in Britain, consists of a steel-jawed trap fixed on top of a pole in a ride or a woodland clearing. Raptors frequently choose such isolated, convenient perches, and a painful lingering death too often results. There is ample evidence that the use of pole traps has survived until quite recent times. In 1972 the Royal Society for the Protection of Birds investigated 69 estates in Britain after

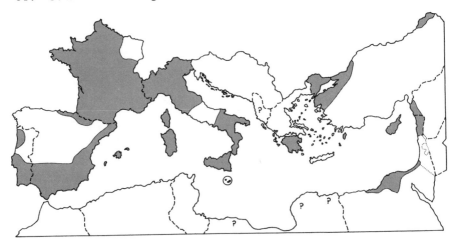

SHOOTING – parts of Mediterranean countries where shooting of migratory birds is most intensive – not indicated are the wetlands where severe shooting of waterfowl occurs (after Woldhek 1979)

receiving reports of the alleged destruction of birds of prey, and 90 pole traps were found. In the eleven-year period, 1970–80, a total of 195 pole-trapping incidents involving birds of prey was reported to the RSPB, including 47 cases in which owls were the victims. The species involved were: Tawny (22), Barn (7), Short-eared (4), Little (3), Long-eared (2), unidentified (7). Most of these incidents were reported in 1971–73 when the RSPB was mounting its pole trap campaign.

In the period 1970–80 a total of 316 instances of killing, by shooting or poisoning, was also reported to the RSPB, many of them involving owls. The victims were: Little (23), Tawny (21), Barn (13), Short-eared (4), Long-eared (3), unidentified (1). Even when such illegal destruction of wildlife has been reported to the relevant authority, conversion of incidents into prosecutions is low. Richard Porter, Species Protection Officer of the RSPB, writes (*in litt.*) that it is 'a product of (a) the difficulty of proving who shot the bird/set the trap, and (b) the size of our Investigation Section (just me until 1975!)'.

Many Italians, exploiting their wildlife to the full, not only shoot large numbers of raptors annually for 'sport' (such as migrating Honey Buzzards in Sicily and Calabria in April and May), but they also trap and sell them in quantity. A photograph reproduced in Everett (1977) shows cages full of Little Owls, part of a batch of a hundred for sale in a market. Lovari (1973) estimated that on average 170 birds of prey and owls were delivered each shooting season to each of several taxidermists known to him, the majority of the victims being Kestrels, Buzzards, Sparrowhawks, Barn Owls and Little Owls. According to Lovari, hundreds of thousands of owls and birds of prey are killed every year by the one-and-three-quarter million hunters in Italy. A chink of light in this black situation is the recent tightening up in the laws relating to the protection of owls in Italy. One hopes that the local authorities will act to enforce these stricter laws, though this is certainly not always the case, as the continuing slaughter of Honey Buzzards, a protected species, proves (Stefano Allavena, *in litt.*). Lovari writes that: 'Italians have little respect for the law and least

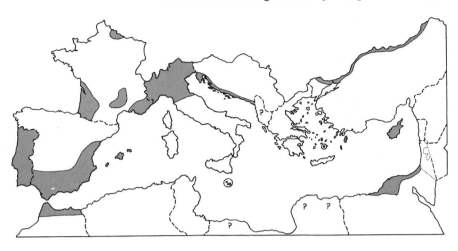

CATCHING – parts of Mediterranean countries where catching of migratory birds with nets, traps and bird-lime is most intensive (after Woldhek 1979)

of all for laws that cannot be enforced. Game wardens are still few in numbers and are often ignorant of the fundamentals of ecology and conservation.'

In Malta, full protection was given to all nocturnal and diurnal raptors in 1980. Until then many hundreds of owls were killed annually in the island group, the species concerned being Long-eared, Short-eared, Scops and Barn Owl.

The peoples of Greece, Turkey, the Near East and North Africa do not, for the most part, treat predatory birds particularly badly, and owls are probably left largely alone, a situation helped by the birds' nocturnal habits. However, the use of pesticides is increasing in these countries and this must pose a serious threat to owls and other birds of prey. This is already the case in Israel, where chlorinated hydrocarbon and organo-phosphorus pesticides, as well as thallium sulphate, fluoroacetamide, gluco-chloralose, alphachloralose and, more recently, azodrin, have had a devastating effect on owls and other birds (Mendelssohn 1972, Mendelssohn, Schlueter and Aderet 1979).

Two threats that do not recognise national boundaries emanate from egg collectors and taxidermists. The laws generally discriminate against the destructive activities of these people in Europe, but a persistent, usually underground trade, international in its scope, flourishes for eggs and mounted specimens of owls. Until the private possession of eggs and skins is made illegal, this trade will continue and may grow.

Another cause for alarm affecting virtually all birds of prey in Europe and the Mediterranean region, especially the Eagle Owl and the Brown Fish Owl, is the continuing drainage of wetlands. The former species traditionally hunts in reed beds and around marshes and lakes in many areas and the latter is totally dependent on the presence of water. Conservationists have long been decrying the tendency to 'drain, drain, drain', because the short-term gain of a few hundred hectares here and there may well prove to be in man's own worst interests, as well as the creatures with which he shares this planet's resources. Lakes and marshes, in the words of Dr Vagliano, writing in the 1977 ICBP Bird of Prey Conference Report, are 'not only reservoirs of incomparable avian fauna but also sources of fish proteins invaluable to man.'

All the European owls offer a certain degree of self-protection in the sense that they are cryptically coloured and, furthermore, most are nocturnal. A number of species, notably Hawk, Ural, Great Grey and Tawny Owl may violently attack a human intruder at their nesting places, but they have no protection against guns, traps and poisons, used against them from a mixture of greed and ignorance. Much of the mindless persecution of these fine creatures, often far less harmful to our interests than many people are prepared to accept, especially game shooters and gamekeepers, has disappeared or is waning. It is a hopeful sign, though, as witnessed by the shameful results of the pole trap enquiry carried out by the RSPB in highly enlightened Britain in the early 1970s, there is every reason for naturalists, conservation organisations and the law-makers to be ever-vigilant.

Nevertheless, the future for European owls does not appear completely hopeless because, at least in parts of their range, we still have healthy populations of all 13 species. Compared with certain raptors (White-tailed Eagle and Peregrine, for example) the feeding habits of owls have, so far, saved them from being particularly vulnerable to pesticide contamination. A recent study by Stanley and Elliott (1976) has indicated that the use of mercurial seed dressings in Britain has not led to any significant contamination of the Tawny Owl and the Barn Owl.

This book seeks to win new friends for owls. As long as there are increasing numbers of owl-watchers and people keen to know more about the ecology of owls, then those who are killing owls indiscriminately may be forced to stop their illegal activities. Our knowledge of owl ecology is certainly incomplete but enough is known to enable us to learn how to protect owls in order to guarantee their continued existence.

Summary of the legal status of owls in Europe, North Africa and the Near East

The following outline is based on the findings of the World Working Group on Birds of Prey whose survey on raptor legislation began in 1970, and the European Committee for the Prevention of Mass Destruction of Migratory Birds (founded 1976). As far as it has been possible to check, the outline is correct to January 1983, and most of the information has been extracted from the ICBP Report on the Proceedings of the World Conference on Birds of Prey, Vienna 1975, and Dr S. Woldhek's report on Bird Killing in the Mediterranean, with additional information from R. F. Porter, Species Protection Officer, RSPB.

It has proved impossible to obtain information on any conservation laws from Albania, Algeria (although it is known that few raptors are killed), Andorra, Libya, San Marino and Syria.

Complete protection to all owls is afforded in the following countries:

AUSTRIA
BELGIUM
BULGARIA
CHANNEL ISLANDS
CYPRUS
CZECHOSLOVAKIA

DENMARK
FRANCE
GIBRALTAR
HUNGARY
ISRAEL
JORDAN
LEBANON
LIECHTENSTEIN
LUXEMBOURG
MALTA
MOROCCO
THE NETHERLANDS
NORWAY
POLAND
PORTUGAL
ROMANIA
SPAIN
SWEDEN (owls may not be used as decoys)
SWITZERLAND
TUNISIA
TURKEY
UNITED KINGDOM (under the Wildlife and Countryside Act 1981 Snowy Owl
   (very rare) and Barn Owl (widespread but declining) receive special
   protection, even from birdwatchers and photographers).
WEST GERMANY
YUGOSLAVIA

In the following countries either no protection or partial protection is afforded or, in
the case of East Germany, the picture appears to be incomplete:

EAST GERMANY
The only owl species known to be protected are Eagle Owl and Pygmy Owl

EGYPT
No protection exists for owls at all. Woldhek makes the sombre observation that 'there is some
demand for taxidermy, particularly for colourful and big birds.' It is not known how many owls
are killed for this purpose, if indeed any at all, or how many fall victim to those hunters who
shoot birds purely for fun, comparing tallies of the numbers shot.

FINLAND
All owls are fully protected, except for Eagle Owl outside the breeding season on the grounds
of alleged damage to game. The Union of Finnish Ornithological Societies has recently made an
official proposal to the Ministry of Agriculture and Forestry that the Eagle Owl should be fully
protected before the next open hunting season. If accepted in the Ministry, as now seems
possible, this will end that shameful situation in the field of owl protection in my own country.

GREECE
Ornithological societies within the country are trying to reform the law which protects all owls

except those within breeding, hunting and wildlife reserves where they are regarded as harmful. Complete protection at all times is being sought.

ITALY

All owls are protected throughout the year with the exception of Little Owls which can be caught by certain people in order to use them as decoys to shoot Skylarks and other small birds! The Little Owls are supposed to be released at the end of the hunting season but many die before then (Allavena, *in litt.*).

USSR

Complete protection exists for all owl species except that special licences may be issued for killing for scientific purposes and a few other special reasons.

Flying Squirrels breeding in Tengmalm's Owl nest box

Selected bibliography

There follows a selected bibliography for those readers who would like to read more about owls, but are not so deeply interested that they would wish to read through all the many reference sources consulted when writing this book. The more exhaustive list of the latter references follows this selected list.

GENERAL BOOKS ON OWLS

Angell, T. 1974. *Owls*. University of Washington Press, Seattle.
Brüll, H. 1977. *Das Leben europäischer Greifvögel*. Gustav Fisher, Stuttgart.
Burton, J. A. (Ed.) 1973. *Owls of the world*. Eurobook, London.
Clark, R. J., D. G. Smith and L. H. Kelso. 1978. *Working bibliography of owls of the world*. Nat. Wildlife Federation Sci., Tech. Ser. 1, Washington.
Baudvin, H. 1976. *Les chouettes et les hiboux*. Atlas visuels. Payot, Lausanne.
Eck, S. and H. Busse. 1973. *Eulen. Die rezenten und fossilen Formen*. Neue Brehm-Bücherei 469, Ziemsen Verlag, Wittenberg-Lutherstadt.
Géroudet, P. 1965. *Les rapaces diurnes et nocturnes d'Europe*. Éditions Delachaux & Niestlé, Neuchatel (Suisse).
Eckert, A. W. 1974. *The Owls of North America*. Doubleday & Co., Garden City, N.Y.
Everett, M. A. 1977. *A Natural History of Owls*. Hamlyn, London.
Grossman, M. L. and J. Hamlet. 1965. *Birds of Prey of the World*. Cassell & Co., London.
Hosking, E. J. and C. W. Newberry. 1945. *Birds of the night*. Collins, London.
Mebs, Th. 1966. *Eulen und Käuze*. Franckh'she Verlagshandlung, Stuttgart.
Sparks, J. and T. Soper. 1970. *Owls: their natural and unnatural history*. David & Charles, Devon.
Tyler, H. and D. Phillips. 1977. *Owls by Day and Night*. Naturegraph Books: 987, Happy Camp, California.
Uttendörfer, O. 1952. *Neue Ergebnisse über die Ernährung der Greifvögel und Eulen*. Eugen Ulmer Verlag, Stuttgart.
Wahlstedt, J. 1969. *Ladrikets fåglar*. A. Bonniers, Stockholm.

ORNITHOLOGICAL MONOGRAPHS ON EUROPEAN OWLS

EAGLE OWL:
März, R. 1958. *Der Uhu (Bubo bubo L.)*. Neue Brehm-Bücherei 108, A. Ziemsen Verlag, Wittenberg.
März, R. and R. Piechocki. 1976. *Der Uhu*. 3 Aufl. N. Brehm-Büch. 108, A. Ziemsen Verlag, Wittenberg.

SNOWY OWL:
Portenko, L. A. 1972. *Die Schnee-eule Nyctea scandiaca*. N. Brehm-Büch. 454, A. Ziemsen Verlag, Wittenberg.

GREAT GREY OWL:
Mikkola, H. 1983. *Der Bartkauz Strix nebulosa*. N. Brehm-Büch. 538, A. Ziemsen Verlag, Wittenberg.

URAL OWL:
Mikkola, H. 1983. *Der Habichtskauz Strix uralensis.* N. Brehm-Büch. (MS), A. Ziemsen Verlag, Wittenberg.

SHORT-EARED OWL:
Gerber, R. 1960. Die Sumpfohreule *Asio flammeus.* N. Brehm-Büch. 259. A. Ziemsen Verlag, Wittenberg.

BARN OWL:
Bunn, D. S., A. B. Warburton and R. D. S. Wilson. 1982. *The Barn Owl.* Poyser, Calton.
Schneider, W. 1964. Die Schleiereule *Tyto alba.* N. Brehm-Büch. 340, A. Ziemsen Verlag, Wittenberg.

TAWNY OWL:
Guérin, G. 1932. La Hulotte et son régime. Encyclopédie ornithologique. P. Lechevalier, Paris.

SCOPS OWL:
Koenig, L. 1973. Das Aktionssystem der Zwergohreule *Otus scops scops* (Linné 1758). Paul Parey Verlag, Berlin.

TENGMALM'S OWL:
März, R. 1968. Der Rauhfusskauz *Aegolius funereus.* N. Brehm-Büch. 394, A. Ziemsen Verlag, Wittenberg.

PYGMY OWL:
Schönn, S. 1978. Der Sperlingskauz *Glaucidium passerinum passerinum.* N. Brehm-Büch. 513, A. Ziemsen Verlag, Wittenberg.

LITTLE OWL:
Schönn, S. 1982. *Der Steinkauz Athene noctua.* N. Brehm-Büch. (MS), A. Ziemsen Verlag, Wittenberg.

Regional books on European owls

FINLAND:
Collin, O. 1886. *Suomessa tavattavien pöllöjen pesimissuhteista.* Hämeenlinna, Hämeen Sanomain kirjapaino.

DENMARK:
Rosendahl, S. 1973. *Ugler i Danmark.* D.O.C.S. Forlag, Skjern.

SWEDEN:
Lindblad, J. 1967. *I ugglemarker.* A. Bonniers, Stockholm.

NORWAY:
Hagen, Y. 1952. *Rovfuglene og Viltpleien.* Gyldendal Norsk Forlag, Oslo.

ESTONIA:
Randla, T. 1976. *Eesti röövlinnud, kullilised ja kakulised.* Valgus, Tallinn.

USSR:
Pukinsky, J. B. 1977. *Ziznj Sov.* Leningrad.

GDR:
Schiemenz, H. 1964. *Die Greifvögel und Eulen der DDR und ihr Schutz.* Tier um Umwelt 1.

GERMANY:
Kleinschmidt, O. 1958. *Raubvögel und Eulen der Heimat.* A. Ziemsen Verlag, Wittenberg.

SPAIN:

Morillo, C. 1976. *Guia de las rapaces ibericas*. Instituto Nacional para la Conservacion de la Naturaleza, Madrid.

Works consulted in preparing the World Distribution Maps
(apart from the correspondents and works mentioned in relation to European distribution)

Bundy, G. 1976. *Checklist of the Birds of Libya*. British Ornithologists' Union.
Bundy, G. and E. F. Warr. 1980. *A Checklist of the Birds of the Arabian Gulf States*. Sandgrouse No. 1.
Burton, J. A. (Ed.). 1973. *Owls of the World*. Eurobook. London.
Cheng Tso-Hsin. Rev. edition 1973. *Distributional List of Chinese Birds*. Peking Institute of Zoology, Academia Sinica.
Dement'ev, G. P., N. A. Gladkov and E. P. Spangenberg. 1969. *Birds of the Soviet Union*. Israeli Program for Scientific Translations.
Etchécopar, R. D. and F. Hüe. 1967. *The Birds of North Africa*. Oliver & Boyd. Edinburgh and London.
Etchécopar, R. D. and F. Hüe. 1970. *Les Oiseaux du Proche et du Moyen Orient*. Editions N. Boubée et Cie. Paris.
Flint, V. E. and Bome, R. L. *et al* 1968: *Ptitsy CCCP*. Izd mysl' Moskva.
Gallagher, M. D. Undated. Birds of Jabal Akdhar. Reprinted from the Scientific Results of the Oman Flora and Fauna Survey 1975 contained in The Journal of Oman Studies.
Gallagher, M. D. and T. D. Rogers. 1980. On Some Birds of Dhofar and Other Parts of Oman. Reprinted from Journal of Oman Studies. Special Report No. 2.
Gallagher, M. D. and M. W. Woodcock. 1980. *The Birds of Oman*. Quartet Books, London.
Glutz von Blotzheim, R. Bauer and E. Bezzel. 1981. *Handbuch der Vogel Mitteleuropas*. Band 9, Strigiformes. Frankfurt am Main.
Jennings, M. C. 1981. *The Birds of Saudi Arabia: A Checklist*. Cambridge.
King, B. 1978. April Bird Observations in Saudi Arabia. Journal of the Saudi Arabian Natural History Society. No. 21, January 1978.
King, B., M. W. Woodcock and E. C. Dickinson. 1975. *A Field Guide to the Birds of South-east Asia*. Collins, London.
McLachlan, G. R. and R. Liversidge. 1976. *Robert's Birds of South Africa*. Trustees of the John Voelcker Bird Book Fund, Cape Town.
Meinertzhagen, T. 1954. *The Birds of Arabia*. Oliver & Boyd. Edinburgh and London.
Nero, R. 1980. *The Great Grey Owl. Phantom of the Northern Forest*. Smithsonian Institute Press. Washington D.C.
Ornithological Society of Turkey. Turkish Bird Reports 1966–1975.
Ornithological Society of Turkey. 1971. *Checklist of the Birds of Turkey*.
Peterson, R. T. 1947. *A Field Guide to the Birds*. Houghton Mifflin, Boston.
Peterson, R. T. 1961. *A Field Guide to Western Birds*. Houghton Mifflin, Boston.
Pizzey, G. and R. Doyle. 1980. *A Field Guide to the Birds of Australia*. Collins, Sydney.
Schauensee, R. M. de. 1971. *A Guide to the Birds of South America*. Oliver & Boyd, Edinburgh.
Scott, D. A., H. M. Hamadani and A. A. Mirhosseyni. 1975. *The Birds of Iran*. Department of the Environment, Tehran.
Serle, W., G. J. Morel and W. Hartwig. 1977. *A Field Guide to the Birds of West Africa*. Collins, London.
Vaurie, C. 1965. *The Birds of the Palearctic Fauna. Non-Passeriformes*. Witherby, London.
Warr, F. E. 1978. Birds recorded in the Arabian Gulf States. (Cyclostyled.)
Williams, J. G. 1963. *A Field Guide to the Birds of East and Central Africa*. Collins, London.

List of References

Aarnio, H. and Häyrinen, U. 1967: Hyrynsalmen lapinpöllöt. Suomen Luonto 26: 134–138.

Adair, P. 1892: The Short-eared Owl (*Asio accipitrinus* Pallas) and the Kestrel (*Falco tinnunculus* Linnaeus) in the vole plague districts. Ann. Scott. Nat. Hist. 1892: 219–231.

Ahlbom, B. 1971: Kattugglans föda. Fåglar i Sörmland 4: 59–62.

Ahlén, I. and Larsson, T. B. 1972: Slagugglans *Strix uralensis* boplats- och biotopval inom södra delen av utbredningsområret i Sverige. Inst. Forest Zoology Res. Notes 11: 1–34.

Aho, J. 1964: The autumn food of *Asio f. flammeus* Pontopp. in the vicinity of the city of Tampere, South Finland. Ann. Zool. Fenn. 1: 375–376.

Alaja, P. and Lyytikäinen, A. 1972: Lapinpöllö (*Strix nebulosa*) pesinyt Vesannolla. Savon Luonto 4: 38–39.

Alho, P. 1971: Katsaus Päijät-Hämeen pöllökantoihin vuosien 1966–70 havaintoaineiston valossa. Päijät-Hämeen Linnut 2: 74–79.

Ali, S. and Ripley, S. D. 1969: *Handbook of the Birds of India and Pakistan. Vol. 3.* Oxford University Press.

Amadon, D. 1943: Bird weights as an aid in taxonomy. Wilson Bull. 55: 164–177.

Amadon, D. 1959: The significance of sexual differences in size among birds. Proc. Amer. Phil. Soc. 103: 531–536.

Andersen, T. 1961: En nordsjaellandsk Natugle-bestand (*Strix aluco* L.) i yngletiden. Dansk Ornith. Foren. Tidsskr. 55:1–55.

Andersson, N. Å. and Persson, B. 1971: Något om fjällugglans *Nyctea scandiaca* näringsval i Lappland. Vår Fågelvärld 30: 227–231.

Araujo, J., Rey, J. M., Landin, A., and Moreno, A. 1973: Contribucion al estudio del Buho Chico (*Asio otus*) en España. Ardeola 19: 397–428.

Armstrong, W. H. 1958: Nesting and food habits of the Long-eared Owl in Michigan. Mich. St. Univ. Publ. Mus. Biol. Ser. 1: 61–96.

Aronson, L. 1979: The Hume's Tawny Owl *Strix butleri* in Israel. Dutch Birding 1: 18–20.

Arvola, A. 1959: Über die Lautäusserungen und die Bedeutung der Lautsignale der erwachsenen Waldkauzes (*Strix aluco*) auf Grund experimenteller Untersuchungen. Ornis Fennica 36:10–20.

Balgooyen, T. C. 1972: Behaviour and ecology of the American Kestrel (*Falco sparverius*). Ph.D. Dissertation, University of California, Berkeley. Pp. 169.

Bakker, D. 1957: De Velduil in de Noordoostpolder. Levende Natuur. 60: 104–105.

Banz, K. and Degen, G. 1975: Zur Gegenwärtigen Verbreitung und Ernährung des Uhus (*Bubo bubo* L.) im Westteil der VR Polen. Beitr. Vogelkd. 21: 258–265.

Barnard, C. C. 1981: Buzzard Preying on Short-eared Owl. Brit. Birds 74:226.

Barrows, W. B. 1912: Michigan bird life. Spec. Bull. Dept. Zool. and Physio., Mich. Agric. Coll. Pp. 822.

Barth, E. K. 1963: Tårnugla, *Tyto alba*, i Norge. Sterna 5: 283–287.

Bäsecke, K. 1951: Vom Harzer Uhu. J. Orn. 93: 66–68.

Bauch, W. 1964: Ungewöhnliche, erfolgreihe Uhu-Brut im Bezirk Gera. Beitr. Vogelkd. 9: 396–401.

Baudvin, H. 1975: Biologie de reproduction de la chouette effraie (*Tyto alba*) en Côte d'Or: Premiers résultats. Jean le Blanc 14: 1–50.

Baudvin, H. 1976: *Les chouettes et les hiboux.* Série 'Comment vivent-ils?', vol. 5. Atlas visuels Payot, Lausanne.

Baudvin, H. 1976: La reproduction de la Chouette Effraie (*Tyto alba*) en Cote d'Or en 1975. Jean le Blanc 15:9–13.

Baudvin, H. 1978: Le cannibalisme chez l'Effraie *Tyto alba*. Nos Oiseaux 34: 223–231.

322

Bauer, W., Helversen, O. V., Hodge, M. and Martens, J. 1969: *Catalogus Faunae Graeciae. Part 2: Aves.* Thessaloniki.

Bauer, W., Böhr, H. J., Mattern, U. and Müller, G. 1973: 2. Nachtrag zum 'Catalogus Faunae Graeciae: Pars Aves.' Die Vogelwelt 94: 1–21.

Baumgart, W., Simeonov, S. D., Zimmermann, M., Bünsche, H., Baumgart, P., and Kühnast, G. 1973: An Horsten des Uhus (*Bubo bubo*) in Bulgarien 1. Der Uhu im Iskerdurchbruch (Westbalkan). Zool. Abh. Mus. Tierk. Dresden, 32: 203–247.

Baumgart, W. 1975: An Horsten des Uhus (*Bubo bubo*) in Bulgarien II. Der Uhu in Nordostbulgarien. Zool. Abh. Mus. Tierk. Dresden, 33: 251–275.

Bayldon, J. M. 1978: Daylight hunting by Long-eared Owls. Brit. Birds 71: 88.

Beacham, T. D. 1979: Selectivity of avian predation in declining populations of the vole *Microtus townsendii.* Canad. J. Zool. 57: 1767–1772.

Belopolsky, L. 1975: Migration peculiarities of some species of owls (Strigiformes) on the basis of trapping and ringing data obtained on the Courland Spit in 1957–1968. Commun. Baltic Comm. Study Bird Migr. 8: 51–71.

Bengtsson, G. 1962: Sparvuggla och pärluggla häckande i Halland 1961. Vår Fågelvärld 21: 210–211.

Benson, S. Vere 1970: Birds of Lebanon and the Jordan Area. ICBP/Frederick Warne, London.

Bent, A. C. 1938 (1961): Life Histories of North American Birds of Prey. Part 2: Falconiformes and Strigiformes. Bull. U.S. nat. Mus. 170: 1–482.

Berggren, V. and Wahlstedt, J. 1977: Lappugglans *Strix nebulosa* läten. Vår Fågelvärld 36: 243–249.

Bergman, S. 1939: Brutbiologische Beobachtungen beim Sperlingskauz *Glaucidium passerinum* L. Beitr. Fortpfl. Vögel 15: 181–189.

Bergmann, H-H. and Ganso, M. 1965: Zur Biologie des Sperlingskauzes (*Glaucidium passerinum* (L)). J. Orn., 106: 255–284.

Bergstedt, B. 1965: Distribution, reproduction, growth and dynamics of the rodent species *Clethrionomys glareolus* (Schreber), *Apodemus flavicollis* (Melchior) and *Apodemus sylvaticus* (Linné) in southern Sweden. Oikos 16: 132–160.

Berlin, O. G. W. 1963: The probable origin and evolution of the order Strigiformes based on the study of the hind limb musculature of three species of owls. Amer. Zool. 3: 488.

Berndt, R. 1959: Sperbereule (*Surnia ulula*) bei Braunschweig. Orn. Mitt. 11: 237.

Beven, G. 1965: The food of Tawny Owls in London. London Bird Rept. 29: 56–72.

Beven, G. 1967: The food of Tawny Owls in Surrey. Surrey Bird Rept. 1966: 32–39.

Beven, G. 1969: Tawny Owl. Pp. 1340–1344 in: Birds of the World (ed. J. Gooders) Vol 4, Part 12. IPC Magazines, London.

Bezzel, E. and Wildner, H. 1970: Zur Ernährung bayerischer Uhus (*Bubo bubo*). Die Vogelwelt 91: 191–198.

Bezzel, E., Obst, J. and Wickl, K-H. 1976: Zur Ernährung und Nahrungswahl des Uhus (*Bubo bubo*). J. Orn. 117: 210–238.

Bianki, V. V. and Koshkina, T. V. 1960: O pitanii iastrevinoi sovy. Trudy Kandalakshskogo Zapovednika 3: 113–117.

Blair, H. M. S. 1962: Studies of less familiar birds: Great Grey Owl. Brit. Birds 55: 414–418.

Blaker, G. B. 1934: *The Barn Owl in England and Wales.* RSPB, London.

Blondel, J. 1967: Reflexions sur les rapports entre predateurs et proies chez les rapaces. I. Les effets de la predation sur les populations de proies. Terre et la Vie (new series): 5–62.

Blondel, J. and Badan, O. 1976: La biologie du Hibou grand-duc en Provence. Nos Oiseaux 33: 189–219.

Bocheński, Z. 1960: Pokarm puchacza *Bubo bubo* (L.) w Pieninach. Acta Zool. Cracoviensia 5 (8): 1–23.

Bocheński, Z. 1966: Contribution to the knowledge of the diet of the Eagle Owl in the Pieniny Mts. Przeglad Zool. 10: 64–65.

Bock, W. J. 1968: A radial proprioceptive organ in the wings of owls. Amer. Zool. 8: 810.

Bock, W. J. and McEvey, A. 1969: The radius and relationship of owls. Wilson Bull. 81: 55–68.

Bogucki, Z. 1967: O pokarmie puszczyka (*Strix aluco* L.) gnieżdżacego sie w śródmiesciu Poznania. Przeglad Zool. 11: 71–73.

Böhme, G. 1971: Brutversuch einer Sumpfohreule in Baumnest. Der Falke 18: 355.

Bonora, M. and Chiavetta, M. 1975: Contribution à l'étude du Faucon lanier *Falco biarmicus feldeggi* en Italie. Nos Oiseaux 33: 153–168.

Boonstra, R. 1977: Predation on *Microtus townsendii* populations: impact and vulnerability. Canad. J. Zool. 55: 1631–1643.

Borowski, S. 1961: Kilka spostrzeżeń c sóweczce *Glaucidium passerinum* (L.) i puszcyku mszarnym *Strix nebulosa* Forst. z Bialowieskiego Parku Narodowego. Przeglad Zool. 5: 59–60.

Borrero, H. J. I. 1962: Notas varias sobre *Asio flammeus bogotensis* en Colombia. Rev. Biol. Trop. Costa Rica 10: 45–59.

Bottomley, J. B. 1972: Two photographers in Finland. Brit. Birds 65: 158–164.

Boyle, G. L. 1974: Kestrel taking prey from Short-eared Owl. Brit. Birds 67: 474–475.

Braaksma, S. and De Bruijn, O. 1976: De Kerkuilstand in Nederland (New data on Barn Owls *Tyto alba* in The Netherlands). Limosa 49: 135–187

Brady, A. 1976: Possible transportation of young Great Horned Owls by parent. Cassinia 56: 30–31.

Brauner, A. 1908: Vom Winternisten der Sumpfohreule. Orn. Jahrb. 19: 55.

Brdicka, I. 1969: Eurasian Eagle Owl. Pp. 1314–1316 in: Birds of the World (ed. J. Gooders). Vol 4, Part II. IPC Magazines, London.

Brewster, W. 1925: Short-eared Owl. In: Bull. Mus. Com. Zool. 1925: 211–402.

Brock, J. 1969: Eurasian Pygmy Owl. In: Birds of the World (ed. J. Gooders). Vol. 4, Part 12. IPC Magazines, London.

Brock, J. 1969: Tengmalm's Owl. In: Birds of the World (ed. J. Gooders). Vol. 5, Part 1. IPC Magazines, London.

Brown, L. and Amadon, D. 1968: *Eagles, Hawks, and Falcons of the World*. 2 vols. Hamlyn, Feltham.

Brown, L. 1970: *African Birds of Prey*. Collins, London.

Brown, L. 1976: *Birds of Prey, their Biology and Ecology*. Hamlyn, London.

Brüll, H. 1964: Das Leben deutscher Greifvögel. Gustav Fischer Verlag, Stuttgart.

Brunton, D. F. and Pittaway Jr., R. 1971: Observations of the Great Grey Owl on winter range. Canad. Field-Nat. 85: 315–322.

Buckley, J. and Goldsmith, J. G. 1972: Barn Owls and their prey in East Norfolk. Trans. Norfolk & Norwich Nat. Soc. 22: 320–325.

Bühler, P. 1970: Schlupfhilfe-Verhalten bei der Schleiereule (*Tyto alba*). Die Vogelwelt 91: 121–130.

Bunn, D. S. 1972: Regular daylight hunting by Barn Owls. Brit. Birds 65: 26–30.

Bunn, D. S. 1974: The voice of the Barn Owl. Brit. Birds 67: 493–501.

Bunn, D. S. 1976: Eyesight of Barn Owl. Brit. Birds 69: 220–222.

Bunn, D. S. 1977: Voice of the Barn Owl. Brit. Birds 70: 171.

Bunn, D. S. and Warburton, A. B. 1977: Observations on breeding Barn Owls. Brit. Birds 70: 246–256.

Bunn, D. S., Warburton, A. B. and Wilson, R. D. S. 1982: *The Barn Owl*. Poyser, Calton.

Burton, J. A. 1970: Little Owl. Pp. 1336–1339 in: Birds of the World (ed. J. Gooders). Vol. 4, IPC Magazines, London.

Burton, J. A. (ed.) 1973: *Owls of the World*. Peter Lowe/Eurobooks, London.

Burton, J. F. 1950: Probable digging by Tawny Owl for Coleoptera. Brit. Birds 43: 301–302.

Busse, H. and Busse, E. 1976: Erfolgreiche künstliche Aufzucht von Schnee-Eulen (*Nyctea scandiaca* L.) im Tierpark Berlin. Zool. Garten N. F., Jena 46(3): 145–156.

Bussmann, J. 1935: Der Terragraph am Schleiereulenhorst. Orn. Beobachter 32: 175–179.

Bussmann, J. 1937: Biologische Beobachtungen über die Entwicklung der Schleiereule. Schweiz. Archiv für Orn. 1: 377–390.

Cade, T. J. 1960: Ecology of the Peregrine and Gyrfalcon populations in Alaska. Univ. California Publ. Zool. 63: 151–290.

Cais, L. 1963: Badania nad skladem pokarmu kilku gatunków sów. Zesz. nauk. Univ. im A. Mickiewicza w Poznainiu (Biol.) 4: 1–21.

Campbell, B. and Ferguson-Lees, J. 1972: *A Field Guide to Birds' Nests*. Constable, London.

Carlyon-Britton, R. 1928: Tawny Owl feeding young on Kestrel. Brit. Birds 22: 161.

Catling, P. M. 1972: A study of the Boreal Owl in Southern Ontario with particular reference to the irruption of 1968–69. Canad. Field-Nat. 86: 223–232.

Catuneanu, I., Hamar, M., Theiss, F., Korodi, G. and Manolache, L. 1970: Importanta economică a Ciufului de Pădure *Asio otus otus* L. în lupta împotriva dăunătorilor agricoli. Analele I.C.P.P. 6: 433–445.

Cavé, A. J. 1968: The breeding of the Kestrel, *Falco tinnunculus* L., in the reclaimed area Oostelijk Flevoland. Netherlands Zool. J. 18: 313–407.

Chaline, J., Baudvin, H., Jammot, D. and Saint Girons, M.-C. 1974: *Les proies des rapaces, petits mammifères et leur environnement*. Doin, Paris.

Chapin, J. P. 1939: Birds of the Belgian Congo. Part 2. Bull. Amer. Mus. Nat. Hist. 75.

Chitty, D. 1938: A laboratory study of pellet formation in the Short-eared Owl (*Asio flammeus*). Proc. Zool. Soc. Lond. 108A: 267–287.

Choussy, D. 1971: Etude d'une population de Grands-ducs *Bubo bubo* dans le Massif Central. Nos Oiseaux 31: 37–56.

Christie, H. H. V. 1931: Buzzard killing Little Owl. Brit. Birds 24: 367.

Clark, R. 1975: A field study of the Short-eared Owl, *Asio flammeus* (Pontoppidan) in North America. Wildlife Monographs 47: 1–67.

Clark, R., Smith, D. and Kelso, L. 1978: Working Bibliography of Owls of the World. Nat. Wildlife Fed. (Washington), Sci./Techn. Ser. 1: 1–319.

Clegg, T. M. and Henderson, D. S. 1971: Kestrel taking prey from Short-eared Owl. Brit. Birds 64: 317.

Collin, O. 1886: Suomessa tavattavien pöllöjen pesimissuhteista. Hämeen Sanomat, Hämeenlinna.

Craighead, J. J. and Craighead, F. C. 1956 (1969): *Hawks, Owls and Wildlife*. Dover Publications, New York.

Croze, H. 1970: Searching image in Carrion Crows. Z. Tierpsychol. 5: 1–85.

Curio, E. 1976: The ethology of predation. Zoophysiology and Ecology 7: 1–250. Springer-Verlag, New York.

Curry-Lindahl, K. 1950: Berguvens, *Bubo bubo* (L.), förekomst i Sverige jämte något om dess biologi. Vår Fågelvärld 9: 113–165.

Curry-Lindahl, K. 1958: Photographic studies of some less familiar birds: Pygmy Owl. Brit. Birds 54: 72–74.

Curry-Lindahl, K. (ed.). 1960: *Våra Fåglar i Norden*. Stockholm.

Curry-Lindahl, K. 1961: Conservation and predation problems of birds of prey in Sweden. Brit. Birds 54: 297–306.

Czarnecki, Z. 1956: Obserwacje nad biologia sowy uszatej (*Asio otus otus* (L.)). Prace Kom. Biol. Poznań 18: 1–42.

Danko, Š. and Švehlik, J. 1971: Poznámky k výskytu, hniezdnej bionómii a etológii sovy dlhochvostej (*Strix uralensis* Pallas) na východnom Slovensku. Československá Ochrana Prirody 12: 79–91.

Davis, A. H. and Prytherch, R. 1976: Field identification of Long-eared and Short-eared Owls. Brit. Birds 69: 281–287.

Delibes, M., Calderon, J. and Hiraldo, F. 1975: Seleccion de presa y alimentacion en España del Aguila Real (*Aquila chrysaetos*). Ardeola 21: 285–303.

Delmée, E., Dachy, P. and Simon, P. 1978: Quinze années d'observations sur la reproduction d'une population forestière de Chouettes hulottes. Gerfaut 68: 590–650.

Dement'ev, G. P. and Gortchakovskaya, N. N. 1945: On the biology of the Norwegian Gyrfalcon. Ibis 87: 559–565.

Dement'ev, G. P., Gladkow, N. A., Ptushenko, E. S., Spangenberg, E. P. and Sudilovskaya, A. M. 1951: Ptitsy Sovetskogo Soyuza. Vol. I. Moscow. (English language translation, Birds of Soviet Union, Jerusalem 1966.)

Desfayes, M. 1951: Nouvelles notes sur le Grand-duc. Nos Oiseaux 21: 121–126.

Diamond, J. M. 1973: Distributional ecology of New Guinea birds. Science 179: 759–769.

Diamond, J. M. 1978: Niche shifts and the rediscovery of interspecific competition. Amer. Sci. 66: 322–331.

Dice, L. R. 1945: Minimum intensities of illumination under which owls can find dead prey by sight. Amer. Nat. 79: 385–416.

Dice, L. 1947: Effectiveness of selection by owls of deermice (Peromyscus maniculatus) which contrast in colour with their background. Contrib. Lab. Vert. Biol. Univ. Mich. (Ann Arbor) 34: 1–20.

Dickson, R. C. 1972: Daylight hunting by Barn Owls. Brit. Birds 65: 221–222.

Dor, M. 1947: Examinations of the food of the Barn Owl in Israel. Hateva ve Haaretz 7: 337–344, 414–419. (In Hebrew.)

Dowell, A. 1979: Tawny Owl nesting in abandoned car. Scott. Birds 11 (6): 196.

Duke, G. E., Jegers, A. A., Loft, G. and Evanson, O. A. 1975: Gastric digestion in some raptors. Comp. Biochem. Physiol. 50A: 649–656.

Dunsire, C. and B. 1978: Barn Owl on dead Hedgehog. Scott. Birds 10: 56.

Earhart, C. M. and Johnson, N. K. 1970: Size dimorphism and food habits of North American Owls. Condor 72: 251–264.

Eck, S. and Busse, H. 1973: Eulen, die rezenten und fossilen Formen. Die Neue Brehm Bücherei 469. A. Ziemsen Verlag, Wittenberg Lutherstadt.

Edberg, R. 1955: Invasionen av hökuggla (Surnia ulula) in Skandinavien 1950–51. Vår Fågelvärld 14: 10–21.

Eiberle, K. 1970: Zur Wahl des Brutplatzes durch den Waldkauz im Lehrrevier der ETH. Schweiz. Zeitschrift für Forstwesen 121: 148–150.

Eliasson, U. 1958: En undersökning rörande pärlugglans (Aegolius funereus) bytesval. Vår Fågelvärld 17: 250–252.

Emmett, R. E., Mikkola, H., Mummery, L. and Westerhof, G. 1972: Prey found in Eagle Owls' nest in central Sweden. Brit. Birds 65: 482–483.

Eriks, A. 1952: Winter-broedgevallen van de velduil (Asio flammeus). Limosa 25: 86.

Erkert, H. G. 1969: Die Bedeutung des Lichtsinnes für Aktivität und Raumorientierung der Schleiereule (Tyto alba guttata Brehm). Z. Vergl. Physiologie 64: 37–70.

Erkinaro, E. 1969: Free-running circadian rhythm in Wood Mouse (Apodemus flavicollis Melch.) under natural light-dark-cycle. Experientia 25: 649.

Erkinaro, E. 1969: Der Phasenwechsel der lokomotorischen Aktivität bei Microtus agrestis (L.), M. arvalis (Pall.) und M. oeconomus (Pall.). Aquilo, Ser. Zool. 8: 1–31.

Erkinaro, E. 1972: Precision of the circadian clock in Tengmalm's Owl Aegolius funereus (L.), during various seasons. Aquilo, Ser. Zool. 13: 48–52.

Erkinaro, E. 1973: Seasonal variation of the dimensions of pellets in Tengmalm's Owl Aegolius funereus and the Short-eared Owl Asio flammeus. Aquilo, Ser. Zool. 14: 84–88.

Ern, H. 1958–59: Ornithologische Beobachtungen während einer Wanderung durch Jugo-slawien. Larus 12–13: 107–121.

Errington, P. L. 1932: Food habits of southern Wisconsin raptors. Pt. I: Owls. Condor 34: 176–186.

Errington, P. L. 1956: Factors limiting higher vertebrate populations. Science 124: 304–307.

Eskelinen, O. and Mikkola, H. 1972: Lehto-, viiru- ja lapinpöllön ravinnosta Pohjois-Karjalassa ja Savossa. Pohjois-Karjalan Luonto 1972: 24–25.

Etchécopar, R. D. and Hüe, F. 1964: *The Birds of North Africa*. Oliver and Boyd, Edinburgh.

Etchécopar, R. D. and Hüe, F. 1970: *Les Oiseaux du Proche et du Moyen Orient*. Boubée, Paris.

Everett, M. 1977: *A Natural History of Owls*. Hamlyn, London.

Everett, M. and Sharrock, J. T. R. 1980: The European atlas: owls. Brit. Birds 73: 239–256.

Fairley, J. S. 1966: Analyses of Barn Owl pellets from an Irish roost. Brit. Birds 59: 338–340.

Fairley, J. S. 1966: An indication of the food of the Short-eared Owl in Ireland. Brit. Birds 59: 307–308.

Fairley, J. S. 1967: Food of Long-eared Owls in North-east Ireland. Brit. Birds 60: 130–135.

Fairley, J. S. and Clark, F. L. 1972: Food of Barn Owls *Tyto alba* (Scopoli) over one year at a roost in Co. Galway. Irish Nat. Journal 17: 219–222.

Fedor, T. and Babay, K. 1962–63: Urali bagoly fèszkelése a Sátorhegységben. Aquila 69–70: 252.

Feduccia, A. and Ferree, C. E. 1978: Morphology of the bony stapes (Columella) in owls: evolutionary implications. Proc. Biol. Soc. Wash. 91: 431–438.

Fellowes, E. C. 1967: Kestrel and Barn Owl sharing entrance to nest-sites. Brit. Birds 60: 522–523.

Ferguson-Lees, I. J. 1969: Eurasian Scops Owl. Pp. 1303–1306 in: Birds of the World (ed. J. Gooders). Vol. 4. IPC Magazines, London.

Ferguson-Lees, I. J. 1969: Ural Owl. Pp. 1347–1349 in: Birds of the World (ed. J. Gooders). Vol. 5. IPC Magazines, London.

Festetics, A. 1959: Gewölluntersuchungen an Steinkäuzen der Camargue. Terre et la Vie 106: 121–127.

Festetics, A. 1968: Zweiphasenaktivität bei der Schleiereule (*Tyto alba*). Z. Tierpsychologie 25: 659–665.

Finnilä, C. 1916: Studier öfver fjällvråken (*Archibuteo lagopus*) i finska Lappland. Fauna och Flora 11: 165–172.

Fischer, W. 1956: Vom Uhu (*Bubo bubo*) in Südost-Thüringen. Beitr. Vogelkd. 6: 395–407.

Fischer, W. 1959: *Die Seeadler*. Die Neue Brehm-Bücherei 221. A. Ziemsen Verlag, Wittenberg-Lutherstadt.

Fischer, W. 1967: *Der Wanderfalk*. Die Neue Brehm-Bücherei 380. A. Ziemsen Verlag, Wittenberg-Lutherstadt.

Fischer, W. 1970: Vergleichende Beobachtungen an zwei Habichtspaaren in Südostthüringen. Beitr. Vogelkd. 16: 94–100.

Fisher, A. K. 1893: The Hawks and Owls of the United States. Bull. U.S. Dept. Agric. 3: 1–210. Washington.

Fisher, B. M. 1975: Possible intra-specific killing by a Great Grey Owl. Canad. Field-Nat. 89: 71–72.

Fitzpatrick, J. W. 1973: Response by a Long-eared Owl to Barred Owl calls. Wilson Bull. 85: 334–335.

Flegg, J. J. M. 1969: Long-eared Owl. Pp. 1357–1361 in: Birds of the World (ed. J. Gooders). Vol. 5. IPC Magazines, London.

Flint, V. E. and Bome, R. L. *et al* 1968: *Ptitsy CCCP*. Izd. mysl', Moskva.

Forsman, D. *et al* 1980: Pöllöjen pesintä Suomessa 1979. Lintumies 15: 2–9.

Förstel, A. 1977: Der Uhu *Bubo bubo* im Frankenwald und Bayerischen Vogtland. Anz. orn. Ges. Bayern 16: 115–131.

Forster, B. 1955: The Short-eared Owl at Churchill, Manitoba. Ontario Field Biologist 9: 15–17.

Fredga, K. 1964: En undersökning av pärlugglans (*Aegolius funereus*) bytesval i Mellansverige. Vår Fågelvärld 23: 103–118.

Fretwell, S. D. 1977: The regulation of plant communities by the food chains exploiting them. Perspectives in Biology and Medicine 20: 169–185.

Frey, H. 1973: Zur Ökologie niederösterreichischer Uhupopulationen. Egretta 16: 1–68.

Frey, H. 1976: Notizen über einen freilebenden, flugunfähigen Uhu (*Bubo bubo*) aus dem Waldviertel (Niederösterreich). J. Orn. 117: 465–468.

Frey, H. and Scherzinger, W. 1969: Künstliche Niststätten für Waldohreulen. Natur und Land 55: 83–84.

Frey, H., Scherzinger, W. and Walter, W. 1974: Künstliche Nistplätze für den Uhu (*Bubo bubo*). Orn. Mitt. 26: 173–174.

Frey, H. and Walter, W. 1977: Brutvorkommen und Nahrungsökologie des Uhus (*Bubo bubo*) im Burgenland. Egretta 20: 26–35.

Fritz, R., Sander, J., Sander, A., Norgall, A. and Norgall, T. 1977: Zur Kopulation der Waldohreule (*Asio otus*). Charadrius 13: 105–110.

Frylestam, B. 1971. Tornugglans *Tyto alba* invandring, utbredning och häckning i Sverige. Vår Fågelvärld 30: 185–193.

Frylestam, B. 1972. Über Wanderungen und Sterblichkeit beringter skandinavischer Schleiereulen *Tyto alba*. Ornis Scandinavica 3: 45–54.

Gallagher, M. D. and Rogers, T. D. 1980: On some birds of Dhofar and other parts of Oman. J. Oman Stud. Spec. Rep. 2: 347–85.

Ganya, I. and Zubkov, N. 1975: Food of the Little Owl (*Athene noctua*) in Moldavian S.S.R. Ecology; Birds and Mammals of Moldavia. Sbornik 1975: 63–72. (in Russian.)

Garner, D. J. 1982: Nest-site provision experiment for Long-eared Owls. Brit. Birds 75: 376–377.

Gause, G. F. 1934: *The Struggle for Existence*. Williams and Wilkins, Baltimore.

Géroudet, P. 1965: *Les Rapaces Diurnes et Nocturnes d'Europe*. Delachaux & Niestlé, Neuchatel.

Ghiselin, M. T. 1966: On semantic pitfalls of biological adaptation. Philosophy of Science 33: 147–153.

Ghiselin, M. T. 1974: *The Economy of Nature and the Evolution of Sex*. London.

Gilliard, E. T. 1958: *Living Birds of the World*. Hamish Hamilton. London.

Glue, D. E. 1967: Prey taken by the Barn Owl in England and Wales. Bird Study 14: 169–183.

Glue, D. E. 1969: Owl pellets. Pp. 1368–1370 in: Birds of the World (ed. J. Gooders). Vol. 5. IPC Magazines, London.

Glue, D. E. 1971: Avian predator pellet analysis and the mammalogist. Mammal Rev. 1: 53–62.

Glue, D. E. 1971: Ringing recovery circumstances of some small birds of prey. Bird Study 18: 137–146.

Glue, D. E. 1972: Bird prey taken by British owls. Bird Study 19: 91–95.

Glue, D. E. 1973: Owl pellets. Pp. 193–196 in: Owls of the World (ed. J. A. Burton). Peter Lowe Eurobooks, London.

Glue, D. E. 1974: Food of the Barn Owl in Britain and Ireland. Bird Study 21: 200–210.

Glue, D. E. 1976: Long-eared Owl invasion. BTO News 78: 5.

Glue, D. E. 1976: Feeding ecology of the Short-eared Owl in Britain and Ireland. Bird Study 23: 70–78.

Glue, D. E. 1977: Breeding biology of Long-eared Owls. Brit. Birds 70: 318–331.

Glue, D. E. 1977: Feeding ecology of the Short-eared Owl in Britain and Ireland. Bird Study 24: 70–78.

Glue, D. E. and G. J. Hammond 1974: Feeding ecology of the Long-eared Owl in Britain and Ireland. Brit. Birds 67: 361–369.

Glue, D. E. and Scott, D. 1980: Breeding biology of the Little Owl. Brit. Birds 73: 167–180.

Glutz von Blotzheim, U. N. 1962: Die Brutvögel der Schweiz. Aarau.

Glutz von Blotzheim, U. 1964: Höchstalter schweizerischer Ringvögel. Orn. Beobachter 61: 115.

Glutz von Blotzheim, U. N., Bauer, K. M. and Bezzel, E. (eds). 1971: Handbuch der Vögel Mitteleuropas. Vol. 4, Falconiformes. Akademische Verlagsgesellschaft, Frankfurt am Main.

Glutz von Blotzheim, U. N. and Bauer, K. 1980: Handbuch der Vögel Mitteleuropas. Vol. 9, Columbiformes-Piciformes. Akademische Verlagsgesellschaft, Wiesbaden.

Goddard, T. R. 1935: A census of Short-eared Owl (*Asio f. flammeus*) at Newcastleton, Roxburghshire, 1934. J. Anim. Ecol. 4: 113–118, 289–290.

Godfrey, W. E. 1966: The Birds of Canada. Nat. Mus. Canada Bull. 203. Ottawa.

Godfrey, W. E. 1967: Some winter aspects of the Great Grey Owl. Canad. Field-Nat. 81: 99–101.

Goloduško, B. Z. and Samusenko, E. G. 1961: Pitanie vorob' inogo syčika v Belovežskoj Pušče. Pp. 135–140 in: Ekologija i Migracii Ptic Pribaltiki. Riga.

Gordon, S. 1955: *The Golden Eagle*. Collins, London.

Green, J. C. 1969: Northern owl invasion winter 1968–69. Loon 41: 36–39.

Grembe, G. 1965: Beiträge zur Ernährungsbiologie des Sperlingskauzes (*Glaucidium passerinum*) im östlichen Europa (Sammelreferat). Orn. Mitt. 17: 197–199.

Grembe, G. 1966: Über die Winternahrung des Sperlingskauzes im Moskauer Gebiet (Referat). Orn. Mitt. 18: 84.

Greschik, J. 1910: Magen- und Gewöllenuntersuchungen unserer einheimischen Raubvögel. Aquila 17: 2–13.

Grimm, R. J. and Whitehouse, W. M. 1963: Pellet formation in a Great Horned Owl: a roentgenographic study. Auk 80: 301–306.

Grönlund, S. and Mikkola, H. 1969: On the ecology of the Short-eared Owl in Lapua Alajoki in 1969. Suomenselän Linnut 4: 68–76.

Grönlund, S. and Mikkola, H. 1974: Huuhkajan ravinnosta Kymenlaaksossa. Kymenlaakson Luonto 15: 13–17.

Grönlund, S. and Mikkola, H. 1977: Sarvipöllön pesimäbiologiasta ja ravinnosta Pohjanmaalla ja Suomenselällä 1962–69. Suomenselän Linnut 12: 77–83.

Grönlund, S. and Mikkola, H. 1978: Sarvipöllön pesintäaikaisesta esiintymisestä ja ravinnosta sekä pesimäbiologiasta Kymenlaaksossa 1970–1976. Kymenlaakson Luonto 19: 7–14.

Grönlund, S. and Mikkola, H. 1979: Lehtopöllön pesintäaikaisesta vuorokausirytmiikasta. Kymenlaakson Luonto 20: 1–6.

Grossman, M. L. and Hamlet, J: 1965: *Birds of Prey of the World*. Cassell, London.

Grote, H. 1949: Der südlichste Brutplatz des Bartkauzes: Bialowies in Polen. Die Vogelwelt 70: 20.

Gruzdev, L. V. and Likhachev, G. N. 1960: Contribution to feeding habits of *Strix aluco* in the Tula Zaseki. Zool. Zhurnal 39: 624–627. (In Russian.)

Guérin, G. 1928: Régime et Croissance de l'Effraye Commune (*Tyto alba alba* Scop.) en Vendée. Paris.

Guérin, G. 1928: *La Vie des Chouettes*. Régime et Croissance de l'Effraye Commune. Lechevalier, Paris.

Guérin, G. 1932: *La Vie des Chouettes*. II. La Hulotte et son Régime. Fontenay-le-Compte.

Guérin, G. 1932: La Hulotte et son Régime. *Encyclopédie ornithologique*. Lechevalier, Paris.

Gunston, D. 1948: Little Owl as prey of Tawny Owl. Brit. Birds 41: 388.

Haartman, L. G. v., Hildén, O., Linkola, P., Suomalainen, P. and Tenovuo, R. 1963–72: Pohjolan Linnut Värikuvin, 8. Otava, Helsinki.

Haensel, J. and Walther, H. J. 1966: Beitrag zur Ernährung der Eulen im Nordharz-Vorland unter besonderer Berücksichtigung der Insektennahrung. Beitr. Vogelkd. 11: 345–358.

Haftorn, S. 1971: *Norges Fugler*. Universitetsforlaget, Oslo.

Hagen, Y. 1942: Totalgewichts-Studien bei norwegischen Vogelarten. Arch. Naturgesch. 11(1): 1–173.

Hagen, Y. 1948: Fra norske undersøkelser over uglenes og rovfuglenes ernaering. Sveriges Natur, Årboken 1948: 73–107. Göteborg.

Hagen, Y. 1952: Rovfuglene og Viltpleien. Byldendal Norsk Forlag, Oslo. Pp. 603.

Hagen, Y. 1956: The irruption of Hawk Owls (*Surnia ulula* (L.)) in Fenno-scandia 1950–51 with some remarks on recent micro-rodent cycles. Sterna 24: 3–22.

Hagen, Y. 1959: Pärlugglan. Pp. 160–165 in: Nordens Fugle i Farver (ed. N. Blaedel). Vol. 3. Copenhagen.

Hagen, Y. 1960: Snøugla på Hardangervidda sommeren 1959. Papers Norwegian State Game Research 2 (7): 1–25.

Hagen, Y. 1965: The food, population fluctuations and ecology of the Long-eared Owl *Asio otus* (L.) in Norway. Medd. Statens Viltundersøkelser (2) 23: 1–43.

Hagen, Y. 1968: Noen iakttagelser over slagugla (*Strix uralensis* Pall.) i Østerdalen. Sterna 8: 161–182.

Hagen, Y. and Barth, E. K. 1950: Iakttagelser over haukuglen. Fauna 3: 1–12.

Hakala, A., Kaikusalo, A. and Rikkonen, M. 1974: Skuolfin vuosi-tunturipöllö palasi. Suomen Luonto 33: 278–280.

Hakala, A., Kaikusalo, A. and Rikkonen, M. 1981: Tunturipöllön (*Nyctea scandiaca* L.) esiintymisestä, pesimisestä ja ravinnosta Suomessa v. 1974–1978. Unpubl. MS, Dept of Zoology, University of Oulu, Finland.

Hansen, L. 1952: Natuglens (*Strix a. aluco* L.) døgn- og årsrytme. Dansk Ornith. Fören. Tidsskr. 46: 158–172.

Hardin, G. 1960: The competitive exclusion principle. Science, N.Y. 131: 1292–1297.

Harrison, C. J. O. 1960: The food of some urban Tawny Owls. Bird Study 7: 236–240.

Harrison, C. 1975: *Nests, Eggs and Nestlings of European Birds*. Collins, London.

Hautala, H. 1977: *Kololinnut ja muut pökkelöpesijät*. Suomen Luonnonsuojelun Tuki Oy, Helsinki.

Haverschmidt, F. 1934: Het broeden van Kerkuilen (*Tyto alba guttata* Brehm) in boomholten. Ardea 23: 212.

Haverschmidt, F. 1946: Observations on the breeding habits of the Little Owl. Ardea 34: 214–246.

Haverschmidt, F. 1946: Notes on the nest-sites of the Oystercatcher and the Long-eared Owl as a hole breeder. Brit. Birds 34: 334–336.

Hawley, R. G. 1966: Observations on the Long-eared Owl. The Sorby Record: J. Sorby Nat. Hist. Soc. 2 (3) 95–114.

Heinonen, E., Kellomäki, E. and Tiainen, H. 1970: Helmipöllö pesinyt kaksi kertaa samana kesänä Virroilla. Suomenselän Linnut 5: 15–17.

Heinroth, O. 1922: Beziehungen zwischen Vogelgewicht, Eigewicht, Gelegegewicht und Brutdauer. J. Orn. 70: 172–285.

Heitkamp, U. 1967: Zur Ernährungsökologie der Waldohreule (*Asio otus*). Orn. Mitt. 19: 139–143.

Helo, P. 1971: Hiiripöllön (*Surnia ulula*) käyttäytymisestä ja äänistä pesimäaikana. Lintumies 7: 44–45.

Helo, P. 1975: Pöllöjen pesintä Kainuussa keväällä 1974. Kainuun Linnut 3: 65–72.

Helo, P., Leinonen, A. and Ruuskanen, J. 1980: Pöllöjen pesintä kainuussa vuosina 1975–78. Kainuun Linnut 4: 33–48.

Herrera, C. M. 1973: Regimen alimenticio de *Tyto alba* en España sudoccidental. Ardeola 14: 359–394.

Herrera, C. M. 1974: Trophic diversity of the Barn Owl *Tyto alba* in continental Western Europe. Ornis Scandinavica 5: 181–191.

Herrera, C. M. and Hiraldo, F. 1976: Food-niche and trophic relationships among European owls. Ornis Scandinavica 7: 29–41.

Hibbert-Ware, A. 1936–38: Report of the Little Owl Food Inquiry. Brit. Birds 29: 302–305; 31: 162–187, 205–229, 249–264.

Hildén, O. and Helo, P. 1981: The Great Grey Owl *Strix nebulosa* – a bird of the northern taiga. Ornis Fennica 58: 159–166.

Hiraldo, F., Andrada, J. and Parreño, F. F. 1975: Diet of the Eagle Owl (*Bubo bubo*) in Mediterranean Spain. Doñana Acta Vertebrata 2: 161–177.

Hirons, G., Hardy, A. and Stanley, P. 1979: Starvation in young Tawny Owls. Bird Study 26: 59–63.

Hjeljord, O. and Ø. Mobråten, Ø. 1975: Hubroen i Numedal. Sterna 14: 127–129.

Höglund, N. H. 1964: Über die Ernährung des Habichts (*Accipiter gentilis* Lin.) in Schweden. Viltrevy 2: 271–328.

Höglund, N. H. 1966: Über die Ernährung des Uhus *Bubo bubo* Lin. in Schweden während der Brutzeit. Viltrevy 4: 43–80.

Höglund, N. H. and Lansgren, E. 1968: The Great Grey Owl and its prey in Sweden. Viltrevy 5: 360–421.

Högstedt, G. and Ulfstrand, S. 1976: Hur många fåglar häckar i Sverige? Anser 15: 1–32.

Holland, T. R. 1974: Behaviour of Long-eared Owls in presence of dog. Brit. Birds 67: 212–213.

Hollom, P. A. D. 1962: *The Popular Handbook of British Birds*. 3rd Edition. Witherby, London.

Holmberg, T. 1972: Automatisk registering av dygnsaktiviteten hos kattuggla under häckning-stiden. Fauna och Flora 67: 246–249.

Holmberg, T. 1974: En studie av slaggugglans *Strix uralensis* läten. Vår Fågelvärld 33: 140–146.

Holmberg, T. 1974: Pärlugglehona *Aegolius funereus* födde ensam upp fem ungar. Vår Fågelvärld 33: 299–300.

Holmberg, T. 1976: Variationer i kattugglans (*Strix aluco*) bytesval. Fauna och Flora 71: 97–107.

Holmes, J. C. and Bethel, W. M. 1972: Modification of intermediate host behaviour by parasites. Behav. Asp. Parasite transmissions. Zool. J. Linnean Soc. 51: 123–149.

Holt, G., Frøslie, A. and Norheim, G. 1979: Mercury, DDE, and PCP in the Avian Fauna in Norway 1965–1976. Acta Vet. Scandinavica, Supplementum 70: 1–28.

Hölzinger, J., Mickley, M. and Schilhansl, K. 1973: Untersuchungen zur Brut- und Ernährungsbiologie der Sumpfohreule (*Asio flammeus*) in einem süddeutschen Brutgebiet mit Bemerkungen zum Auftreten der Art in Mitteleuropa. Anz. orn. Ges. Bayern 12: 176–197.

Horn, H. S. and May, R. M. 1977: Limits to similarity among coexisting competitors. Nature 270: 660–661.

Hörnfeldt, B. 1978: Synchronous population fluctuations in voles, small game, owls and tularemia in Northern Sweden. Oecologia (Berl.) 32: 141–152.

Hortling, I. 1929: *Ornitologisk Handbok*. Helsinki.

Hortling, I. 1952: *Lintukirja*. Otava, Helsinki.

Høst, P. 1935: Norsk Jaeger- og Fiskerfor. Tidsskrift 64: 302–317. Oslo. (Cited in Hagen 1960.)

Hubl, H. 1952: Beiträge zur Kenntnis der Verhaltensweisen junger Eulenvogel in Gefangen-schaft: (Schleiereule *Tyto alba*, Steinkauz *Athene noctua* und Waldkauz *Strix aluco aluco*). Z. Tierpsychologie 9: 102–119.

Hublin, P. and Mikkola, H. 1977: Nesting of the Hawk Owl (*Surnia ulula*) in Kuopio in 1976. Savon Luonto 9: 6–8.

Hudson, R. 1975: *Threatened Birds of Europe*. Macmillan, London.

Huhtala, K., Finnlund, M. and Korpimäki, E. 1976: Huuhkajan pesimäaikaisesta ravinnosta Vaasan läänissä. Suomenselän Linnut 11: 4–13.

Huhtala, K., Rajala, P. and Sulkava, S. 1976: Uusin tieto kotkan ravinnosta. Suomen Luonto 1976 (1): 25–29.

Huhtala, K., Korpimäki, E. and Mikkola, H. 1979: On the activity and food of the Ural Owl *Strix uralensis* during the breeding season. Unpubl. MS, Department of Zoology, University of Oulu, Finland.

Hummitzsch, E. 1950: Starke Schleiereulenbruten. Orn. Mitt. 2: 102.

Hummitzsch, E. 1953: Zur Fortpflanzungsbiologie der Schleiereule. Beitr. Vogelkd. 3: 248–249.

Hutchinson, G. E. 1957: Concluding remarks. Cold Spring Harbor Symposium of Quantitative Biology 22: 415–427.

Hutchinson, G. E. 1959: Homage to Santa Rosalia, or why are there so many kinds of animals? Amer. Nat. 93: 145.

ICBP 1977: *Proceedings of the World Conference on Birds of Prey, Vienna 1975*. Ed. R. D. Chancellor. ICBP, London.

Imaizumi, Y. 1968: Analysis of Ural Owl Pellet Contents. Zool. Mag. (Dobutsugaku Zasshi) 77: 402–404.

Ingram, C. 1959: The importance of juvenile cannibalism in the breeding biology of certain birds of prey. Auk 76: 218–226.

Ingritz, G. 1969: Slagugglans (*Strix uralensis*) biotop- och boplatzval i nedre Västerdalarna. Vår Fågelvärld 28: 253.

Iso-Iivari, L. 1979: Havaintoja Inarin Lapin satunnaislajistosta. Lintumies 14: 78–81.

Itämies, J. and Mikkola, H. 1972: On the diet of the Tawny Owl (*Strix aluco*) in Rauma. Porin Lintutiet. Yhd. Vuosikirja 3: 25–26.

Jabloński, B. 1976: Estimation of bird abundance in large areas. Acta Ornithologica 16(2): 1–76.

Jäderholm, K. 1981: Helmipöllö viirupöllön saaliina. Siivekäs 1981 (3).

Jäkkel 1891: Cited in Schneider, W. 1964.

Jánossy, D. and Schmidt, E. 1970: Die Nahrung des Uhus (*Bubo bubo*) Regionale und erdzeitliche Änderungen. Bonn. Zool. Beitr. 21: 25–51.

Jansson, E. 1964: Anteckningar rörande häckande sparvuggla (*Glaucidium passerinum*). Vår Fågelvärld 23: 209–222.

Järvinen, O. and Väisänen, R. 1978: Miksi aikaisemmin tehtyjä pesimälinnuston laskentoja kannattaa toistaa? Lintumies 13: 1–6.

Jeal, P. E. C. 1976: Prey of Short-eared Owls in breeding quarters in the Outer Hebrides. Bird Study 23: 56–57.

Jennings, M. C. 1977: 'More about Desert Liliths': Hume's Tawny Owl. Israel Land and Nature 2 (4).

Jennings, M. C. 1981: *The Birds of Saudi Arabia:* checklist. Cambridge.

Jensen, S., Johnels, A. G., Olsson, M. and Otterlind, G. 1969: DDT and PCB in Marine Animals from Swedish Waters. Nature 224: 247–250.

Johansson, H. 1978: Något om slagugglans *Strix uralensis* boplatzval. Fauna och Flora 73: 207–210.

Johnsen, S. 1933: Notes on the Birds of Svalbard. Bergens Museums Årbok 1933 (3): 1–53.

Johnston, R. F. 1956: Predation by Short-eared Owls on a Salicornia salt marsh. Wilson Bull. 68: 91–102.

Jokinen, M., Kaikusalo, A. and Korpimäki, E. 1982: Pöllöjen pesintä Suomessa vuonna 1980. Suomenselän Linnut 17: 15–22.

Joutsamo, E. 1969: Pöllötakseeraus Varsinais-Suomessa keväällä 1968. Lintumies 5: 43–46.

Jussila, E. 1974: Joitakin havaintoja varpuspöllön pesältä Lahdessa 1974. Päijät-Hämeen Linnut 5: 87–90.

Jussila, E. and Mikkola, H. 1973: Varpuspöllön pesinnästä, pesintäaikaisesta käyttäytymisestä ja ravinnosta Lahden ympäristössä 1966–73. Päijät-Hämeen Linnut 4: 73–80.

Juvonen, A. 1976: Sarvipöllön (*Asio otus*) pesimäbiologiasta ja esiintymisestä Outokummussa vuosina 1969–1976. Siipirikko 3: 13–18.

Kaakinen, K. and Mikkola, H. 1972: Varpuspöllön syys- ja talviravinnosta Oulun seudulla ja Kainuussa 1962–1971. Kainuun Linnut 2: 78–79.

Källander, H. 1964: Invasionen av pärluggla (*Aegolius funereus*) i Mellansverige 1958 samt nagot om artens förekomst i Sverige. Vår Fågelvärld 23: 119–135.

Källander, H. 1977: Food of the Long-eared Owl *Asio otus* in Sweden. Ornis Fennica 54: 79–84.

Kaufman, D. W. 1974: Differential predation on active and inactive prey by owls. Auk 91: 172–173.

Kaus, D. 1977: Zur Populationsdynamik, Ökologie und Brutbiologie der Schleiereule *Tyto alba* in Franken. Anz. orn. Ges. Bayern 16: 18–44.

Kazama, T. 1974: Cage observation of wounded Ural Owls and their egg-laying in captivity. Misc. Repts. Yamashina Inst. Orn. 7(3): 83–99.

Kellomäki, E. 1966: Havaintoja varpuspöllöstä Suomenselän alueella. Lintumies 2: 39–43.

Kellomäki, E. 1969: Varpuspöllön ravintobiologiasta Etelä- ja Keski-Suomessa 1960-luvulla. Suomenselän Linnut 4: 54–55.

Kellomäki, E. 1969: Varpuspöllön (*Glaucidium passerinum*) ravintobiologiasta Etelä- ja Keski-Suomessa 1960-luvulla. Unpubl. MS, Dept. of Zool., University of Turku, Finland.

Kellomäki, E. 1970: Havaintoja varpuspöllöstä. Suomenselän Linnut 5: 64–70, 99–103.

Kellomäki, E. 1971: Lintuhavaintoja Virroilta v. 1970. Suomenselän Linnut 6: 28–29.

Kellomäki, E. 1977: Food of the Pygmy Owl *Glaucidium passerinun* in the breeding season. Ornis Fennica 54: 1–29.

Kenward, R. E. 1976: The effect of predation by Goshawk, *Accipiter gentilis*, on Woodpigeon, *Columba palumbus*, populations. D.Phil. thesis, Oxford University.

Keve, A. 1960: Magyarország madarainak névjegyzéke. A Madártani Intézet Kiadványa, Pp. 90. Budapest.

Keve, A., Kohl, I., Matoušek, F., Mošanský, A. and Rucner-Kroneisl, R. 1960: On the taxonomic position of the Little Owl, *Athene noctua* (Scop.) of South-east Europe. Larus 14: 26–74.

Kiefer, J. 1892: Schleiereulen und Turmfalken kämpfend. Die Vogelwelt 1892: 290–291.

Kirkpatrick, C. M. and Conway, C. H. 1947: The winter foods of some Indiana owls. Amer. Midl. Nat. 38: 755–766.

Kislenko, G. S. 1967: On the food habits of the Ural Owl. Ornitologiya 8: 357. (Translated from the Russian by Dr. O. Semenov-Tian-Shanski.)

Kivirikko, K. E. 1930: Huuhkajan ateriatunkiot ja mitä ne todistavat. Ornis Fennica 7: 95–101.

Kivirikko, K. E. 1947: *Suomen Linnut*, I. Porvoo and Helsinki.

Klaas, C. 1949: Zur Lebens- und Verhaltensweise des Habichts. Natur und Volk 79: 68–75.

Klaas, C. 1957: Vom Roten Milan. Natur und Volk 87: 228–233.

Klaas, C. 1967: Lebensstätte und Beauteauswahl dreier Habichtspaare. Natur und Volk 97: 347–353.

Klaus, S., Vogel, F. and Wiesner, J. 1965: Ein Beitrag zur Biologie des Sperlingskauzes. Zool. Abhandl. 28: 165–204.

Klaus, S., Mikkola, H. and Wiesner, J. 1975: Aktivität und Ernährung des Rauhfusskauzes *Aegolius funereus* (L.) während der Fortpflanzungsperiode. Zool. Jb. Syst. 102: 485–507.

Klemetsen, A. 1967: Analyse av jorduglegulp fra lavlandet. Sterna 7: 293–294.

Koenig, L. 1973: Das Aktionssystem der Zwergohreule *Otus scops scops* (Linné 1758). Fortschritte der Verhaltensforschung. Advances in Ethology 13: 1–124. Verlag Paul Parey, Berlin und Hamburg.

Koivusaari, J. 1980: Merikotkan (*Haliaeetus albicilla* L.) ravintobiologiasta. Phil. lic. thesis, University of Kuopio, Finland.

Koivusaari, J., Lahti, E., Mikkola, H., Pelkonen, K. and Takkinen, P. 1977: Tunturipöllön ravinnonkäyttö, oksennuspallot ja niiden soveltuminen ravintotutkimuksiin. Savon Luonto 9: 39–42.

Kolunen, H. and Pietiäinen, H. 1978: Pöllövuoden 1978 tilinpäätös. Päijät-Hämeen Linnut 9: 102–106.

König, C. 1968: Lautäusserungen von Rauhfusskauz (*Aegolius funereus*) und Sperlingskauz (*Glaucidium passerinum*). Die Vogelwelt, supplement: 115–138.

König, C. 1969: Sechsjährige Untersuchungen an einer Population des Rauhfusskauzes, *Aegolius funereus* (L.). J. Orn. 110: 133–147.

König, C. 1972: Mobbing of small passerine birds in response to the song of the Pygmy Owl. Proc. Int. Orn. Congress 15: 661–662.

König, H. and Haensel, J. 1968: Ein Beitrag zum Vorkommen und zur Biologie des Uhus (*Bubo b. bubo* (L.)) im Nordharzgebiet. Beitr. Vogelkd. 13: 335–365.

Konishi, M. 1970: Comparative neurophysiological studies of hearing and vocalisations in songbirds. J. Vergl. Physiol. 66: 257–272.

Konishi, M. 1973. How the owl tracks its prey. Amer. Sci. 61: 414–424.

Konishi, M. 1973: Locatable and nonlocatable acoustic signals for Barn Owls. Amer. Nat. 107: 775–785.

Konishi, M. and Kenuk, A. S. 1975: Discrimination of noise spectra by memory in the Barn Owl. J. Comp. Physiol. 97: 55–58.

Korpimäki, E. 1972: Hiiri- ja helmipöllön pesinnästä sekä ravinnosta samalla biotoopilla. Suomenselän Linnut 7: 36–40.

Korpimäki, E. 1978: Havaintoja seitsemän petolintulajin saalistustavoista. Suomenselän Linnut 13: 40–44, 86–89.

Korpimäki, E. 1978: Pöllöjen pesimäaikaisesta esiintymisestä Suomenselällä v. 1978. Suomenselän Linnut 13: 100–107.

Korpimäki, E. 1981: On the ecology and biology of Tengmalm's Owl (*Aegolius funereus*) in Southern Ostrobothnia and Suomenselkä, Western Finland. Acta Univ. Ouluensis (A) 118: 1–84.

Korpimäki, E. 1981: Pöllöjen esiintyminen Suomenselällä v. 1980. Suomenselän Linnut 16: 21–28.

Korpimäki, E., Ikola, S., Haapoja, R. and Kirkkomäki, J. 1977: Sarvi-, suo- ja helmipöllön, tuuli- ja sinisuohaukan ekologiasta Lapuan-Kauhavan Alajoella v. 1977. Suomenselän Linnut 12: 100–117.

Koskela, K. 1978: Pöllöt 1977 Pohjois-Karjalassa. Siipirikko 5: 2–13.

Koskela, K. 1979: Pöllöt 1978 Pohjois-Karjalassa. Siipirikko 6: 15–18.

Koskela, K. and Koskela, K. 1975: Pöllöt 1974 Pohjois-Karjalassa. Siipirikko 2: 8–11.

Koskela, P. 1975: The annual cycle in the life of the common frog, *Rana temporaria* L., in northern Finland. Oulu. Ph.D. thesis, Dept of Zoology, Univ. of Oulu.

Koskimies, P. 1976: Pöllöjen esiintymisestä Etelä-Karjalassa. Ornis Karelica 3: 10–23.

Koskimies, P. 1979: Pöllöjen esiintymisestä Etelä-Karjalassa 1976–1978. Ornis Karelica 5: 21–30.

Kramer, V. 1950: Die Ernährung des Wanderfalken (*Falco peregrinus germanicus* Erlanger) in zwei verschiedenen Landschaftsformen der Oberlausitz. Syllegomena Biologica 1950: 213–216.

Kramer, V. 1955: Habicht und Sperber. Die Neue Brehm-Bücherei 158.

Krampitz, H. E. 1956: Die Brutvögel Siziliens. J. Orn. 97: 310–334.

Kranz, P. 1971: Något om berguvens aktivität och föda. Fåglar i Sörmland 4: 13–23.

Kucera, L. 1970: Die Vögel des mittleren Böhmerwaldes (Sumava). Orn. Mitt. 22: 223–242.

Kuhk, R. 1949: Aus der Fortpflanzungsbiologie des Rauhfusskauzes, *Aegolius funereus* (L.) Pp. 171–172 in: *Ornithologie als Biologische Wissenschaft:* Festschr. Erwin Stresemann (ed. E. Mayr & E. Schüz). Universitetsverlag, Heidelberg.

Kuhk, R. 1953: Lautässerungen und jahreszeitliche Gesangtätigkeit des Rauhfusskauzes, *Aegolius funereus* (L.). J. Orn. 94: 83–93.

Kuhk, R. 1969: Schlüpfen und Entwicklung der Nestjungen beim Rauhfusskauz (*Aegolius funereus*). Bonn. Zool. Beitr. 20: 145–150.

Kuhlman, E. & K. Koskela 1980: Lehto- ja helmipöllön pesintäaikaisesta ravinnosta. Siipirikko 7: 46–50.

Kulczycki, A. 1964: Badania nad skladem pokarmu sów z Beskidu Niskiego. Acta Zool. Cracoviensia 9: 529–559.

Kulczycki, A. 1966: Przyczynek do znajomości pokarmu sowy blotnej, *Asio flammeus flammeus* (Pontop, 1763). Przeglad Zool. 10: 218–221.

Kulves, H. 1973: Haliaetus albicilla. Skrifter Utgivna av Ålands Kulturstiftelse 9: 1–126.

Kumerloeve, H. 1968: Gewöllstudien an einem Sumpfohreulen-Brutpaar auf der Insel Amrum. Orn. Mitt. 20: 33–34.

Kunttu, H. 1978: Viirupöllön (*Strix uralensis*) pesimäaikaisesta ravinnosta. Päijät-Hämeen Linnut 9: 14–19.

Lack, D. 1946: Competition for food by birds of prey. J. Anim. Ecol. 15: 123–129.

Lack, D. 1954: *The Natural Regulation of Animal Numbers.* Blackwell, Oxford.

Lack, D. 1971: *Ecological Isolation in Birds.* Blackwell Sci. Publ., Oxford.

Lagerström, M. 1969: Viirupöllön (*Strix uralensis*) sukukypsyydestä. Ornis Fennica 46: 31–32.

Lagerström, M. 1978: Helmipöllön ja viirupöllön yhteispesintä. Ornis Fennica 55: 183–184.

Lagerström, M. 1978: Huuhkajan *Bubo bubo* saalislajeista Pirkanmaalla. Lintumies 13: 146–147.

Lagerström, M. and Syrjänen, J. 1969: Varpuspöllö (*Glaucidium passerinum*) lehtopöllön (*Strix aluco*) saaliseläimenä. Ornis Fennica 46: 86–87.

Lahti, E. 1972: Nest sites and nesting habitats of the Ural Owl *Strix uralensis* in Finland during the period 1870–1969. Ornis Fennica 49: 91–97.

Lahti, E. and Mikkola, H. 1974: Nest sites and nesting habitats of the Ural, Tawny and Great Grey Owls. Savon Luonto 6: 1–10.

Lambrecht, K. 1917: Die Ausbildung und Geschichte der europäischen Vogelwelt. Aquila 24: 191–221.

Lammin-Soila, R. and Uusivuori, P. 1975: Pöllöjen esiintymisestä Itä-Uudellamaalla 1970–73. Lintumies 10: 109–117.

Lange, H. 1948: Sløruglens Føde belyst gennem Undersøgelser af Gylp. Dansk Ornith. Foren. Tidsskr. 42: 50–84.

Langvatn, R. 1977: Characteristics and relative occurrence of remnants of prey found at nesting places of Gyrfalcon *Falco rusticolus*. Ornis Scandinavica. 8: 113–125.

Laurie, W. A. 1971: The food of the Barn Owl in the Serengeti National Park, Tanzania. J. East Afr. Nat. Hist. Soc. 28: 1–4.

Law, C. 1960: The Great Gray Owl of the woodlands. Blue Jay 18: 14–16.

Lawrence, A. G. 1926: Chickadee Notes – Kismet, Breeding records. Winnipeg.

Leibundgut, H. 1973: Studien über das Verhalten von Uhus in der Gefangenschaft. Z. Jagdwiss. 19: 122–131.

Leinonen, A. 1980: Lapinpöllön *Strix nebulosa* talvisesta käyttäytymisestä. Kainuun Linnut 4: 9–13.

Lepiksaar, J. 1954: Berguvens matsedel. Dalajägaren 1954: 26–31.

Leppänen, H. 1970: Lehtopöllön pesiminen ja ravinto Tampereen seudulla. Unpbl. MS, Dept. of Zoology, University of Oulu.

Leshem, Y. 1974a: Lilit Ha' Midbar. Teva Va' Aretz 16: 66–67.

Leshem, Y. 1974b: Hume's Tawny Owl – Lilith of the Desert. Israel Land and Nature 1974: 12–14.

Lettesjö, A. 1974: Äldsta berguven i världen. I Kikaren 15: 12–13.

Levin, S. A. 1970. Community equilibria and stability, and an extension of the competitive exclusion principle. Amer. Nat. 104: 413–423.

Levin, S. A., Levin, J. E. and Paine, R. T. 1977: Snowy Owl predation on Short-eared Owls. Condor 79: 395.

Lewontin, R. C. 1976: Evolution and the theory of games. Amer. Sci. 64: 41–45.

Lichačev, G. N.1951: Zimny zapas pišči vorob'inogo syčika. Pridoga 40: 63–64.

Lindberg, P. 1966: Invasionen av sparvuggla (*Glaucidium passerinum*) i södra Skandinavien 1963–64. Vår Fågelvärld 25: 106–142.

Lindberg, P. 1975: *Pilgrimsfalken i Sverige*. Stockholm.

Lindblad, J. 1967: *I ugglemarker*. Bonniers, Stockholm.

Lindhe, U. 1966: En undersökning av pärlugglans (*Aegolius funereus*) bytesval i SV Lappland. Vår Fågelvärld 25: 40–48.

Lindqvist, O. V. 1978: Biologista maailmaa kuvaavien teoriain yleisestä luonteesta. Teoreettisen Biologian Seminaari, Lammi 1977. Suomen Akatemian julkaisuja. 1978 (2): 7–17.

Linkola, P. 1963: Beobachtungen über die Nahrung des Rauhfusskauzes (*Aegolius funereus*) während des Herbstzuges auf Signilskär, Åland. Ornis Fennica 40: 69–72.

Linkola, P., Kellomäki, E. and Ruohomäki, T. 1967: Viirupöllön (*Strix uralensis*) uusia pesimäympäristöjä ja pesäpaikkoja. Ornis Fennica 44: 25–26.

Linkola, P. and Myllymäki, A. 1969: Der Einfluss der Kleinsäugerfluktuationen auf das Brüten einiger kleinsäugerfressender Vögel im südlichen Häme, Mittelfinnland 1952–1966. Ornis Fennica 46: 45–78.

Lockie, J. D. 1955: The breeding habits and food of Short-eared Owls after a vole plague. Bird Study 2: 53–69.

Lönnberg, E. 1928: Rovfåglar som byte för andra rovfåglar. Fauna och Flora 23: 236–237.

Lopez Gordo, J. L. 1973: Sobre la alimentacion del carabo (*Strix aluco*) en España Central. Ardeola 19: 429–437.

Lovari, S. 1973: Shooting and the Preservation of Wildlife in Italy. Conservation Around the World 5: 235–236.

Lovari, S. 1974: The feeding habits of four raptors in central Italy. Raptor Research 8: 45–57.

Lovari, S. 1978: Sex differences in the diet of the Barn Owl. Avocetta 1: 61–63.

Lovari, S., Renzoni, A. and Fondi, R. 1976: The predatory habits of the Barn Owl (*Tyto alba* Scopoli) in relation to the vegetation cover. Boll. Zool. 43: 173–191.

Løvenskiold, H. L. 1947: *Handbok over Norges Fugler*. Oslo.

Lowther, E. H. N. 1949: *A Bird Photographer in India*. Oxford University Press.

Lund, H. M-K. 1951: A contribution to the knowledge of the biology of *Glaucidium passerinum* in the breeding season. Nytt Mag. for Naturvidenskapene 88: 247–262.

Lundberg, A. 1974: Taxering av slaguggla *Strix uralensis* i Uppland – metoder och resultat. Vår Fågelvärld 33: 147–154.

Lundberg, A. 1976: Breeding success and prey availability in a Ural Owl *Strix uralensis* Pall. population in Central Sweden. Zoon 4: 65–72.

Lundberg, A. 1977: Slaugugglans föda vid låg smågnagaretillgång under häckningstiden. Fåglar i Uppland 4: 11–17.

Lundberg, A. 1979: Residency, migration and a compromise: adaptations to nest-site scarcity and food specialisation in three Fennoscandian owl species. Oecologia (Berl.) 41: 273–281.

MacArthur, R. H. 1960: On the relation between reproductive value and optimal predation. Proc. Nat. Acad. Sci. 46: 143–145.

MacArthur, R. H. 1972: *Geographical ecology*. Harper and Row, New York.

MacArthur, R. and Levins, R. 1964: Competition, habitat selection, and character displacement in a patchy environment. Proc. Nat. Acad. Sci. 51: 1207–1210.

MacArthur, R. H. and Pianka, E. R. 1966: On optimal use of a patchy environment. Amer. Nat. 100: 603–609.

MacDonald, D. W. 1976: Nocturnal observations of Tawny Owls *Strix aluco* preying upon earthworms. Ibis 118: 579–580.

MacFarlane, A. M. 1977: Song of Tawny Owl. Brit. Birds 70: 348.

McInvaille, W. B. and Keith, L. B. 1974: Predator-prey relations and breeding biology of the Great Horned Owl and Red-tailed Hawk in Central Alberta. Canad. Field-Nat. 88: 1–20.

McLachlan, G. R. and Liversidge, R. 1970: *Roberts' Birds of South Africa*. South African Bird Book Fund, Cape Town.

MacNaughton, S. J. and Wolf, L. L. 1973: *General Ecology*. Holt, Rinehart and Winston, New York.

Mackworth-Praed, C. W. and Grant, C. H. B. 1952: *African Handbook of Birds*, series I: Birds of Eastern and North-Eastern Africa. Vol. 1. Longman, London.

Macura, A. 1959: Delayed reactions in the Tawny Owl (*Strix aluco aluco* L.). Folia Biologica 7: 329–348.

Makatsch, W. 1969: *Wir bestimmen die Vögel Europas*. Verlag J. Neumann (Neudamm Melsungen), Basel und Wien.

Makatsch, W. 1976: *Die Eier der Vögel Europas*. Neumann Verlag, Leipzig-Radebeul.

Martin, C. and Saint-Girons, M-C. 1973: Evolution d'un dortoir hivernal de hiboux brachyotes, *Asio flammeus* (Pontoppidan, 1783), au cours d'une pullulation de campagnols des champs, *Microtus arvalis* (Pallas, 1779). Oiseau et R.F.O. 43: 51–54.

Martin, G. R. and Gordon, I. E. 1974: Visual acuity in the Tawny Owl (*Strix aluco*). Vision Res. 14: 1393–1397.

März, R. 1936: Der Uhu auf Åland. Ornis Fennica 13: 23–34.

März, R. 1954: Jagdweise und Ernährung des Seeadlers. Falke 1: 168–170.

März, R. 1954: Neues Material zur Ernährung des Uhus. Die Vogelwelt 75: 181–188.

März, R. 1957: Rupfungs- und Gewöllaufsammlung bei Darfeld/Westfalen. Die Vogelwelt. 78: 105–115.

März, R. 1957: Ernährung eines Harz-Uhus. Die Vogelwelt. 78: 32–34.

März, R. 1958: *Der Uhu.* Die Neue Brehm-Bücherei 108. Wittenberg-Lutherstadt.

März, R. 1964: Zur Ernährung des Sperlingskauzes. Die Vogelwelt 85: 33–38.

März, R. 1968: *Der Rauhfusskauz.* Die Neue Brehm-Bücherei 394. Wittenberg-Lutherstadt.

März, R. 1972: *Gewöll- und Rupfungskunde.* Akademie-Verlag, Berlin.

März, R. and Piechocki, R. 1976: *Der Uhu.* 3 Aufl., Neue Brehm-Bücherei 108, A. Ziemsen Verlag. Wittenberg-Lutherstadt.

May, R. M. 1973: *Stability and Complexity in Model Ecosystems.* Univ. Press, Princeton (New Jersey).

May, R. M. 1974: On the theory of niche overlap. Theoret. Pop. Biol. 5: 297–332.

May, R. M. and MacArthur, R. H. 1972: Niche overlap as a function of environmental variability. Proc. Nat. Acad. Sci. USA. 69: 1109–1113.

Mayol, J. 1971: Sobre nidificación de *Asio otus* en Mallorca. Ardeola 15: 148.

Mayol, J. 1973: Nuevo dato de cria del *Asio otus* en Mallorca. Ardeola 19: 25.

Mead, C. 1969: Short-eared Owl. Pp. 1362–1365 in: Birds of the World (ed. J. Gooders). Vol. 5. IPC Magazines, London.

Mebs, T. 1959: Beitrag zur Biologie des Feldeggsfalken (*Falco biarmicus feldeggi*). Die Vogelwelt 80: 142–149.

Mebs, T. 1964: Zur Biologie und Populationsdynamik des Mäusebussards (*Buteo buteo*). J. Orn. 105: 247–306.

Mebs, T. 1966: *Eulen und Käuze*, Strigidae. Kosmos-Naturführer. Franckh'sche Verlagshandlung, Stuttgart.

Mebs, T. 1972: Zur Biologie des Uhus (*Bubo bubo*) im nördlichen Frankenjura. Anz. Orn. Ges. Bayern 11: 7–25.

Meinertzhagen, R. 1930: *Nicoll's Birds of Egypt.* H. Rees, London.

Meinertzhagen, R. 1954: *Birds of Arabia.* Oliver and Boyd, Edinburgh and London.

Meinertzhagen, R. 1959: *Pirates and Predators.* Oliver and Boyd, Edinburgh and London.

Mendelssohn, H. 1972: Effect of toxic chemicals on bird life: the impact of pesticides on bird life in Israel. Bull. Int. Council Bird Pres. 11: 75–103.

Mendelssohn, H., Yom-Tov, Y. and Safriel, U. 1975: Hume's Tawny Owl *Strix butleri* in the Judean, Negev and Sinai Deserts. Ibis 117: 110–111.

Mendelssohn, H., Schlueter, P. and Aderet, Y. 1979: Report on Azodrin poisoning of birds of prey in the Huleh Valley in Israel. Bull. Int. Council Bird Pres. 13: 124–129.

Merikallio, E.: Archives in Department of Zoology, University of Oulu, Finland.

Merikallio, E. 1955: Suomen lintujen levinneisyys ja lukumäärä. Otava, Helsinki.

Merikallio, E. 1958: Finnish birds, their distribution and numbers. Fauna Fennica 5: 1–181.

Mikkola, H. 1968: Suopöllön ekologiasta. Unpubl. MS, Dept. of Zoology, University of Oulu, Finland.

Mikkola, H. 1968: Lehtopöllöt ovat yksilöllisiä. Suomenselän Linnut 3: 4–5.

Mikkola, H. 1969: Pöllökannat Suomenselällä ja Pohjanmaalla vv. 1965–68. Suomenselän Linnut 4: 4–7.

Mikkola, H. 1969: Viirupöllön pesintä- ja ei pesintäaikaisesta ravinnosta. Suomenselän Linnut 4: 41–44.

Mikkola, H. 1969: Katsaus kesän 1969 pöllökantoihin. Suomenselän Linnut 4: 81.

Mikkola, H. 1969: On the nest-sites of the Great Grey Owl (*Strix nebulosa*). Ornis Fennica 46: 141.

Mikkola, H. 1970: Lehtopöllöstä ja sen ravinnosta Pohjois-Savossa. Savon Luonto 2(1): 8–9.

Mikkola, H. 1970: On the ecology of the Great Grey Owl (*Strix nebulosa*). M.Sc. Thesis, Dept. of Zoology, University of Oulu, Finland.

Mikkola, H. 1970: Milloin ja millä säällä pöllöt huutelevat? Kainuun Linnut 1: 52–55.

Mikkola, H. 1970: On the activity and food of the Pygmy Owl *Glaucidium passerinum* during breeding. Ornis Fennica 47: 10–14.

Mikkola, H. 1970: Zur Ernährung des Sperlingskauzes (*Glaucidium passerinum*) zur Brutzeit. Orn. Mitt. 22: 72–75.

Mikkola, H. 1970: On the food of the Great Grey Owl (*Strix nebulosa*), the Ural Owl (*Strix uralensis*) and the Eagle Owl (*Bubo bubo*) in Finland during summer. Suomen Riista 22: 97–104.

Mikkola, H. 1971: Population crash of the Great Grey Owl in Finland in 1971. Suomen Luonto 30: 177–179, 213.

Mikkola, H. 1971: Uralkauz oder Bartkauz? Orn. Mitt. 23: 40–41.

Mikkola, H. 1971: Zur Ernährung der Sperbereule (*Surnia ulula*) zur Brutzeit. Angewandte Orn. 3: 133–141.

Mikkola, H. 1971: On the food of Hawk, Ural and Short-eared Owls in Päijät-Häme in the nesting season. Päijät-Hämeen Linnut 2: 8–11, 32.

Mikkola, H. 1971: Helmipöllön pesintäaikaisesta ravinnosta Pohjois-Savossa. Savon Luonto 3: 11–12.

Mikkola, H. 1971: On methods used in studying the diet of raptors. Lintumies 7: 40–43, 73–75.

Mikkola, H. 1972: Neue Ergebnisse über die Ernährung des Uralkauzes (*Strix uralensis*). Orn. Mitt. 24: 157–163.

Mikkola, H. 1972: Hawk Owls and their prey in northern Europe. Brit. Birds 65: 453–460.

Mikkola, H. 1972: Zur Aktivität und Ernährung des Sperlingskauzes in der Brutzeit. Beitr. Vogelkd. 18: 297–309.

Mikkola, H. 1972: Food of Great Grey Owls in the Lapland Reserve, U.S.S.R. Brit. Birds 65: 31–32.

Mikkola, H. 1973: Der Bartkauz und seine Nahrung in Finnland. Falke 20: 183, 196–204, 216.

Mikkola, H. 1973: Wood owls *Pulsatrix, Ciccaba, Strix, Rhinoptynx* and *Asio*. Pp. 116–146, in: *Owls of the World* (ed. John A. Burton). Eurobook/Peter Lowe, London.

Mikkola, H. 1974: Owl of the taiga. Wildlife 16: 320–322.

Mikkola, H. 1974: Kuopion huuhkajien ravinnosta 1890- ja 1970-luvuilla. Savon Luonto 6: 21–22.

Mikkola, H. 1974: Late nesting of Tengmalm's Owl. Lintumies 9: 31.

Mikkola, H. 1974: The Wren sheltered by the Eagle Owl. Lintumies 9: 32.

Mikkola, H. 1974: Lehto- ja lapinpöllön ravinnosta Joensuun ympäristössä. Siipirikko 1 (2): 16–18.

Mikkola, H. 1976: Great Grey Owls of Konnevesi. Savon Luonto 8: 13–22.

Mikkola, H. 1976: Owls killing and killed by other owls and raptors in Europe. Brit. Birds 69: 144–154.

Mikkola, H. 1977: Pöllöjen esiintyminen ja ravinto Vilppulassa. Suomenselän Linnut 12: 42–47.

Mikkola, H. 1978: Pöllöjen suhteet päivänvaloon (Owls of Finland). Suomen Luonto 37: 312–321.

Mikkola, H. 1979: On the eye structure and vision of the Eagle Owl. Lounais-Hämeen Luonto 62: 47–50.

Mikkola, H. 1981: Der Bartkauz *Strix nebulosa*. Die Neue Brehm-Bücherei 538. Wittenberg-Lutherstadt.

Mikkola, H. 1981: Lapinpöllöjen talviravinnosta suurvaelluksen aikana 1981. Savon Luonto 13: 30–33.

Mikkola, H. and Jussila, E. 1974: Varpuspöllön pesintäaikaisesta ravinnosta Lahden ympäristössä. Päijät-Hämeen Linnut 5: 19–21.

Mikkola, H. and Jussila, E. 1974: Lehto-, viiru- ja sarvipöllön ravinnosta Lahden ympäristössä. Päijät-Hämeen Linnut 5: 84–87.

Mikkola, H. and K. 1974: Viirupöllön poikasajan ravinnosta Vilppulassa ja Virroilla. Suomenselän Linnut 9: 103–107.

Mikkola, H. and Sulkava, S. 1969: On the occurrence of the Great Grey Owl (*Strix nebulosa*) in Finland 1955–68. Ornis Fennica 46: 126–131.

Mikkola, H. and Sulkava, S. 1969: On occurrence and feeding habits of Short-earned Owl in Finland 1964–68. Ornis Fennica 46: 188–193.

Mikkola, H. and Sulkava, S. 1970: Food of Great Grey Owls in Fenno-Scandia. Brit. Birds 63: 23–27.

Mikkola, H. and Sulkava, S. 1972: Mitä syö tunturihaukka. Suomen Luonto 31: 183–185.

Miller, A. H. 1934: The vocal apparatus of some North American owls. Condor 36: 204–213.

Moltoni, E. 1949: Alcuni dati sul peso e sulla longevita degli uggeli rapaci italiana. Riv. Ital. Ornithol. 19: 95–122.

Montell, J. 1917: Fågelfaunan i Muonio socken och angränsande delar af Enontekis och Kittilä socknar. Acta Soc. Fauna Flora Fenn. 44: 1–260.

Moore, N. W. 1957: The past and present status of the Buzzard in the British Isles. Brit. Birds 50: 173–197.

Morillo, C. 1976: Guia de las Rapaces Ibericas. Instituto Nacional para la Conservacion de la Naturaleza, Madrid.

Muir, R. C. 1954: Calling and feeding rates of fledged Tawny Owls. Bird Study 1: 111–117.

Müller, H. C. 1975: Hawks select odd prey. Science 188: 953–954.

Munyer, E. A. 1966: Winter food of the Short-eared Owl (*Asio flammeus*) in Illinois. Trans. Ill. Acad. Sci. 59: 174–180.

Murray, G. A. 1976: Geographic variation in the clutch size of seven owl species. Auk 93: 602–613.

Myers, J. H. and Krebs, C. J. 1971: Sex ratios in open and enclosed vole populations: demographic implications. Amer. Nat. 105: 325–344.

Mysterud, I. 1969: Biotop or reirforhold ved en hekking av slagugle ved Elverum i 1967 (*Strix uralensis* Pall.). Sterna 8: 369–382.

Mysterud, I. 1970: Hypotheses concerning characteristics and causes of population movements in Tengmalm's Owl *Aegolius funereus* (L.). Nytt Mag. Zool. 18: 49–74.

Mysterud, I. and Hagen, Y. 1969: The food of the Ural Owl (*Strix uralensis* Pallas) in Norway. Nytt Mag. Zool. 17: 165–167.

Nagel, B. and Frycklund, I. 1965: Invasionen av fjälluggla (*Nyctea scandiaca*) i södra Scandinavien vintrarna 1960–1963. Vår fågelvärld 24: 26–55.

Nero, R. 1969: The status of the Great Gray Owl in Manitoba with special reference to the 1968–69 influx. Blue Jay 27: 191–209.

Nero, R. 1970: Additional Great Gray Owl records for Manitoba and adjacent Minnesota. Blue Jay 28: 72–73.

Nero, R. 1970: A visit to a Great Gray Owl nest. Ontario Naturalist 8: 4–7.

Nero, R. W. 1971: Spirit of the Boreal Forest: the Great Grey Owl. Beaver 302: 25–29.

Nero, R. 1980. *The Great Gray Owl: Phantom of the Northern Forest.* Smithsonian Inst. Press, Washington D.C.

Nero, R., Sealy, S. G. and Copeland, W. R. 1974: Great Gray Owls occupy artificial nest. Loon 46: 161–165.

Neuhaus, W., Bratting, H. and Schweizer, B. 1972: Morphologische und funktionelle Untersuchungen über den 'lautlosen' Flug der Eulen (*Strix aluco*) im Vergleich zum Flug der Enten (*Anas platyrhynchos*). Biol. Zentralbl. 92: 495–512.

Newton, I. 1976: Breeding of Sparrowhawks (*Accipiter nisus*) in different environments. J. Anim. Ecol. 45: 831–849.

Newton, I. 1979: *Population Ecology of Raptors.* Poyser, Berkhamsted.

Nicholl, M. K. Mc. and Scott, V. H. 1973: Great Gray Owl captures Vole by means of Bill. Canad. Field-Natural. 87: 184–185.

Niethammer, G. 1967: Vom Uhu in der Eifel. Bonn. Arbeitsgem. 3: 195–196.

Nilsson, I. N. 1977: Aktivitet och biotoputnyttjande hos två kattugglor. Fauna och Flora 72: 156–163.

Nilsson, I. N. 1978: Hunting in flight by Tawny Owl *Strix aluco*. Ibis 120: 528–531.

Norberg, A. 1964: Studier över pärlugglans (*Aegolius funereus*) ekologi and etologi. Vår Fågelvärld 23: 228–244.

Norberg, A. 1968: Physical factors in directional hearing in *Aegolius funereus* (Linné) (Strigiformes), with special reference to the significance of the asymmetry of the external ears. Arkiv för Zoologi 20 (10): 181–204.

Norberg, A. 1970: Hunting techniques of Tengmalm's Owl *Aegolius funereus* (L.). Ornis Scandinavica 1: 51–64.

Norberg, R. Å. 1977: Occurrence and independent evolution of bilateral ear asymmetry in owls and implications on owl taxonomy. Phil. Trans. Royal Soc. Lond. 280(973): 375–408.

Norberg, R. Å. 1978: Skull asymmetry, ear structure and function, and auditory localisation in Tengmalm's Owl, *Aegolius funereus* (Linné). Phil. Trans. Royal Soc. Lond. 282(991): 325–410.

Obst, J., Stich, A. and Wickl, K-H. 1977: Todesfälle und Todesursachen beim Uhu (*Bubo bubo*) in Bayern. Garmischer Vogelkundliche Berichte 3: 24–29.

Ødegaard, H. 1969: Noen nyere hekkefunn av jaktfalk. Sterna 8: 360–368.

Odsjö, T. and Olsson, V. 1975: Kvicksilverhalter i en population av berguv *Bubo bubo* i sydöstra Sverige efter 1966 års alkylkvicksilverförbud. Vår Fågelvärld 34: 117–124.

Oeming, A. F. 1955: A preliminary study of the Great Grey Owl (*Scotiatex nebulosa nebulosa*) in Alberta. Dissertation, University of Alberta, Edmonton.

Ogilvie, M. A. 1976: Birds in Ireland during 1970–74. Brit. Birds 69: 91–103.

Oksanen, L. 1979: On the role of food quality in the regulation of herbivores – a critique of White's theory. Oecologia.

Oksanen, L., Fretwell, S. D. and Järvinen, O. 1979: Interspecific aggression and the limiting similarity of close competitors: the problem of size gaps in some community arrays. Amer. Nat. 114: 117–129.

Oles, T. 1961: Obserwacje nad obyczajami pokarmowymi pójdźki. Przeglad Zool. 5(4): 377–378.

Olofsson, V. 1910: Något om lappugglans fortplantning. Fauna och Flora 5: 180–183.

Olsson, V. 1967: Berguvinventeringen 1965: Sveriges Natur, Årsboken 1967: 78–88.

Olsson, V. 1976: Berguven *Bubo bubo* i Sverige 1974–1975: Vår Fågelvärld 35: 291–297.

Olsson, V. 1979: Studies on a population of Eagle Owls, *Bubo bubo* (L.) in Southeast Sweden. Viltrevy 11: 1–99.

O'Neill, J. P. and Graves, G. R. 1977: A new genus and species of owl (Aves: Strigidae) from Peru. Auk 94: 409–416.

Ornithological Society of Turkey Bird Reports no. 3 (1970–1973), no. 4 (1974–1975).

Osmolowskaja, W. I. 1948: Ecology of birds of prey and owls in the Yamal Peninsula. Trudy Inst. Geogr. Akad. Nauk SSSR 41: 5–77. (In Russian.)

Otto-Sprunck, A. 1967: Übersprungsschlafen beim Habichtskauz (*Strix uralensis*). Ornis Fennica 44: 78.

Parslow, J. 1973: *Breeding Birds of Britain and Ireland: a historical survey*. Poyser, Berkhamsted.

Paterson, A. 1964: Tawny Owl attacking Fox in winter. Brit. Birds 57: 202–203.

Payne, R. S. 1961: Acoustic orientation of prey by the Barn Owl *Tyto alba*. Charles Walcott Division of Engineering and Applied Physics (Harvard Univ.), Tech. Rept. 1: 1–67.

Payne, R. S. 1962: How the Barn Owl locates prey by hearing. Living Bird 1: 151–159.

Payne, R. S. 1971: Acoustic location of prey by Barn Owls (*Tyto alba*). J. Exp. Biol. 56: 535–573.

Pearson, O. P. and Pearson, A. K. 1947: Owl predation in Pennsylvania, with notes on the small mammals of Delaware county. J. Mammal. 28: 137–147.

Pedroli, J-C., Berthoud, G., Jousson, M., Monnier, C. and Mathey, J. 1975: Répartition géographique, habitat et densité de la Chouette de Tengmalm *Aegolius funereus* (L.) dans le Jura suisse. Nos Oiseaux 33: 49–58.

Persson, K. 1978: Fågelobservationer i Norrbottens län 1977–1978. Norrbottens Natur 34: 20–24.

Peters, J. L. 1940: *Check-list of Birds of the World*. Vol. 4. Harvard University Press, Cambridge (Mass.).

Peterson, R. L. 1966: *The Mammals of Eastern Canada*. Toronto.

Pianka, E. R. 1972: r and K selection or b and d selection? Amer. Nat. 106: 581–588.

Pianka, E. R. 1974a. Niche overlap and diffuse competition. Proc. Nat. Acad. Sci. USA 71: 2141–2145.

Pianka, E. R. 1974b. *Evolutionary Ecology*. Harper & Row, New York.

Picozzi, N. and Hewson, R. 1970: Kestrels, Short-eared Owls and Field Voles in Eskdalemuir in 1970. Scott. Birds 6: 185–190.

Piechocki, R., Stubbe, M., Uhlenhaut, K. and Dawka, N. 1977: Die Ernňrungsökologie des Uhus *Bubo bubo yenisseensis* Buturlin in der Mongolischen Volksrepublik. Zool. Jb. Syst. 104: 539–559.

Pietiäinen, H. 1975: Pöllöhavaintoja Päijät-Hämeestä 1975. Päijät-Hämeen Linnut 6: 104–110.

Pietiäinen, H. and Kolunen, H. 1979: Pöllöjen pesinnästä 1979. Päijät-Hämeen Linnut 10: 92–97.

Pihlainen, J. 1977: Lintuhavaintoja, tammi-elokuu 1977. Suomenselän Linnut 12: 93–96.

Pitelka, F. A., Tomich, P. Q. and Treichel, G. W. 1955: Ecological relations of jaegers and owls as lemming predators near Barrow, Alaska. Ecol. Monogr. 25: 85–117.

Pittaway, R. and Brunton, D. F. 1969: The Great Gray Owl: fact and fiction. Trial and Landscape 3: 94–97.

Plucinski, A. 1966: Beobachtungen an einem neuen Brutplatz des Rauhfusskauzes (*Aegolius funereus*) im Harz. Orn. Mitt. 18: 49–54.

Portenko, L. A. 1972: *Die Schnee-Eule*. Die Neue Brehm-Bücherei 454: A. Ziemsen Verlag, Wittenberg Lutherstadt.

Prestt, I. 1965: An enquiry into the recent breeding status of some smaller birds of prey and crows in Britain. Bird Study 12: 196–221.

Prestt, I. and Wagstaffe, R. 1973: Barn and Bay Owls. Pp. 42–60 in: *Owls of the World* (ed. J. A. Burton). Peter Lowe/Eurobooks, London.

Price, P. W. 1975: *Insect Ecology*. New York.

Psenner, H. 1960: Die Zwergohreule, *Otus scops scops* (Linnaeus, 1758) in Freiheit und Gefangenschaft. Unpubl. MS.

Ptušenko, E. S. and Inozemcev, A. A. 1968: Biologija i chozjajstvennoe značenie ptic Moskovskoj oblasti i sopredel'nych territorij. Moskva. (Pages 174–176.)

Pukinskii, Yü. B. 1977: *Life of the Owls*. Leningrad. (Translated from the Russian.)

Pulliainen, E. 1971: Behaviour of a nesting Capercaillie (*Tetrao urogallus*) in north-eastern Lapland. Ann. Zool. Fennici 8: 456–462.

Pulliainen, E. 1974: Nesting biology of a pair of Rough-legged Buzzards (*Buteo lagopus lagopus*) in north-eastern Lapland. Ann. Zool. Fennici 11: 259–264.

Pulliainen, E. 1975: Choice of prey by a pair of Gyrfalcons *Falco rusticolus* during the nesting period in Forest-Lapland. Ornis Fennica 52: 19–22.

Pulliainen, E. and Loisa, K. 1977: Breeding biology and food of the Great Grey Owl, *Strix nebulosa*, in a north-eastern Finnish forest, Lapland. Aquilo, Ser. Zool. 17: 23–33.

Pulliainen, E. and Rajala, P. 1973: Observations on the nesting of birds in the snow. Ornis Fennica 50: 89–91.

Quine, D. B. and Konishi, M. 1974: Absolute frequency discrimination in the Barn Owl. J. Comp. Physiol. 93: 347–360.

Raczyński, J. and Ruprecht, A. L. 1974: The effect of digestion on the osteological composition of owl pellets. Acta Ornithologica 14 (2) 25–37.

Rajala, E. 1976: Lapinharakan ja helmipöllön ravinnosta samalla biotoopilla. Suomenselän Linnut 11: 41–43.

Randla, T. 1976: *Eesti Röövlinnud*. Valgus, Tallinn.

Ratcliffe, D. A. 1962. Breeding density in the Peregrine *Falco peregrinus* and Raven *Corvus corax*. Ibis 104: 13–39.

Ratcliffe, D. A. 1963: The status of the Peregrine in Great Britain. Bird Study 10: 56–90.

Ratcliffe, D. A. 1970: Changes Attributable to Pesticides in Egg Breaking and Eggshell Thickness in Some British Birds. J. Appl. Ecol. 7: 67–115.

Ratcliffe, D. A. 1980: *The Peregrine Falcon*. Poyser, Calton.

Rauhala, P. 1980: *Kemin-Tornion seudun linnusto*. Pohjolan, Sanomat, Kemi.

Rendall, T. E. 1925: Abnormally large clutches of eggs of Short-eared Owl (*Asio flammeus*). Canad. Field-Nat. 39: 194.

Rensch, B. 1950: Die Abhängigkeit der relativen Sexualdifferenz von der Körpergrösse. Bonn. Zool. Beitr. 1: 58–69.

Renzoni, A. and Lovari, S. 1977: The food habits of the Barn Owl in an area of Central Italy. Pp. 276–280 in: Proc. World Conference on Birds of Prey, Vienna 1975 (ed. R. D. Chancellor). ICBP, London.

Rich, P. V. and Bohaska, D. J. 1976: The world's oldest owl: a new Strigiform from the Paleocene of southwestern Colorado. Smithson. Contrib. Paleobiol. 27: 87–93.

Richard, A. 1923: Le Grand-duc dans les Alpes. Nos Oiseaux 55–56: 65–74.

Rikkonen, P., Helsten, H. and Moilanen, P. 1976: Suopöllön (*Asio flammeus*) pesinnästä Riihimäen Vankilanpellolla 1973. Päijät-Hämeen Linnut 7: 88–93.

Ritter, F. 1972: Untersuchungen über die Fütterungsaktivität des Waldkauzes (*Strix aluco* L.) während einer Brutperiode. Beitr. Vogelkd. 18: 156–161.

Ritter, F. 1973: Erster Nachweis eines Nachgeleges beim Waldkauz (*Strix aluco*). Beitr. Vogelkd. 19: 465–466.

Ritter, F. and Görner, M. 1977: Untersuchungen über die Beziehung zwischen Fütterungsaktivität und Beutetierzahl bei der Schleiereule. Der Falke 24: 344–348.

Ritter, F. and Zienert, W. 1972: Bemerkungen zum Schutz des Rauhfusskauzes (*Aegolius funereus*). Landschaftspfl. u. Natursch. in Thüringen 9: 12–16.

Roberts, M. W. and Wolfe, J. L. 1974: Social influence on susceptibility to predation in cotton rats. J. Mammal. 55: 869–872.

Rockenbauch, D. 1971: Die Ernährung südwestdeutscher Wanderfalken (*Falco peregrinus*). J. Orn. 112: 43–60.

Rockenbauch, D. 1978: Brutbiologie und den Bestand steuernde Faktoren bei Waldkauz (*Strix aluco*) und Waldohreule (*Asio otus*) in der Schwäbischen Alb. J. Orn. 119: 429–440.

Rockenbauch, D. 1978: Untergang und Wiederkehr des Uhus *Bubo bubo* in Baden-Württemberg. Anz. orn. Ges. Bayern 17: 293–328.

Rörig, G. 1910: Arb. Kaiserl. Anst. Land- u. Forstwirtsch. IV, V and VII. Berlin.

Rosendahl, S. 1973: *Ugler i Danmark*. DOCS Forlag, Skjern.

Røv, N. 1971: Fugleobservasjoner fra Over Pasvik 1969. Sterna 10: 159–170.

Ruprecht, A. 1964: Analiza skladu pokarmu płomykówki *Tyto alba guttata* (C. L. Br.) z Aleksandrowa Kuj., Ciechocinka i Raciazka w latach 1960–1961. Zesz. Nauk. Univ. Mikolaja Kopernika Toruniu Biol. 7: 45–66.

Saarinen, R. 1979: Ei aina korpikuusien kätkössä. Suomenselän Linnut 14: 115.

Sandman, J. A. 1897: Om lappugglan (*Syrnium lapponicum* Sparrman). Tidsskr. Jägare Fiskare 5: 79–85.

Saurola, P. 1978: Pöllöjen rengastus Suomessa. Lintumies 13: 7–12.

Saurola, P. 1979: Rengastettujen petolintujemme löytymistavat. Lintumies 14: 15–21.

Schaaning, H. T. L. 1916: *Norges Fugle Fauna*. Oslo.

Schaaning, H. T. L. 1916: Bidrag til Novaja Semljas fauna. Dansk Orn. Foren. Tidsskr. 10: 145–190. (Cited in Portenko 1972.)

Schaefer, H. 1970: Womit ernährt der Uhu (*Bubo bubo*) in Lappland seine Jungen? Bonn. Zool. Beitr. 21: 52–62.

Schaefer, H. 1971: Beutetiere des Uhus *Bubo bubo* aus Karpaten und Lappland. Bonn. Zool. Beitr. 22: 153–160.

Schaefer, H. 1973: Die Fledermäuse vom Muran in der Hohen Tatra (Tschechoslowakei). Die Höhle 24: 51–58.

Schaefer, H. 1975: Ein Frosch- und Käfer-Waldkauz (*Strix aluco*) im Wendland. Vogelkund. Ber. Niedersachsen 7(3): 79–84.

Schäfer, H. and Finckenstein, G. 1935: Zur Kenntnis des Lebensweise des Uralkauzes. Orn. Monatsberichte 43(6): 171–176.

Scherzinger, W. 1968: Bemerkenswerte Paarbildung beim Waldkauz (*Strix aluco*). Egretta 11: 56.

Scherzinger, W. 1970: Zum Aktionssystem des Sperlingskauzes (*Glaucidium passerinum*, L.). Zoologica 41: 1–130.

Scherzinger, W. 1974: Zur Ökologie des Sperlingskauzes *Glaucidium passerinum* im National-park Bayerischer Wald. Anz. orn. Ges. Bayern 13: 121–156.

Scherzinger, W. 1974: Zur Ethologie und Jugendentwicklung der Schnee-Eule (*Nyctea scandiaca*) nach Beobachtungen in Gefangenschaft. J. Orn. 115: 8–49.

Scherzinger, W. 1974: Habichtskauznachzucht im Nationalpark Bayerischer Wald gelungen. Zool. Garten N. F., Jena 44: 59–61.

Scherzinger, W. 1974: Die Jugendentwicklung des Uhus (*Bubo bubo*) mit Vergleichen zu der von Schneeule (*Nyctea scandiaca*) und Sumpfohreule (*Asio flammeus*). Bonn. Zool. Beitr. 25: 123–147.

Scherzinger, W. 1980: Zur Ethologie der Fortpflanzung und Jugendwicklung des Habicht-kauzes (*Strix uralensis*) mit Vergleichen zum Waldkauz (*Strix aluco*). Bonn. Zool. Mono-graphien 15: 1–66.

Schifferli, A. 1949: Schwankungen des Schleiereulenbestandes *Tyto alba* (Scopoli). Orn. Beobachter 46: 61–75.

Schifferli, A. 1957: Alter und Sterblichkeit bei Waldkauz (*Strix aluco*) und Schleiereule (*Tyto alba*) in der Schweiz. Orn. Beobachter 54: 50–56.

Schládek, J. 1961–62: Doterajšie poznatky o potravnej ekológii sovy dlhochvostej karpatskej (*Strix uralensis macroura* Wolf). Sborník Východoslovenského Múzea, 2–3 A: 221–236.

Schmidt, A. 1977: Zur Ernährungsökologie der Schleiereule, *Tyto alba* Scopoli. Beiträge Vogelkd. 23: 235–244.

Schmidt, E. 1960: A réti fülesbagoly (*Asio flammeus*) költése és vonulása a Kárpát-medence területén. Aquila 66: 89–98.

Schmidt, E. 1968: Der Haussperling (*Passer domesticus* (L)) und der Feldsperling (*Passer montanus* (L.)) als Nahrung der Schleiereule (*Tyto alba* (Scop.)) in Ungarn. Internat. Stud. on Sparrows 2: 96–101. Warszawa.

Schmidt, E. 1970: Über die geographische Verbreitung und Wohndichte der Hausmaus (*Mus musculus* L.) in Europa nach Gewölanalysen von Schleiereulen (*Tyto alba* Scop.). Z. Angewandte Zoologie 57: 137–143.

Schmidt, E. 1972: Über die Vogelnahrung der Schleiereule *Tyto alba* und der Waldohreule *Asio otus* in Ungarn. Ornis Fennica 49: 98–102.

Schmidt, E. 1973: Die Nahrung der Schleiereule (*Tyto alba*) in Europa. Z. Angewandte Zoologie 60: 43–70.

Schmidt, E. and Szlivka, L. 1968: Adatok a réti fülesbagoly (*Asio flammeus*) téli táplálkozásához a Bácskában (Észak-Jugoszlávia). Aquila 75: 227–229.

Schneider, W. 1964: *Die Schleiereule*. Die Neue Brehm-Bücherei 340. Wittenberg-Lutherstadt.

Schnurre, O. 1950: Wandlungen in Bestand und Ernährung norddeutscher Wanderfalken und Habichte. Syllegomena Biologica 1950: 396–401.

Schnurre, O. 1954: Vom norddeutschen Uhu. Die Vogelwelt 75: 229–233.

Schnurre, O. 1956: Ernahrungsbiologische Studien an Raubvögeln und Eulen der Darsshal-binsel (Mecklenburg). Beitr. Vogelkd. 4: 211–245.

Schnurre, O. 1956: Über einige strittige Fragen aus dem Leben der beiden Milanarten. Die Vogelwelt 77: 65–74.

Schnurre, O. 1961: Lebensbilder märkischer Waldkäuze (*Strix aluco* L.). Milu 1: 83–124.

Schnurre, O. 1963: Lebensbilder märkischer Habichte (*Accipiter gentilis* L.). Milu 3: 221–238.

Schnurre, O. 1964: Berliner Habichts-Chronik 1963/64. Milu 4: 403–407.

Schnurre, O. 1966: Zur Ernährung märkischer Wanderfalken (*Falco peregrinus*). Beitr. Vogelkd. 11: 368–378.

Schoener, T. W. 1968: Sizes of feeding territories among birds. Ecology 49: 123–141.

Schoener, T. W. 1969: Models of optimal size for solitary predators. Amer. Nat. 103: 277–313.

Schoener, T. W. 1974: Resource partitioning in ecological communities. Science 185: 27–39.

Schönn, S. 1976: Vierjährige Untersuchungen der Biologie des Sperlingskauzes, *Glaucidium p. passerinum* (L.), im oberen Westerzgebirge. Beitr. Vogelkd. 22: 261–300.

Schönn, S. 1980: Käuze als Feinde anderer Kauzarten und Nisthilfen für höhlenbrütende Eulen. Der Falke 27: 294–299.

Schuster, L. 1930: Ueber den Nestbau bei den Eulen. Beitr. Fortpfl. Biol. Vögel 6: 53–58.

Seierstad, A., Seierstad, S. and Mysterud, I. 1960: Et lite bidrag til kjennskapet til spurveugla, *Glaucidium passerinum* (L.). Sterna 4: 153–168.

Selander, R. K. 1966: Sexual dimorphism and differential niche utilisation in birds. Condor 68: 113–151.

Sharrock, J. T. R. (ed.). 1976: *The Atlas of Breeding Birds in Britain and Ireland*. Poyser, Berkhamsted.

Short, H. L. and Drew, L. C. 1962: Observations concerning behavior, feeding and pellets of Short-eared Owls. Amer. Midl. Nat. 67: 424–433.

Short, L. L. and Horne, J. F. M. 1981: Bird observations along the Egyptian Nile. Sandgrouse 3: 43–61.

Siivonen, L. 1943: Ist unsere Eulenfauna im Begriff einen hochborealen Charakter anzunehmen? Ornis Fennica 20: 16–21.

Siivonen, L. 1967 (1972): *Pohjolan nisäkkäät*. Otava, Helsinki.

Siivonen, L. 1972: *Suomen nisäkkäät I*. Otava, Helsinki.

Šilov, J. A. and Smirin, J. M. 1959: O zimnem pitanii vorob'inogo syčika v Podmoskov'e. Proc. 2nd Soviet Ornithol. Congress, Moscow 1959. Part 2: 93–94.

Simeonow, D. 1963: Nahrungsuntersuchungen des Waldkauzes im Losengebirge. Acta Mus. Maced. Sci. Nat. Skopje 9: 35–50.

Simson, C. 1966: *A Bird Overhead*. Witherby, London.

Skovgaard, P. 1920: Gylp af jydske Skovhornugler (*Otus vulgaris*). Danske Fugle 1: 33–42.

Skuratowicz, W. 1950: Badania nad skladem pokarmu puszczyka (*Strix aluco aluco* L.) w latach 1946/48. Poznanskie Towarzystwo Przyjaciol Nauk 12: 1–10.

Sládek, J. 1961: Príspevok k poznaniu potravnej ekológie myšiaka lesného *Buteo buteo* (L.). Zool. Listy 10: 331–344.

Sládek, J. 1961–62: Doterajšie poznatky o potravnej ekólgii sovy dlhochvostej karpatskej (*Strix uralensis macroura* Wolf.). Sborník Východoslovenského Múzea II–IIIA: 221–236.

Sládek, J. 1963: Príspevok k potravnej ekólgii jastraba obyčajného (*Accipiter gentilis* L.). Zool. Listy 12: 98–106.

Slobodkin, L. B. 1968: How to be a predator. Amer. Zool. 8: 43–51.

Slobodkin, L. B. 1972: On the inconstancy of ecological efficiency and the form of ecological theories. Trans. Connecticutt Acad. Arts & Sci. 4: 293–305.

Slobodkin, L. B. 1974: Prudent predation does not require group selection. Amer. Nat. 108: 665–678.

Smeenk, C. 1969: Legselgrootte bij de Bosuil (*Strix aluco* L.). Limosa 42: 79–81.

Smeenk, C. 1972: Ökologische Vergleiche zwischen Waldkauz *Strix aluco* und Waldohreule *Asio otus*. Ardea 60: 1–71.

Smith, D. G., Wilson, C. R. and Frost, H. H. 1974: History and Ecology of a Colony of Barn Owls in Utah. Condor 76: 131–136.

Smith, J. 1976: Tawny Owl male breeding at one year old. Avicultural Mag. 82: 194–196.

Smith, K. D. 1965: On the birds of Morocco. Ibis 107: 493–526.

Smith, V. W. and Killick-Kendrick, R. 1964: Notes on the breeding of the Marsh Owl *Asio capensis* in northern Nigeria. Ibis 106: 119–123.

Snyder, N. F. R. and Wiley, J. W. 1976. Sexual size dimorphism in hawks and owls of North America. AOU Orn. Monographs 20: 1–96.

Soikkeli, M. 1964: Über das Überwintern und die Nahrung der Waldohreule (*Asio otus*) in Südwestfinnland 1962/63. Ornis Fennica 41: 37–40.

Sonerud, G. A., Mjelde, A. and Prestrud, K. 1972: Spurveuglehekking i fugleholk. Sterna 11: 1–12.

South, R. G. 1966: Food of Long-eared Owls in south Lancashire. Brit. Birds 59: 493–497.

Southern, H. N. 1954: Tawny Owls and their prey. Ibis 96: 384–410.

Southern, H. N. 1959: Mortality and population control. Ibis 101: 429–436.

Southern, H. N. 1969: Prey taken by Tawny Owls during the breeding season. Ibis 111: 293–299.

Southern, H. N. 1970: The natural control of a population of Tawny Owls *Strix aluco*. J. Zool. Lond. 162: 197–285.

Southern, H. N. and Lowe, V. P. W. 1968: The patterns of distribution of prey and predation in Tawny Owl territories. J. Anim. Ecol. 37: 75–97.

Southern, H. N., Vaughan, R. and Muir, R. C. 1954: The behaviour of young Tawny Owls after fledging. Bird Study 26: 101–110.

Sparks, J. and Soper, T: 1970: *Owl: their natural and unnatural history*. David & Charles, Newton Abbot.

Stanley, P. I. and Elliott, G. R. 1976: An assessment based on residues in owls of environmental contamination arising from the use of mercury compounds in British agriculture. Agro-Ecosystems 2: 223–234.

Staton, J. 1947: Little Owl as prey of Tawny Owl. Brit. Birds 40: 279.

Stefansson, O. 1978: Lappuggla (*Strix nebulosa*) i Norrbotten 1975–78. Norrbottens Natur 34: 49–63.

Stafansson, O. 1979: Lappugglan *Strix nebulosa* i Norrbotten 1975–78. Vår Fågelvärld 38: 11–22.

Stewart, P. A. 1952: Dispersal, breeding behavior, and longevity of banded Barn Owls in North America. Auk 69: 227–245.

Steyn, P. 1973: Observations on the Tawny Eagle. Ostrich 44: 1–22.

Steyn, P. 1975: Observations on the African Hawk-Eagle. Ostrich 46: 1–19.

Storer, R. W. 1952: Variation in the resident Sharp-shinned Hawks of Mexico. Condor 54: 283–289.

Storer, R. W. 1966: Sexual dimorphism and food habits in three North American accipiters. Auk 83: 423–436.

Streaten, E. van der and Asselberg, R. 1973: Het voedsel van de Kerkuil, *Tyto alba*, in België. Gerfaut 63: 149–159.

Sulkava, P. 1965: Vorkommen und Nahrung der Waldohreule, *Asio otus* (L.), in Ilmajoki (EP) in den Jahren 1955–1963. Aquilo, Ser. Zool. 2: 41–47.

Sulkava, P. 1972: Varpushaukan, *Accipiter nisus* (L), pesimisbiologiasta ja pesimisaikaisesta ravinnosta. Phil. Lic. study., Dept. of Zool., Univ. of Helsinki, Finland.

Sulkava, P. and Sulkava, S. 1971: Die Nistzeitliche Nahrung des Rauhfusskauzes *Aegolius funereus* in Finnland 1958–67. Ornis Fennica 48: 117–124.

Sulkava, S. 1964: Zur Nahrungsbiologie des Habichts, *Accipiter g. gentilis* (L.). Aquilo, Ser. Zool. 3: 1–103.

Sulkava, S. 1966: Feeding habits of the Eagle Owl (*Bubo bubo*) in Finland. Suomen Riista 18: 145–156.

Sulkava, S. 1966: Zur Nahrung des Steinadlers, *Aquila chrysaetos* (L.), in Finnland südlich vom Rentierzuchtgebiet. Aquilo, Ser. Zool. 5: 1–13.

Sulkava, S. 1968: A study on the food of the Peregrine, *Falco p. peregrinus* Tunstall, in Finland. Aquilo, Ser. Zool. 6: 18–31.

Sulkava, S. and Rajala, P. 1966: Diet of the Golden Eagle (*Aquila chrysaetos*) during the nesting period in the Finnish reindeer husbandry area. Suomen Riista 19: 7–19.

Sulkava, S. and Sulkava, P. 1967: On the small-mammal fauna of Southern Ostrobothnia. Aquilo, Ser. Zool. 5: 18–29.

Suomalainen, E. W. 1915: Tietoja erään ison-huuhkajan (*Strix bubo* L.) pesän vaiheista ja sen asukkaiden ruokalistoista Pohjois-Savossa. Medd. Soc. Fauna et Flora Fennica 41: 88–94.

Thiollay, J-M. 1967: Ecologie d'une population de rapaces diurnes en Lorraine. Terre et la Vie 114: 116–183.

Thiollay, J-M. 1968: Essai sur les rapaces du midi de la France, distribution – écologie. Hibou Grand Duc, *Bubo bubo bubo* L. Alauda 36: 179–189; 37: 15–27.

Thiollay, J. M. 1968: Le régime alimentaire de nos rapaces: quelques analyses françaises. Nos Oiseaux 29: 249–269.

Thompson, D. Q. 1955: Ecology of the lemmings. Arct. Inst. North Amer.: Final Rept. Proj. ONR-133.

Landsborough Thomson, A. (ed.) 1964: *A New Dictionary of Birds*. Nelson, London.

Tinbergen, L. 1936: Gegevens over het voedsel van Nederlandse Haviken (*Accipiter gentilis gallinarum* (Brehm)). Ardea 25: 195–200.

Tinbergen, L. 1946: De Sperwer als Roofvijand van Zangsvogels. Ardea 34: 1–213.

Tinbergen, L. 1960: The natural control of insects in pine woods. 1. Factors influencing the intensity of predation by songbirds. Arch. néerl. Zool. 13: 265–336.

Tinbergen, N. 1933: Die ernährungsökologischen Beziehungen zwischen *Asio otus otus* L. und ihren Beutetieren, insbesondere den Microtus-Arten. Ecol. Monogr. 3: 443–492.

Tomialojć, L. 1972: *Ptaki Polski*. Wykaz Gatunków i Rozmieszczenie. PWN, Warszawa.

Trann, K. 1974: Short-eared Owls near Edmonton, 1970–1973. Blue Jay 32: 148–153.

Trap-Lind, I. 1965: *De Danske Ugler*. København.

Tubbs, C. R. 1967: Analysis of nest record cards for the Buzzard. Brit. Birds 60: 381–395.

Tulloch, R. J. 1968: Snowy Owls breeding in Shetland in 1967. Brit. Birds 61: 119–132.

Tulloch, R. J. 1969: Snowy Owls breeding in Shetland. Brit. Birds 62: 33–36.

Tulloch, R. J. 1969: Snowy Owls breeding in Shetland. Scott. Birds 5(5): 244–257.

Tulloch, R. J. 1975: Fetlar's Snowies. Birds (RSPB) 5, (8): 24–27.

Udvardy, M. D. F. 1951: The significance of interspecific competition in bird life. Oikos 3: 98–123.

Ulfstrand, S. and Högstedt, G. 1976: Hur många fåglar häckar i Sverige? Anser 15: 1–32.

Ullrich, B. 1973: Beobachtungen zur Biologie des Steinkauzes (*Athene noctua*). Anz. Orn. Ges. Bayern 12: 163–175.

Ullrich, B. 1975: Zu Legeabstand, Brutbeginn, Schlupffolge und Brutdauer beim Steinkauz (*Athene noctua*). J. Orn. 116: 324–325.

Uttendörfer, O. 1939: *Die Ernährung der deutschen Raubvögel und Eulen und ihre Bedeutung in der heimischen Natur*. Neudamm.

Uttendörfer, O. 1952: *Neue Ergebnisse über die Ernährung der Greifvögel und Eulen*. Verlag Eugen Ulmer, Stuttgart.

Valkeila, V. 1976: Pesivien viirupöllönaaraiden ikärakenteesta. Päijät-Hämeen Linnut 7: 80–82.

Vaurie, C. 1960: Systematic notes on Palearctic birds No. 43. Strigidae: The genera Otus, Aegolius, Ninox and Tyto. Am. Mus. Novit. No. 2021: 1–19.

Vaurie, C. 1965: *The Birds of the Palearctic Fauna: Non-Passeriformes*. Witherby, London.

Vernon, C. J. 1971: Owl foods and other notes from a trip to South-West Africa. Ostrich 42: 153–154.

Vernon, C. J. 1972: An analysis of owl pellets collected in southern Africa. Ostrich 43: 109–123.

Vieweg, A. 1979: Der Waldkauz – eine Gefahr für den Rauhfusskauz? Der Falke 26: 392–393.

Vilhunen, L. 1977: Viirupöllö *Strix uralensis* kanahaukan *Accipiter gentilis* saaliina. Lintumies 12: 23.

Village, A. 1981: The diet and breeding of Long-eared Owls in relation to vole numbers. Bird Study 28: 215–224.

Viscian, A. 1932: Studen über die Ernährung der Waldoreula. Ornithologische Msschr. 58: 173–182.

Vladimirskaya, M. 1948: Ptitsy Laplanskogo Zapovednika. Trudy Laplandskogo Gos. Zapovednika 3.

Voous, K. H. 1950: On the distributional and genetical origin of the intermediate populations of the Barn Owl (*Tyto alba*) in Europe. Pp. 429–443 in: Syllegomena Biologica (O. Klein-schmidt). Leipzig.

Voous, K. H. 1960: *Atlas of European Birds*. Nelson, London.

Voous, K. H. 1966: The distribution of owls in Africa in relation to general zoogeographical problems. Ostrich, Suppl. 6: 499–506.

Voous, K. H. 1977: *List of Recent Holarctic Bird Species*. BOU Academic Press, London.

Vorob'ev, K. A. 1952: Zapasy vorob'inogo syčika. Priroda 41: 115–116.

Voroncov, N. N., Ivanova, O. and Šemjakin, M. F. 1956: Materialy po zimnemu pitaniju vorob'inogo syča. Zoologičeskij Žhurnal 35: 615–618.

Voskár, J., Mošanský, A. and Palásthy, J. 1969: Zur Bionomie und ökologischen Verbreitung des Steinadlers (*Aquila chrysaetos* L.) in der Ostslowakei. Zool. Listy 18: 39–54.

Vries, T. de. 1973: The Galapagos Hawk. Ph.D. Thesis, Univ. of Amsterdam.

Wagner, G. and Springer, M. 1970: Zur Ernährung des Uhus *Bubo bubo* im Oberengadin. Orn. Beob. 67: 77–94.

Wahlstedt, J. 1959: Ugglornas spelvanor. Fauna och Flora 54: 81–112.

Wahlstedt, J. 1969: Jakt, matning och läten hos lappuggla *Strix nebulosa*. Vår Fågelvärld 28: 89–101.

Wahlstedt, J. 1974: Lappugglan *Strix nebulosa* i Sverige 1973. Vår Fågelvärld 33: 132–139.

Wahlstedt, J. 1976: Lappugglan *Strix nebulosa* i Sverige 1974. Vår Fågelvärld 35: 122–125.

Walker, C. A. 1973: The origins of owls. Pp. 27–33 in: *Owls of the World* (ed. J. A. Burton). Peter Lowe/Eurobooks, London.

Walker, F. J. 1981: Notes on the birds of Dhofar, Oman. Sandgrouse. 2: 56–85.

Wallace, G. J. 1948: The Barn Owl in Michigan; its distribution, natural history and food habits. Michigan Agr. Exp. Stat. Tech. Bull. 208: 1–61.

Wallace, G. J. 1955: *An Introduction to Ornithology*. Macmillan, New York.

Warga, K. 1962. The nesting of the Short-eared Owl at the Kisbalaton. Aquila 67: 254.

Warncke, K. 1961: Beitrag zur Brutbiologie von Habicht und Sperber. Die Vogelwelt 82: 6–12.

Watson, A. 1957: The behaviour, breeding and food-ecology of the Snowy Owl *Nyctea scandiaca*. Ibis 99: 419–462.

Watson, A. and Jenkins, D. 1968: Experiments on population control by territorial behaviour in Red Grouse. J. Anim. Ecol. 37: 596–614.

Watson, D. 1972: *Birds of Moor and Mountain*. Scottish Academic Press, Edinburgh and London.

Watson, D. 1977: *The Hen Harrier*. Poyser, Berkhamsted.

Wendland, V. 1957: Aufzeichnungen über Brutbiologie und Verhalten der Waldohreule (*Asio otus*). J. Orn. 98: 241–261.

Wendland, V. 1963: Fünfjährige Beobachtungen an einer Population des Waldkauzes (*Strix aluco*) im Berliner Grunewald. J. Orn. 194: 23–57.

Wendland, V. 1972: 14 jährige Beobachtungen zur Vermehrung des Waldkauzes (*Strix aluco* L.). J. Orn. 113: 276–286.

Wendland, V. 1972: Zur Biologie des Waldkauzes (*Strix aluco*). Die Vogelwelt 93: 81–91.

Westermark, T., Odsjö, T. and Johnels, A. G. 1975: Mercury Content of Bird Feathers Before and After Swedish Ban on Alkyl Mercury in Agriculture. Ambio 4(2): 87–92.

White, T. C. R. 1978: The importance of a relative shortage of food in animal ecology. Oecologia (Berl.) 33: 71–86.

Whittaker, R. H., Levin, S. A. and Root, R. B. 1973: Niche, habitat, and ecotope. Amer. Nat. 107: 321–338.

Wickl, K-H. 1979: Der Uhu (*Bubo bubo*) in Bayern. Garmischer Vogelkundliche Berichte 6: 1–47.

Wikan, S. 1972: Fuglefaunan i Øvre Pasvik. Fauna 25: 136–180.

Wille, H-G. 1972: Ergebnisse einer mehrjährigen Studie an einer Population des Waldkauzes (*Strix aluco*) in West-Berlin. Orn. Mitt. 24: 3–7.

Willgohs, J. F. 1961: The White-tailed Eagle *Haliaetus albicilla albicilla* (Linné) in Norway. Årbok for Univ. i Bergen, Mat.-Naturv. Ser. 12: 1–212.

Willgohs, J. F. 1969: Hubroen. Fauna (Oslo) 22: 129–131.

Willgohs, J. F. 1974: The Eagle Owl *Bubo bubo* (L.) in Norway. Part I: food ecology. Sterna 13: 129–177.

Wilson, D. S. 1975: The adequacy of body size as a niche difference. Amer. Nat. 109: 769–784.

Winde, H. 1977: Vergleichende Untersuchungen über Proportionalität und Sexualdimorphismus im Skelett von *Asio otus otus* (L.). Zool. Abhand., Dresden 34: 143–146.

Winter, J. 1980: Status and distribution of the Great Gray Owl in California. Resources Agency, Californian Dept. of Fish and Game. Pp. 37.

Winter, J. 1981: Some aspects of the ecology of the Great Gray Owl in the central Sierra Nevada. Final Report for U.S. Forest Service. Pp. 22.

Witherby, H. F., Jourdain, F. C. R., Ticehurst, N. F. and Tucker, B. W. 1940: *The Handbook of British Birds*. Witherby, London. (Revised edition 1943.)

Woldhek, S. 1979: Bird Killing in the Mediterranean. European Committee for the Prevention of Mass Destruction of Migratory Birds, Zeist, Netherlandsæ.

Wolk, K. 1965: Z badań nad odżywianiem sie plomykówki, *Tyto alba* (Scop.). Przeglad Zool. 9: 404–407.

Wood, C. R. 1976: Piratical Short-eared Owl. Brit. Birds 69: 272.

Wooltorton, G. C. 1957: Buzzard killing Tawny Owl. Brit. Birds 49: 149.

Wortelaers, F. 1950: De Havik als nestplunderaar en enkele gegevens in verband met de aard van zijn prooien. Gerfaut 40: 17–27.

Wortelaers, F. 1959: De Havik, *Accipiter gentilis* (L.), in Meerdaelwoud. Gerfaut 49: 363–368.

Wuttky, K. 1963: Beutetier-Funde in Greifvogelhorsten des Hakel. Beitr. Vogelkd. 9: 140–171.

Wuttky, K. 1968: Ergebnisse 10jähriger Beobachtungen an der Greifvogel-population des Wildforschungsgebietes Hakel (Kr. Aschersleben). Beitr. Jagd. – und Wildforschung 6, Tag.-Ber. Deutsche Akad. Landw. Wiss. (Berlin) 104: 159–173.

Yalden, D. W. and Jones, R. 1971: The food of suburban Tawny Owls. The Naturalist 914: 87–89.

Yeatman, L. 1976: *Atlas des Oiseaux Nicheurs de France de 1970 à 1975*. Société Ornithologique de France, Paris.

Zastrov, M. 1946: Om kungsörnens (*Aquila chr. chrysaetos* L.) utbredning och biologi i Estland. Vår Fågelvärld 5: 64–80.

Zeuthen, E. 1947: Body size and metabolism in the animal kingdom. C.R. Lab. Carlsberg, Serchin 26: 17–162.

Zeuthen, E. 1953: Oxygen uptake as related to body size in organisms. Quart. Rev. Biol. 28: 1–12.

Zeuthen, E. 1955: Comparative physiology (respiration). Ann. Rev. Physiol. 17: 459–462.

Ziesemer, F. 1973. Siedlungsdichte und Brutbiologie von Waldohreule, *Asio otus*, und Turmfalk, *Falco tinnunculus*, nach Probeflächenuntersuchungen. Corax 4: 79–92.

Tables 1–69

TABLE 1: *Temporal distribution of early fossil owls in Europe. (From: Eck and Busse 1973, Walker 1973).*

CAENOZOIC ERA	PLIOCENE	*Asio pygmaeus* *Bubo florianae*	Ukraine Hungary	
	MIOCENE	*Tyto edwardsi* *Tyto sanctialbani* *Otus winterhofensis* *Strix brevis* *Tyto ignota* *Prosbybris antiqua* *Bubo arvernensis* *Bubo poirrieri*	France France Germany Germany France France France France	— 10 — 20
	OLIGOCENE	*Asio henrici* *Necrobyas harpax* *Necrobyas rossignoli* *Necrobyas edwardsi* *Strigogyps dubius* *Strigogyps ninor* *Bubo incertus*	France France France France France France France	— 30 — 40
	EOCENE			— 50
MESOZOIC ERA	PALEOCENE	*Strigiformes sp.*	France	— 60 — 70
	CRETACEOUS	*Strigiformes sp.*	Rumania	—135

Millions of years

349

TABLE 1(A): *European owls found as fossils at Pleistocene sites. (From Burton et al 1973).*

Tyto alba	*Athene noctua*
Tyto melitensis from Malta (Upper Pleistocene)	*Strix aluco*
Otus scops	*Strix uralensis*
Bubo bubo	*Strix nebulosa* from Rumania
Bubo africanus from Sardinia	*Asio otus*
Nyctea scandiaca	*Asio flammeus*
Surnia ulula	*Aegolius funereus*
Glaucidium passerinum	

TABLE 2: *Wing-loading (total weight in g per cm² wing area) of owls compared with that of some other birds.*

	Wing-loading (g/cm²)	Source
Eagle Owl *Bubo bubo*	0.71	Brüll 1964
Great Grey Owl *Strix nebulosa*	0.35	Mikkola, this study
Ural Owl *S. uralensis*	0.34	Mikkola, this study
Tawny Owl *S. aluco*	0.40	Mikkola, this study
Short-eared Owl *Asio flammeus*	0.34	Brüll 1964
Long-eared Owl *A. otus*	0.31	Brüll 1964
Barn Owl *Tyto alba*	0.29	Brüll 1964
Tengmalm's Owl *Aegolius funereus*	0.29	Mikkola, this study
Pygmy Owl *Glaucidium passerinum*	0.26	Mikkola, this study
Golden Eagle *Aquila chrysaetos*	0.65	Brown 1976
Peregrine *Falco peregrinus*	0.63	Brown 1970
Carrion/Hooded Crow *Corvus corone*	0.42	Sparks & Soper 1970
Black Grouse *Tetrao tetrix*	1.34	Mikkola, this study

TABLE 3: *Minimum intensities of illumination (in foot candle) under which different owl species can find dead prey by sight (after Lindblad 1967).*

Long-eared Owl	0. 000 000 25	Tengmalm's Owl	0. 000 015
Ural Owl	0. 000 000 24	Pygmy Owl	0. 000 145
Tawny Owl	0. 000 000 16	Man (Lindblad)	0. 000 075

TABLE 4: *Pellet sizes (mm) of eleven species of European owls studied by H. Mikkola. Barn Owl pellets were collected from a nest-site in southern England, 1971–74, and pellets of other species from Finland, 1966–76. The length and height of the intact pellets were measured, and the width always measured at the widest point (cf. Mikkola 1971).*

	length	*height*	*width*	*av. size*	*pellets*
Barn Owl	29–74	21–35	17–28	50 × 27 × 22	80
Eagle Owl	43–129	22–44	19–42	77 × 31 × 28	100
Snowy Owl	52–113	25–43	20–30	78 × 34 × 26	5
Hawk Owl	30–76	17–35	13–23	41 × 22 × 19	40
Pygmy Owl	17–40	8–19	6–14	27 × 11 × 9	100
Tawny Owl	34–84	17–30	11–28	55 × 24 × 20	45
Ural Owl	35–94	17–36	13–29	62 × 25 × 22	100
Great Grey Owl	35–110	18–44	15–33	63 × 29 × 25	100
Long-eared Owl	19–77	13–27	11–25	40 × 21 × 18	59
Short-eared Owl	22–82	13–32	11–25	48 × 22 × 18	200
Tengmalm's Owl	20–40	10–17	9–14	30 × 13 × 12	42

TABLE 5: *Food of Barn Owls in Europe throughout the year. Data sources: Glue (1974), Haensel and Walther (1966), Herrera (1973), Lange (1948), Lovari et al (1976) and Thiollay (1968).*

	Denmark %	E. Germany %	England %	France %	Spain %	Italy %
Bats	0.12	0.04	0.03	0.02	0.95	0.05
Moles	0.16	0.08	0.18	0.38	—	0.08
Shrews	38.03	12.89	31.88	23.90	17.32	18.46
Voles	22.22	67.60	49.51	51.10	12.00	36.93
Short-tailed *Microtus agrestis*	15.10	0.47	45.44	6.94	—	—
Common *M. arvalis*	7.00	65.73	—	34.69	—	—
Pine *Pitymys sp.*	—	—	—	0.76	11.90	26.74
Rats	1.40	0.19	1.96	0.44	0.93	0.46
Mice	32.22	17.91	13.55	19.13	55.67	37.64
*Other small mammals	—	0.06	+	0.34	0.19	2.34
Mammals total	94.15	98.77	97.11	95.31	87.06	95.96
Birds	5.05	0.93	1.99	0.57	4.31	2.02
Frogs and Lizards	0.66	0.11	0.17	3.76	4.36	—
Invertebrates	0.10	0.20	0.72	0.33	4.28	2.02
Total	38,899	8,535	48,207	31,259	14,806	3,672

+ = less than 0.005

* Other mammals = Hamsters, Rabbits, Weasels, Stoats, Dormice and Birchmice.

TABLE 6: *Nesting sites of Barn Owls in Holland according to Braaksma and de Bruijn (1976).*

Nest site	Before 1963 %	After 1963 %	Difference ± %
Churches	29.9	24.7	−5.2
Castles	9.6	8.5	−1.1
Farms and barns	39.6	39.1	−0.5
Nest boxes	3.9	12.2	+8.3
Windmills	3.1	3.5	+0.4
Other buildings	8.0	9.7	+1.7
Hollow trees	4.1	1.5	−2.6
Other more or less natural nest sites	1.8	0.8	−1.0
Number of nests	639	599	

TABLE 7: *Average clutch size of Barn Owls in various European countries.*

	Av. clutch size	Nests	Source
Sweden	4.63	33	Frylestam (1971)
Denmark	5.55	74	Trap-Lind (1965)
East Germany	5.77	126	Hummitzsch (1953)
	5.95	15	Schneider (1964)
West Germany	5.51	354	Kaus (1977)
Switzerland	5.33	63	Schifferli (1949, 1957)
Holland	4.03	705	Braaksma & Bruijn (1976)
France	6.22	269	Baudvin (1975, 1976)
Total	4.99	1,639	

TABLE 8: *Average brood size of Barn Owls in various European countries. Brood size refers to number of young leaving nest.*

	Av. brood size	Nests	Source
Sweden	2.15	36	Frylestam (1971)
East Germany	3.84	141	Hummitzsch (1953) & Schneider (1964)
West Germany	4.38	354	Kaus (1977)
Holland	3.20	507	Braaksma & Bruijn (1976)
Switzerland	4.50	182	Schifferli (1949, 1957)
France	4.54	512	Baudvin (1975, 1976)
Total	4.00	1,732	

TABLE 9: *Wing lengths (mm) of all sub-species of Eagle Owl. Compiled from Dement'ev et al 1951 and Vaurie 1965. Larger, northernmost birds head table.*

	female wing (mm)				male wing (mm)			
	max.	min.	average	numbers	max.	min.	average	numbers
B. b. ruthenus	515	471	485.4	22	468	430	445.6	17
B. b. sibiricus	515	472	492	14	465	438	451	7
B. b. yenisseensis	518	473	487	18	463	443	456	18
B. b. jakutensis	495	475	484	5	468	452	458	3
B. b. ussuriensis	502	470	483	11	465	430	448	10
B. b. borissowi			470	1			465	1
B. b. kiautschensis	485	440	455.5	20	448	410	428.8	15
B. b. tarimensis	475	465	471.2	4	455	450	452.5	2
B. b. tibetanus	505	490	498.8	9	485	450	461	13
B. b. hemachalana	508	473	485.5	16	466	433	450.7	15
B. b. auspicabilis	508	455	483.8	22	482	415	450.5	13
B. b. turcomanus	492	470	481.5	17	468	420	442.5	20
B. b. omissus	460	425	445	15	424	404	415	7
B. b. gladkovi	500	495	497.5	2	440	470	451.2	2
B. b. bubo	520	475	485.4	20	465	430	452.5	29
B. b. interpositus	502	468	480	19	463	428	447.7	25
B. b. hispanus	475	445	453	8	450	420	430	7
B. b. nikolskii	465	410	437.8	9	430	405	419	9
B. b. bengalensis	403	376	387	12	391	358	370	10
B. b. ascalaphus B. b. desertorum*	390	340	367	20	368	325	346.5	20

* Vaurie, from whose work these figures were extracted, does not separate these distinctive races.

TABLE 10: *Eagle Owl's diet during breeding season. Data: Estonian SSR, Randla 1976; Finland, Suomalainen 1915, Kivirikko 1930, März 1936, Sulkava 1966, Mikkola 1974, Grönlund and Mikkola 1974, Huhtala et al 1976, Lagerström 1978; Norway, Willgohs 1974; Sweden, Olsson 1979.*

Prey items (%)	Estonia	Finland	Norway	Sweden	% total
Shrews Soricidae	0.08	0.4	0.09	0.06	0.1
Bats Chiroptera sp.	—	—	—	0.03	0.03
Hedgehog Erinaceus europaeus	2.4	2.7	0.6	0.5	1.3
Mole Talpa europaea	0.1	0.02	—	—	0.02
Hares Lepus timidus, L. europaeus	0.8	2.9	2.0	3.9	2.7
Mice (Mus, Micromys and Apodemus)	1.5	0.8	0.2	1.8	1.1
Rats (Rattus norvegicus and R. rattus)	0.08	23.0	9.2	8.9	11.1
Voles Microtus agrestis, arvalis, ratticeps	14.1	10.5	15.0	9.5	11.8
„ Clethrionomys, glareolus, rufocanus	5.7	2.0	4.3	0.6	2.6
„ Arvicola terrestris	53.6	26.7	3.6	23.8	23.6
Voles, sub-total	(73.4)	(39.2)	(32.9)	(33.9)	(38.0)
Lemming Lemmus lemmus	—	—	1.5	—	0.4
Muskrat Ondatra zibethica	0.8	2.0	—	—	0.6
Red Squirrel Sciurus vulgaris	4.0	3.4	0.9	1.2	2.1
Flying Squirrel Pteromys volans	—	2.1	—	—	0.5
Microrodentia sp.	—	0.2	3.2	0.3	1.0
Mink, Stoat and Weasel Mustelidae	0.2	0.8	0.4	0.2	0.4
Pine Marten Martes martes	0.04	0.07	—	0.02	0.03
Badger Meles meles	0.04	—	—	—	0.00
Raccoon Dog Nyctereutes procyonoides	0.04	—	—	—	0.00
Fox Vulpes vulpes	—	0.1	0.1	0.2	0.1
Domestic Cat Felix catus	—	0.02	0.05	0.03	0.03
Roe Deer Capreolus capreolus	0.04	—	—	0.03	0.02
Sheep (lamb) Ovis aries (juv)	—	—	0.2	—	0.05
Unidentified mammals	—	0.4	0.1	0.2	0.2
Mammals, total	(83.5)	(78.2)	(41.4)	(51.2)	(59.7)
Corvidae	7.6	2.9	2.6	2.5	3.3
Galliformes	3.6	5.3	3.3	1.4	3.1
Anatidae	0.8	3.2	10.3	14.4	8.7
Charidriiformes	0.4	1.0	5.5	6.5	4.1
Laridae, Sternidae, Alcidae	0.3	0.5	20.8	10.3	9.2
Strigidae, Falconiformes	0.8	1.7	1.2	3.7	2.2
Other birds	0.8	3.1	7.3	6.6	5.2
Birds, total	(14.3)	(17.7)	(51.0)	(45.4)	(35.8)
Reptiles (Laceridae and Viperidae)	0.04	—	—	0.03	0.02
Frogs (Rana, Bufo)	2.1	2.9	6.4	1.7	3.2
Fish	0.08	0.5	0.8	1.5	0.9
Beetles (Coleoptera)	—	0.7	0.4	0.2	0.4
Total number prey animals	2,490	4,226	4,476	6,423	17,615

TABLE 11: *Causes of death of Eagle Owls in West Germany (Wickl 1979), Sweden (Olsson 1979) and Finland (Saurola 1979).*

	W. Germany	Sweden	Finland	Total	%
Unnatural causes					
collided with traffic	23	13	10	46	15.5
electrocuted (wires, etc.)	50	20	12	82	27.7
shot or otherwise killed	35	4	—	39	13.2
trapped in buildings, caught on barbed wire, or caught in traps for other animals	9	5	11	25	8.4
poisoned	9	12	2	23	7.8
Natural causes					
starvation	2	18	—	20	6.8
drowning	1	2	2	5	1.7
preyed upon	6	4	4	14	4.7
sickness or injury	17	21	—	38	12.9
fallen down	2	—	—	2	0.7
bitten by snake (Adder)	—	1	—	1	0.3
oesophagus perforated when eating leg of raptor	—	1	—	1	0.3
	154	101	41	296	100.0
Unknown causes	57	—	34	91	
Total of deaths	211	101	75	387	

TABLE 12: *Population sizes of Eagle Owl in northern and western Europe from recent estimates.*

	pairs minimum	pairs maximum	Source
Austria		200	K. Bauer and H. Frey
Bulgaria		50	S. Dontchev
Czechoslovakia	350	520	J. Švehlik and K. Hudec
Estonian SSR	100	120	Randla 1976
East Germany	35	42	H. Knobloch
Finland	300	1,000	H. Mikkola (300); v. Hartmann *et al* (1967: 1,000)
France	<100	>300	J-F. Terrasse (1975); Yeatman 1976: <100)
Hungary	25	30	E. Schmidt
Italy	50	100	Hudson 1975
Lithuanian SSR	400	420	Curry-Lindahl 1950
Norway	500	>1,000	J. Willgohs (>1,000); Hudson (1975: 500)
Poland	70	100	L. Tomialojć
Spain		2,000	J. Garzon
Sweden	171	350	Olsson (1976: 171); B. Helander (350)
Switzerland		60	Glutz v. Blotzheim and Bauer 1980
West Germany	160	180	K-H. Wickl
Total	4,571	6,472	

TABLE 13: *Size of Snowy Owl pellets (mm).*

	Koivusaari et al 1977 (test conditions)		Hagen 1960 (in the wild)	
	length (mm)	thickness (mm)	length (mm)	thickness (mm)
Largest pellet	90	35	153	39
Smallest	35	22	55	32
Average	59	30	92	33
Number of pellets	20	20	19	19

TABLE 14: *Food of Snowy Owls at nest sites in Fenno-Scandia. Data sources: Løvenskiold 1947, Hagen 1960, Andersson and Persson 1971 and A. Hakala, A. Kaikusalo and M. Rikkonen (in litt.).*

	Norway	Sweden	Finland	Total
Research years	1934/1959	1969–70	1974–75	1934–75
No. of prey animals	1,686	206	834	2,726
Norway Lemming *Lemmus lemmus*	29.2%	90.3%	30.7%	34.3%
Voles *Clethrionomys sp.*	0.1	1.0	27.2	8.4
Voles *Microtus sp.*	68.6	7.3	24.8	50.6
Ground Vole *Arvicola terrestris*	0.2	—	0.4	0.2
Unidentified voles	0.1	—	12.5	3.9
Shrews *Soricidae*	0.3	0.5	0.4	0.3
Weasel *Mustela nivalis*	0.1	—	0.1	0.1
Red Squirrel *Sciurus vulgaris*	—	—	0.2	0.1
Blue Hare *Lepus timidus*	—	—	0.4	0.1
Mammals total	98.6%	99.1%	96.7%	98.0%
Birds	1.2	1.0	1.8	1.5
Frogs	—	—	1.1	0.3
Fish	0.1	—	0.5	0.2
Insects	0.2	—	—	0.1
Total	100.1%	100.1%	100.1%	100.1%

TABLE 15: *Food of Snowy Owls outside the breeding season in Finland. Data sources: Sulkava and Sulkava 1967, A. Kaikusalo (in litt.) and Mikkola (unpublished material).*

	Lapland	S. Finland	Total
Research years	1975	1961–74	1961–75
No. of prey animals	226	95	321
Norway Lemming *Lemmus lemmus*	34.5%	—%	24.3%
Voles *Clethrionomys sp.*	31.0	6.0	23.3
Voles *Microtus sp.*	21.7	78.0	38.4
Unidentified voles	11.5	—	8.1
Shrews *Soricidae*	0.4	5.0	1.9
Hares *Lepus sp.*	0.5	2.0	0.9
Mammals total	99.6%	91.0%	96.9%
Birds	0.4	8.0	2.8
Insects	—	1.0	0.3
Total	100.0%	100.0%	100.0%

TABLE 16: *Food of Hawk Owls at nest sites in northern Europe during 1949–76. Data from Norway (Hagen 1952), Finland (Mikkola 1972, Hublin and Mikkola 1977) and Murmansk Province, northern Russia (Bianki and Koshkina 1960).*

	Norway	Finland	Russia	Total
Research years	1949	1958–76	1957	1949–76
Number of nests	4	12	1	17
Number of prey animals	525	774	174	1,473
Voles (*Microtus*)	7.4%	57.1%	12.6%	34.2%
Voles (*Clethrionomys*)	54.5	34.1	75.9	46.3
Water voles (*Arvicola*)	—	0.6	3.4	0.7
Lemmings (*Lemmus, Myopus*)	5.9	1.7	—	3.0
Unidentified voles	30.5	—	5.8	11.5
Total voles (Microtidae)	98.3%	93.5%	97.7%	95.7%
Shrews (*Soricidae*)	0.2	2.5	—	1.4
Birds	1.0	2.6	1.7	1.9
Other prey	0.5	1.4	0.6	1.0

TABLE 17: *Food of Hawk Owls outside the breeding season in Finland and Russia during 1912–77. These figures are based on 37 stomach-contents: 35 from Finland during 1912–77 (this study) and two from Murmansk Province, northern Russia, in 1956 (Bianki and Koshkina 1960).*

	Total	%
Pygmy Shrew *Sorex minutus*	1	2.3
Common Shrew *Sorex araneus*	3	6.8
Water Shrew *Neomys fodiens*	1	2.3
Total Shrews (Soricidae)	5	11.4
Bank Vole *Clethrionomys glareolus*	10	22.7
Ground Vole *Arvicola terrestris*	1	2.3
Short-tailed Vole *Microtus agrestis*	9	20.5
Root Vole *Microtus ratticeps*	3	6.8
Unidentified voles	2	4.5
Total Voles (Microtidae)	25	56.8
Willow Grouse *Lagopus lagopus*	8	18.2
Hazel Hen *Tetrastes bonasia*	2	4.5
Mistle Thrush *Turdus viscivorus*	1	2.3
Crossbill *Loxia curvirostra*	1	2.3
Redpoll *Acanthis flammea*	1	2.3
Total birds	13	29.6
Beetle *Carabus* sp.	1	2.3
Grand Total	44	100.1

TABLE 18: *Evidence of the decrease of Hawk Owls in northern and central Finland.*

1930/31	60	1958/59	2	1965/66	1
1931/32	21	1959/60	2	1966/67	–
1932/33	8	1960/61	4	1967/68	–
1933/34	7	1961/62	7	1968/69	–
1934/35	6	1962/63	1	1969/70	–
1935/36	6	1963/64	–	1970/71	1
1936/37	7	1964/65	5	1971/72	3

Figures given are numbers of corpses sent to A. Hellemaa, a Finnish taxidermist, autumn/winter 1930–37, and to the Department of Zoology, University of Oulu, autumn/winter 1958–72.

TABLE 19: *Food of Pygmy Owls in Finland in 1962–73. Sources: Jussila and Mikkola 1973, Kaakinen and Mikkola 1972, Kellomäki 1969 and 1977, Mikkola 1970 and Mikkola and Jussila 1974. All figures are percentages of prey numbers.*

	Breeding season	Outside breeding season
Research years	1962–1973	1962–1971
Number of nests studied	34	—
Number of prey animals	2,761	1,297
Voles (*Microtus*)	19.9%	21.4%
Voles (*Clethrionomys*)	29.6	24.7
Lemmings (*Myopus*)	—	0.1
Unidentified voles	—	1.8
Total voles	49.5%	48.0%
Mice (*Muridae*)	1.0	2.6
Mice or voles	—	4.8
Shrews (*Soricidae*)	3.6	12.4
Other mammals (bats and weasels)	0.1	0.1
Total mammals	54.2%	67.9%
Small birds, weight 5–35 g	37.7	24.9
Medium-sized birds, weight 35–88 g	1.3	1.7
Unidentified birds	5.0	5.5
Total birds	44.0%	32.1%
Other prey (lizards, insects, fish)	1.8	0.1

TABLE 20: *Comparison of Pygmy Owl's food outside breeding season in Finland (this study), in Norway (Hagen 1952), in USSR in the Moscow area (cf. Grempe 1965, 1966) and in the forest of Bielowieza (Grempe 1965), and in Central Europe (Uttendörfer 1952).*

	Finland	Norway	Moscow	Bielowieza	Cent. Europe
Small rodents	55.5%	24.6%	74.7%	26.5%	24.2%
Shrews	12.4	44.0	20.2	51.6	14.2
Birds	32.1	31.4	5.1	21.9	61.6
Total material	1,297	418	446	252	250

TABLE 21: *Food of Little Owls during breeding season in Europe. Data from Moldavian SSR (Ganya and Zubkov 1975), East Germany (Haensel and Walther 1966), Holland (Haverschmidt 1946), France (Thiollay 1968) and Spain (Herrera and Hiraldo 1976).*

	Moldavian SSR	E. Germany	Holland	France	Spain
	%	%	%	%	%
Rodents	39.2	26.0	0.7	3.1	2.5
Shrews, Bats	1.5	0.4	0.7	2.5	0.3
Birds	1.4	0.8	2.5	—	0.4
Amphibians	1.3	0.5	6.9	—	0.2
Reptilians	0.1	—	—	—	0.5
Invertebrates	56.5	72.3	89.2	94.4	95.9
Total prey items	855	2,993	277	323	5,018

TABLE 22: *Food of Little Owls outside breeding season in France (Thiollay 1968), in Italy (Lovari 1974) and in Moldavian SSR (Ganya and Zubkov 1975).*

	France	Italy	Moldavian SSR
	%	%	%
Rodents	5.0	0.7	70.7
Shrews and Bats	0.6	1.4	2.2
Birds	—	0.1	2.2
Reptilians	—	0.1	—
Amphibians	—	0.1	—
Invertebrate prey	94.4	97.6	24.9
Total prey items	340	733	406

TABLE 23: *Breeding habitats of 486 Little Owls in England and Wales (Glue and Scott, 1980).*

Habitat type	No. of nests	%
Farmland	361	74.3
Woodland	59	12.1
Gardens and habitations	51	10.5
Heath and moor	6	1.2
Wetlands	6	1.2
Coastal	3	0.6
Totals	486	100.0

TABLE 24: *Nest sites of 526 Little Owls in England and Wales (Glue and Scott, 1980).*

Nesting site	No. of nests	%
Holes in deciduous trees[1]	482	91.6
Buildings and other structures	35	6.7
Rock clefts or rabbit burrows	6	1.1
Others[2]	3	0.6
Totals	526	100.0

[1] Holes in trees including at least 14 nests in wooden nestboxes, and some old nests of Magpie *Pica pica* or dreys of Grey Squirrel *Neosciurus carolinensis*; exact numbers not stated by Glue and Scott, 1980.
[2] Little Owls have nested once in gravel- and sand-pit tunnels and inside stacked peat on moorland.

TABLE 25: *Wing length (mm) comparison of Tawny Owl races in western Eurasia. Data: Dement'ev et al 1951, Vaurie 1965.*

	sylvatica (England)	aluco (Sweden)	aluco (W. USSR)	siberiae (N.E. USSR)
females	256–272 (265.6)	272–298 (284.5)	277–311 (296.4)	301–307 (303.3)
males	250–273 (259)	265–283 (274)	268–295 (283.2)	280–300 (290.6)
numbers ♀ and ♂	10/10	25/25	66/53	3/4

	mauritanica (Morocco)	Sancti-nicolai (Iraq/S.W. Iran)	wilkonskii (Caucasus)
females	272–305 (285)	270–285 (279.3)	282–305 (296.2)
males		255–273 (266)	266–296 (276.2)
numbers ♀ and ♂	17	7/12	33/17

TABLE 26: *Comparison of the diet of a Tawny Owl family according to pellet and nest floor analysis (Mikkola 1977). Pellets represent adult diet, mainly that of the male during spring; the nest floor items are prey remains left by the female and young. Prey animals listed in order of increasing size.*

	% in pellets	% nest floor	difference
Common Shrew *Sorex araneus*	6.2	2.0	−4.2
Harvest Mouse *Micromys minutus*	12.3	—	−12.3
Water Shrew *Neomys fodiens*	—	2.0	+2.0
House Mouse *Mus musculus*	9.2	—	−9.2
Bank Vole *Clethrionomys glareolus*	6.2	—	−6.2
Small birds (15–20 g)	1.5	14.0	+12.5
Field Vole *Microtus agrestis*	43.1	40.0	−3.3
Frogs (Rana sp.)	9.2	8.0	−1.2
Thrush-size birds (−75 g)	1.5	12.0	+10.5
Brown Rat *Rattus norvegicus*	4.6	6.0	+1.4
Water Vole *Arvicola terrestris*	6.2	16.0	+9.8
Number of prey items	65	50	

TABLE 27: *Diet of Tawny Owl in Fenno-Scandia and in England. Data: England: Southern 1954; Finland: Eskelinen and Mikkola 1972, Itämies and Mikkola 1972, Leppänen 1970, Kuhlman and Koskela 1980, Mikkola 1968, 1970, 1974, 1977, Mikkola and Jussila 1974; Norway: Hagen 1952; Sweden: Ahlbom 1971, Holmberg 1976, Källander 1977.*

	Fenno-Scandia (%)	England (%)
Mole *Talpa europaea*	0.01	4.1
Shrews (Soricidae)	10.2	12.9
Bats (Chiroptera)	0.1	0.04
Mice (Apodemus, Mus, Micromys)	15.8	26.4
Rat *Rattus norvegicus*	2.1	0.8
Rattus or *Arvicola* spp.	1.6	—
Voles – *Arvicola* spp.	3.3	0.1
Voles – *Microtus* spp.	27.1	12.0
Voles – *Clethrionomys* spp.	11.6	27.7
Microtus or *Clethrionomys* spp.	1.9	—
Squirrels (Sciurus, Pteromys)	0.1	—
Rabbits and Hares – *Oryctolagus, Lepus* spp.	0.01	1.6
Weasels (Mustelidae)	0.1	0.04
Lemmings – *Lemmus, Myopus* spp.	0.3	—
Birds	14.4	4.6
Frogs	9.2	—
Lizards	0.1	—
Fish	0.3	—
Insects	1.8	9.7
Number of prey items	9,369	10,533

TABLE 28: *Diet of Tawny Owl during breeding season 1973 and in spring 1974, in the New Forest and at Sunbury, Middlesex, England (Mikkola).*

	New Forest	Sunbury	Total
Common Shrew *Sorex araneus*	2	—	2
Wood Mouse *Apodemus* spp.	22	4	26
House Mouse *Mus musculus*	—	1	1
Bank Vole *Clethrionomys glareolus*	4	—	4
Field Vole *Microtus agrestis*	4	1	5
Grey Squirrel *Sciurus carolinensis*	1	—	1
Rabbit *Oryctolagus cuniculus*	3	1	4
Birds	9	11	20
Frogs	2	21	23
Insects	7	—	7
Totals of prey items	54	39	93
Number of earthworm pellets	—	4	4

TABLE 29: *Comparison of vertebrate diets Long-eared, Tawny and Barn Owls in Britain. Data: Long-eared Owl, Glue and Hammond 1974, Village 1981; Tawny Owl, Southern 1954, Beven 1965, 1967, Yalden and Jones 1971, Harrison 1960, Mikkola Table 28; Barn Owl, Glue 1974. Similarity Index formula according to McNaughton and Wolf 1973.*

(%)	Long-eared	Tawny	Barn Owl
Mole *Talpa europaea*	0.12	4.1	0.2
Common Shrew *Sorex araneus*	3.0	10.8	25.6
Pygmy Shrew *Sorex minutus*	1.8	1.6	5.3
Water Shrew *Neomys fodiens*	0.07	0.4	1.2
Bats (Chiroptera)	0.06	0.05	0.03
Edible Dormouse *Glis glis*	0.01	0.01	—
Harvest Mouse *Micromys minutus*	0.01	—	0.5
House Mouse *Mus musculus*	0.1	0.3	1.3
Wood Mouse *Apodemus* spp.	16.9	27.6	11.8
Brown Rat *Rattus norvegicus*	2.8	1.3	2.0
Bank Vole *Clethrionomys glareolus*	10.3	27.7	3.9
Orkney Vole *Microtus arvalis orcadensis*	0.6	—	—
Field Vole *Microtus agrestis*	49.4	13.6	45.8
Water Vole *Arvicola amphibius*	0.3	0.2	0.2
Grey Squirrel *Sciurus carolinensis*	0.02	0.01	—
Rabbit *Oryctolagus cuniculus*	0.18	1.6	0.01
Weasel *Mustela nivalis*	0.05	0.04	0.002
Stoat *M. erminea*	0.01	—	—
Birds	14.2	10.2	2.0
Frogs	0.06	0.5	0.2
Lizards	—	—	0.002
Fish	—	0.02	—
Total numbers of prey	8,272	10,936	47,864
Similarity Index	0.65	0.46	

0.71

TABLE 30: *Percentage distribution of Tawny Owl nest sites at different periods in southern Finland. Data: Alho 1971, Lahti and Mikkola 1974, Pietiäinen 1975, Koskela and Koskela 1975.*

	1940–1959	1960–1969	1970–1975	Total
Nest boxes	33	75	95	77
Holes in trees	48	14	3	15
Buildings	15	1	1	4
Tree stumps	4	5	1	3
Stick nests	—	4	—	1
	100	99	100	100
Number of nests observed	46	73	123	242

TABLE 31: *Average clutch size and average brood size of Tawny Owl in Finland, Central Europe and Britain. Data: Finland, Linkola and Myllymäki 1969, Koskela 1978, Kolunen and Pietiäinen 1978, Forsman et al 1980; Central Europe, Schifferli 1957, Rockenbauch 1978, Glutz von Blotzheim and Bauer 1980; Britain, Southern 1970, including British Trust for Ornithology's nest record cards.*

	Clutch size	Nests	Brood size	Nests	Difference
Finland	3.81	378	3.05	601	−0.76
Central Europe	3.29	361	2.61	131	−0.68
Britain	2.67	252	2.27	181	−0.40

TABLE 32: *Food of Hume's Owl in the Negev desert in Israel in 1978 (Yossi Leshem, in litt.).*

	Numbers consumed
Mammals	
Rock Gerbil *Gerbillus dasyurus*	22
A gerbil *Gerbillus henleyi*	5
Meriones crassus	14
Bushy-tailed Jird *Sekeetamys calurus*	3
Golden Spiny Mouse *Acomys russatus*	1
A spiny mouse *Acomys sp.*	1
Lesser White-toothed Shrew *Crocidura suaveolens*	2
	48
Birds	
Desert Lark *Ammomanes deserti*	1
House Sparrow *Passer domesticus*	1
Unidentified Passerine	1
	3

TABLE 32 (*continued*)

Reptiles	
Fan-toed Gecko *Ptyodactylus hasselquistii*	2
Starred Agama *Agama stellio*	1
	3
Arthropods	
A grasshopper (?) *Sphodromerus pilipes*	29
Jericho Scorpion *Nebo hierochonticus*	6
Unidentified *Arthropoda*	12
	47
Total	101

TABLE 33: *Food of Ural Owls during breeding season in Finland (data from Eskelinen and Mikkola 1972, Kunttu 1978, Mikkola 1969, 1971, 1972, Mikkola and Jussila 1974, Mikkola and Mikkola 1974), in Sweden (Lundberg 1976, 1977), in Norway (Mysterud and Hagen 1969) and in Germany (Schäfer and Finckenstein 1935, Uttendörfer 1952). Figures are % of total consumed.*

	Finland	Sweden	Norway	Germany	Total
Research years	1965–78	1969–76	1949–67	1929–44	1929–78
Number of prey animals	1,895	1,123	133	282	3,433
Moles *Talpidae*	1.2	?	—	0.4	0.7
Shrews *Soricidae*	7.7	9.3	12.0	7.1	8.3
Voles *Microtus*	31.1	24.1	36.8	41.5	29.9
Voles *Clethrionomys*	16.7	16.3	29.3	14.9	16.9
Water voles *Arvicola*	11.0	33.3	0.8	0.4	17.0
Lemmings *Myopus*	0.1	—	0.8	—	0.1
Muskrat *Ondatra zibethicus*	0.1	—	—	—	0.03
Mice and rats *Muridae*	2.0	0.7	—	11.7	2.5
Northern Birch Mouse *Sicista betulina*	—	—	—	1.8	0.1
Stoats and weasels *Mustelidae*	0.3	—	0.8	—	0.2
Small mammals unidentified	—	2.0	3.7	—	0.6
Squirrels *Sciuridae*	3.9	0.5	0.8	0.4	2.4
Hares *Leporidae*	0.7	—	—	0.7	0.5
Total mammals	74.8	86.2	85.0	78.9	79.2
Birds	17.6	11.3	15.0	7.4	14.6
Frogs *Rana*	5.7	2.5	—	5.3	4.4
Lizards *Lacerta*	0.1	—	—	—	0.03
Fish *Perca fluviatilis?*	—	—	—	0.4	0.03
Insects mostly *Coleoptera*	1.8	—	—	8.1	1.7
	100.0	100.0	100.0	100.1	100.0

TABLE 34: *Food of Ural Owls outside breeding season in Finland (H. Mikkola, this study), in Norway (Mysterud and Hagen 1969) and in Central Europe (Sládek 1961–62). Figures (%) are based on contents of 208 stomachs.*

	Finland	*Norway*	*Cent. Europe*	*Total*
Research years	1961–78	1873–1962	1902–60	1873–1978
Number of stomachs	45	11	152	208
Moles *Talpidae*	—	—	2.1	1.4
Shrews *Soricidae*	38.5	26.6	7.1	17.8
Voles *Microtus*	1.7	6.7	37.8	25.1
Voles *Clethrionomys*	17.1	6.7	4.6	8.6
Pine Vole *Pitymys subterraneus*	—	—	1.3	0.8
Water voles *Arvicola*	—	6.7	0.8	0.8
Mice and rats *Muridae*	3.4	13.3	11.8	9.2
Dormouse *Muscardinus*	—	—	0.7	0.5
Stoats and weasels *Mustelidae*	0.8	—	1.7	1.4
Squirrels *Sciuridae*	1.7	—	0.4	0.8
Hares *Leporidae*	—	6.7	3.8	2.7
Mammals unidentified	—	13.3	4.3	3.3
Total mammals	63.2	80.0	76.4	72.4
Birds	8.6	20.0	10.9	10.6
Frogs *Rana*	27.4	—	1.7	9.7
Insects mostly beetles	0.8	—	10.9	7.3
	100.0	100.0	99.9	100.0
Number of prey animals	117	15	238	370

TABLE 35: *Ural Owl nest-sites in Finland (Lahti 1972, Lahti and Mikkola 1974) and in Sweden (Ingritz 1969, Ahlen and Larsson 1972). The percentage distribution of Finnish nests presented at different periods and in South and North Finland separately.*

	Finnish nests			*S. Finland*	*N. Finland*	*Total*	
	1870–1949	1950–1959	1960–1969	(up to 63°N)	63°N–67°N	*Finland*	*Sweden*
	%	%	%	%	%	%	%
Boxes	—	—	42	42	13	33	11
Twig nests	15	34	28	25	23	28	14
Stumps	59	52	20	11	51	27	40
Holes in trees	26	14	6	19	6	10	34
Buildings	—	—	2	2	4	2	—
Flat ground	—	—	1	—	3	1	—
Rock face	—	—	1	1	—	0	1
Total	100	100	100	100	100	101	100
Number of nests	27	29	194	170	80	250	74

TABLE 36: *Food of Great Grey Owls at 61 nest sites in Fenno-Scandia, 1955–1974 (cf. Mikkola 1981).*

	%
Mole *Talpa europaea*	0.02
Pygmy Shrew *Sorex minutus*	0.50
Common Shrew *S. araneus*	2.80
Taiga Shrew *S. isodon*	0.04
Masked Shrew *S. caecutiens*	0.17
Least Shrew *S. minutissimus*	0.04
Water Shrew *Neomys fodiens*	0.19
Unknown shrews *Sorex sp.*	0.73
Insectivores total	4.50
Wood Lemming *Myopus schisticolor*	1.84
Bank Vole *Clethrionomys glareolus*	10.30
Grey-sided Vole *C. rufocanus*	2.94
Unknown *Clethrionomys sp.*	3.23
Short-tailed Vole *Microtus agrestis*	66.16
Common Vole *M. arvalis*	0.14
Root Vole *M. oeconomus*	7.07
Unknown *Microtus sp.*	0.12
Ground Vole *Arvicola terrestris*	1.66
Muskrat *Ondatra zibethicus*	0.02
Red Squirrel *Sciurus vulgaris*	0.08
Harvest Mouse *Micromys minutus*	0.29
Brown Rat *Rattus norvegicus*	0.02
Rodents total	93.84
Pygmy Weasel *Mustela rixosa*	0.08
Mammals total	98.42
Birds total	1.02
Frogs *Rana sp.*	0.50
Invertebrates *Coleoptera* and *Gastropoda*	0.06
Total	100.00
Number of prey animals	5,177

TABLE 37: *Weight distribution of Great Grey Owl prey animals during breeding season (n = 5,177; 169,170 g). Weights of mammals are from Siivonen (1967); those of birds from v. Haartman et al (1963–72).*

Weight (g)	number (%)	weight (%)
<10.0	1.80	0.33
10.0– 49.9	95.17	87.72
50.0– 99.9	0.97	1.64
100.0–499.9	2.05	9.64
>500.0	0.02	0.68
Total	100.01	100.01

TABLE 38: *Trapping results compared with food composition of Great Grey Owl's diet in (A) Konnevesi, Central Finland and (B) Salla, Finnish Lapland. Small mammals were caught in Konnevesi during 433 trapping nights, 14th April to 30th July 1972 (Mikkola 1976) and in Salla during 700 trapping nights, 21st July to 1st August 1974 (Pulliainen and Loisa 1977), near Great Grey Owl nests in places where owls were seen hunting.*

	(A)		(B)	
	Food	*Traps*	*Food*	*Traps*
	%	%	%	%
Ground Vole *Arvicola terrestris*	4.5	—	—	—
Root Vole *Microtus oeconomus*	—	—	19.0	50.9
Short-tailed Vole *Microtus agrestis*	71.2	15.2	68.6	35.1
Bank Vole *Clethrionomys glareolus*	12.9	65.2	9.9	8.8
Sorex spp.	—	—	2.5	5.3
Common Shrew *Sorex araneus*	8.7	13.6	—	—
Pygmy Shrew *Sorex minutus*	1.5	—	—	—
Least Shrew *Sorex minutissimus*	0.4	—	—	—
Brown Rat *Rattus norvegicus*	0.4	—	—	—
Yellow-necked Field Mouse *Apodemus flavicollis*	—	6.1	—	—
Harvest Mouse *Micromys minutus*	0.4	—	—	—
Total	100.0	100.1	100.0	100.1
No. of animals	264	66	121	?

TABLE 39: *Winter food of Great Grey Owls in Finland in 1981 (Mikkola 1981).*

	%
Common Shrew *Sorex araneus*	4.3
Taiga or Common Shrew *S. araneus/isodon*	0.5
Taiga Shrew *S. isodon*	0.5
Pygmy Shrew *S. minutus*	5.3
Short-tailed Vole *Microtus agrestis*	75.4
Short-tailed or Common Vole *M. agrestis/arvalis*	1.4
Common Vole *M. arvalis*	4.8
Bank Vole *Clethrionomys glareolus*	4.3
Ground Vole *Arvicola terrestris*	1.0
Harvest Mouse *Micromys minutus*	0.5
House Mouse *Mus musculus*	0.5
Yellow-necked Field Mouse *Apodemus flavicollis*	0.5
Red Squirrel *Sciurus vulgaris*	0.5
Pygmy Weasel *Mustela rixosa*	0.5
Total	100.0
Prey items	207

TABLE 40: *Percentage distribution of Great Grey Owl nest sites in different parts of Finland (Mikkola 1981 and this study).*

	S. Finland 60–63°N	C. Finland 63–66°N	N. Finland 66–69°N	Total 60–69°N
Twig nests	65.7	85.7	88.5	82.7
Stumps	25.7	10.2	9.6	13.0
Flat ground	2.9	4.1	—	2.7
Rock face	—	—	1.9	0.5
Barn roof	2.9	—	—	0.5
On a large stone	2.9	—	—	0.5
Nests observed	35	98	52	185

TABLE 41: *Diet of Long-eared Owl in seven European countries throughout the year. All figures are percentages of prey numbers. Data: Araujo et al (1973), Catuneanu et al (1970), Chaline et al (1974), Glue and Hammond (1974), Grönlund and Mikkola (1977, 1978), Haensel and Walther (1966), Källander (1977), Mikkola (1977), Soikkeli (1964), Sulkava (1965), Thiollay (1968).*

	Britain	Finland	France	E. Germany	Spain	Sweden	Rumania
Shrews (Soricidae)	4.0	7.0	0.1	0.4	3.7	2.3	1.2
Moles (Talpidae)	0.1	+	−	0.1	+	−	+
Bats (Chiroptera)	0.1	−	−	+	+	+	−
Rabbits, Hares (Leporidae)	0.2	+	−	+	+	−	+
Squirrels (Sciuridae)	+	+	−	−	−	−	+
Voles (Microtidae)	59.3	83.1	91.4	80.7	79.8	67.4	28.0
Common *M. arvalis*	(0.6)	(25.6)	(83.7)	(78.0)	(36.2)	−	(27.0)
Field *M. agrestis*	(47.4)	(47.2)	(4.5)	(1.6)	−	(65.2)	+
Pine *Pitymys* spp.	−	−	(1.5)	−	(41.8)	−	(0.6)
Other Voles	(11.3)	(10.2)	(1.7)	(1.1)	(1.5)	(2.2)	(0.4)
Mice, Rats (Muridae)	21.2	7.4	6.3	16.9	10.0	28.4	56.7
Dormice (Gliridae), Birch Mice (Zapodidae), Mole Rats (Spalacidae)	+	−	−	+	0.3	−	+
Hamsters (Cricetidae)	−	−	−	0.1	−	−	1.7
Stoats, Weasels (Mustelidae)	+	−	−	−	−	−	+
Mammals total (%)	84.9	97.5	97.8	98.2	93.9	98.1	87.6
Birds	15.0	1.9	2.1	1.6	4.6	1.9	12.4
Frogs and fish	0.1	0.1	−	+	−	−	−
Insects	★	0.5	0.1	0.2	1.5	★	★
Total (numbers)	7,761	2,678	3,504	6,547	7,052	13,917	26,346

★ = no exact figure
+ = less than 0.5% eaten
− = not eaten

TABLE 42: *Twig nests of other species used by Long-eared Owls in Britain (Glue 1977) and Finland (Mikkola, this study).*

	Britain (%)	Finland (%)
Carrion/Hooded Crow *Corvus corone*	37	46
Magpie *Pica pica*	47	38
Woodpigeon *Columba palumbus*	5	—
Sparrowhawk *Accipiter nisus*	8	—
Kestrel *Falco tinnunculus*	1	—
Buzzard *Buteo buteo*	—	1
Honey Buzzard *Pernis apivorus*	—	1
Grey Heron *Ardea cinerea*	0.5	—
Jay *Garrulus glandarius*	0.5	—
Squirrels *Sciurus sp.*	1	14
Total number of nests	239	95

TABLE 43: *Tree nest sites of Long-eared Owls in Britain (Glue 1977) and Finland (Mikkola, this study). Average nest height in metres in brackets.*

	Britain		Finland	
	%	m	%	m
Pine	48	(7.9)	66	(9.1)
Fir or spruce	12	(7.6)	32	(6.5)
Larch	10	(6.7)	1	(15.0)
Other coniferous	4	(7.6)	—	
Hawthorn	14	(4.9)	—	
Willow	3	(4.6)	1	(2.2)
Other broad-leaved	7	(6.1)	—	
Unidentified trees	2	(5.5)	—	
Total number of nests	198	(6.7)	101	(8.2)

TABLE 44: *Brood sizes of Long-eared Owl during an average micro-rodent cycle. Data sources: Hagen (1965), Linkola and Myllymäki (1969) and Ziesemer (1973). Number of nests studied in brackets.*

Vole cycle	Peak − 2 years		Peak − 1 year		Peak year		Peak + 1 year	
Norway	0	(1)	2.1	(7)	3.4	(12)	1.7	(3)
Finland	2.4	(9)	3.3	(14)	3.6	(22)	2.8	(4)
Germany	—	—	3.0	(10)	3.5	(19)	1.0	(2)

TABLE 45: *Food of Short-eared Owls at nest-sites in Finland (Grönlund and Mikkola 1969, Mikkola and Sulkava 1969 and Mikkola, this study), in Norway (Hagen 1952), in Germany (Hölzinger et al 1973) and in Hungary (Kulczycki 1966).*

	Finland	Norway	Germany	Hungary
Research years	1958–69	–1950	1964–71	1963
No. of prey animals	2,520	510	1,307	118
	%	%	%	%
Voles *Clethrionomys sp.*	5.2	9.0	—	2.4
Voles *Microtus sp.*	78.9	65.1	94.6	21.1
Ground Vole *Arvicola terrestris*	0.8	—	0.1	—
Unidentified and other voles	—	20.6	—	0.8
Mice *Muridae*	4.0	—	5.0	4.8
Shrews *Soricidae*	6.5	2.9	—	69.9
Stoats and Weasels *Mustelidae*	0.1	—	—	—
Small mammals total	95.5	97.6	99.7	99.0
Birds	1.8	1.8	0.1	0.8
Frogs	0.1	—	—	—
Lizards	0.1	0.2	0.1	—
Insects	2.5	0.4	0.1	?
Total	100.0	100.0	100.0	99.8

TABLE 46: *Autumn food of Short-eared Owls in Finland. Table is based on 291 autumn pellets (August to October) studied by Aho (1964) in 1958 at Tampere, and the contents of 36 stomachs studied by Mikkola (this study) 1961–1977.*

	In pellets %	In stomachs %
Common Shrew *Sorex araneus*	1.6	19.0
Pygmy Shrew *Sorex minutus*	—	5.0
Masked Shrew *Sorex caecutiens*	—	1.0
Unidentified shrews *Sorex sp.*	0.2	—
Water Shrew *Neomys fodiens*	0.1	—
Northern Bat *Vespertilio nilssoni*	0.2	—
Bank Vole *Clethrionomys glareolus*	0.4	10.0
Ground Vole *Arvicola terrestris*	0.1	1.0
Common Vole *Microtus arvalis*	73.5	—
Short-tailed Vole *Microtus agrestis*	12.6	31.0
Voles *Microtus sp.*	7.5	—
Harvest Mouse *Micromys minutus*	1.1	14.0
Yellow-necked Field Mouse *Apodemus flavicollis*	0.2	—
Brown Rat *Rattus norvegicus*	0.5	—
House Mouse *Mus musculus*	0.2	4.0
Mammals total	98.2	85.0

TABLE 46 (*continued*)

Yellow Wagtail *Motacilla flava*	—	1.0
Warblers *Sylvia spp.*	0.2	—
Whinchat *Saxicola rubetra*	0.5	—
Unidentified small birds	0.4	—
Birds total	1.1	1.0
Geotrupes spp.	0.4	14.0
Dytiscus spp.	0.2	—
Carabus sp.	0.1	—
Insects total	0.7	14.0
Total number of prey items	820	74

TABLE 47: *Food of Short-eared Owls at wintering areas in Britain (Glue 1977), in France (Martin and Saint Girons 1973), Germany (Uttendörfer 1952), Ireland (Fairley 1966 and Glue 1977) and in Yugoslavia (Schmidt and Szlivka 1968).*

	Britain %	France %	Germany %	Ireland %	Yugoslavia %
Common Vole *Microtus arvalis*	—	98.3	94.8	—	66.9
Short-tailed Vole *Microtus agrestis*	52.5	0.3	0.3	—	—
Wood Mouse *Apodemus spp.*	13.4	1.1	?	32.4	14.6
Brown Rat *Rattus norvegicus*	16.4	—	0.1	39.1	—
Birds	14.3	0.2	0.6	17.1	15.5
Others	3.4	0.1	4.2	11.4	3.0
Total material	2,076	1,950	2,612	105	239

TABLE 48: *Effect of the weather on the hooting activity of Tengmalm's Owls (60 observations in Finland). Number of hooting males expressed in percentages.*

Wind speed			Cloud cover (0/10–10/10)			Temperature °C					
(Beaufort scale)											
0	1–2	2–5	0/10	1–5/10	5–10/10	−20	−15	−10	−5	0	+5
68%	27%	5%	58%	27%	15%	8%	16%	17%	24%	31%	4%

TABLE 49: *Food of Tengmalm's Owls at nest sites in different natural provinces in Finland 1958–1977. Provinces and their identifying number used in this table are shown in Fig. 34. Data sources: Heinonen et al 1970, Helo, P. (unpublished material), Klaus et al 1975, Korpimäki 1972, Mikkola 1971, Rajala 1976 and Sulkava & Sulkava 1971. Numbers of prey species expressed as percentages of total prey animals taken.*

Natural province number	1	2	3	4	5	6	Total
Research years	1960–67	1970–72	1970–72	1960–69	1958–74	1977	1958–77
Number of nests	12	4	2	10	52	15	95
No. of prey animals	1,158	501	130	1,298	5,665	946	9,698
Voles:							
Microtus agrestis	6.8	62.7	44.6	11.0	16.3	34.1	19.0
Microtus arvalis	1.6	—	—	—	2.2	—	1.5
Clethrionomys glareolus	41.6	25.8	14.6	48.0	43.4	57.8	43.9
Microtidae sp.	10.2	0.2	2.3	12.9	6.8	5.2	7.5
Total Voles	60.2	88.7	61.5	71.9	68.7	97.1	71.9
Mice (*Muridae*)	4.9	2.0	1.6	3.9	1.4	—	2.1
Other Rodents	0.1	—	—	0.2	0.0	—	0.0
Shrews (*Soricidae*)	28.8	5.8	19.2	17.5	24.1	1.9	20.6
Bats (*Chiroptera*)	0.1	0.4	—	0.1	—	—	0.0
Birds	5.9	3.2	17.7	6.0	5.8	1.0	5.4
Frogs	—	—	—	—	0.0	—	0.0
Insects	—	—	—	0.4	—	—	0.1
Total	100.0	100.1	100.0	100.0	100.0	100.0	100.1

TABLE 50: *Food of Tengmalm's Owls during the breeding season in Europe. Studies included are mentioned in the text and in Table 49. All figures as percentages of prey numbers.*

	Finland	Norway	Sweden	C. Europe
	%	%	%	%
Insectivora*	20.6	10.1	19.9	23.2
Bank Vole *Clethrionomys glareolus*	43.9	30.5	18.1	15.9
Grey-sided Vole *Clethrionomys rufocanus*	—	7.1	6.8	—
Short-tailed Vole *Microtus agrestis*	19.0	18.0	37.3	10.4
Common Vole *Microtus arvalis*	1.5	—	—	4.0
Microtidae sp.	7.5	17.2	3.8	9.0
Mice (*Muridae*)†	2.1	9.2	11.7	32.6
Small mammals total	94.6	92.1	97.6	95.1
Birds	5.4	7.7	2.4	4.8
Others	0.1	0.3	—	0.1
Total number of prey items	9,698	338	2,045	2,081

* Insectivora includes shrews, bats and moles *Talpidae*
† Mice includes Northern Birch Mouse *Sicista betulina* and dormice *Gliridae*

TABLE 51: *Food of Tengmalm's Owls outside the breeding season in Finland in the years 1928–76. These figures are based on the contents of 29 stomachs (8 of which were empty).*

	Total	%
Pygmy Shrew *Sorex minutus*	3	10.7
Common Shrew *Sorex araneus*	7	25.0
Taiga Shrew *Sorex isodon*	1	3.6
Unidentified Shrew *Sorex sp.*	1	3.6
Total shrews	12	42.9
Short-tailed Vole *Microtus agrestis*	5	17.9
Root Vole *Microtus ratticeps*	1	3.6
Bank Vole *Clethrionomys glareolus*	7	25.0
Total voles	13	46.4
Harvest Mouse *Micromys minutus*	3	10.7
Grand total	28	100.0

TABLE 52: *Wing length (mm) of European owls in decreasing order, by sex (F = female, M = male). Note that the order is not the same as in Table 53. Sources: 1. Dement'ev et al 1951, 2. Department of Zoology, University of Oulu, Finland, 3. Voous 1950, and 4. Keve et al 1960.*

	Source	Sex	Number	Range	Average
Eagle Owl	1	F	20	475–520	485.4
		M	29	430–465	452.5
Great Grey Owl	1	F	57	438–480	464.8
		M	21	405–436	432.5
Snowy Owl	1	F	63	428–462	437.9
		M	86	384–423	405.4
Ural Owl	1	F	26	357–382	366.5
		M	21	342–368	354.0
Short-eared Owl	1	F	88	285–335	310.2
		M	90	281–329	307.7
Long-eared Owl	1	F	150	282–320	298.6
		M	125	276–309	294.8
Tawny Owl	1	F	66	277–311	296.0
		M	53	268–295	283.0
Barn Owl	3	F	164	263–305	286.7
		M	174	259–309	285.8
Hawk Owl	1 + 2	F	27	224–250	237.0
		M	22	222–244	235.0
Tengmalm's Owl	1	F	34	163–181	174.7
		M	21	154–170	163.0
Little Owl	4	F	23	152–170	162.9
		M	20	151–170	160.9
Scops Owl	1	F	11	146–163	154.2
		M	11	143–161	150.6
Pygmy Owl	1	F	41	100–112	103.8
		M	29	92–102	97.8

TABLE 53: *Body weight (g) of European owls in decreasing order, by sex (F = Female, M = male). Sources of information: 1. Dement'ev et al 1951, 2. v. Haartman et al 1967, 3. Baudvin 1975, 4. Keve et al 1960, 5. Géroudet 1965 and 6. Koenig 1973.*

	Source	Sex	Number	Range	Average
Eagle Owl	1 + 2	F	27	2,200–4,000	3,056
		M	28	1,620–3,000	2,275
Snowy Owl	1 + 2	F	27	1,700–2,950	2,239
		M	13	1,280–2,300	1,726
Great Grey Owl	1 + 2	F	24	995–1,900	1,242
		M	31	650–1,100	871

TABLE 53 (*continued*)

	Source	Sex	Number	Range	Average
Ural Owl	1 + 2	F	19	630–1,020	871
		M	11	650– 800	720
Tawny Owl	1 + 2	F	22	410– 800	583
		M	13	410– 550	474
Short-eared Owl	1	F	4	400– 430	411
		M	10	320– 385	350
Barn Owl	3	F	55	290– 450	362
		M	17	280– 365	312
Long-eared Owl	1 + 2	F	20	280– 390	327
		M	22	200– 360	288
Hawk Owl	1 + 2	F	20	270– 380	324
		M	22	215– 375	282
Little Owl	4	F	16	120– 207	175
		M	17	108– 210	172
Tengmalm's Owl	5	F	100	150– 197	168
		M	89	116– 133	123
Scops Owl	6	F	8	86– 140	112
		M	8	80– 118	96
Pygmy Owl	1 + 2	F	14	55– 79	67
		M	7	47– 62	57

TABLE 54: *Dimorphism indices of wing length and cube root of body weight in European owls. See text for method of calculation. Species are in decreasing order of body weight.*

	D.I. wing	D.I. $\sqrt[3]{weight}$
Eagle Owl	+7.02	+ 9.83
Snowy Owl	+7.71	+ 8.68
Great Grey Owl	+7.20	+11.80
Ural Owl	+3.47	+ 6.35
Tawny Owl	+4.49	+ 6.89
Short-eared Owl	+0.81	+ 5.36
Barn Owl	+0.31	+ 4.95
Long-eared Owl	+1.28	+ 4.24
Hawk Owl	+0.85	+ 4.63
Little Owl	+1.24	+ 0.61
Tengmalm's Owl	+6.93	+10.42
Scops Owl	+2.36	+ 5.13
Pygmy Owl	+5.95	+ 5.60
Average	+3.82	+ 6.50
S.D.	2.84	3.02

TABLE 55: *Percentages of prey found in stomachs of male and female Great Grey, Ural and Tengmalm's Owls. All owls had been killed illegally by hunters or found dead during autumns and winters in Finland. Average weight (g) of small mammals according to Siivonen (1972), and of birds according to v. Haartman et al (1963–1972).*

	Av. weight	Great Grey Owl		Ural Owl		Tengmalm's Owl	
		(F)	(M)	(F)	(M)	(F)	(M)
Dorbeetle *Geotrupes sp.*	1.5	—	—	—	2.2	—	—
Least Shrew *Sorex minutissimus*	2.6	—	5.1	1.6	—	—	—
Pygmy Shrew *Sorex minutus*	4.0	2.7	—	—	—	11.8	9.1
Harvest Mouse *Micromys minutus*	6.5	—	—	3.3	—	5.9	18.2
Common Shrew *Sorex araneus*	8.8	37.3	48.1	40.3	42.2	17.7	45.5
Taiga Shrew *Sorex isodon*	10.5	1.3	—	—	—	—	9.1
Water Shrew *Neomys fodiens*	14.5	1.3	—	—	—	—	—
House Mouse *Mus musculus*	15.0	1.3	—	—	—	—	—
Bank Vole *Clethrionomys glareolus*	20.0	12.0	13.9	24.2	8.9	35.3	9.1
Yellow-necked Field Mouse *Apodemus flavicollis*	26.5	—	—	1.6	—	—	—
Grey-sided Vole *Clethrionomys rufocanus*	29.5	5.3	—	—	—	—	—
Short-tailed Vole *Microtus agrestis*	39.9	22.7	27.9	1.6	—	23.5	9.1
Root Vole *Microtus ratticeps*	45.0	12.0	3.8	—	—	5.9	—
Common Frog *Rana temporaria*	50.0	—	1.3	16.1	33.3	—	—
Unidentified bird *Aves sp.*	50.0	—	—	3.3	—	—	—
Waxwing *Bombycilla garrulus*	55.5	—	—	1.6	—	—	—
Fieldfare *Turdus pilaris*	106	—	—	1.6	—	—	—
Ground Vole *Arvicola terrestris*	150	2.7	—	—	—	—	—
Stoat *Mustela erminea*	195	—	—	—	2.2	—	—
Red Squirrel *Sciurus vulgaris*	290	—	—	—	4.5	—	—
Hazel Grouse *Bonasia bonasia*	350	—	—	1.6	4.5	—	—
Carrion Crow *Corvus corone*	525	—	—	—	2.2	—	—
Willow Grouse *Lagopus lagopus*	620	1.4	—	1.6	—	—	—
Black Grouse, male *Tetrao tetrix*	1,260	—	—	1.6	—	—	—
Total		100.0	100.1	100.0	100.0	100.1	100.1
Number of owls studied		29	25	26	20	20	9
Number of prey animals		75	79	62	45	17	11
Average weight (g) of prey		34	20	58	67	21	12
Similarity Index: Female/Male		0.76		0.67		0.51	

TABLE 56: *Owls killed by other owls in Europe. Predators and prey are listed in decreasing order of size (maximum total length). A dash indicates that although the prey species is smaller than the predator there is no record of its being killed by the larger species. Note the lack of records of Short-eared, Little, Scops or Pygmy Owls as predators of other owls. The totals include 17 Asio/Strix sp., seven unidentified owls, five Asio sp. and two Strix sp. taken by Eagle Owl (2+ means 'at least twice').*

OWLS AS PREY

OWL PREDATORS	Great Grey Owl	Snowy Owl	Ural Owl	Hawk Owl	Tawny Owl	Short-eared Owl	Long-eared Owl	Barn Owl	Tengmalm's Owl	Little Owl	Scops Owl	Pygmy Owl	Totals
Eagle Owl	1	4	6	17	286	42	768	46	36	48	7	3	1,288
Great Grey Owl		—	1	—	—	—	—	—	1	—	—	—	2
Snowy Owl			—	—	—	1	—	—	—	—	—	—	1
Ural Owl				1	2	—	1	—	12	—	—	2	18
Hawk Owl					—	—	—	—	3	—	—	—	3
Tawny Owl						—	3	1	6	23	2+	3	38
Long-eared Owl							—		1	2	—	1	4
Barn Owl								—		7	—	—	7
Tengmalm's Owl										—	—	2	2
Totals	1	4	7	18	288	43	772	47	59	80	9	11	1,363

TABLE 57: *Diurnal raptors killed by owls in Europe. Predators and prey are each listed in decreasing order of size (maximum total length). A dash indicates that although the prey species is smaller than the predator there is no record of its being killed by the larger species. Eagle Owl/White-tailed Eagle records appear in brackets because they are not conclusive and because the eagles were well-grown young in the nest; and the Ural Owl because there was no proof that it killed the Honey Buzzard. (2+ means 'at least twice').*

DIURNAL RAPTORS AS PREY

OWL PREDATORS	White-tailed Eagle Haliaeetus albicilla	Red Kite Milvus milvus	Goshawk Accipiter gentilis	Rough-legged Buzzard Buteo lagopus	Accipiter sp.	Osprey Pandion haliaetus	Honey Buzzard Pernis apivorus	Buteo or Pernis	Buzzard Buteo buteo	Buteo sp.	Black Kite Milvus migrans
Eagle Owl	(2+)	2	55	18	2	8	12	4	327	2	1
Snowy Owl		—	—	1	—		—	—	—		—
Ural Owl				—	—	—	(1)	—	1	—	—
Tawny Owl			1								
Barn Owl											
Little Owl											
Totals	(2+)	2	56	19	2	8	13	4	328	2	1

	Gyr Falcon Falco rusticolus	Booted Eagle Hieraaetus pennatus	Hen Harrier Circus cyaneus	Peregrine Falco peregrinus	Saker Falco cherrug	Montagu's Harrier Circus pygargus	Sparrowhawk Accipiter nisus	Hobby Falco subbuteo	Kestrel Falco tinnunculus	Merlin Falco columbarius	Falco sp. (small)	Totals
Eagle Owl	1	1	1	22	3	3	35	3	194	5	4	705
Snowy Owl	1	—	—	—	—	—	—	—	—	—	—	2
Ural Owl	—	—	—	—	—	—	—	—	—	—	—	2
Tawny Owl							15	1	15	1	—	33
Barn Owl									3	—	—	3
Little Owl							1		2			3
Totals	2	1	1	22	3	3	51	4	214	6	4	748

TABLE 58: Owls killed by diurnal raptors in Europe. Predators and prey are listed in decreasing order of size (maximum total length). A dash indicates that although the prey species is smaller than the predator there is no record of its being killed by the larger species. The totals include four Asio sp. taken by Goshawk.

OWLS AS PREY

RAPTOR PREDATORS	Eagle Owl	Great Grey Owl	Snowy Owl	Ural Owl	Hawk Owl	Tawny Owl	Short-eared Owl	Long-eared Owl	Barn Owl	Tengmalm's Owl	Little Owl	Scops Owl	Pygmy Owl	Totals
White-tailed Eagle *Haliaeetus albicilla*	1	—	—	1	—	—	1	—	—	1	—	—	1	5
Golden Eagle *Aquila chrysaetos*	4	4	—	5	1	1	14	2	1	1	—	—	—	33
Imperial Eagle *Aquila heliaca*	—	—	—	—	—	—	1	—	—	—	—	—	—	1
Tawny Eagle *Aquila rapax*	—	—	—	—	—	—	—	—	—	—	1	—	—	1
Long-legged Buzzard *Buteo rufinus*	—	—	—	—	—	—	1	—	—	—	—	—	—	1
Rough-legged Buzzard *Buteo lagopus*	—	—	—	—	1	—	5	1	—	—	1	—	—	8
Red Kite *Milvus milvus*	—	—	—	—	—	4	—	4	1	—	4	—	—	13
Goshawk *Accipiter gentilis*	—	2	—	2	1	100	66	317	13	26	32	—	10	573
Black Kite *Milvus migrans*	—	—	—	—	—	—	1	6	—	—	—	—	—	7
Buzzard *Buteo buteo*	—	—	—	—	—	16	2	24	3	—	2	—	—	47
Gyr Falcon *Falco rusticolus*	—	—	1	—	1	—	4	—	—	1	—	—	1	8
Booted Eagle *Hieraaetus pennatus*	—	—	—	—	—	—	—	—	—	—	1	—	—	1
Peregrine *Falco peregrinus*	—	—	—	—	1	5	17	5	2	2	4	—	—	36
Hen Harrier *Circus cyaneus*	—	—	—	—	—	—	2	—	—	—	—	—	—	2
Pallid Harrier *Circus macrourus*	—	—	—	—	—	—	1	—	—	—	—	—	—	1
Lanner *Falco biarmicus*	—	—	—	—	—	1	—	—	1	—	2	—	—	4
Eleonora's Falcon *Falco eleonorae*	—	—	—	—	—	—	—	—	—	—	—	2	—	2
Sparrowhawk *Accipiter nisus*	—	—	—	—	—	1	—	3	—	1	1	—	3	9
Totals	5	6	1	8	5	128	115	362	21	32	48	2	15	752

TABLE 59: *Food items of Fenno-Scandian owls during the breeding season. Percentages based on the number of food items. The proportion of Microtidae from the total amount is presented in brackets. Sources of information are listed in Appendix (see Table 60).*

	Pygmy Owl	Tengmalm's Owl	Hawk Owl	Long-eared Owl	Short-eared Owl	Tawny Owl	Ural Owl	Great Grey Owl	Snowy Owl	Eagle Owl	Average
Mammals	54.2	94.5	97.7	97.0	97.9	61.8	74.0	98.4	98.0	73.3	84.7
(Microtidae)	(49.5)	(71.9)	(95.7)	(81.4)	(91.3)	(47.3)	(56.5)	(93.5)	(97.4)	(43.9)	(72.8)
Birds	44.0	5.4	1.9	2.2	1.1	28.6	15.8	1.0	1.5	22.0	12.4
Amphibians and Reptilians	1.3	0.04	0.2	0.04	—	6.7	8.1	0.5	0.3	3.3	2.0
Fishes	0.1	—	0.1	0.1	—	0.3	—	—	0.2	1.4	0.2
Invertebrates	0.4	0.1	0.1	0.7	1.0	2.6	2.2	0.1	0.1	0.04	0.7
Materials	2,761	9,698	1,473	2,216	1,209	2,049	1,037	5,177	2,726	1,079	29,425

TABLE 60: *Diet of Mediterranean owls during breeding season. Percentages based on number of food items. The proportion of* Microtidae *from total amount is given in brackets. Sources of information are listed in Appendix, below.*

	Scops Owl	Little Owl	Barn Owl	Long-eared Owl	Hume's Owl	Tawny Owl	Eagle Owl	Average
Mammals	1.2	2.8	86.7	93.9	48.0	28.5	65.1	46.6
(*Microtidae*)	(—)	(0.2)	(12.0)	(79.8)	(—)	(0.7)	(2.7)	(13.6)
Birds	0.6	0.4	4.3	4.6	3.0	8.9	25.9	6.8
Amphibians and Reptilians	3.7	0.7	4.4	—	3.0	5.3	1.0	2.6
Fishes	—	—	—	—	—	—	2.7	0.4
Invertebrates	94.3	95.9	4.3	1.5	46.0	57.2	5.1	43.5
Material	159	5,018	14,806	7,052	101	1,033	3,392	31,561

APPENDIX: *Information sources used for Tables 59 and 60.*

PYGMY OWL: Kellomäki 1969; 1977
    Jussila and Mikkola 1973
    Mikkola and Jussila 1974
TENGMALM'S OWL: Heinonen *et al* 1970
    Klaus *et al* 1975
    Korpimäki 1972
    Mikkola 1971
    Rajala 1976
    Sulkava and Sulkava 1971
HAWK OWL: Mikkola 1972
    Hublin and Mikkola 1977
LONG-EARED OWL: Fennoscandian: Sulkava 1965; Mikkola 1977;
                Grönlund and Mikkola 1977; 1978
    Mediterranean: Araujo *et al* 1973
SHORT-EARED OWL: Mikkola and Sulkava 1969
TAWNY OWL: Fennoscandian: Itämies and Mikkola 1972
                 Mikkola 1968; 1970; 1970
    Mediterranean: Herrera and Hiraldo 1976
URAL OWL: Mikkola and Mikkola 1974
GREAT GREY OWL: Mikkola 1972; 1973; 1974; 1976
    Mikkola and Sulkava 1970
    Pulliainen and Loisa 1977
SNOWY OWL: Hagen 1960; Andersson and Persson 1971; Hakala *et al* (*in litt.*)
EAGLE OWL: Fennoscandian: Mikkola 1970, Sulkava 1966
    Mediterranean: Herrera and Hiraldo 1976
SCOPS OWL: Herrera and Hiraldo 1976
LITTLE OWL: Herrera and Hiraldo 1976
BARN OWL: Herrera and Hiraldo 1976
HUME'S OWL: Leshem (*in litt.*)

TABLE 61: *Daily food intake of owls kept in captivity. Sources of information: Eck and Busse 1973, Koivusaari* et al *1977, Scherzinger 1970 and Schmidt 1977. Mean weight (g) of both sexes has been calculated from Table 53. Owls in increasing order of weight.*

	Mean weight (g)	Food intake per day
Pygmy Owl *Glaucidium passerinum*	62	30
Scops Owl *Otus scops*	104	40
Tengmalm's Owl *Aegolius funereus*	145	65
Little Owl *Athene noctua*	173	65
Hawk Owl *Surnia ulula*	303	105
Long-eared Owl *Asio otus*	308	105
Barn Owl *Tyto alba*	337	95
Short-eared Owl *Asio flammeus*	381	105
Tawny Owl *Strix aluco*	529	180
Ural Owl *Strix uralensis*	796	180
Great Grey Owl *Strix nebulosa*	1,057	250
Snowy Owl *Nyctea scandiaca*	1,983	315
Eagle Owl *Bubo bubo*	2,665	435
Average	680	152

TABLE 62: *Relative sizes of European owls. Weight ratios have been calculated from the male and female average weights presented in Table 53. Owls in decreasing order by larger sex (i.e. female). (— = no significant overlap in body size, i.e. weight ratio more than 2.0.)*

	Eagle Owl	Snowy Owl	Great Grey Owl	Ural Owl	Tawny Owl	Short-eared Owl	Barn Owl	Long-eared Owl	Hawk Owl	Little Owl	Tengmalm's Owl	Scops Owl	Pygmy Owl	Number of competitive species
Eagle Owl	1.3	—	—	—	—	—	—	—	—	—	—	—	—	1
Snowy Owl		1.9	—	—	—	—	—	—	—	—	—	—	—	2
Great Grey Owl			1.3	2.0	—	—	—	—	—	—	—	—	—	3
Ural Owl				1.5	—	—	—	—	—	—	—	—	—	2
Tawny Owl					1.3	1.6	1.7	1.7	—	—	—	—	—	6
Short-eared Owl						1.2	1.3	1.3	—	—	—	—	—	4
Barn Owl							1.1	1.1	1.9	—	—	—	—	5
Long-eared Owl								1.0	1.8	—	—	—	—	5
Hawk Owl									1.8	—	—	—	—	5
Little Owl										1.4	1.7	—	—	5
Tengmalm's Owl											1.3	—	—	2
Scops Owl												1.7	—	3
Pygmy Owl														1

TABLE 63: *Ecological segregation in distribution ranges of European owls. Distribution comparison has been made from maps in this book, as well as those in Makatsch (1976).*

	Great Grey Owl	Snowy Owl	Ural Owl	Tawny Owl	Short-eared Owl	Hawk Owl	Long-eared Owl	Barn Owl	Tengmalm's Owl	Little Owl	Scops Owl	Pygmy Owl
Eagle Owl	R	—	R	R	R	R	R	R	R	R	R	R
Great Grey Owl		—	R	L	R	R	L	—	R	—	—	R
Snowy Owl			—	—	L	—	—	—	—	—	—	—
Ural Owl				R	R	R	R	L	R	L	L	R
Tawny Owl					R	L	R	R	R	R	R	R
Short-eared Owl						R	R	L	R	L	L	R
Hawk Owl							L	—	R	—	—	R
Long-eared Owl								R	R	R	R	R
Barn Owl									L	R	R	L
Tengmalm's Owl										L	L	R
Little Owl											R	L
Scops Owl												L
Pygmy Owl												

L = limited overlap (less than 50%)
R = European distribution range overlapping more than 50% of range of less distributed species
— = no contact

TABLE 64: *Breeding habitat selection by three* Strix *owls in Finland. For basic data cf. Lahti and Mikkola (1974) and Mikkola (1981).*

	Ural Owl	Tawny Owl	Great Grey Owl
Damp heath forests	67	63	45
Dry heath forests	21	3	11
Spruce mires	10	—	35
Pine bogs	1	—	6
Herb-rich forests	1	33	3
Totals	100	99	100
Number of nests observed	87	30	106
*Similarity Index**		0.67	0.47
		0.65	

* Similarity Index $= \dfrac{\Sigma(2\,m_i)}{\Sigma(a_i + b_i)}$, where

a_i = percentage share of habitat *i* by the owl *a*
b_i = percentage share of habitat *i* by the owl *b*
m_i = minimum %-value of habitat *i* in any of those two lists compared

TABLE 65: *Nest site similarity of three* Strix *species in Finland. Basic data taken from Lahti and Mikkola 1974 and Mikkola 1981.*

	Ural Owl	Tawny Owl	Great Grey Owl
Nest boxes	27	59	—
Twig nests	27	3	84
Stumps	33	5	12
Holes in trees	10	27	—
Buildings	2	7	1
Ground	1	—	2
Rock face	1	—	1
Totals	101	101	100
Number of nests observed	250	119	168
Similarity Index		0.47 0.09	
		0.42	

TABLE 66: *Similarity of feeding activity of some Central European owls. Similarity index as developed by MacNaughton and Wolf (1973): 1 signifies a complete overlap of activity, and 0 signifies no similarity of activity patterns. Pygmy Owl's activity studied by Scherzinger (1970) in Austria 26th May–1st July; Tengmalm's Owl in Jena, GDR, 10th March–30th May (Klaus, Mikkola, Wiesner 1975); Tawny Owl in Jena, GDR, 8th April–18th May (Ritter 1972) and Barn Owl in Jena, GDR, 9th June–14th September (Ritter and Görner 1977).*

	Pygmy	Tengmalm's	Barn	Tawny	Average
Pygmy Owl		0.48	0.23	0.47	0.39
Tengmalm's Owl	0.48		0.71	0.83	0.67
Barn Owl	0.23	0.71		0.70	0.55
Tawny Owl	0.47	0.83	0.70		0.67
					x̄ 0.57

TABLE 67: *Similarity of feeding activity of some North European owls. Similarity index as in Table 64. Pygmy Owl's feeding activity studied in Oulu, Finland between 2nd June and 20th June (Mikkola 1970); Tengmalm's Owl in Oulu 2nd May–3rd June (Klaus, Mikkola, Wiesner 1975); Tawny Owl in Valkeala, Finland 13th May–31st May (Grönlund and Mikkola 1979); Ural Owl in Lappajärvi, Finland 15th May–13th June (Huhtala, Korpimäki, Mikkola, unpublished); Great Grey Owl in Salla, Finland 6th May–21st June (Pulliainen and Loisa 1977) and Eagle Owl in Sörmland, Sweden June–August (Kranz 1971).*

	Pygmy	Tengmalm's	Tawny	Ural	Great Grey	Eagle	Average
Pygmy Owl		0.39	0.43	0.71	0.69	0.43	0.53
Tengmalm's	0.39		0.83	0.62	0.46	0.76	0.61
Tawny Owl	0.43	0.83		0.64	0.50	0.74	0.63
Ural Owl	0.71	0.62	0.64		0.74	0.67	0.68
Great Grey	0.69	0.46	0.50	0.74		0.57	0.59
Eagle Owl	0.43	0.76	0.74	0.67	0.57		0.63
							x̄ 0.61

TABLE 68: *Similarity in composition of diet in Fenno-Scandian owls. The index of similarity of diet is based on the Index of Community Similarity developed by MacNaughton and Wolf (1973). Index is 0 when there are no similarities or overlap of food niches and 1 if the food niches completely overlap. Basic data presented in Table 59.*

	Pygmy Owl	Tengmalm's Owl	Hawk Owl	Long-eared Owl	Short-eared Owl	Tawny Owl	Ural Owl	Great Grey Owl	Snowy Owl	Eagle Owl	Average	Range
Pygmy Owl		0.60	0.57	0.57	0.56	0.85	0.72	0.56	0.56	0.78	0.64	0.56–0.85
Tengmalm's Owl	0.60		0.97	0.97	0.96	0.67	0.80	0.96	0.96	0.79	0.85	0.60–0.97
Hawk Owl	0.57	0.97		0.99	0.99	0.64	0.76	0.99	1.00	0.76	0.85	0.57–1.00
Long-eared Owl	0.57	0.97	0.99		0.99	0.65	0.77	0.98	0.99	0.76	0.85	0.57–0.99
Short-eared Owl	0.56	0.96	0.99	0.99		0.64	0.76	0.99	0.99	0.74	0.85	0.56–0.99
Tawny Owl	0.85	0.67	0.64	0.65	0.64		0.87	0.63	0.64	0.87	0.72	0.63–0.87
Ural Owl	0.72	0.80	0.76	0.77	0.76	0.87		0.76	0.76	0.92	0.79	0.72–0.92
Great Grey Owl	0.56	0.96	0.99	0.98	0.99	0.63	0.76		0.99	0.75	0.85	0.56–0.99
Snowy Owl	0.56	0.96	1.00	0.99	0.99	0.64	0.76	0.99		0.75	0.85	0.56–1.00
Eagle Owl	0.78	0.79	0.76	0.76	0.74	0.87	0.92	0.75	0.75		0.79	0.74–0.92

x̄ 0.80

TABLE 69: Similarity in composition of diet of Mediterranean owls. The index of similarity of diet is based on the Index of Community Similarity developed by MacNaugton and Wolf (1973). Index is 0 when there are no similarities or overlap of food niches, and 1 if the food niches completely overlap. Basic data presented in Table 60.

	Scops Owl	Little Owl	Barn Owl	Long-eared Owl	Hume's Owl	Tawny Owl	Eagle Owl	Average	Range
Scops Owl		0.97	0.10	0.03	0.51	0.63	0.08	0.39	0.03–0.97
Little Owl	0.97		0.08	0.05	0.50	0.61	0.09	0.38	0.05–0.97
Barn Owl	0.10	0.08		0.93	0.58	0.42	0.75	0.48	0.10–0.93
Long-eared Owl	0.03	0.05	0.93		0.53	0.35	0.71	0.43	0.03–0.93
Hume's Owl	0.51	0.50	0.58	0.53		0.81	0.57	0.58	0.50–0.81
Tawny Owl	0.63	0.61	0.42	0.35	0.81		0.44	0.54	0.35–0.81
Eagle Owl	0.08	0.09	0.75	0.71	0.57	0.44		0.44	0.08–0.75
								$\bar{x}\,0.46$	

Index